FRANCE

HOW TO USE THIS GUIDE

The first section consists of useful general information—Facts at Your Fingertips—designed to help you plan your trip, as well as local facts, business hours, local holidays, time zones, and customs that will be of use while you are traveling.

Next are essays to help you with the background of the area that this Guide covers—the cultural scene, some historical insights, regional food and drink, and so on.

Following these essays comes the detailed breakdown of the area, geographically. Each chapter begins with a description of the place or region, broadly describing its attraction for the visitor; this is followed by Practical Information to help you explore the area—detailed descriptions, addresses, directions, phone numbers, and so forth for hotels, restaurants, tours, museums, historical sites, and more.

Two vital ways into this book are the Table of Contents at the beginning and the Index at the end.

FODOR'S TRAVEL GUIDES

are compiled, researched, and edited by an international team of travel writers, field correspondents, and editors. The series, which now almost covers the globe, was founded by Eugene Fodor in 1936.

OFFICES
New York & London

FRANCE:

Area Editor: VIVIENNE MENKES
Editor: RICHARD MOORE
Assistant Editor: THOMAS CUSSANS
Editorial Contributors: JOHN ARDAGH, ANDREW HERITAGE, FRANCES HOWELL, MAUREEN MONMARCHÉ, DAVID TENNANT, ELIZABETH VENANT
Maps: C. W. BACON, KEN McCREITH
Drawings: GRAHAM BYFIELD

SPECIAL SALES

Fodor's Travel Guides are available at special quantity discounts for bulk purchases (100 copies or more) for sales promotions or premiums. Special travel guides or excerpts from existing guides can also be created to fit specific needs. For more information write Special Marketing, Fodor's Travel Guides, 2 Park Avenue, New York, N.Y. 10016.

FODOR'S
FRANCE
1984

FODOR'S TRAVEL GUIDES
New York

Copyright © 1984 by FODOR'S TRAVEL GUIDES
ISBN 0-679-01004-1 (Traveltex edition)
ISBN 0-340-34068-1 (Hodder and Stoughton edition)
No part of this book may be reproduced in any form without permission in writing from the publisher.

All the following Guides are current (most of them also in the Hodder and Stoughton British edition.)

CURRENT FODOR'S COUNTRY AND AREA TITLES:

- AUSTRALIA, NEW ZEALAND AND SOUTH PACIFIC
- AUSTRIA
- BELGIUM AND LUXEMBOURG
- BERMUDA
- BRAZIL
- CANADA
- CARIBBEAN AND BAHAMAS
- CENTRAL AMERICA
- EASTERN EUROPE
- EGYPT
- EUROPE
- FRANCE
- GERMANY
- GREAT BRITAIN
- GREECE
- HOLLAND
- INDIA
- IRELAND
- ISRAEL
- ITALY
- JAPAN
- JORDAN AND HOLY LAND
- KOREA
- MEXICO
- NORTH AFRICA
- PEOPLE'S REPUBLIC OF CHINA
- PORTUGAL
- SCANDINAVIA
- SCOTLAND
- SOUTH AMERICA
- SOUTHEAST ASIA
- SOVIET UNION
- SPAIN
- SWITZERLAND
- TURKEY
- YUGOSLAVIA

CITY GUIDES:

- BEIJING, GUANGZHOU, SHANGHAI
- CHICAGO
- DALLAS AND FORT WORTH
- HOUSTON
- LONDON
- LOS ANGELES
- MADRID
- MEXICO CITY AND ACAPULCO
- NEW ORLEANS
- NEW YORK CITY
- PARIS
- ROME
- SAN DIEGO
- SAN FRANCISCO
- STOCKHOLM, COPENHAGEN, OSLO, HELSINKI, AND REYKJAVIK
- TOKYO
- WASHINGTON, D.C.

FODOR'S BUDGET SERIES:

- BUDGET BRITAIN
- BUDGET CANADA
- BUDGET CARIBBEAN
- BUDGET EUROPE
- BUDGET FRANCE
- BUDGET GERMANY
- BUDGET HAWAII
- BUDGET ITALY
- BUDGET JAPAN
- BUDGET MEXICO
- BUDGET SCANDINAVIA
- BUDGET SPAIN
- BUDGET TRAVEL IN AMERICA

USA GUIDES:

- ALASKA
- CALIFORNIA
- CAPE COD
- COLORADO
- FAR WEST
- FLORIDA
- HAWAII
- NEW ENGLAND
- PENNSYLVANIA
- SOUTH
- TEXAS
- USA (in one volume)

MANUFACTURED IN THE UNITED STATES OF AMERICA
10 9 8 7 6 5 4 3 2 1

FOREWORD

France, often regarded as the world's most civilized nation, has for centuries exerted a powerful influence on travelers. Today, as ever, it is a most delightful and rewarding country to visit—whether for a full holiday or a briefer sight-seeing tour. Many Americans and Britons see it as their natural first choice for a Continental tour.

In the four decades since the end of the war, the old slow-moving France of peasant farms and sleepy market towns has been substantially transformed into a brisk, modern industrial nation, one of the richest and most successful in Europe. Yet the old France also remains: and so two societies, two ways of life, co-exist, producing contrasts that any visitor will find exciting.

In Paris, new skyscraper blocks tower above the picturesque old squares with their chestnut-trees. Ritzy American-style hypermarkets stand beside the little corner-shops where housewives still go to buy a loaf of bread and enjoy a neighborhood gossip. In the provinces, smart new factories and scientific centers have been planted down in landscapes dotted with lovely old châteaux or terraced with vineyards. And along country lanes, you see village girls in the latest international 'pop' fashions, walking beside their beshawled, black-smocked grandmothers.

These changes brought social conflicts, as new generations tried to work out a new French identity. The student flare-up of May 1968 showed how close their anxieties were to the surface. Yet for many years it seemed that the basic conservatism of the French would prevent a move away from the right wing and center governments of General de Gaulle, Georges Pompidou and Valéry Giscard d'Estaing. The change finally came in 1981, when the Socialist Party leader, François Mitterrand, won a convincing victory in the presidential elections, followed by a virtual landslide for his party in the ensuing parliamentary elections. Yet many of the reforms promised by the new government could be implemented only very slowly, if at all, as France sank deeper into recession. By 1983 there were serious signs of disaffection even among those who had most welcomed the change, and much disillusionment with Socialist policies.

For the tourist, France has almost everything to offer—a wonderful variety of beautiful scenery, romantic old cities with some of Europe's finest art treasures, the best food and wines in the world, and an elegant, zestful and sophisticated way of life. Go into any small-town *bistrot* with its smell of garlic, stroll along a leafy Paris boulevard or visit a noisy seaside resort in high summer—and you will be rubbing shoulders with a people who, maddening and mercurial though they sometimes may be, have that vital and precious quality: style.

This edition of our Guide provides the most thorough coverage of the attractions that make France a major tourist goal. Recent developments in resort areas such as Languedoc-Roussillon have extended the variety of vacation possibilities, and increased the range of the less expensive places to explore. In fact, the generally accepted myth of the high cost of visiting France is really just that—a myth. Paris is certainly a pricey destination, but less so than Brussels and even London. Once away from the main centers, life and prices relax. You can have a gourmet meal in an atomspheric country spot for a remarkably low cost.

We would like to thank the staff of the following organizations for giving us such ready aid in the preparation of this edition: the Secrétariat d'Etat au Tourisme; the Office de Tourisme de Paris; the Mission Interministérielle pour l'Aménagement Touristique du Littoral Languedoc-Roussillon; the Maison de Normandie; the Direction du Tourisme and Comité Interprofessionnel des Vins de Touraine in Tours; and the staff of many tourist offices. We also wish to express our thanks the Mrs. Pauline Hallam of the French Government Tourist Office in London for her continued assistance.

All prices quoted in this Guide are based on those available to us at time of writing, mid-1983. Given the volatility of European costs, it is inevitable that changes will have taken place by the time this book becomes available. We trust, therefore, that you will take prices quoted as indicators

FOREWORD

only, and will double-check to be sure of the latest figures. In particular, the seesawing of exchange rates during 1983, made forecasting even more difficult than usual.

*

We are deeply grateful to John Ardagh for putting his considerable knowledge and expertise at our disposal, and to Vivienne Menkes, our Area Editor, for her tireless work, without which this edition would not have been possible.

Errors are bound to creep into any Guide. Hotels and restaurants can suffer instant decline in the quality of their service, acts of governments or God can change the travel picture overnight, and in many smaller ways we can find items that we have given as gospel appear to be untrue. For these reasons we greatly appreciate letters from our readers, telling us of their travel experiences or chastising us for apparent—or actual—errors. Not only do such letters help to keep us on the straight and narrow path, but they also give us a traveler's eye view that might have escaped our professional revisors.

Our addresses for such letters are –

in the US: Fodor's Travel Guides, 2 Park Avenue, New York, NY 10016;

in the UK: Fodor's Travel Guides, 9-10 Market Place, London W1N 7AG.

CONTENTS

FOREWORD v

FACTS AT YOUR FINGERTIPS
Planning your trip; How to reach France;
Arriving in France; Staying in France;
Traveling in France; Leaving France 3

THE FRENCH SCENE

THE FRENCH WAY OF LIFE—A sophisticated, stimulating, often exasperating people *John Ardagh* 53

A MINI HISTORY OF FRANCE—An aide-mémoire to monarchs and moments 65

CREATIVE FRANCE—Mecca of the arts *Andrew Heritage* 70

DINING—The noble art of gastronomy *John Ardagh* 82

THE FACE OF FRANCE

INTRODUCING PARIS—A promenade in three days *Dan Behrman* 91

GETTING SETTLED IN PARIS—Where to stay and what to do 97
Map of Paris Arrondissements 99
Map of Paris Métro 118-119

EXPLORING PARIS—A voyage of discovery 138
Map of Paris 142-143

THE CAPITAL OF FOOD—Over 8,000 restaurants—pick your own 165

PARIS BY NIGHT—Painting the Moulin Rouge 187

FREE!

To find out how to get your *free* brochure on "Avoiding the Hassles of Travel" open this flap.

Detach here

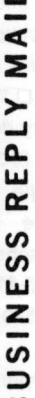

BUSINESS REPLY MAIL
FIRST CLASS   PERMIT NO. 9260   NEW YORK, N.Y.

Postage will be paid by addressee —

FODOR'S TRAVEL GUIDES
2 Park Avenue
New York, NY 10016

NO POSTAGE
NECESSARY
IF MAILED
IN THE
UNITED STATES

CONTENTS ix

SAVOIR FLAIR—Shopping in Paris	198
ILE DE FRANCE—Heartland of a nation *Georgianna Pouzzner*	210
BRITTANY—Land's end with Celtic folklore *John Ardagh*	238
NORMANDY—Beachheads and abbeys *Vivienne Menkes*	255
THE LOIRE VALLEY—Château country *Vivienne Menkes*	274
THE NORTH—Ferry boats and Flanders' fields *John Ardagh*	292
CHAMPAGNE—Sparkle from the chalk	304
ALSACE AND LORRAINE—The Marseillaise and Joan of Arc	314
THE JURA AND FRANCHE-COMTÉ—Forested mountains, eastern bastion	331
BURGUNDY—The treasure house of history	344
THE RHÔNE VALLEY—Gastronomy, gorges and craftsmanship *Map of Lyon* 361	359
THE FRENCH ALPS—One area, two countries	373
THE RIVIERA—High life with a suntan *Map of Nice* 409	397
MONACO—Glittering principality *Map of Monoco* 435	432
PROVENCE AND THE CAMARGUE—Rome away from Rome	442
LANGUEDOC AND ROUSSILLON—Modern resorts and ancient fortresses *John Ardagh*	459

CONTENTS

TOULOUSE AND THE CENTRAL PYRENESS—Tradition as rugged as the mountains *John Ardagh* 477

THE ATLANTIC COAST—Two thousand years of wine 495

AROUND THE DORDOGNE—Rural valleys and prehistoric paintings 516

THE AUVERGNE—France's volcanic heart 531

CORSICA—The scented isle 544

SUPPLEMENTS

ENGLISH-FRENCH TOURIST VOCABULARY 559

INDEX 569

Map of France 580-581

FACTS AT YOUR FINGERTIPS

FACTS AT YOUR FINGERTIPS

Planning your Trip

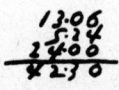

WHAT IT WILL COST. This is the most difficult travel question to answer in advance, because much depends on individual requirements of comfort and the outlay the tourist is able to make. The basic minimum in France, unfortunately, is already rather high. In 1983 inflation was running at around 10%. However, the poor performance of the French franc against the dollar during 1983, and for much of the time against the pound too, made what is basically an expensive country seem slightly easier on the pocket for both British and US tourists. There seemed little prospect of the franc improving in the short term at our press time, but we must stress that it is essential for you to check the current position when planning your trip.

How much your vacation in France will cost you depends a great deal on where you spend it. Generally speaking, it is safe to say that prices in regional capitals (Bordeaux, Marseille, Toulouse, etc.) are between 30 and 40% lower than in Paris; in rural areas 40–50% lower. Fashionable resorts such as Deauville, La Baule or Biarritz are about the same price as Paris. Even the Riviera (Cannes, Nice, St-Tropez) in season can be considerably cheaper than Paris if you don't insist on patronizing the deluxe spots. As for holidays in such delightful areas as Brittany, Alsace, the Alps, the Auvergne or the Basque country, these can be, in comparison, quite inexpensive. The new resorts along the Languedoc-Roussillon coast are considerably cheaper than the Riviera and are equipped with every amenity.

HOTEL ROOM
(prices, for a double room, in French francs)

	Major city	Major resort	Small town	Budget resort
Deluxe (L)	600–1000	600–1500	—	—
Expensive (E)	350–550	400–600	200–350	—
Moderate (M)	250–350	250–400	150–250	150–250
Inexpensive (I)	100–250	100–250	75–150	65–150

Few hotels nowadays have more than an occasional single room and it will usually be poky and depressing. Out of season a single occupant of a double room may be able to go below the rates we give here. On the other hand many double rooms now have an extra single bed, for which you will only need to pay about 35–60 frs extra if there are three of you. *For Paris rates see Paris chapter.*

RESTAURANT PRICES
(including wine, in French francs)

	Major city	Major resort	Small town	Budget resort
Expensive (E)	250–450	250–450	200–250	—
Moderate (M)	150–250	150–250	150–200	100–160
Inexpensive (I)	80–150	80–150	60–120	60–100

For Paris restaurants see 'Paris' chapter. For a choice of moderate to inexpensive ways to vacation in France, see under 'Staying in France' later in this chapter.

A TYPICAL DAY IN PARIS FOR TWO
(moderate outlay)

Hotel room and breakfast, tax and service incl.	250 francs
Lunch, incl. tax, service, and wine	220
Dinner, ditto	300
Transportation, 1 taxi, 2 public, each 3 km	55
Pack best local cigarettes	6
Two coffees in a chic café	20
Two beers in a local café	15
Miscellaneous	50
Approx.	916

FACTS AT YOUR FINGERTIPS

Miscellaneous items. A ticket for the opera costs between 80 and 300 frs (except in the gallery); a theater seat 50–150; a tot of whisky or gin, around 25 frs, liqueur or cognac 15–25, an American-style cocktail, around 30. A woman's shampoo and set is 65–150 frs, a man's haircut, 60–120. To launder and iron a shirt, around 25 frs, to press a suit or dress, around 30. A foreign newspaper costs 6–20 frs, a French one 4–6. At a chic café, a sandwich costs around 10 frs, a croissant around 5 frs.

At museums throughout France, senior citizens (women over 60, men over 62), teachers, students and children (but age limit varies here) pay half-price entry fee. Senior citizens do not pay at any time at City of Paris museums. State-owned museums (*musées nationaux*) are now free on Wednesdays, but this applies only to the regular collections, not to special exhibits.

Anyway, if you really budget yourself carefully, and stay only at the least expensive hotels (listed in our Paris section); eat at self-service cafeterias (or student restaurants if you have a student card); take the Métro and buses; and do all the things that Paris offers for free or almost free: walks in the lovely parks; museums, window-shopping; wandering through the Marché aux Puces or the flower markets—you can manage remarkably well.

WHEN TO GO. The main tourist season in France runs from Easter to the end of Sept.; the peak comes in July and Aug., when the weather is best. However, as practically all of France is on vacation in Aug., higher prices and crowded roads and accommodations are apt to be encountered around this time and many shops and restaurants are closed in cities that are not primarily tourist centers, where closures are more likely in June or September. But summer is the time when you must come if you want to take in the events designed especially for tourists.

The exception used to be Paris, because so many theaters, restaurants and small shops close for at least a month during July or Aug. They still do, but on the other hand the recent reinstatement of the office of mayor of Paris has led to an upsurge of summer happenings in the capital. The dynamic mayor, Jacques Chirac, a former prime minister, and his staff are constantly staging *fêtes* of all kinds throughout the summer months, plus firework displays, flower shows and the like. You may not find many Parisians in town, but at least that means less traffic congestion!

Things have changed, too, on the Riviera, not least because of changing weather patterns over the whole of Europe. The winter season used to be the smartest and liveliest there, but now, with the exception of Nice's brilliant carnival in February—still a big attraction—the only real 'season' is in the summer. Riviera beaches are as crowded as Paris is deserted, particularly in Aug., when the beaches sometimes resemble Coney Island or Blackpool; and rooms at one of Monte Carlo's top hotels cost nearly twice as much in July and Aug. as they do Oct. through April.

Do not on any account travel on 1, 13/14 or 31 July, or 1, 14/15 or 31 Aug., or the nearest weekends to these dates, unless you absolutely have to. Many

French people take at least a month's holiday in July or Aug. and as schools and factories all close at the same time, on those peak dates major roads, trains and coaches are unbearably crowded.

For Corsica, spring and fall are the best seasons, and particularly June when the days are longest (though evenings can be cool). In high summer, the resorts are crowded.

The winter sports season in France and Corsica starts in Nov. and continues until mid-April. Resorts are crowded during the week-long half-term holidays in February. You can ski all year round in the high-altitude resorts of the Mont Blanc region, such as Super-Tignes, Val d'Isère (the Col d'Iséran), Val Thorens and Chamonix, but summer skiing, although fun, is not taken seriously by true skiers.

Off-season travel. This has become increasingly popular in recent years as tourists have come to appreciate the advantage of avoiding the crowded periods.

The French Government Tourist Office has organized a series of campaigns to encourage hoteliers and restaurants to offer lower prices in June, in an attempt to prevent the hideous overcrowding prevalent in July and August. 'The South-West in June' and 'Brittany in June' have already been launched. More campaigns are expected to follow. Some areas, such as the Languedoc-Roussillon coast, have persuaded hotels that are normally shut for much of the year to remain open, with lower prices, April through October, and have made sure that all the usual summer amenities are available throughout this period. Considerable reductions (up to 40%) on train fares to participating resorts are also offered. Ask at government or national tourist offices for details (see addresses).

But do bear in mind that in spring and fall (and even more in winter, except in winter sports resorts) many hotels and restaurants are closed in holiday centers.

CLIMATE. Average maximum daily temperatures in degrees Fahrenheit and Centigrade

	Jan.	Feb.	Mar.	Apr.	May	June	July	Aug.	Sept.	Oct.	Nov.	Dec.
North												
F°	42	45	52	60	67	73	76	75	69	59	49	43
C°	5	7	11	16	19	23	24	23	21	15	9	6
Riviera												
F°	56	56	59	64	69	76	81	81	77	70	62	58
C°	13	13	15	18	21	24	27	27	25	21	17	14

PUBLIC HOLIDAYS. January 1, Easter Monday, May 1 (Labor Day), May 8 (VE Day), Ascension Day (5 weeks after Easter), Whit Monday, July 14 (Bastille Day, national holiday), August 15 (Assumption), November 1 (All Saints' Day), November 11 (Armistice Day), December 25.

FACTS AT YOUR FINGERTIPS

WHERE TO FIND OUT. The best place for getting information about local events, sports opportunities, etc., as well as hotels and restaurants, is in the *syndicat d'initiative* or *office du tourisme*, which you will find in all sizeable towns and in resorts both inland and by the sea. The former (often abbreviated to *SI* and pronounced *essi*) are often manned by helpful volunteers and in many cases are open in the summer months only. They are gradually being superseded in larger places by the latter, which are well-organized bodies run by the local council or regional administration, usually open year-round and brimful of brochures and booklets on their town or area. They're a key address for you, and we've given main ones in our regional chapters. Each of France's 22 administrative regions also has a 'welcome information office' *(France-Accueil)* but obviously the staff won't have the same detailed knowledge of a particular town or village as the local office. The Welcome Information offices can normally make hotel reservations in other areas for you. Other, alternative, names to watch out for: *Maison du Tourisme, Pavillon du Tourisme, Centre d'Accueil.*

Many tourist offices now have slot machines outside so that you can obtain hotel lists and other leaflets even out of opening hours. You may also find a large board with light-up signs indicating hotels that have rooms available.

Information Overseas. Information while planning your trip may be obtained from the *French Government Tourist Office* at: 610 Fifth Ave, New York 10020; 645 N. Michigan Ave, Chicago 60601; 323 Geary St, San Francisco 94102; 9401 Wilshire Bd, Beverly Hills, Calif. 90212; 1840 Sherbrooke St West, Montreal; 372 Bay St, Toronto; 178 Piccadilly, London W1; 127, av. des Champs-Elysées, 75008, Paris.

SPECIAL EVENTS. The visitor to France is never short of special events and festivals to entertain him. We've given details of regional events in our individual chapters, but here is a brief list of the main attractions that bring tourists to the country at specific times of year: **January** Monte Carlo Motor Rally; **February** Fashion shows in Paris, carnival in Nice, Mardi Gras carnivals in many parts of France, especially the southwest and the Nord-Pas-de-Calais area; **March** International Fairs in Nice and Lyon (continues into April); **April** The Paris Fair (sometimes in May), ready-to-wear fashion shows in Paris; **Easter** the Prix du Président de la République at Paris's Longchamp racecourse; Good Friday processions in many places, especially Corsica, galas in Deauville; **May** Normandy's apple blossom, International Fair in Bordeaux, gypsy pilgrimage to Stes-Maries-de-la-Mer, Monaco Grand Prix, International Tennis Championships at Paris's Roland Garros tennis stadium (continue into June); **June** The Prix de Diane at Chantilly's racecourse, Air Show at Le Bourget (takes place every other year), fireworks and other celebrations in Paris and towns and villages beginning with St Jean (St-Jean-de-Luz, St-Jean-Cap-Ferrat and so on) on June 24 (Feast of John the Baptist), the traditional 'Grand Fénétra' fair in Toulouse, 'Les 24 Heures du Mans' motor race; **July** French Grand Prix, Tour de France cycle race (sometimes starts in June), dancing in the streets, military parade on the Champs-Elysées in Paris and fairs and celebrations all over the country for the *Fête Nationale* (Bastille Day) on July 14, Battle of Flowers in Nice (also in August); **August** 'Musical Saturdays' in Chartres (continues to Oct.), Assumption Day pilgrimage to Lourdes (August 15), Wine Fair in Colmar, bullfights (but without putting the bulls to death) in the Camargue and the southwest, Galléa Cup tennis in Vichy, 'Les Grandes Heures de Cluny', *Pardon de Notre-Dame-de-la-Clarté* in Perros-Guirec, Napoleon's birthday celebrations in Ajaccio (August 15), Lavender Fair in Digne, Provençal Folklore Fair in St-Rémy-de-Provence; **September** Beginning of the fishing and shooting seasons, International Fairs in Marseille and Strasbourg, grape harvest fairs and celebrations in the major wine regions (especially Bordeaux and Burgundy), *Fête de la Vigne* in Dijon, and Champagne Wine Fair in Bar-sur-Aube, Autumn Pilgrimage to Mont-St-Michel, pilgrimage to Moustiers-Ste-Marie (September 8); **October** Prix de l'Arc-de-Triomphe at Longchamp, Auto Show in Paris (even-numbered years), ready-to-wear fashion shows in Paris, international Wine Fair in Montpellier, Rosary Pilgrimage to Lourdes, international horse jumping event in Poitiers; **November** International Fair in Dijon, 'Les Trois Glorieuses' in Burgundy (Nuits-St-Georges, Beaune, Meursault)—wine auction in Hospices de Beaune, dancing in the streets, celebrations of all kinds; 'Tour de Corse', international motor race in Corsica, Santons Fair in Marseille; **December** midnight masses on Christmas Eve all over France, the most picturesque in Provence and the Alpes Maritimes, in Pérouges, and a famous one in Beaune, special street lighting and window displays in all big towns, especially Paris, with big dinners on Christmas Eve (after midnight mass) and New Year's Eve.

Note: French Government Tourist Offices now issue a special brochure, *France in a Holiday Mood*, listing special events planned.

FESTIVALS. It sometimes seems as if there's a festival for every day of the year in France these days, from the huge ones in the big cities to picturesque local ones devoted to local folklore, puppets or what have you. You can get details from the French National Tourist Office (see addresses section) or from local tourist offices, but the following list will give you an idea of the major festivals:

April Spring Music Festival in Paris, Contemporary art in Royan, young soloists in Antibes/Juan-les-Pins (continues into May and June). **May** Theater in Nancy, music, dance and theater in Bordeaux (plus International Young Soloists Festival), music week in the abbey of Fontfroide, music in Toulon (continues into June), Cannes International Film Festival.

June Marais Festival in Paris (continues into July), music in Strasbourg, Bastia in Corsica (organ music), Ile de France (with concerts in the region's

Make Your Trip More Enjoyable

"Try to speak the local language; it's really great fun. . . .

"The natives, who may not speak your language, will be proud and appreciative of your efforts to use *their* language.

"I can't think of a better way to break the ice---"

—*Eugene Fodor*

Fodor's / McKay has a wide list of Teach Yourself language and phrase books and foreign-language dictionaries. Most cost only a few dollars. If your local bookstore doesn't have the language book you need, write to us for a complete list of titles and prices.

Write to:
Sales Director
FODOR'S / McKAY
2 Park Avenue
New York, NY
10016

✺Maupintour
Quality tours at home and abroad.

ESCORTED TOURS are fun. You enjoy yourself when you tour with a Maupintour group...and you have a choice of over 100 escorted holidays.

BETTER HOTELS, resorts, fine dining, special events, entertainment, luggage handling, tips, transfers...these are included with Maupintour.

NEW MAUPINTOUR BROCHURES. Be sure to read through the Maupintour brochures before you decide. Just write or phone for a copy. Then ask your Travel Agent for reservations on the Maupintour of your choice.

- ☐ Africa
- ☐ Alaska/Yukon
- ☐ Alps
- ☐ Arizona
- ☐ Australia
- ☐ Bavaria/Austria
- ☐ Belgium
- ☐ British Isles
- ☐ California
- ☐ Canada
- ☐ China
- ☐ Christmas Tours
- ☐ Colorado
- ☐ Cruise Tours
- ☐ Egypt/The Nile
- ☐ Europe
- ☐ Fall Foliage
- ☐ France
- ☐ Germany
- ☐ Greece/Aegean
- ☐ Hawaii
- ☐ Historic East
- ☐ Holland
- ☐ Iceland
- ☐ India/Nepal Kashmir
- ☐ Israel
- ☐ Italy
- ☐ Japan
- ☐ Middle East
- ☐ Morocco
- ☐ National Parks
- ☐ New Zealand
- ☐ Nile Cruise
- ☐ Opera Tours
- ☐ Orient
- ☐ Pacific N.W.
- ☐ Scandinavia
- ☐ South Pacific
- ☐ Spain/Portugal
- ☐ Switzerland
- ☐ USA East
- ☐ USA South
- ☐ USA West

✺Maupintour
quality escorted tours since 1951

Maupintour, P.O. Box 807, Lawrence, Ks. 66044. Telephone 800-255-4266.

FACTS AT YOUR FINGERTIPS

châteaux continuing throughout the summer), Versailles, Angers (also dance and theater), Abbeville, Nice (religious music), Evian, Divonne-les-Bains; also Gascony Festival in Auch, and Lyon Festival. **July** Summer festival in Paris, with fireworks displays, theater, music and dance (continues into Sept.), jazz in Bergerac, Antibes, La Grande-Motte, and Nîmes, music all along the Aquitaine (i.e. Atlantic) coast, and in Vézelay, Ajaccio (Millelli Festival), Villeneuve-lès-Avignon, Uzès, Gourdon, Albi, Mont-St-Michel, St-Tropez, Antibes, Menton, Valence, Orange and Loire Valley châteaux.

August The famous Avignon Festival, with theater especially, but also dance and music (sometimes starts in July); and the International Aix-en-Provence Festival, mostly music; theater in Albi, Aigues-Mortes, La Baule, Montauban, Carcassonne; music in Bergerac, Menton and the Vaucluse (Gordes, Cavaillon, Apt, etc.), jazz in La Grande Motte and Salon-de-Provence; many of the July festivals continue into the first half of August.

September Chamber music in Paris and at Royaumont château, other music festivals in the Basque country (Bayonne, Biarritz, St-Jean-de-Luz, etc.), Dijon, Chartres (Saturdays only), Besançon (International Young Pianists' Competition), Mazamet, St-Pons; Haute-Provence Festival in Forcalquier; 'Living Book' Festival in Fougères, with plays, tableaux, etc. **October** International Dance Festival in Paris; theater in Nancy. **November** Music in Metz, theater and café-theater in Rennes. We advise you to check dates, as last-minute changes can occur.

Son-et-Lumière. The success of the original 'sound and light' shows in the Loire Valley châteaux led to so many shows being put on throughout France that, with costs escalating, it is now very hard for the organizers to make money out of them. As a result they are often staged only at weekends, or at a handful of times every year, and few shows start before June or continue after early September. Check at local or regional tourist offices for shows available and details of times. An increasing number of shows now include actors (usually local amateurs), dressed in period costumes.

HOW TO GO. When you have decided where you want to go, your next step is to consult a good travel agent. If you haven't one, the *American Society of Travel Agents,* 4400 MacArthur Blvd., N.W., Washington, D.C. 20007, or the *Association of British Travel Agents,* 55–57 Newman St, London W1P 4AH, will advise you. Whether you select *Maupintour Associates, Havas, American Express, Cook's,* or a smaller organization is a matter of preference. They all have branch offices or correspondents in the larger European cities. There are good reasons why you should engage an agent.

Travel abroad today, although it is steadily becoming easier and more comfortable, is also growing more complex in its details. As the choice of things to do, places to visit, ways of getting there, increases, so does the problem of *knowing* about all these questions. A reputable, experienced travel agent is a specialist in details, and because of his importance to the success of your trip, you should inquire in your community as to which organization has the finest reputation.

If you wish your agent to book you on a package tour, reserve your transportation and even your first overnight hotel, his services should cost you nothing.

If, on the other hand, you wish him to plan for you an individual itinerary and make all arrangements down to hotel reservations and transfers to and from rail and air terminals, you are drawing upon his skill and knowledge of travel as well as asking him to shoulder a great mass of detail and correspondence. His commissions from carriers won't come close to covering his expenses, and thus he will make a service charge on the total cost of your planned itinerary. This charge may amount to 10 or 15% but it will more than likely *save* you money on balance. A good travel agent can help you avoid costly mistakes due to inexperience. He can help you take advantage of special reductions in rail fares and the like that you would not otherwise know about. Most important, he can save you *time* by making it unnecessary for you to waste precious days abroad trying to get tickets and reservations.

There are four principal ways of traveling: (1) The group tour, in which you travel with others, following a prearranged itinerary hitting all the high spots, and paying a single all-inclusive price that covers everything—transportation, meals, lodging, sightseeing tours, taxis, guides. And here your travel agent can book you with a special interest group, thus you needn't spend a high proportion of your tour trotting round museums if you would much rather be wandering round botanical gardens or pot-holing, and you will be among people with similar interests to yours. (2) The prearranged individual tour, following a set itinerary planned for you by the travel agent, with all costs paid in advance. (3) The individual tour where you work out the itinerary for yourself, according to your own interests, but have your agent make transportation and hotel reservations, transfers, sightseeing plans. (4) The freelance tour, in which you pay as you go, change your mind if you want to, and do your own planning. You'll still find a travel agent handy to make your initial transport reservation and book you for any special event where long advance booking is essential.

Short trips from the UK. One advantage of living in Great Britain, and being so close to the Continent, is that in winter and spring you can almost literally hop over to northern France for a long weekend (in summer, the ferries and airplanes are too crowded for such impulsive actions). Obviously, for a two- or three-day holiday, there is no point making the long Le Havre–Southampton sea crossing: better take the short, classical Dover–Calais or Folkestone–Boulogne routes. All the ferry companies—*Sealink, Townsend Thoresen, Normandy Ferries, Brittany Ferries,* etc.—have special weekend- to four-day deals (with four passengers the car goes free). So do the hovercraft services. Many British tourist agencies also specialize in inclusive three- to five-day budget trips to Paris: for instance, *Cook's, Cosmos, Havas, Time Off, Travelscene, Paris Travel Service* (who also arrange tailor-made holidays, etc.). Be careful, however, when you read the brochures, to see what actually is included.

A new system called *Service Loisirs Accueil* has been introduced to help people looking for accommodations or all-in holidays in France. About 20 *départements* are now in the scheme. They provide details of hotels, *gîtes,* vacation villages etc, plus package deals for riding holidays, craft lessons and what have you, and make the reservations for you. (Central office at BP 52, 75022 Paris Cedex 01.)

SPECIAL INTEREST TOURS. More and more, special interest tours are gaining in popularity, especially among younger travelers who feel that travel should be purposeful, and among others who plan to roam Europe often and with a more intimate view of life abroad. Travel agencies in the US, Britain and France offer a staggering variety of special interest tours ranging from the most luxurious château-gourmet trips in Rolls-Royces to rugged archeological work camps in little-known regions of France. Antiques, architecture, music, photography, pilgrimage, railways, river and canal barge travel, singles, and wine tasting are some of the categories that are particularly appropriate to France. In the field of architecture and gardening, for example, many private châteaux, manor houses and gardens are open to visitors in France.

Maupintour, for instance, specializes in unhurried tours of France, taking in the highlights of past and present French life and culture, plus gourmet dining. The 12-day trip provides a look at northwestern France, the Loire and Burgundy, while the 26-day comprehensive trip takes in about every principal historic and scenic spot in the country.

If you are looking for a special interest tour, begin by contacting your hometown travel agent. The French Government Tourist Office publishes, early in each year, an issue of its Travel Newsletter devoted to a consolidated list of tours offered by both US and French tour operators for the forthcoming season.

There are many agencies specialized in study-and-travel—or just travel—for students and young people (usually up to 21, although students may be older if they really are bonafide students) at extremely reasonable rates. Your high school or college, the local French club or Alliance Française are good places to begin investigating the possibilities. The airlines also have numerous charter groups for youngsters, and the Paris *International Herald Tribune* classified ads run notices about special flights, buses, jeep trips, even bicycle tours.

In Britain, schools and universities are active in arranging trips for youngsters, as are some of the travel agencies.

As for agencies specialized in special interest tours, you can count them by the dozens, so we can name only some of the best-known, such as: *Heritage Travel,* 22 Hans Pl., London SW1; *Club Méditerranée,* 62 South Moulton St, London W1Y 1HH; *Continental Waterways Ltd,* 127 Albert Bridge Rd, SW11 4QH; *Cosmos Tours,* 1 Bromley Common, Bromley, Kent; also, *American Express, Thomas Cook* and *Havas. Tower Travel's* Flexi-Plan tours make possible a wide variety of vacation arrangements at prices from budget up. Britain's *Twickenham Travel* has budget rail tours, and *Waymark* offers walking tours. *British Airways* has expanded its 'French Leave' program: now includes fly-drive, motoring, canal cruising holidays.

One slightly unusual way to see the country is by barge—hotel barge, to be exact. These floating hostelries meander through the canals and waterways of Burgundy, Champagne, Charentes, Brittany and Anjou from April to October, offering all the luxuries of a first-class tour—deluxe accommodations, hoity-toity food and drink, and the like. The barges leave on the average about once a week, and travel for anywhere from two to seven days. Cost depends on the barge and the length of its trip, but runs from $440 (for a weekend) up to $1,300 for a full week's float. For more information, talk to your travel agent, or write *Salt and Pepper Tours* (the U.S. booking agent for the barges) at 59 E. 54th St., New York, N.Y. 10022.

Tours starting from Britain are often much cheaper than those beginning in the US (we are talking about the tour itself here, not the transportation, which is obviously more expensive from North America). The British put less store on obvious luxury, and are willing to settle for very modest, not to say rugged, accommodation, in order to have more money for actual sightseeing. So, if you are counting your pennies, take a cheap charter flight across the Atlantic to London, and arrange your tour from there.

The *Touring Club de France,* which is the largest and most diversified association of its kind in France, has sections for camping, yachting, sports, mountain climbing, and all sorts of special interest activities.

Cookery courses. For those who would like to learn something of *haute cuisine,* or just family French cooking, you can include a short course at one of France's top schools during an ordinary vacation. A one-week course at *La Varenne* costs about $500, classes in English. You can also watch a demonstration by a master chef for 80 frs (or 850 frs for 12 demonstrations). If you're staying longer, courses at various levels (orientation, intermediate, advanced, graduate) are available. For instance, a 6-week course costs around $3000. *Rising Stars of Nouvelle Cuisine* course (1 week, $550) includes demonstrations by up-and-coming chefs of some of Paris's most interesting restaurants. Specialized classes include *charcuterie* and preserving, and an 'Escoffier' course devoted to classical cuisine. La Varenne Ecole de Cuisine, 34 rue St-Dominique, Paris 75007. The *Marie-Blanche de Broglie cooking* school has morning sessions costing 1200 frs for a series of six three-hour practical sessions including lunch, or 250 frs per session, and demonstrations costing 125 frs each. Classes in cheese and wine tasting and flower arranging have also been introduced. The school is closed in August and September; write Princess Marie-Blanche de Broglie, 18 av. de la Motte Picquet, Paris 75007.

Mme de Broglie also offers an exciting one-week package called *La Cuisine au Château,* which is available in August and the first half of September. Groups of eight are introduced to Norman cuisine, history and landscape, with classes (in English and French) at Mme de Broglie's family château near Rouen. Accommodations are in an 18th-century building. 1983 cost was 3000 francs a week. Write the above address for further details.

Art Classes. The *Académie de Port-Royal* (4 rue Mont-Louis, 75011 Paris, tel: 373–90–33) is the place to know about if you want to include painting and drawing sessions in an ordinary vacation. It is closed July, August and the first half of September, but the rest of the year the studios are open to people of any age and nationality, at all levels including beginners. Run by painters Claude Schurr and Jean-Maxime Relange, the school charges the lowest rates of all the private art academies in Paris but offers the added bonus of a friendly international atmosphere (Jean-Maxime Relange's wife, who helps to run the school, is English, so there are no language problems). Prices for the 1983/4 academic year: six half-day sessions cost 440 frs, 12 sessions 800, unlimited attendance for a month cost 1050 frs, or only 840 if you're under 25. Providing the school isn't fully booked, you can enrol any time except during the summer break.

ROUGHING IT. Of recent years, foreign visitors to France, especially youngsters, have been participating in increasing numbers in the cheapest and most rugged form of traveling. This means moving about the country on bicycles, in boats or on foot, carrying your luggage on your back, and sleeping under canvas or in youth hostels. If you elect to travel in bourgeois fashion by train or bus, you can often get reduced rates through the youth hostel organizations. France has about 300 youth hostels where hikers or cyclists (not motorists) may spend the night in fair comfort and get meals at comparably cheap rates, while camping sites offering facilities of varying degrees of convenience exist throughout the country.

The *Fédération Unie des Auberges de Jeunesse* (Youth Hostels Federation) is at 6 rue Mesnil, 75016 Paris; and the French branch of the *Federation of International Youth Travel Organizations* is at 20 rue J.-J. Rousseau, 75001 Paris.

A mixture of tents, hotels, cookouts, restaurants, sightseeing and informal bus travel is the formula of *Continental Coach Tours,* 139 Earls Court Rd, London SW5; or c/o University Travel Co., 129 Mount Auburn St, Cambridge, Massachusetts 02138. Thirty days around Western Europe for about $835, 22 days for about $650, plus airfare.

Trailer (caravan) travel and camping are popular: there are numerous trailer camps—but these are so crowded in July and August that we strongly urge you (and so do the police and tourist authorities) to avoid these months, especially on the Riviera. There is nothing to stop a trailer from pulling up at a camp site patronized chiefly by humble plodders, and if you really want peace and quiet, you can pull up at a farmhouse, and ask the farmer if he will rent you a corner of his field for an evening or two. Tent cities mushroom in summer. *The Cortell Group,* 3 East 54 St, New York, NY 10022 rents VW Joker, James Cook and Hymer campers in Frankfurt. All cross-Channel boats have special rates for caravans, except on weekends. Townsend-Thoresen, Sealink and Normandy Ferries rent out camping equipment and even caravans.

Ample information about this type of travel can be obtained from: *The American Youth Hostels, Inc.,* 1332 I St NW, Washington DC 20005; *Canadian Hostelling Assn,* 333 River Rd, Vanier City, Ottawa, Ont. K1L 8B9.

FACTS AT YOUR FINGERTIPS

In England the addresses are: *Camping Club of Great Britain and Ireland,* 11 Lower Grosvenor Pl., London, SW1; *Youth Hostels Association International Travel Bureau,* 14 Southampton St, London, WC2.

STUDENTS. One of the most economical ways of spending a holiday in France is to attend a summer course in the French language or French civilization. In addition to special summer sessions arranged at the university and the Alliance Française in Paris, there are any number of programs for foreign students at such pleasant locations as Nice (Centre International d'Etudes Françaises), Grenoble (Université de Grenoble), Nîmes (Ecole Antique de Nîmes), Boulogne-sur-Mer (Université de Lille), Cap d'Agde (Institut de Langues Cap d'Agde), Tours (Université d'Orléans-Tours and Institut de Touraine) and Montpellier (Université de Montpellier), to mention only a few. Tuition fees are modest, lodging can be arranged in private homes or simple *pensions,* and special reductions are granted on rail tickets. Write the *Office National des Universités et Ecoles Françaises,* 96 bld Raspail, 75006 Paris, for details. The cultural services of the French embassies or consulates in your country publish special booklets describing summer courses available.

In the United States, there are three main sources of information; *French Cultural Services,* 972 Fifth Ave, New York NY 10021; *Council on International Educational Exchange,* 205 East 42 St., New York, NY 10017; *Institute of International Education,* 809 United Nations Plaza, New York, NY 10017.

Two other organizations in the US are: *Franco-American Committee for Educational Travel and Study* (FACETS), 220 Park Ave. South, New York, NY 10003; and *French Federation of Alliances in the US,* 22 East 60 St, New York, NY 10022.

In France, sources of information, facilities, programs and help are: *Alliance Française,* 101 bld Raspail, 75014 Paris; *American Center for Students and Artists,* 261 bld Raspail, 75014 Paris; *Office National des Universités et Ecoles Françaises,* 96 bld Raspail, 75006 Paris.

Student package tours of Europe, gaining in popularity, are organized by several American companies, including *American Express, Educational Travel Assoc.,* c/o Columbia Tours Intl. Inc., 535 Fifth Ave., New York, NY 10017, *US Student Travel Service, Inc.,* 801 Second Ave, NY 10017, and *University Travel,* 129 Mt. Aubon St., Cambridge, Mass. 02138, who have tours that include sessions at various universities.

The Paris American Academy, 9 rue des Ursulines, 75005 Paris offers courses in French and English in various aspects of French civilization and culture, in the fine and performing arts, and in fashion and design.

WHAT TO TAKE. The first principle is to travel light, and fortunately for the present-day traveler this is really possible due to the manufacture of strong, lightweight luggage and drip-dry, crease-resistant fabrics for clothing. Airline baggage allowances are now based on size rather than weight.

FACTS AT YOUR FINGERTIPS

Economy class passengers between France and the United Kingdom may take free one piece of baggage provided that the sum of its dimensions—height plus length plus width—is not over 62 in. For first class the allowance is two pieces up to 62 in. each. In both classes you are also allowed one piece of hand baggage the total dimensions of which do not exceed 39 in. Any piece of baggage exceeding the maximum dimensions, or each piece in excess of the free allowance, is charged at 5% of the first-class one-way fare. From the US, most airlines allow you two pieces of baggage, but the sum of their dimensions must not exceed 62 inches and neither must weigh more than 62 pounds. You are allowed a third piece of hand baggage, but this must not be larger than 21 by 16 by 8 inches and again must not weigh more than 62 pounds. In any case, traveling light simplifies going through customs, makes registering and checking baggage unnecessary, and is a lifesaver if there are no porters available.

Porters are increasingly scarce in these days of European prosperity, and you will face delays every time you change trains (or hotels) or go through customs if you have a lot of baggage. Motorists need to be frugal, too. You should limit your luggage to what can be locked into the trunk or boot of your car when you make daytime stops.

Almost inevitably you will find yourself accumulating gifts, souvenirs, extra clothing, picture books, etc., on your travels. To avoid excess baggage charges it's a good idea to mail books back home.

Major purchases such as furniture, sets of china and the like have to be shipped specially, of course. Before you do this, however, consider the pros and cons carefully. Unless you deal with a thoroughly reliable and experienced store, you run the risk that the goods you ordered either won't be sent at all or else will be so poorly packed that they are damaged in transit. Assuming that you are dealing with a reputable firm, insist on finding out exactly what the shipping charges will amount to. In many cases, shipments such as these are handed over to customs brokers and freight forwarders in your country whose charges may be in addition to what you have already paid. Make sure, too, that your shipment is insured and the proper customs documents are attached.

Clothing. If you are wisely limiting yourself to one average-size suitcase it's obvious that your clothes must be carefully selected. The first considerations are the season of the year and the regions you plan to visit. Paris can be sizzling in summer and chilly in winter, although neither extreme will likely be as great as transatlantic visitors might be inclined to expect. Both men and women will feel less conspicuous if they avoid the sportier kind of clothing in Paris and other major cities (sneakers, bermuda shorts and flashy ties or jackets), though the young and slim can get by in the internationally worn jeans (and Paris-cut jeans have a chic that American and others do not). At Mediterranean and Atlantic beach resorts, especially along the Riviera, dress in summer is as casual as anywhere in the world—and more elegant.

Women. More basic is the problem of versatility, particularly for women, so you need to select outfits that can be combined in different ways.

Dresses made of materials that resist crushing are practical and easy to care for. Bare-shoulder models should have jackets for cool evenings or less formal occasions. Several cocktail dresses should be included if you move in dressy circles; otherwise you can get by with a dressier suit, a dress with jacket, or an elegant pants suit with appropriate blouse. A handsome jacket, sweater or lightweight woolen or jersey jacket is useful and comfortable. Unless you are planning to attend gala performances at the Paris Opéra or at Monte Carlo, you do not need formal evening dress: in fact, people are dressing less and less, even for theater and concerts. But if you're invited to a dinner party in a private home, the golden rule is: 'If in doubt, dress up rather than down.' French women take a great deal of trouble with their appearance and tend to dress up (except in very young or bohemian circles). As a result you won't feel silly even if you're dressier than most of the guests, but you will feel awkward if you're in casual clothes and no one else is. Long dresses and skirts are rarely worn in France, even for dances, so your best bet is a smart cocktail dress or a really pretty silk or chiffon blouse or shirt with a fairly dressy black skirt (knee-length or closer to midi depending on your taste).

Practical, low-heeled shoes may be less flattering than dainty pumps, but they're better suited to wet weather, cobbled streets and long hours on your feet. Don't on any count bring your best suede shoes, as they're bound to get spoiled, especially in Paris, where large areas of the sidewalks are made of a mixture of clay and gravel that turns into a sea of mud when it's been raining. A pair of soft slippers may be a lifesaver during long plane or train rides. You do need one pair of dressy (but not evening) shoes. A folding umbrella and good-looking raincoat that doubles as a coat are advisable.

Handbags can be another problem. While it's wiser to select a model big enough to hold your passport, travelers checks, sunglasses, tickets, cosmetics, and other necessities, something really outsized may seem like a millstone dangling from your shoulder after you've carried it day after day for weeks or months. More to the point is a handbag with enough interior pockets (at least one with a zipper closing for your money) to keep things in some kind of order. Something with a positive fastening is protection against pickpockets. Take along another smaller flat bag for daytime sightseeing (you can leave passport and money in hotel safe). Pack an evening bag unless you plan to buy one in Paris.

Men. Men's clothing problems are less complex. A dark business suit is adequate for most functions. A lightweight suit, a sportscoat, two or three pairs of slacks that can be mixed with the sportscoat, and a couple of sweaters will complete your outer wardrobe, except for a light overcoat/raincoat that you'll likely prefer to carry over your arm.

Wash-yourself shirts of dacron, orlon, etc., are marvelous conveniences when you're traveling light or making many one-night stops. The same considerations apply to socks, underwear and pyjamas. A lightweight dressing gown is useful for excursions to and from the bathtub. Handkerchiefs and neckties are good buys in France, so take the minimum and supplement your supplies with local purchases. Many men now carry shoulder bags—youngsters go in for folklore from Morocco, Greece and Afghanistan, but older men can buy a handsome leather bag in Paris.

FACTS AT YOUR FINGERTIPS

You will probably be visiting a lot of churches and cathedrals in France, and you may be refused admittance unless you dress respectably (no shorts, either for men or women). However, just for a visit, a jacket is not necessary, nor do women need to cover their heads, even in the provinces. Of course, if you are planning to attend services, dress as you would at home.

PASSPORTS. It is best to give obtaining a passport priority in your plans. **US residents** must apply in person to the US Passport Agency in Boston, Chicago, Detroit, Honolulu, Houston, Los Angeles, Miami, New Orleans, New York, Philadelphia, San Francisco, Seattle, Stamford (Conn.), or Washington, DC, or the local County Courthouse. In some areas selected post offices are also able to handle passport applications. If you have a passport issued within the past eight years you may use this to apply by mail. Otherwise, you will need 1) proof of citizenship, such as a birth certificate, 2) two identical photographs, in either black and white or color, on non-glossy paper and taken within the past six months; 3) $35 for the passport itself plus a $7 processing fee if you are applying in person (no processing fee when applying by mail) for those 18 years and older, or if you are under 18, $20 for the passport plus a $7 processing fee if you are applying in person (again, no extra fee when applying by mail); 4) proof of identity such as a driver's license, previous passport, any governmental ID card, or a copy of an income tax return. Adult passports are valid for 10 years, others for five years. When you receive your passport, write down its number, date and place of issue separately; if it is later lost or stolen, notify either the nearest American Consul or the Passport Office, Department of State, Washington D.C. 20524, as well as the local police.

If a resident-alien, you need a Treasury Sailing Permit Form 1040C, certifying that all federal taxes have been paid. You will have to present a blue or green alien registration card (Form I-151), passport, travel tickets, most recently filed Form 1040, W2 forms for the most recent full year, most recent payroll stubs—and maybe more, so check. To return to the United States, you need a re-entry permit only if you are planning to stay outside the US more than one year. Apply for it at least six weeks before departure in person at the nearest office of the Immigration and Naturalization Service, or by mail to the Immigration and Naturalization Service, Washington, DC. Or, six weeks before leaving, inquire whether an Alien Registration Card (green card) would suffice in your case.

British subjects. Application forms are obtainable from your travel agency or from the main post office in your town. The application should be sent to the Passport Office in your area (as indicated on the guidance form) or taken personally to your nearest main post office. Apply at least five weeks before the passport is required. The regional passport offices are located in London, Liverpool, Peterborough, Glasgow and Newport (Gwent). The application must be countersigned by your bank manager, or by a solicitor, barrister, doctor, clergyman or Justice of the Peace who knows you personally. You will need two photos. Fee is £11 for the standard 30-page 10-year validity passport.

National Travel Club

Over 75 Years of Service To Our members

Membership brings you 14 money-saving benefits and services INCLUDING a subscription to TRAVEL-HOLIDAY magazine AND $35,000 travel accident insurance coverage ($50,000 IMMEDIATELY with an initial 2-year membership) for ALL your travels ANY-WHERE in the world and for the ENTIRE TERM of your membership. You enroll JUST ONCE (at incredibly low annual dues) — No monthly payments to make or bother about.

NO OTHER TRAVEL CLUB GIVES YOU SO MUCH FOR SO LITTLE

Over a HALF MILLION members consider these benefits indispensable:

- $35,000 Travel Accident Insurance ($50,000 on renewal; Immediately with initial 2-year membership
- Subscription to TRAVEL-HOLIDAY magazine
- Travel Information Service
- Book Discounts (25% savings)
- Routing Service
- Travel Digest Evaluation Program
- Avis & National Car Rental Discounts
- Mediguide Service
- Discount travel film Library
- Mail Forwarding Service
- Discount Pharmaceutical Service
- Discount Film Processing
- Car/Puter-Discount Auto Pricing & Buying Service
- Membership Card & Club Emblems

*Accident insurance provided by
Nationwide Insurance Company, Columbus, Ohio.*

YOU ARE CORDIALLY INVITED TO JOIN!

LLOYD BRIDGES *(Popular Actor)*
"I'm a traveling man...on business or for pleasure...the information offered makes life not only easier, but lots more fun."

DOROTHY KIRSTEN *(Metropolitan Opera Soprano)*
"TRAVEL/HOLIDAY has become a great favorite in my home."

YEHUDI MENUHIN *(Renowned Concert Violinist)*
"I recommend TRAVEL/HOLIDAY for the best information, clearly, concisely and directly to the point."

Taken separately, NTC services would total up to many times the modest dues...if you could get them elsewhere. But these unique privileges are not obtainable apart from the Club! You can't get travel service like this at such incredibly low dues anywhere else on earth. And whether you're traveling on a shoestring or plan a big vacation NTC experts promise you the best vacation ever!

National Travel Club

Travel Building, Floral Park, N.Y. 11001

Please enroll me as a member for the term indicated:
- ☐ 1 Year (**$35,000** travel accident insurance) $12.00
- ☐ 2 Years (**$50,000** travel accident insurance) $23.00
- ☐ **I enclose remittance**

Charge to my ☐ Mastercard ☐ Visa
☐ Diner's ☐ American Express

Acct. # _____ Exp. Date _____

Name _____
(Signature if charging)

Address _____

City _____ State _____ Zip _____

FG-2A

FACTS AT YOUR FINGERTIPS

British visitor's passport. This simplified form of passport has advantages for the once-in-a-while tourist to France and most European countries. Valid for one year and not renewable, it costs £5.50. Application must be made in person at a post office and two passport photographs are required.

Canadian citizens entering France must have a valid passport, application forms for which may be obtained at any post office; send to regional passport offices or to the Passport Office, Dept. of External Affairs, Ottawa, Ont. A $20 fee and two photographs are required.

VISAS. Not required for nationals of the United States, Canada, United Kingdom and most countries of the British Commonwealth for a stay of less than three months. If that period is about to expire and you wish to stay longer, go to the Préfecture de Police, and apply for a *carte de séjour*. The préfecture in Paris is located on the Ile de la Cité, near Notre-Dame. Ask at tourist offices for the address of the Préfecture in other parts of the country.

HEALTH CERTIFICATES. Not required for entry into France. Neither the US nor Canada requires a certificate of smallpox vaccination on re-entry, unless coming from an area where infection was recently reported, but in our opinion, you'd be wise to have it. The simplest way is to be vaccinated before you leave. Have your doctor fill in the standard form which comes with your passport, or obtain one from a steamship company, airline or travel agent. Take the form with you to present on re-entering. It is also wise for any visitor to Mediterranean areas to have anti-typhoid, cholera and polio jabs.

PET AND ANIMAL LICENSES. Check with your travel agent on the current requirements, but *best leave your pet at home.* Rabies is now gaining ground in France and some other European countries. Restrictions are rigid on taking animals from one country to another, and contravention means heavy fines, or prison, and sometimes destruction of the animal.

MEDICAL SERVICES. The *IAMAT* (International Association for Medical Assistance to Travelers) offers you a list of approved English-speaking doctors who have had postgraduate training in the US, Canada or Gt. Britain. Membership is free; the scheme is worldwide with many European countries participating. An office call costs $25, a hotel call is $30, a night or holiday call is $35. For information and a directory of physicians and hospitals apply in the US to 736 Center St., Lewiston, NY 14092; in Canada, 123 Edward St, Toronto M5G 1E2. In France, *IAMAT* has 29 member hospitals and clinics. A similar service is offered by *Intermedic,* 777 Third Ave, New York, NY 10017. *Intermedic* charges an initial membership fee of $6 per person or $10 per family, its subsequent fare schedule is somewhat higher than *IAMAT*'s. It is also less well represented in France than *IAMAT*.

Europ Assistance Ltd offers unlimited help to its members. There are two plans: one for travelers using tours or making their own trip arrangements, the

FACTS AT YOUR FINGERTIPS

second for motorists taking their cars abroad. Multilingual personnel staff a 24-hour, seven days a week telephone service which brings the aid of a network of medical and other advisors to assist in any emergency. Special medical insurance is part of the plan. Up to 12 days personal coverage for £7.15; with vehicle £19.35. Write to Europ Assistance Ltd, 252 High St, Croydon, Surrey CR0 1NF, for details. *Note:* only available to residents of the UK.

Free medical care (or reduced cost treatment) for *British* residents who are employed (*not* those who are unemployed or self-employed) is available in France: obtain from your local office of the Department of Health and Social Security, Form CMI, at least one month before leaving Britain. Fill this in and return it, when you will get Form E111 to take with you. In France, you pay doctors on the spot and reclaim between 10 and 90% of the cost by taking Form E111 to the local Caisse Primaire de Sécurité Sociale (address from the town hall or tourist office or telephone book). Names of English-speaking doctors available from tourist offices.

How to reach France

FROM NORTH AMERICA

BY AIR. In spite of many cutbacks caused by ever-increasing oil prices, there are still plenty of flights between Paris and North America. Flying time from the east coast is just 6½ hrs in a subsonic jumbo jet; 3¾ hrs by supersonic *Concorde*.

Important Note: Roissy/Charles de Gaulle airport now has two terminals, called Roissy 1 and Roissy 2 (or CDG 1 and 2). Terminal 2 is used by Air France for its CDG flights, plus those of Air Inter. Some Orly flights by other airlines have now switched to Roissy/CDG 1. *Check your ticket carefully to make sure that you go to the right airport and terminal.*

From New York. *Air France*, one of the world's largest airlines, has twice-daily Boeing 747s, some into the ultra-modern airport north of Paris, Roissy/Charles de Gaulle (terminal 2), and with daily Concorde services to Roissy/CDG as well. Both *Pan Am* and *TWA* have direct flights from New York to Roissy/CDG; a number of other carriers including *El Al* and *Pakistan International* operate into Orly.

From Boston. *TWA* maintains a daily wide-body TriStar to Paris (Roissy/CDG 1).

From Chicago. *TWA* and *Air France* both fly daily to Paris.

From Los Angeles. *Air France* currently have an 'over the pole' service into Roissy/CDG daily.

From Washington. *TWA* has a daily service.

From Miami. *Pan Am* and *Aeromexico* fly DC-10s to the French capital several times weekly.

From Montreal and Toronto. *Air France* and *Air Canada* have daily services.

20 FACTS AT YOUR FINGERTIPS

For *Air France* and all transatlantic airlines the free baggage allowance is now based on *size* rather than weight: in first class, two pieces up to 62 in. overall measure, each piece; in economy class, two pieces, neither one over 62 in., both together no more than 106 in. Underseat baggage up to 45 in.

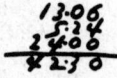

AIR FARES. There are only two classes, first and economy, on the regularly scheduled transatlantic route, but many different price levels, depending on how and when you fly. Although fares and accommodations are regulated by the International Air Transport Association, and are subject to change, it is safe to say that almost nobody (except business travelers) pays the listed IATA rates, because of the numerous reduced-fare offers. Your travel agent can advise you on the most economical rates and times to travel, as well as help to unravel and explain the complex and frequently mystifying world of charter and excursion fares and the many other fare possibilities.

As an indication, here are some approximate return air fares from New York: First class, $4,100; Business class, $1,350; APEX, $635–$800. All under constant change so do check with your travel agent.

The whole transatlantic fare structure was being completely reviewed as we went to press, and several new ideas regarding cheaper rate fares are likely to emerge. Details of these for 1984 were not available in time to incorporate in this text, but they will be based on three "levels"—first, full-fare economy (ie. a business class of some kind) and cut-price economy. In the last one advance booking will be essential and there will be no stop-overs or changes in plans without financial penalties. We estimate that such a ticket at high season for the round trip—New York to Paris—will be about $635 to $800. But please note these are estimates and you should keep in touch with your travel agent to find out what the exact position is when you wish to travel.

Since there are some 20,000 charter flights a year from the United States alone, we shall spare you the details. They are well covered in a specialized publication, Jens Jurgen's *How to Fly for Less, a Consumers' Guide to Low Cost Air Charters and Other Travel Bargains,* published annually by *Travel Information Bureau,* 44 County Line Road, Farmingdale, NY 11735.

Then these is the whole area of package tours, in which you get generally a very advantageous airfare, which is frequently some kind of charter, plus some degree of land arrangements. Hundreds of these are offered each year, and the best you can do here is consult a good travel agent.

Children between the ages of 2 and 12 travel at half the adult tariff, but are entitled to a full luggage allowance. Infants under 2 not occupying a seat and accompanied by an adult are charged 10% of the full fare. Although they are not entitled to a free luggage allowance, their food, clothing and other supplies needed in flight are not weighed. Most airliners provide special bassinets if notified in advance. Students and military personnel are entitled to certain additional reductions at specified seasons of the year.

FACTS AT YOUR FINGERTIPS

Airline tickets can be bought on the instalment plan. A down payment of as little as 10% secures the reservations, and the balance can be paid off, after your trip, during the next 12 months.

Bonus stopovers to France. If you are going to the French Riviera, you can stopover *en route* at Milan or Lisbon, London or Dublin. These and many other European points may be visited without any extra charge when you purchase a regular first-class or economy ticket from New York to Nice. No stopovers are permitted on the various APEX or regular excursion tickets, or the affinity groups; but limited stopovers are allowed on other types of tickets.

When you buy a ticket to Nice, you are entitled to 7,810 km (4,854 miles) transportation in each direction. This allows you to add many cities which lie off the direct route and saves you paying for separate side trips. Here are some sample stopover combinations: New York, Glasgow, Edinburgh, London, Nice; New York, Amsterdam, Brussels, Paris, Nice; New York, Milan, Nice; New York, London, Brussels, Cologne, Frankfurt, Stuttgart, Zürich, Milan, Nice.

Instead of traveling via London, after leaving Glasgow, you can be routed direct to Hamburg. Let's examine some sample routings. One itinerary takes you to Bremen, Hanover, Frankfurt, Stuttgart, Zürich and Milan before arrival in Nice, while the other includes Bremen, Düsseldorf or Cologne and Geneva *en route* to the Riviera.

Through-plane service is offered from New York to Nice not only via Paris but also by way of Lisbon and Barcelona.

Leaving New York, you can fly first to Lisbon. Then follows a short trip to Madrid. Barcelona, gateway to the Costa Brava, is a popular port of call as is Palma de Mallorca. Both towns may be visited *en route* from Madrid to Nice. Geneva also can be included in itineraries entering through Lisbon. It is an approved stopover between Madrid or Barcelona and Nice.

The wide range of routings makes circle trips based on Nice a very attractive proposition. You may visit Britain, the Netherlands and Germany, for instance, on your outward trip and return by way of Switzerland, Spain and Portugal.

BY SEA. Sad to say, the days of the leisurely Atlantic crossing are long since gone, and Cunard's *QE2* is the only luxury vessel making regular crossings to Southampton (England) and Cherbourg (France). Write 555 Fifth Ave, New York, NY 10017.

However, there are also a number of smaller lines that have fairly regular trips, though none from the US. *Polish Ocean Lines* and the *Baltic Shipping Co.* both have sailings from Montreal to London and on to other destinations in Europe, though not France. Both have modern, airconditioned and stabilized ships. Contact both of these c/o March Shipping Passenger Services, One, World Trade Center, Suite 5257, New York, NY 10048. At the same address is the *Gdynia America Line*, which offers limited passenger accommodations on some 210 freighters going all over the world.

Recently, however, some cruise lines have begun to feature transatlantic crossings after they've completed their winter and spring Caribbean services.

EUROPE AND
DON'T MISS

Now you can sail the legendary QE2 to or from Europe—and fly the other way, free! That means you can begin or end your European vacation with five glorious days and nights on the last of the great superliners. And get a free British Airways flight between London and most major U.S. cities. (Specially reserved flights of the Concorde are open to QE2 passengers at incredible savings.)

Only the QE2 offers four top restaurants and five lively nightspots. A glittering disco, a glamorous casino, and a 20,000-bottle wine cellar. The famed "Golden Door" spa, with saunas and Jacuzzi® Whirlpool Baths. And your choice of yoga, aerobic dance, jogging, swimming, hydrocalisthenics and massage.

- Regular crossings between England and New York, some also calling at other U.S. ports. Sail roundtrip at big savings.
- Cunard's choice European tours—varying in length, attractively priced, either escorted or independent—all include a QE2 crossing.
- Big discounts at all of Cunard's London hotels—including the incomparable Ritz.
- Enchanting QE2 European cruises, which may be combined with a crossing.

For all the facts, including any requirements and restrictions, contact your travel agent or Cunard, P.O. Box 999, Farmingdale, NY 11737; (212) 661-7777.

CUNARD

Certain restrictions apply to free airfare and Concorde programs. See your travel agent.

The QE2:
The Magic.

British Registry

Queen Elizabeth 2
Getting There Is Half The Fun.

For example, Norwegian America Line does the same for its *Sagafjord* or *Vistafjord* (whichever ship is in Caribbean service; they alternate). The sailings, also in late spring are from both Fort Lauderdale (Port Everglades), Florida and New York. Check with the lines for schedules, fares and details of transatlantic crossings. Write to: *Paquet French Cruises, Inc.,* 1370 Ave of the Americas, New York, NY 10019; *Norwegian America Line,* 29 Broadway, New York, NY 10006.

Fares. There is a very wide range of fares for crossing the Atlantic by sea. These range from around $850 to a staggering $16,500 for the best deluxe cabins. But there are often bargain rates for off-peak sailings and also sail-one-way, fly-the-other. Children between 2 and 12 inclusive go half fare.

Transatlantic passengers who embark or disembark at a French port pay a port tax of around 30 frs in addition to the tourist or first-class fares.

FROM BRITAIN

BY AIR. From London (Heathrow) to Paris (Roissy/Charles de Gaulle) there is a virtual air bridge—the closest thing to an international shuttle service—operated jointly by *Air France* and *British Airways* on an hourly basis.

Important: see note in our FROM NORTH AMERICA section about new Roissy/CDG terminal. At our presstime Air France was using Roissy/CDG 2 for London flights, British Airways was using Roissy/CDG 1, but check before departure in case the position has changed. It is always wise to book well in advance. Almost all flights are operated by wide-body aircraft; TriStars in the case of *BA,* Airbuses by *Air France.* Flying time is just under an hour.

Other airlines with a service between London and Paris in 1983 were: Air India, Aerolineas Argentinas, Gulf Air, Japan Airlines, Singapore Airlines.

Air France also flies from Manchester to Paris and from London to Nice, Bordeaux, Toulouse, Lyon, Marseille, Strasbourg, Lille and Nantes. *British Airways* links London with the French cities of Nice, Bordeaux, Biarritz, Marseille and Lyon. *British Caledonian* has several daily flights from London's Gatwick airport to Paris (Roissy/Charles de Gaulle 1). Other flights from London Gatwick to France include *Dan Air* to Strasbourg, Clermont-Ferrand, Montpellier, Dijon, Perpignan and a *Skyways* coach-air service from London to Paris via Lydd and Beauvais. *TAT* (Touraine Air Transport) flies from Gatwick to Rouen, Béziers, and Le Havre; *Brymon Airways* operating from Plymouth and other points in the southwest fly to Paris; *Aurigny Air Services* in the Channel Islands go to Cherbourg; and *Jersey European Airways* fly from Jersey/Guernsey to Paris, Lille and Dinard. *Britair* has small planes flying between London Gatwick and Caen, Le Havre, Morlaix and Quimper.

Fares. *British Caledonian, Air France* and *British Airways* have a basic two fare price structure with variations within the lower rates. From London to Paris the *Club Class,* which is roughly the same as the old first class and currently costs £180 return; and *Economy Class,* where the seats are closer together and there is no drink or newspaper service. Ordinary fare is £110 return. These have restrictions according to the rate, but it is well worthwhile checking on what the current rates and offers are before making your booking. British Caledonian fares are around the same, but conditions are not identical to the BA/Air France services. Best consult with your travel agent.

BY TRAIN AND BOAT TO PARIS. Services from London (Victoria station) vary according to the season, with the greatest frequency in July, August and early September, when there are eight trains (two overnight) daily connecting the two capitals. The fastest year-round service is the 9.58 A.M. (earlier on weekends) from London, via Folkestone–Calais (1¾ hrs), arriving at Paris Gare du Nord at 6.20 P.M. Or the afternoon service departing at 1.58 P.M., reaching Paris about 10.30 P.M. Another route is London–Newhaven–Dieppe (4-hr crossing)–Paris Gare St-Lazare. First- and second-class cars on all these.

Fares vary widely according to service. First class (one class only on ferry) is about £72 one way, second class is around £45 to £50; there are also special returns in second class, though there are many variations, which range from around £40 to £60.

To the Riviera. From London the best route is via Folkestone–Calais and then on the *Flandre–Riviera Express* via Paris. It has through sleeping cars and through couchette cars (first and second class in both cases) from Calais and/or Lille to Ventimiglia calling at all Riviera resorts. You can leave London early afternoon and reach Nice, for example, by mid-morning the following day. Also via Paris, but changing trains (and stations) and using the couchette and sleeping-car train; with this you leave London mid-morning and reach Nice around 8 A.M. next day. The train carries first and second class sleepers and second class couchettes and there is a refreshment service between Paris and Dijon and vice versa. There is also *L'Esterel* which leaves Paris about 10.15 P.M. and offers a similar service, arriving in Nice around 9 A.M.

BY CAR AND BOAT TO PARIS. There are many ferry routes across the Channel which have drive-on/off facilities for cars and also carry non-motorists. All have daily services each way the year round. Many run several times daily over the short Channel crossing, but with greatly reduced winter service (Nov.–Apr.). *Sealink* operates from Dover and Folkestone to Boulogne, Calais and Dunkirk, from Newhaven to Dieppe and from Weymouth to Cherbourg. *Townsend Thoresen* also operates Dover–Calais and *P&O Ferries* to Boulogne. Standard one-way rate on these crossings for two passengers in a 14-ft car averages around £58. *Sealink* from Newhaven costs £72. *Townsend Thoresen* also plies from Southampton and Portsmouth to Le Havre/Cherbourg, and

P&O Ferries to Le Havre. Comparable fares average £63–£77. The new *Sally Viking Line* operates between Ramsgate and Dunkirk; the cost is £46.

There are daily services from Plymouth/Portsmouth to Roscoff/St Malo in Brittany, a 6–7 hr crossing. Both fares are £91; cabins are an extra £22. Both run by *Brittany Ferries*.

All of the ferries, which each year get bigger and more comfortable, offer sleeping accommodation during their night crossings—either cabins with berths and wash-basins, or reclining seats. However, on a crowded trip, there are not enough to cater for everybody, except in *P&O* ships, hence the uneasy slumbering figures in the public rooms. Moral: if you don't want to have a grim night, book your accommodation early, particularly during the height of the summer season. Facilities include restaurant, cafeteria, bar (where there is dancing at times), duty-free boutiques, television, nursery, ship-to-shore phones, money-changing offices. Be prepared, however, in season, to queue for everything, and beware of the closing hours of the boutiques: some are open only a short time; some are just a rip-off anyway.

All these companies also have special package rates for short vacations. They also rent out tow-caravans and camping equipment from their depots at Dover or Southampton.

For complete tariffs, inquire of the AA, RAC, AAA London office, or direct to: *Sealink Car Ferry Centre,* PO Box 303, 52 Grosvenor Gdns, London SW1; *Townsend/Thoresen Car Ferries,* 127 Regent St, London W1; *P&O Ferries,* Beaufort House, St Botolph St, London EC3; and Eastern Docks, Dover (London tel. no. for inquiries and reservations: 623 1505); *Brittany Ferries,* 2 Endell St, London WC2 (tel. 01-836 5885). *Sally Viking Line,* 81 Piccadilly, London W1 (tel. 01-409 0536).

BY HOVERCRAFT. *Hoverspeed* (operated by British Rail and the SNCF) takes 400 passengers and 65 cars. Crossing time is about 35 mins (more in rough weather). Frequent flights throughout the year: fewest is four flights per day in Jan. and Feb., most frequent is 16 per day in Aug. (17 on Fri. and Sat.). All flights leave from Dover, with some landing in Calais, others in Boulogne. Around five departures every day (only four in January and February) connect with trains at either end for passengers without cars; all these land in Boulogne. If you're taking your car you check in at the hoverports 45 mins before departure time at the latest. Otherwise if you're coming from London the special train from Charing Cross takes you to Dover Priory station, from where a free bus gets you to the check-in building at the hoverport; from elsewhere, check in 45 mins before departure. On the other side of the Channel, the train for Paris leaves from immediately outside the hoverport building. Fares are a little higher than for the ferries, again with special excursion fares.

Hoverspeed information—Sealink Center, 52 Grosvenor Gdns., London SW1.

Motoring package tours. For the first-timer, this mode of traveling is useful. It may not be the cheapest way to travel, but it avoids the chance of making horrible mistakes, saves time, and eases the path. Various agencies sell prepared

FACTS AT YOUR FINGERTIPS

packages: AA's *Argosy, Canvas Holidays, Cook's. Car Holidays Abroad* will prepare a custom-built trip for you.

FROM THE CONTINENT

BY AIR. Getting to France from other major European countries is simple, as every airline flies to Paris, and many operate into Nice. *Air France* has the most services, obviously, with the national airlines of the country of departure next most convenient. There are also a number of flights from other countries into Lyon, Marseille and Lourdes. Otherwise, provincial cities can be reached through Paris, though this can mean a change of airport—from Roissy/Charles de Gaulle to Orly—or a change from terminal 1 to terminal 2 at Roissy; and changing planes.

BY TRAIN. Paris is the destination of many of Europe's best trains, and is well served by the TEE (Trans Europ Express) and various other international networks. With the completion of the High Speed Train (TGV) network in 1983, you can now travel to Paris from Geneva in under 3¾ hours. Here is a selection of leading trains and routes:

Trans-Europ Express Services. *Ile de France* and *Etoile du Nord.* Amsterdam – Hague – Rotterdam – Antwerp – Brussels – Paris. Daily, about 5 hrs.

Rubens, Oiseau Bleu, Brabant, Memling. Brussels–Paris. Daily, about 2½ hrs.

Cisalpin. Milan – Lausanne – Dijon – Paris. Daily, about 8½ hrs. Operates from/to Venice summer only.

Other express services. *Nord.* Copenhagen–Hamburg–Cologne–Liège–Paris. Overnight, about 16 hrs.

Barcelona Talgo. Barcelona–Gerona–Perpignan–Paris–Austerlitz. Overnight service only. Daily, 12½ hrs.

Arlberg Express. Vienna–Innsbruck–Zurich–Basle–Paris. Daily, about 22 hours.

Madrid Talgo. Madrid–Paris–Austerlitz non-stop overnight. Daily 13 hrs.

Palatino. Overnight fast service Rome–Paris, sleeping cars all the way, dining car attached for dinner and breakfast.

BY CAR. Europe's excellent highways leading into France are too numerous to describe here, but the best routes into Paris are the A1 *autoroute* from Lille (for traffic from the Low Countries and northern Germany), or from Dunkerque or St. Omer (from Britain); A4 from Metz and A34 from Strasbourg (from central Germany); A6 from Beaune (A41 from Geneva); A6/A7 from the Riviera and Italy. Also A13 from Le Havre or Dieppe (from Britain).

Arriving in France

CUSTOMS. Visitors over 15 coming directly from **America** or other non-European countries may bring in 400 cigarettes, 100 cigars or 500g of pipe tobacco. Visitors arriving from a **Common Market (EEC) country** (including the United Kingdom) by air or sea may bring in 300 cigarettes, 75 cigars or 400g of pipe tobacco. Visitors arriving from **other European (non-EEC) countries** are allowed only 200 cigarettes, 50 cigars, or 250g of pipe tobacco. Your tobacco allowance must be in your hand baggage to escape payment of duty.

Passengers arriving from **non-EEC countries** are allowed 2 liters of wine *plus* 1 liter of spirits over 22° *or* 2 liters of spirits up to 22°. For those entering from **EEC countries** it's 3 liters of wine *plus* 1½ liters of spirits over 22° *or* 3 liters up to 22°.

You're also allowed 50g of perfume and ¼ liter of toilet water if you're coming from **outside the EEC**; 75g and ⅜ liter if you're coming from **an EEC country**.

You may bring in two cameras of different makes if they're not new, ten rolls of film or 24 plates (black or color) for each, an amateur motion picture camera and ten reels of film (black or color). The duty on additional film is 41% for rolls and 47% for reels.

In general, everything obviously for personal use, not for re-sale, comes in duty free. Aside from hunting guns (two, plus 100 cartridges per gun), firearms and ammunition cannot be brought in at all. No restrictions on the entry of pets, provided you have certificates of health and anti-rabies vaccination.

MONEY. The current basic exchange rate as we go to press is around 7.30 francs to the US dollar, around 6 to the Canadian dollar, and about 11.30 francs to the pound sterling. But exchange rates change so frequently these days that you must *check near the time of your trip*. Visitors to France are allowed to take out 5,000 French francs and other currency to the value of 5,000 francs without any formalities. You can take out more foreign currency than this if you fill in a form called 'Declaration of the Entry of Foreign Bank-notes into France' and have it signed and certified by the customs office when you arrive in France. There are currently no take-out restrictions on travelers checks or letters of credit obtained outside France.

Travelers checks are the best way to safeguard travel funds, but remember that hotels charge a high rate for cashing them: best to go to a bank. They are sold by various banks and companies in terms of American and Canadian dollars and pounds sterling. *American Express* and *Cook's* and major British banks will supply checks in French currency, on which you will get face value in France, even if the dollar or pound has slipped since you bought them. Checks issued by *Bank of America* are widely used. In the US only checks issued by

FACTS AT YOUR FINGERTIPS

Barclay's and *Perera* are entirely free of charge; all others require a commission, usually 1%. For a list of branches, write to *Barclay's Bank of New York,* Traveler's Cheques Division, 120 Broadway, New York, NY 10006.

Best known and easily exchanged British travelers checks are those issued by *Thos. Cook & Son* and these banks: *Barclay's, National Westminster, Lloyd's* and *Midland.*

Credit Cards. Holders of American Express credit cards can cash up to $1,000 at one time (some in currency, the rest in travelers checks of your choice) upon presentation of their Amexco card, a personal check and passport. This transaction can be repeated in three weeks. British travelers can cash checks abroad for up to £100 per day on production of a Eurocheque Enchashment Card. Nearly all European banks will accept these cards. However, hotels and restaurants in France will rarely accept a credit card, though car hire companies normally will.

HOW TO GET TO TOWN FROM THE AIRPORT. From Roissy (Charles de Gaulle) airport, Paris, buses leave every 15 mins between 5.30 A.M. and 11 P.M. for the Centre International de Paris, Porte Maillot; from Orly to Les Invalides city air terminal. Special buses are put on for flights arriving during the night. Fare from Roissy and Orly, around 30 frs. The regular 351 bus will take you from Roissy to either the Nation or Vincennes metro stops. Regular buses 215 and 183A will take you from Orly to Denfert Rochereau and Porte de Choisy respectively (both in southern Paris). There are bus shuttle services between the two airports, but beware the rush-hours and weekend departures, particularly to Roissy.

If you don't have too much baggage you can avoid rush-hour traffic by making use of the Orly Rail and Roissy Rail train services, which are now conveniently slotted in to the express metro (RER) system and will take you to many points in central Paris. Each involves a short bus trip (free) between airport and station.

A taxi from one of the airports to a central spot in Paris will cost about 120–160 frs including tip.

Lyon Satolas international airport has regular buses to the city center. From Nice airport, there are bus services to the center and to Cannes and other spots on the Riviera. At the smaller airports you'll have to ask for a taxi to be called to get you to the town center or your hotel.

Staying in France

HOTELS. France has many comfortable hotels in all price categories. They are required by law to post the price of each room on its wall and cannot legally charge more than that rate, which is fixed by the government. This is not true of deluxe hotels, where prices are not subject to government control. In a few hotels, the posted prices do not include the service charge or taxes, which together can increase your hotel bill about 25%. The letters TTC, which you will see in many places, mean *toutes taxes comprises* (ie. inclusive of all forms of tax).

Rates for Paris hotels are given in the 'Getting settled in Paris' chapter. Outside Paris, rates are lower, except of course in top resort spots such as Nice, Cannes and Biarritz. In most provincial towns or average vacation localities, you can usually find a good hotel where a double room with bath, dinner and breakfast will cost 200–250 frs per person. Many hotels offer special rates for stays of three days and longer, as well as off-season weekend and weekly all-inclusive rates that may be 30% off high-season rates. Special family rates are offered by many seaside and inland resorts. Half-board *(demi-pension)* and full-board *(pension)* rates are always advantageous, but this obviously deprives you of the delights of trying out local restaurants.

A useful service called *SOS Hotels France* offers a central reservations service covering the whole of France. Main office is in Paris, at 51 rue Notre-Dame de Lorette, 9e (tel. 526–08–07; telex 650697), with additional offices at rail stations in Avignon, Montpellier and Tours (open daily, including Sundays and public holidays), in Strasbourg and Toulouse; and on the following motorways: A4 (Rheims), A6 (Nemours) and A7 (Mornas and Sorgues). You can pay for the first night when you reserve, using a Visa credit card if you wish to, and are therefore sure of finding a bed even if you reach your destination late.

Hotel chains. Reliable, fairly reasonable hotel chains to be found in France, often resembling American motels, include *Frantel* (the best and most expensive), *Sofitel, Novotel, Holiday Inns, Arcade, Ibis* and *Mercure*, the cheapest. They are often sited at airports, or at strategic motor route crossways outside cities, though increasingly you will find them in town centers. *France-Accueil* hotels are a friendly 1- and 2-star chain that now covers the whole of France.

Relais et Châteaux. This is a chain of châteaux, inns and country manors covering the whole of France with an emphasis on regional character. Each hotel thus has a distinct atmosphere of its own, which makes for a very pleasant stay, where the accent is on relaxation, peaceful surroundings and fine cuisine. Hotels range from the luxurious (including the Ritz in Paris and the fabulous Oustau de Baumanière in Provence) to far more modest establishments. A booklet listing all member establishments is obtainable from *Relais et Châteaux* at their new office in the Hôtel Crillon, 10 pl. de la Concorde, 75008 Paris; it is published in nine languages. For many of these delightful hotels you need a car, and some of them are so secluded that you may have trouble finding them, so ask for clear instructions before setting out.

Château-Accueil. An association of privately owned châteaux offering rooms inside the château itself or in other buildings within the grounds, (sometimes a whole cottage). The accent is on friendly hospitality and an introduction to local architecture, culture and gastronomy. Brochure and information from Mme la Vicomtesse de Bonneval, Château de Thaumiers, Thaumiers, 18210 Charenton-du-Cher.

FACTS AT YOUR FINGERTIPS

Relais du Silence. A chain of peaceful hotels, mostly in the country, somewhat similar to the Relais et Châteaux, but far less expensive. You can make reservations from one member of the chain to another. Write: Hôtel des Oiseaux, 38640 Claix, France, for free booklet.

Pensions. In these, you pay for your room and all or some of your meals in one package, according to the arrangements you make, and if you do not turn up to eat all of them, the loss is yours, not the *pension* keeper's. Information from the *French National Tourist Office* at 127 av. des Champs-Elysées, 75008 Paris, where you can get a list of *pensions* in Paris with prices and minimum-stay requirements, or at the *Office du Tourisme Universitaire et Scolaire,* 137 bld St-Michel, 75005 Paris. The latter specializes in serving students and teachers, who can inquire there about special reduced-rate lodging and eating facilities.

Residence-hotels. Currently mostly in Languedoc-Roussillon, these are a cross between a hotel and a furnished apartment or villa (called in French *hôtel-résidence de tourisme* or *résidence hôtelière*). Each room, or pair of rooms, has kitchenette, though self-service restaurant is also available. Minimum stay is normally one week.

Logis de France and Auberges de France. Well over 3000 small and medium-sized family-run hotels belong to the excellent *Logis de France* association. Most of them are in small towns or in the countryside and they normally have one- or two-star grading. They must conform to conditions laid down by the Logis de France 'Quality Charter', which puts the accent on comfortable bedrooms, well-prepared family-style cooking, with some regional dishes, and all-inclusive room rates (no extras in the way of taxes or service charge). However, a few do not have restaurants. The *Auberges de France* belong to the same association as the Logis. The accommodations are more modest (they are not usually graded as starred tourist hotels) and they are generally very small and in rural districts. But they too must comply with minimum standards of friendliness, comfort, amenities and regional cuisine. For a complete list of both groups, apply to the *Fédération Nationale des Logis et Auberges de France,* 25 rue Jean-Mermoz, 75008 Paris, or to your local French Government Tourist Office. Regional lists are available from many tourist offices.

Monasteries and convents. There are about 100 monasteries and convents all over France that accept paying guests. Two directories are available: *Petit Guide des Haltes de Prière,* published by Cahiers du Livre, 37110 Chambray-les-Tours, France, available from ordinary bookshops; and *Répertoire de l'Hospitalité Monastique en France,* available from L'Imprimeur Monastique, St Julien, 86800 Vienne, France.

Gites ruraux de France. The *Fédération Nationale des Gîtes Ruraux de France* lists furnished rooms, apartments or small houses in rural areas of the country that can be rented by the month, or for a fortnight or a week. Once invariably modest and inexpensive, *gîtes* have become so popular that prices have inevitably risen and owners of larger and grander houses (even châteaux sometimes) are now letting out rooms or wings to visitors. Prices are considerably higher in July and August.

FACTS AT YOUR FINGERTIPS

For detailed information, write to the *Fédération Nationale des Gîtes Ruraux de France*, 34 rue Godot de Mauroy, 75009 Paris, indicating the region in which you are interested. Regional tourist offices can usually supply local brochures. However, it is essential to reserve your *gîte* well ahead of time, especially for the mid-July to mid-September period. *Gîtes de France* have a booking service in London. Write to or call at the French Government Tourist Office, 178 Piccadilly, London W1, for brochure. Although around 1000 *gîtes* are set aside specifically for British holidaymakers, it is still essential to reserve well in advance.

A British agency, *Vacances Franco-Britanniques,* 15 Rodney Rd, Cheltenham GL50 1HX, specializes in rentals similar to the *gîtes*. Also, regional tourist offices can often supply lists of furnished rooms, apartments or houses for holiday lets.

Farm Holidays. Similar to *gîtes,* but run by the local Chamber of Agriculture in each region (contact *Agriculture et Tourisme, Maison des Chambres d'Agriculture,* 9 av. George V, 75008 Paris, for brochure giving lists of local offices and organizers). Some areas offer special farm holidays for children.

Lodging with families. *Central Bureau for Educational Visits and Exchanges,* 44 Dorset St, London W1. The US, *Council on International Educational Exchange (CIEE),* 205 E 42nd St, New York NY 10017. Operating a more personal scheme are *Chez des Amis,* 139 West 87th St, New York 10024.

Villas. The French Government Tourist Offices in London and New York publish extensive lists of agencies specializing in villa rental. Or write to *Interhome,* 297 Knollwood Rd., White Plains, N.Y. 10607, *Rent-A-Villa Ltd.,* 422 Madison Ave., New York, N.Y. 10017, or *Variety Leisure,* 1525 Walnut St., Philadelphia, PA 19102. You can also write to *Fédération Nationale des Agents Immobiliers,* 163 rue du fbg St-Honoré, 75008 Paris, for their brochure *Allo Vacances,* which lists real estate agents throughout the country. *Swiss Chalets Interhome,* 88 bld Latour Maubourg, 75007 Paris, has a large choice of weekly rentals.

With changing holiday patterns in France, 1-week and 2-week stays are available everywhere. In Paris it still isn't easy to find short-stay accommodations though. A welcome new find is the résidence Charles-Dullin, 10 pl. Charles-Dullin, 75018 Paris, in Montmartre. Has 64 studios and a few 2-room and 3-room apartments, all of which can be reserved for a week. *Inter-Urbis,* 1 rue Mollien, 75008 Paris, will handle month-long vacation rentals, but is quite expensive. You might place an advertisement in the *International Herald Tribune*.

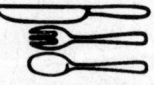

RESTAURANTS. French cooking is world famous and the high standards of this country mean that you can eat almost anywhere with the assurance of getting a reasonably good meal.

Traditional *haute cuisine* is now complemented by what is called *la nouvelle cuisine* or 'new' cooking. This relies less on rich sauces than on the fresh flavor of natural ingredients, often combined in unorthodox ways. It is much less fattening than classical French cuisine: in fact one version calls itself *cuisine minceur* ('slimmers' cooking'). In the hands of a talented chef it is a delightful gastronomic experience, but you may find the combination of ingredients (such as veal with raspberries) not to your taste, and bear in mind that in the 'new cuisine' fish and shellfish are served very underdone—still pink in the middle— or even raw in the case of scallops. We must also warn you that there has been something of a backlash against *nouvelle cuisine:* increasing numbers of critics and visitors feel that it has been over-praised and has led to absurdly high prices plus absurdly small portions. However, there is no doubt that French cuisine will continue to feel the effects of this culinary revolution, and many American and British visitors are enthusiastic about the new note of lightness and freshness that is its hallmark. In our restaurant lists we tell you if you can expect classical or 'new' cuisine.

Breakfast at your hotel may not be included in the room-rate quoted: make sure, when you reserve, to clarify this point. Where breakfast is not included, and depending on the class of hotel and what you eat, it will cost 15–50 frs. An American or British breakfast will cost much more than a French *café complet, chocolat complet* or *thé complet,* (a couple of rolls, croissants or pieces of bread, butter and jam, plus the beverage of your choice). In large modern hotels you will probably have to come down to a breakfast room; in old established and family-type hotels breakfast will be served on a tray in your room.

For lunch or dinner *à la carte,* you can easily pay 250–550 frs per person, wine and service included, in an expensive (E) restaurant. A moderate (M) meal will cost 150–250; an inexpensive (I) one, 70–150. A small carafe of wine with a meal will cost 10–15 frs; a bottle from 25 to as high as you care to go; a glass of beer around 7–8 frs for French, 10–15 for imported; a cocktail 20 frs and up; coffee from 7–15 frs; all this plus about 15% for service.

All except luxury-class restaurants are required by law to post their menus outside—so you have an ally in keeping your gustatory budget within reason. Study it carefully before you go in and you'll know what you're letting yourself in for. Virtually all non-luxury restaurants outside Paris and many inside Paris have at least one fixed-price menu (called a *menu* in French) (in fact in country districts there probably won't be a *carte* at all). The cheapest one, usually called a *menu touristique,* will often include some local specialties and is invariably good value. The *menu gastronomique* is, needless to say, at the other end of the price scale and will almost always have an *hors d'oeuvres,* an *entrée* and a main course, not to mention cheese and fruit or a dessert. The lower-price menus probably won't have the *entrée.* These fixed-price menus vary considerably in price, even between restaurants in the same category, but they do often include service charge, and sometimes wine too at the bottom end of the scale (though of course it won't be the finest vintage). Look at the menu carefully to see if the words *prix nets* or *service compris* (including service) are used.

Fixed-price menus are virtually always better value than eating *à la carte,* especially as it is customary in France to eat at least a starter, a main course and cheese or a dessert. You will be thought odd if you don't have a starter in restaurants at any price level (though not in pizzerias, *crêperies* or snackbars) and may not receive such friendly service—not really because of the money, but because it seems barbaric to the food-loving French! Similarly skipping the cheese or dessert course may provoke the condescending stares that foreign visitors sometimes complain of, though they too are usually more a sign of surprise than of disdain. ('When in Rome, do as the Romans do' is always a good motto to carry about when you're traveling, but it's particularly true in France.)

However, if you're short on time and money all big towns are now full of cafeterias, *crêperies,* pizzerias and Tunisian pastry shops. A free booklet listing selected restaurants in Paris, ranging from luxury establishments to cafeterias, may be obtained from any French Government Tourist Office. Regional and city tourist offices also issue restaurant lists. Another precious aid for those wishing to eat cheaply and well is the yearly *Guide des Relais Routiers* ('Truckdrivers' Guide'), which you can obtain from bookshops or at 8 rue de l'Isly, 75008 Paris. This guide lists not only restaurants, but also inexpensive lodging places. An English-language edition is produced by Routiers (British Isles & Commonwealth) Ltd of 354 Fulham Rd, London SW10 9UH. It can be found in some London bookshops. Members are marked by a red and blue shield bearing the logo *les Routiers.*

Drinks or coffee at the bar-counter of cafés are up to 50% cheaper than if you have waiter service at a table or outside on the terrace. But don't do as you would in an English pub and pay for your drink at the bar, then go and sit at a table.

TIPPING. This is widely practised in France, as in most parts of Europe. Most people doing something for you professionally will expect a tip, but a service charge is generally added automatically nowadays to your bill in hotels, restaurants and cafés. The words *prix nets, service compris* or the letters t.t.c. (*toutes taxes comprises,* or 'including all taxes') tell you that service is included. When in doubt, ask. If service is included there is no obligation to leave anything additional. But it is customary to add a little extra to the service charge, especially in expensive restaurants.

In hotels, the service charge covers everybody except the baggage porter (the bell boy), who expects a small tip (it might be anywhere from 5 to 20 frs, depending on the number of bags and the class of the hotel) and the hotel porter *(concierge),* whose tip varies so much, depending on the length of your stay and the extent of the service you demand, that you will have to work it out for yourself on an instinctive basis. If you have made special demands on the telephonist's services, she will not take it amiss if you tip her also. If you stay longer than two or three days in a hotel, you should leave 50–100 frs for the chambermaid; otherwise, she is covered by the service charge. Of course, if you ask her to do anything special for you, like pressing, a small tip is in order for the service rendered. The room service waiter expects at least 2 frs, even if there is a service charge included in the bill; the same goes for the doorman when he calls a taxi. It is a good rule of thumb to say that anyone who delivers anything to your room (message, telegram, laundry, etc.) automatically should be given at least 2 frs.

FACTS AT YOUR FINGERTIPS

In restaurants, as we have said, the service charge is added to your bill nowadays. When there is a separate wine waiter, he gets a minimum of 2 frs, much more in a deluxe restaurant. Barmen get 12–15%. In restaurant cloakrooms, where there is a special attendant, you customarily give at least 2 frs, but not when a waiter helps you into your coat. Washroom attendants get at least 2 frs.

Rail porters get a fixed fee, which is stated on a metal tag on their overalls; you needn't give more, though an extra 50 centimes is often added. In theater cloakrooms, the price per object is generally posted on the wall.

In theaters and movies, you tip the usher 2–5 frs for two. This also applies to the rather forbidding ladies who show you to your reserved seat at sports events (e.g. tennis matches).

Service charges are usually included in barber shops, except in the fancier ones, but rounding out the amount on top of the service is usual. If the service isn't included, 15% should do. In ladies' hairdressers, tip about 15%.

Give 15% plus in taxis. Museum guides get around 5–10 frs for an extended visit as you file out the door on leaving, and if you take a bus tour, the guide expects a tip, which can vary considerably, depending on the length of the trip and the number in your party.

TOURIST DISCOUNT ROUNDUP. Tourists normally residing outside France can be excused from the French Value Added Tax on certain goods. The standard deduction is 13%, but on some luxury items and perfumes can be 23%. This is not a legal obligation for shopkeepers, but a great many shops in Paris and the large cities do this, though only if the total value of the purchases exceeds 800 frs (1030 *for a single item* if you live in an EEC country) and if all the purchases have been made in one shop and paid in a recognized strong currency (dollars, pounds, Swiss francs, German marks, yen, etc.). The store fills out a form in quadruplicate, gives three copies to the tourist, who must then present two copies to customs when he leaves the country.

However, the business is complicated and demands quite some time when presenting the papers to customs officials at port of exit, especially in summer. For this reason you may feel it is simply not worth the time and trouble, unless it is for a large purchase, in which case, insist on the store making out the papers properly (in particular, if you don't live in an EEC country make sure you haven't been given an EEC form, and vice versa, and make sure you've given details of your bank account or that of friends in France—shop assistants often forget to tell you that reimbursements can't be made to private addresses), and be sure to leave time at the airport to arrange everything correctly with the customs officials. (If you live in Britain or any other EEC country, the countersigning of the papers is done by the customs official *when you get back home,* not at the exit port or airport.) Also, you may find that all or most of what you've saved on the VAT is taken away again in customs duty when you return home.

CONVENIENT CONVENIENCES. Most cafés in France have public toilets of varying standards of cleanliness. (It is normal practice to have at least a coffee or a drink if you are making use of a café's services). If there is an attendant, leave 1 to 2 frs. Public lavatories are to be found in Métro stations, in the larger underground garages, and tucked away in side streets, but tend to be rather smelly.

Paris now proudly sports a breed of public convenience known as a *sanisette*, very modern and sophisticated and certainly less smelly than their forerunners. But there have been some nasty accidents with children playing in and around them and getting caught up in the automatic cleaning system, so do beware. Conveniences in rail stations and at gas stations on *autoroutes* are usually reasonably clean. In inexpensive restaurants in Paris (even quite fashionable ones), and sometimes in moderate-priced restaurants in country districts, as well of course as inexpensive ones, lavatories may be of the hole-in-the-ground variety, so be prepared.

ELECTRICITY. France has almost finished changing over to 220 volts (50 cycle). This is what you will find in all modern hotels both in Paris and the provinces. A few old hotels may still be on 110, so check before plugging in your electric razor. You should also bring adapters to fit the different size lamp sockets and plug receptacles of France. For electric razors, some hotels have 2-pin sockets, some 3-pin. Remember that clocks, phonographs, electric hair rollers and other apparatus designed for 60-cycle current will not operate properly in France.

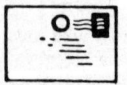

MAIL. If you are staying in a large hotel, complete with porter, the easiest way to take care of your mail is to hand it to him. Street pillarboxes are yellow and are surprisingly few and far between. Stamps may be purchased at post offices and the cigarette counter in cafés. Many stationers, bookshops and souvenir shops will sell you stamps in basic denominations if you buy postcards from them. At the time of publication, letters weighing up to 20g (¾ oz) cost 1.80 frs within France, 2.60 frs abroad (EEC countries 1.80 frs, except Britain, Ireland and Denmark, 2.10 frs); postcards 1.60 frs for France, all EEC countries, Switzerland and Canada, and 2 frs elsewhere, unless the message on the card is not more than five words, then it goes anywhere abroad for 1.60 fr. Airmail to the US is 3.25 frs for 5g, plus 65 centimes for each extra 5g. The rate to Canada is 2.45 frs for 5g, plus 65 centimes for each extra 5g. Don't put airmail postage on letters to Britain. It goes airmail anyway. Aerograms to all destinations cost 3.10 frs. However, check current rates locally.

FACTS AT YOUR FINGERTIPS

TELEPHONES. The French telephone service, which used once to be a sick joke, has now greatly improved and is almost on a par with other advanced countries. Virtually the whole network is now automatic, and linked to the international dialing system. Public pay stations can be found in post offices, in cafés (these can be used without your having to buy a drink) and, more rarely than in some countries, in the street (often attached to bus stops).

For local calls in Paris you sometimes need a token *(jeton),* which can be bought from a café cashier or post office counter. Put in your slug, wait for the dial tone, dial your number, and when you hear your party answer (not before) push the button on the front of the phone. The more modern public telephones take coins, not slugs, and from these you can make long-distance or international calls. Coins taken are 50 centimes, and 1 and 5 frs. If you want to call home, we recommend you make a quick call from an international call box and ask to be called back. Alternatively, you can make a *préavis* (person to person) call for a stated time, or ask for a PCV (reversed charge) call; but both methods involve much waiting, plus operators are reluctant to handle them. Your hotel porter can put in long distance calls but check carefully beforehand what the surcharge will be. European hotels are notorious for marking up the cost of long-distance calls, especially overseas calls, sometimes by several hundred percent. There are English-speaking operators on the international switchboards. Calls to the US and Canada are cheaper between 10 P.M. and 10 A.M., French time and all day Sunday and holidays; calls to Britain are cheaper 9 P.M. –8 A.M. and on Sundays and holidays.

To call outside the *département* you're in, or to call anywhere from Paris, dial 16, wait for a second tone, then dial the area code and your number. To call Paris, dial 16, then 1, then the number. For international calls, dial 19, wait for the second tone, then continue with the country code.

TELEGRAMS AND CABLES. Cables, telegrams and wireless messages are sent from post offices.

GOLF. There are facilities for playing golf at all principal resorts. The more important golf links in France are those at Aix-les-Bains, La Baule, Biarritz, Bordeaux, Cannes, Chantaco, Chantilly, Chamonix, Deauville, Dinard, Divonne, Etretat, Fontainebleau, Hossegor, La Nivelle, Le Lys, Lyon, Marly, Marseille, Monte Carlo, Morfontaine, Nantes, Ozoir-la-Ferrière, Pau, Pruneville, Rheims, Rouen, St-Cloud, St-Cyprien, St-Germain, St-Raphaël, Strasbourg, Tignes, Toulouse, Le Touquet, Tours, Valenciennes, Versailles, Vichy. You can usually play on any course on weekdays by payment of green fees, but on crowded weekends you must be invited by a club member. Write the *Fédération Française de Golf,* 11 rue de Bassano, 75016 Paris.

FACTS AT YOUR FINGERTIPS

SWIMMING. Thanks to France's extensive coasts along both the Atlantic and Mediterranean, swimming can be enjoyed at any number of resorts. There is usually a charge for the use of a sun umbrella, beach hut, etc., and sometimes for just going on the beach, except on the public (municipal) beaches, which are very crowded (and often dirty) in July and August.

POLLUTION REPORT. Beaches In high summer, between Menton and St-Raphaël, the water is dirty, and occasionally (unofficially) polluted; at times bathing is not allowed—*Baignade Interdite* signs. Similar problems on the Basque coast, particularly at Biarritz. Eastward Corsican beaches suffer from Italian chemical plants. A private consumer group has declared Trouville, Cherbourg, La Rochelle, Marseille, St-Jean-de-Luz and Arromanches, among others, to be above the pollution danger limit, though Marseille is at last to get its much-needed purification plant.

Although 12 out of the 18 Mediterranean countries recently signed an agreement on protection against sea pollution, it will be years before the Mediterranean becomes truly clean. Despite popular opinion some of the Atlantic and Normandy beaches are equally dangerous. The new resorts along the Languedoc-Roussillon coast are mostly pollution-free.

River and lakes The Seine, Gironde, Loire and Garonne, along with other rivers running through large towns, are unsuitable for swimming. The rivers Lot, Lys, Vire, Somme, Sèvre-Nantaise and Adour are considered clean. Lake Annecy is now clean, Lac du Bourget (Aix-les-Bains) is now a great deal cleaner. Lac Leman is clean at certain spots, but not near the big cities; and it is cold.

TENNIS. In recent years tennis has been enjoying a boom in France and courts are being built all over the place. The sport's sudden popularity means that the tennis championships at Roland-Garros stadium in Paris in May and June are now as popular as Wimbledon or Flushing Meadow. So do bring your racket if you like playing, as you stand a reasonable chance of finding a court, and many first-class hotels now have one or two for guests' use. The *Fédération française de Tennis* is at 2 av. Gordon-Bennett, 75016 Paris. For details of Cap d'Agde's Tennis Village see Languedoc-Roussillon chapter.

FISHING. For *trout* and *salmon,* the streams of Brittany, the Pyrenees, the Alps, Auvergne and Corsica are best. The coast of Brittany is excellent for sea fishing, while near St-Jean-de-Luz is the place for *tuna*. Other possibilities include the Gironde river for *sturgeon;* Lac du Bourget for *whitefish;* and *pike, perch, carp* and *black bass* almost anywhere in rivers and streams. The Languedoc-Roussillon resorts specialize in tuna fishing. For further details write the *Touring Club de France,* 65 av. de la Grande-Armée, 75016 Paris, or the *Conseil Supérieur de la Pêche,* 10 rue Péclet, 75015 Paris.

FACTS AT YOUR FINGERTIPS

Underwater fishing. This adventurous sport can be enjoyed along the entire French coast. Use of diving suits is forbidden (unless you simply wish to explore without doing any fishing). A hunting permit must be obtained. The best thing is to join one of the many *Clubs des Chasseurs et Explorateurs Sous-Marins de France.* Write or visit the *Fédération Française d'Etudes et de Sports Sous-Marins,* 34 rue du Colisée, 75008 Paris, for details. The membership fee includes not only the hunting permit (issued at once without formality upon presentation of passport and four identification photos) but insurance, weekly training sessions in a Paris swimming pool throughout the winter months, and viewing films of underwater hunting.

BOATING. Canoeing and kayaking opportunities are available in the Bay of Biscay, in the numerous rivers in the Pyrenees, the Loire valley, the Jura, the Ardèche and Auvergne. Yachting is popular along the Riviera and at Biarritz and Deauville. For information on travel by water in France, write the *Touring Club de France,* 65 av. de la Grande-Armée, 75016 Paris; *Fédération française Motonautique,* 8 pl. de la Concorde, 75008 Paris; *Fédération Française de la Voile,* 55 av. Kléber, 75016 Paris; *Ministère de L'Equipement,* Direction des Ports Maritimes et des Voies Navigables, 244 bld St-Germain, 75007 Paris.

Cruising, both on inland waterways and on the sea, is becoming extremely popular. The most attractive inland areas are Burgundy (the Burgundy Canal), southwestern France (Canal du Midi) and the Rhône valley (Canal du Rhône). Companies renting boats, with or without crew, are too numerous to list fully here, but some of the better known are: *Nautour,* in Auxerre; *Nautic Voyage,* 8 rue de Milan, 75009 Paris; *Blue Line Cruises,* 11400 Castelnaudary. Or write to the *Syndicat National des Loueurs de Bateaux de Plaisance,* Fédération des Industries Nautiques, Port de la Bourdonnais, 75007 Paris, for a list of rental agents.

For the real *dolce vita,* you can rent a yacht with crews: *Camper Nicholson's* and *Glenmot et Cie,* Cannes; *Aureglia,* in Monaco; *Cie Générale Transatlantique,* Tour Winterthur, 92085 La Défense.

For considerably less money, however, you can enjoy good food, wine, marvelous scenery and peace in converted hotel barges operated by *Continental Waterways Ltd,* 127 Albert Bridge Rd, London SW11 4QH, who have leisurely cruises covering some 240 km (150 miles) of inland waterways in the Burgundy and Champagne countryside. *Air France Holidays,* 158 New Bond St, London W1X 7AA, do weekly canal cruises on the Canal du Midi and the Canal Latéral à la Garonne. You can also sail down the Rhône river from Lyon to Valence: this tour is handled by *Compagnie Le Rhône,* 9 rue du Président Carnot, 69000 Lyon.

One of the best sailing schools in the world is the *Centre Nautique des Glénans,* in Brittany. For information, write *Ponton des Glénans,* quai Louis-Blériot, 75781 Paris, cedex 16.

Windsurfing. The craze for this new sport shows no sign of dying down and you'll find boards for hire in resorts on all coasts, as well as in some inland lakes and reservoirs. La Grande Motte in Languedoc-Roussillon has a Festival of Windsurfing in July. The *Association Française de Windsurfers* is at 19 rue Neuve-Sainte-Catherine, 13007 Marseille.

 **CAMPING AND MOUNTAIN CLIMBING.** Camping opportunities are numerous; write the *Fédération Française de Camping et de Caravanning,* 78 rue de Rivoli, 75004 Paris, or contact the *Touring Club de France,* 178 Piccadilly, London W1, for details. Two useful camping guides are Michelin's *Camping Caravaning France* and the *FFCC Guide Officiel Camping Caravanning.* Mountain climbing centers on the Alps, with the Pyrenees, Massif Central, Jura and Corsica also popular. Both the *Union Nationale des Centres Sportifs de Plein Air,* 62 rue de la Glacière, 75013 Paris and the *Club Alpin Français,* 7 rue de la Boétie, 75008 Paris, organize schools of mountain climbing and skiing. The latter also has a special section devoted to pot-holing or caving, an increasingly popular sport in the Pyrenees, Provence, Grande Chartreuse and Dordogne, or contact the *Fédération Française de Spéléologie,* 130 rue St-Maur, 75011 Paris. The *Comité National des Sentiers de Grande Randonnée,* 92 rue de Clignancourt, 75018 Paris, deals with hiking and publishes a series of maps and booklets covering GR (*grande randonnée* or hiking) routes.

 **HORSEBACK RIDING.** For riding enthusiasts, it is possible to have a vacation on horseback. The *Touring Club de France* organizes both stay-put and trekking holidays in various parts of France. There are many centers in almost every part of France which offer riding holidays. For information write the *Association Nationale pour le Tourisme Equestre* (ANTE), 12 rue du Parc Royal, 75003 Paris, or the *Touring Club de France,* Groupe Hippique, 65 av. de la Grande-Armée, 75016 Paris. The *Club Méditerranée* has an enormous riding center at Pompadour, with instruction ranging from beginners to top riders. The ANTE publishes an annual booklet giving addresses of regional riding associations, details of riding holidays and so on, and many regional tourist offices have special leaflets.

 **WINTER SPORTS.** France has a number of Europe's best ski resorts, and new facilities are constantly being added to meet the growing demand both from the French themselves and from foreign skiers, whose numbers have multiplied within recent years. This popularity is of course partly due to favorable climate and terrain, but also to the fact that the French winter sports centers are well organized and well equipped, offering a unified system of instruction that has proved its worth in international competition, as well as an increasingly wide variety of accommodations and entertainment. The most important centers are easy to reach; many have their own airports, from which planes make connections with international lines at Geneva or direct to Paris.

FACTS AT YOUR FINGERTIPS

The most popular resorts in the *Alps* are Megève, Chamonix, Méribel-les-Allues, Super-Tignes, Avoriaz, La Plagne, Flaine, Serre-Chevalier, Chamrouse, Val d'Isère, Courchevel and Alpe de Huez. The high slopes of Mont Blanc above Chamonix provide summer skiing, as do the peaks above Val d'Isère and Tignes.

Further south, in the *Alpes-de-Haute-Provence* and the *Alpes Maritimes,* are La Foux d'Allos, Auron and Valberg-Beuil, which are easily accessible from the Riviera, so that you can ski one day and swim the next. Chief among the *Pyrenees* resorts are Font-Romeu, Barèges, La Mongie and Superbagnères; near the Spanish frontier, these take the longest to reach from Paris. Nearest to Paris are resorts in the *Massif Central,* the best being Le Mont-Dore. In the *Jura* and *Vosges* are secondary centers, of interest primarily to local enthusiasts.

Further details of skiing facilities are given in the regional practical information chapters of this guide, most notably in the *French Alps* chapter. Full particulars can be obtained from the *Fédération Française du Ski,* 34 rue Eugène Flachat, 75017 Paris. Ask for the booklet *Winter Sports in France,* available also at French government tourist offices abroad. You can check snow conditions in the Savoie resorts by calling 523–26–14 when you are in Paris.

To make skiing easier and safer, a system of route markings *(balises)* has been adopted that includes both numbers and colors. The numbers indicate the sequence of a certain route, the color indicates the degree of difficulty.

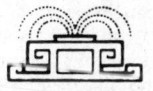

SPAS AND DRINKING WATER. Ordinary tap water is normally safe in France, but there are occasional mishaps when even a major town's system may break down; so do ask for advice locally before drinking tap water. The water *(eau minérale)* that bubbles up from France's many springs has an importance second only to wine itself. If you don't care for wine or if you want to give your liver a rest (the French do sometimes) or are suspicious of the local tap water, try one or another of France's bottled waters. Vittel is still, Badoit semi-gaseous, and Vichy quite gaseous (carbonated). Evian makes a pleasant morning refresher for the night before, and Perrier can be drunk straight or with whisky or brandy.

You can always take the waters directly (instead of in bottles) at one of France's hundred odd thermal resorts and spas. In some the water is primarily for drinking and is helpful for specific illnesses or medical conditions. In others the emphasis is on bathing, massage and hydrotherapy. Although medical staffs and clinics are part of every major spa, many of the guests are there for a treat rather than a treatment. The more sophisticated spas have casinos, nightclubs, concerts and similar diversions. Best known are Vichy, Evian-les-Bains, Aix-les-Bains, Divonne, Enghien, Vittel, Royat and La Bourboule. Salt water cure *(thalassotherapie)* centers are also very popular. They can be found at Le Touquet, Quiberon, Biarritz among many other places.

CASINOS AND GAMBLING. Symbolic of the social transformation that has brought upper-class vices within the reach of (almost) everyone is the introduction, a few seasons ago, of craps at the Monte Carlo casino. Except for a few *salles privées* (where minimum stakes can be high) in the larger casinos, the average tourist patronizes what is popularly called the 'kitchen' where roulette, baccara or boule are played from noon (or 4 P.M. in some cases) until dawn and minimum stakes are around 5–10 frs. Admission requires presentation of a passport and payment of 25 frs upwards a day. Minors, military personnel in uniform, civil servants and bank employees are excluded.

The most important casinos are at Divonne-les-Bains (in the Jura), Nice, Cannes, Deauville, Evian-les-Bains, Le Touquet, Trouville, Vichy, Biarritz, Aix-les-Bains, Juan-les-Pins, Enghien, Annecy, Dieppe, Forges-les-Eaux, Beaulieu and Monte Carlo in Monaco. Unfortunately, several casinos have been closed for long periods as a result of financial scandals, so check first.

Traveling in France

BY AIR. *Air Inter*, France's dynamic domestic airline, provides an elaborate service within the country. They offer good reductions, which are now based on such factors as time of year, time of day and destination rather than a straight percentage as formerly (percentage now ranges between 30 and 60%). Their calender has red, white, and blue days just like the SNCF. The red periods, when no reductions are allowed, run roughly 7–9.30 A.M. and 5–7 P.M. weekdays. During the blue periods the following reductions are offered: couples traveling together (valid only for parents plus children below 25, or 27, if full-time students), young people aged under 25, students up to 27, families of 3 or more traveling together, women aged over 60 and men over 65, and honeymooners (within 60 days of the wedding). Reductions are now available to Corsica as well as to mainland destinations.

Air Inter also offers various all-inclusive golf, fishing, riding and sailing holidays, as well as 'just relaxing' holidays. Air Inter's good-value Nice package gives you a weekend with 2 nights in a hotel (bed and breakfast) for the price of a return ticket: operates year-round Fri–Sun or Sat–Mon. Alternatively, you can have a weekend with free car hire (unlimited mileage) and insurance thrown in. Sat and Sun year-round.

Air Alpes is active in connecting ski resorts with larger centers in the Alps; *Air Littoral* serves the French Mediterranean coast, hopping from town to town with its nine-seaters; *Rousseau Aviation* operates in Brittany and eastern France; *Touraine Air Transport* now covers most of the country. *Brit Air* covers Normandy and Britanny.

FACTS AT YOUR FINGERTIPS 41

BY TRAIN. One of the most progressive systems in the world, French Railways (Société Nationale des Chemins-de-Fer Français, known usually by the initials SNCF) are both owned and operated by the State. In the last few years they have been completely modernized in every respect, with the majority of main lines electrified. Because of the high operating speeds it is possible to travel to any part of France from Paris without resorting to an overnight journey. SNCF tickets can now conveniently be bought with American Express, Visa and Mastercard credit cards.

The SNCF now has the fastest passenger trains in Europe since the introduction of the TGV service (*Train à grande vitesse* or High Speed Train), which can reach speeds of about 170 mph. The service currently goes to Lyon, Valence, Geneva, Aix-les-Bains, Chambery, Avignon, Nimes, Montpellier and Marseille. By the end of the eighties it is expected to go via Tours and Bordeaux to the Atlantic coast—and may even go through to Britain one day. Journey time from Paris to the Mediterranean coast is only 5½ hours, and the use of the new track for part of the Paris-Lyon route means that it is just as quick to go to Lyon by train as by air with the journey time down to 2 hrs. TGVs can be boarded without paying a supplement, except at peak times, but you must reserve (this is possible up to 5 mins before departure time).

The first-class only TEE (Trans Europ Express) trains are invariably excellent, but you must pay a supplement to travel in them. The regular *Trains Corail* are sleek and comfortable, with self-closing doors and air conditioning in both first and second class; if you have a choice, always pick a *Corail* (they are indicated in timetables). Some ordinary Corail trains require a supplementary payment in both first and second class (you can save money by buying it before you board the train).

French Railways have for some years run a successful car-hiring system bookable when you purchase your ticket. The car awaits you at the station on arrival and the network covers all the main cities and holiday resorts. Bookings can be made at any rail station or travel agent. Telephone inquiries at 292-0292. They also run a very useful registered baggage service in which the luggage is picked up from where you're staying and delivered back there. This of course applies only in big towns. Otherwise registering baggage at stations is subject to a maximum of 30 kg per item; you are allowed three pieces of baggage per traveler.

The key to the new reductions system operated by the SNCF is a calendar showing blue, white and red days, or parts of days. It is obtainable from all stations and most travel agents. All the following reductions apply *only* when you travel during the blue periods. This means any time except 3 P.M. Fri. to Sat. noon and 3 P.M. Sun. to Mon. noon (white periods), plus a few public holidays and key summer holiday departure and return dates (red period).

Round trip tickets for journeys of more than 1000km (620 miles) cost 25% less than twice the one way fare, provided the whole trip lasts five days or more. Family tickets are advantageous when two or more persons of the same family travel together; all but one of the family get reductions of 50%. And for senior citizens of any nationality, the *Carte Vermeil* gives a 50% reduction to men over 62 and women over 60. The pass costs around 60 frs. Couples traveling together benefit from a 50% reduction on one of their tickets (you don't have to be married, but must be able to show proof you live together). Children between 4 and 10 years old travel half fare; infants travel free if they do not occupy seats. All SNCF tickets are valid 2 months only. Group reductions are available on some trains for 10 or more persons. To benefit from the 'Family' and 'Couple' reductions you must acquire a *Carte Famille* or *Carte Couple* from a rail station or SNCF tourist office. You'll need identification and two passport-sized photos per person. Special rates are often offered, e.g. winter weekend (Oct-mid Mar) service to Normandy seaside resorts; 'day-by-the-sea' tickets, also to Normandy; day return tickets to races at Chantilly. But there are no ordinary day returns.

For extensive rail travel we certainly recommend the runabout *France Vacances* tickets. These are issued for 7, 15 and 30 days costing respectively in 1st class approximately $195, $250, and $380; and in 2nd class $135, $170, and $265. Children aged 4 to 11 get 60% reduction. Gives unlimited travel on all French Railways services plus special concessions on the Paris transport network and reduced car hiring. Details from French Railways, 610 Fifth Avenue, New York 10020 or French Railways, 179 Piccadilly, London W1. If you're staying for some time in France you might find it worth your while to buy a half-price season ticket *(abonnement demi-tarif)*, entitling you to half-price travel either over a specific route or within a specific area. Available for six months or a year and good value if you're planning to do a lot of traveling.

If you travel at night (thus saving time for sightseeing), the cheapest way (aside from sitting up) is to rent a couchette, a very simple form of sleeper, really bunks, where you are provided with a blanket and pillow (six-person compartment in second class, four in first). Berths in regular sleeping cars, mostly now in the Western European sleeping car pool, are for one, two or three (the last in tourist cars). Here, you have a full-sized bed and wash basin. The sexes aren't segregated in couchettes, but they are in sleepers (though of course couples can travel together.

The SNCF has package deals covering train fare, hotel and breakfast to Nice, Cannes, Lyon and Strasbourg from Paris (see regional chapters). There are also self-catering holidays on the Côte d'Azur, in Chamonix, and in Najac in the Rouergue.

A helpful new scheme for selling train tickets in post offices in rural areas may be functioning in 1984.

Note. It is absolutely essential to have your ticket punched in one of the orange machines *(Composter votre billet)* on the station *or you get fined.* Put the ticket in then move it slightly to the left till you hear a click. If you break your journey *on the same day* you don't have to have your ticket repunched, but you *must* if you do an overnight stop.

EURAILPASS. A *Eurailpass* is a convenient, all-inclusive ticket that can save you money on over 160,900 km (100,000 miles) of railroads and railroad-operated buses, ferries, river and lake steamers, etc., in 15 countries of Western

FACTS AT YOUR FINGERTIPS

Europe (including France). It provides the holder with unlimited first-class travel at rates of: 15 days, $260, 21 days, $330, 1 month, $410, 2 months, $560, 3 months, $680, and second-class Youthpass (anyone up to age 26) second-class fare of 2 months for $370. Children under 12 go half-fare, under 4 go free. The prices cover first-class passage, reservation fees, and TEE surcharges. It is also valid on the High-Speed Trains (TGV).

Available only if you live outside Europe or North Africa, the pass must be bought from an authorized agent *before* leaving for Europe. Apply through your travel agent, or to: French National Railroads, Eurailpass Div., 610 Fifth Ave, New York 10020. For complete details, write to Eurailpass, c/o WBA, 51 Ridgefield Ave, Staten Island, NY 10304. If you plan to travel in France exclusively, the *France Vacances French Railpass* is somewhat cheaper and comes with a variety of discounts including bus and subway travel in Paris, as well as car rental. Apply as for Eurailpass.

Bige Transalpino tickets, available to those under 26, are very good value, but can normally only be used during 'blue' periods.

BY BICYCLE. The SNCF now rents bikes at around 18 frs for half a day, around 25 frs a day, with lower rates if you hire for 3 or more days, from 172 stations in France (list posted up in all main stations). Best call the station from which you want to pick up the bike ahead of time and reserve. You have to put down a returnable deposit of around 170 frs, and you must show your passport too. Holders of various credit cards (Access, Visa, Eurocard, Mastercard) or of *France Vacances* or *Vermeil* tickets need not put down a deposit. You must return the bike to the same station, or occasionally to one within the same region. On some local trains you don't pay extra to travel with your bike; look for details posted in stations.

BY BUS. There are very few long-distance bus services in France, though there are local services between some towns and cities. French Railways (SNCF) has a number of combined rail and coach tours, most leaving from Paris and returning there, but usually each tour runs only three or four times a year. They also have a few one-day all-coach tours, again each one running only three or four times a year. The most extensive regular service is provided by *Europabus*, which has two different routes between Paris and Nice (via Grenoble and the Alps or via the Rhône valley), leaving once a week between late June and mid-Sept.; and Antwerp (Belgium) to Menton service via Brussels, Rheims, Dijon, Orange, Cannes and Nice; Toulouse–Barcelona via Carcassonne and Perpignan. Also one-day tours from Strasbourg (the Wine Road in Alsace), from Tours (the Loire châteaux), from Avignon (Arles, Les Baux, etc.), from Chamonix (Mont Blanc tour), the Camargue (from Avignon), the Valais (from Thonon) and one or two others. Also a four-day tour from Paris of Normandy and the Mont St-Michel and the Loire valley, and a seven-day Best of Brittany tour; 3-day tour of Mont St-Michel and Loire châteaux; 2-day tour of Normandy and Mont St-Michel; all of these May–Oct. only, whereas one-day tours usually start in March. You can pick up the regular services at many different points *en route,* but this does not apply to the tours.

Paris Vision has half-day and one-day tours in the Paris area, plus a one- or two-day tour of the Loire châteaux or of Normandy, and a three- or four-day tour of the Loire *and* Normandy. This operator now offers a 12-day *'Tour de France'*, similar to Cityrama's mammoth tour (see below). There are around seven departure dates (May through September only) and the cost for half-board, staying in 3-star hotels, all rooms with bath or shower, was 7525 frs in 1983. Optional extras are for single rooms and full-board terms. Includes Mon St-Michel, St-Malo, Rennes, Loire Valley châteaux and Tours, Poitiers, Cognac, Angoulême, Bordeaux, St-Emilion (with wine-tasting), Toulouse, Carcassonne, Montpellier, Nîmes, Aigues-Mortes, Arles, Les Baux, Avignon, Aix-en-Provence, Marseille, Cannes, Nice, Grasse, Route Napoléon, Grenoble, Lyon, Beaune, Dijon, Colmar, the Alsace Wine Road, Strasbourg, Nancy, World War I battlefields, Reims (champagne tasting included). *Cityrama's* long-established 'Magnificent France' 12-day tour costs around 7000 frs for full board and follows a somewhat different itinerary: including Rouen, Honfleur, Arromanches, Bayeux, Caen, Mont St-Michel, Loire valley châteaux, Limoges, Cognac, Bordeaux, Lourdes, Biarritz, Albi, Carcassonne, Montpellier, Nîmes, Arles, Les Baux, Marseille, Riviera resorts right through to Monaco and Menton, the Route Napoléon and Grenoble, and Lyon. Both these long tours are totally exhausting, but very rewarding too if you want to get a good idea of the country in a short space of time. Cityrama also has shorter tours to the Loire Valley, Normandy and occasionally Burgundy. *Europe Autocar* have a wide range including Normandy seaside resorts, Nice carnival, châteaux and abbeys in the Limousin (see regional chapters).

BY CAR. Bringing your own car requires only proof of third-party insurance. You may use your home driving license for a period of one year. For information, contact your travel agency or automobile association: *Royal Automobile Club,* 8 pl. Vendôme, 75001 Paris; *Automobile Club de France,* 6 pl. de la Concorde, 75008 Paris; *Touring Club de France,* 65 av. de la Grande-Armée, 75016 Paris.

Motorail services. Many hundreds of miles of tiring driving and hours of time can be saved by using one of these express trains for transporting your car and your party. In summer only, they run—with the exception of the daily Nice service—from one to three times a week in both directions, and all carry first- and second-class sleepers and couchettes. Most useful are: Boulogne to Avignon, Biarritz, Narbonne, St-Raphaël; Calais to Nice; Paris to Avignon, Biarritz, Evian, Gap, Grenoble, Narbonne, Toulon, Nice. Orléans-Toulouse is also handy.

Car-hire. Car-hire firms with branches all over the country and at major airports are *Avis, Hertz* and *Europcar.* There are many smaller local firms too. At present writing, a small car (Renault 5, Ford Fiesta) costs about 98 frs a day, plus 1.11 frs per km. A week's hire with unlimited mileage costs about 1260 frs.

FACTS AT YOUR FINGERTIPS

(All prices inclusive of VAT and other taxes.) Inquire about special weekend rates and about fly-drive packages.

Road and traffic conditions. France is an easy and delightful country for the motorist—thanks both to the scenery and to the excellence of the road network, one of the best in Europe. After a slow start the building of motorways is going ahead fast, and France now has more miles of motorway than any European country except West Germany. A ringway *(boulevard péréphérique)* circles central Paris and links with motorways that radiate from the capital to Lille, Brussels, Strasbourg (and Germany); Lyon/Marseille and on to Nice (for Italy) or Perpignan (for Spain); Tours and Bordeaux, Le Mans and Caen. Motorways linking provincial cities are improving rapidly and it is now feasible to drive the 1,126 km (700 miles) from Calais to Marseille in one day, if you must. But it is wise to time your journey so that you circle the Paris and Lyon ringways at a quiet time as at rush hours congestion can cause delays of an hour or more.

There are tolls on all French motorways, except in urban areas. Keep 50 centime and 1 franc coins handy for automatic toll machines. Toll charges depend on the size of the car and the distance traveled. At regular intervals along the motorways are gasoline (petrol) stations and other facilities, including quick-service snack and grill restaurants of indifferent quality—the French do not excel at this kind of modern catering.

There are speed limits of 130 kph (81 mph) on motorways, 110 (68) on dual carriageways, 90 (56) on other non-urban roads and usually 60 (37) in towns. When it is raining (officially defined as when you have to use your windscreen wipers) speed limits are lower. Check locally as they were subject to variation as we went to press. The network of traditional main roads *(routes nationales)* is good, but the speed limits can be frustrating—and a motorist caught speeding is liable to have to pay a fine of several hundred francs. Also, many towns on these roads have inadequate by-passes, and traffic jams are frequent at exits from towns, especially on tourist routes in summer. For all these reasons, we recommend that if you're not in too much of a hurry you should take the secondary roads (marked in yellow on Michelin maps). These are sometimes winding but are nearly always well-surfaced, often scenically beautiful and relatively free of heavy traffic. Mountain roads in France are generally very well engineered.

In France, British drivers will have to get used to driving on the right, but after 30 minutes or so of discomfort, it starts coming naturally. The rule-of-thumb as far as traffic regulations go is: priority of traffic from the right. When a small road crosses a main one, this is not true, but it is always signalled by one of the international traffic signs with which you should be familiar. You might purchase a French *Code de la Route* from a garage when you arrive. Yellow car lights, though not obligatory, are a good idea. It is mandatory to wear seat belts in front seats all the time. Be very sure to belt up as there are severe penalties for failure to do so. Children under 12 are not allowed to travel in the front passenger seat. Flashing warning lights and a red warning triangle are also compulsory.

The breathalyser (referred to in France as the *'alcootest'*) is a relatively recent feature in French motoring and is much feared. Heavy on-the-spot fines are common, and you can even go to prison for a first offence in extreme cases, so keep off the drink if you're driving.

If, in spite of our earlier warning, you have to drive on one of the peak holiday dates, keep an eye open for *Bison Futé* ('Cunning Bison'), a nationwide scheme designed to relieve some of the congestion and keep motorists smiling. Brandishing horrifying statistics (over the six days at the end of July and the beginning of August, no fewer than six million French people set off on holiday and four million come home!), the scheme's Red Indian mascot with his feather head-dress and attendant squaw is constantly broadcasting advice on how to avoid the worst of the jams. Watch out for posters and detour signs; ask at tourist offices and gas (petrol) stations for maps of alternative routes (such as the delightful, though slow, Blue Road or *Route Bleue* between Paris and the Mediterranean).

Parking. Towns and cities of any size have now installed parking meters, with charges ranging from 1 franc for a half hour to 6 frs for two hrs, a little less expensive than the underground garages. Meters do not usually need to be fed on Sundays, on Saturdays in business districts, and between around 12 and 2 in many districts (but not Paris). Check carefully, as times vary widely. In some places (such as outside rail stations), there is often a 15-minute limit.

Motor fuel. Gasoline (petrol) costs about 5.50 frs per liter for the best grade *(super)*, around 5 frs for the regular *(essence)*. Most British cars demand premium grade. At our presstime the government was pledged to keep petrol prices down, but they may well shoot up again during 1984.

Maps and guide books. Several different small-scale maps of the French main road network are in print. If you want a larger-scale and more detailed map of a particular area, by far the best are the 1/200,000 Michelin maps. These are inexpensive, clearly printed and mark all roads, villages and other features. The Blay series of city plans, with alphabetical street gazetteer, bus routes and list of places of interest, are a good buy. The famous annual red Michelin guide contains clear street-plans of many towns, and gives fuller lists of hotels and restaurants than we can in our guide. Gault-Millau is another popular guide.

FRENCH TIME. French summer time runs roughly from April to Sept. and is one hour ahead of French winter time, which is itself one hour ahead of GMT. Therefore, French clocks are one hour ahead of British clocks, and either six or seven ahead of US Eastern Standard Time.

ON THE ROAD. One of the most confusing experiences for many motorists is their first encounter with the metric system. The following quick conversion tables may help to speed you on your way.

Motor fuel. An Imperial gallon is approximately 4½ liters; a US gallon about 3¾ liters.

Liters	Imp. gals.	US gals.
1	0.22	0.26
5	1.10	1.32
10	2.20	2.64

THE BEST WAY TO SEE THE "REAL" EUROPE IS TO CRUISE THROUGH ITS TIMELESS WATERWAYS.

See France as you always thought it would be.

Picture perfect canals are surrounded by a land unequaled in scenic delights and gourmet pleasures. Whether your cruise takes you along the 17th-century Canal du Midi, through the vineyards of Champagne country or into the heart of Burgundy's Cote d'Or wine district, tasting the wines and meeting the families who grow the grapes, you'll see the France most travelers never see. On board our intimate luxury hotel barges, enjoy stimulating conversation, gourmet food and the little touches we provide—fresh flowers, chocolates on your pillow, classical music.

This is a Europe seldom seen, presented in an ambience seldom experienced. And it's only one of 26 different 3-night and 6-night cruises offered throughout the year in ENGLAND, FRANCE, HOLLAND and BELGIUM. Send for a free, colorful brochure on all our luxury hotel barge cruises.

Floating Through Europe, Inc.
Leisurely, luxurious, hotel barge cruises.
271 Madison Ave., New York, NY 10016   (212) 685-5600

Name _____

Address _____

City_____ State _____ Zip _____

LANGUAGE/30

For the Business or Vacationing International Traveler

In 24 languages! A basic language course on 2 cassettes and a phrase book... Only $14.95 ea. + shipping

Nothing flatters people more than to hear visitors try to speak their language and LANGUAGE/30, used by thousands of satisfied travelers, gets you speaking the basics quickly and easily. Each LANGUAGE/30 course offers:
- approximately 1½ hours of guided practice in greetings, asking questions and general conversation
- special section on social customs and etiquette

Order yours today. Languages available:

ARABIC	GREEK	JAPANESE	RUSSIAN
CHINESE	HEBREW	KOREAN	SERBO-CROATIAN
DANISH	HINDI	NORWEGIAN	SPANISH
DUTCH	INDONESIAN	PERSIAN	SWAHILI
FRENCH	ITALIAN	PORTUGUESE	SWEDISH
GERMAN	TURKISH	VIETNAMESE	TAGALOG

To order send $14.95 per course + shipping $2.00 1st course, $1 ea. add. course. In Canada $3 1st course, $2.00 ea. add. course. NY and CA residents add state sales tax. Outside USA and Canada $14.95 (U.S.) + air mail shipping: $8 for 1st course, $5 ea. add. course. MasterCard, VISA and Am. Express card users give brand, account number (all digits), expiration date and signature.
SEND TO: FODOR'S, Dept. LC 760, 2 Park Ave., NY 10016-5677, USA.

20	4.40	5.28
40	8.80	10.56
100	22.01	26.42

Tire pressure measured in kilograms per square centimeter instead of pounds per square inch; the ratio is approximately 14.2 pounds to 1 kilogram.

Lb per sq. in.	Kg per sq. cm.	Lb per sq. in.	Kg per sq. cm.
20	1.406	26	1.828
22	1.547	28	1.969
24	1.687	30	2.109

Kilometers into miles. This simple chart will help you to convert to both miles and kilometers. If you want to convert from miles into kilometers read from the center column to the right, if from kilometers into miles, from the center column to the left. Example: 5 miles = 8.046 kilometers, 5 kilometers = 3.106 miles.

Miles		Kilometers	Miles		Kilometers
0.621	1	1.609	37.282	60	96.560
1.242	2	3.218	43.496	70	112.265
1.864	3	4.828	49.710	80	128.747
2.485	4	6.347	55.924	90	144.840
3.106	5	8.046	62.138	100	160.934
3.728	6	9.656	124.276	200	321.868
4.349	7	11.265	186.414	300	482.803
4.971	8	12.874	248.552	400	643.737
5.592	9	14.484	310.690	500	804.672
6.213	10	16.093	372.828	600	965.606
12.427	20	32.186	434.967	700	1,126.540
18.641	30	48.280	497.106	800	1,287.475
24.855	40	64.373	559.243	900	1,448.409
31.069	50	80.467	621.381	1,000	1,609.344

BY BOAT. Europe's inland waterways network is highly developed. Barge holidays on the canals and rivers of Burgundy and the south of France are offered by *Continental Waterways Ltd,* 127, Albert Bridge Rd, London SW11 4QH (tel. 228 8671). Gourmet meals and bicycles for shore excursions are included. Cruises in central France are offered by *Inland Voyages,* Guildford Boat House, Millbrook, Guildford, Surrey, England. And in the US, a company specializing in all types of European waterway travel is *Floating Through Europe, Inc.,* 271 Madison Ave, New York, NY 10016 (in the UK, Hemingway PR, Barclay House, Chapel Ash, Wolverhampton). *Hoseasons* offer self-catering canal cruises in Brittany, the Yonne and the south. Many French companies also offer inland waterway cruises or boats for hire. Ask in tourist offices for *Tourisme Fluvial* brochures.

FACTS AT YOUR FINGERTIPS

TRAVEL FOR THE HANDICAPPED. Literally millions of handicapped people who are able to travel do so enthusiastically when they know that they can move about with safety and comfort. Generally their tours parallel those for the non-handicapped, but at a more leisurely pace.

For Americans, important sources of information about this type of travel: the *Travel Information Center,* Moss Rehabilitation Hospital, 12th St and Tabor Rd, Philadelphia, Penn. 19141; the *Easter Seal Society for Crippled Children and Adults,* Director of Education and Information Service, 2023 West Ogden Ave, Chicago, Illinois 60612; the book, *Access to the World,* by Louise Weiss, published by Facts on File, 460 Park Ave. South, New York, N.Y. 10016 ($14.95), the book, *Travelability,* by Lois Reamy, published by Macmillan; and the *Society for the Advancement of Travel for the Handicapped,* 26 Court Street, Brooklyn, New York 11242, which publishes a list of commercial tour operators who arrange tours for the handicapped. UK residents should contact the *Royal Association for Disability and Rehabilitation* (RADAR), 25 Mortimer St, London W1, England.

Two leading tour operators in this field are *Flying Wheel Tours,* P.O. Box 382, Owatonna, Minn. 55060; *Evergreen Travel Service, Inc.,* 19505-L 44th Ave. West, Lynnwood, WA 98036.

A series of excellent paperbacks, brimful of useful advice on getting around, hotels, etc., is available from Mr G. R. Couch, 68b Castlebar Rd, Ealing, London W5 2DD. 300 or so rail stations throughout France have wheelchairs and special mobile steps. Advisable to ask for this service ahead of time. Details are given in official timetables, or ask the *Centre des Voyages en Groupes,* 50 rue d'Alsace, 75010 Paris, to supply them.

Leaving France

CLEARING CUSTOMS. You may take anything out, except original works of art, for which you need a license. In fact, as an extra inducement to you to buy and export, you can purchase certain items for foreign currency and take them out of the country without paying the heavy excise taxes levied on French citizens. These include automobiles, which must be exported within a year to escape payment of tax, and wine or brandy, of which you may buy 500 frs worth free of tax, but you must have an *acquit à caution* (ask the seller). But inquire about the restrictions on entry of these purchases in your own country before you buy liquor.

CUSTOMS ON RETURNING HOME. If you propose to take on your holiday any *foreign-made* articles, such as cameras, binoculars, expensive time-pieces and the like, it is wise to put with your travel documents the receipt from the retailer or some other evidence that the item was bought in your home country. If you bought the article on a previous holiday abroad and have

FACTS AT YOUR FINGERTIPS

already paid duty on it, carry with you the receipt for this. Otherwise, on returning home, you may be charged duty (for Britons, VAT as well).

US residents may bring in $400 worth of foreign merchandise as gifts or for personal use without having to pay duty, provided they have been out of the country more than 48 hours and provided they have not claimed a similar exemption within the previous 30 days. Every member of a family is entitled to the same exemption, regardless of age, and the exemptions can be pooled. For the next $1,000 worth of goods, inspectors will assess a flat 10% duty based on the price actually paid, so it is a good idea to keep your receipts.

Included in the $300 allowance for travelers over the age of 21 are one liter of alcohol, 100 cigars (non-Cuban) and 200 cigarettes. Any amount in excess of those limits will be taxed at the port of entry, and may additionally be taxed in the traveler's home state. Only one bottle of perfume trademarked in the US may be brought in. However, there is no duty on antiques or art over 100 years old—though you may be called upon to provide verification of the item's age. Write to US Customs Service, Washington, DC 20229 for information regarding importation of automobiles and/or motorcycles. You may not bring home meats, fruits, plants, soil or other agricultural items.

Gifts valued at under $50 may be mailed to friends or relatives at home, but not more than one per day (of receipt) to any one addressee. These gifts must not include perfumes costing more than $5, tobacco or liquor.

If you are traveling with such foreign-made articles as cameras, watches or binoculars that were purchased at home, it is best either to carry the receipt for them with you or to register them with US Customs prior to departing. This will save much time (and potentially aggravation) upon your return.

British Customs. There are two levels of duty free allowance for people entering the U.K.; one, for goods bought outside the EEC or for goods bought in a duty free shop within the EEC; two, for goods bought in an EEC country but not in a duty free shop.

In the first category you may import duty free: 200 cigarettes or 100 cigarillos or 50 cigars or 250 grammes of tobacco (*Note* if you live outside Europe, these allowances are doubled); plus one liter of alcoholic drinks over 22% vol. (38.8% proof) or two liters of alcoholic drinks not over 22% vol. or fortified or sparkling wine; plus two liters of still table wine; plus 50 grammes of perfume; plus nine fluid ounces of toilet water; plus other goods to the value of £28.

In the second category you may import duty free: 300 cigarettes or 150 cigarillos or 75 cigars or 400 grammes of tobacco; plus 1½ liters of alcoholic drinks over 22% vol. (38.8% proof) or three liters of alcoholic drinks not over 22% vol. or fortified or sparkling wine; plus four liters of still table wine; plus 75 grammes of perfume; plus 13 fluid ounces of toilet water; plus other goods to the value of £120 (*Note* though it is not classified as an alcoholic drink by EEC countries for Customs' purposes and is thus considered part of the "other goods" allowance, you may not import more than 50 liters of beer).

In addition, no animals or pets of any kind may be brought into the U.K. The penalties for doing so are severe and are strictly enforced; there are *no* exceptions. Similarly, fresh meats, plants and vegetables, controlled drugs and firearms and ammunition may not be brought into the U.K. There are no restrictions on the import or export of British and foreign currencies.

Canadian Customs. In addition to personal effects, the following articles may be brought into Canada duty-free: a maximum of 50 cigars, 200 cigarettes, 2 lb of tobacco and 40 oz of liquor, provided these are declared to customs on arrival. The total exemption is $300 a year, and unsolicited gift mailings may be up to $25 in value. The regulations are strictly enforced, so check on what your allowances are and make sure you have kept receipts for whatever you bought abroad.

DUTY FREE is not what it once was. You may not be paying tax on your bottle of whiskey or perfume, but you are certainly contributing to somebody's profits. Duty free shops are big business these days and mark ups are often around 100 to 200%. So don't be seduced by the idea that because it's duty free it's a bargain. Very often prices are not much different from your local discount store and in the case of perfume or jewelry they can be even higher.

As a general rule of thumb, duty free stores on the ground offer better value than buying in the air. Also, if you buy duty free goods on a plane, remember that the range is likely to be limited and that if you are paying in a different currency to that of the airline, their rate of exchange often bears only a passing resemblance to the official one.

THE FRENCH SCENE

THE FRENCH WAY OF LIFE

A sophisticated, stimulating, often exasperating people

by
JOHN ARDAGH

(A leading British writer and broadcaster on French and European affairs, John Ardagh is a former correspondent of The Times *in Paris and author of the much-acclaimed study* The New France *(originally published as* The New French Revolution), *which has become a classic, of* A Tale of Five Cities: Life in Provincial Europe Today *and of* France in the 1980s, *published in 1982.)*

An arrogant Parisian executive, impeccably dressed, applying his quick, élite-trained mind to *le marketing,* in some glossy modern office;

a Socialist-voting schoolteacher, quoting Marx as he heatedly denounces the 'capitalist bosses' at a political rally in a village hall; a provincial, working-class housewife, enjoying a gossip as she buys her *baguette* of crispy bread in the corner shop, or loads her trolley in the hypermarket; a red-cheeked peasant farmer, sipping his *vin du pays* on a sunlit café terrace above the lush valley of the Dordogne—what is the indefinable 'Frenchness' that these four, and a hundred other stereotypes, have in common?

France is a land of immense diversity, both scenic and human. This is part of its charm. The dour industrial plains of the north are a world apart from the pine groves and mimosa scents of the sunny Riviera; it is an equally far cry from the ski slopes of the Alps to the rocky headlands and lonely stone churches of Brittany. Yet this diversity adds up to its own harmony, and the same is true of the French themselves. City and country dwellers, rich and poor, have many traits in common, some paradoxical. They are extrovert and talkative, yet suspicious of neighbors and unwilling to suffer fools gladly; individualistic, yet deeply conservative in many of their habits and attitudes; materialistic, with bourgeois property-owning instincts, yet zestful hedonists with a creative flair and a rare sense of style. They work devotedly (the myth of the Frenchman as a lazy, lolling Latin is false), yet dissipate much of their energy on struggling with each other, for teamwork is not their *forte*. Though resentful of authority and of the State as an institution, they love *la douce France* almost as if she were a person, and so attached are they to the French way of life that they will seldom emigrate. A second loyalty is to their own province or birthplace, in a land where city immigrants retain a strong awareness of their regional roots. '*Moi, je suis Auvergnat,*' a Parisian may tell you, with fierce pride.

In short, the French are complex, sophisticated, stimulating, often exasperating—a people with whom many foreign francophiles have built up over the years an intense love-hate relationship.

Today, in the mid-1980s, a Socialist Government under President Mitterrand has been forced to apply austerity measures to cope with a difficult economic situation. But these troubles may be only a temporary setback, and they have certainly not negated the tremendous rise in prosperity since the war. Indeed France has changed dramatically since 1945, from a sluggish agriculture-based society to a modern industrial state. For good or ill, the towering new Paris skyscrapers stand as symbols of this change, as do the new freeways and hypermarkets, the futuristic resorts along the Languedoc coast, and much else that will rapidly strike the visitor. The French themselves have been almost schizophrenic in their reactions to this modernism. In some ways, they have been adapting eagerly to a new world of wealth, glamor and technical efficiency; in others, they cling for security to old rituals and habits. An example of this conservatism: the new franc (100 old ones) was introduced in 1959, but over 20 years later many people are still unable or unwilling to calculate in anything but old francs, including youngsters born *after* the change! Yet look elsewhere and you see that the French have been embracing modern innovations, mostly American, then using their own creativity to lend them a special French flavor—the so-called 'drugstores' in Paris and other cities are not imitations of their American namesakes but modernized *brasseries* with boutiques added, very French. Continuity amid change is the keynote of France today. A new, brash, materialistic France has arisen that may not be to every tourist's taste. Yet the old picturesque France still survives, for those who care to seek it out—the France of old châteaux amid vineyards, of Romanesque churches lost in silent valleys, of street markets in the heart of cities, of old men playing dominoes in backstreet *bistrots*. Can France manage to combine the best of old and new? To preserve her traditions, while also completing the modernization that is essential for her continued prosperity? It is quite a challenge. Let us explore it.

Changing habits of the affluent society

France, 'mother of the arts,' had by the 1970s come to seem more a land of big business. It had zoomed ahead of Britain in standard of living to become the world's fourth exporting nation. Today, scores of new managerial schools have sprung up, and a new breed of young executives and planners have eagerly embraced a different business ethos and show an ingenuous faith in technical progress. Hard-working state technocrats parade their plans for creating new ports, airports or industrial estates in 'Europe's Texas', while young business managers return from study courses in the United States and enthuse about *le merchandising*, many staying at their desks till eight or later. Paris bristles with new banks, consultancy firms, multinational HQs, and suddenly has discovered *le public-relations*. Even many of the new Socialist rulers have embraced these trends.

American influences have been invading daily life, as witness the vogue that grew in the 1960s for the newspeak of *franglais*, whereby a couple offer *un drink* to their friends in *le living* of their flat, after which in *le dressing-room* they discuss *le planning* for *le weekend*, which is sure to include *le shopping*, perhaps for *une tee-shirt* or *un smoking* (dinner jacket). The *franglais* craze infuriated the French purists, and today is on the wane. It is no more than a facet of a much more profound phenomenon: prosperity rose steadily in the boom years before the oil crisis (it has since levelled off) and has been changing the way of life of millions of families. The percentage of homes with refrigerators has risen since 1954 from 7 to 93; with television, from 1 to 88; with cars, from 21 to 68 (the level of car ownership is one of the highest in Europe). Affluence has been pushing the French closer to Anglo-American habits: they spend as much as ever on food and drink, but as a proportion of the total family budget this item has dropped since 1939 from 50 to 23%, while spending on health and hygiene has risen from 6 to 12.3% (witness how the métro smells less!).

The French are also becoming more house-proud, readier to spend their weekends on the new pastime of *le bricolage* (do-it-yourself). It is true that until about 15 years ago France's housing shortage was scandalous, and though matters are now much improved, the French today are still less comfortably housed than the Germans or British. Older middle-class apartments usually spurn thick carpets and cosy sofas in favor of the austere elegance of spindly, straight-backed chairs and parquet floors. But a younger generation is now caring more for home comfort and amenities. People are spending more of their time at home, drawn above all by the lure of television. And this television craze has led to a decline of that great French tradition, café-going. The cafés and *bistrots* are still busy at apéritif time, up till 8 or so. But later, after dinner, they mostly tend to be half-deserted, save those in tourist areas or city centers. On the big new housing estates, where the aerials sprout thickest, there are hardly any cafés at all.

But these suburbs do have hypermarkets. The French, who do nothing by halves, have moved in one swoop from the little local shop to the biggest modern stores in Europe, some with up to 50 checkout desks and 20,000 square meters of selling space—brash emporia, with musak, where the whole family comes to load up the car with anything from an off-the-peg suit to a packet of frozen snails. Thousands of little shops have been pushed out of business. Another portent of modernization: the French telephone service, for so long a sick joke, has at last improved. A family may still have to wait months to get a machine installed (such is the backlog, notably in Paris) but at least the whole country is now on the international automatic, and public booths have at last been set up on sidewalks, so no longer are you so dependent on the cramped cubby-hole of some noisy café for making a call when the post office is closed.

Traditionally lovers of good eating above all else, the French have now been discovering other interests too. *Le weekend* has become a cult. The French adapt ill to the strains of big-town living, especially in frenetic Paris, and they feel the urge to get away. Many a middle-class family today have their second residence, maybe a cottage or converted farmhouse in Normandy or the Seine valley, where they bolt for refuge at the weekend—thus blocking the city's exits with giant

Friday-night and Sunday-night jams. And an even stronger cult is the new holiday mania. The French work so hard, year round, that they yearn for their holidays, and take the longest in Europe. All firms are now legally obliged to give five weeks' annual paid leave, while for the affluent classes six weeks in summer plus two weeks' winter skiing is not unusual. The individualistic French do not shine at team sports (save rugby football), but in other respects they have become passionately *sportifs*—witness the crowded ski slopes, the marinas crammed with sailing boats, the rash of new riding stables. Millions go camping —everywhere, in summer, superbly equipped sites are packed with blue and orange tents—while an adventurous minority trek off to maybe Yukatan or Samarkand (that is, if they can find ways of getting round the stringent limitations on taking money abroad, imposed for economic reasons in 1983). The major postwar holiday phenomenon is of course the flamboyant success of the Club Méditerranée, with its scores of 'villages' around the globe where jaded executives escape from their city selves to play the noble savage, with Tahitian *pareos,* straw huts, and beads for money. This idyll offers them a brief compensation for the rigidities of French society.

Snobbery, sex and students

France's new prosperity has been filtering slowly down the social scale, but is still unevenly shared. Wage differentials are among the widest in Western Europe. Between manager and unskilled worker they average 6:1 in France, against 4:1 in West Germany and only 3½:1 in Britain. Doctors, lawyers, bankers and the like have achieved American levels of affluence—but many peasant families are still near the breadline; so are older people living on fixed incomes. However, since 1981 the Socialists have done a little to reduce the gulf between rich and poor.

This is still a class-divided society, even though the divisions are slowly blurring. At one end of the scale is the aristocracy, the grand old families whose names begin with '*de.*' Largely ignored today by the rest of France, they cling together in their own exclusive little social world, inviting each other to formal cocktail parties, or to an occasional ball or banquet with echoes of past glories. But many live in genteel semi-poverty, struggling to keep their centuries-old châteaux from tumbling into ruin. Only in a few rural areas do they retain some feudal influence. A far more powerful social category is the 'upper' bourgeoisie, the class that provides France with the bulk of its élite civil servants, financiers, and fashionable lawyers and surgeons. They tend to live in big apartments in the better Paris districts such as Passy, or in Neuilly, endlessly discuss property, status, politics, and look down snobbishly on the 'lower' bourgeoisie, the shopkeeper class. 'So sorry I'm late,' says Marie-Chantal, archetypal Parisian débutante, in a well-known joke, 'but brother Xavier took the Jag, brother Arnaud took the Mercedes, so I had to take the Métro—do you know it?'

Rising prosperity has, however, reduced the visible gulf in lifestyles between bourgeois and worker, and between country and city dweller. Peasant farmers drive to town in their new Citroëns, village girls in the garb of Chelsea walk beside their beshawled, black-smocked grandmothers. A new blue-collar élite of skilled workers and technicians, with money to spend, is acquiring the property-owning instincts, the habits and material aspirations of the bourgeoisie; television programmes and glossy magazines such as *Elle* are spreading middle-class taste more widely, so that a working girl will often dress with as much *chic* as the boss's wife. And yet, though the classes may *appear* to be drawing closer, the psychological barriers remain. It may be easier than 50 years ago for the gifted son of a member of the working class to penetrate up the social ladder, but it is still harder than in Britain and far harder than in the United States. The ambitious *nouveaux riches* (and there are plenty) soon find that money alone will not buy them entry to a higher social class. Family connections and the right education still matter hugely.

Family ties, though becoming less rigid, remain far closer than in the English-speaking world. The family is still a supreme focus of loyalty, more than the State: 'I cannot pay my taxes. You see, I have a duty to support Aunt Louise,' has long been a stock French attitude. Many a young Frenchman still spends as much of his time with uncles, cousins or grandmothers as with chums of his own age, and will still dutifully attend those clan gatherings of the extended family that have featured in ten thousand French novels or movies, from Balzac to *Cousin Cousine*. But the wind of change is blowing. The accent of loyalty is shifting from the extended to the nuclear family, the home cell of parents and children—and here, too, there are new tensions. In the wake of the May 1968 explosion, teenagers have been rebelling against the old tradition of tight parental authority, and no longer is it quite so much the norm for a son or daughter to live at home until wed. Some even go off flat-sharing with friends, though far less often than in New York or London.

Rebellion against authority has marked the education system, too, since May 1968. The old, confident order has been smashed. Teachers and university students go on strike; so sometimes do *lycée* pupils, or else they argue in class with teachers, or demand a say in the running of the school. The result of all this has been a decline in the quality of education. Probably the old classical system *was* too rigid and academic; but the reformers do not seem quite sure what kind of more humane, liberal system to put in its place. Only in the élitist senior colleges, the Grandes Ecoles (led by the Polytechnique), are standards being fully maintained; in the ordinary campus faculties, overcrowded, underfunded, shabbily equipped, a student *Lumpenproletariat* muddles along amid confusion, racked by growing fears about job outlets. Of France's expected 2 million unemployed in 1983, nearly half were under-25s.

Many young people also feel a sense of insecurity through the weakening, as in other Western countries, of the old code of established moral values. So much is under question, including religion. The Catholic Church has been liberalizing and moving to the Left, and many priests now put as much stress on social action as on liturgy. But this has not enabled the Church to win back the dechristianized urban millions (in Paris, only 10% attend mass each week, and in some towns the figure is even lower). And meanwhile, the leftward lurch has provoked a backlash by the 'integrist' diehard minority, led by the notorious Archbishop Lefebvre who has insisted on such measures as a return to the mass in Latin. Only in certain rural areas, notably in the west, does the parish priest retain his traditional role as leader of society. Elsewhere the Church has become a kind of militant pressure-group within a lay society. In other words, today a man or woman is a practising Catholic not so much through social or family convention, as in the past, but through sincere personal conviction. Not an entirely negative trend.

It follows that France has become a more permissive society, though less blatantly so than Britain or many parts of the United States. The taboo of public silence about abortion and birth control has finally been broken, and both have recently been legalized. Many young couples now live together before getting married (though this is less acceptable in the provinces than in Paris) or they go on holiday together, while even girls from good families are kept on much less tight a rein than in the past.

It was only in 1964 that women finally won the same legal rights as men, over such matters as property ownership and grounds for divorce. A women's movement has made its mark recently, and is fighting to secure better job opportunities for women in some professions that are still male-dominated. And yet it is far from certain that the average Frenchwoman, at heart, really desires full emancipation in the sense of wanting to be the same as a man in a man's world. She wants to be equal, yes—but different. She prizes femininity far more than feminism. She enjoys using her female charm and sex appeal; and her ideal today is to live with her man in a state of intimate equality where each preserves his/her seductive role. She despises the bra-burning type of feminist who seeks to bury her attractiveness. In short, this is a society of smouldering sexuality and romanticism, where flirtatiousness is never far from the surface in any man-woman encounter. French women as a whole are not especially pretty, compared, say, with Swedes or Italians, but they know how to make up for it, with that indefinable quality of *chic* and allure, helped along with hours spent over cosmetics and *coiffure*.

Formalities, friends and Parisian frenzy

While an American calls a new acquaintance 'Bill' or 'Bob', a Frenchman calls him *'Monsieur'*, and shakes hands on greeting and parting. The French set store by social formalities, and to an English-speaking visitor their respect for hierarchies may seem almost Germanic—any ex-chairman expects to be addressed all his life as Monsieur le Président. Letters still end, 'Please agree, Dear Sir, to the assurance of my most distinguished sentiments'. But such formality should not be mistaken for coldness. Though courtesy may be stylized, it can still be a means of expressing warmth. The common *cher Monsieur* does not mean 'dear Sir': an older Frenchman may often call his buddies just that, cordially. And in any case younger French people are today breaking with many of the old formalities, and are moving over to the first-name habit. They are also beginning to entertain at home more casually, thus defying the bourgeois convention that a dinner party should be given with ceremonial lavishness or not at all.

Paradoxically the French, though loquacious, are socially reserved when it comes to making new friends. They will easily start up a chat with a stranger in a bus or café, and maybe debate with him passionately. But direct personal questions will not be asked, mutual privacy will be respected, there will be no presumption of new friendship. Real friendship is highly selective, but deep, and usually long standing. The French are wary of making new friends casually, in this society traditionally based on mistrust. Thus, for example, they are slow to become pally outside the office with their work colleagues. This reticence inevitably involves unneighborliness, and has made it harder for the French to adapt to life in the big modern suburbs. They may have moved from dingy slums to airy new apartments, but there they hug their family privacy and do little to create a new caring community. Feeling wary of each other, and isolated, they seldom group together spontaneously for such self-help activities as baby minding that might make life easier. Any resident who tries to organize voluntary work of this kind may be suspected of ulterior motives, often political. When a housewife on a new middle-class estate tried to start up a crèche, the neighbors whispered suspiciously, 'What's she getting at? She must be a Communist' —though she merely wanted to help them.

In these and many other matters there is a vast difference between Paris and the provinces, which are two worlds apart. Paris is a deceptive city, where life can be very exciting, or very lonely. It has its passionate little cliques of intellectuals, artists, politicians and others; and it has its brilliant society world of *'le Tout Paris'*, the rich and famous few, for whom life is one long round of opera first nights, art gallery *vernissages,* exclusive *salons,* or visits to the races at Longchamp or to modish nightclubs such as Castel. But for the average middle-class Parisian, life is by no means a social whirl. In this congested city, the tempo is fast and nerves fray easily, so it is small wonder that Parisians tend to be brusque and tense. Overtired by work they save their leisure for family and a few close friends, so there is noticeably less gregarious casual party giving than in London or New York. To have fun in Paris it is best either to be rich, or young and single—but not to be a middle-class couple aged 40 with two kids. In the provinces, people are more gentle and the pace of life is more human. In fact, most complaints by foreigners about French inhospitality are based on periods spent in Paris. Go to other towns and you will often find a warm welcome.

Provincial renewal, and 'quality of life'

The postwar decades have brought a vital renewal of the provinces, economic, social and cultural. This is the result both of France's industrial growth and of the farming revolution. Since the war, technical progress on the farms has led to a rural exodus of about six million people (the percentage of French people working on the land has fallen from 35 to 9%). Many farmers have become prosperous and dynamic, and have grouped into powerful cooperatives: the old-style peasant, drunken, reactionary, illiterate, living little better than his animals, is still to be found in parts of the Massif Central or Brittany, but he is a dying species. The farm emigrants have made for the towns, and this and other factors have led to the kind of rapid growth of cities that Britain, for instance, knew 100 years ago. Many cities have doubled or trebled in size. Towns that in prewar days looked so quaint and charming, but in fact were sluggish and inward-looking, are now vibrating with new industry, culture, and links with other lands. Some, such as Marseille, are even beginning to catch the Parisian disease of over-frenetic activity and congestion. But in most cases provincial towns today offer a happy and harmonious balance between new-style animation and old-style *douceur de vivre*. A man can find a villa with a garden only ten minutes' drive from his office; he has time to linger over a *pastis* with friends in his favorite café; he can fit in a game of tennis or a swim on a summer evening after work—as the Parisian can rarely do.

In fact after centuries of Parisian contempt for provincials, a curious reversal is today taking place. Parisians are coming to realize that their noisy, hectic city is not the only place to live in, and that the provinces might even be more fun. Today, more young middle-class Parisians and their families are actually migrating to new jobs in the regions, especially the south, than are following the classic route of Stendhal's Julien Sorel, to seek fame and fortune in the capital. It is almost *more* chic now to say that you live and work in Avignon or Annecy than in Montparnasse—a remarkable inversion of snobberies!

In wider terms, too, the dramatic urbanization of the '50s and '60s is today producing a counter-swing: some of those who emigrated to the towns are now beginning to yearn for a return to their roots, not to the farms but at least to small towns. Young people are rejecting big-city life, and would rather stay near their rural background, so long as they can find work there. And little groups of pioneers are trying to find ways of bringing new life to dying country areas: executives, tired of Paris tensions, come to remoter areas such as the Massif Central uplands with a sense of mission. In one remote village, a young engineer has created an electronics workshop, employing 12. Some young people go a stage further and virtually drop out, moving to rural regions to herd sheep, weave rugs, spin and make pottery, or farm. A few tentative communes have formed.

These are fringe cases, concerning only a tiny minority. But they are symptomatic of a much more general new French concern for environment, ecology and a return to traditional values. During the postwar decades, the French were fired with an ardent faith in material expansion as a cure for all ills; but this credo is now losing ground. The accent today is on better quality of life. This slogan is now official policy and it reflects a true public mood. More greenery and traffic-free piazzas in city centers; better protection of coastlines and other natural assets; an end to the fearful shortage of sports equipment in schools; stronger measures against pollution; low-rise housing amid trees, in place of towering city blocks—these are among the new preoccupations. After the 1960s vogue for apeing the Texas ethos that big is best, the French are now beginning to believe that small can be beautiful. While ardent ecologists protest against nuclear power projects, in the cities a trend is emerging that is new to the French, a break with French tradition: local neighborhood associations are appearing, devoted to consumer protection or to better communal use of local amenities. Is the French citizen, finally, learning the virtues of community spirit?

Mitterrand as President: hopes and hazards

The golden era of post-war economic progress in France was during the presidency of Charles de Gaulle, 1958–69. He also ended the cruel war in Algeria by granting freedom to that country; and he restored French self-confidence, as well as France's voice in world affairs (albeit by an assertive nationalism that angered some of her allies). His policies were broadly continued by his successor, Georges Pompidou, and subsequently by Valéry Giscard d'Estaing. But Giscard proved a disappointing President. He came to power as a liberal reformist, then veered towards a somewhat cynical autocracy. By the end of his mandate, in 1981, the French were also growing bored with 23 years of much the same Right-of-center rule and were hankering for change. Yet the normal alternation of power that is healthy in a democracy was hazardous for France. The only alternative on offer was a Left with a large Communist element. Several times the electorate had already baulked at so radical a change.

However, in May 1981 they finally took the risk. They voted in as President the veteran Socialist leader François Mitterrand, and in June they gave his party a huge majority in the National Assembly. The democratic transition passed off far more smoothly than many people had feared, and Mitterrand reassuringly appointed a Government led by moderates, with the affable Pierre Mauroy as Prime Minister. However, Mitterrand also gave the Communists four junior posts in the Government, for he wanted to secure their acquiescence: he did not want them constantly sniping at him. The move caused some anxious raising of eyebrows, notably in Washington. But in practice the Communist Ministers have behaved loyally and efficiently. And as their Party's share of the French vote has slumped recently, from roughly 20 to 15%, the Communists as a whole no longer pose such a threat.

Abroad, Mitterrand's Government has provided continuity in foreign policy, notably in loyalty to the Atlantic Alliance. At home, it has been trying to offer the French a 'new deal,' to bring more equality to French society and cure some of its basic blockages. Some of its reforms are anti-capitalist and Socialist-inspired. Others, less specifically Left-wing, are intended to update and liberalize public life. Here above all they have set about dismantling France's Napoleonic legacy of centralization, through sweeping reforms of local government that are intended to transfer much power from the Paris-appointed prefects to elected councils in the cities, départements and regions. This move is quite popular with the French, who recognize that France has long been too centralized. The Socialists have also carried out other liberal measures, such as reducing State control over radio and television, and abolishing the death penalty. And they are studying ways of modifying France's elitist education system, whereby much of the real power in French public life is held by technocrats graduating from a few exclusive colleges, recruited mainly from 'good' Paris families.

In a bid to weaken the role of capitalism, the Socialists have extended France's already large nationalized sector by taking over nine big industrial groups and almost all private banks. It is debatable whether this ideologically inspired move has done much to help the economy. However, the Socialists' attempts to reduce inequalities of income are probably less open to criticism. In 1981–2 they slapped new taxes on the rich and enacted various measures to make life easier for workers—big rises in basic wages and welfare allowances, retirement at 60, a 39-hour working week, a fifth week of paid holidays, and so on. In terms of greater social justice, these were commendable steps. But alas they proved very costly for France's budget at a time when her economy was in growing trouble, with world recession hitting her later but more severely than many other countries. At first the new Government tried to combat this with the unfashionable remedy of neo-Keynesian reflation: but this largely failed. Inflation stayed in double figures, while a horrendous annual trade deficit built up (and France has no oil of her own to help her deal with this). Clearly the nation was living above its means.

So in 1983 the Socialists were forced to face realities. They backtracked by imposing an all-round austerity programme that included big cuts in welfare spending and higher taxes for poor as well as rich. This angered many on the Left wing of the Party, who accused Mitterrand of 'betraying Socialist ideals.' By the spring of 1983 the mood in France was tense and anxious, with numerous strikes and protest movements. The Socialists themselves were deeply split as to what economic course to follow, while the Right was angrily accusing them of 'leading the nation to catastrophe.' France was more profoundly politicized, and polarized, than for many years. Compounding Mitterrand's difficulties, many of the Government's sympathisers were beginning to lose confidence in his competence in handling the economy. So is Mitterrand's brave new deal threatened with failure?

France today has been moving into uncharted waters, a fascinating but perilous adventure. Can the Socialists succeed? It is far from certain. And yet, change *is* needed, and many of their ideas are good ones. Basically this is still a prosperous country, with vast resilience and human resources. It can afford to experiment. So long as Western civilization survives, France seems well placed to be a leader of that survival—and, despite the hectic modernism, she will remain gloriously French.

A MINI HISTORY OF FRANCE

An aide-mémoire to monarchs and moments

Reigning monarch or regime	Dates	Important events
	390 BC	The Gauls sack Rome, first of many conflicts
	58–51 BC	Caesar's conquest of Gaul
	5th c.	End of Roman influence in Gaul
	496	Conversion of Clovis I to Christianity
	481–768	Various kings (of Paris, of Orléans, of Burgundy, etc.)
Charlemagne, *Carolingian dynasty* 768–814	800	Charlemagne becomes Holy Roman Emperor

THE FRENCH SCENE

Reigning monarch or regime	Dates	Important events
Louis the Pious 814–840		King of Aquitaine and Holy Roman Emperor
Lothair I 840–855		Holy Roman Emperor
Louis II 855–875		Holy Roman Emperor
Charles the Bald 875–877		Holy Roman Emperor
Louis II 877–879		Demoted from Emperor, now 'King of France'
Louis II 879–882		Rival 'King of France' was Carloman, 879–884
Charles II (the Fat) 884–887		Holy Roman Emperor from 881–887 and King of France
Arnulf 887–899		Holy Roman Emperor, but not King of France
Charles III (the Simple) 893–923		King of France
Louis IV 936–954		King of France
Lothair II 954–986		King of France
Louis V 986–987		King of France
Hugh Capet, *House of Capet* 987–996		First to achieve principle of hereditary kings, not elected ones; began unification of France
Robert II (the Pious) 996–1031		
Henry I 1031–1060		
Philip I 1060–1108	1066	William of Normandy invades England, defeating Harold at Battle of Hastings
	1099	Capture of Jerusalem by Crusaders
Louis VI (the Fat) 1108–37	early 12th c.	*Chanson de Roland* written
Louis VII (the Young) 1137–80	late 12th c.	Cathedrals of Chartres and Notre-Dame begun
Philip II 1180–1223		'The Maker of Paris' began the Louvre
Louis VIII 1223–26		Louis conquers the south of France
Louis IX (St Louis) 1226–70	1257	Founding of the Sorbonne

A MINI HISTORY OF FRANCE

Reigning monarch or regime	Dates	Important events
Philip III (the Bold) 1270–85		Walls of Carcassonne built
Philip IV (the Fair) 1285–1314	1302 1309–78	Summoning of first Estates General The Pope in Avignon
Louis X (the Quarrelsome) 1314–16		His uncle was the real ruler
Jean I 1316		Jean I died one week after birth
Philip V (the Tall) 1316–22		
Charles IV (the Fair) 1322–28		Last Capetian of the direct line
Philip VI, (*Valois line* 1328–50	1337–1453	Hundred Years' War
Jean II (the Good) 1350–64	1356	The English advance; Jean defeated by the Black Prince at Poitiers
Charles V (the Wise) 1364–80	1360–69 1378	Peaceful lull in Hundred Years' War The Great Schism in Church
Charles VI 1380–1422	1396–1416	Charles often insane Twenty-year truce in war
Charles VII 1422–61	1431 1453	Joan of Arc burned; from lowest point, French nation revived End of Hundred Years' War with English retreat to Calais
Louis XI (the Spider) 1461–83	1477 1480	Defeat of Burgundian pretenders Extinction of the house of Anjou
Charles VIII 1483–98		Charles conquers Naples but later forced to withdraw
Louis XII 1498–1515		Continues attempts to conquer Italy
François I 1515–47	1517 1519	Luther publishes Wittenberg Protest A Hapsburg (Charles I of Spain) elected Holy Roman Emperor (as Charles V), beginning Franco-German rivalry of 450 years
Henri II 1547–59	1547	Mary, Queen of Scots, taken to France; Henri marries Catherine de Médicis
François II 1559–60		Married Mary, Queen of Scots, but no children
Charles IX 1560–74	1572	St Bartholomew Massacre of Protestants
Henri III 1574–89 (assassinated)	1580–87	Montaigne's *Essays*
Henri IV, *Bourbon line* 1589–1610 (assassinated)	1594	Henri renounces Protestant faith, becomes a Catholic

THE FRENCH SCENE

Reigning monarch or regime	Dates	Important events
Henry IV (continued)	1608	Champlain founds Quebec
Louis XIII 1610–43	1614	Estates General summonded; Richelieu to the fore
	1618–48	Thirty Years' War
	1643	Founding of Académie Française
Louis XIV 1643–1715	1685	Revocation of Edict of Nantes, causing emigration of Huguenots
	late 17th c.	Works of Molière, Racine, etc.
Louis XV 1715–74		Mme de Pompadour, Mme du Barry, but also Voltaire, Montesquieu, Diderot, Rousseau; Fragonard, Watteau and Boucher; the zenith of French enlightenment and influence
	1756–63	Seven Years' War
Louis XVI 1774–92 (beheaded)		Louis married Marie Antoinette
	1776 ff.	French assistance for American War of Independence
	1789–92	The French Revolution, beginning with calling of Estates General, ending with founding of a Republic
First Republic 1792–1804	1792–95	The Convention (Robespierre, Danton, Marat, etc.) in control; The Terror
	1795–99	The Directory, with Napoleon Bonaparte as its champion
	1799–1804	The Consulate, with Napoleon First Consul
Napoleon I, First Empire 1804–14 (abdicated)	1805	French defeated at Battle of Trafalgar
	1805–12	Napoleon conquers large part of Europe but is defeated in Russia
	1807	*Code Napoléon*
Louis XVIII 1814–24	1815	Return of Napoleon for 100 days; defeated at Waterloo; his second abdication (St Helena)
Charles X 1824–30 (abdicated)		Victor Hugo's works
Louis-Philippe 1830–48 (abdicated)	1846–7	Severe industrial and agricultural depression
Second Republic 1848–52		Louis Napoleon, nephew of Bonaparte, elected president
Napoleon III, Second Empire		Colonial expansion into Indochina, Syria, Mexico

A MINI HISTORY OF FRANCE

Reigning monarch or regime	Dates	Important events
1852–70 (exiled)	1870	Franco-Prussian War; France defeated; but Flaubert and Baudelaire writing
Third Republic 1870–1944		16 presidents in 75 years
	1871	Alsace-Lorraine ceded to Germany
	1894–1906	Dreyfus Affair
	1904	Entente Cordiale signed
	1914–18	First World War
	1940	French surrender to German army
Vichy Government 1940–44		German-sponsored government under Marshal Pétain
Provisional Government 1944–46		Charles de Gaulle president; resigns 1947
Fourth Republic 1947–58	1946–54	Indochinese War, trouble in Africa, independence for Morocco and Tunisia
Fifth Republic 1958–	1958	General de Gaulle elected president, proposes new constitution with presidential form of government
	1962	New constitution approved; Algeria granted independence
	1967	France leaves NATO
	1968	Widespread disruption initiated by student uprisings in Paris (generally known as the 'Events of May 1968') brings the country to a standstill, but President de Gaulle manages to reassert his authority
	1969	April referendum against de Gaulle's civic proposals; he resigns and is succeeded by Georges Pompidou
	1974	Pompidou dies and is succeeded by Valéry Giscard d'Estaing
	1981	Mitterrand leads Socialist party to election victory.

CREATIVE FRANCE

Mecca of the arts

by
ANDREW HERITAGE

France has traditionally benefited from its geographical location at the heart of Western Europe. Having coasts on the Atlantic and the Mediterranean, access to the North Sea, the Alpine passes, and exclusive control of the passes of the Pyrenees, France has always played a key role in European trade, travel and politics, as well as intellectual and artistic development. Within its present boundaries France encompasses Latin, Germanic, Celtic and Flemish racial types. These factors have combined to determine the nature of French culture—an interaction of ideas and influences from all over Europe, and, in the days of Empire, the world.

CREATIVE FRANCE

Early traces of French culture include the cave paintings of wild beasts and hunters at Lascaux, in the Dordogne (c.1,500 BC), and the slightly earlier fertility figures found in neighboring regions, such as the Venus of Lespugue. France even boasts its own Stonehenge, in the megalithic stone complexes at Carnac in Brittany (c. 3,500 BC).

The first known racial group to occupy France were the Celts, who inhabited most of northwest Europe during the last millennium BC. Regarded as barbarians by the Romans, they were nonetheless skilled in metalwork and carving and produced beautiful artefacts and ornaments. Soon, however, these peoples were to be subjugated by the classical civilizations of the Mediterranean.

Traces of Greek trading colonies from the 5th century BC have been found at Marseilles and Perpignan; however, it was not until the Roman Empire spread suddenly and rapidly north of the Alps, occupying southern France by 120 BC and penetrating the northern forests by 49 BC, that the first unified culture was established, albeit by invaders.

Many examples of Roman architecture are found in the south, from the well-preserved amphitheaters at Arles and Nîmes, to the monumental arch at St Remy and the functional beauty of the Pont du Gard at Nîmes. France, more than any other country north of the Alps, inherited a substantial foundation of classical Roman civilization, and although much was destroyed in the Dark Ages, enough remained to dominate the development of early Christian art and architecture. The cathedral baptisteries at Aix and Marseille owe much to this inheritance. It is no accident that the most famous modern example of a Roman triumphal arch—the Arc de Triomphe—should have been built in Paris.

The Franks and Charlemagne

By the 7th century AD, Christianity was well established throughout France. Its interaction with an inherited classical tradition produced the first great indigenous French culture, the Frankish or Merovingian. The Franks, originally a group of Germanic tribes, established a huge empire over Western Europe, finally expelling the Romans from French soil.

Although most of the architecture of this period has been lost, Frankish sophistication is reflected in the ornate damascene silver and bronze work found in the many warrior cemeteries of Northern France. France was soon to become part of the central core of Catholicism, and would remain so until the French Revolution. Many of the great monastic centers—Tours, Limoges, Auxerre, Reims, Chartres and Corbie—were established at this time.

Under Charlemagne (c.742–814) not only did the Frankish Empire expand into Northern Italy, but the axis of European power shifted north of the Alps, to the newly constituted Holy Roman Empire, centered around Charlemagne's huge palace at Aix-la-Chapelle, regarded by contemporaries as a 'second Rome'. His chapel at Aix, now part of Aachen cathedral, was modeled on San Vitale in Ravenna. Little of the complex now remains, but Charlemagne, supported by his friend and teacher Alcuin, also promoted a renaissance of classical learning and creativity. He imported bronzes from Italy and numerous small votive pieces from Asia Minor as models for Frankish craftsmen working in gold, ivory, bronze and cloisonné. His interest in the written word led to the production of illuminated manuscripts in nearly all major monastic centers, especially at Reims and Tours. The Ebbo Gospels and the Utrecht Psalter (both at Reims) display a vivacity and technique not usually associated with early Medieval art. Following the achievements at Aachen, Carolingian architecture flowered, with its distinctive slender piers, round-headed arches and groin vaults; the oratory of Germigny des Prés (c.820, restored) is a fine example of the period. In tandem with the rise of manuscript illumination and architecture was the development of fresco painting, based on the rather heavy style of Byzantine mosaics, such as at St Germain in Auxerre.

Romanesque and Gothic

The more settled conditions in Europe during and after the 10th century saw the increasing prosperity of the church and the flowering of Romanesque, a style that developed under the protective wing of reformist monastic orders such as the Benedictines at Cluny in Burgundy. The rapid expansion of such orders, strategically placed on pilgrim routes, led to a profusion of building, painting and sculpture. Languedoc, Burgundy and the Loire valley have the best examples—the first fully-vaulted European church can be found at Saint-Benoît-sur-Loire (1083).

Romanesque architecture was an almost exclusively ecclesiastical style, characterized by immensely solid buildings, whose rounded arches are set on powerful columns with ornate floral capitals. Each region had its own variations, that of the south being quite different from that of Normandy, for example. During the 12th century a greater range of materials and techniques were developed; smoothly finished stone and ornate reliefs appear and the individual artist, as opposed to the mere anonymous artisan, became important—Giselbertus, who worked at Autun Cathedral, was one such. The wonderfully sculpted relief of Christ in Majesty over the main Autun doorway is combined with a wealth of spontaneous detail. A similar vitality also marks the few

CREATIVE FRANCE

remaining examples of Romanesque painting, in which detailed narrative was developed; although the best example of this story-telling power remains the famous tapestry at Bayeux (c. 1070).

The desire to span greater areas with stone and to admit more light to the building was to lead to the development of the pointed arch and the rib vault. The essentially skeletal structure that was produced could then contain large areas of glass. This style, the Gothic, first appeared at Saint-Denis (1140), today on the outskirts of Paris, but was soon to gain currency throughout Europe. It subsequently dominated ecclesiastical architecture from Portugal to Poland for the next four hundred years. First fully developed at Notre Dame, Paris (from 1163), Chartres (from 1200), Reims (from 1211) and Amiens (from 1220), these cathedrals all contain distinctive Gothic forms; delicate filigree-like rose windows, tall lancet windows—both usually of richly-stained glass—and elaborately carved doorways and facades.

The Gothic style was long-lived and went through distinct evolutions. Conceived as organic wholes, the cathedrals took many years to build, and consequently reflect changes both in architecture and society as a whole. Often a single building demonstrates the progression from the purity of early Gothic line and form to the intricate tracery of the Flamboyant style (developed after about 1375), and so on to the highly complex and possibly febrile over-decoration of Late Gothic, from the 15th century. The best examples of the late style are in Normandy.

In secular buildings, ecclesiastical Gothic forms were combined with the more popular elements of wooden gable and round-spired turret, as in the Palace of Justice at Rouen (1499). Like its ecclesiastical counterpart, this style spread throughout France in the wake of the monarchy's gradual unification of the country, supplanting the many regional styles, especially in the south—a mirror both of the imposition of a central power and a slow progress towards national identity.

Renaissance to Revolution

From the late 15th century into the 16th, the golden light of the Italian Renaissance slowly dawned over France. In its wake there came a significant increase in secular artistic activity. The Renaissance in France received its greatest impetus under François I, who imported many Italian artists and craftsmen—among them Leonardo da Vinci, who lived at Cloux from 1507. The climax of this process was the building, under the supervision of the Venetian Serlio, of the Palace of Fontainebleau (from 1528). For the decoration of the Palace a workshop was developed, whose members included such Italian painters and sculptors as Cellini, Primaticcio and Rosso, as well as jewelers and tapestry weavers. The school developed a distinct late Renaissance (or

Mannerist) style in obvious competition to its Italian contemporaries, characterized by a use of rich colors, flowing, elongated forms and a concentration upon allegory and eroticism. An earnest desire to rival and outdo Italy in cultural pursuits was to dominate French culture for the next two hundred years.

Massive building programs were started, although constantly disrupted by the religious wars of the 16th century they saw a rigorous rejection of Gothic and vernacular forms in favor of classical models. The first great examples of this development were the châteaux around Paris and in the Loire valley. They were hybrid creations, combining daring interpretations of Italian forms with more traditional spired skylines. Fine examples are those at Blois (from 1498) and Chambord (from 1519). The rebuilding of the Louvre, begun in 1546, marked the final assimilation of Italian classical architecture into France.

This was also the age of the rise of the French court, and with it came the appearance of the independent, free-thinking courtier, whose cultural antecedents can be found in the works of the sceptical essayist Montaigne (1533–92), the political theorist Jean Bodin (1530–96) and the poet courtier Pierre de Ronsard (1524–85); Ronsard in particular was to contribute much to the reformation and modernization of the French language by reference to and borrowings from the classics. The establishment of humanist learning is probably best illustrated by the philosophical works of René Descartes (1596–1650) and Blaise Pascal (1623–62). The clarity, reason and severity of the Cartesian school marked the ascendancy of France in the academic world.

By the beginning of the 17th century the strongly Italianate flavor of the 16th had been replaced by something more distinctly French, although the urge to better their southern neighbors was still pronounced. The formal and dramatic lessons of Roman Baroque architecture, for example, were fully absorbed by Salomon de Brosse in his facade for St Gervais, and were to be developed in Bruant and Mansart's church of Les Invalides (1679). Similarly, in the reign of Henri IV, much emphasis was placed on one of the most characteristic of Baroque architectural concerns, the development of large scale town planning. Under Henri IV the Place des Vosges was built, the first of a number of *places* (squares) forming focal points within a city. The *place* continued as a central ideal in Parisian town planning until the 19th century.

However, it was under Louis XIV that the most grandiose schemes of post-Renaissance France were to be realized. In considering these massive works one should remember that France had, by the 17th century, regained its former position as the preponderant power of Europe—fully unified, heavily armed and defended, and administered by a carefully-ordered aristocratic bureaucracy which radiated from

CREATIVE FRANCE

the absolutist court of the Sun King at Versailles. This was the golden age, in which patronage of the arts enjoyed almost equal expenditure to that lavished on Louis's continual wars. The palaces of the Louvre (1546–1878) and Versailles (1661–1756) bear witness to this in sheer scale, if nothing else. They were built as demonstrations of France's power and, more specifically, that of Louis. In their profusion of painted and sculpted decoration were performed the intellectually exquisite plays of Corneille (1606–84), and were hung the opulent portraits of their creators by painters such as Philippe de Champaigne (1602–74). Indeed, under Louis's patronage and the auspicious eye of his treasurer Colbert, the Académie des Beaux-Arts was established, by which the state could control the nature and quality of the Arts, often as a propaganda machine. It held sway as arbiter of taste until the famous Salon des Refusés in 1863.

It was perhaps unfortunate that the two greatest French painters of the age spent most of their working lives in Rome—Nicolas Poussin (1594–1665) reflects Corneille's admiration for classical order and Stoicism in his severe figure compositions and landscapes, whereas Claude Lorraine (1600–82) surveys a lost world of classical idyll in his pictorial imagination.

However, this was also the age of the Counter-Reformation, and of the persecution of the Huguenots—not all was lofty and grand. The devotional paintings of Georges de la Tour (1593–1652) and the genre pieces of the Le Nain brothers display a concern for the spiritual existence of the common man which seems far removed from the glories of Versailles. The fables of La Fontaine (1621–95) and Perrault (1635–88) have retained their popular appeal, as have many of the products of the popular theater which flourished in the 17th century, none more so than the satirical comedies of Molière (1622–73). Less universally enduring, but as popular at the time were the tragic masterpieces of Racine (1639–99).

The beginning of the 18th century found France on the verge of bankruptcy; the court withdrew from the splendors of Versailles, and their cultural life reflected a taste for domesticity, albeit tempered by a pronounced taste for fantasy. It was in their elegant Parisian boudoirs and reception rooms that the French Rococo style of decoration and ornamentation developed—the grand gesture on a small scale. The theatrical fantasies and *fêtes champêtres* of the painters Watteau (1684–1721) and Fragonard (1732–1806), the intimate eroticism of Boucher (1703–70), and the dreams realized in stone by Clodion (1738–1814), provided civilized diversions for an aristocracy now withdrawn from the stage of power politics. A more social diversion which was to have lasting appeal was the development of the comic opera, a misnomer for the most popular and accessible art form of the century.

However, the age also produced artists given less to providing diversions for a pampered and frivolous aristocracy. The paintings of Chardin (1699–1779) display a placid stillness comparable with the solidity of Poussin. Houdon's sculpture, at its best, combines a profound classicism with a remarkable veracity, as his portrait of Voltaire (1778) shows. The development of the novel from its early picaresque form can be seen in the work of Abbé Prévost (1697–1763) whose *Manon Lescaut* looks forward to the sophisticated form of Laclos's *Les Liaisons Dangereuses,* probably the finest mirror of French aristocratic dalliance.

It was in the realm of literature that a new force was first apparent. The beady eye of Voltaire (1694–1778) surveyed contemporary society and declared, in novels such as *Candide* (1759), that maybe this wasn't the best of all possible worlds. Similar seeds of doubt were voiced by other writer/philosophers. The 18th century had seen the rise—not only in France—of a wealthy entrepreneurial middle class whose values were based in the main upon logic and empirical reason, whether in commerce, the arts or in science. The spokesmen were Voltaire, Diderot (1713–84), who recorded the state of human achievement in his *Encyclopaedia* (published from 1751) and J.-J. Rousseau (1712–78), who more than anyone defined the paradox at the heart of mid-18th-century France. In *La Nouvelle Héloïse* (1760) and *Confessions* (c.1770) he used a careful examination of the individual's faults and needs as a natural being as a basis for arguing for social and political reform—the need for Revolution.

The Modern Age

As often happens, art was one step ahead of history. Notions of political identity for the common man had made the novellas of Beaumarchais (1732–99), including the *Marriage of Figaro* and the *Barber of Seville,* popular works. The design for the Panthéon by Soufflot (1757–90), Gabriel's refined Petit Trianon at Versailles (1762), and the paintings of Greuze (1725–1805) and David (1748–1825) display a concern for moral order in great contrast to the flippancies of Fragonard. The clear, apparently simple, frieze-like structure of David's *Oath of the Horatii* (1784), the first masterpiece of Neo-classicism, touched an artistic nerve which was to explode in the French Revolution five years later.

Many of the ideals of the French Revolution proved impracticable and short-lived, but the renewed taste for classicism remained a touchstone for the Establishment until the late 19th century—a tradition, best exemplified in the work of Ingres (1780–1867), which was to degenerate in a matter of 50 years into a voyeuristic justification for painting nudes.

CREATIVE FRANCE

With the rise to power of Napoleon from the ashes of the Revolutionary Directoire, a new intellectual force and esthetic mode came to the fore—Romanticism. While respecting many of the genuine tenets of the classical world, its adherents rejected the slavish emulation of them. The subject matter of Romanticism was the modern world, seen in all its heroism, adventure and horror, or more precisely the artist's means of expressing his reaction to it. Never strictly formulated—the very idea was against the Romantic grain—its dye spread to all the arts, demanding an immediacy to technique, emotionalism and the ability to convey the doubts and uncertainties of the human condition. It found its most successful outlet in literature, in the morbid speculations of Chateaubriand (1768–1848), the amoral and intensely psychological novels of Stendhal (1783–1842), and the all-encompassing fiction and dramatic works of Victor Hugo (1802–1885), Dumas (1802–70) and Balzac (1799–1850). In painting, its early master was Géricault (1791–1824), whose powerfully Romantic *Raft of the Medusa* (1819), at once hopeful and despairing, inspired Delacroix (1798–1863), the master of the expressive brush-stroke whose emotive use of color epitomized Romantic aspirations. In music, it found expansive expression in the works of Berlioz (1803–69). His *Symphonie Fantastique* is perhaps the most widespread and accessible of all Romantic works. On a smaller scale, but with no less intensity, the music of the expatriate Pole, Chopin (1810–49), crystalized the movement's lucid introspection.

The nebulous nature of Romanticism, which made it so adaptable to various art forms, reflected both the political turmoil of France in the 19th century, and the withdrawal of the artist from politics, growing industrialization and urbanization into a more subjective world. It also led to a rapid fragmentation of Romanticism into many different movements. Adherents of 'Art for Art's Sake', for example, promoted extreme estheticism and intuitive psychological investigation; its major literary exponents were the poets Baudelaire (1821–67) and Théophile Gautier (1811–72), who combined a taste for the exotic with a concern for the extreme refinement of their art. This approach was to develop through the 19th century into the Symbolist movement, in which the wilder shores of art were explored by the poets Mallarmé (1842–98), and Verlaine (1844–96), and by painters such as Moreau (1826–98) and Redon (1840–1916).

Another development from Romanticism was Realism, often carrying strong social overtones. The close observation of life in a supposedly non-stylized fashion was taken up by Flaubert (1821–80)—probably the finest French writer of the century—and in a more sensational fashion by Zola (1840–1903), whose Rougon-Macquart series (inspired by Balzac's *Comédie Humaine*) set out to examine the consciousness of modern man in all its manifestations. The conclusions were inevitably depressing. Pictorially, however, the results were quite different. The Barbizon School of landscape painters approached their subjects with a fresh eye, using clear, bright colors to produce paintings in which atmospheric effects and naturalistic observation replaced the idealized classicism prevalent in previous centuries.

It was primarily from the work of these painters that the Impressionist movement evolved. Taking modern life as their subject matter, Monet (1840–1926), Renoir (1841–1919) and Pissarro (1831–1903) proceeded to break down their visual perceptions in terms of light and color, an interpretation of 'realism' which was to have lasting effect, culminating in Monet's late series of *Waterlily* paintings (from 1916).

The breaking down of established cultural barriers in favor of a new perception was not solely the province of the Impressionists, indeed they played only a small part in the process. The political commitment apparent in the work of Courbet (1819–77) looked forward to the republican ideals of the 1870s, and Manet's (1832–83) rejection of pictorial tradition in both subject matter and treatment caused great scandal in 1863 when, due to the number of works rejected at the annual Salon of the Academy, an alternative, the Salon des Refusés, was held. It was this period of disruption, in both politics and the arts, which gave rise to the popular myth of the Parisian Bohemian artist, the disaffected idealist kicking at the shins of tradition.

The term Impressionism also implies the pinning down of movement, of the ephemeral. This was to find its most successful expression in the exquisite paintings and sculpture of Degas (1834–1917) and the weighty sculpture of Rodin (1840–1917). A similar end was also achieved in music by the composers Debussy (1862–1918) and Ravel (1875–1937), who sought to capture mood and resonance rather than narrative development.

If the middle of the 19th century saw the dissolution of form—which, in pictorial terms had been a sine qua non from the Renaissance onwards—in the work of the Impressionists, it also saw the introduction of new solid forms in the environment. Baron Haussmann (1809–91), under the direction of Napoleon III, continued the re-shaping of Paris as a modern, planned city, opening large boulevards connecting strategic *places*. Much of his planning was dominated by new considerations; a large, industrial population, modern materials, modern communications, especially railways—and the need for mob control, which, though not new, was now tackled on a large scale. The French ability to adapt to modernism was underlined by a series of World Exhibitions held in Paris, and it was the experience of these which propelled the nation so forcibly into the 20th century. The most potent symbol of this startling progress was the Eiffel Tower, built for the

Paris Exhibition of 1889, and a work in which industrial engineer, architect and sculptor suddenly and radically unite.

The Twentieth Century

The diffusion of Romanticism in the second half of the 19th century led to a splintering of cultural direction. The avant garde of the mid-century had become the Establishment of the *fin de siècle*, while younger artists on the other hand were dominated by one concept—modernism. In painting the many implications of Impressionism are illustrated by the developments that led from it, ranging from the broad color fields of Gauguin (1848–1903), the technical detail and structural contrivance of Seurat (1859–91), and most influentially in the flat modulations of Cézanne (1839–1906). The most controlled assessment of the ferment, and probably the greatest masterpiece of Post-Impressionism, was Proust's novel *Remembrance of Things Past* (from 1913), which, in combining a dissolution of subject matter with a restructuring of material in an equally convincing and yet artificial manner, pointed towards the future.

The ferocious flat colors used by the Fauves, led by Matisse (1869–1954) and Derain (1880–1954), caused an outrage in 1905. But barely two years later the development of Cubism by Braque (1882–1963) and the Spaniard Picasso (1881–1973)—which rejected all established notions of the relationship between object, artist and audience—heralded a valid and frightening view of the world, adapted to 20th century needs. Similar trends were developed by the poet Apollinaire (1880–1918) and in the novel by Gide (1869–1951). However, the assurance and confidence of this generation of artists was shattered by the experience of the Great War.

For four years French soil soaked up the blood of Europe's youth, and France suffered almost more than her foe in bearing the brunt of subsequent economic and moral disaster in this, the second of three German invasions within 80 years. The Romantic dream of a modern Europe turned into a senseless nightmare. However, during the Great War young men from all over the Western world had a taste of French culture, which, in its wake, they were keen to renew. Paris and its environs were to attract painters, writers and dilettantes as a result of its role both as a cultural center and as a resort of liberalism. Russian artists such as Kandinsky (1866–1944) and Chagall (b. 1887), the composer Stravinsky (1882–1971), the Romanian sculptor Brancusi (1876–1957), and various writers including Gertrude Stein (champion of the Cubists), Anaïs Nin, Hemingway and Joyce only formed the vanguard of a creative torrent.

Paris was to form a focal point and context for most of the major inter-war artistic movements; Constructivism, Dadaism and Surrealism each found their French spokesmen, notably in the writers André Breton (1896–1966) and Aragon (1897–1966). There was a great fecundity and cross-fertilization of ideas, so well brought to life in the novels of Colette (1873–1954). The career of say, Picasso, reflects the wealth of influences of the time.

Nonetheless, French culture itself remained somewhat directionless, and at best eclectic. The work of the so-called School of Paris emphasizes this; it is difficult to envisage the high Expressionist Soutine sharing a Montmartre studio with the delicate Modigliani, but he did. It was a time when monumental classical works could be created side by side with Cubist-inspired constructions. Perhaps the most consistent vision of the time was that of the Swiss-born architect Le Corbusier (1887–1966) whose chapel at Ronchamp (1950–54) and Unité d' Habitation at Marseilles (1947–52) are high points in a career dedicated to the combination of esthetically satisfying form and a theoretical social utility.

Overall, the most important aspect of inter-war French culture was the development of the doctrine of Existentialism by Jean-Paul Sartre (1905–80). In the novels *Nausea* and *The Roads to Freedom* he underlined the individual's need to abstract himself from his immediate surroundings, and in doing so to develop his own moral and ethical code. Sartre's example was taken up by Albert Camus, the criminal-poet Jean Genet and Simone de Beauvoir, each of whom modified the doctrine by introducing broader moral and critical questions. The age of the creative individual, rather than the member of a 'movement', had arrived.

A foil to Sartre's vision can be found in the writings of the historian and Gaullist Minister for Culture André Malraux (1901–76); his ability to digest and redefine the national cultural heritage from a world view provided a vital central vortex about which the strands of modern French creative thought could orbit. This motion was most characteristically expressed in an urge towards art as experiment. The novels of Robbe-Grillet and Marguerite Duras embody this in their enigmatic structure. A similarly radical move occurred in the theatrical work of Ionesco, Anouilh and the Irish expatriate Samuel Beckett, musically in the structural preoccupations of Messiaen (b. 1908) and his pupil Pierre Boulez (b. 1925).

However, it was probably the cinema which realized the greatest steps. An ideal existential medium, the form also fascinated the Surrealists. France has often been regarded as the home of the cinema; the popular trickeries of the Lumière brothers in the early years of the century enjoyed international success, and were the outcome of a long-standing French fascination with photography. The portraits by Nadar (1820–1910) are among the first masterpieces of photography, and the mechanical imagery of the camera had fascinated the painters Manet, Degas and Toulouse-Lautrec.

Between the wars the cinema industry boomed, and by 1930 had reached a remarkable maturity in the work of Jean Renoir (1894–1979)—*Une Partie de Campagne* (1936) and *La Règle du Jeu* (1939) represent the 20th-century flowering of a humorous and humane tradition stretching back to Montaigne and Molière. The work of Marcel Carné (b. 1903) and his collaborator Jacques Prévert—especially the magical *Les Enfants du Paradis* (1944), made illicitly in German-occupied Paris—represents the modernization of another French tradition, the *opéra comédie*. A strong Romantic sense permeates the films of the Surrealist poet Jean Cocteau (1889–1963), from the lyrical *Beauty and the Beast* (1946) to the masterly *Orphée* (1950), (yet another example of France's empathy with classical themes).

The 1950s saw a truly remarkable development, initially through the auspices of the critical journal *Cahiers du Cinema*. Its editors, including Godard (b. 1930), Truffaut (b. 1932) and Chabrol (b. 1930) inaugurated a new wave of self-conscious cinema, based on the immediacy of American B-movies, and a commitment to the unique political and expressive qualities of film. Truffaut's *Four Hundred Blows* (1959) and *Jules et Jim* (1961), and Godard's *Breathless* (1960) and *Weekend* (1967) remain dominant masterpieces of modern French cinema. In their wake, the six 'Moral Tales' of Rohmer (b. 1920) and the playful narrative games of Rivette (b. 1928) are outstanding.

Modern France has sloughed off many of its traditional bohemian associations, and has adopted rather the lofty role of *maîtresse* of Euro-culture; its position is one of conservatism. Even the vigorously modern Pompidou complex in Paris represents primarily an ambitious (and successful) assertion of France's place at the heart of European creativity. The annual Cannes film and television festivals in early summer inexplicably remain the major world marketplace and arbiters of good taste in each medium. In contrast to the serious work of Boulez, French popular musical taste remains distinctly old hat. Nonetheless, France does remain the most enriched of European countries—with the possible exception of Italy—and the maintenance of local museums, galleries and folk festivals put the rest of Europe to shame.

DINING

The noble art of gastronomy

by
JOHN ARDAGH

(The author is a former managing editor of The Good Food Guide, *Britain's leading gastronomic guide.)*

Marvelous meals with good wines will rank for many visitors among the keenest pleasures of a trip to France, a land virtually synonymous with gastronomy. Blessed with a fertile soil the French have evolved an agriculture of amazing variety, and to this they have applied their creative flair and their zestful hedonism to produce a *cuisine* of a range and subtlety with no equal—not even in China. The French have gastronomy in their bones. It is less a conscious cult than an accepted part of daily life, a heritage taken for granted; a good housewife will no more mix the wrong ingredients in her family's *coq au vin* than a good doctor will prescribe the wrong drugs or a car worker fit the wrong parts to a new Renault.

Gastronomy is also regarded as one of the noble arts. Great chefs become celebrated national figures (Escoffier yesterday, Bocuse today) as much as leading actors or singers. Older people, especially, talk and think about food in a detailed way that an Anglo-Saxon might find boring, or even in bad taste: eavesdrop on a conversation in street or bus, and it might well be two men enthusing over the flavor of the *quenelles de brochet* in their local *bistrot,* or working wives comparing the subtleties of ten cheeses. The French like to linger over a good meal, and many regard it as one of life's finer enjoyments, roughly halfway, say, between listening to Mozart and making passionate love.

It is true that this glorious tradition is today under assault from a modern nation in a hurry. *But* this decline is very relative. The French, when they want to, still eat far better than any other race on earth—and so therefore can their visitors.

Choosing your restaurant, and your meal

The range of *good* eating-places is staggering, from the Tour d'Argent in Paris at $100 a head, down to a truckdriver's pull-in serving a copious dish-of-the-day for $5. Under each town, this book lists a brief selection to suit most purses, but it is by no means complete: for fuller details, you might choose to buy a French guide, such as the red *Michelin,* or *Gault-et-Millau.*

The first rule: it is not necessarily in the smart places that you eat best, for the French usually set less store by gloss and comfort than by what happens in the kitchen. Do not judge a restaurant by its swanky façade, nor by the number of waiters in tails. Look first at the menu, posted outside, then poke your nose inside: if it is full, of people who seem *French,* that is a good sign. If not in the guidebooks, a pricey place on a tourist route may be a clip-joint—alas, there are all too many.

Paris restaurant menus are mostly *à la carte;* in the provinces they usually have fixed-price meals too, of three, four or five courses, and these offer the best value. The French traditionally eat four courses, including cheese and sweet. Indeed you may not be popular if you take just one dish, and anyway it will be a false economy, costing as much as the full *table d'hôte.* In the provinces, in family-run *bistrots,* it is still possible to have a good meal with wine for only $10 to $15; and the dispensable paper tablecloths, on which the waitress maybe scrawls the bill, are all part of the fun. A *brasserie* is a downtown café-restaurant, often large, bright and noisy, with solid cooking of a routine kind; an *auberge* (inn) is more cosily characterful, but not always better. If you don't mind roughing it a bit, the truckdrivers' main-road pull-ins *(relais routiers)* often give excellent value (the French working man is a discriminating food lover).

Once the language barrier is overcome, there is a special mystique about ordering a meal. Staff may seem brusque at first, especially in Paris—that is their style—but will generally be helpful if you show an interest in their dishes. If in France you want to do as the French do, then you will eat cheese *before* sweet, and accept that meat is generally served on its own or with just one vegetable, not smothered by several in the Anglo-Saxon manner. Many restaurants offer copious *hors d'oeuvres* at lunch (*crudités,* mixed raw vegetables with dressing can be delicious), but at dinner the French are more likely to start with soup. A warning: French taste is to eat meat rare *(saignant)* or semi-rare *(à point),* and a serious restaurateur may refuse to serve a 'barbarian' who insults him by asking for it well-done *(bien cuit).*

From regional tradition to Paul Bocuse's new wave

De Gaulle once asked, 'How can you govern a nation with 300 cheeses?' He need not have been so sceptical: the French still hang together, politically, despite their 300 cheeses and umpteen thousand recipes. The diversity of French cooking beggars belief. While some dishes are common in most of France, each region also has its own complex array of specialties, rooted deep in peasant history, and these are described in our regional chapters.

The Lyon area, with its elaborate ways of preparing pork, chicken, pike and crayfish, is often considered the heartland of French gastronomy. The cooking of Burgundy is equally rich, with the accent on meat in wine sauces. In fact France's cuisine is closely allied to its regional wines: for example Alsace uses its white wines for the cooking of *choucroute* and *coq au riesling,* while Touraine simmers its poultry in a red Chinon or Bourgeuil. From Périgord to the Pyrenees they savor the subtleties of truffles and *foie gras,* while the rougher, spicier cuisine of Provence is noted for its garlicky fish stews, charcoal-grilled meat with aromatic herbs, and pungent vegetable dishes such as *ratatouille.* The non-vinegrowing north of France may not at first sight seem so gastronomic, yet the Normans do wonderful things with veal or chicken cooked in cream, cider or calvados, and the Bretons have devised fascinating recipes for the fish and shellfish from their seas. Some French towns are famous for their own special dishes: Toulouse for *cassoulet,* Caen for its way with tripe; Nice for tuna-fish salad, and of course Marseille for *bouillabaisse.*

Most provincial restaurants feature some local dishes—so why not try them? Paris has no dishes of its own (unless you count new imports like *le hamburger*), but many of its best restaurants are run by émigrés from the regions who have kept their local connections and still cook their local dishes. So you can savor a wide range of good regional cooking without straying more than five miles from the Arc de Triomphe. Also, it is worth asking for the speciality of the house, often a dish the *patron* has invented himself and is proud of. Or try the dish of the day *(plat du jour)*. But, except in large international restaurants, beware of lengthy, standardized menus, which usually betray precooking and reheating, and too much use of the deep-freeze or can. The French believe in fresh ingredients freshly cooked, and the best menus are thus very often the shorter ones.

Most regional cooking falls into the category of *cuisine bourgeoise* (good ingredients, well prepared in the middle-class way) or else *cuisine paysanne* (peasant fare: simple materials, maybe scrags or leftovers, cleverly freshened up to maximize their flavors, as poor peasants, perforce, have learned to do). These dishes are often heavy and spicy. In the southeast, olive oil is the basis of much cooking, and everywhere south of the Loire garlic is used to succulent effect. But do not be led to suppose that all French cooking is rich, and thus indigestible. Its secret is in many cases simplicity, allied to careful preparation—in many a country *auberge* you can eat deliciously without needing to attempt anything more exotic than, say, *crudités* or fresh vegetable soup, omelets, grilled farmyard chicken with rosemary or roast lamb, French beans lightly tossed in butter, Brie, and a homemade apple or cherry tart.

In the great classic restaurants, such as Lasserre or Le Grand Véfour in Paris, you will find *haute cuisine*. This is the refined, expensive style of cooking that was elaborated for smart society in the 19th century, with lavish use of rich sauces based on butter, cream, egg yolk, and maybe brandy. Today it is going out of fashion. A new generation of gourmets has become more diet-conscious, thus providing a ready clientele for the great culinary revolution of the past two decades, known as *la nouvelle cuisine française* (the 'new French cooking'). This inventive style marks a return to a lighter, purer manner. It spurns most heavy sauces that mask the taste of the meat; spurns flour and carbohydrates too. It relies on very fresh ingredients, rapidly cooked in their own juices, almost in the Chinese manner, so as to bring out their true flavors. Vegetables are served crispy, half-cooked. It encourages the chef to deviate from classic recipes and try out daring new blends: for instance a purée of mixed spinach and pear preserves the fresh taste of both.

The style was pioneered by the late and great Fernand Point, of the Pyramide restaurant at Vienne. Today its leading exponent and propagandist is Paul Bocuse, owner-chef of a famous restaurant just outside

Lyon. This ebullient showman has become the ringleader of a whole new school of restaurateurs dedicated to *la nouvelle cuisine,* and today probably more than half the best restaurants in France follow this style. You can find the 'new cooking' today in many different places. But it is nearly always expensive, for it demands much time and skill, and quality ingredients. And some gourmets consider it a little chi-chi and over-refined, preferring the more robust tastes of traditional if less healthy dishes, such as *cassoulet.*

One well-known chef, Michel Guérard, has taken the new style even further by inventing what he calls *la cuisine minceur* (slimmers' cooking), and is now running a kind of luxury health-farm for gourmet slimmers in a country hotel near Pau, where you can combine exquisite eating with an intake of less than 500 calories per four-course meal.

Invasion of the 'drugstore' and the deep freeze

The 'new cooking' is a typical symptom of the present confused transitional phase in the world of French eating habits. All is relative: depending on how you look at it, the French can seem to be steadfast in their gastronomic traditions, or fast deserting them. In their own homes, as in restaurants, they are today eating lighter meals: four courses are no longer a ritual, and the young middle-class wife may as soon toss a couple of steaks under her new electric grill as spend a couple of hours on a complex stew. Lunch is traditionally the main meal of the day, especially in the provinces, where schoolkids and bread-winners return home for the leisurely family meal. However, in Paris and other big cities, many firms are moving over to the shorter lunch break, Anglo-Saxon style, and this has given rise to a rash of new snackbars and fast eateries, most of them horrid. The vogue for Anglo-American gimmicks has thrown up scores of so-called 'pubs' and 'drugstores', but these bear little relation to their originals (some of them do in fact serve perfectly authentic French food, in a ritzy modern setting).

The younger urban middle classes are developing new tastes in dining out. They want not only good food but also 'amusing' décor and atmosphere. Hence, in the wake of London, a recent vogue for candlelit *bistrots,* and rustic or arty-crafty décor, with music. There are scores of such places on the Paris Left Bank, and on the Riviera. The food is generally far better than in their London or New York equivalent, for the French do still *care* what they eat, but gourmets treat this trend with scorn. The French are also discovering, belatedly, that theirs is not the world's only worthwhile cuisine. From their foreign holidays they have now acquired a taste for *paella, moussaka,* kebabs, and so on, so that foreign restaurants are multiplying, in Paris and many other cities. Vietnamese and Chinese lead the way, followed by Italian, Spanish,

Greek, Moroccan, Tunisian and others. There are also a number of modest-priced pizza houses, many of them run by Corsicans, as well as many restaurants serving North African specialties such as *couscous*, mostly cooked by French repatriates from Algeria.

The French are at last also thawing towards frozen foods. These were shunned for many years by a nation that cares for flavor and freshness, and even today the French consume only a third as much frozen produce as the British or Germans. But sales are now rising 20% a year, and the hypermarkets' deep-freeze counters are expanding. But with a difference: the French are not interested in the freezing of basic foods such as peas and fish fingers: they prefer more complex, and costly, precooked dishes such as *bouillabaisse, coq-au-vin,* or even frogs' legs *provençale*. In other words, they are harnessing modern deep-freeze techniques to their own gastronomy. And many gourmets accept that very little flavor is lost, so long as the precooking and then the thawing are done correctly. This could offer French gastronomy an eventual way out of its current dilemma: how to preserve tradition and quality in an age of rising costs and hectic tempo. Answer—make modern science your ally, not your enemy.

Choosing the right wine

What do the French drink with, or before, their meals? One golden rule: if you are about to enjoy a fine meal, do not dull your palate by drinking too many dry martinis or other cocktails. You will be too woozy, and your taste buds too anesthetized, to appreciate the food. Best stick, as the French do, to one simple apéritif. Try, for example, an anisette-based *pastis* (Pernod or Ricard), drunk with water which clouds it whitish; or one of the sweet French apéritifs, such as Byrrh or St-Raphaël. The French drink little sherry, but *le gin-tonic* is catching on and they are as avid for whisky *(le scotch)* as any kilted Highlander.

The range of French wines is so vast that choosing the right one for your meal may seem intimidating. But in fact it can be simple. For most tastes, a dry white wine goes best with shellfish, a slightly softer white with other fish, red wine with meat and cheese, and a sweet white with a rich dessert. But there are no set rules. In fact it has now become *à la mode* to drink a light red wine with some fish, such as sole. Much will depend on your own taste—and the weather. Either red or white goes well with roast chicken, so why not try a red Burgundy in winter and a fruity Riesling on a hot day? For a large, formal meal of the banquet type, the French will change wines three or four times, but for an ordinary meal it is not unusual to stick to the same wine.

The vinegrowing industry is subject to strict government controls, and wines are carefully graded and labeled. For some assurance of quality, look for the phrase *'Appellation Contrôlée'* on the label—this means that the wine comes from a particular area, as designated, and is not a mixture of cheap blends from various vineyards. A slightly lower grade, but still very drinkable, is labeled 'VDQS' *(vin de qualité supérieure)*. In most restaurants you will find the range of prices enormous. The better vintage wines have rocketed in price in recent years and are now just as expensive in France as abroad (due partly to a tacit conspiracy of high mark-ups by restaurateurs). But, unless you are very rich, there is no need to drink a special vintage wine every day. Most good restaurants offer a respectable house wine at a reasonable price, and often their carafe wines are pleasant (though in cheaper places they can be nastily acid). When in doubt, consult the *patron* or the *sommelier* (wine waiter).

Americans may be used to Californian wines which, because of climate, and production methods, vary little from year to year, or from one area to another. But in France, with erratic climate and manifold kinds of soil and vine, the wines vary hugely from year to year and even from acre to acre. Connoisseurs have written thousands of books on the subject. In a few lines, all we can say of the better wines is that the choice between Bordeaux and Burgundy reds is a matter of taste; the former are lighter and subtler, the latter more full-bodied and earthy. Both, especially Bordeaux, improve with age, whereas a Beaujolais is best drunk young. Finest among the non-sparkling whites are Burgundies such as Meursault or Chablis, or the wines of the Loire valley and Alsace; if your taste is for a sweet white, try Monbazillac or Sauternes (above all, the ambrosial Château-Yquem).

Many other areas of France produce pleasant wines that are much cheaper, partly because they are less fashionable, than the fine wines quoted above. If you want to save a few francs but still drink well, then look on the wine list for reds such as Côtes du Rhône, Corbières, Cahors, whites such as Muscadet, Gros Plant, Listel, or the *rosés* of Anjou, Provence and Béarn (our regional chapters give more details). Wine is grown over nearly all of France south from Paris, and as with food it is not a bad idea to order what is produced locally.

Or you need not drink wine at all. France is not a great beer country like Belgium or Germany, but its lagers such as Kronenbourg or Kanterbrau are good thirst-quenchers. And it has the world's best range of mineral waters, from sparkling Perrier via the effervescent Vichy to the still, spring-like Evian or Badoit. Many French people no longer drink wine, especially the young, and few restaurateurs will frown if you opt for beer or water. But he may explode if you insult his delicate cooking by seeking to wash it down with some unsuitable sugary concoction.

THE
FACE
OF
FRANCE

INTRODUCING PARIS

A promenade in three days

by
DAN BEHRMAN

A gifted American journalist and author, Dan Behrman was for a long period a contributor to the English-language edition of Réalités, *and writes for several other periodicals. His many years of residence equip him admirably to present the highlights of Paris to the first-time visitor.*

There is no shortcut to Paris. Whether you spend three days or three months in this city, it will always have something new to offer you (that is why the most assiduous explorers of Paris are the Parisians themselves).

92 **THE FACE OF FRANCE**

If you are pressed for time, don't hesitate to take a Cook's or American Express guided tour of the city. This provides you with a general impression, a synopsis, and then you need only pick your favorites and return to them at your leisure. Another effective introduction to Paris is the *bateau mouche* service on the Seine. While it cannot take in such land-locked *quartiers* as Montmartre or Montparnasse, it does give an admirable perspective of the city's development along the river banks.

Nothing can replace walking in Paris, however. Distances are suprisingly short, because nearly all the Paris that you will want to see is concentrated in one corner of the city. Here we offer an itinerary for seeing Paris, mainly on foot, in three days.

First day

Morning. Starting point is the Arc de Triomphe and its star of 12 avenues forming the place de l'Etoile, now renamed place Charles de Gaulle (if the weather is clear, take the elevator up to the top of the arch; you will have Paris at your feet). Then stroll down the Champs-Elysées on the north side (even-numbered side) where everyone walks. The film palaces, the cafés and the sidewalks clogged with parked cars end at the Rond-point des Champs-Elysées, and you find yourself in a delightful park. Halfway down to the place de la Concorde, there is one of Paris's famed perspectives: at the place Clemenceau, a glance to the right offers you the Grand Palais and the Petit Palais, the Pont Alexandre-III across the Seine (all three a pompous 1900 ensemble, but grandiose enough to get away with it) and, at the very end, the vast hulk of the Invalides.

Then you reach the place de la Concorde and, once you have succeeded in reaching the safety of the obelisk, you have another perspective to reward you: on your left, the church of the Madeleine balanced perfectly on your right by the National Assembly. Crossing the place de la Concorde, you escape the Paris motorist once again in the graceful Tuileries Gardens ending at the Arc de Triomphe du Carrousel. Here, turn around and take in the most royal perspective of them all: the obelisk bisecting the Arc de Triomphe as it rises out of the green haven of the gardens of the Champs-Elysées at your starting point. Beyond, in the distant haze, rise the skyscrapers of the new business Défense area.

Afternoon. The Carrousel arch is also the gateway to the Louvre (which requires a separate visit). Then cross the Seine by walking along to the Pont-Neuf (unfortunately the Pont des Arts, a wrought-iron bridge for pedestrians only with a perfect view of the Ile de la Cité has had to be partly demolished in preparation for extensive restoration work; it is unlikely to reopen until the late 1980s. On the Left Bank,

INTRODUCING PARIS

prowl along the Seine past the booksellers' stalls and then double back over the Pont-Neuf to the Ile de la Cité.

The green prow of this island formed by the place du Vert Galant can be seen from the Pont-Neuf behind the statue of good King Henri IV ('a chicken in every pot'). Then, cut into the middle of the island to the delightful place Dauphine slumbering in the shadow of the Palais de Justice. A left turn brings you to the quai de l'Horloge and, continuing along the Seine, past the Conciergerie, you reach the boulevard du Palais where the Sainte Chapelle lies hidden behind the sprawling Palais de Justice. The Sainte Chapelle deserves a visit and don't hesitate to ask directions, for it is invisible from the street. Then, return to the Seine, take the quai de Corse to the rue d'Arcole, and suddenly you see before you the magnificent bulk of Notre-Dame.

After walking past the façade of the cathedral, turn into the square Jean-XXIII, with its pretty garden, and then on to the square de l'Ile-de-France, at the tip of the Ile de la Cité, to visit the moving Memorial to the Deported in a sort of crypt by the water's edge. After this, cross the footbridge to the Ile St-Louis, which still retains something of the flavor of 17th-century Paris, though it is now one of the smartest (and most expensive) places to live in the capital. Turning right, follow the quai d'Orléans on this island, which has remained largely unchanged since the 17th century, to the Pont de la Tournelle with its connoisseur's view of Notre-Dame. Walk down to the quai de la Tournelle, the quai de Montebello and the quai St-Michel until you reach the place St-Michel, the beginning of the Latin Quarter. Then turn student and walk up the boulevard St-Michel, past Cluny, the Sorbonne and the Panthéon, all lying on your left. The narrow streets around St-Séverin are full of exotic restaurants, some cheap, some horribly expensive. (There have been some nasty incidents of mugging and even murder around this area at night, so best to avoid it after dark, though there's no problem in the daytime.) The place St-Michel, the place de l'Odéon, the pedestrian-only rue St-André-des-Arts with its avant-garde boutiques, St-Germain-des-Prés with its cafés, and the surrounding streets bursting with art galleries, all teem with life. Up on top of the 'Boul' Mich', all you have to do is sit down . . . in the Luxembourg Gardens.

Another fascinating walk in the same neighborhood takes you behind the Panthéon, up the hilly rue de la Montagne-Ste-Geneviève, named for Paris's patron saint, where you'll see buildings that till recently housed France's most celebrated school, the Ecole Polytechnique (which has now been transferred to the suburbs); down to the remarkable 17th-century church of St-Etienne du Mont. In the same area is the famous and colorful rue Mouffetard—best to go in the morning to see the raucous centuries-old street market. From there wander up to the place de la Contrescarpe: during the day it is peaceful and almost provincial with its quiet cafés—after dark it is a center of youthful nightlife.

Then complete your rest cure by strolling through the Luxembourg Gardens to the rue Vavin exit, walk down the rue Vavin to the boulevard Montparnasse and sit down again on the terrace of the Dôme or the Coupole. A short walk down the boulevard Montparnasse takes you to the Tour Montparnasse.

Second day

Morning. After breakfast, you can either return to St-Germain-des-Prés and walk to the Invalides along the rue de l'Université, drinking in the fading aristocratic glory of the faubourg St-Germain, or else start directly at the Invalides. In either case, the pilgrimage to Napoleon's tomb should not be omitted. A bus will take you to Champ de Mars, or else you can walk the short distance along the avenue de Tourville.

From here you won't have any trouble finding your next objective, the Eiffel Tower, which lies smack in the middle of another miraculous perspective formed by the 18th-century Ecole Militaire, the 19th-century tower and, across the Seine, the 20th-century Palais de Chaillot. After visiting the tower, cross the Pont d'Iéna and walk through the Trocadéro gardens up to the place du Trocadéro for the view. If you're in an expansive—and expensive—mood, have lunch in the restaurant on the first floor of the Eiffel Tower. Otherwise, take a bus down the avenue Kléber back to the Etoile for lunch in the Champs-Elysées district.

Afternoon. In either case, start your afternoon at the Etoile by walking down the avenue Foch into the Bois de Boulogne and spend as much time in the Bois as you need to recuperate from the preceding. (Avoid the Bois on Sundays, it's not very restful.) On the way out, take the Métro at the Porte Dauphine on the avenue Foch back to the Etoile. Here you have a choice: the easy way is a 73 bus down the Champs-Elysées to the Concorde. The expensive way, if you're with your wife, is to get off the 73 at the Rond-Point des Champs-Elysées and walk over on the rue Jean Mermoz to the rue du faubourg St-Honoré, window-shopping all the way down to the rue Castiglione and the place Vendôme. From the place Vendôme, the rue de la Paix leads you to the Opéra and the Café de la Paix.

Third day

Morning. Picking up where you left off the day before, walk down the avenue de l'Opéra to the place du Palais Royal and prowl through

INTRODUCING PARIS

the gardens of the Palais-Royal and the old rue de Beaujolais. Then, from the Palais-Royal, take a 74 bus to the place Clichy. From here, the heart of Pigalle, you can scale Montmartre on foot via the rue Caulaincourt and the rue Lepic, or continue your climb aboard an 80 bus, getting off at Lamarck-Caulaincourt. The rue des Saules will lead you in a 45 degree angle past Paris's last surviving vineyard to the place du Tertre and the Sacré-Coeur at the top of Montmartre and of all Paris. Lunch, of course, on the place du Tertre.

Afternoon. Take a 74 bus from place Clichy to the Palais-Royal and, from here, a 72 bus to the place du Châtelet. Walk up boulevard Sebastopol, turn left on the tiny rue de la Grande Truanderie, and explore the old Halles area, with its glittering boutiques and cafés around the Forum center. This is a good chance to have a look at the controversial architecture of the new Pompidou Center (usually known as the Centre Beaubourg) by taking the rue Aubry-le-Boucher eastwards. Be prepared for a shock when you see it—it looks rather like a vast oil refinery! (You'll want to make a special visit to the museum and exhibition galleries.) After this experience walk to the Hôtel de Ville, Paris's neo-Renaissance city hall. Then walk down the rue de Rivoli, which becomes the rue St-Antoine, and take the first tiny street left after the rue de Turenne. This leads you into the place des Vosges and the fascinating Marais district, once the most aristocratic neighborhood of Paris, and now back in fashion after centuries of neglect.

Go to the Centre d'Information des Monuments Historiques in the Hôtel de Sully, 62 rue St-Antoine, for maps of the area, suggested itineraries, programs of festivities, etc. One place not to be missed is the Hôtel Carnavalet (from the edge of the place des Vosges, turn left on the rue des Francs-Bourgeois), now a museum devoted mainly to the history of Paris and well worth a visit if only for a glimpse of its magnificent interior courtyards. Work your way back to the rue St-Antoine and then you may either take a 72 bus back from the Hôtel de Ville to the Palais Royal or the Concorde or else push on along the rue St-Antoine to the Bastille. All that's left of the Bastille is a column and a huge nondescript square, but this leg of your trip will give you a glimpse of the people's Paris.

From the Bastille there's a Métro back to the Champs-Elysées, or you can walk down the boulevard Henri IV, cross the Seine at the Ile St-Louis, and, turning left, reach the Jardin des Plantes, the botanical gardens. Right behind the Jardin des Plantes on the rue Geoffroy St-Hilaire lies the one and only mosque in Paris, with a Moslem tearoom attached. If you continue down the rue Geoffroy St-Hilaire, you reach the rue Jussieu and the Latin Quarter, but you will probably prefer to take a train at the Jussieu Métro stop and rest up for a final night out in Paris.

WE WANT AND APPRECIATE YOUR COMMENTS

Errors are bound to creep into any guidebook. Hotels and restaurants can suffer instant or gradual decline in the quality of their service, acts of governments or God can change the travel picture, and in many ways, items that we presented as gospel will now appear to be untrue.

For these reasons we greatly appreciate letters from you, the reader, telling us of your travel experiences, chastising us, if you will, for our errors, or advising us of our oversights. We want to know! (We also appreciate words of praise, and we receive a lot of those too.) Your letters help us improve our coverage, but they also give us that essential "consumer's eye view," which is so helpful. We want to produce the best-possible travel guide series—and you can help us do it.

Please send your comments to
> Research Director
> Fodor's Travel Guides
> 2 Park Avenue
> New York, N.Y. 10016

GETTING SETTLED IN PARIS

Where to stay and what to do

One thing you'll soon be aware of in Paris is that the city is divided into twenty districts (called *arrondissements*), each with its own *mairie* or town hall. You won't have any difficulty remembering them, because they're simply called 'the first', 'the second' and so on. (Apart from the first, which is *le premier,* you just add the letters *ième* on to the number—*deuxième, troisième* etc.) You'll find that people are always talking in terms of these districts, and will say: 'I live in the seventh', or 'There are lots of new restaurants in the tenth these days.' And if you're studying a list of museums or suchlike, don't be puzzled because it doesn't seem to be in any apparent sequence, alphabetical or otherwise—it'll be arranged in the order of the *arrondissements,* though this won't be mentioned. If you've followed our advice and bought the pocket-sized and very useful *Plan de Paris par Arrondissement,* you'll see that each district has its own map (or occasionally two maps for the larger ones), so you'll soon get the feel of the geography of the capital.

Our hotel and restaurant lists are clearly divided into districts, but to help you get to grips with the system, we pinpoint below the features of each district that you might like to bear in mind. As you'll see from the map overleaf, the numbering starts in the heart of Paris, then spirals round like a swiss roll or a snail shell, finishing up with the *vingtième* in the far east. To the west lie two suburbs that are normally thought of as part of Paris proper, Boulogne-Billancourt and Neuilly-sur-Seine.

The **first** includes the Louvre and the Palais-Royal, the Tuileries Garden and the elegant place Vendôme, the Ritz and the Comédie Française; it crosses the Seine by the Pont-Neuf and contains half of the Ile de la Cité, with the Sainte-Chapelle. This is tourist country *par excellence,* and even the area round the former Les Halles food market, once rather working-class, is now getting smarter all the time. Many of the capital's super-deluxe hotels are here, close to the expensive shops in the rue de Rivoli area; but you'll also find a number of inexpensive hotels in the side streets. The **second** lies north of the first and can be divided roughly into two halves: the Opéra area, the avenue de l'Opéra and the exclusive rue de la Paix, with its famous jewelers' shops, plus the major banks, the stock exchange *(Bourse)* and the famous Bibliothèque Nationale; this area has quite a few expensive hotels and is also full of theaters and movies; the other half, to the east, is mush less exclusive and has many reasonably priced hotels for those who like browsing in the expensive areas but want to keep hotel costs to a minimum. The **third** is a good hunting ground for those who love exploring old Paris—it includes part of the renovated Marais district, with the National Archives and the excellent Musée Carnavalet, but there are virtually no hotels here suitable for foreign tourists. The **fourth** covers the rest of the Marais, with the beautiful place des Vosges, but it also includes the new Beaubourg/Pompidou Center in an area that is becoming smarter every day, with attractive little restaurants and boutiques, and the Hôtel de Ville, with its popular department stores (La Samaritaine and the Bazar de l'Hôtel de Ville), plus the other half of the Ile de la Cité, including Notre-Dame, and the whole of the delightful Ile St-Louis, a wonderful place to stay if you can get into one of its peaceful hotels.

The first four *arrondissements* are north of the Seine (or on the Right Bank, as the Parisians say), but when we come to the **fifth** we have to cross over to the Left (i.e. south) Bank and the Latin Quarter. Here we are in student territory, with the Sorbonne and the Panthéon, the lively boulevard St-Michel and, further away, the Jardin des Plantes; there are many inexpensive hotels in the streets around the Sorbonne, and

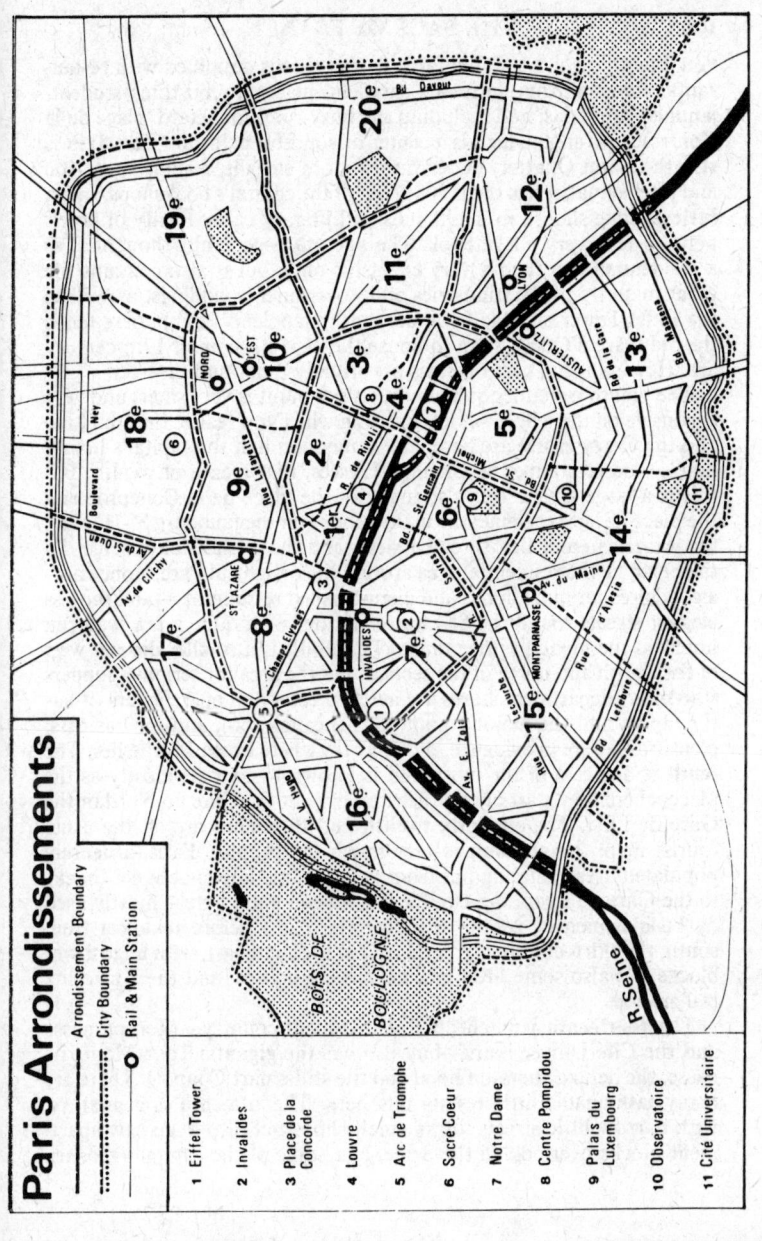

you'll never go short of food in a district that is crammed with restaurants, ranging from intimate candlelit places to bustling student-jammed cafeterias, and including the busy rue Mouffetard/place de la Contrescarpe area, which is a center of youthful nightlife. The **sixth** is still the Latin Quarter, but is rather more elegant; resolutely artistic and intellectual, it has the lion's share of the capital's bookshops, smart little antique shops, 'in' nightclubs and literary cafés. Plenty of hotels here, to suit every pocketbook. The **seventh** is generally thought of as a residential area (and a very exclusive one), but it also contains the great majority of the ministries and government buildings, as well as the Eiffel Tower and the Invalides, with Napoleon's tomb; here too is the old Gare d'Orsay, soon to house the new museum of 19th-century art. Hotels in this part of Paris are usually quiet and discreet.

The **eighth** is neither quiet nor discreet, but it is very smart and very expensive on the whole—not surprising when you realize that the Lido and the Crazy Horse are here, not to mention half the capital's luxury hotels, and of course the Champs-Elysées, that mecca of wealth. But this is a large area and it also includes the place de la Concorde and the place de la Madeleine, the luxury shops on the faubourg St-Honoré, the American and British embassies—and the presidential palace. To the north lie the residential area around the delightful Parc Monceau—a good area for quiet hotels and distinguished restaurants—and the less elegant streets round the St-Lazare station, with quite a few well-run hotels in the medium price range. The **ninth** is a smaller district west of the eighth and north of the second. It's the area for serious shoppers (the smart department stores are here), theater and opera lovers (it has the Opéra and the major commercial theaters too), and for business; pleasure is more in evidence in the north, where brash Pigalle lies. The **tenth** is due east of the ninth and is known to tourists mostly as the place where they start or end their travels—at the Gare du Nord or the Gare de l'Est. The eleventh, twelfth and thirteenth are off the usual tourist map: the **eleventh** is very much the people's Paris, a densely populated area radiating out from the place de la République; thanks to the Gare de Lyon, the **twelfth** has several good hotels, mostly used by businessmen or people spending the night before taking a train south; the **thirteenth** is a large district in the southeast, with huge tower blocks but also some little provincial-type houses, and the Austerlitz rail station.

The **fourteenth** is intellectual and student country—Montparnasse and the Cité Universitaire—but also has the gigantic Tour Montparnasse, the deluxe Sheraton hotel and the still-smart Coupole. There are many fashionable little restaurants here. The **fifteenth** is a mixture, with narrow little streets full of small shops but also huge new apartment blocks overlooking the Seine, and some of the capital's modern

GETTING SETTLED IN PARIS

luxury hotels, while the **sixteenth** is still, as it always has been, a fashionable residential area; it includes the Bois de Boulogne, the village-like Auteuil district and the aristocratic avenue Foch. There are many comfortable hotels, with good old-fashioned service. The **seventeenth**, too, has this type of hotel, usually in the quiet and dignified residential avenues, but it also has vast modern hotels grouped around the international congress center at the Porte Maillot. The Sacré-Coeur is the major landmark in the **eighteenth,** which covers the Montmartre district (more sex shops than can-can these days). Finally the **nineteenth** and the **twentieth,** in the northeast and east, are working class districts with no tourist hotels, though there are some good meat restaurants near the old slaughterhouses in the nineteenth.

As for the two inner suburbs, **Boulogne** has smart residential streets inhabited by wealthy middle-class families, as well as more modest small shopkeepers, while aristocratic **Neuilly** is increasingly becoming a major business area, with many advertising agencies and the headquarters of several multinational companies, but still has spacious, leafy avenues.

Cititel. Over 50 of Paris's top hotels have now installed an electronic information service known as *Cititel,* which will provide answers to a huge range of questions about Paris and the Ile de France, including airline and rail timetables, hotel room availability, cultural events and so on.

HOTELS. There are hundreds of hotels in Paris, many of them good, though it is always advisable to reserve well ahead, especially at the times when major shows (the air show in June, the auto show in October, the ready-to-wear collections) attract many visitors to Paris. We can list only a small sample here, classified as 'super-deluxe' (extremely expensive, among the world's best-known hotels), 'luxurious', 'expensive', 'moderate', and 'inexpensive'. The official grading is in terms of stars, based partly on price and partly on such details as whether rooms have telephones, and the number of bathrooms; roughly speaking, the hotels we refer to as inexpensive are graded with one or two stars; moderate have two or three stars; and expensive have three or four stars. But prices and facilities vary considerably within each category. Where you stay will obviously depend on your interests as well as your pocketbook, so we've given an idea of where hotels are situated within each district.

The great majority of hotels nowadays quote a price inclusive of service and all taxes, but just to make sure, check the price posted up in the room (this is compulsory, except in super-deluxe hotels). The letters *ttc (toutes taxes comprises)* or *prix nets* mean that there'll be nothing extra to pay. Breakfast is normally extra, costing from around 15 to as much as 70 frs per person, depending on the class of hotel. It will always be a continental breakfast of coffee, tea or chocolate plus limited quantities of rolls or bread, butter and jam. Avoid the temptation to add fruit juice, eggs or cereal if you're interested in keeping extras to a minimum on your final bill. Until recently breakfast has normally been served in your room, but increasingly the modern hotels are charging extra for this service and encourage you to come down to a breakfast room or restaurant; the smaller and older hotels still generally serve it in your room.

A double room with bath in a super-deluxe hotel will cost at least 850 frs. Suites cost more of course, and can go up to 10,000 frs (at the Ritz). Luxurious hotels will charge 550–800; Expensive, 350–550; Moderate 250–350; and Inexpensive 80–220. However, rates charged by Paris hotels change with amazing frequency, as they modernize and redecorate, or alternatively decide to aim for a lower income bracket, so we urge you to check a hotel's rates before making a reservation.

The bottom categories include many hotels that have been recently modernized, and far more hotels in these categories now have attractive, functional little bathrooms than a few years ago. In particular, hotels near the Champs-Elysées, the Opéra and the Madeleine are used to dealing with English-speaking tourists. On the whole Left Bank hotels are smaller and less formal, but often more picturesque than their staider Right Bank counterparts.

In the following list we give the super-deluxe hotels first, grouped together, since if you're able to stay in this category it'll be the hotel rather than the district that you go for. All the other hotels are grouped according to *arrondissement*. Hotels listed don't have a restaurant unless we mention this.

Super-deluxe

Bristol, 112 fbg St-Honoré, 8e, one of the most elegant in Paris and the most expensive; it is near both the British Embassy and the Elysée Palace. Rooms and suites are luxurious. Extremely chic clientele: British, German and American diplomats; distinguished foreigners. 205 rooms, including 50 suites. Has restaurant overlooking lovely garden, heated pool on top floor and sauna.

Crillon, 10 pl. de la Concorde, 8e, in a grandiose location with views across to the National Assembly building on the far side of the Seine. 206 rooms and suites. Excellent cuisine. Along with the George V, this is the headquarters for wealthy Americans in Paris (and has been since the time of Benjamin Franklin and Thomas Jefferson, when they visited it as a private palace). During the early 1980s was given a no-expense-spared facelift and is now as dazzlingly magnificent as when it was a private residence. The cuisine, too, has been rejuvenated and is now probably the best of any Paris hotel.

George V, 31 av. George V, 8e, off the Champs-Elysées. 292 rooms and suites, some furnished with antiques, as are the reception halls. Modern art displays in *Les Princes* restaurant. Fashionable, and often used by rich Arab businessmen. Its bar is almost a club for visiting US impresarios, starlets, businessmen and the press.

Grand, 2 rue Scribe, 9e, with 600 rooms, it is the largest in the area. It has cheerful bars (with pianist in the early evening), salons and boutiques. US guests are invited to a party on the *Café de la Paix* terrace on July 4.

GETTING SETTLED IN PARIS

Intercontinental-Paris, 3 rue de Castiglione, 1er, superb comfort. An assortment of pleasant restaurants, cafeterias and grill-rooms. The nightclub can be entered from the street side as well as from inside the hotel. 500 rooms.

Lotti, 7 rue de Castiglione. Restaurant, bar, 130 rooms. Front rooms can be noisy. Otherwise quiet and elegant.

Meurice, 228 rue de Rivoli, 1er, halfway between the Ritz and the Crillon, it was once known as the hotel of kings, because so many of them stopped here. Kings are scarcer now, but it's still one of the top-notchers. 221 rooms and suites (recently airconditioned). Good restaurant is now open non-stop from 12 A.M. to 11 P.M.

Nova-Park Elysées, 51 rue François-1er, 8e, Paris's latest super-deluxe hotel, just off the av. George-V close to the Champs-Elysées. 73 extremely expensive rooms and suites, very good restaurant, roof gardens, sauna, gym, bars, pool—and all of them the last word in luxury.

Plaza-Athénée, 25 av. Montaigne, 8e, just far enough off the Champs-Elysées to escape the noise and the glitter. A favorite of South Americans, it is very elegant. Its *Régence* restaurant is where you'll see some of the prettiest girls in town at lunch, and the *Relais-Plaza* is just right for an expensive after-theater supper. Or try the smart snackbar for a single main dish. On winter evenings the downstairs *Bar Anglais* becomes an intimate discotheque. 218 soundproofed rooms and suites.

Prince de Galles, 33 av. George V, 8e, 164 rooms, and suites, restaurant (open air buffet lunches in summer). Friendly, attractive and under the same management as the Meurice. Both now belong to the British Grand Metropolitan Hotels group.

Ritz, 15 pl. Vendôme, 1er, in 17th-century square midway between Opéra and Tuileries Gardens. Under its dynamic young German manager and Egyptian ownership this stately spot has undergone a facelift yet has lost none of its old-world charm and legendary service. Many of its 163 rooms and 46 suites have been redecorated throughout and some suites have been renamed after famous guests such as Coco Chanel, Proust and Edward VII of England. The cuisine has been upgraded too. The *Espadon Grill* and *Vendôme* restaurant are now in the hands of top-flight chefs and the head wine waiter was lured away from the Tour d'Argent restaurant. There are also two small and select bars, a pretty courtyard garden and attractive boutiques. Secretarial services available.

FIRST ARRONDISSEMENT

Luxurious

Louvre-Concorde, pl. André-Malraux, 219 rooms, 214 with bath. Just by the Comédie-Française and the Palais-Royal.

Mayfair, 3 rue Rouget-de-l'Isle. 53 rooms, all with bath or shower. On quiet side street, off the rue de Rivoli.

Régina, 2 pl. des Pyramides. 126 rooms, 124 with bath or shower. Facing Tuileries Gardens.

Expensive

Burgundy, 8 rue Duphot. 92 rooms, all with bath or shower. Restaurant. Just off the pl. de la Madeleine.

Madeleine-Palace, 8 rue Cambon. 104 rooms, all with bath or shower. On quiet street, has popular bar and restaurant.

Normandy, 7 rue de l'Echelle. 138 rooms, 123 with bath. Comfortable, recently renovated.

Moderate

Continent, 30 rue du Mont-Thabor. 28 rooms, most with bath or shower.

Duminy, 3 rue du Mont-Thabor. 62 rooms, 30 with bath or shower. Good value for this expensive area.

Family, 35 rue Cambon. 25 rooms, most with bath or shower. Has long-established clientele. Friendly.

Londres Stockholm, 13 rue St-Roch. 28 rooms, 26 with bath or shower.

Sainte-Anne, 10 rue Ste-Anne. 95 rooms, all but 2 with bath or shower. In the Bourse area.

Violet, 7 rue Jean-Lantier. 30 rooms, all with bath or shower. Attractive rooms. Close to pl. du Châtelet.

Inexpensive

Nantes, 55 rue St-Roch. 19 rooms, only 6 with bath or shower.

Palais, 2 quai de la Mégisserie. 19 rooms, a few with bath or shower. Close to the Seine and opposite the Sainte-Chapelle on the Ile de la Cité.

SECOND ARRONDISSEMENT

Luxurious

Edouard-VII, 39 av. de l'Opéra. 81 rooms, all with bath or shower. Close to the Opéra. Has good restaurant, the *Delmonico* (E).

Westminster, 13 rue de la Paix. 102 rooms, all with bath or shower.

Expensive

Cusset, 95 rue de Richelieu. 115 rooms, all but 15 with bath or shower. In the Bourse area.

Etats-Unis Opera, 16 rue d'Antin. 52 rooms, all with bath or shower. Recently modernized, just by the Opéra.

Gaillon-Opéra, 9 rue Gaillon, 26 rooms all with bath or shower.

Métropole-Opéra, 2 rue de Gramont. 51 rooms, two-thirds of them with bath or shower. Recently redecorated. Friendly service. Off the blvd des Italiens.

Moderate

Etna, 61 rue Ste-Anne. 27 rooms, all but 8 with bath or shower.

Vivienne, 40 rue Vivienne. 44 rooms, all with bath or shower.

GETTING SETTLED IN PARIS

FOURTH ARRONDISSEMENT

Moderate

Deux-Iles, 59 rue St-Louis-en-l'Ile. 17 rooms, all with bath and/or shower. Attractive small hotel in a 17th-century house on the Ile St-Louis, with bar and sitting-room in the old cellars. At top end of price range.

Lutèce, 65 rue St-Louis-en-l'Ile. 23 rooms, all with bath or shower. Another small and delightful hotel on the Ile St-Louis, peaceful and with some rooms arranged as duplexes.

Saint-Louis, 75 rue St-Louis-en-l'Ile. 25 rooms, 17 of them with bath or shower. Attractive rooms on five floors (the top floor has marvelous view, but there's no elevator), with good modern bathrooms. Good value, with some inexpensive single rooms.

Inexpensive

France, 40 rue de Rivoli, 33 rooms, 19 with bath or shower. Close to the Hôtel de Ville.

FIFTH ARRONDISSEMENT

Expensive

Colbert, 7 rue de l'Hôtel Colbert. 40 rooms, all with bath or shower. By the river, just opposite Notre-Dame; an 18th-century building with attractive, smallish rooms.

Moderate

Collège de France, 7 rue Thénard. 29 rooms, all with bath or shower. A new arrival on the Paris scene, in the heart of the Latin Quarter, yet quiet. Some rooms have old beams.

Esmeralda, 4 rue St-Julien-le-Pauvre. 19 rooms, 16 with bath or shower. A 17th-century building, again with smallish rooms, but pleasantly furnished. Just by the pretty sq. Viviani.

Saint-Jacques, 35 rue des Ecoles. 39 rooms, 15 of them with bath or shower.

Inexpensive

Avenir, 52 rue Gay-Lussac. 47 rooms, only 6 with bath or shower. A modest budget hotel. On six floors but no elevator.

Nevers-Luxembourg, 3 rue Abbé-de-l'Epée. 29 rooms, all but 4 without bath or shower. Attractively decorated, yet very inexpensive.

Sorbonne, 6 rue Victor-Cousin. 37 rooms, 22 of them with bath or shower. Another modest budget hotel in this student area.

SIXTH ARRONDISSEMENT

Luxurious

L'Hôtel-Guy-Louis-Duboucheron, 13 rue des Beaux-Arts. 27 rooms. Attractive, very 'in'. Furnished with antiques, including Mistinguett's mirror-lined bed. (You can also sleep in the room where Oscar Wilde died!) Some rooms at super-deluxe prices.

Lutétia-Concorde, 45 bld Raspail, near Bon-Marché department store, 300 rooms, 280 with bath. Restaurant, bar. Pleasant atmosphere, good service.

Expensive

L'Abbaye Saint-Germain, 10 rue Cassette. 45 rooms, all with bath or shower. Quiet and attractive hotel in what was once a monastery.

Angleterre, 44 rue Jacob. 31 rooms, all with bath or shower. Once the home of the British ambassador, and Hemingway used to live here too. Excellent service, traditional.

Littré, 9 rue Littré. 100 rooms, all with bath or shower. Same management as the Victoria Palace; popular with the wealthier publishers.

Odéon, 3 rue de l'Odéon. 34 rooms, all with bath. Apparently this mansion once belonged to Madame de Pompadour.

Pas-de-Calais, 59 rue des Sts-Pères. 41 rooms, all with bath or shower. Has been here since the early 19th century and is still popular. Built around a tiny courtyard, but try to get a room away from the street.

Saints-Pères, 65 rue des Sts-Pères. 35 rooms, all with bath or shower. Old favorite.

Victoria Palace, 6 rue Blaise-Desgoffe. 113 rooms, all with bath or shower. In a tiny street, well run, good service. Same management as Littré.

Moderate

Ferrandi, 92 rue du Cherche-Midi. 42 rooms, all with bath or shower.

Louisiane, 60 rue de Seine. 79 rooms, all but 5 with bath or shower. Jean-Paul Sartre and Juliette Greco once lived here.

Madison, 143 bld St-Germain. 56 rooms, all with bath or shower. Set back from the boulevard slightly, in tiny square facing the church; front rooms have delightful view, but are rather noisy; popular with publishers.

Marronniers, 21 rue Jacob. 37 rooms, all with bath or shower. Quiet and friendly, with pretty leafy courtyard-cum-garden. Rooms small, but comfortable.

Michelet-Odéon, 6 pl. de l'Odéon. 43 rooms, most with bath or shower.

Molière, 14 rue de Vaugirard. 15 rooms, all with bath or shower.

Principautés-Unies, 42 rue de Vaugirard. 29 rooms, 25 with bath or shower. Recently redecorated, some suites with mini-kitchen. Friendly.

Rennes—Montparnasse, 151 bis rue de Rennes. 38 rooms, 23 with bath or shower. Close to Panthéon, recently redecorated.

Saint-André-des-Arts, 66 rue St-André-des-Arts. 32 rooms all but 4 with bath or shower.

Saint-Paul, 43 rue Monsieur-Le-Prince. 29 rooms, all but 4 with bath or shower. Attractively furnished.

Scandinavie, 27 rue de Tournon. 22 rooms, all with bath. Attractive mansion with fine Louis XIII furniture, close to Luxembourg Gardens. Must reserve well ahead. Good value.

Inexpensive

Académies, 15 rue de la Grande-Chaumière. 21 rooms, 17 with bath or shower.

Avenir, 65 rue Madame. 35 rooms, 12 with bath or shower. Well-run hotel, with a glimpse of the Luxembourg Gardens from some rooms, quiet.

Bréa, 14 rue Bréa. 26 rooms, only 3 with bath or shower. An old favorite.

Lys, 23 rue Serpente. 21 rooms, all with bath or shower. Very picturesque.

Régent, 61 rue Dauphine. 28 rooms, all but 4 without bath.

Verneuil, 36 rue Dauphine. 27 rooms, 19 with bath or shower. One or two more expensive double rooms.

SEVENTH ARRONDISSEMENT

Luxurious

Pont-Royal, 7 rue Montalembert, 80 rooms, all but 1 with bath or shower, some of them rather cramped for this category, but pleasant atmosphere. Attractive bar is popular with publishers.

Sofitel-Bourbon, 32 rue St-Dominique. 112 rooms, all with bath. Airconditioned, modern, but without the impersonal atmosphere of so many modern hotels. Good restaurant.

Expensive

Beaugency, 21 rue Duvivier. 30 rooms, all with bath or shower. Renovated throughout; near Eiffel Tower and Les Invalides.

Bourgogne et Montana, 3 rue de Bourgogne. 35 rooms, all with bath. Just by the Chambre des Deputes. Restaurant.

Cayre, 4 bld Raspail. 131 rooms, all with bath or shower. Quiet, popular with writers.

Montalembert, 3 rue de Montalembert. 61 rooms, all but 1 with bath. Excellent, next door to Pont-Royal, but a lot cheaper.

Saint-Simon, 14 rue St-Simon. 34 rooms, all with bath or shower. In a little street just off the bld St-Germain.

Saxe-Résidence, 9 villa de Saxe. 52 rooms, all with bath or shower. In quiet cul-de-sac near the Ecole Militaire.

Suède, 31 rue Vaneau. 41 rooms, all but 4 with bath or shower. Attractive, has pretty inner courtyard.

Université, 22 rue de l'Université. 28 rooms, all with bath or shower. In small converted mansion, attractive décor.

Moderate

Bersoly's, 28 rue de Lille. 14 rooms, all with bath or shower. Friendly little hotel in a 17th century building.

Bourdonnais, 111 av. de la Bourdonnais. 60 rooms, all but 4 with bath or shower. Quiet, cheerful bar. Restaurant called *Cantine des Gourmets.*

Quai Voltaire, 19 quai Voltaire. 33 rooms, 26 with bath or shower. Overlooking the Seine, but rooms in front are noisy. Some (I) singles.

San Domenico, 62 rue St-Dominique. 33 rooms, all but one with bath or shower.

Sèvres-Vaneau, 86 rue Vaneau. 46 rooms, 28 with bath or shower.

Solferino, 91 rue de Lille. 35 rooms, all with bath or shower. Attractive décor.

Varenne, 34 rue de Bourgogne. 24 rooms, all with bath or shower. Another converted mansion, peaceful and friendly, with a pretty little patio. Good value.

Inexpensive

Empereur, 2 rue Chevert. 40 rooms, 23 with bath or shower. Close, as its name suggests, to Napoleon's tomb in the Invalides.

Pretty, 8 rue Amelie. 57 rooms, only 6 with bath or shower. Close to Eiffel Tower and Invalides.

EIGHTH ARRONDISSEMENT

Luxurious

California, 16 rue de Berri, near the Etoile. 188 rooms with bath. Restaurant, bar. Best rooms are on inner courtyard. Belongs to Mapotel chain.

Castiglione, 40 rue du fbg St-Honoré. 105 rooms, all with bath. Restaurant, bar. Singles are small, and in (E) price range.

Château-Frontenac, 54 rue Pierre-Charon. 103 rooms, all with bath or shower. Inviting restaurant.

Concorde Saint-Lazare, 108 rue St-Lazare. 324 rooms, all with bath or shower. Large, close to the St-Lazare station and the big stores.

Lancaster, 7 rue de Berri. 67 rooms with bath. Best in category in this area. Movie stars love going incognito here. Charmingly furnished suites overlooking a courtyard. Quiet, a bit overpriced (some rooms at Superdeluxe rates).

Napoléon, 40 av. de Friedland. 140 rooms, 133 with bath. Elegant restaurant, pleasant bar; the sort of charm you don't get in most of the newer hotels.

Royal-Madeleine, 26 rue Pasquier. 70 rooms, all with bath or shower. Belongs to PLM group.

La Trémoïlle, 14 rue de la Trémoïlle. 112 rooms, all with bath or shower. Run by the same management as the Plaza-Athénée; close to the Champs-Elysées and the couture houses, so popular with top models and their escorts. Good service and attractive period furnishings, coupled with all modern facilities.

Vernet, 25 rue Vernet. 63 rooms, all with bath or shower. Very close to the Etoile and the Champs-Elysées.

Warwick, 5 rue de Berri. 150 rooms, all with bath. Restaurant with '30s decor, rooftop terrace. Opened 1983, very comfortable.

Windsor, 14 rue Beaujon. 135 rooms, all with bath or shower. Quiet, close to the Etoile, rather smart but not showy. Has excellent restaurant *(Le Clovis)* with good 'new' cuisine—rare for a big hotel (closed Aug. and weekends).

Expensive

Atala, 10 rue Chateaubriand. 49 rooms, all with bath or shower. Close to the Etoile.

Celtic, 6 rue Balzac, off the Champs Elysées. 80 rooms, all with bath. Restaurant, bar. Mostly for business men.

Mayflower, 3 rue Chateaubriand. 24 rooms, all with bath or shower. Small and cozy. Close to the Etoile.

Powers, 52 rue François 1er. 57 rooms, all but one with bath or shower. Close to the Champs-Elysées, has very pleasant atmosphere.

Royal-Alma, 35 rue Jean-Goujon. 84 rooms, all with bath or shower. Close to the Seine.

Royal, 33 av. de Friedland. 57 rooms, all with bath or shower. Has restaurant and bar, plus friendly service.

San Régis, 12 rue Jean-Goujon. 43 rooms, all with bath or shower. Quite close to the Champs-Elysées, but comparatively quiet. Must reserve well ahead.

Schweizerhof, 11 rue Balzac. 20 rooms, all with bath or shower. Tiny, close to the Champs-Elysées.

Moderate

Angleterre-Champs-Elysées, 91 rue La Boétie. 40 rooms, all but 4 with bath or shower.

Arromanches, 6 rue Chateaubriand. 25 rooms, all with bath or shower. All these three are pleasant small hotels close to the Champs-Elysées.

Bradford, 10 rue St-Philippe-du-Roule. 48 rooms, all but 4 with bath or shower. Large, comfortable rooms, good service, but not expensive for the quality.

Buckingham, 45 rue des Mathurins. 35 rooms, all with bath or shower. Close to the big stores, but quiet.

Céramic, 34 av. de Wagram. 59 rooms, 44 with bath or shower. Popular with businessmen; good value. Close to the Etoile.

Chambiges, 8 rue Chambiges. 30 rooms, 22 with bath or shower. Very pleasant little hotel, close to the Seine and the av. Montaigne.

Folkestone, 9 rue de Castellane. 32 rooms, all with bath or shower. In a side street near the Madeleine and the big stores.

Havre Tronchet, 11 rue Greffulhe. 27 rooms, 18 with bath or shower. Close to the Madeleine.

Madeleine-Plaza, 33 pl. de la Madeleine. 52 rooms, all but 2 bath or shower. Just by the Madeleine church.

Montaigne, 6 av. Montaigne. 33 rooms, all with bath or shower. Good bet if you're visiting the couture houses.

Queen Mary, 9 rue Greffulhe. 36 rooms, all with bath or shower. In a side street close to the big stores.

Résidence Lord Byron, 5 rue de Chateaubriand. 26 rooms, all with bath or shower. Pleasant little hotel close to the Etoile. Has a few (E) rooms.

Rome, 18 rue de Constantinople. 30 rooms, all with bath or shower. Rather out of the way behind the Gare-St-Lazare.

Tronchet, 22 rue Tronchet. 32 rooms, 27 with bath or shower. In the Madeleine district, near the big stores.

Washington, 43 rue Washington. 23 rooms, all with bath or shower. Close to Champs Elysées.

NOTE: The Buckingham is the only hotel in this category with a restaurant, but they're all close to a wide range of restaurants and cafés.

Inexpensive

Bellevue, 46 rue Pasquier. 48 rooms, 16 with bath or shower. In the St-Lazare area.

Champs-Elysées, 2 rue d'Artois. 40 rooms, 19 with bath or shower.

Fortuny, 35 rue de l'Arcade. 32 rooms, 25 with bath or shower. In a side street near Madeleine and big stores.

Newton, 11 bis rue de l'Arcade. 29 rooms, 17 with bath or shower. Again close to the Madeleine.

Royal, 7 rue du Colisée. 37 rooms, all but 1 with bath or shower. Off the Champs-Elysées this time.

Wilson, 10 rue de Stockholm. 37 rooms, only 8 with bath or shower. Near St. Lazare station.

NINTH ARRONDISSEMENT

Luxurious

Ambassador-Concorde, 16 bld Haussmann. 300 rooms, all with bath. Restaurant. Rather impersonal and commercial atmosphere, but convenient for the big stores and the Opéra.

Expensive

Bergère Mapotel, 34 rue Bergère. 93 rooms, all but 6 with bath or shower. Quiet, appears slightly off the beaten track, but it is in fact near the Opéra and the Bourse. Good service. A few (M) rooms.

Caravelle, 68 rue des Martyrs. 32 rooms, all with bath or shower. Also near Pigalle.

Commodore, 12 bld Haussmann. 160 rooms, all with bath. Two restaurants, with one of them a convenient help-yourself buffet. Recently renovated.

Moderate

Blackston, 12 rue de Parme. 40 rooms, all but 2 with bath or shower. In quiet street near pl. Clichy and St-Lazare station. Comfortable and friendly.

Blanche Fontaine, 34 rue Fontaine. 49 rooms, all with bath or shower. In the Pigalle area.

Central Monty, 5 rue de Montyon. 70 rooms, all but 10 with bath or shower. Near the *grands boulevards* and the Bourse.

Corona, 8 Cité Begère. 62 rooms, 50 with bath or shower. In a small side street and surprisingly quiet.

Excelsior-Opéra, 5 rue Lafayette. 53 rooms, all with bath or shower. Almost next door to Galeries Lafayette.

Diamond, 73 rue de Dunkerque. 52 rooms, 40 with bath or shower. Close to the Gare du Nord. At bottom end of price range.

Hollandais, 16 rue Lamartine. 46 rooms, 35 with bath or shower. Quiet and particularly friendly little hotel.

Impérial, 45 rue de la Victoire. 37 rooms, 29 with bath or shower. Small hotel not far from the big stores and with some reasonably priced singles.

London Palace, 32 bld des Italiens. 49 rooms, all but 2 with bath or shower. Reduced rates July and Aug. Well run hotel.

Migny, 13 rue Victor-Masse. 54 rooms, 39 with bath or shower. Pigalle area.

Peyris, 10 rue du Conservatoire. 50 rooms, all with bath or shower. In a side street close to the *grands boulevards*.

Riboutté-Lafayette, 5 rue Riboutté. 24 rooms, all with bath or shower. Charming little hotel, beautifully decorated. Close to a little square halfway between Pigalle and the *grands boulevards*.

Sèze, 16 rue de Sèze. 25 rooms, 13 with bath or shower. Near the Madeleine.

Inexpensive

Cité-Bergère, 4-6 Cite Bergère. 70 rooms, 47 with bath or shower. Close to the *grands boulevards*.

Nil, 10 rue du Helder. 31 rooms, 19 with bath or shower. In a little street between the bld des Italiens and the bld Haussmann.

Paris-Rome, 4 rue de Provence. 38 rooms, 23 with bath or shower. Close to the big stores.

TENTH ARRONDISSEMENT

Expensive

Paris-Est, 4 rue du 8 mai 1945. 31 rooms, all with bath or shower. Near Gare de l'Est; has restaurant.

Pavillon-l'Horset, 36-8 rue de l'Echiquier. 98 rooms, all but 9 with bath or shower. A bit out of the way, but good if you're a china fiend—the rue de Paradis, where all the finest china and porcelain showrooms are, is close by. Restaurant.

Moderate

Londres et Anvers, 133 bld Magenta. 43 rooms, only 13 with bath or shower. Near the Gare du Nord and the Gare de l'Est.

Inexpensive

Europe, 98 bld Magenta. 36 rooms, 24 with bath or shower. Convenient for both the Gare du Nord and the Gare de l'Est.

ELEVENTH ARRONDISSEMENT

Expensive

Holiday Inn, 10 pl. de la Republique. 335 rooms, all with bath or shower. Opened in 1982 and very comfortable, though not very central. Has restaurant and '20s-style oyster bar.

Moderate

Nord et Est, 49 rue de Malte. 44 rooms, all with bath or shower. Near the place de la République.

TWELFTH ARRONDISSEMENT
Moderate

Modern Hôtel Lyon, 3 rue Parrot. 53 rooms, all with bath or shower. Quiet, but close to Gare de Lyon. Popular with businessmen.

Paris-Lyon Palace, 11 rue de Lyon. 128 rooms, all with bath or shower. Also near the Gare de Lyon, but this one has a restaurant.

THIRTEENTH ARRONDISSEMENT
Moderate

Gobelins, 57 bld St-Marcel. 45 rooms, all with bath or shower. Close to the Orléans and Austerlitz stations, yet not far from the Latin Quarter.

FOURTEENTH ARRONDISSEMENT
Luxurious

PLM-Saint-Jacques, 17 bld St-Jacques. 797 rooms, all with bath. Not on the usual tourist track, but convenient for Orly airport (airport bus even stops here). Has a variety of restaurants and bars to suit all tastes and purses plus boutiques and cinema. New reductions system is similar to Air Inter and SNCF's "tricolor" calendar. On blue days (including all July and August) everyone gets a reduction of 20%; women over 60 and men over 65, students, couples, families benefit from even better reductions.

Montparnasse Park Hotel, 19 rue Commandant-Mouchotte. 1000 rooms, all with bath. Large, rather impersonal hotel near the Tour Montparnasse, with restaurants, bars, shops, two skating rinks. Wonderful view from top floors.

Expensive

Royal, 212 bld Raspail. 48 rooms, all with bath. Centrally placed in Montparnasse.

Moderate

Aiglon, 232 bld Raspail. 50 rooms, all with bath. Close to the Coupole and all the Montparnasse restaurants and cinemas, yet quiet.

Carlton Palace, 207 bld Raspail. 63 rooms, all with bath or shower.

Orléans Palace, 185 bld Brune. 92 rooms, all with bath or shower. Near the Cité Universitaire.

Raspail, 203 bld Raspail. 40 rooms, all but one with bath or shower.

Inexpensive

Delambre, 35 rue Delambre. 36 rooms, all but 2 with bath or shower. Close to the Tour Montparnasse.

GETTING SETTLED IN PARIS

Départ, 19 rue du Départ. 32 rooms, 17 with bath or shower. Again close to the monster tower.

Idéal, 108 bld Jourdan. 70 rooms, 60 with bath or shower. Close to the Cité Universitaire.

Nouvel-Orléans, 25 av. Général-Leclerc. 49 rooms, all but 9 with bath or shower.

Royal-Bretagne, 11 bis rue de la Gaîté. 47 rooms, 24 with bath or shower. Convenient for movies and the Montparnasse restaurants, but the street is full of sex shops these days!

Sophie-Germain, 12 rue Sophie-Germain. 38 rooms, only 5 with bath or shower. Off the beaten track, but good for budgeteers.

FIFTEENTH ARRONDISSEMENT

Luxurious

Hilton International Paris, 18 av. de Suffren. 489 rooms, all with bath and balcony. Has rooftop restaurant (closed Aug.) and another restaurant, plus coffee shop, boutiques, hairdresser, bank.

Holiday Inn, 69 bld Victor. 90 rooms, all with bath. Opposite the Exhibit Center at the Porte de Versailles, so convenient if you're visiting one of the fairs, otherwise a bit out of the way.

Nikko de Paris, 61 quai de Grenelle. 778 rooms all with bath. Newish hotel owned by Japan Air Lines, overlooking the Seine to the west of the Eiffel Tower. Mixture of Japanese and French décor; has Japanese restaurant too (and a French one). Pool, sauna, shops, the lot.

Sofitel-Paris, 8–12 rue Louis-Armand. 635 rooms, all with bath. Near the Exhibit Center at the Porte de Versailles. Restaurants, conference rooms, pool, nursery, gym, sauna. A bit out of the way unless you're motorized.

Expensive

Ségur, 34 bld Garibaldi. 34 rooms, all with bath or shower. Near the Ecole Militaire.

Suffren la Tour, 20 rue Jean-Rey. 407 rooms, all with bath. Just by the Eiffel Tower, with restaurant and garden.

Moderate

France, 46 rue Croix-Nivert. 30 rooms, all with bath or shower.

SIXTEENTH ARRONDISSEMENT

Luxurious

La Pérouse, 40 rue La Pérouse. 36 rooms, all with bath or shower. Close to the Etoile, now belongs to Swiss Nova Park group and the last word in luxury. Beautifully furnished, good restaurant (called *Astrolabe*).

Raphaël, 17 av. Kléber. 87 rooms, and suites, all with bath and attractive balcony. Well decorated with period furniture and very comfortable and quiet. Close to the Etoile. Restaurant.

Résidence du Bois, 16 rue Chalgrin. 20 rooms, all with bath. Close to the Etoile, quiet and attractive, with some rooms overlooking peaceful garden. Must reserve well ahead. Belongs to Relaïs et Châteaux group.

Expensive

Kléber, 7 rue de Belloy. 22 rooms, all with bath. Halfway between the Etoile and the Trocadéro. Very well run.

Majestic, 29 rue Dumont-d'Urville. 28 rooms and suites, all with bath. Converted mansion in quiet street near the Etoile; most rooms and suites have period furniture, but a few are very modern.

Victor-Hugo, 19 rue Copernic. 76 rooms, all with bath or shower. Close to the Etoile. With spacious rooms.

Moderate

Queen's, 4 rue Bastien-Lepage. 22 rooms, all with bath or shower. Recently redecorated and now with all modern amenities, but still moderate prices.

Régina de Passy, 6 rue de la Tour. 62 rooms, all but 5 with bath or shower. In Passy, near the Trocadéro.

Sévigné, 6 rue de Belloy. 30 rooms, all with bath or shower. Has been extensively redecorated and modernized, with brasserie (open for lunch only) and good service. Close to the Etoile.

Inexpensive

Poussin, 52 rue Poussin. 20 rooms, all with bath or shower. Close to the Auteuil racecourse.

SEVENTEENTH ARRONDISSEMENT

Luxurious

Concorde-Lafayette, 3 pl. du General-Koenig. 1,000 rooms, all with bath. In a vast complex with conference rooms, secretaries, restaurants for all tastes and most pocketbooks. Smart and expensive shopping arcade, nightclub, movies. Very convenient for Roissy/Charles-de-Gaulle air terminal.

Méridien-Paris, 81 bld Gouvion-St-Cyr. 1,027 rooms, all with bath. Efficient, huge, American-style hotel, with 4 restaurants (including a reasonably priced help-yourself buffet, and one with Japanese cuisine), bar with jazz after 10 P.M., boutiques. Again convenient for Roissy air terminal.

Splendid-Etoile, 1 bis av. Carnot. 61 rooms and suites. Pleasant furnishings, close to the Etoile. Has restaurant (called *Pré Carré*).

Expensive

Cécilia, 11 av. Mac-Mahon. 46 rooms, all but 4 with bath or shower. Again close to the Etoile; has off-season reductions.

Etoile, 3 rue de l'Etoile. Close to the Champs Elysées and also convenient for the air terminal at the Porte Maillot. Modern décor, very pleasant atmosphere.

Regent's Garden, 6 rue Pierre-Demours. 41 rooms, all with bath. In a 19th century mansion near the Etoile, with a pretty garden. Excellent service. Has been extensively modernized.

Moderate

Astrid, 27 av. Carnot. 40 rooms, all but 1 with bath or shower. Close to the Etoile.

Banville, 166 bld Berthier. 40 rooms, all with bath. A bit far out, but quiet and friendly; attractive wallpaper and furnishings (different in each room).

Berthier-La-Tour, 163 bis av. de Clichy. 324 rooms, all with bath or shower. Cheerful modern hotel, sharing restaurant with *Brochant-la-Tour*.

Brochant-La-Tour, 163 bis av. de Clichy. Twin of *Berthier-La-Tour* (see above). Also has 324 rooms, but slightly lower prices.

Inexpensive

Médéric, 4 rue Médéric. 27 rooms, all with bath or shower. Close to the Parc Monceau.

Riviéra, 55 rue des Acacias. 33 rooms, only 13 with bath or shower. Near the Etoile, with low prices for this mostly expensive area.

EIGHTEENTH ARRONDISSEMENT

Expensive

Mapotel Terrass, 12–14 rue Joseph-de-Maistre. 108 rooms, all with bath. Close to Montmartre Cemetery and delightful; surprisingly quiet for this rackety area. Has two restaurants.

Moderate

Residence Montmartre, 10 rue Burq. 46 rooms, all with bath or shower. In cul-de-sac in heart of Montmartre.

NEUILLY

Expensive

Club Méditerranée, 58 bld Victor-Hugo. 335 rooms, all with bath. Run rather differently from an ordinary hotel, in the typically friendly Club Méditerranée style. Pleasant atmosphere, excellent buffet, a bit overpriced.

Jardin de Neuilly, 5 rue Paul-Déroulède. 30 rooms, all with bath or shower. Attractive small hotel near the Bois. Some apartments.

Inexpensive

Maillot, 46 rue de Sablonville. 30 rooms, all but 7 with shower. Friendly little hotel close to the air terminal at the Porte Maillot; very reasonable for this expensive area.

SUBURBS AND AIRPORTS

If central accommodation is scarce, and you have a car, the suburban hotels might suit you. We find them very impersonal, not to say cold, and service for tourists leaves quite a bit to be desired. Not bad for business visitors.

BAGNOLET. Novotel Paris Bagnolet (E), 611 rooms. Has restaurant and pool.

COURBEVOIE. Paris Penta (E), 494 rooms. With (M) restaurant, well-run.

ORLY AIRPORT. Hilton Orly (E), 379 soundproof and airconditioned rooms, *Louisiane* restaurant, coffee shop; **Motel PLM Orly** (M), 200 rooms.

PALAISEAU. Novotel Massy-Palaiseau (M), 151 rooms, with bath, pool, grillroom, close to Orly airport and RER metro stop.

ROISSY (CHARLES-DE-GAULLE) AIRPORT. Sofitel (E), 352 rooms; with pool. **Holiday Inn** (E), 250 rooms. Both have restaurants. **Arcade** (M), 356 soundproofed rooms, grillroom, bars, conveniently sited next to Roissy rail station with its regular service to and from the Gare du Nord; shuttle service to both airport terminals.

RUNGIS (near Orly). 206-room **Frantel** (E); with restaurant and pool. **Holiday Inn Paris-Orly** (E), 171 rooms.

VANVES. Mercure Paris Vanves (E), rue Moulin on the very edge of Paris proper, by the Porte de la Plaine. 387 rooms with bath or shower. Has brasserie for light meals (M).

MONEY. Most Paris banks change foreign money into francs, but most close Sat. All major hotels and many stores accept travelers checks, but they charge a higher rate than banks and official exchange offices. American, British and Canadian banks, and special exchange offices that are open at exceptional hours are given below. These opening times were correct at our presstime, but they are liable to change without warning. Bear in mind that all ordinary banks close at noon the day before a public holiday. Some banks shut their exchange counters between about 11.30 and 1.30, mid-June through Aug. The words 'No change,' frequently seen posted up on bank doors, do not mean that they won't give you change but that they do not change notes or travelers checks into francs!

American Express, 11 rue Scribe, 9e, 9–5 Mon-Fri.
Bank of America, 43 av. de la Grande-Armée, 16e, 9–1, Mon-Fri.
Banque Canadienne Nationale, 47 av. George-V, 8e, 9–5, Mon-Fri.

GETTING SETTLED IN PARIS

Barclay's Bank, 23 rue d'Antin, 2e; 33 rue du 4 Septembre, 2e; 157 blvd St-Germain, 6e; 6 rond-point des Champs-Elysées, 8e; 108 rue St-Lazare, 8e; 24 av. Kléber, 16e; 9–4.30, Mon-Fri.

Chase-Manhattan Bank, 41 rue Cambon, 9–4, Mon-Fri.

CIC, Gare de Lyon, 6.30 A.M. to 11 P.M. daily

Crédit Commercial de France, 115 av. des Champs-Elysées, 8e. Open to 7.45 P.M. Mon-Sat.

Crédit Lyonnais, 55 av. des Champs-Elysees, 8e, 9–11 on Sat.

Drugstore Opéra, 6 blvd des Capucines, 9e, 9–7.15 daily.

Eiffel Tower exchange office, 10–6 daily.

Lloyds Bank International, 43 blvd des Capucines, 9–4 Mon-Fri.

Morgan-Guaranty Trust Co., 14 pl. Vendôme, 1er, 9–4 Mon-Fri.

Royal Bank of Canada, 3 rue Scribe, 9e, 9–4 Mon-Fri.

Société Générale, 29 blvd Haussmann, 8e, 9–12 on Sat; if you have a checking account with the New York branch, you can cash up to $200 per week at any branch, and use ordinary banking facilities.

Union des Banques à Paris, 125 av. des Champs-Elysees, 8e; open all day Sat to 5.30 P.M.

Rail station exchange offices: daily opening hours; Gare d'Austerlitz, 7 A.M. to 9 P.M.; Gare de l'Est, 7.30 A.M. to 8 P.M.; Gare de Lyon, 6.30 A.M. to 11 P.M.; Gare du Nord, 6.30 A.M. to 9.30 P.M.; Gare St-Lazare, 7.30 A.M. to 8 P.M.

Airport exchange offices: Orly, 6.30 A.M. to 1.30 A.M.; Roissy/Charles de Gaulle, 6.30 A.M. to 11.30 P.M.

Travelers can arrange with one of the travel credit organizations for a European charge account that enables them to sign for hotel and restaurant bills, car rentals, and straightforward purchases and pay a monthly bill. Offering this service are *American Express, Diners' Club, Hilton's Carte Blanche, Eurocard International,* among many others.

MAIL. Paris post offices are open from 8–7, Mon. to Fri., and 8–12 only on Sat.; on Sun. one post office is open in each *arrondissement,* from 8–11. Main Paris post office (it never closes) is at 52 rue du Louvre. The post office at 71 av. des Champs-Elysées is open 8 A.M. to 11.30 P.M. Mon-Sat and 8 A.M. to 8 P.M. on Sun. A special fast letter service *(pneumatique)* guarantees delivery in Paris areas within 3 hrs during working hours; ask for special form. Transatlantic mail posted at any post office by 5 P.M. or at main office by 7 P.M. will normally catch the evening flight.

TELEGRAMS. After ordinary post office closing hours, cables and telegrams can be sent from the all-night post office at 52 rue du Louvre 1er, or the telephone and telegram office at 8 pl de la Bourse, 2e. Telegrams and cables can be sent by phone at any time. For telegrams in English, call 233-21-11.

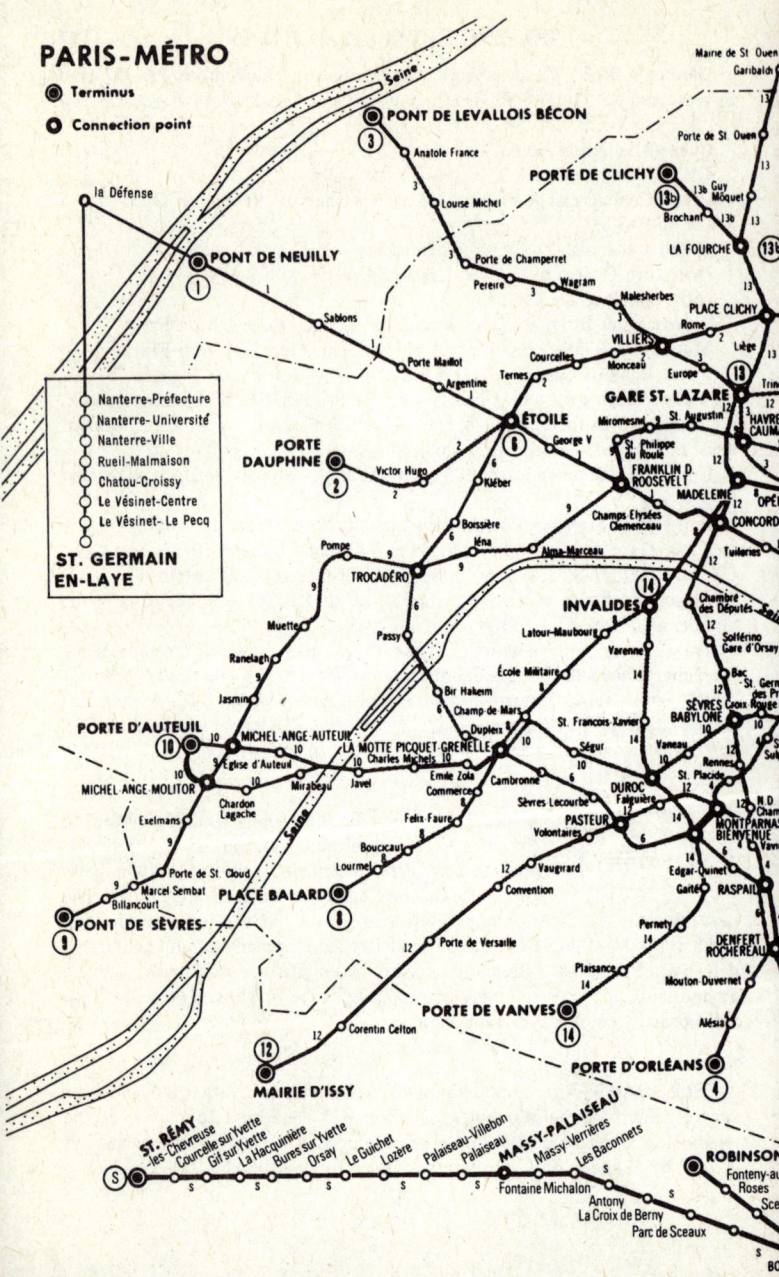

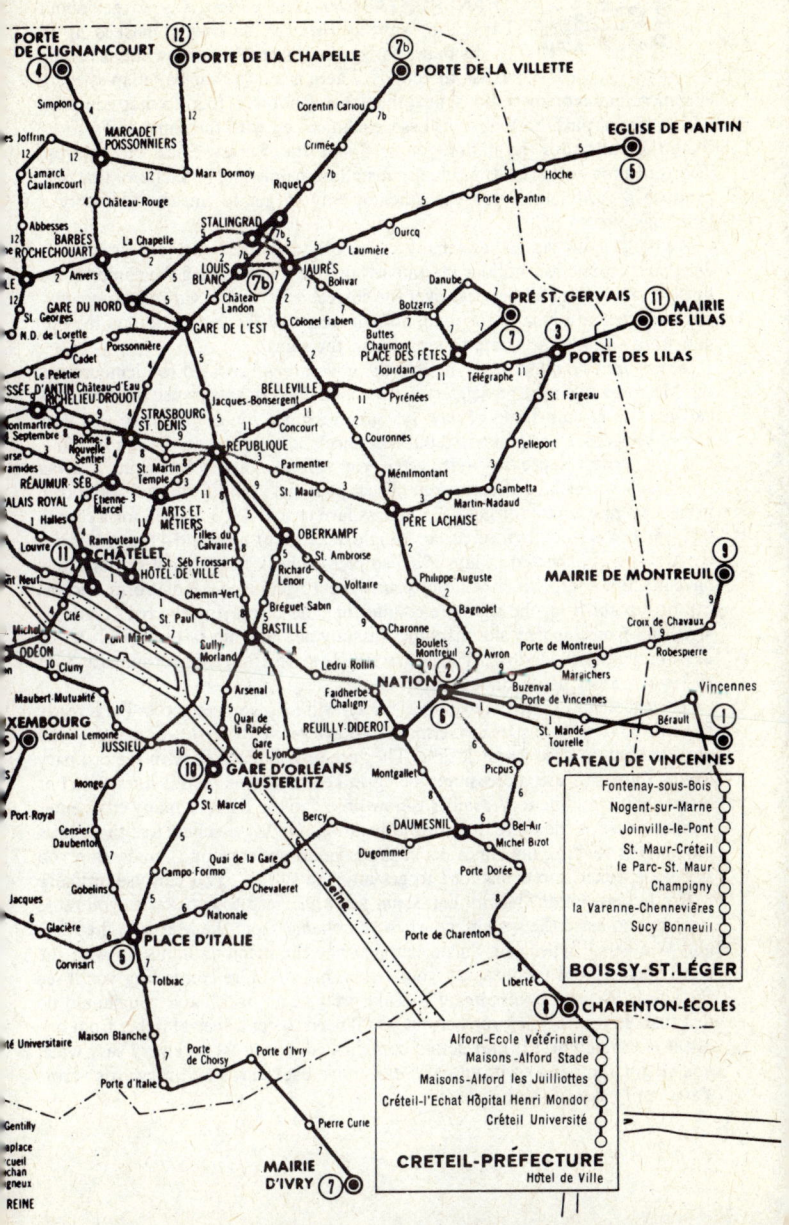

THE FACE OF FRANCE

TRANSPORTATION. The easiest way to get about Paris is by subway (Métro), so clearly marked at all points that a foreigner can find his way without having to ask directions. There is a large subway map at every entrance, and in many stations, near the ticket window, is found a map equipped with a row of push-buttons at its base, each marked with the name of a station. Push the button for the station you need, and the shortest route will light up. The transport authority is gradually installing helpful new machines that will produce a card telling you the quickest way to get to museums, historical buildings and so on.

A change (you can make as many as you please on one ticket) is a *correspondance,* and at junction stations illuminated orange signs bearing the names of the lines to which they lead appear over the correct exits for the various *correspondances.* When you look at the map, note the name of the last station on the line you want—that's the name to look for in the signs.

There are two classes but in 1982 the government decided to 'democratize' the Métro by allowing passengers with second class tickets to use the first class carriages at certain times of day. At our presstime you could do so any time except between 9 A.M. and 5 P.M., but best check before running the risk of a fine.

If you expect to use the Métro often, you will save money by buying a *carnet* (*'car-nay'*) or booklet of ten tickets. Keep your ticket until the end of the trip: inspectors may come through. First-class fare in mid-1983 was 36 for a *carnet;* second-class was 24 frs for a *carnet.* Single tickets cost 6 frs and 4 frs respectively. A rise was expected in late 1983, so please check locally. All stations now have machines into which you slot your ticket to get on to the platform. Tickets can be bought from the cigarette counter in cafés displaying the red 'TABAC' sign, and from the new slot machines (mainly near the big rail stations) as well as from the ticket windows. The Métro service starts from each terminus at 5.30, the last reaches its destination at 1.15 A.M.

The excellent express Métro lines (RER) will help you get across Paris really fast and take you out to St-Germain-en-Laye or St-Rémy-les-Chevreuse well outside Paris in double-quick time. They are fully integrated with the ordinary Métro lines and are increasingly being linked to the main rail lines too. For instance the rail line to Versailles is now linked to the RER at many city-center points and so is the Gare du Nord rail station. Highly mechanized, these lines have ticket vending machines (as in the London underground), and again you slot your ticket into a machine to get into the system. You can use ordinary Métro tickets within the city limits, *but you must keep your ticket* as you reuse it when you leave the system, or when you change from the Métro to the RER and vice versa; when you finish your journey the machine lights up with the word '*Passez*', but swallows up your ticket, but if you're continuing you'll see the words '*Reprenez votre ticket*'—'Take your ticket back', and you should do just that. If you're going further out you'll need to get a special ticket from one of the slot machines. It may sound complicated, but in fact it's very easy when you've got the hang of it, and you can move backwards and forwards across Paris really fast.

GETTING SETTLED IN PARIS

BUSES. These are marked with the destination in front and with the major points they pass along their sides. Clear route maps are now displayed at all bus stops. The second-class Métro tickets are used for bus travel—either one or two at a time, depending on distance you ride. The circular Petite Ceinture (PS) buses have their own fare scales, going up to a maximum of four tickets. Buses start at around 6.30 A.M. but most of them do not run after around 9 P.M. and the majority do not run on Sundays or public holidays at all.

Note. On the Métro and RER you slot all tickets into the machines, but, if you have a *Sesame* ticket, *do not do so on the buses* or it will become demagnetized and unusable. Instead show it to the driver.

A special bargain is the Paris Sesame ticket issued by the Paris Public Transportation System (RATP). Valid for 2, 4 or 7 consecutive days, it entitles you to unlimited travel on the Métro, RER (first class) and all RATP buslines in Paris and environs. The ticket may be purchased in the USA and Canada at official French Tourist Offices (for addresses, see *'Facts at Your Fingertips'*). In Paris, from the RATP Tourist Service, 53 bis quai des Grands-Augustins, at their excursion bureau, 20 pl de la Madeleine (on the right of the church), in any of more than 50 Métro or RER stations (look for the list posted up on Métro platforms); at the six main rail stations and at the rail terminal at the Roissy/Charles-de-Gaulle airport; at the Banque Nationale de Paris, 2 bld des Italiens, 2e, or pl. de Clichy, or the Crédit Commercial de France, 115 av. des Champs-Elysées, 8e. Also available from the French Rail office in your country.

If you are staying for a month, the RATP issues a monthly pass called the *Carte Orange* which entitles the holder to an unlimited number of Métro, RER and bus routes and SNCF lines inside Paris. Can be purchased at a Métro or SNCF (railway) station. A very good bargain. The pass itself is free, but you must produce a passport-sized photo and have it stamped. The monthly coupon is purchased from the ticket window and fits into the card.

Important. As with Paris Sesame tickets, your *carte orange* coupon must be shown to the driver on buses, *not* slotted into the machine.

Recommendation for finding your way about Paris, particularly if you use the best means of getting acquainted with the city, walking: buy a *Plan de Paris par Arrondissement* (a city guide containing separate maps of each district), a directory of all street names, Métro, RER, bus, general and suburban maps, and addresses of many places you will want to visit. Bear in mind that street names are listed alphabetically under the *first* part of the name, so avenue Franklin-Roosevelt will be found under F, not R.

TAXIS. Usually plentiful but often hard to find in rush hours. A taxi with its sign lighted is free, but if the meter flag is covered by a hood, the driver is on his way home and will only take you if you are going in his direction. Cruising cabs (if you can find any) may be hailed, but not within 20 yds of a rank. Fares start at 6 frs, then 1.75 fr per km within Paris. Prices rise steeply between 10 P.M. and 6.30 A.M., and on Sundays and public holidays. If you pick up a cab at a railway station or airport, there is an extra charge of around 4 frs. Luggage also costs extra. Tip 15–20%.

There are different meter rates for places outside the Paris city limits, and the driver will set his meter at a faster rate depending on which outlying district you are heading for; so don't be surprised to see him maneuver his meter. One problem: most Paris taxi drivers won't let anyone sit in a front seat and their saloon cars won't take more than three people in the back. If there are four of you you'll probably have to take two cabs.

Fare to airports To Roissy, about 150 frs (including tip); to Orly, about 130 frs from central Paris. For a complete list of ranks near you, consult the telephone directory; or go to the nearest hotel and tip the doorman to help.

Look out for meterless cabs in front of the big hotels, nightclubs, etc. They are private cars, whose rates are not registered by law, and they can charge anything you let them get away with. If you take one, agree on the price first.

CHAUFFEUR-DRIVEN CARS. You can hire a car with driver on either a time or a trip basis. You will see them lined up, displaying cards announcing their availability, in various centers frequented by tourists. Agree on the price beforehand. Most of these drivers speak English. A reliable firm is *Murdoch Associes,* 59 av. Marceau, 16e (tel. 720–63–28).

SELF-DRIVE CARS. Rates will vary considerably depending upon the car you choose and the length of hire. There is a mileage allowance. Cars are usually insured and your own driver's license is adequate except for long trips or international trips.

Among the hire firms are: *Avis,* central reservations on 609–92–12; main office 5 rue Bixio, 7e; other offices at Rond-Point des Champs-Elysées, 8e and 99 av. Charles-de-Gaulle, Neuilly-sur-Seine; *Hertz,* central reservations on 788–51–51, main office is at 27 rue St-Ferdinand, 17e (574–97–39); *Europcar,* central reservations on 645–21–25, main office at 42 av. de Saxe, 7e (273–35–20). All three also have service at the airports. Other firms include: *Mattei,* 205 rue de Bercy (346–11–50); *Citer,* 180 av. Daumesnil, 12e (345–01–20); *Inter-Touring,* 117 bld Blanqui, 13e (588–52–37).

France Auto-Vacances kit offers special low-cost tax-free all-inclusive car-leasing program for travel in Europe (3 weeks or longer). Works out less expensive than renting and covers delivery in Paris or Nice (you return it to Paris, Nice, Lyon, Marseille, Bordeaux or Toulouse), unlimited mileage, full insurance, new-car warranty, and tax-waiver. 1983 prices were $116–$239 per week if you rented for 3 weeks, slightly less per week if for a longer period. An additional $29 per week is charged for a compulsory collision damage waiver, which includes passenger accident coverage. Apply *France Auto-Vacances,* 420 Lexington Ave, New York, NY 10170 (tel: (212) 867–9820).

PARKING. A parking disc *(disque de contrôle)* must be used in *zones bleues.* They must be displayed on the windscreen when you park, setting the clock to show time of arrival and departure. (Obtain disc from your hotel, garage, or Office du Tourisme.) Time allowed: 1½ hrs, 9–noon and 2.30–7 weekdays. Before 9 A.M. and after 7 P.M., no disc is needed.

In Paris, as well as in major provincial towns, parking meters are found in congested areas. Rates are about 6 frs per hr. It is wise to have a supply of 1 fr and 50 centime pieces on hand—the meter-women in their periwinkle blue suits have been known to stick a ticket on your windshield between the time you park and dash to the nearest café for some change.

Although street parking at night is free, it is usually very hard to find space in any central area, especially in the entertainment districts on the Left Bank. It may be necessary to park in one of the many underground garages, where rates are from around 5 frs an hour. Better still—take a taxi!

CLOSING DAYS. Some small stores in Paris and many food shops are closed on Mon. Many coiffeurs and barbers are closed Mon. The expensive coiffeurs in the Champs-Elysées, fbg St-Honoré, Opéra and Grands Magasins areas open Mon. afternoons. Most museums close Mon. or Tues. Newsstands are usually closed evenings and Sun., though several are open till 10 P.M., and Sun. afternoons; and the drugstores, which sell French and foreign newspapers and magazines as well as pharmaceutical products and gift items, are open till 1 or 2 A.M.

Most theaters have one closing day per week, which varies with the individual establishment, and restaurants close for one or two days. Many restaurants are closed in August.

HORSERACING AND RIDING. Racetracks in the Paris district are: Chantilly (32km/20 miles out), Maisons-Lafitte (16km/10 miles out), Longchamp, St-Cloud, all having flat-racing; Auteuil has steeplechase; Enghien has steeplechase and trotting, and Vincennes has trotting only.

There is racing year round, every day of the week, but the big events are held on Sun. and holidays. In June at Chantilly, two of the richest and most elegant events are the Prix de Diane and Prix du Jockey; at Longchamp, eight major races held over a week end with the Grand Prix de Paris race. Other big events are held at Longchamp from the first Sun. in Sept. to the last Sun. in Oct., the Prix de l'Arc de Triomphe having the biggest purse in France.

Off-track betting is handled by Pari-Mutuel Urbain (PMU), which has tickertape machines in various cafés and offices throughout the city. Results can be found in the morning *Paris-Turf* and in the afternoon *Sport-Complet* as well as in the daily papers. Night races are held in summer.

For those who like to ride themselves, there are several places to hire horses. Here are two addresses: *Fédération Française des Sports Equestres,* 164 rue du fbg St-Honoré, 8e, and *Société d'Equitation de Paris,* Porte de Neuilly, Bois de Boulogne, 16e.

SWIMMING. There are four outdoor pools: *Piscine Georges Valleret,* 148 av. Gambetta, 20e; *Piscine Molitor,* 8 av. de la Porte-Molitor, 16e; *Piscine Deligny,* quai Anatole France, 7e; and *Piscine de l'Ile de Puteaux* at the Parc des Sports, Ile de Puteaux. Recommended indoor pools are: *Blomet,* 17 rue Blomet, 15e; *Pontoise St-Germain,* 19 rue de Pontoise, 5e; *Etoile,* 32 de Tilsitt, 17e; *Inkermann,* 50 rue Pauline Borghèse, Neuilly; *Piscine Municpale de Boulogne,* 165 rue du Vieux-Pont-de-Sèvres; *Molitor,* 10 av. de la Porte-Molitor, 16e; *Henry de Montherlant,* 24 bld Lannes, 16e.

GOLF. There are several courses close to Paris, easily accessible by train and bus. For information, ask at the Fédération Française de Golf, 11 rue de Bassano, 16e. On weekdays, you can play by paying the greens fee, but on weekends you must be invited by a member. There are both 9- and 18-hole courses at Golf de Paris, near Versailles and at St-Germain-en-Laye, and 18-hole courses at Le Lys-Chantilly, Fontainebleau, Marly, Mortefontaine, Ozoir-la-Ferrière, St-Cloud, Le Prieuré and St-Nom-la-Bretèche. For a nominal monthly fee, you can join the Golfers Club, 53 av. Hoche, 8e. *Club British Golf* (33 rue Raffet, 16e) has a delightful rooftop green on the seventh floor of no. 10 in the av. de la Grande-Armée, 16e (marvelous view); they also have a new putting green.

OTHER SPORTS. There are various **tennis** courts in the Paris area, but most are booked up for the entire season, so it is hard to find a free one except during Aug., when most Parisians are away. For information, inquire of the *Fédération Française de Tennis,* 2 av. Gordon-Bennett, 16e. You can go **ice-skating** at the Patinoire Molitor, av. de la Porte Molitor; the Patinoire Gaîté Montparnasse, 27 rue du Commandant-Mouchotte, 14e; the Patinoire des Buttes-Chaumont, 30 rue Edouard-Pailleron, 19e; and the Centre Olympique de Courbevoie, the other side of the Seine from Neuilly. **Roller-skating** at the Patinoir Gaité-Montparnasse, 16 rue Vercingétorix, 14e.

One great French national sport is **cycling**—the biggest single sports event in France is the Tour de France. Shorter races are held in the Parc des Princes and the Piste Municipale, and in winter at the Palais des Sports, where one of the big events is the 24-hr Bol d'Or, held in Nov. You can hire a cycle in the Bois de Boulogne (Métro Sablons), or the Bois de Vincennes. *Paris-Vélo,* 2 rue du Fer à Moulin, 5e (tel. 337–59–22), is another rent-a-bike operation.

Football (soccer) and **rugby** games draw enormous crowds every Sun. afternoon. The big games are held at the large stadiums such as Colombes and the Parc des Princes. For **basketball,** there are courts in the Bois de Boulogne.

GETTING SETTLED IN PARIS

SIGHTSEEING. *Bateaux Mouches* sightseeing boats make numerous daily trips on the Seine all year on a schedule varying by season. There are evening trips and you can dine aboard. Most trips last an hour and a quarter and cost around 20 frs. You can have lunch or dinner on board (fairly expensive); casual clothes are frowned on for dinner. Starting point is the Right Bank end of the Pont de l'Alma. The *Bateaux-Parisiens-Tour Eiffel*, using smaller glass-topped boats, sail from the Pont d'Iéna (near the Eiffel Tower), and from quai Montebello, likewise on a varying schedule. Fares are 15–20 frs. The *Vedettes Pont-Neuf* leave from pl. du Vert-Galant, near Notre Dame, about every 45 mins, for around 20 frs. Evening cruises start at about 9 P.M. Taped commentary in French, English and German.

A novelty is a cruise on Paris's canals on board the flat-bottomed *Patache*. Leaves every day except Mon. (Easter through Oct.) from the quai Anatole France at 9 for a half-day trip to La Villette (you can come back again leaving at 2 P.M.). Half-day, around 85 frs, 45 frs for children aged 6 to 12; children under 6 travel free. Men over 65 and women over 60 are entitled to reductions, except at weekends. Must reserve (tel. 874-75-30).

Cityrama tours in double-decker coaches with tape-recorded English commentary provide a good three-hour introduction to Paris. Starting-point is pl. des Pyramides, near the Tuileries. *Paris Vision* also has Paris tours, with departures from 214 rue de Rivoli (also by the Tuileries), and 'Paris by Night' excursions. Office is at 1 rue Auber, 9e. Magnificent view of Paris from the top of the *Tour Montparnasse*—you're whisked up to the 59th floor by what is claimed to be the fastest elevator in Europe (open 9.30 A.M. to 11.30 P.M.).

Helicopter trips available year-round from the Paris Heliport near the Porte de Versailles (call 557-75-51). Circuits of Paris and Versailles.

Several travel agencies, including *American Express*, have 'Modern Paris' tours, which include a visit to the UNESCO building.

The Ile de la Cité flower market is open daily except Sun. (when it becomes a bird market) from around 8–7. There is a flower market at the Madeleine on Tues., Wed., Fri., and Sat.

The famous flea market *(Marché aux Puces)* is at the Portes de Clignancourt and de St-Ouen, open Sat., Sun., Mon. There is a smaller antique market near the pl. Aligre every morning. And the *Marché de Montreuil*, near the Porte de Montreuil, is well known to bargain hunters who don't mind wading through a lot of pure junk; open Sat., Sun. and Mon. mornings.

You might want to try your luck at one of the official Paris auction houses, such as *Hôtel Drouot* (closed Aug.) in its attractive new building in the rue Drouot, 9e or at the elegant Sun. afternoon auctions at the *Hôtel des Rameaux* in Versailles.

Sun. is the big day for animal markets—birds on the quai de la Cité, cats on the quais either side of pl. du Château, 14e, dogs at 106 rue Brancion, 15e.

The picturesque wholesale markets at *Les Halles*—Zola's 'belly of Paris'— have moved to Rungis. But Les Halles is busy acquiring a new life of its own, centered around the new (opened 1979) and glittering *Forum*, a stylish glass and concrete shopping and leisure center. Many of the streets round about are pedestrian only and filled with fashion boutiques, art galleries, antique shops and the like. The completed scheme (should be ready in 1984) will include a fantastic aquarium and a children's garden.

The fountains in the pl. de la Concorde and other squares are often illuminated at night, especially on weekends and holidays. The floodlighting of Paris buildings is also well worth seeing—especially the pl. de la Concorde, Notre-Dame, the Invalides and Sacré-Coeur.

If you're in Paris on July 14, you won't miss the dancing in the streets, but perhaps you will want to know where to go to see the most authentic popular dancing (pl. de la République), the young student-artist writer groups (pl. de l'Institut), or the Bretons dancing in local costumes to bagpipe music (near the Tour Montparnasse, generally in the rue du Départ). Look out for City of Paris posters telling you about other *bals populaires* and about the magnificent fireworks display, usually let off from the Palais de Chaillot across the river from the Eiffel Tower.

Views over the city may be had from the Eiffel Tower, the Arc de Triomphe, the tower of Notre-Dame, the July Column in the pl. de la Bastille, from the dome of Sacré-Coeur, the Tour Montparnasse (see previous page), and the tops of these department stores: *Printemps, Galeries Lafayette* and *Samaritaine*.

To visit the famous sewers of Paris, be in the pl. de la Résistance (Left Bank end of the Pont de l'Alma) between 2 and 5 on Mon., Wed. or the last Sat. in the month (unless it's a public holiday the day before or after one).

There is a stamp and coin market at corner of av. Gabriel and av. Marigny, 8e, Thurs., Sat., Sun. and holidays, 10–dusk.

The Wine Museum, rue des Eaux, 16e, deserves to be better known. Splendidly set in vaulted 13th- and 14th-century wine cellars, it includes waxwork figures and is open daily (afternoons only). You can enjoy a wine-tasting session, or even attend a class in wine connoisseurship.

 **MUSEUMS.** Paris has well over 100 museums, many of them with good modern presentation of exhibits, though a few still seem a bit old-fashioned. State-owned museums close Tues, as in the rest of the country, but those owned by the City of Paris *(musées nationaux)* close on Mon. Many museums are closed on public holidays (check with *Pariscope* or *L'Officiel des Spectacles* for that week), but virtually all of them are open on Sun., when you get in half-price or even free. *Musées nationaux* offer free admittance on Weds. Children, students, teachers, men over 62 and women over 60 can usually get in half-price at all times. City of Paris museums allow senior citizens in free at all times. Sun. is inevitably a bit too crowded for comfort, so avoid it if you can. But remember that the French rarely skip lunch, and as most museums nowadays are open all day, 12.30 to 2 is always a good time for peaceful browsing both in the week and at weekends. In the following selected list the museums are open every day except Tues. unless otherwise stated. *Opening times are liable to change without warning, so always double-check locally.*

GETTING SETTLED IN PARIS

Arts Décoratifs 107 rue de Rivoli, 1er. In the opposite wing of the Louvre Palace from the Louvre Museum proper, this deals with interior decoration and furniture. However, it is currently being extensively renovated, so check locally to see whether it has reopened.

Archives Nationales and **History of France Museum** 60 rue des Francs-Bourgeois, 3e, 2–5. Documents and other exhibits relating to the history of France.

Art Moderne de la Ville de Paris 11 av. du Président-Wilson, 16e, 10–5.30, except Mon.; Weds, 10–8.30; 20th-century painting, sculpture, engravings, etc., plus temporary exhibits and a special children's museum. City of Paris museum.

Arts et Traditions Populaires 6 rte du Mahatma-Gandhi, Bois de Boulogne, 16e (Sablons entrance); 10–5.15; an astounding variety of objects related to rural activities in pre-industrial environments. Interesting audiovisual presentation makes this a particularly good place to take children, who will be able to press knobs and push buttons to their hearts' content. Also a research lab., library and photo lab.

Balzac's House 47 rue Raynouard, 16e, 10–5.40, except Mon. City of Paris museum.

Bourdelle 16 rue Antoine-Bourdelle, 15e, 10–5.40, closed Mon. and public holidays. Works by the famous sculptor. City of Paris museum.

Carnavalet 23 rue de Sévigné, 3e, 10–5.40, except Mon. and holidays. Costumes through the ages, china, history of Paris. Mementoes of Mme de Sévigné; 17th–18th-century French furniture. City of Paris museum.

Centre National d'Art et de Culture Georges Pompidou (usually known as the Beaubourg Center, or just Beaubourg), rue St-Martin, 4e, 12–10; Sat. and Sun. and public holidays, 10–10. Houses the **National Museum of Modern Art** (formerly in the av. Wilson), plus industrial design, excellent temporary exhibits, vast library with large microfilm and colored slide section; theater, experimental music, children's workshop. This very lively and always crowded arts complex has some excellent temporary exhibits and is full of interesting things for those who aren't put off by the sneers of dyed-in-the-wool Parisians who don't care for the futuristic architecture.

Cernuschi 7 av. Vélasquez, 8e, 10–5.45, closed Mon., holidays. Devoted to Chinese art.

Cluny 6 pl. Paul-Painlevé, off rue des Ecoles, 5e, 9.45–12.30, 2–5.15. Medieval museum in a delightful 15th-century abbey, with remains of Roman baths. Also 17th-century Jewish tombstones and monuments found in the area (you have to ask to see these). Don't miss the 'La Dame à la Licorne' tapestries or the recently discovered fragments of sculptures removed from Notre-Dame during the Revolution.

Cognacq-Jay 25 bld des Capucines, 2e, 10–5.40, closed Mon. Finely furnished 18th-century mansion. City of Paris Museum.

Conciergerie 1 quai de l'Horloge, 1er, in the Palais de Justice, 10–5 in winter, 10–6 in summer (last visits 4 and 5 respectively). Relics of the French Revolution, Marie-Antoinette's cell.

Delacroix's studio pl. de Fürstemberg, 5e, 9.45–5.15. In a charming old square, the painter's studio has been preserved as he left it.

Grand Palais, av. Winston-Churchill, 8e. Splendid glass-domed 19th-century building used to house excellent exhibits, often devoted to one painter (e.g. Cezanne, Manet). 10–8; Wed 10–10.

Guimet 6 pl. d'Iéna, 16e, 9.45–12, 1.30–5.15. Closed Tues and public holidays. Indo-Chinese and other Far Eastern art. Presentation is now modernized.

Histoire Naturelle 57 rue Cuvier, Jardin des Plantes, 5e, 1–5; 10.30–5 on Sun. Botanical, entomological, zoological and paleontological exhibits.

Invalides and **Musée de l'Armée** Esplanade des Invalides, 7e, open daily 10–5 (Oct through Mar) or 10–6 (April through Sept). Napoleon's tomb, military museum, weapons, armor, battle flags. *Son-et-lumière* show, 'The Return of the Ashes', twice nightly in English in summer.

The **Musée des Plans-Reliefs** can be visited on the same ticket, but the opening times are shorter: 10–12, 2–5, closed Sun. morning and Tues.

Jacquemart André, 158 bld Haussmann, 8e. 18th century paintings and furniture, plus Italian Renaissance collection. Good special exhibits too.

Jeu de Paume Tuileries Gardens, pl. de la Concorde, 1er, 9.45–5.15. Houses a famous collection of Impressionists; due to move to the Musée d'Orsay (see below).

Louvre. The most famous, of course, open 9.45–6.30. It is the world's largest museum, in the world's largest palace. The sections include: Greek and Roman; Oriental; Egyptian; sculpture; paintings and drawings; furniture and art objects from the Middle Ages to the 19th century. And, of course, the Mona Lisa (now behind a rather reflective glass frame), and the Venus de Milo. Lecture tours in English and French start daily, except Sun. (and of course Tues.), from the Pavillon Denon at around 10.30 and 3, with additional tours if the demand is great enough. Snackbar in Pavillon Mollien.

Marine Palais de Chaillot, pl. du Trocadéro, 16e, 10–6. Ship models and seafaring objects.

Marmottan 2 rue Louis-Boilly, 16e, 10–6, closed Mon. Magnificent collection of Monet's works.

Musée de l'Homme Palais de Chaillot, pl du Trocadéro, 16e, 10–5. Fine anthropological museum, with modern presentation. Documentary films daily.

Nissim de Camondo 63 rue de Monceau, 8e, 10–12, 2–5, closed Mon., Tues. and holidays. Magnificent 18th-century furniture in former private house.

Orsay, quai Anatole-France, 7e. The Museum of Nineteenth Century Art is being fashioned out of the old Gare d'Orsay and may be open by the end of 1984.

Palais de la Découverte 1 av. Franklin-Roosevelt, 8e, 10–6, daily except Mon. and holidays. Scientific, mechanical, technical exhibits, working models. Several daily demonstrations; planetarium.

Palais de Tokyo 13 av. du Président-Wilson, 16e, 9.45–5.15. This used to be the famous Museum of Modern Art, which is now part of the Beaubourg/Pompidou Center. Its old home now houses an important post-Impressionist collection that will move to the new Musée d'Orsay.

GETTING SETTLED IN PARIS

Panthéon pl. du Panthéon, 5e, 10–4.30. Formerly the church of Ste-Geneviève, now the burial place for Voltaire, Rousseau, Victor Hugo, etc.

Petit Palais av. Winston-Churchill, 8e, across the street from the Grand Palais, 10–5.40, closed Mon. Permanent collections of French painting and art objects, regularly supplemented by important temporary shows. City of Paris museum.

Rodin 77 rue de Varenne, 7e, 10–5 (6 in summer). The most charming of the individual museums, an old house in a garden, filled with Rodin's sculptures.

Victor Hugo's House 6 pl. des Vosges, 4e, 10–5.40, closed Mon. Souvenirs of the writer and paintings and carvings by him. City of Paris museum.

Ossip Zadkine Museum, 100 bis rue d'Assas, 6e; open Weds-Sat only, 10–5.40. The sculptor's house and studio are now open to the public with much of his work on display.

SPECIALIZED MUSEUMS

Affiche et Publicité, 18 rue de Paradis, 10e, 12–6. Closed Mon. and Tues. Devoted to advertising art in general and posters in particular. Attractive premises in what used to be a china showroom.

Archeological Crypt, beneath the Parvis Notre Dame, 4e, 10–5.30. New museum displaying the results of excavations in front of Notre Dame cathedral: foundations of the city's 3rd-century ramparts, remains of medieval houses, ruins of an earlier Merovingian cathedral etc.

Arts Africains et Océaniens 293 av. Daumesnil, 12e, 9.45–12, 1.30–5.15. African (including North African) art and civilization, plus the arts of the South Seas and a tropical aquarium.

Bricard, Musée de la Serrure 1 rue de la Perle, 3e, 10–12, 2–5, closed Sun., Mon., Tues. and holidays. Locks and locksmiths through the ages, displayed in a beautifully restored 17th-century mansion in the Marais.

Fashion and Costume, Palais Galliera, 10 av. Pierre-1er-de-Serbie, 16e. Has over 4000 outfits on display.

Gobelins workshops 42 av. des Gobelins, 13e, 2–3.15 Wed., Thurs. and Fri. for guided tour of shops where tapestries are being made.

Holography 4 rue Beauborg, 4e. 11–7; Sun. and public holidays 2–7. Closed Mon. Includes an incredibly realistic metro carriage.

Légion d'Honneur et des Ordres de Chevalerie 2 rue de Bellechase, 7e, 2–5, closed Mon. Well-displayed collections of French and foreign decorations, with new audiovisual section.

Monnaie 11 quai de Conti, 6e, 11–5, closed Sun., holidays. Medals, coins.

Montmartre, 12 rue Cortot, 18e, 2.30–5.30; Sun 11–5.30. Exhibits associated with Montmartre painters such as Toulouse-Lautrec, plus some of their works.

Musée du Cinéma pl. du Trocadéro, 16e. Tours only, 10, 11, 2, 3 and 4, closed Mon. History and classics of the film industry.

Notre-Dame de Paris 10 rue du Cloître Notre-Dame, 4e, 2.30–6, weekends only (except public holidays). The cathedral treasure, gold plate, embroidery.

Opéra pl. de l'Opéra, 9e, 10–5, closed Sundays and holidays. History of the opera and theatrical costumes.

Postal 34 bld de Vaugirard, 15e, 10–5, closed Sun. and holidays. Stamps, rare and historic, plus other items connected with communications.

CLOSE TO PARIS

Céramiques de Sèvres 4 Grande-Rue, 92410 Sèvres, 9.30–12, 1.30–5.15. Devoted to the famous Sèvres porcelain. The nearby factory can be visited on first and third Thurs. in the month at 1.30 and 3 (go to the museum entrance). Closed July and Aug. No children under 14.

Chantilly 10.30–5.30. The famous Musée Condé has superb paintings, jewelry and books.

Ecouen Museum of the Renaissance. In the Château d'Ecouen, which is set in attractive grounds nearly 20 km (12 miles) north of Paris; 9.45–12.30, 2–5.15. Tapestries, furniture, bronzes, etc., dating from the Renaissance period.

Fontainebleau. 10–12.30, 2–5 (6 in summer).

Malmaison. 10–12, 1.30–4.30 (5.30 in summer). Souvenirs of Napoleon and Josephine.

St-Germain-en-Laye. Prehistory Museum, 9.45–12, 1.30–5.15.

Sceaux. Musée de l'Ile de France, 10–12, 2–5. Closed Tues. all day and Mon and Fri A.M. Painting and documents connected with the Ile de France. Concerts are held in the Orangerie in summer.

Musée de Versailles in the Château de Versailles. Royal apartments, chapel, Galerie des Glaces, queen's bedroom, 9.45–5; Grand Trianon, 9.45–5 Petit Trianon, 2–5.15. Closed weekends. Guided visits at frequent intervals. Everything closed Mon. Fountains play first and third Sun. every month from May through Sept. between 4 and 5.30 P.M. Magnificent *fêtes de nuit* in July and Sept. (must reserve ahead).

PARKS AND GARDENS. The parks and gardens of Paris are varied and beautiful, whether they are the large rambling wooded variety or the formally laid-out open spaces in the center of the city. Some Paris parks are enclosed and are shut at dusk. The Bois de Boulogne and Bois de Vincennes are always open. But *it is not wise* to wander about there alone after dark.

Bois de Boulogne most famous of the Paris woods, at its western edge. It contains 7 lakes, the *Cascade* (waterfall), the Longchamp and Auteuil racetracks, the Roland-Garros tennis stadium, a polo field, a children's zoo (the Jardin d'Acclimatation), camping grounds, the Bagatelle Park, which exhibits spring flowers, roses (June, July) and water lilies, and a Shakespeare Garden.

Bois de Vincennes The working class opposite number to the Bois de Boulogne, on the other side of Paris (southeastern edge), a trifle larger (940 hectares/2,322 acres), containing zoo, a racetrack, three lakes, a couple of museums.

GETTING SETTLED IN PARIS

The **Luxembourg Garden** is famous throughout the world. On the Left Bank, off bld St-Michel, it encloses the Palais du Luxembourg, and the now disused Petit Luxembourg. The terrace, with its statues of the queens of France surrounding the pool on which children sail their boats, is a beautiful sight, as are the formal tree-lined avenues. Excellent enclosed playground for children; puppet shows from 2.30–3 in summer.

Jardin des Plantes Left Bank near the Austerlitz rail station. Contains the botanical gardens with special exhibits of medical plants, an Alpine garden and greenhouses, and the Natural History Museum.

Parc Monceau off bld de Courcelles, 8e, is quiet, charming, frequented mostly by the residents of the well-to-do quarter about it and their children; genuine *Parisien* atmosphere.

Parc des Buttes-Chaumont, 9e. In a middle-class quarter in the northern part of the city, another charming park. On a high mound like that of Montmartre, which it faces, it offers a splendid view from its often-painted Belvedere, and has a lake and a waterfall.

Parc Montsouris bld Jourdan, 14, in the south of Paris. Another charming park, near the Cité Universitaire. Besides the usual lake and waterfall, there is a copy of the palace of the Bey of Tunis in the park; you may be interested in Paris's *other* river, the Bièvre, which is briefly visible here before it ducks underground to join the Seine.

Jardin des Champs-Elysées on the west of pl de la Concorde, 1er, and **Jardin des Tuileries,** on the east, will not escape the tourist, as they are in the heart of Paris. The latter, designed by Le Nôtre, is particularly notable for its two wading pools, its formal gardens embellished with statues, and above all for the magnificent vista that sweeps all the way from the Louvre through the Tuileries to the Arc de Triomphe, with the Défense skyscrapers visible in the distance.

A garden the tourist can easily miss if, unguided, he fails to walk beneath the arches alongside the Comédie-Française, is the historic **Jardin du Palais Royal.** A stroll through it is rewarding if only for appreciation of the architectural harmony which accounts for the fact that some of the most famous residents of Paris, including Paul Valéry, Jean Cocteau and Colette, have at one time occupied apartments overlooking the gardens.

Moorish Gardens in Paris Mosque, 1 pl. du Puits de l'Ermite, 5e. Can be visited between 2 and 5. Don't go Fri., the Moslem holy day.

Jardin du Musée Rodin rue de Varenne, 7e, can be seen at the same time as you visit this spot, listed under 'museums'. It contains 2,000 rose bushes, representing 100 different varieties as well as sculptures by Rodin. Also special exhibits by other sculptors in summer.

CEMETERIES. The cemeteries in Paris are remarkable for their statues and beautifully designed tombs of famous people. They are open about 7.30–6 in summer; 8–4.30 in winter. The most visited are:

Montmartre av. Rachel, 18e (Métro: pl. Blanche or pl. Clichy). Tombs of famous authors and writers and of the composer Berlioz.

Montparnasse 3 bld Edgar-Quinet, 14e (Métro: Edgar Quinet). Tombs of scholars, artists and writers, including Baudelaire.

Passy 2 rue du Commandant-Schloesing, 16e (Métro: Trocadéro). Graves of the painter Edouard Manet, the actress Réjane, the composers Gabriel Fauré and Debussy.

Père-Lachaise 16 rue du Repos, 20e (Métro: Père-Lachaise or Philippe-Auguste). The most famous, with the tombs of Héloïse and Abélard, Balzac, Delacroix, Sarah Bernhardt, Chopin and Oscar Wilde.

Picpus 35 rue de Picpus, 12e (Métro: Picpus), in a convent. Open only 1–4.30, Nov.–Feb.; 1–7, Mar.–Oct. Contains the grave of General Lafayette (look out for the US flag flying over it).

American Cemetery 190 bld Washington, Suresnes, just outside Paris, contains the graves of American soldiers who died in World War I. Open 8–6.

CHURCHES. There are a number of churches in Paris with services in English, as well as branches of sects of English or American origin whose services are in French. Services in English are usually on Sunday.

American Church in Paris 65 quai d'Orsay (Métro: Invalides). Nondenominational.

American Pro-Cathedral of the Holy Trinity 23 av. George-V, 8e (Métro: Alma-Marceau). Episcopal, but welcomes all Protestants.

British Embassy Church 5 rue d'Aguesseau, 8e (Métro: Madeleine). Church of England.

St George's Anglican Church 7 rue Auguste Vacquerie, 16e (Métro: Kléber).

Baptist Church 49 rue de Lille, 7e (Métro: Rue du Bac).

Wesleyan Methodist Church 4 rue Roquépine, 8e (Métro: St-Augustin).

St Joseph's Roman Catholic English-speaking church, 50 av. Hoche, 8e (Métro: Etoile).

Scots Kirk 17 rue Bayard, 8e (Métro: F.-D. Roosevelt).

Christian Science 58 bld Flandrin, 16e (Métro: Dauphine), 45 rue La Boëtie (Métro: Miromesnil).

Centre Pastoral Halles Beaubourg 78 rue St-Martin, 4e (Métro: Châtelet). Roman Catholic masses in English and French.

Great Synagogue 44 rue de la Victoire, 9e (Métro: Le Peletier).

Liberal Synagogue 24 rue Copernic, 16e (Métro: Victor Hugo).

International Religious Center Palais des Congrès, Porte-Maillot, 17e, has masses in nearby chapel but will also provide a priest or minister for non-Catholic religions; information on religious activities in the Paris area; sells religious books; English spoken (open 10–8 Mon-Sat, 3–8 Sun).

CHILDREN. Paris has three zoos—the big and modern open-range type at the Bois de Vincennes; a smaller more old-fashioned zoo in the Jardin des Plantes; and a children's zoo in the Bois de Boulogne (the Jardin d'Acclimatation) with animals to ride. There are two aquariums, the principal one

GETTING SETTLED IN PARIS 133

in the park below the Palais de Chaillot (just across the Seine from the Eiffel Tower) and one of tropical fish in the Musée des Arts Africains et Océaniens, near the Porte de Vincennes. The *Popular Art and Traditions Museum* (see museums list) is also a good place to take children.

If you are planning to travel in France, and want someone to help with the children, you can find a foreign student through the *American College in Paris,* 31 av. Bosquet, 7e (tel. 555–91–73); a French student through the *French Medical Students Association,* 105 bld de l'Hôpital, 5e, tel. 586–19–42 or *Crous,* 39 av. Georges-Bernanos, 5e (tel. 329–12–43). An organization called *Volontaires pour enfants handicapes* will look after handicapped children free of charge between 9 A.M. and midnight. See under 'Guides' (later in this section) for a useful service taking your children to places of interest.

For babysitters, best look in *L'Officiel des Spectacles* or *Pariscope* for the 'Gardes d'Enfants' section, as the telephone numbers change frequently.

Apart from the museums listed earlier, children may like to visit the Grévin waxworks museum, 10 bld Montmartre, 9e (1–7 daily; 12–7 during school holidays), the Paris counterpart of London's Madame Tussaud's; or the Historial de Montmartre (daily 10.30–5.30), 11 rue Poulbot, 18e, with its history of Montmartre in wax dioramas.

They might like to visit the animal cemetery on the Ile d'Asnières, just beyond Neuilly.

Another marvelous excursion for children (and grownups) is the African game reserve in the grounds of the château of Thoiry in the Yvelines. Zebras, giraffes, lions and other large and small beasts wander around freely. There is also a regular zoo of baby animals, and the château can be visited.

There are several children's theaters in Paris operating all year round (French-speaking only). For details consult *Pariscope* or *L'Officiel des Spectacles.*

Punch and Judy shows are given in the Champs-Elysées gardens, av. Gabriel side, in the Luxembourg Garden, in the Champ-de-Mars (near the Eiffel Tower), in the Tuileries and the Jardin d'Acclimatation in the Bois de Boulogne. Shows are usually at about 3.30 or 4 on Sat., Sun.; also Weds. in term time.

READING MATTER. One local English-language paper is available in Paris, the *International Herald Tribune,* published Mon. through Sat. Numerous daily and Sun. papers from Britain are flown to Paris. Most of the larger newsstands carry a supply of English and American periodicals.

EMERGENCIES. American Hospital, 63 bld Victor-Hugo, Neuilly, 747–53–00. American staff. Out-patients received 9–12, 2–6; emergencies only on Sun. Dental clinic, facilities for contagious, infectious, or tubercular patients. Issues accident identity cards. British Hospital, 48 rue de Villiers, Levallois-Perret, 758–13–12, a small unit, open 24 hrs a day. All-night pharmacy, *Dhéry,* Galerie des Champs, 84 av. des Champs-Elysées, 8e (562–02–41). The

Pharmacie Anglaise des Champs-Elysées, 62 av. des Champs-Elysées, 8e, 225-25-13, carries British and American products.

For the 24-hour medical emergency service: 707-77-77 or 542-37-00.

Emergency dentists: 337-50-00 (between 8 P.M. and 8 A.M. weekdays, and all day weekends and public holidays).

For medical or pharmaceutical services at night, contact the nearest Commissariat of Police, which can supply you with names and addresses. *Pharmacie des Arts,* 106 bld Montparnasse, 14e, is open to midnight Mon.–Sat. and 8 P.M. to midnight on Sun. *Pharmacie Michelon,* 5 pl. Pigalle, 9e, is open till 1 A.M. On Sundays chemists normally display a list of doctors and chemists available in the area. Automatic call boxes are located at main cross-roads for use in instances requiring police *(Police-Secours)* or first-aid *(Services Médicaux).*

If stranded, try American Aid Society, at the US Embassy (296-12-02), mornings only. The embassy also has its own Welfare Service, open all day. For Britons in distress, there's the British Embassy (266-91-42).

For emergencies, call 723-80-80 after 7 P.M. This is a volunteer SOS service for English-speaking people, and the charming people at the other end of the telephone will make the greatest effort to help you, whether you are just lonely, have lost all your money, or have discovered you suffer from a peculiar disease.

If you've lost your keys, try 707-99-99.

GUIDES. The *Agence Nationale pour l'Emploi,* 50 rue de Malte, 11e (tel: 355-44-05), has a special Tourist Service providing English-speaking guides and interpreters. In 1983 cost was 260 frs for 3 hrs, 300 frs for half a day (approx. 4 hrs), 500 frs for a day (approx. 6 hrs). A guide to show you round the illuminated parts of Paris (starting at 9 P.M.) will cost 300 frs and a long day (perhaps to Chartres and Versailles as well as Paris), 550 frs. Each additional hour 60 frs. These are all official guides and it's best to reserve one a week ahead if possible. Either write in advance or telephone any weekday morning in June, July, Aug., or on Tues. or Thurs. morning the rest of the year (no callers at the office). Some guides have cars; otherwise you travel by public transport, in your own car, or, if you're in a group, by coach. The *École Française d'Hôtesses de Tourisme,* 11 bis rue de Milan, 75009 Paris (tel. 526-79-88) can often supply guides who are completing their training; all are fluent in English.

The *RATP* (Paris Transport Authority) has various guide-accompanied excursions both within and outside Paris. Inquire at their Tourist Service in the pl. de la Madeleine, 8e, or at 53 quai des Grands-Augustins, 6e; both offices are open on Sun. and holidays as well as in the week.

La Demeure Historique, 55 quai de la Tournelle, 5e, 329-02-86, publish a useful leaflet called 'Gardens and Castles Open to the Public' and will give you information on visits to private châteaux. *Centre d'Information des Monuments Historiques,* 62 rue St-Antoine, 4e, 274-22-22, provides a wealth of free documentation about France; programs, visit-conferences and special festivities in historic monuments. Hostesses will help visitors plan trips throughout the coun-

GETTING SETTLED IN PARIS

try. For guided visits only, call 887-24-14. Details of daily visits to places of interest in Paris can be found in *Pariscope, L'Officiel des Spectacles, Le Monde, Le Figaro,* etc. English-speaking guides also available on request.

Other semi-private agencies who arrange visits to places of interest outside Paris are: *Arts et Voyages,* 58 rue St-Lambert, 15e, 828-15-08, and *Paris et Son Histoire,* 82 rue Taitbout, 9e, 526-26-77.

Meet the French, at 11 rue Mesnil, 16e (tel. 727-26-10), arranges really personal service, both for tours in Paris and the countryside; idea is to make guest feel he has a 'friend in Paris'. They will even take your children to places such as the Eiffel Tower, the Grévin Waxworks Museum or the zoo, leaving you a whole morning or afternoon free to visit Paris at your leisure.

INTERNATIONAL FRIENDSHIP ORGANIZATIONS. *Union Interalliée,* 33 fbg St-Honoré, 8e. Exclusive club devoted to cultural exchanges and social activities linking French and English-speaking groups. Admits visitors as members.

Association France-Etats-Unis, 6 bld de Grenelle, 15e, is devoted to arranging contacts between French citizens and American citizens.

Association France-Grande-Bretagne, 17 rue Philibert-Delorme, 17e, has branches throughout France.

The *British Council,* 9 rue Constantine, 7e, has good library and organizes lectures, meetings and film showings.

Association France-Canada, 5 rue de Constantine, 7e; organizes outings, get-togethers, and exhibits at Canadian Cultural Center in same building.

USEFUL ADDRESSES. Embassies and Consulates *United States Embassy,* 2 av. Gabriel, 8e; Consulate, 2 rue St-Florentin, 1er, tel. 296-12-02. *British Embassy,* 35 fbg St-Honoré, 8e; Consulate, 109 fbg St-Honoré, 8e, tel. 266-91-42. *Australian,* 4 rue Jean Rey, 15e, tel. 575-62-00. *Canadian,* 35 av. Montaigne, 8e, tel. 723-01-01. *New Zealand,* 9 rue Léonard da Vinci, 16e, tel. 500-24-11. *South Africa,* 59 quai d'Orsay, 7e, tel. 555-92-15.

General information. *Information Office,* Paris official tourist office, 127 av. des Champs-Elysees, 8e (tel: 723-61-72). 9 A.M.–10 P.M. Mon.–Sat. (Sun and hols 9–8). Branch offices at Austerlitz, Est, Lyon, Nord rail stations (but these are closed Sun and holidays). *American Express,* 11 rue Scribe, 9e. *Thomas Cook & Son,* 2 pl. de la Madeleine, 8e.

Cleanliness-is-next-to-Godliness department. Laundromats are a fairly new phenomenon in France but you'll find them all over Paris now. Best look for *laverie automatique* in the telephone book (*laverie* on its own means a laundry) and pick one convenient for where you're staying.

Weather forecast. For the Paris area call 555-95-90; for the rest of the country: 555-91-09.

THE FACE OF FRANCE

FOR TEACHERS AND STUDENTS. For general information: *Centre d'Information et de Documentation Jeunesse,* 101 quai Branly, 15e. *Service d'Accueil des Etudiants Etrangers Boursiers du Gouvernement Français,* 4 rue Jean Calvin, 5e, publishes guides, finds housing and part-time jobs, etc.

Other useful addresses are: *Bureau des Renseignements,* Sorbonne, 47 rue des Ecoles, 5e; *Office National des Universités et Ecoles Françaises,* 96 bld Raspail, 6e; *American Student Advisory Service,* 261 bld Raspail, 14e.

For accommodations (students only, who must have an international student card): *Accueil des Jeunes en France* (AJF) specializes in lodging and tours throughout the country, accommodates young people in places ranging from dormitories to private rooms. Main office is at 119 rue Saint-Martin, 4e. It provides an information service for young people and offers good-value, special-interest holidays throughout France. Two branch offices, at the Gare du Nord and the Pont Louis-Philippe, deal with accommodations only. Accommodations at youth centers throughout France are very good value. Other useful addresses are: *Centre Régional des Oeuvres Universitaires et Scolaires* (CROUS), 39 av. Georges-Bernanos, 5e, *Office de Coopération et d'Accueil Universitaires,* 69 quai d'Orsay, 7e.

You can also be a paying guest with a French family: contact the Paris Tourist Office, 127 av. des Champs-Elysées, 8e, for lists and prices. Or, in Gt Britain, the *Central Bureau for Educational Visits and Exchanges,* 43 Dorset St., London W1; in the US at 777 United Nations Plaza, New York 10017.

Organizations that plan vacations and travel for students and teachers are: *Office du Tourisme Universitaire,* 137 bld St-Michel, 5e; *Concordia* (work camp holidays, archeological digs), 27 rue Pont-Neuf, 1er, *Jeunesse et Reconstruction,* 10 rue Trévise, 9e, plans holiday work, including fall grape harvesting, as does *Loisirs-Jeunes,* 36 rue de Ponthieu, 8e, and *CROUS,* 39 av. Georges-Bernanos, 5e.

YOUTH GROUPS. *Comité de Coordination des Associations d'Echanges Internationaux,* 26 rue Cabanis, 14e. *Centre d'Echanges Internationaux,* 21 rue Béranger, 3e. *Council on International Educational Exchange,* 49 rue Pierre-Charron, 8e. *Vacances Studieuses,* 3 fbg St-Honoré, 8e, arranges exchanges for children from the age of seven. A complete list of youth and student organizations can be obtained from the Office de Tourisme, 127 av. des Champs-Elysées, 8e. *Allostop* provides a well-organized service putting motorists with room to spare in touch with people who wish to travel in the same direction. You can pay per ride or for a year's use of the service. For details contact the office in Paris: Allostop-Provoya, 84 passage Brady, 75010 Paris (tel. 246-00-66). There's a number to ring in many other towns, such as Bordeaux (tel. (56) 81-24-59), Grenoble (tel (76) 96-72-99), Lyon (tel. (7) 842-38-29), and Strasbourg (tel. (88) 37-13-13).

GETTING SETTLED IN PARIS

There are two *Youth Hostels* in Paris. First is open year round at 8 bld Jules-Ferry, 10e (Métro: République), with 100 beds divided 2–6 per room. The second is only open July, Aug and first half of Sept: Maison des Arts et Métiers, 1 rue Pierre-Massé, 14e (Métro:Gentilly) and has 180 beds, all in single rooms.

For Motorists. *Royal Automobile Club,* 8 pl. Vendôme, 1er. *Automobile Club de France,* 6 and 8 pl. de la Concorde, 16e. *Touring Club de France,* 65 av. de la Grande-Armée, 16e.

FOR THE HANDICAPPED. A most useful guide to Paris, listing accessibility to buildings and with several plans as well as general information essential to the handicapped person, is available from Mr G. R. Couch, 68B Castlebar Rd, Ealing, London W5 2DD. Called *Access in Paris,* it is free, but a contribution to cover postage would be appreciated.

A helpful organization in Paris is the *Association des Paralysés de France* (APF), 17 bld Auguste-Blanqui, 13e, tel. 580-82-40, which publishes a useful hotel list. Also the *Comité de Coordination de l'Action en Faveur des Handicapés,* 36 rue de Prony, 75017, Paris, tel. 227-78-51. A free service for looking after physically handicapped children and teenagers between 9 A.M. and midnight is provided by *Volontaires pour Enfants Handicapes,* 42 rue du Louvre, 1er, tel. 508-45-15 (10-12.30 and 2-6 weekdays).

SAFETY WARNING. We have to say it, but mugging and other attacks on tourists have reached epidemic proportions in major tourist areas such as the Champs-Elysées, near the Louvre and around the Beaubourg/Pompidou Center. So take great care, particularly after about 10 P.M. Pickpockets have also become a major nuisance, both in tourist areas and even more in the metro. Police warn visitors to be on the alert for groups of small ragged-looking children, mostly gipsies, who offer to tell your fortune, sell you flowers or generally attract your attention while their 'colleagues' help themselves to your purse or wallet. As the children are (or claim to be) under 13, they can't be prosecuted and seem to go from strength to strength.

EXPLORING PARIS

A voyage of discovery

A town cannot be classified like a zoological or a marine specimen: 'Paris, the city of light' is inadequate, especially as Paris is much less brilliantly lit than many other great cities. Nor is it enough to choose some well-known place, Gothic Notre-Dame or the steel lacework of the Eiffel Tower, the red marble tomb in which Napoleon lies, or the venerable stones of Cluny, and to make of this a synthesis of Paris. That might be excellent for a poster, but otherwise is quite inadequate.

Neither is it by contrast that the problem is resolved: the Grande Galerie of the Louvre, and the little galleries of modern art on the Left Bank; the concerts in the Palais des Congrès, and the noisy sporting events at the Palais des Sports; the impeccable straight lines of the boulevards drawn by Haussmann, and the twisted complications of the little streets of the Marais; the tiny fashionable shops and the enormous

Marché aux Puces, where they sell old iron, antique furniture and American surplus goods; the rue Mouffetard, with its noisy street traders, and the Champs-Elysées; the 59-story Montparnasse Tower with its satellites of glassy boutiques in the shopping center jutting above the grey rooftops of old Paris; the new business center at La Défense with its tall skyscrapers and wide vistas, right across the Seine from fashionable, conservative Neuilly with its aristocratic town houses.

On our voyage of discovery we must invent new itineraries: the Royal Road from the Louvre to the Etoile, now baptized place Charles-de-Gaulle: the Embankment Road from the Bois de Boulogne to the Jardin des Plantes with its zoo; the Latin Road, which climbs across the students' quarter to Montparnasse, and then dives down to St-Germain-des-Prés, where a strange and way-out crowd perambulate day and night; the Milky Way of the *grands boulevards,* sprinkled with constellations of neon lights; the Evening Road, which goes down the Champs-Elysées and ascends the heights of Montmartre.

The Etoile

The Etoile! The Star! Twelve avenues radiate from the central circle, dominated by the triumphal arch designed by Napoleon in honour of his victorious army (it was not completed until 1836). But although the names of 384 of his campaigns are carved in its stone, although his mortal remains passed under its huge arch in 1840, having been returned from Elba, the Arc de Triomphe is much more than a monument to the glory of Napoleon. It is the very symbol of France. The sculpture groups represent four great episodes in the life of a people who often went to war in spite of their dislike of it: Departure, Resistance, Triumph, Peace. The finest is the Departure, where the Motherland, her wings spread wide, seems to be exhorting her sons with the stirring strains of the *Marseillaise.* Flickering in the wind, but never extinguished, is the flame burning before the tomb of the unknown soldier of the 1914-18 war, symbolically relit every evening at 6 by groups of veterans who march solemnly up the Champs-Elysées.

This arch, noble in its grandeur 50 meters/164 ft high, 45 meters/148 ft wide and 22 meters/72 ft thick, has a quality that makes it eminently suitable for great occasions such as the lying in state of Victor Hugo in 1885, before his body, followed by 800,000 mourners, was carried away on a common hearse; or on July 14, 1919, when, bedecked with flags, the victory procession led by Joffre, Foch, Pershing and Haig passed under its vaulted roof, a ceremony repeated with even more joy in 1944 when Charles de Gaulle, flanked by his faithful

Resistance followers (many of whom later became his bitter enemies), led *his* victory procession.

The Champs-Elysées, originally designed by Le Nôtre as a garden sweeping away from the Louvre, was for long a fashionable promenade where carriage-driven ladies and their elegant escorts rode beneath the chestnut trees (of which only a few remain at the Rond-Point). The 19th and 20th centuries turned this green haven into one of the widest and busiest avenues in the world, a symbol of all that Paris means to people in the remotest parts of the earth, who have never seen and may never see the City of Light. With its numerous café terraces, airline and tourist offices, car displays and shopping arcades, newspaper and commercial offices, cosmopolitan crowds, the Champs-Elysées *is* Paris.

At the Rond-Point the avenue widens and at the end of the afternoon all the automobiles in Paris seem to converge here. Then it continues towards the Concorde. On either side are chestnut trees and thickets behind which are old fashioned pavilions used as theaters or restaurants. Children stare at the Punch and Judy show while three times a week stamp and coin dealers hold their sales.

On the other side of the wide roadway are the Grand Palais and the Petit Palais. The latter houses a collection of modern French paintings, as well as medieval objects and porcelain. Both are also used for temporary exhibitions. Both were constructed for the 1900 Exhibition. The Grand Palais is due to become, after essential repairs and modernization of facilities, a large concert hall as well as the site of major art exhibitions. At the end of the avenue, as it opens onto the place de la Concorde, are the famous equine sculptures of Marly, now restored and free from their protective metal casing, though by about 1987 they will have been replaced by copies and removed to some pollution-free museum.

Place de la Concorde

We are now in the place de la Concorde. Consecrated to the glory of Louis XV, it was here that his successor, Louis XVI, and Marie-Antoinette were guillotined. Here, also, the chemist Lavoisier was beheaded ('The République does not need scientists,' said the judge who condemned him). And here it was that Madame Roland cried, 'Liberty, what crimes are committed in thy name!'

When the blood of the victims had been washed away, and the rolling of the drums and the yells of the *sans-culottes* had died down, the *place* was renamed 'Concorde'. And, since the statue of Louis XV had been overturned during the Revolution, it was decided to erect another monument, free from any political significance. The Viceroy of Egypt had offered France an obelisk—a monolith 23 meters/75 ft long, weighing 230 tonnes. It was considered that its venerable age, 3,300 years, protected it from any tendentious interpretation. The French went to Luxor to fetch it, and brought it back intact despite innumerable difficulties in 1833. With its cryptic hieroglyphics, it now symbolizes concord among men.

The place de la Concorde is, undoubtedly, one of the most beautiful in the world. Everything in it is balanced and harmonious, its huge perspective (it is the second largest square in France; the esplanade des Quinconces in Bordeaux is the first) is a perfect example of the classical French penchant for refined proportions. Two 18th-century palaces by Gabriel (who also built the Petit Trianon) frame in their impressive but gracious structures the rue Royale, which is terminated by the columns and frieze of the Madeleine. Opposite, beyond the Seine, is the colonnade of the Palais Bourbon. There is the same perfect symmetry in the east-west axis; on the one hand, the horses from château Marly emerging from the foliage of the Champs-Elysées, on the other, the horses of Coysevox from that of the Tuileries, whose green depths are enclosed by the triumphal arch of the Carrousel on one side, and by that of the Etoile on the other. Two Roman fountains, two Grecian-style temples, an Egyptian obelisk and eight statues of lovely women, representing French cities, ornament this truly Parisian well-planned *place*.

Behind a richly decorative iron railing, between the pavilions of the Jeu de Paume and the Orangerie, lies the Tuileries Garden: yet another work by Le Nôtre, one of the finest of French landscapists, it is a perfect example of what is called 'a French-style garden'. Well balanced, with fountains and ornamental basins designed to harmonize with the general architecture, it is filled with statues of gods and horses, nymphs and sylphs. A playground for children by day, although rather dusty and a bit unkempt now, it is an ideal tranquil spot for courting couples of an evening in spring when there are lots of other people around. It is not advisable to walk alone through the Tuileries after dark when the park looks empty: alas, Paris is beginning to discover some of the unpleasantness of urban living.

Here, close to the Palais Royal, Louis XIV organized an enormous carrousel to celebrate the birth of the Dauphin. The *place* takes its name from this event. After Austerlitz, Napoleon ordered the building of two triumphal arches in honor of the French success, that of the Carrousel and that of the Etoile, and set aside one million francs for the purpose.

We can see from here the splendid perfection of the perspective that sweeps across the Tuileries, past the obelisk of the Concorde, up to the Etoile and beyond and across the Seine to the tall towers of the new Défense neighborhood. It is the Royal Way of Paris, for close at hand is the Louvre.

Two wings of gray stone form the pavilions of Flore and Marsan. The effect is theatrical, with successive backgrounds merging finally into a highly decorated façade behind a garden courtyard, with statues of Lafayette and a gesticulating Gambetta, whom Rémy de Gourmont described as a gentleman always hailing a cab and never getting one.

The Louvre

This is the largest palace in the world, begun in 1200 and finished in 1870. Before becoming the royal residence it was a fortress. Today it houses seven museums that form one of the most important artistic collections in the world; Greek and Roman antiquities, Egyptian and Oriental antiquities, paintings and drawings (beginning, in classical art-history tradition, with the 12th-century Italians, and following along in a most orderly manner through the European Renaissance, and ending with 19th-century French and English schools), sculpture, furniture, *objets d'art* (in the wing running by the Seine). The Museum of Decorative Art is housed in the wing running along the rue de Rivoli. In the Tuileries, at the place de la Concorde end, the Museum of the Jeu de Paume displays the work of the Impressionists (Manet, Monet, Degas, Renoir, Cézanne, Van Gogh, Gauguin and others), while its twin museum, the Orangerie, is due to reopen in 1983 after renovation to make it a fit home for a splendid collection of 19th- and 20th-century paintings bequeathed to the nation. In a special room in the basement are Monet's famous *Waterlilies* series of paintings.

The principal entrance of the Louvre Museum is the Porte Denon in the vast Court of the Carrousel. Once past the threshold, your route will be marked by your preferences, your curiosity, or, more simply, by your guidebook.

The *Victory of Samothrace,* wings outstretched, thrusts forward its magnificent bulk like a superb prow. The *Venus de Milo* remains the classical model of beauty, and the most photogenic star in the world. On the ground floor squats the celebrated Egyptian *Crouching Scribe,* another masterpiece in the Louvre's collection of antique sculpture.

For equivalent wonders in painting, go upstairs to the first floor. In the Grande Galerie: French School: the *Sacre* by David, the romantic and revolutionary *Barricade* by Delacroix. Italian School: to the left of the French School, heading towards the Pavillon de Flore, suave Fra Angelico, the *St Anne* by Leonardo da Vinci, four Raphaels, three Titians, and, in the Salle des Etats, against a background of wine-colored velours, the eternal, enigmatic, ironic smile of the *Mona Lisa.*

In the Pavillon de Flore is the Spanish School: El Greco, Murillo, Velasquez, Ribera. On the second floor, in the Galerie Medicis, and what are known as the *'petits cabinets',* the Flemish School, with the

EXPLORING PARIS

famous *Virgin* by Van Eyck, a triptych by Roger van der Weyden and, in addition to Memling, Brueghel, Quentin Massys and Van Dyck, the magnificent portrait by Rubens of his second wife, Hélène Fourment. Dutch School: four Rembrandts, the *Bohémienne* by Frans Hals, a classical landscape by Ruysdael. German School: the famous *Erasmus* by Holbein. English and American Schools: Bonington's *Versailles* and Whistler's *Mother*.

In the Galerie d'Apollon are the crown jewels, including the *Régent*, a diamond that weighs 137 carats.

The genius of successive generations of architects, under François I, Henri II, Henri III, Catherine de Médicis, Henri IV, Louis XIII, Louis XIV, Napoléon I and Napoléon III, was responsible for the superb transformation of this ancient fortress, dating from the Crusades, into the most important palace in the world. The building survived the years after Louis XIV abandoned it: during this period, when the king sought the pleasures of Versailles, many artists, Boucher among them, installed themselves without ceremony in the great *salons*, and stovepipes often poked through the admirable colonnade built by Claude Perrault in the time of the *Roi Soleil*.

This colonnade is opposite St-Germain-l'Auxerrois, the parish church of the illustrious inhabitants of the Louvre. From its belfry, on the night of August 24, 1572, Catherine de Médicis gave the signal for the massacre of the Huguenots. The atrocious night of St Bartholomew is commemorated by the statue of Coligny, not far away.

Iles de la Cité and St-Louis

But the Seine summons us, the Seine, which, with a tender gesture, seems to enclose its precious islands, the Cité and St-Louis, within its arms. These islands seem to be gliding downriver like a boat with a painter trailing in its wake. At the river's edge, anglers keep their eyes on their floats, except occasionally when they look up at the massive towers of Notre-Dame, the golden spire of the Sainte Chapelle, the slate turrets of the Conciergerie, and, at the very tip of the Ile de la Cité, a garden where silver willow leaves trail in the water. A stone bridge crosses the river: it is the Pont-Neuf—the New Bridge, which in fact is Paris's oldest—called 'new' because, in 1604, it was the first to be lined with houses and shops (now all torn down), to have pavements, and to be distinguished by a statue (of Henri IV, erected only four years after his death). The present equestrian statue of Henri IV, cast in the bronze of Napoleon's statue in the place Vendôme, turns its back on the Seine to appreciate the peaceful old-world façades of the place Dauphine's ancient dwellings, and the monumental Palais de Justice. Formerly a royal palace, this building became the seat of parliament, and, after the Revolution, the Court of Justice. A Capetian king built the Sainte Chapelle, and it was in one of the courts of the Palais, that, on the day that World War II ended, Marshal Pétain was condemned to death, only to be reprieved immediately and the death sentence changed to life imprisonment on a desolate Breton island.

Many famous people have lived on the Ile St-Louis: Helena Rubenstein, Baudelaire at 17 quai d'Anjou, Cézanne at no. 15 and Daumier at no. 19: Voltaire at 2 rue St-Louis-en-l'Ile, but he died at 27 quai Voltaire—another famous street where Ingres, Delacroix and Corot had their studios.

Sainte Chapelle

The Sainte Chapelle is a Gothic jewel. In its stone lacework are set the most ancient stained-glass windows of Paris, an enormous display in which 1,130 scenes from the Bible are shown in color. St Louis, having acquired from the Venetians the true crown of thorns, decided to build in the heart of his palace a chapel in which to place the holy relic, together with nails and pieces of wood from the cross of Calvary, and it was built in less than three years. Today it is enclosed within the walls of the Palais de Justice, and represents a treasure even more precious than the hoard that the king kept in the Tour d'Argent, which, together with the Tour de César, guards the entrance to the Conciergerie on the quai opposite the Ile de la Cité. Romantic, candlelit concerts are held here.

The Conciergerie is the Museum of the Terror. In the Salle d'Armes more than 1,000 persons were herded together; in one cell Marie-Antoinette lived for two and a half months, spied upon day and night, by leering jailers; nearby, Danton, and then Robespierre, passed their last night. In the women's courtyard, the highborn captives did their washing and tried to approach the iron railings that separated them from the male prisoners. Here, in the shadow of the guillotine, love still played its part, although many of the liaisons were sordid enough, for pregnant women were not executed. The last moments were passed at the 'Greffe' (on the spot where the buffet of the 'Palais' stands today) where the executioner's assistants ripped the shirts of the condemned, cropped their hair, and then hustled them into the fatal cart that carried, in turn, a queen, Marie-Antoinette; a former court favorite, Madame du Barry; Charlotte Corday, who assassinated Marat; a scientist, Lavoisier; a poet, André Chénier, and many others.

Close by are the fresh colors of the flower market, which on Sunday mornings becomes a bird market. It extends as far as the Châtelet bridge, and fills the little street that winds around the hospital of Hôtel Dieu with chirping and perfume.

Notre-Dame and the islands

Notre-Dame de Paris was built in the early Gothic style between 1163 and 1330, the task of building going on without interruption. It stands on the site where originally there was a Roman temple, followed by the first Christian church, built in the 4th century. The Notre-Dame of today is, however, largely reconstruction work of the original, for in the 17th and 18th centuries it was despoiled of much of its beauty. It was not until 1844 that work on its restoration was started, under the architect Viollet-le-Duc. Working from old plans, and with detailed knowledge, he brought the building back to its original concept, with some new—but apt—embellishments (such as the gargoyles). Of the three beautiful and richly hued rose windows, the first from the main doorway on the north side is the original, that on the south side was restored in 1726 by Viollet-le-Duc, who also created the one above the main façade.

Notre-Dame cannot fail to entrance. Kings and princes married before its great altar; Napoleon crowned himself emperor here, and it was he who restored the cathedral to its proper function. In front of the great cathedral you can now visit the fascinating Archeological Museum in what was once a crypt; it displays exhibits dating from Roman, medieval and more recent times, all discovered during excavations for a car park.

The statue of St Geneviève, patron saint of Paris, stands by the Pont de la Tournelle and overlooks the two islands she saved by her prayers from Attila. Ile de la Cité, with its cathedral, law courts and hospital, overshadows by its brilliance the Ile St-Louis, built up in the 12th century, which now has something of the calm of a provincial city.

Ile St-Louis seems to be towed by the Cité, joined to it by a ridiculous iron bridge in strange contrast to the dignity of the venerable plane trees and the beautiful houses whose façades have been softened by the passage of time. Here the old streets must be explored on foot to discover the noble old mansions of Lambert or Lauzun, with their green courtyards and great staircases, or the quais endowed with the names of the great families of Bourbon, Anjou and Orléans. From here, and from the garden of the Left Bank church of St-Julien-le-Pauvre, with its famous false acacia, the oldest tree in Paris (1601), you will have your most memorable views of Notre-Dame.

The Seine, swollen by the waters of the Marne, runs between sheds and warehouses, past the glassy new office buildings rising on the Right Bank quais, on past the Jardin des Plantes and its captive beasts, and past the recent buildings of Paris University's science faculty, which, after a long battle succeeded in displacing the cellars and warehouses, moved across the river and further down to the quai de Bercy. And finally, the Seine opens two great arms to enclose the very heart of Paris.

Quartier Latin

The spirit of Paris lives on the *Rive Gauche,* the Left Bank. In the third century the Romans chose the Left Bank, opposite the Island of Lutetia, to build baths, theater, arena, forum and temple. The arena still exists and the remains of the baths can be seen in the ruins of Cluny where Roman relics still turn up. On the site where the theater and the forum stood, you now find the Sorbonne, the Collège de France and the Bibliothèque St-Geneviève. For this is the Latin Quarter. Latin, because professors and students were obliged to use this language for lectures and even for the necessities of daily life. Today all languages are spoken in the Latin Quarter. Young men and young women, of all nationalities and colors, come from the four corners of the earth, not only to take their places in the lecture rooms of the university, but also to spend their time at the cafés discussing politics and sex as well as literature and art.

The heart of the Latin Quarter is the famous boulevard St-Michel, scene of violent street fighting between students and police in 1968. Constantly crowded with street vendors, students, hippies, Arabs and Africans from the former French colonies. We advise you to keep away from the little streets west of the place Saint-Michel late at night, as there have been some nasty incidents.

Since ancient times this quarter has detested the bourgeoisie, for here walks the ghost of Villon, that great poet and rapscallion who died sordidly in a tavern brawl. Verlaine lived a stone's throw from the Panthéon, among the shopkeepers of rue Mouffetard, drinking absinthe and writing poetry. He was not, however, buried in the Panthéon, that Temple of Fame dedicated by the Revolution to receive the ashes of the great. In the crypt, Rousseau, Voltaire, Victor Hugo and Zola lie side by side with Marceau the soldier, Jean Jaurès the politician, and Berthelot the scientist. Their tombs may be visited, but it is no longer possible to visit the dome, whose 'columned crown' is most effectively seen from the Luxembourg Gardens.

The Luxembourg Gardens are a magnificent site for the palace that Marie de Médicis built in memory of her native Tuscany. Later she was evicted by her son, Louis XIII, and the palace became the property of the crown. Successively, it has since served as a prison, as the headquarters of the Directory, as Senate, House of Lords, and today it houses the Council of the Republic. But the councillors insist on calling it the

EXPLORING PARIS

Senate. For the Parisians it remains 'the Luxembourg,' and so the conference held within its walls by the victorious powers in 1946 was called the Luxembourg Conference.

The avenue de l'Observatoire, which runs from the Luxembourg Gardens to the Observatory, is bordered by chestnut trees, statues and columns. This district was formerly the home of convents and abbeys. Of these there now remain Val de Grâce, whose dome is surpassed only by those of the Invalides and the Panthéon, and the abbey of Port-Royal, where Pascal visited his sister, who converted him to Jansenism. Near the Jardin des Plantes, and dominated by its minaret, is the Great Mosque. In this veritable miniature Moslem city, you can refresh yourself with a mint tea in the mosque gardens.

The boulevard Montparnasse is ordinary enough in appearance, and joins the boulevard Raspail at a crossroads that is the real center of Montparnasse. The very name of Montparnasse (Mount Parnassus) predestined this district to be the haunt of artists and poets. It was on the moleskin-covered benches of the little cafés of Montparnasse that Lenin meditated on his great crusade against the Czars, that Foujita, having no rice, was hungry enough to eat his chopsticks, and that Kisling devoured the art critics because he had no money to buy a steak. Here, too, Ernest Hemingway, happy haunter of the Dôme and the Coupole, boozed and wrote his way to fame.

All around sprang up the studios of painters and sculptors, where salesgirls, waitresses and art-students disrobed to pose for the pure love of art. The hotel or restaurant bill was often paid with a picture: some are now worth millions of francs, some worth less than their frames. Cafés like the Dôme and the Rotonde (now in a revised version beside a modern movie house) proudly exhibited on their walls these blank checks signed by artists who made them famous. At the Luxembourg end of the boulevard Montparnasse is the famous Closerie des Lilas, oldest literary café-restaurant in the *quartier,* now a chic restaurant.

The most eye-catching landmark today is the 59-story Tour Maine-Montparnasse, an ugly slab of tinted glass and steel that is visible from everywhere in Paris, jutting above the domes and spires of the ancient city. On the first floor is an ultra-modern shopping center, including a branch of the Galeries Lafayette department store, convenient but not as picturesque as the Breton *crêperies* and *bistrots* in the side streets. Nevertheless, the area remains the rallying place for Paris's Bretons. Fortunately, nor far away, the St. Stanislas church still stands, as does the Café Select, one of the last hold-outs of the good old days. And the magnificent view from the top of the monster tower is worth seeing.

Today, the artists have come down from their hill, and have settled either beyond Montparnasse, towards Denfert-Rochereau and the

Portes d'Orléans and d'Italie where living is cheaper and community spirit still thrives, in the lofts and courtyards of the faubourg St-Antoine and the rue de Charonne, or, if they are on their way up in the world, St-Germain-des-Prés.

St-Germain-des-Prés

To many, the name of St-Germain-des-Prés still carries the same echoes as Greenwich Village in New York or Soho in London, standing for a world of fun and games, for the bohemian life; for cafés, restaurants, nightclubs, which are, according to the whim of the moment, either crammed to suffocation or entirely deserted. In part all this is still true, but basically, St-Germain-des-Prés, once the citadel of France's intellectual life, is suffering from anemia. Invaded by provincials and foreigners who think they are rubbing shoulders with the intelligentsia on the terraces of its Café Flore and Deux Magots, it is but a pale reflection of its former self. True, the streets are still stuffed with expensive antique shops, avantgarde art galleries and new boutiques, but most of the artists and writers have migrated to less expensive haunts, and the nights are populated by a curious and occasionally vicious motley crowd, to such an extent that it is inadvisable for a lone woman—or even a man—to roam the streets late.

However, this romantic old area has many permanent charms. Don't miss, for instance, the Romanesque bell tower of St-Germain-des-Prés church, the oldest of its size in Paris, founded in the 8th century by Benedictine monks; it has suffered many vicissitudes during its long history, and during the Revolution was even used as a saltpeter refinery.

In the immediate vicinity you find modest, quiet streets, and the enchanting place de Fürstemberg with its catalpa trees, its old lamps, and its atmosphere of old-world operetta. These streets were occupied by the aristocracy and the dignitaries of the church before the fine mansions of the faubourg St-Germain were built. The latter, now that these noble families lack the money necessary for their maintenance, have become ministries or embassies. This 'suburb of the nobility' has lost much of its brilliance since the 18th century, when it was considered indispensable to have a house in the rue de Varenne or the rue de Grenelle, but you can still glance in the doors of private houses, the Palace of the Légion d'Honneur and the Palais-Bourbon (constructed from the stones of the Bastille) where the French Assemblée Nationale now holds its meetings. This building was erected by a daughter of Louis XIV, who insisted that the façade should not overlook the Seine. The present Greek peristyle, in front of which are two goddesses and six statesmen, was built by Napoleon Bonaparte, that superb town

EXPLORING PARIS

planner, who wished to perfect the symmetry of the Concorde and, at the same time, to make the Palais-Bourbon the complement of the Madeleine. In this area, American painter James McNeill Whistler had his studio, at 110 rue de Bac, writer Antoine de St-Exupéry lived at 5 rue de Chanaleilles, and General de Gaulle's headquarters were at 5 rue Solférino, which now houses a library of books by and about him.

The Tomb of Napoleon

The mortal remains of Napoleon lie in the Invalides in a tomb of red marble under the highest dome in Paris. The church of the Invalides, whose principal façade is more than 180 meters (600 ft) in length and stands before an enormous esplanade, dominates its majestic surroundings. A palace, two chapels, an army museum and several military buildings together form a homogeneous unity. A 'triumphal battery', composed of old bronze cannons surrounding two tanks from the last war, stands guard over the monument. Beyond the door, in front of which stands the equestrian statue of the Sun King, is the Cour d'Honneur, and by the stairway of the right wing is one of the old taxis of the Marne, which, in September 1914, carried the reinforcements that saved Paris, a true museum piece worthy to take its place among the hundreds of flags taken from the enemy, and the swords, crossbows, culverins, and muskets.

The church of St-Louis-des-Invalides and that of the Dôme are both consecrated to the glory of those who won immortality on the field of battle. In the crypt of the church of St-Louis, near the tomb of the illustrious Turenne, lie the mortal remains of some of the heroes of the 1914–18 war together with General Leclerc—who set out as colonel of a unit of lorries in the Chad and finished as a general commanding the armored division that invested Hitler's eyrie in Berchtesgaden—and General Giraud, whom the Americans imported into North Africa at the time of their landings in 1942. But France's greatest soldier, Napoleon, rests in the crypt of the Eglise du Dôme.

The tomb is surrounded by twelve enormous figures and guarded by two statues of bronze. The outer shell of porphyry encloses six coffins, the innermost of which contains the body of the emperor. The remains of the famous Corsican, having lain in a tomb on St Helena since 1821, were transferred to Paris in 1840 at the request of Louis-Philippe. He rests in a monument built by Louis XIV to exalt the grandeur of his reign. Next to the church is a public garden, the Garden of the Intendant. It has a lovely avenue of lime trees and was laid out as a formal French garden with a statue of Jules Hardouin-Mansart, who built the Hôtel des Invalides.

The Eiffel Tower

If the Statue of Liberty is New York, if Big Ben is London, if the Kremlin is Moscow, then the Eiffel Tower is Paris. For two years a French engineer, Gustave Alexandre Eiffel, worked to erect this strange monument, which was designed to exalt the technical era that had begun with Edison and Bell. Eiffel used 5,000 sheets of paper, each a meter square, for his full-scale plans of this enormous construction. It was opened on June 10, 1889, by Edward VII, then Prince of Wales. For years it was considered the right thing to say that the tower was hideous, and to compare it to a giraffe, a giraffe that weighed 6,810,000 kg (15,000,000 lb) and whose head soared 300 meters (1,000 ft) high. Then gradually, the tower became part of the Parisian landscape, and paperweights, ashtrays and other souvenirs were manufactured to spread its reputation throughout the world.

Moreover, it was discovered to be useful, and wireless experiments were carried out between the Panthéon and its first floor. After years of faithful service as a radio broadcasting tower, its top was rebuilt and heightened in 1957 for use as a television transmitting mast, and it is now 230 meters (984 ft 6 in) high. Since 1981 a local radio station called Radio Tour Eiffel has broadcast from the tower, which has undergone a drastic slimming-down operation and refurbishment and reopened all its floors in 1982, with a new range of restaurants and bars and shops—even an exchange office. In 1983 a museum and slide projection show will also open here.

During the German occupation Paris trembled when it was suggested that its 12,000 pieces of metal and 2,500,000 rivets should be requisitioned. But the Germans hesitated at this sacrilege, and, like good tourists, climbed up to its summit (the elevators had been sabotaged) to enjoy the sight of the capital of France lying at their feet.

They saw also the shadow of the tower falling across the enormous Champ de Mars, where Napoleon used to review his troops. At one end of it stands the Ecole Militaire, which has an interesting history. A financier, Pâris-Duverney, a royal favorite, Madame de Pompadour and a writer, Beaumarchais (who, before writing the *Mariage de Figaro*, taught the harp to the royal princesses), got together to arrange the building of the Ecole Militaire. But it required a tax on playing cards and a national lottery to pay for its completion. Here the officers of the French army are now trained. From the heights of the Eiffel Tower can be seen a narrow island at the tip of which is a statue more usually associated with New York and its harbor—a replica of Bartholdi's famous *Liberty enlightening the World.* This statue symbolizes the unity of ideals uniting these two peoples, which induced Lafayette to

EXPLORING PARIS

fight under the orders of Washington and, two centuries later, Pershing and Eisenhower to fight in France.

Now the eye also takes in the skyscrapers of the new Front de Seine development. Some consider them unesthetic, but they are an improvement on the crumbling warehouses that formerly lined this section of the banks of the Seine.

Near here Lafayette used to visit Benjamin Franklin, then an ambassador sent to plead the American cause before Louis XVI. The aged Franklin watched the trials of his balloons on the banks of the Seine, publicly embraced Voltaire, and bombarded the minister Vergennes with letters and petitions. In the end he achieved what he had been sent to France to obtain: official recognition of the United States and a loan of several million francs. A statue and a road bearing his name commemorate Franklin's stay on the hill of Chaillot.

The hill forms a magnificent terrace overlooking the Seine, the Eiffel Tower, the Champ de Mars and the Ecole Militaire. The Palais de Chaillot is divided in two, to frame the superb perspective of statues, aquariums, gardens and ornamental fountains that prove that the 20th century has also contributed to the glory of Paris. Built at the time of the 1937 Exhibition, it houses several museums. In the rue Franklin wing are the Musée de l'Homme and the Musée de la Marine, and in the wing in the avenue du Président Wilson are the Théâtre National de Chaillot and the Musée des Monuments Français, with plaster casts of some of the more representative statues from the beginning of the Roman period to the end of the 19th century. The United Nations were housed in this wing during the 1948 meeting, and in the underground theater of the Palais de Chaillot, the Security Council discussed the Berlin blockade. Later NATO moved in and occupied their ugly 'temporary' buildings until 1960. Now, once more, the Palais de Chaillot has recovered all its rather chilly glory, and in spring and summer visitors and Parisians can look out at the impressive panorama of the great fountains playing, with the Eiffel Tower in the background.

The Bois de Boulogne

Of the six avenues that converge at the place du Trocadéro, the avenues Henri-Martin and Georges-Mandel lead directly to the Bois de Boulogne. The Bois is shaped, appropriately, like a lung. For, with its thousands of tall trees, it is a lung through which Paris breathes. Stretching from the city to the Seine, the Bois has over 96 km (60 miles) of roads, avenues, lanes and footpaths and is crowded with seekers of fresh air, tranquility, and (very relative) solitude. In recent years, however, the Bois has become literally infested with prostitutes of varying ages and sexes, who meander about even in the morning, but more particularily after 5.30, when suburbanites begin to return home from their Paris offices. Sometimes, in fact, there are so many cars suddenly stopped along the roads that accidents are caused. It is not wise to stroll alone in the Bois after dark, and many women do not even care to drive alone there after 8 o'clock.

However, during the daytime, walk around the lakes, between the racecourses of Auteuil and Longchamp, or in the Jardin d'Acclimatation and the flower gardens of Auteuil, the Pré Catalan and Bagatelle. The Bois is also a place for watching sport, with the Roland Garros tennis stadium playing host to the French tennis championships in May or June, polo near Bagatelle, cross-country races from time to time, and of course horseracing.

The Madeleine and Opéra

The church of Ste-Marie-Madeleine, with its elegant columns 18 meters (60 ft) high, is a copy of the Parthenon, erected to the glory of Napoleon's Grande Armée. The Madeleine—where a special service is held for Americans on Thanksgiving Day—is one of the most famous buildings in Paris, largely owing to its site, facing the Concorde. It is also the beginning of the boulevards.

The time is past when everything happened on the boulevards. Alphonsine Duplessis, immortalized by Dumas in *The Lady of the Camelias,* lived in one of the houses on the boulevard de la Madeleine. Revolutionary barricades crossed the boulevard des Capucines, and here, in a cellar, the brothers Lumière held their first performance of the animatograph, the forerunner of the modern cinema. Today this district has been taken over by the travel agencies, and the avenue de l'Opéra, which runs from the Comédie-Française to the Opéra itself, is becoming known as the avenue des Japonais, due to the countless Japanese stores, department stores and travel agencies that have sprung up in the past few years. Visitors who come from the ends of the earth to this extraordinary spot where the boulevard des Capucines meets the place de l'Opéra, neglect the Cognacq-Jay Museum (with its paintings by Boucher, Fragonard, Reynolds, Gainsborough, Canaletto, Guardi, Rubens and Rembrandt) to sit at the terrace of the Café de la Paix, where only the waiters speak French. This is indeed Paris, this noisy corner where, against the great backdrop of the Opéra, sellers hawk flowers, newspapers, chestnuts or ice cream, depending on the season.

The Opéra building, built by Gabriel, with its rather odd green roof, can be criticized for its many inconsistencies of style, material, detail and taste. There are as many as five different tones of marble used. But taken as a whole, the building has beauty and balance. The white marble staircase, the magnificent *grand foyer,* and the ceiling painted by Chagall are attractions that often surpass what happens on stage. Its history can be studied in the library and museum, which contain 40,000 volumes and 60,000 engravings dealing with the dance, singing, and the stage, scores, model sets, costumes and instruments. A piano that belonged to Massenet, Rossini's clock, and the blood stained bandages of the duc de Berri, who was stabbed as he left the theater, are among the curiosities of this museum. The Salle Favart (which is the brand-new name for the Opéra-Comique) is not far away, in a side street of the boulevard des Italiens, so named for the singers and *castrati* who performed here. A little further away, on the boulevard Montmartre, the American Robert Fulton (who invented submarines and developed the steamship) installed his 'Panoramas', showing Paris, London, Naples, Jerusalem, Babylon and St. Helena. Today on this same boulevard is the Musée Grévin, which, like Madame Tussaud's in London, resuscitates in wax the Old Testament and the history of France, and brings together the notables and notorious of today.

There are countless cinemas and cafés, becoming less luxurious as we proceed. The two monumental gates of St-Denis and St-Martin were consecrated to the glory of the armies of Louis XIV. At the end of the boulevard Sébastopol, the Gare de l'Est brings back memories of departure for the front in 1914–18. Beyond the boulevard Sébastopol the *grands boulevards* degenerate rapidly. To clean up this district Baron Haussmann, the prefect of Paris under the Second Empire, demolished the theaters and cheap dancehalls, and designed a large open space to relieve the congestion of traffic. Barracks for the Garde Républicaine were built here, and later an enormous statue of the Republic was also erected.

Very characteristic of Paris, a matter-of-fact, hardworking Paris, is the Canal St-Martin, littered with barges that exude an odor of tar, ropes and sawn wood. It is an area now becoming popular with hard-up artists and young out-of-funds foreigners.

The boulevard Beaumarchais was named after the author of the *Mariage de Figaro,* who lost his fortune in a deal to furnish munitions and uniforms to the army in the American War of Independence.

The Bastille

We have reached a place famous in the history of France: the Bastille. On the morning of July 14, 1789, 600 rioters attacked this grim fortress. Its prisoners then included four forgers, two lunatics, and a young nobleman imprisoned at the request of his father. There were no political prisoners, and the Bastille had no claim to strategic importance. Its garrison consisted of 32 Swiss and 82 disabled soldiers, and its artillery of 15 cannon (without cannonballs) and three fieldpieces.

Its demolition had been under discussion for some time, but historic events were faster than the slow process of bureaucratic change. The Bastille had become a symbol of tyranny in the minds of the rioters, a looming reminder of the evils of arbitrary power—and so it was taken by the people of Paris in the name of Liberty. Immediately afterwards its long-delayed demolition began.

Its construction was begun in 1370 to serve as a prison to the man who built it, and behind its walls some of the most somber dramas in the history of France, like the mystery of the man in the iron mask, have been enacted. But most of the prisoners in the Bastille, imprisoned for debt, or as the result of some amorous intrigue, had their own cook and valet, received visitors, and even gave banquets. One of the towers was actually called the Tower of Liberty.

On July 14, 1790 the people of Paris danced in front of the gutted Bastille, and, since then, this custom is repeated each year at the Bastille, Montparnasse and other places in the city. But in 1793, 73 heads fell under the guillotine that had taken the place of the fortress. In the place de la Bastille today stands the Colonne de Juillet (the July Column) on top of which the *Génie de la Liberté* poses with the grace of a ballerina. In the foundations are the bodies of the victims of the 1830 insurrections and of those who fell in the fighting of 1848. Their names are engraved in golden letters on the column.

Many of them came from the faubourg St-Antoine, a once-charming quarter inhabited by carpenters, silversmiths, upholsterers and cabinet-makers, but now lined with furniture shops, some hideously modern and some old and aristocratic, like the famous Mercier. In recent years the old buildings in the little side streets have been cleaned and restored and you will find any number of craft boutiques and workshops, antique or junk shops and so on. Particularly attractive is the Village St-Paul, a series of little shops grouped in and around the renovated buildings leading off the rue des Jardins St-Paul between the rue du fbg St-Antoine and the river. The rue St-Antoine has its aristocratic memories, for it was here, in a fatal tournament, that King Henri II was killed by a lance thrust in the eye. His widow, Catherine de Médicis, conceived a hatred for this place and so it was abandoned until Henri IV decided to develop a piece of waste ground nearby. In effect it was the first attempt at town planning in Paris, for the king and his architects decided that this would be more than an ordinary market place: it would be a residential area and a pleasure ground. All the houses in the enormous square were built of brick or of white stone, with tall slate roofs. Covered arcades made it possible to linger in front of the shops even in bad weather. It was inaugurated by a 'Carrousel' in which a thousand noblemen took part, and soon became the center of society.

The Marais

Its popularity gone, the place Royale was renamed the place des Vosges in the 18th century in honor of the department that had paid its taxes first. Here Madame de Sévigné was born, and Bossuet and Richelieu lived. Under its windows the young Montmorency fought a duel and paid for his audacity with his head, despite the prayers of his beautiful mistress, Marion Delorme. This adventure served as the inspiration for a romantic drama by Victor Hugo, who lived for many years in the house that is now the Victor Hugo museum, where you may see drawings and furniture made by his own hand, together with many articles used by him in his everyday life.

Over the last few years most of the houses in the place des Vosges have been restored and it has now recovered much of its former glory. At night, when the apartments are lit up, you can glimpse the ancient ceiling beams and the high, carved walls.

At the Musée Carnavalet, home of Madame de Sévigné, maps, prints, engravings and numerous historic exhibits give a picture of the eternal yet ever-changing face of Paris throughout the ages.

The labyrinth of streets in the Marais is a goldmine for those interested in the architecture and history of Paris, with its magnificent mansions (known in French as *hôtels particuliers*), many of which have recently been restored with loving care. After centuries of neglect this whole area is no longer grimy and impoverished but is becoming an increasingly fashionable place to live and work. It is well worth an extended visit. Street-corner maps and arrows point out the principal monuments to the stroller in this area, or you can obtain a map of the many *hôtels particuliers,* churches and other monuments from the Caisse Nationale des Monuments Historiques in the Hôtel de Béthune-Sully, 62 rue St-Antoine.

The handsome Hôtel de Sully is used as a dramatic setting for ballets and plays during the Marais Festival, as is the more austere Hôtel d'Aumont. In the palatial mansion of the Rohan-Soubise are the National Archives, while alongside is the Museum of French History. Here also are the severe Hôtel Lamoignon and the Hôtel d'Albret, where Louis XIV's favorite, Madame de Montespan, found the widow of the poet Scarron, soon to replace her in the king's favor and become Madame de Maintenon and later on, the morganatic wife of Louis XIV.

The Hôtel de Sens is, along with the Cluny Museum, the only great private residence dating from the Middle Ages that still exists in Paris. Here Queen Margot, sister of François I, carried on her passionate and often tragic love affairs. Not far from here the Hôtel Salé is being restored and in 1983 will house a brand-new Picasso museum.

Around many of the noble mansions—including the Hôtel Chalons-Luxembourg, whose ravishing courtyard you can look into—wretched hovels had sprung up. But demolition and the wiping out of many unhealthy blocks have re-endowed the Hôtel de Sens with its former elegance. It is to be the Museum of the Craftsmen of Paris, a well-merited honor for, since the Middle Ages, it is around here that typical *articles de Paris* have been made. Today, in tiny workshops on the streets named St-Merri, Archives and Temple, are made ribbons, braid, feather flowers, artificial pearls and jewelry, and all the other trifles that come under this heading; in quiet courtyards, patient craftsmen lovingly repair bent silver, cracked crystal, ebony and ivory, continuing a way of life hardly changed since medieval times. In the neighborhood of Réamur-Sentier, the center of wholesale cotton and silk materials, the tie was invented in 1840.

Near the venerable church of St-Nicolas-des-Champs is a museum of industry, the Musée National des Techniques, containing models of early airplanes, locomotives and other machines. This humble, hardworking district hums with the activity of little workshops. In the narrow labyrinthine streets, miscellaneous articles, cheap, readymade clothes, fancy-dress and masks are manufactured at low prices to be sold in the Carreau du Temple, where sometimes extraordinary bargains can be found buried under heaps of nondescript clothing. It is called 'Carreau' because the merchandise used to be spread out on the *carreaux,* or flagstones, and 'du Temple' because this market is built on the site of the sinister Tour du Temple, where Louis XVI and his family were imprisoned until their death.

Unfortunately, the old Carreau du Temple, built in 1853, is gradually making way for a vast building housing an old people's home, nursery, school, library, etc., and, on the ground floor, a market place for clothes, which is less grubby, but also less colorful, than the Carreau.

The rue des Rosiers is the main street of the Jewish quarter of Paris. The shop signs are in Hebrew, unleavened bread and stuffed carp are plentiful, and the shops close on Saturday to reopen on Sunday. In recent years, since the exodus of French families, many of them of Jewish origin, from Algeria, the Eastern European atmosphere of this vibrant and picturesque area of Paris has become rather more North African. Nearby, in the vicinity of the great Jesuit church of St-Paul, is a small Polish and Hungarian neighborhood, where tiny shops sell delicious spicy sausages, barrels of sauerkraut and black bread.

The City Hall

On the edge of this part of old Paris stands the Hôtel de Ville. This vast neo-Renaissance city hall is almost theatrical with its 136 statues, an impression heightened when—as frequently happens—it is gaily decorated with flags.

Until the middle of the last century the place de l'Hôtel de Ville was called the place de Grève *(grève* meaning strand, river beach). In the Middle Ages unemployed workmen used to meet here, so *faire grève* soon came to mean 'not to work'. Today, by a further distortion, *faire la grève* means 'to go on strike'. Criminals were also executed here. The first city council sat in the Châtelet in the 13th century, but in the 14th moved to a colonnaded house on place de Grève, the Maison aux Piliers. Within a century the building had so deteriorated that François I ordered the building of the Hôtel de Ville (1558). Two centuries later Louis XVI was forced to accept the revolutionary cockade at the Hôtel de Ville.

Red, white and blue! Red and blue, the colors of Paris, to which Lafayette added white, the color of royalty. As Louis passed under an archway of crossed swords, the people cried: 'Long live the king!' but soon the cry was changed to 'Death to the king!' The guillotine was erected and did not spare even Robespierre who, hunted by the mob, took refuge in the Hôtel de Ville, only to be dragged out, taken to the Conciergerie, and thence to the scaffold.

The Second and Third Republics of 1848 and 1870 were proclaimed from the Hôtel de Ville. The present Hôtel de Ville dates from the end of the last century. Curiously, for over 100 years (from 1871 to 1977) Paris was the only French city without a mayor in charge of its affairs in the city hall. It was administered instead by a prefect, assisted by municipal councillors. Today the post of mayor has been revived and the man who holds this powerful office is the dynamic Gaullist leader and former prime minister Jacques Chirac, who dominates Parisian life.

Not far away is the pure Gothic form of the Tour St-Jacques. This tower is all that remains of the church that, in the 16th century, stood on the route of the pilgrims from the north on their way to Santiago de Compostela, in Spanish Galicia.

Four sphinxes spurting out water crouch at the foot of the Colonne de la Victoire in the place du Châtelet. It is difficult, however, for the passer-by to see this column palm-tree and the fountain, for two theaters (the fascinatingly modern Théâtre de la Ville and the new Théâtre Musical de Paris, a reincarnation of the old Châtelet Theater staging subsidized performances of ballet, opera and concerts) dominate the square with their inelegant bulk.

Les Halles/Beaubourg area

Near here the voracious tentacles of the Paris market, Les Halles, 'the belly of Paris', as Zola wrote with repugnance and admiration, drew in, until late 1968, the best of France's produce in as rowdy and picturesque a scene as you could wish. Now, the market is at Rungis, near Orly airport.

The old iron pavilions of Les Halles, built during the reign of Napoleon III, were demolished in 1971, despite protests from lovers of the city's history. Close by, the enormous ultra-modern Georges Pompidou Center opened in 1977. Generally known as the Beaubourg Center (from the area where it is built), this extraordinary building—it has been likened to, among other things, an oil refinery—was the most-visited monument in Europe during its first year of existence and is still extremely popular. Be prepared for a shock when you see it, with all its pipes, elevators and so on visible in all their naked glory, but do go inside and see the collection of the National Museum of Modern Art and all sorts of exciting temporary exhibits, not to mention a popular library, children's workshop, cinemathèque and many other 'happenings'. Close by is the stylish new Forum, an eye-catching glass and concrete shopping and leisure center, well worth a visit. Round and about here the area is gradually developing a new character of its own, though some of the old restaurants serving onion soup to the nostalgic Parisians and tourists are still open. The side streets are full of fashion boutiques, art galleries and antique shops, and the remainder of the 'Hole' where the market used to be will be filled by the mid-eighties with a 'magic garden' for children only and an aquarium.

In the midst of this change rises the church of St-Eustache, second only to Notre-Dame in beauty. Begun in the middle of the 16th century, it was not consecrated until 1637, and it is now noted for its religious music.

A few fine houses still remain in this area, most notably the one built by Mansart for the count of Toulouse, which is now the Bank of France. The place des Victoires, with the equestrian statue of Louis XIV, is also the work of Mansart. Nearby is the rue Vide-Gousset, which has only two numbers. On the almost provincial place des Petits-Pères you'll find shops specializing in candles and religious objects, for it is close to the church of Notre-Dame-des-Victoires, which is celebrated for its pilgrimages to the Virgin; 30,000 ex-votos adorn its walls, and candles burn unceasingly before its altar. Recently, several avant-garde fashion boutiques opened, somewhat changing the character of this lovely round little *place*.

At the northern edge of the district are the Stock Exchange and the National Library (with six million volumes and manuscripts). On the rue Réamur, an impersonal boulevard bordering Les Halles, stand the great newspaper offices and news agencies.

The Palais-Royal

Not far away is the peaceful garden of the Palais-Royal in the midst of dense blocks of buildings. Richelieu built himself a palace opposite the Louvre. It became a royal palace when Anne of Austria moved in with her son. During the Revolution it became the Palais-Egalité (the Palace of Equality) because its owner, Louis-Philippe d'Orléans, the king's cousin, professed revolutionary ideals and called himself 'Philippe-Egalité'. Before the Revolution he had lived so extravagantly that, in order to earn some money, he had built blocks of apartments and shops to let around the garden behind the palace. Cafés and clubs sprang up under the arcades and in the middle of the garden there was a circus that was turned into a theater and a ballroom. Fashionable under the Directory, of ill repute during the Empire, the palace regained its prestige and dignity with the Restoration. Louis-Philippe lived there modestly, and the Second Empire attempted to restore it as a fashionable center. Today the Palais-Royal is an oasis of tranquility. André Malraux, Jean Cocteau and Colette lived in the apartments that Philippe-Egalité built.

On the other side of the rue de Valois, Richelieu presided over the first meetings of the Académie Française, near the modest room where Molière created his major works and where his sudden death prevented him from finishing his performance in *Le Maladie Imaginaire*. It is only fitting that the fine theater, built in one corner of the Palais-Royal, should have been given the name of Maison de Molière (the House of Molière).

This crossroads is very Parisian. The rue St-Honoré runs into it at the beginning of the avenue de l'Opéra, and the short rue de Rohan leads to the Louvre and to the rue de Rivoli that Napoleon built by knocking down the buildings that stood in the way. One of these buildings was the Manège Royal des Tuileries, where Louis XVI was condemned to death and where the First Republic was proclaimed. The rue de Castiglione, which joins the rue de Rivoli to the place Vendôme, brings back memories of the Second Empire. Its name is that of the beautiful woman Cavour sent to plead the cause of Italian unity with the emperor.

Napoleon III was susceptible to feminine charms (it was said that the Empress Eugénie won her crown as a beauty prize). He allowed himself to be persuaded, and the name of Castiglione was given to this corner of Paris.

Place Vendôme, the rue de la Paix and the rue St-Honoré have long been bywords for all that is fashionable elegance and luxury, with their world-famous jewelers, perfume shops and luxury hotels. Yet this part of Paris is changing and you will find that in many places smart restaurants are giving way to self-service bars and cafés as the concept of *chic* moves on to new pastures. The smart young *Parisienne* is not as likely to be found around here as her mother might have been, and most of the customers in the still-elegant shops are foreigners.

The place Vendôme, which was intended to outshine the place des Victoires, dedicated to Louis XIV, had its statue of the Sun King even before the surrounding buildings were constructed. It soon became fashionable. Eugénie de Montijo lived there before becoming empress. The Ritz became a symbol of luxury. Fashions change, but the place Vendôme maintains firmly its high tradition of luxury. The statues in the place Vendôme change also. As the equestrian statue of Louis XIV had been overthrown during the Revolution, Napoleon ordered the construction of a column made of the bronze of captured enemy cannons. On top was set his statue as a Roman emperor, his right hand resting on a sword, the left hand holding a globe ornamented with a winged victory, and his head crowned with a laurel wreath. In 1814 the Roman Napoleon was in its turn melted down and replaced by a flag with the *fleur de lys*. Louis-Philippe put Napoleon back, but this time without a toga, clothed in his greatcoat and well-known hat, his hand placed in its traditional position inside the waistcoat. Napoleon III replaced the 'Little Corporal' in 1863 with another Roman-emperor Napoleon, which the Commune knocked down in 1871 as being 'a barbarous monument, symbolic of brute force and false glory'. A week later order was re-established in Paris, but four more years passed by before Napoleon, again in his toga, was replaced on the column, where he still stands.

Behind the Madeleine, in the direction of St-Augustin and the Gare St-Lazare, is a district of banks, department stores and business premises, bustling during the day, completely deserted at night. But in front of the Gare St-Lazare there is always movement.

Little-known areas, virtually off the tourist track, are the 'villages' of Gobelins, at the southern end of the city, and Charonne, between faubourg St-Antoine and Père Lachaise cemetery, with its ancient sanctuary church of St-Germain-de-Charonne. To the northeast are the popular districts of Bellevue and Menilmontant, whose narrow gas-lit streets, running up and down hill, preserve the aura of earlier days. See

Montmartre

Montmartre, or Mont des Martyrs (the Mountain of the Martyrs), was so named because in the year 272 three saints were beheaded on the road to the Temple of Mercury, which stood on the crest of the hill. One of them, St Denis, picked up his head, which had rolled on the ground, washed off the blood and dirt at a nearby fountain, and set off on foot, only to collapse 6 km (4 miles) farther on at the spot where the fine basilica of St-Denis now stands. All the kings of France, except three, are buried there. Today, with its streets with feminine names—Antoinette, Berthe, Gabrielle; with its Moulin (Mill) de la Galette, which seems destined to mill only rice powder; with the feverish and slightly drunken animation of the place Blanche; with neon lights spelling out Eve with Venus and 'L'Enfer' (Hell) with 'Le Ciel' (Heaven), Montmartre is the citadel of those who seek amusement, or who seek to amuse others.

But to know Paris intimately we must climb up the holy hill where the blood of the martyrs of Paris was spilled. In the crypt of the chapel built on the place of execution—and where today the Chapelle des Auxiliares du Purgatoire stands—Ignatius Loyola and six of his companions met on Assumption Day in 1534 and swore solemnly to fight against the enemies of religion, by this act creating the Society of Jesus. Here the bloody Commune of 1871 began, when the soldiers fraternized with the crowd and shot two generals.

The itinerary of Old Paris must also pass by Montmartre and linger there. You should wander in the narrow streets, climb the steep stairways where noisy urchins slide down the balustrades, and pause in the winding little streets.

You will find the celebrated vineyard that still produces its annual quota of wine, and, hidden behind a tree, the cabaret 'Lapin Agile', made famous by two generations of poets and artists. It is known throughout the world by this name, which means 'nimble rabbit', but that wasn't what it meant to the obscure painter who unwittingly baptized it. He had his studio in the same building, and to advertise it, he placed a sign over the entrance that read: 'Là peint A. Gill', or, allowing for a certain grammatical license on the part of André Gill, 'A. Gill paints here'. The corrupting process of time did the rest and today thousands of persons who have never heard of Gill the painter know the restaurant of the Nimble Rabbit.

All the streets and lanes of the Commune Libre of Old Montmartre lead to the place du Tertre, which unfortunately has lost most of its old village-like charm. Frankly, it is in many ways a mere tourist trap. But it is pleasant to dine outdoors here on a warm evening.

Just across the place du Tertre, and within a stone's throw of the basilica of the Sacré-Coeur, is the church of St-Pierre—neighbors in space, but with 14 centuries separating them in time. In the latter are the earliest pointed arches in Paris, while the basilica of the Sacré-Coeur is the most modern of the capital's great churches. Built just after Sedan by national subscription—40 millions—'in witness of repentance and as a symbol of hope', Sacré-Coeur, has become, since 1919, part of the Parisian landscape. Its cupolas, dome and bell tower (102 meters/336 ft) stand out chalk-white against the silver-gray sky. From this vantage point the view of the City of Light is incomparable, particularly on a clear summer night.

THE CAPITAL OF FOOD

Over 8,000 restaurants—pick your own

If you were to ask half a dozen longtime residents of Paris to name the 100 restaurants each one considered the best, it is probable that not more than a score of names would be duplicated in all the different lists. Except for a few distinguished establishments that everyone knows about, the good restaurants of Paris are so numerous and so varied that everyone builds up his own private list, and though its author is likely to argue valiantly that his choices, and his alone, are the best, the fact is that all of them are likely to be good.

There is plenty of opportunity for compiling series after series of recommendations—more than 8,000 restaurants, many of them excellent. In other words, if you ate out two meals a day, going to a different place each time, it would take you nearly 11 years to get through them! As even in Paris people do eat at home once in a while, you can take it for granted that nobody knows all Paris's eating places. Anyone can make gastronomic finds in Paris. There are so many to find. And even after you've found them, new ones keep turning up.

The following list is therefore not to be taken as comprehensive. But we shall try to include most of the places that visitors to Paris should not miss and to pass on hints to save you time experimenting. There will be some omissions that some will consider heinous—it can't be helped.

For the tourist in Paris, the restaurant question breaks down into two sections—first, there are the places to which he goes deliberately to sample the artistry of Paris cooks. For these restaurants, it doesn't matter where they are or where you are—you do whatever is necessary to get to them. The second part of your problem comes when you are regarding your next meal, not as a pilgrimage to a temple of gastronomy, but just as a place to relax and enjoy a pleasant repast. In this case, you want to know what good restaurants are handy.

A word of warning to start with: *le fast food* (or its alliterative equivalent, *le repas rapide*) has undoubtedly taken its toll in Paris and you may well hear people complaining that the traditional little family-type restaurant is being driven out. It's certainly true that you can't be sure of eating well more or less anywhere in Paris, as you once could. But if you avoid the fast food places and choose restaurants where the menu is handwritten or typed and dated, rather than printed, you'll still enjoy the market-fresh cuisine that is what Parisian eating should be all about.

In the listing that follows *(hotel restaurants are not included),* restaurants are divided into Paris's 20 *arrondissements,* plus the semi-suburbs of Neuilly and Boulogne. They're marked with the letters, *E, M* and *I,* meaning expensive, moderate or inexpensive. But what you pay for a meal depends almost as much on what you order and the wine you drink as on the price category of the restaurant, so this classification can only be approximate. If the restaurant has a fixed-price menu this will invariably work out cheaper.

Many restaurants close for a month or so (usually in the summer) and for one day a week. We have given these closing times in our list, but they do sometimes change without warning, so it's always a good idea to check first. You'll soon see that the great majority of restaurants are closed on Sunday, so you may well feel that this is a good time to try out one of the restaurants in the countryside close to Paris; our Ile de France chapter gives you some suggestions.

You'll find a useful menu translator list in the vocabulary section at the end of this guide.

THE CAPITAL OF FOOD

FIRST ARRONDISSEMENT

L'Absinthe, 24 pl. du Marché-St-Honoré, friendly service in this smart little restaurant near the pl. Vendôme and the av. de l'Opéra. The cooking is mostly 'new', with the delectably fresh ingredients from the market opposite. Attractive décor with *Art Nouveau* bits and pieces (M). Closed Sat. for lunch and Sun.

Barrière Poquelin, 17 rue Molière. Light and airy nouvelle cuisine served in a little street near that bastion of French classical theater, the Comédie-Française (E). Closed Sat. for lunch and Sun.

Baumann-Baltard, 9 rue Coquillière. Beside the Forum; sister-restaurant of well-known Alsatian restaurant in the 17e. Good *choucroute* served in what was once a butcher's shop. Has excellent Alsace wines. Surprisingly reasonable prices (M). Open daily until 2 A.M.

Bistro de La Gare, 30 rue Saint Denis. New link in this successful chain (I). Open to 1 A.M.

Bistro d'Hubert, 36 pl. du Marché-St-Honoré, is very fashionable so you must book. Good 'new' cooking, with new fixed-price menus at lunchtime. (A recent development is the take-away boutique that has opened next door, so you can always buy something there if you can't afford to eat in the restaurant!) (E). Closed Sun. and Mon.

L'Escargot Montorgueil, 38 rue Montorgueil (in the middle of what used to be the Les Halles food market). Opened in the 1930's and still going strong, with delightful 19th-cent. décor of mirrors and traditional wall sofas. Smart clientele, with a sprinkling of well-known politicians. Snails of course, but other well-cooked dishes too (mostly classical French cuisine) (E). Closed Mon. and Aug.

Faure, 40 rue du Mont-Thabor, near the Tuileries Gardens and the pl. de la Concorde, is a good place for a simple, home-style lunch or a special 'farmhouse dinner'. Lunchtime trade includes models from the nearby fashion houses (I). Closed Sun. and Aug.

Le Grand Véfour, 17 rue du Beaujolais, behind the Palais-Royal gardens. One of Paris's finest restaurants and run by one of France's best-known chefs, Raymond Oliver (though he no longer cooks himself), so you'd expect it to be expensive, and it is. But the food is very good indeed, with some imaginative dishes among the perfectly cooked traditional ones, so it's worth paying for (E). Attentive service. Closed Sat. evening, Sun. and during Aug. The ground floor and entrance are officially listed as "Historical monuments."

Le Jardin du Louvre, in the Louvre des Antiquaires, a newish antiques hypermarket in the rue de Rivoli, opposite the Louvre and just by the Palais-Royal. This chic restaurant is garden-like, with plants and flowers all over the place. Elegant setting, newish cuisine, open to 1 A.M., closed Sun. and Mon. (M).

Le Lodi, 30 rue du Mont-Thabor. Very simple little restaurant with a good but inexpensive fixed-price meal. The sort of place you should go to if you want to know where the French eat on ordinary days. (I).

Le Mercure Galant, 15 rue des Petits-Champs. Fashionable restaurant with turn-of-the-century décor. Good and inventive nouvelle cuisine (M). Closed Sat. lunch and Sun.

Chez Paul, 15 pl. Dauphine, in a charming little square behind the law courts and the Sainte Chapelle. A crowded, unpretentious bistro with genuine marble counter and straightforward home cooking, presided over by a very Parisienne *patronne*. A few tables outside (I). Closed Wed.

Chez Pauline, 5 rue Villedo, no relation, in spite of the similarity of the names, but another old Paris bistro that has undergone something of a facelift recently (the cooking, not the bistro-style décor). Excellent home-style dishes, fine house-bottled wines (E). Closed Sat. evening and Sun.

Le Pharamond, 24 rue de la Grande Truanderie, in the Les Halles area, specializes in tripe, but has plenty of other good dishes to tempt you too. Turn-of-the-century décor (M). Closed Sun.; lunchtime Mon. and July.

Au Pied de Cochon, 6 rue Coquillière, never closes, though it has inevitably lost some of its charm now that the food market has disappeared to the suburbs. But you can still enjoy the grilled pig's trotters and onion soup that made it famous (M).

Pierre-Traiteur, 10 rue de Richelieu. A small, friendly restaurant, with good traditional cooking plus a few innovations, just behind the Comédie-Française. Always crowded (E). Closed weekends and Aug.

Potager des Halles, 15 rue du Cygne. Owned by Gérard Vié whose restaurants in Versailles *(Les Trois Marches* and *Potager du Roy)* are a huge success. Carefully prepared home-style dishes in a street leading off Les Halles (M). Open daily to 1 A.M.

Prunier-Madeleine, 9 rue Duphot. After a number of vicissitudes this famous restaurant is back on form again, serving marvelous nouvelle cuisine fish dishes to a chic and cosmopolitan clientele (E). Closed August.

Au Roy Gourmet. This long-standing restaurant is in the attractive setting of the pl. des Victoires, at no. 4. Specializes in *andouillettes* (chitterling sausages) (M). Closed weekends.

Le Soufflé, 36 rue du Mont-Thabor, specializes, as its name suggests, in soufflés of all kinds, both sweet and savory (M). Closed Sun.

Le Vert Galant, 42 quai des Orfèvres, close to the law courts, has a delightful view over the Seine, but the smart diners—with, inevitably, quite a few legal bigwigs—come for the beautifully cooked classical dishes (E). Closed Sat.

SECOND ARRONDISSEMENT

L'Amanguier, 110 rue de Richelieu, near the Bourse and quite close to the Opéra. The delightful green-and-white décor—with parasols and garden chairs —is like a summer's day in the garden or by the sea. Short but imaginative menu, very reasonably priced, with particularly good desserts. (I).

L'Assiette au Boeuf, 9 bld des Italiens. One of a series of attractive but very inexpensive restaurants with a rigid formula of green salad with pine kernels, steak and excellent French fries (chips) and delicious homemade pastries or

THE CAPITAL OF FOOD

desserts. The atmosphere is far from rigid, however, and you can dine here till 1 A.M. (I).

Drouant, 18 pl. Gaillon. A long-established, comfortable restaurant, popular with old faithfuls, though not very exciting. Perfect service, classical cooking, well known for seafood, including oysters in season (E). Also has grill room (M), which is open to 1 A.M. Closed Sat. and second half of Aug.

Gérard, 4 rue du Mail, bustling bistro, often full of journalists. Good traditional home-style cooking (I–M). Closed Sun. and Aug.

Le Petit Coin de la Bourse, 16 rue Feydeau, now owned by Claude Verger. Lively atmosphere, mostly new cuisine, (M).

Ruc'Univers, pl. André-Malraux, diagonally opposite Comédie-Française. Typically Parisian old-style restaurant, spacious and comfortable; specializing in excellent oysters. Good for a late supper after the theater or opera, as it's open to 2 A.M. (M).

THIRD ARRONDISSEMENT

L'Ambassade d'Auvergne, 22 rue du Grenier-St-Lazare. Copious peasant fare, beautifully served, in the unlikely but delightful setting of a spacious and elegant tavern near the Centre Beaubourg/Pompidou. Open to 11 P.M. (M). Closed Sun.

L'Ami Louis, 32 rue du Vertbois. Long-standing and excellent bistro, with huge portions of traditional French cuisine, rich wines and plenty of atmosphere (E). Closed August.

Bateau Beaubourg, 60 rue Rambuteau. On the spot where the famous Ciboulette used to be, and under same ownership. Delicious fish dishes, cooked new-style, attractive setting (E). Serves dinners only (no lunches), closed Sun. and Mon.

Guirlande de Julie, 25 pl. des Vosges. Pleasant atmosphere in this flower-filled restaurant in the lovely place des Vosges in the heart of the Marais (M). Good value lunch *menu.* Closed Sun. for dinner, Mon. and Feb.

FOURTH ARRONDISSEMENT

Bofinger, 5 rue de la Bastille, claims to be the oldest *brasserie* in town, though it tends to be pricey, which is rare for a *brasserie.* Genuine *art nouveau* décor. Good for after-theater suppers as it's open to 1 A.M. (M).

La Brasserie de l'Ile, 55 quai Bourbon, Ile St-Louis. Crowded *brasserie* with cheerful, lively waiters who manage to keep smiling in spite of the crush. Traditional Alsatian dishes with particularly good *tripes au riesling* and *choucroute,* and deliciously fruity Alsatian wines. Popular for Sun. lunch, when you must get there early. A good place to go after visiting Notre-Dame (I). Closed Weds. and Aug.

La Ciboulette, 141 rue Saint-Martin, one of Paris's top restaurants, can now be found opposite the Beaubourg/Pompidou Center and has spawned a whole range of ultra-chic eating places housed in a single building; the ground floor has a cafe for people-watching, two bars and a garden-like bistrot serving traditional home cooking every day of the week (M); the first floor restaurant offers superb nouvelle cuisine in a most elegant setting (E); and on the floor above you can dine in the privacy of a series of rooms each decorated in a different style, where you must order your meal (nouvelle cuisine again) in advance, and naturally be prepared to pay accordingly. Closed weekends.

Coconnas, 2 bis pl. des Vosges, is under the same management as the Tour d'Argent but has remarkable-value fixed-price menu served in lovely setting. Cuisine is basically nouvelle (M). Closed Mon., Tues. and mid-Dec. to mid-Jan.

La Colombe, 4 rue de la Colombe, is tucked away in a little street near Notre-Dame with open-air dining beneath a vine trellis. It's apparently the oldest bistro in Paris and no attempt has been made to follow fashion in modernizing the cuisine, which is inveterately traditional—and none the worse for that. You can linger till midnight in the delightful atmosphere and then wander romantically back past Notre-Dame (M). However, the service can be slapdash. Closed Sun., Mon. for lunch, Feb. and part of Aug.

Au Gourmet de l'Ile, 42 rue St-Louis-en-l'Ile, a delightful and good-value little restaurant on the unspoilt Ile St-Louis. Popular and therefore crowded (I). Closed Mon., Tues. and all of Aug.

Petit Gavroche, 15 rue Ste-Croix-de-la-Bretonnerie. Typically Parisian bistrot with low prices and cheerful atmosphere (I). Closed Sun. and Aug.

Quai des Ormes, 72 quai de l'Hotel-de-Ville. Attractive setting by the Seine and close to the Hotel de Ville; beautifully served nouvelle cuisine, discreeet ambience. A very welcome addition to Paris's gastronomic scene. (M). Closed weekends and Aug.

Le Tourtour, 20 rue Quincampoix, a fashionable restaurant near the Beaubourg/Pompidou Center. Charming, spacious, candlelit at night. Service can be a trifle condescending if you're not as 'in' as the people at the next table, but the food is good and the prices are reasonable. Open to 1 A.M. (M).

Ursins dans le Caviar, 3 rue de la Colombe. Marvelous old house on the Ile de la Cité, near Notre Dame, with old beams and lots of atmosphere. New cuisine and antique furniture. (M). Closed Sun.

FIFTH ARRONDISSEMENT

Auberge des Deux Signes, 46 rue Galande, in a wonderful medieval setting with views over Notre-Dame. The cooking's good too, with some Auvergnat dishes (M). Closed Sun. and Aug.

Balzar, 49 rue des Ecoles. Genuine brasserie with waiters in long white aprons and traditional home-style cooking (I). Closed Tues. and Aug.

La Bûcherie, 41 rue de la Bûcherie, is an old favorite with log fires, classical music and relaxed atmosphere. Good 'new' cooking, though some people find the portions on the small side. Lovely view of Notre Dame from window tables. Rather chic clientele, who throng here till 1 A.M. (M). Closed July.

Le Coupe-Chou, 11 rue Lanneau. Fashionable, attractive restaurant in an old house with beams. The cooking can be uneven but you're bound to enjoy a meal here. Open 1 A.M. (M). Closed Sun. for lunch.

THE CAPITAL OF FOOD

Dodin Bouffant, 25 rue Frédéric-Sauton, is one of the best restaurants in Paris, with inspired 'new' cuisine and superb, yet reasonably priced, wines. Very fashionable, and not too expensive; but you must reserve ahead (M). Closed weekends, Aug. and over Christmas and New Year.

Le Mange-Tout, 30 rue Lacépède, has interesting, inventive cuisine in plain, modern surroundings. Specializes in the dishes of the Aveyton and Rouergue regions of rural France. Always crowded, so do reserve ahead (M). Closed Sun., Mon. for lunch, Aug. and Christmas period.

La Marée Verte, 9 rue de Pontoise. Has fixed price menu which, though moderately priced, includes *foie gras* and oysters in season. Mostly fish. Mixture of new and classical cooking, rather smart (M). Good value. Closed Sun, Mon and Aug.

Moissonnier, 28 rue des Fossés-St.-Bernard. Excellent rich cuisine from the Lyon region (M). Closed Sun. for dinner, Mon. and Aug.

Au Pactole, 44 bld St-Germain. Carefully cooked dishes blending new and classical cuisine. Deserves to be better known. Discreet atmosphere. Good value lunchtime *menu*. (M). Closed Sat. for lunch and Sun.

La Tour d'Argent, 15 quai de la Tournelle. A world-famous restaurant that really does live up to its reputation. Extremely expensive, of course, but worth it if you can afford it, for the elegant service and décor, the attention to detail at every level, the magnificent wines and not least the cooking, which, though not in the fashionable 'new' mode, is French *haute cuisine* at its best. Now serving excellent fixed-price menus (Tues.–Sat. only) as well as the famous *carte;* not cheap, but it works out at about half the price of an *à la carte* meal. Closed Mon.

Villars-Palace, 8 rue Descartes. In the rue Mouffetard area and a fashionable place to be seen; mostly fish, cooked new-style (i.e. very lightly poached or steamed). Good-value *menu,* otherwise (E). Closed Sat. for lunch.

SIXTH ARRONDISSEMENT

Chez Allard, 41 rue St-André-des-Arts. One of the most authentic bistro-type restaurants in Paris, close to the pl. St-Michel. Traditional cooking (E). Closed weekends and Aug.

Les Assassins, 40 rue Jacob, cheerful atmosphere, good-value cooking (I).

L'Assiette au Boeuf, 22 rue Guillaume Apollinaire. The same formula as in the other restaurants of the same name elsewhere in Paris—green salad with pine kernels, steak and French fries (chips) and a wide choice of desserts. Excellent value (I).

Le Bistro de la Gare, 59 bld Montparnasse, close to the monster tower. A short but imaginative menu with superb desserts, served in a huge room with newly renovated turn-of-the-century décor. However, it's always crowded and so is no place to linger over a meal. Nonetheless fine value and really rather chic. Open to 1 A.M. (I).

Au Charbon de Bois, 16 rue du Dragon. Attractive and fashionable patrons (especially for lunch on Sat.) add to the pleasure of a meal in this busy yet intimate restaurant, which specializes in charcoal-grilled dishes. Open till 11.30 P.M. (M). Closed Sun and Aug.

Aux Charpentiers, 10 rue Mabillon. Typically Parisian bistro, unpretentious and altogether delightful. Used to be the headquarters of the Carpenters' Guild (the walls are covered with fascinating period photographs of the guild members at their get-togethers). The food's good too—plain, straightforward, homely dishes, very reasonably priced (I). Closed Sun. Open till midnight

Claude Sainlouis, 27 rue du Dragon, another pleasant little haven, lively but away from the raucousness of some spots in St-Germain-des-Prés. Excellent value, with simple but well-prepared meat dishes. Popular with 'in' journalists (I). Closed Sun., Easter, Aug. and Christmas period.

La Closerie des Lilas, 171 Bld du Montparnasse. Some people find it overrated, but this is still a very popular spot in Paris, especially with writers, artists and actors, and is always crowded to 1.30 A.M. Lovely openair terrace is as delightful as it was in the thirties. The food is good, if unoriginal, but the atmosphere is what counts (E). Terrace dining is less expensive.

Echaudé St-Germain, 21 rue de l'Echaudé. Very pretty restaurant in the heart of St-Germain-des-Prés. Chic and lively, newish cuisine, with good-value *menus* (M). Open till at least 1 A.M.

La Grosse Horloge, 22 rue St-Benoît. Get a table upstairs if you can in this good fish restaurant (the room up there has attractive old beams). The cooking's traditional, which is a relief to those who find the 'new' method of presenting fish (still pink and therefore almost raw) more than they can take. (M).

Jacques Cagna, 14 rue des Grands-Augustins, has imaginative 'new' cooking in a pretty setting, but you have to pay for it (E). Closed weekends, Aug. and between Christmas and New Year.

Lipp, 151 bld St-Germain. A Paris institution, but still a favorite haunt of politicians, writers and film people. Fair home-style cooking of the *brasserie* type (marvelous *pot-au-feu*) and very reasonably priced. Very typical of one aspect of Paris and always crowded. Reserve ahead (M). Closed Mon., Easter, July and New Year.

Chez Maître Paul, 12 rue Monsieur-le-Prince. A tiny little place with dishes from the Franche-Comté region of France (M). Closed Sun, Mon. and Aug.

Le Muniche, 27 rue de Buci. Another *brasserie,* another crowded spot, but the patrons are more bohemian than *chez* Lipp. Much more French than German, despite its name. A bit noisy (M). Open till 3 A.M. Some tables outside.

La Petite Cour, 10 rue Mabillon. Delightful little courtyard set below street level in a narrow road a bit away from the bustle of boulevard St-Germain makes for perfect summer meals. Mostly new cuisine, good value (M). Closed Sun. and Mon.

Petit St-Benoît, 4 rue St-Benoît. Amazingly low prices in this popular bistrot in the heart of St-Germain-des-Prés (I). Closed weekends and about mid-July to mid-Aug.

Petit Zinc, 25 rue de Buci. An old favorite, ever-popular, ever-crowded right through to 3 A.M. Traditional home-style dishes, plus excellent oysters (M).

Polidor, 41 rue Monsieur-le-Prince. Old-established Parisian bistro with literary associations (André Gide and Paul Valéry used to come here, among many others). This charming friendly spot near the Luxembourg Gardens and the bld St-Michel still offers good home cooking at amazingly reasonable prices (I). Closed Sun., Mon. and Aug.

Porte Fausse, 72 rue du Cherche-Midi. Just the place to try genuine Niçoise specialties and the pleasant wines of Provence (M). Closed Sun., Mon., Easter, Aug. and part of Sept.

Le Procope, 13 rue de l'Ancienne Comédie. Large crowded, bustling café-restaurant with a famous past (Voltaire and Blazac knew it as a coffee house). Open till 1.30 A.M. (I). Closed July.

Saint-Germain-de-la-Mer, 2 rue du Sabot. A large, bustling, Club Méditerranée-type place, with help-yourself *hors d'oeuvres* and goodish fish at low prices. Lantern-slide show and sailor waiters are accompanied by marine noises off (seagulls' cries etc)! All in all, very Parisian, new-style (I).

Restaurant des Saints-Pères, 175 bld St-Germain. Another old favorite, though perhaps a little overpriced these days. But you'll love the traditional marble counter, the bentwood hat stand, the small tables ranged against the walls, the little dishes of *crudités* carefully arranged to make a symphony of colors, the baskets of walnuts in season, the glass panels—in other words a genuine Parisian bistro. Go soon—there aren't many of them left, and the slightly grumpy waitresses in their black dresses can't go on for ever (M). Closed Weds for dinner, Thurs and around mid-Aug. to mid-Sept.

Les Trois Marmites, rue Mazarine, specializes in beautifully cooked *pot-au-feu*. Popular with the neighboring publishers at lunchtime (I).

Vagénende, 142 bld St-Germain. Charming turn-of-the-century décor in this popular restaurant which is a favorite with our readers. They boast of providing good old-fashioned fare and you can dine off their generous portions till 2 A.M. Good game in season (I).

SEVENTH ARRONDISSEMENT

Chez les Anges, 54 bld de Latour-Maubourg. Spacious and comfortable restaurant near the Invalides with a judicious mixture of classical and 'new' dishes. (E). Closed Sun. evening, Mon. and most of Aug.

L'Archestrate, 84 rue de Varenne, is generally considered to be one of the top five or six restaurants in France. Chef-owner Alain Senderens produces truly imaginative 'new cuisine'. It is very expensive, but you'll be lucky if you ever eat such a meal again (E). Closed weekends, most of Aug. and at Christmas. Essential to reserve well ahead.

Le Bellecour, 22 rue Surcouf. Mostly classical Lyonnais cuisine (M). Closed weekends in summer months, but open Sat. for dinner in winter.

Bistrot de Paris, 33 rue de Lille. Run by Michel Oliver, son of the great Raymond Oliver of Grand Véfour fame, this is a fashionable restaurant frequented by writers and publishers (E). Closed weekends.

Le Bourdonnais, 113 av. de la Bourdonnais. Chic little restaurant with 'new' cooking. (M). Closed Sun. and for lunch on Mon.

La Chaumière, 35 rue de Beaune. Peaceful, rustic décor (the name means 'the Cottage') with beams and ochre walls (I). Closed weekends and Aug.

La Ferme Saint-Simon, 6 rue Saint-Simon. Chef used to be assistant to the great Gaston Lenôtre and his decorative wife is a well-known television announcer, but diners come here for the food. New cuisine at its light and delicious best. Good value lunchtime menu (M). Closed Sat. for lunch, Sun. and part of Aug.

La Fontaine de Mars, 129 rue St-Dominique. Typically French little restaurant near the Eiffel Tower, plain and very popular with local residents in this chic area. No frills, but good straightforward home cooking and friendly service. Tables outside in summer beside a delightful fountain set in a little square (I). Closed Sat. evening, Sun. and August.

Le Galant Verre, 12 rue de Verneuil. Fashionable restaurant popular with publishers. 'New' cooking (M). Closed Sat. for lunch, Sun. and most of Aug.

Chez Marius, 5 rue de Bourgogne. Mostly fish, popular with the deputies from the nearby National Assembly (E). Closed Sat. and August.

Le Mémorial, 19 rue Las-Cases. Small bistro near the Chambre des Députés, with simple but delicious food at amazingly reasonable prices (I).

Pantagruel, 20 rue de l'Exposition. Tiny and crowded little restaurant where the great *Archestrate* used to be is a worthy successor with its fine 'new' cooking (E). Closed Sun. and Aug.

Petits Oignons, 20 rue de Bellechasse. Lively little place, with good value, pleasantly light cuisine and exceptionally pretty tablecloths and decor (I). Closed Sun., part of Aug. and over Christmas.

La Petite Chaise, 36 rue de Grenelle. Charming, slightly shabby, traditional, always full—not surprisingly since it is excellent value. (I).

Au Quai d'Orsay, 49 quai d'Orsay. This pleasant spot has long been fashionable and never seems to lose its popularity. Carefully cooked nouvelle cuisine. Good value (M). Closed Sun. and Aug.

Le Récamier, 4 rue Récamier. Intimate and elegant, with first-class food, mainly Burgundian, but not entirely (M). Closed Sun.

Thoumieux, 79 rue St-Dominique. Typically French home cooking in typically French bistrot (I). Closed Mon. and roughly mid-July to mid-Aug.

EIGHTH ARRONDISSEMENT

Alsace, 39 av. des Champs-Elysées. Chic brasserie with excellent *choucroute*, beautifully fresh seafood and superb fruit tarts, as well as the delicious wines for which the Alsace region is famous. (The regional tourist office is next door, if you are inspired to travel there to sample more of its delights.) (M). Open all day and all night.

André, 12 rue Marbeuf. Red-checked tablecloths, lots of noise and bustle in this cheerful bistro very close to the Champs-Elysées. Quieter in the evening. Good home cooking (M). Closed Tues. and Aug.

Androuët, 41 rue d'Amsterdam. There are no fewer than 300 cheeses and cheese dishes on offer in this restaurant attached to a celebrated cheesemonger's. Excellent wines to bring out their full flavor (I). Closed Sun.

L'Assiette au Boeuf, 123 av. des Champs-Elysées. The same set menu as in the other restaurants of the same name *(see sixth arrondissement)*. Fashionable décor (I). Open to 1 A.M.

Barrière des Champs, 18 av. Franklin-Roosevelt. Another venture by the excellent chef-owner Claude Verger, opened 1982 and an immediate success. Good traditional cooking (M).

Le Bar des Théâtres, 6 av. Montaigne, opposite the Plaza-Athénée hotel. This is theater and couture land, so there's a liberal sprinkling of models, actresses and their admirers. You'll enjoy the food too, if you can bear to take your eyes off your neighbors! Unpretentious, always full, just right for after the theater (I). Closed Sun.

La Boutique à Sandwiches, 12 rue du Colisée. Generally thought to be the best sandwich place in town, but it does have other things too, such as cold meat platters. Open till 12.30 A.M., always crowded (I). Closed Sun. and Aug.

Chiberta, 3 rue Arsène-Houssaye. Owner and chef are both passionate exponents of the *nouvelle cuisine*. Results are sometimes unexpected, mostly delicious, but anyway this is one of Paris's best restaurants, so go there if you can afford it (E). Closed weekends and Aug.

Chez Edgard, 4 rue Marbeuf. Always crowded and particularly popular with the after-theater crowd. Straightforward cooking, but pretty good nonetheless (M). Closed Sun. Open till 1 A.M.

La Fermette, 5 rue Marbeuf, is another useful address when you're going to the theater or cinema. Good-value set menu (I). A room at the back has marvelous *art nouveau* decoration, discovered during recent redecoration.

Fouquet's, 99 av. des Champs-Elysées. Prices are high, but the food is basically good in this eternal landmark. A place to be seen (M).

L'Hippopotamus, 6 av. Franklin-Roosevelt, is one of a menagerie of four beasts known for their good meat, their ridiculously low prices, their cheerful atmosphere. Not a gastronomic experience, but fun. Open to 1 A.M. (I).

Lamazère, 23 rue de Ponthieu. Chic and expensive, with particularly good dishes from the southwest of France, including splendid *cassoulet* (E). Closed Sun. and Aug.

Lasserre, 17 av. Franklin-Roosevelt. One of Paris's finest restaurants, very pretty and smart, and correspondingly expensive. Especially good on summer evenings because it has (excellent idea) a sliding roof. Classical cuisine (E). Closed weekends and Aug.

Laurent, 41 av. Gabriel. Fashionable restaurant overlooking the gardens running down the Champs-Elysées to the Concorde. Splendid *hors d'oeuvres* trolley, fine wine list, rather grand atmosphere (E). Closed Sat. for lunch and Sun.

Le Lord Gourmand, 9 rue Lord-Byron, in a quiet side street off the Champs-Elysées and surprisingly little known. The still-lifes of game and fish on the walls seem to spring to life as you contemplate your food! Delicious *pot-au-feu de la mer,* basically 'new' cuisine. (M). Closed weekends.

Lucas-Carton, 9 pl. de la Madeleine. This old favorite has been rather left behind by a wave of new restaurants, but it's still good, if unexciting. Classical cuisine (E).

La Marée, 1 rue Daru, is one of Paris's top restaurants for superbly cooked classical dishes. (E). Closed weekends and Aug.

Marius et Janette, 4 av. George-V. Excellent fish restaurant, smart, though not 'in'. Specializes in Mediterranean dishes like *bouillabaisse,* and *bourride* and *aïoli* (E). Closed Sun., Aug. and over Christmas and New Year.

Maxim's, 3 rue Royale. Turn-of-the-century and world-famous. Now belongs to couturier Pierre Cardin and is being renovated and revitalized from head to toe. It is still very smart, the food is better than ever—lighter and more imaginative—and you still have to be very rich, or have rich friends, to go there (E). However, now serves (M) meals on first floor. Open to 1 A.M. Closed Sun.

Le Moulin du Village, Cité Berryer, just behind 25 rue Royale. Smart, attractive, tables outside in quiet cul-de-sac. Serves *nouvelle cuisine* (M). Closed Sat. for dinner and Sun.

Petit Montmorency, 5 rue Rabelais. Delectably light nouvelle cuisine, though the prices are on the heavy side. Chic and charming atmosphere (E). Closed weekends and Aug.

La Poularde Landaise, 4 rue St-Philippe-du-Roule. A comfortable spot off the Champs-Elysées specializing in the cooking of southwestern France. Crowded at lunchtime (M). Closed weekends.

Savy, 23 rue Bayard. Old-fashioned bistro, warm and friendly, with country-style cooking from the Auvergne. (M). Closed weekends and Aug.

Taillevent, 15 rue Lamennais. One of France's top restaurants, it has changed over from basically classical to basically 'new' cooking, and has managed the transition perfectly. (E). Closed weekends and Aug.

La Truite, 30 rue du fbg St-Honoré. Hidden in a courtyard behind Lanvin and close to the window-shopper's paradise of the fgb St-Honoré. (M). Closed Sun.

NINTH ARRONDISSEMENT

L'Antre de Bacchus, 1 rue Papillon. Friendly, traditional little bistro with sturdily classical dishes. (I). Closed Sat. for lunch, Sun. and around mid-July to mid-Aug.

Auberge Landaise, 23 rue Clauzel, specializes in cooking from the Bordeaux region and does it beautifully. Rustic décor to go with the food, though the cooking's full of subtlety too (M). Closed Sun. and Aug.

Bistro de la Gare, 38 Bld des Italiens. Same formula as its namesake in the sixth *arrondissement.*

Le Bistrot Papillon, 6 rue Papillon. Another friendly bistro opposite l'Antre de Bacchus. Traditional French dishes, peaceful (I). Closed weekends.

THE CAPITAL OF FOOD

Chartier, 7 rue fbg Montmartre. Turn-of-the-century décor and incredibly low prices (I).

Le Grand Café, 4 bld des Capucines, close to the Opéra. Excellent seafood restaurant, very typical of Paris with its aproned waiters and splendid display of shellfish outside. Open day and night (M).

Ty-Coz, 35 rue St-Georges. Well-known Breton fish restaurant (M). Closed Sun. and Mon.

TENTH ARRONDISSEMENT

Brasserie Flo, 7 cour des Petites-Ecuries. In a courtyard, this is one of the most authentic *brasseries* in Paris, with Alsatian décor and sound Alsatian cooking. Always full, so reservation is essential. (M). Open to 1.30 A.M. Closed Aug.

Julien, 16 rue du fbg St-Denis. Fashionable *art nouveau* décor and interesting food, so very popular (must reserve). Clientele is fashionable too, especially in the evening, when it stays open till 1.30 A.M. (M). Closed Sun. and July.

Nicolas, 12 rue de la Fidélité. This very popular restaurant close to the Gare de l'Est maintains high standards of cuisine and service. Classical traditional dishes, with delicious tarts (M). Closed Sat. and Aug.

Terminus Nord, 23 rue de Dunkerque. Very lively and popular bistrot decorated in outrageous *art nouveau* style and under same ownership as the Brasserie Flo and Julien. Good value, but you may have to wait for your table (M). Closed July. Service until 12.30 A.M.

ELEVENTH ARRONDISSEMENT

Cartet, 62 rue de Malte. Off the beaten tourist track near the pl. de la République, but worth the journey as you'll find one of the few female chefs in Paris busy cooking delicious traditional French dishes. (M). Closed weekends and Aug.

St-Germain-de-la-Mer, 9 blvd Voltaire. Useful place to know in this not very gastronomic area. Similar to restaurant of same name in the 6e. (I).

Sousceyrac, 35 rue Faidherbe. Bustling family-run restaurant serving genuine country cooking but definitely not peasant fare—sumptuous, perfectly cooked hare, *cassoulet*, etc. Not for tiny appetites! Excellent service too (E). Closed weekends and Aug.

TWELFTH ARRONDISSEMENT

Le Morvan, 22 rue de Chaligny. Very French little restaurant such as you find more often in provincial towns, but in fact near the Gare de Lyon and the Bastille. Traditional cooking at very reasonable prices (I). Closed weekends and Aug.

Le Train Bleu isn't a train but it is inside the Gare de Lyon station, and, what's more, it's a classified 'monument' with magnificent Belle Epoque décor.

The cooking (specialties from the Massif Central) doesn't always live up to the décor, though the wines are always good. (M).

Trou Gascon, 40 rue Taine. Inventive 'new' variants on the traditional cuisine of the Gascony region of southwestern France. Marvelous wine list too. Good value *menu* at lunchtime, otherwise high (M). Closed weekends.

FOURTEENTH ARRONDISSEMENT

Chez Albert, 122 av. du Maine. An old favorite for fish cooked in classical style. (E). Closed Mon. and most of Aug.

Aux Armes de Bretagne, 108 av. du Maine. Excellent service in this restaurant with ultra-Victorian décor. Mostly seafood. Mixture of rich classical cooking and some lighter dishes (E). Closed Sun. evening, Mon. and mid-July to mid-Aug.

La Coupole, 102 bld Montparnasse. The whole of Paris and their guests seem to meet for lunch or supper at this famous and longstanding *brasserie* that looks like an arty rail station. Fun people, sound classical cooking. Open more or less non-stop from 12 noon to 2 A.M. (I). Closed Aug.

Le Duc, 243 bld Raspail, is probably Paris's finest seafood restaurant, firmly anchored in the 'new' cuisine. Don't come here if you're against the idea of raw scallops or underdone *loup de mer,* but we're willing to bet that chef Jean Minchelli will convert you if you're prepared to try. Anyway, nouvelle cuisine addicts will adore it, but do make sure to reserve (E). Closed weekends and Mon.

Hippopotamus, 12 av. du Maine. Yet another hippo from the same menagerie as its namesakes. Very good value (I).

Lous Landès, 157 av. du Maine. Excellent cooking from the Bordeaux region, with tables outside in summer. (E). Closed Sun., Mon. lunch and most of June.

Le Jardin de la Paresse (Restaurant du Parc Montsouris), 20 rue Gazan. Friendly restaurant overlooking the delightful Parc Montsouris near the Cité Universitaire. Good value newish cuisine, served in very pretty setting. Service can be a bit haphazard, but it's so delightful you won't mind waiting (M). Closed Sun for dinner and Mon. (winter only). Open to midnight in summer. Special low prices for children.

FIFTEENTH ARRONDISSEMENT

L'Amanguier, 51 rue du Théâtre. Identical to its twin-restaurant in the second arrondissement—equally pretty, equally interesting menu, equally reasonable prices. (I).

L'Aquitaine, 54 rue de Dantzig. An all-female staff led by Christiane Massia, perhaps Paris's most interesting woman chef, run this airy and delightful restaurant down by the Porte de Versailles exhibition center. Imaginative fish dishes and excellent dishes from southwestern France. Openair dining (M). Closed Sun. and Mon.

Bistro 121, 121 rue de la Convention. Bistro with a mixture of traditional and new cooking (E). Closed Sun. eve. and Mon. and mid-July to mid-Aug.

Olympe, 8 rue Nicolas-Charlet. Another excellent woman chef runs this inventive and fashionable restaurant. 'New' cooking. Well worth the rather high prices, but be prepared for small portions. Evenings only, but it's open till midnight (E). Closed Mon., Aug. and Christmas period.

SIXTEENTH ARRONDISSEMENT

Brasserie Stella, 133 av. Victor-Hugo. The 'Lipp' of this fashionable area. Particularly lively after-theater crowd, but be prepared to be rather cramped (M). Open to 2 A.M. Closed Aug.

Les Deux Stations, bld Murat. No frills here, a very modest little café-restaurant with no attempt at décor, but genuine country-style dishes (rabbit, *pot-au-feu,* braised mutton) at ridiculously low prices for this expensive area. For those who want to see how ordinary French people eat—and who share their preference for food over atmosphere. (I).

Faugeron, 52 rue de Longchamp, is one of the very best restaurants in Paris, with delicious 'new' cuisine. Smart and popular, so do reserve. Good wine list too (E). Closed weekends (but open for Sat. dinner Oct. through April), Aug. and over Christmas and New Year.

La Grande Cascade, in the Bois de Boulogne. Attractive leafy setting near the famous Longchamp racecourse, with the refreshing sound of the nearby waterfall that gives it its name. Built like a spacious garden pavilion, it seems to belong to a more leisurely era (which probably explains why the service can be very slow). Good classical cooking, with some 'new' dishes too, but also a good place for a delicious ice cream after the races or a stroll in the Bois. Much used for society weddings, so excellent for people-watching (E). Lunch only in summer. Closed mid-Dec. to mid-Jan.

Guy Savoy, 28 rue Duret. Another excellent nouvelle cuisine restaurant. Must reserve (E). Closed weekends and part of July.

L'Ile de France, port Debilly (opposite 32 av. de New-York). A barge-restaurant moored opposite the Eiffel Tower and bearing a distinct resemblance to a Mississippi paddle steamer with its colonial-style décor. Rather unexpectedly, you can eat well here too (though for a price), as well as admiring the delightful view (E). Closed Sat. lunch and Sun.

Jenny Jacquet, 136 rue de la Pompe. Very popular with those who live in this chic neighborhood, so reserve ahead. Good value nouvelle cuisine, nice ambience (M). Closed Sat. for lunch, Sun. and Aug.

Paul Chêne, 123 rue Lauriston. You'll enjoy the new note of lightness and airiness that has crept in. Must reserve ahead (M). Closed weekends and Aug.

Pré Catalan, route de Suresnes, Bois de Boulogne, is now run by Gaston Lenôtre, France's most famous pastry cook, who's turned it into one of Paris's best and most sought-after restaurants for nouvelle cuisine. Lovely décor (E). Closed Sun. for dinner, Mon. and Feb.

Prunier Traktir, 16 av. Victor-Hugo. Long-established classical seafood restaurant (no longer run by the same people as the other Prunier) with elegant clientele and twenties décor (E). Closed Mon. and July.

Ramponneau, 21 av. Marceau. Quiet and distinguished. Good, carefully prepared home-style cooking. Openair tables are very pleasant for an unhurried lunch (E). Closed Aug.

Robuchon, 32 rue de Longchamp. Old Paris hands may remember this as Jamin and it is still just as memorable as when the great Jamin was alive. Young chef-owner Joël Robuchon is an excellent practitioner of the nouvelle cuisine. Good value menus, otherwise (E). Closed weekends and July.

Le Vieux Galion, 10 av. du Bord-de-l'Eau. A huge galleon moored opposite the Longchamp racecourse and just right for openair dining in summer (though it's open year-round), with a view over the Seine. Specializes in fish. Open to 1 A.M. (E).

Le Vivarois, 192 av. Victor-Hugo. One of Paris's top restaurants, with marvelous 'new' cuisine. Chef Claude Peyrot is endlessly inventive. Recently redecorated from top to toe (E). Closed weekends and Aug.

SEVENTEENTH ARRONDISSEMENT

L'Amanguier, 43 av. des Ternes. Another sister restaurant to the original restaurant of the same name (see 15e *arrondissement*), deservedly popular for its good value meals, nice atmosphere and friendly service (I).

Auberge Saint-Jean-Pied-de-Port, 123 av. de Wagram. Well-known Basque restaurant close to the Etoile, with good *paella* and *cassoulet* and cheerful atmosphere. Good-value fixed-price meal includes apéritif, wine, coffee and service, so there's no danger of the bill ruining your digestion. Also has free parking, which is an added bonus. (M). Closed Sun.

La Barrière de Neuilly, 275 bld Péreire. Owned by lively restaurateur Claude Verger; serves newish cuisine at not too horrific prices (M).

Baumann, 64 av. des Ternes. A lively crowd patronizes this cheerful restaurant busily eating *choucroute* till 1 in the morning. So many different versions you won't know which to choose. Other Alsatian dishes too (M). Closed most of May.

Le Bernardin, 18 rue Troyon, near the Arc de Triomphe. Don't come to this fashionable restaurant if you don't like seafood. If you do, you'll rave over the deliciously fresh fish and shellfish, though the portions are apt to be small. Run by lively brother and sister from Brittany. (E). Closed Sun., Mon. and Aug.

La Coquille, 6 rue du Débarcadère. Ultra-traditional cooking, beautifully done. Rather elegant (E). Closed Sun., Mon. and Aug.

Grosse Tartine, 91 bld Gouvion-St-Cyr. Good place for a reasonably priced lunch near the Porte Maillot air terminal (dinners on Wed., Fri. and Sat. only). Home style cooking, good wines (owner is a wine merchant) (I). Closed Sun. and Aug.

Chez Petrus, 12 pl. du Maréchal-Juin (which you may know as the old pl. Péreire). Specializes in seafood, cooked in the 'new' way. Friendly (E). Closed Sun., Mon. and Aug.

Michel Rostang, 20 rue Rennequin. Well known for nouvelle cuisine versions of homely dishes, so must reserve (E). Closed Sat. for lunch, Sun. and Aug.

EIGHTEENTH ARRONDISSEMENT

L'Assommoir, 12 rue Girardon. Tourist-frequented Montmartre has very few good restaurants, alas. But this is one of them, with some imaginative dishes and reasonable prices. (M). Closed Sun. evening and Mon. and around mid-July to mid-Aug.

Beauvilliers, 52 rue Lamarck. Elegant atmosphere in normally rackety Montmartre, and deliciously light nouvelle cuisine to match (E). Closed Sun., Mon. for lunch and Sept.

Clodenis, 57 rue Caulaincourt. Inventive cooking here too. Also has the turn-of-the-century décor that is so fashionable in Paris at the moment. Some tables outside (M). Closed Sun. Mon.

La Crémaillière 1900, 15 pl. du Tertre. Newish restaurant with Mucha posters and a delightfully tiny garden. Food surprisingly good now, though atmosphere is what counts here. Remember that the pl. du Tertre is very crowded in summer (M). Closed Mon., part of Jan. and part of Aug.

Marie-Louise, 52 rue Championnet. Long-standing bistro, off the beaten track but good-value traditional French cuisine. (I). Closed Sun., Mon. and Aug.

Le Relais de la Butte, 12 rue de Ravignan. An old favorite. Friendly, good-value (I). Closed Mon. and Aug.

Semailles, 3 rue Steinlen. Serves sparklingly inventive nouvelle cuisine (E). Open for dinner only, but closed Sun., Mon.

Tartempion, 15 bis rue du Mont-Cenis. Not very imaginative, but pleasant and surprisingly peaceful (except on Sun.) considering the number of tourists converging on this area. Good-value fixed-price menu (M).

Chez Toi ou Chez Moi, 8 rue de Marché-Ordener. Attractive, popular, with imaginative versions of traditional dishes. Serves only one set menu, and you don't know what you're getting in advance! (M). Must reserve.

Le Tournant de la Butte, 46 rue Caulaincourt. Very inexpensive fixed-price menu, cheerful atmosphere. Crowded, even though this isn't the touristy part of Montmartre (I). Closed Mon. and Sept.

Wepler, 14 pl. Clichy. This is a long-standing thoroughly professional restaurant in the old and rather grand style. Useful as a change from the touristy haunts in Montmartre (M). Open to 1.30 A.M.

NINETEENTH ARRONDISSEMENT

The av. Jean-Jaurès, close to the old slaughterhouses has no fewer than five restaurants close together and all except *La Mer* specializing in—of course—meat. They call themselves the Villette Five, and here they are:

Au Boeuf Couronné, at no. 188. Large and cheerful with huge portions of traditional French meat dishes (M). Closed Sun.

Au Cochon d'Or, at no. 192, has even bigger portions and is generally thought to be the best of the five (E). Open all week.

Dagorno, at no. 190, serves generous helpings. (E). Closed Sat.

Ferme de la Villette, at no. 184. Long-established. Still meat, though not quite as good as the first two (M). Closed Sun. and Aug.

La Mer, at no. 192 as well, and run by the same management as Cochon d'Or, though a more modest version. Specializes in fish this time. (M). Open all week.

Pavillon du Lac, in the Parc des Buttes-Chaumont. Delightful setting, excellent for lunch if you are visiting this lovely park (M). Closed Wed. and Aug., no dinners.

TWENTIETH ARRONDISSEMENT

You really are off the beaten track here, but here's one suggestion in case you find yourself stranded in the Far East:

Le Relais des Pyrénées, 1 rue du Jourdain. Traditional fare from southwestern France, which means *confit d'oie, foie gras,* etc. (E). Closed Sat. and Aug.

NEUILLY

Amanguier, av. de Madrid. Yet another offshoot of this very popular group of restaurants (see Second Arrondissement).

Bourrier, 1 pl. Parmentier. Set in a pretty square well away from the Porte Maillot traffic. Fine "new" cuisine cooked in front of you, rather chic, yet good value (M). Closed weekends, over Christmas and New Year and part of August.

La Boutarde, 4 rue Boutard. This may look like a modest provincial café, but in fact it has a very unprovincial clientele. Straightforward home-style cooking; very tasty, though the portions can be small. Delicious *oeufs à la neige* to round off your meal. You can eat outside in summer. Crowded with expense-accounters at lunchtime. Cheerful waiters (M). Closed Sat. lunch and Sun.

Jacqueline Fénix, 42 av. Charles-de-Gaulle. Pretty, charming service, smart. Excellent 'new' cuisine (E). Closed weekends and mid-July to early Sept.

Sébillon-Paris-Bar, 20 av. Charles-de-Gaulle, just by the Porte Maillot. Longstanding and always busy restaurant near the Porte Maillot. Good traditional cooking, at reasonable prices (M). Closed Aug.

BOULOGNE-BILLANCOURT

La Bretonnière, 120 av. J.-B.-Clément. Rustic décor and new cuisine, with good value *menu* (M). Closed weekends.

Au Comte de Gascogne, at no. 89 in the same avenue, is one of the best restaurants in the Paris area, also with 'new' cuisine, with specialties from southwestern France (E). Closed weekends and Aug.

Gérard Pangaud, 1 rond-point Rhin-et-Danube. The restaurant moved out to these attractive new premises in Boulogne after a brilliant career in cramped surroundings in the rue Montmartre. Excellent nouvelle cuisine and still one of the very best restaurants in the Paris area (E). Closed weekends.

THE CAPITAL OF FOOD

Laux à la Bouche, 117 av. J.-B.-Clément. Despite its punning title (the chef-owner is Monsieur Laux), this is a serious little restaurant with carefully cooked traditional French dishes (I–M). Closed weekends (in the summer months) and for a couple of weeks in the middle of Aug.

JUST FOR A CHANGE

Even the most determined gourmet seeking new delights in French cuisine, *nouvelle* or otherwise, occasionally feels like a change, so here are some suggestions for places to sample other cuisines. As before, the letters *E, M* and *I* stand for expensive, moderate and inexpensive.

Chinese and Vietnamese

Au Jardin de Printemps, 32 rue de Penthièvre, 8e, subtle and elegant (M). Closed Sun. and August.

Ling Nam, 10 rue de Mazagran, 10e, has delicious *dim sum* (I).

La Petite Tonkinoise, 56 rue du fbg Poissonière, 10e, is often said to be the best in Paris. Mouthwatering *pigeonneau laqué* instead of the usual duck. (I). Closed Sun., Mon., Aug. and part of Sept.

Tan Dinh, 60 rue de Verneuil, 7e, became so popular in its old premises in the rue de Navarre that it had to move to these more spacious surroundings. A Vietnamese version of the nouvelle cuisine, served with fine French wines. Expensive by Vietnamese restaurant standards (M). Closed Sun. and Aug.

Filipino

Aux Iles Philippines, 17 rue Laplace, 5e. Exotic and delicious, with unexpectedly elegant clientele. Has pretty little garden (M). Closed Mon. and over Christmas.

German

Vieux Berlin, 32 av. George-V, 8e. Good sauerkraut and game in season (M). Closed weekends.

Greek

Diamantaires, 60 rue la Fayette, 9e. Genuine Greek dishes, carefully cooked (I). Closed Mon. for dinner, Tues. all day and Aug.

Indian

Vishnou, 11 bis rue Volney, 2e. There are not many Indian restaurants in Paris but this is a good one, specializing in tandoori dishes (M). Closed Sun.

Irish

Ferme Irlandaise, 30 pl. du Marché-St-Honoré, 1er. A new arrival on the Paris scene and very popular. Friendly atmosphere, particularly good smoked salmon (I). Closed Sun. for dinner and Mon. all day.

Italian

Le Chateaubriant, 23 rue de Chabrol, 10e. Probably the best Italian restaurant in Paris, with huge portions slightly at odds with the *nouvelle cuisine* tendency. Modern paintings on the walls. (E). Closed Sun. and Mon. and Aug.

Conticini, 4 rue Pierre-Leroux, 7e. Another candidate for the best Italian place in Paris. Very popular (must reserve); good value *menus* (M). Closed Sun. and Aug.

Le Grand Vénise, 171 rue de la Convention, 15e. Exuberantly Italian service, Venetian specialties (E). Closed Sun. and Mon., Aug. and part of Sept.

Da Graziano, 83 rue Lepic, 18e. Charming little restaurant, overshadowed by Montmartre's Moulin de la Galette. Very good food and delightful garden.

La Main à la Pâte, 35 rue St-Honoré, 1er. Marvelous freshly made pasta just by the Les Halles district (M). Closed Sat. for lunch and Sun.

Japanese

Suntory, 13 rue Lincoln, 8e. Rather chic and correspondingly expensive (E). Closed Sun.

Yakijapo Mitsuko, 8 rue du Sabot, 6e. Simple food, carefully cooked. (I).

North African

Chez Bébert, bld Montparnasse, 6e, opposite the monster tower, and also at 33 rue Marbeuf, 8e and 92 bld St-Germain, 5e, has delicious *couscous,* beautifully presented. Magnificent display of fruit, but you'll probably be too full to touch it. Crowded, fun (M).

Le Caroubier, 8 av. du Maine, 15e. Good *tagines* as well as *couscous* (I). Closed Sun., Mon. and Aug.

Charly de Bab-el-Oued, 215 rue de la Croix-Nivert, 15e. Cheerful and lively, good spit-roasted lamb. (M). Closed Mon. and Aug. Another branch has now opened beside the Palais de Congrès at the Porte Maillot (95 bld Gouvion St-Cyr, 17e).

Martin Alma, 44 rue Jean-Goujon, 8e. Very different from Chez Bébert, but good cooking in a plainer and quieter ambiance. (I). Closed Sun. for dinner, Mon. and Aug.

Le Timgad, 21 rue Brunel, 17e, has good *pastilla* and *tagines* and good choice of wines (E). Closed Sun and Aug.

Russian

Dominique, 19 rue Bréa, 6e. The best-known Russian restaurant in town, started 50 years ago and still going strong, though many of its thirties patrons have died long since, and the atmosphere is perhaps more Parisian than Russian these days. But the caviar and the blinis are still good (M). Closed July.

Turkish

Uludag, 24 rue d'Enghien, 10e. Said to be very genuine Turkish cuisine by those in the know. Good kebabs (M). Closed for lunch on Sun.

United States

Conway's, 73 rue St-Denis, 1er. Near Les Halles and Beaubourg, so rather 'in'. Sunday brunches are surprisingly popular with the French (I). Closed Mon., otherwise keeps going until 1 A.M.

Joe Allen, 30 rue Pierre-Lescot, 1er, is a favorite with homesick Americans but also popular with Paris's smart young things. Generous helpings (I). Non-stop service from 12 noon to 1 A.M.

WINE BISTROS

Often run by old-timers from the provinces, these jolly, unpretentious places serve top-flight regional wine by the glass, plus cheeses, charcuterie (ham, sausages and pâtés) and country-style bread. They're ideal spots for a light, inexpensive lunch, a round or two of wine-tastings and lively barside conversation.

Bar des BOF, 5 rue des Innocents, 1 er. This three-table bistro is just on the lip of the Les Halles hole, where the Paris food market used to be. Long a hang-out of market merchants, the BOF *(Bons Ouvriers Français)* is still a favorite with local workers and, more recently, an American discovery of working-class chic. Specialties here are vintage apéritifs, bottled and by-the-glass wines, accompanied by Burgundy, cheese and *charcuterie.* The *coup de grâce* is delivered from a bottle of Marc de Beaujolais, the house's grain alcohol, in which a viper floats. Open till 1 A.M. Closed Sun.

L'Ecluse, 15 quai des Grands-Augustins, 6e. This tiny newcomer, close by the pl. St-Michel, is the slickest of the wine bistros, decorated with Belle Epoque posters and converted gas lamps, and catering to a well-heeled clientele. The specialties are Bordeaux, with by-the-glass selection, with prices running as high as you'll want. Open till 2 A.M. Closed Sun.

Petit Bacchus, 13 rue du Cherche-Midi, 6e. This new wine bistro, across the street from Au Sauvignon, is set up and run like a wine shop. Over 100 bottles of wine, for take-out sale or table service, are stacked on shelves around the room and a half-dozen wines are available by the glass. With wicker chairs and colorful table mats, this is a bright, cozy lunch spot. Platters of *charcuterie* and cheese are generous, and owner Jean-Marie Picard gives friendly and helpful advice on wines. Closed Sun. and Mon.; closed for lunch Sat. (but bar and shop open).

Le Rubis, 10 rue du Marché St-Honoré, 1er. Just near the fashionable pl. Vendôme, this lively bistro is in high spirits after 6 P.M. and jammed at lunch. But you can sandwich yourself in at the old zinc bar, between, say, a fireman and a fahion model, for your choice of omelets, usually a hot *plat du jour,* tasty home-made *rillettes,* and pies for dessert—not to mention the usual *charcuterie* and cheeses. Léon Gouin, who has run Le Rubis unchanged for 35 years, stocks plenty of Meilleur Pot Beaujolais, Rhône, Loire, Bordeaux and some Burgundy wines. And he can tell you most anything you might want to know about them. Closed Fri. at 4 P.M., Sat., Sun., Easter week and Aug.

Au Sauvignon, 80 rue des Saints-Pères, 6e. This small blue and yellow bistro, on a smart Left Bank shopping street, is covered with wine posters and full of merriment. A mix of secretaries, shopkeepers, workers and literary types variously sip and chat the time away with Henri and Alice Vergnes, the vivacious owners from the Auvergne. The Vergnes, who set up business in 1954, were early winners of the Coupe du Meilleur Pot, a prize annually awarded to the bistro with the year's best Beaujolais. There are also good white summer wines and two or three minuscule sidewalk tables where you can enjoy them. Open till around 10 P.M. Closed Sun. and Aug.

La Tartine, 24 rue de Rivoli, 4e. Another old-timer of the Meilleur Pot, this casual and comfy place, with mirrored walls and faded red banquettes, is about as Parisian as you can get. Located on the edge of the newly renovated Marais quarter, it brings in a regular clientele of young artists and students in jeans and capes, a tweedy English writer and a prominent archeologist. Jean Bouscarel, the *patron* for over 25 years, carries a selection of more than 20 wines, from an inexpensive Loire valley choice to Châteauneuf-du-Pape. Open till around 10 P.M. Closed Tues. and Aug.

PARIS BY NIGHT

Painting the Moulin Rouge

You won't have any trouble finding a way of spending your evenings in Paris. In fact your major problem may well be how to decide what to pick with so many possibilities on offer. Maybe a show? Or a concert? Or what about a quiet dinner followed by a spot of dancing? Or watching the world go by from a café terrace? Your decision will obviously depend on a number of different factors, such as how much you want to spend, how good your French is, and of course how you enjoy your nights out.

Your first move should be to see what's going on during your visit. Head for the nearest drugstore or newspaper kiosk and buy one of the weekly 'What's on in Paris' publications, *Pariscope* or *L'Officiel des Spectacles.* They come out Wednesdays and are so packed with information you should allow yourself plenty of time to study them. Your hotel may have a copy of the Paris Tourist Office's *Paris Sélection*. A new aid to successful planning is the *Sélection Loisirs* telephone service. Call 720–88–98 for the English version (though you may need to listen to it twice round, as the English pronunciation sometimes leaves a lot to be desired). The recording covers the week's happenings and includes concerts, ballet, *son-et-lumière*, exhibits, parades, special events of all kinds.

In this chapter we give you plenty of ideas, but keep your eyes skinned for posters advertising one-off events that we can't know about in advance.

Opera and ballet

Fortunately you don't need a knowledge of French to enjoy the excellent productions at the *Paris Opéra*, now generally considered to be one of the world's great houses after a long period in the doldrums. When the controversial director Swiss Rolf Liebermann completed his eight-year reign in 1980—his successor is a Frenchman, Bernard Lefont—he had somehow managed to restore its fortunes and you'll probably have great trouble getting tickets. The Palais Garnier, the official name given to the opulent building in the place de l'Opéra, has now been renovated throughout.

The *Salle Favart* is the new name given to what used to be called the 'Opéra Comique', Paris's second opera house specializing in opera with spoken dialogue (which is what the term *opéra comique* means in French).

The Opéra is also the home of the state-subsidized ballet company, which has a fairly high reputation, and now has Rudolf Nureyev, no less, as director. But you'll find that much of the most interesting ballet in Paris comes during the annual October-December Ballet Festival held in the Théâtre des Champs-Elysées in the avenue Montaigne. Major foreign companies and guest stars perform during this excellent festival. Other places where ballet is staged are the Théâtre de la Ville, the huge Palais des Congrès and the Palais des Sports at the Porte de Versailles—not as atmospheric as the Opéra, but able to seat thousands of people. The huge *Théâtre Musical de Paris*, formerly the *Théâtre du Châtelet*, has been converted into an opera and ballet house, but with much lower seat prices than at the Opéra.

Keep an eye open for ballet performances during the Festival du Marais in the early summer and the Festival Estival (Summer Festival), which runs from mid-July to around mid-September. And, outside Paris, opera (and occasionally ballet) is staged in the pretty opera house in Versailles.

Theater

Paris's best-known 'national' (i.e. state-subsidized) theaters are:
The Comédie Française, in the delightful Salle Richelieu in the place André-Malraux. The company specializes in performances of the great dramatists of the seventeenth century, Corneille, Molière and Racine. The theater ranges well beyond the seventeenth-century repertoire, however, staging plays by modern playwrights from France and all over the world. Seats cannot be reserved more than a week in advance.
The Théâtre de Chaillot, in the place du Trocadéro, doesn't have the cachet it enjoyed in the days when Jean Vilar's TNP (Théâtre National Populaire) attracted theater lovers from all over the world, but it has some interesting experimental shows from time to time.
The Odéon, in the place de l'Odéon, is used mainly as an overspill for the Comédie Française, but also houses visiting companies, including major foreign troupes (such as Britain's Royal Shakespeare Company) playing in their own language.
The Théâtre de la Ville in the place du Châtelet stages a major international theater festival, plus opera and ballet at times. It usually presents two programs daily, with ballet or a well-known popular singer early in the evening and theater later.

For the many commercial theaters you'll need to study lists of what's currently on. A surprising number of plays turn out to be translations of American or British hits, but you may find such well-known French dramatists as Jean Anouilh, Henri de Montherlant or the ever-green Ionesco running. Paris also has some lively experimental theater: the *Lucernaire-Forum,* 53 rue Notre-Dame-des-Champs, 6e, and the various theaters making up the *Cartoucherie,* route de la Pyramide, 12e, are particularly good bets, but there are many others too.

Concerts

Paris is one of Europe's liveliest cities for contemporary music these days, thanks partly to the influence of Pierre Boulez, France's greatest living composer-conductor, who returned to the country to head the contemporary music section at the Pompidou/Beaubourg Center. Interesting concerts are given there most of the year. Classical music is generally thought to be below the standard set in New York and London, but fine concerts are often held in the city's concert halls and, perhaps more interestingly for foreign visitors, in her historic churches. This is a splendid way of combining the delights of sightseeing with listening to music. Have a look to see if there is a concert being performed in *Notre-Dame, Saint-Louis-des-Invalides, Saint-Germain-l'Auxerrois, Saint-Merri* or the *Sainte Chapelle,* all of which provide the most stunning settings. The concerts in the marvelous Gothic Sainte-Chapelle are out of this world, especially if you're lucky enough to hit a time when they're performed by candlelight. Leaflets covering six months of programs can be obtained from the Paris Tourist Office or the Sainte Chapelle itself, and you'd be well advised to reserve well ahead if possible.

In the summer months the excellent Festival de l'Ile-de-France stages fine concerts of classical music in churches, abbeys, châteaux and town halls all over the Ile de France. This again gives you an opportunity to combine an evening's concert going with a spot of sightseeing. And during the Festival du Marais in Paris concerts are often performed in the courtyards of the area's beautifully restored mansions.

Café-theaters

Originally an import from the United States, café-theaters have now been thoroughly absorbed into the cultural life of Paris and often display a spark of invention that is missing in more conventional theater. They're usually crowded, often uncomfortable, but at some of them you can get a good dinner too. Again, they tend to come and go, but the following are usually reliable:

Au Bec Fin, 6 rue Thérèse, 1er; here you can get a good dinner before, after or between the shows (usually three different ones nightly). **Blancs-Manteaux,** 15 rue des Blancs-Manteaux, 4e;—**Le Café d'Edgar,** 58 blvd Edgar-Quinet, 14e;— **Le Café de la Gare,** 41 rue du Temple, 3e;— Le Fanal, 85 rue Saint-Honoré, 1er;— **Soupap,** 3 rue Ste-Croix-de-la-Bretonnerie, 4e;— **La Vieille Grille,** 1 rue Puits-l'Hermite, 5e.

The Chansonniers

These have been largely superseded by the café-theaters, but are still very popular with Parisians. The material is topical and frequently satirical, so you'll need to be pretty familiar with the current French political and social scene, as well as knowing French really well. The best two are **Caveau de la République,** 1 blvd Saint-Martin, 3e, and **Deux-Anes,** 100 blvd de Clichy, 18e.

Movies

Paris has hundreds of movie houses, some huge and palatial, some tiny and uncomfortable. The letters 'v.f.' (*version française*) beside a foreign film in a newspaper or magazine listing mean that it has been dubbed into French; the letters 'v.o.' (*version originale*), that it is showing in the original language. The bigger and more expensive movie houses are mostly on the Champs-Elysées or around the Opéra, the smaller 'art' houses in the Latin Quarter or Saint-Germain-des-Prés.

Paris has two cinémathèques, showing classics from all over the world, one in the Beaubourg/Pompidou Center, 4e, the other at the Palais de Chaillot in the Place du Trocadéro, 16e.

Circuses

The circus is a popular form of entertainment in Paris and has the great advantage that you don't need to know the language. Don't miss Sylvia Monfort's **Cirque Gruss à l'Ancienne** if it's playing when you're in town. This is true traditional circus, with the emphasis on brilliant equestrian acts. The **Cirque Bouglione** is another first-rate troupe.

Other nightlife ideas

Sailing along the Seine in a *bateau-mouche* while enjoying a good dinner is an excellent way of spending the evening. From Palm Sunday through October departures every evening at around 8.30 P.M. and there's a musical accompaniment too. You should be fairly formally dressed. Occasionally full-scale concerts are held on board, usually on Saturdays (look out for the posters in Métro stations).

The startlingly modern Pompidou/Beaubourg Center is one of *the* centers of Paris by Night these days. It's open to 10 P.M. every night except Tuesday and you may well enjoy the novelty of visiting an exhibit in the evening. Concerts, plays, ballet and movies are all staged here, and the huge notice board on the ground floor will tell you if there's some other happening due to take place. The whole of this area attracts street entertainers of all kinds, some of them really talented, even a fully fledged circus sometimes. An evening spent strolling round here and the nearby Les Halles district will give you a good taste of contemporary Paris. (However, do beware of pickpockets!)

Don't forget the splendid *son-et-lumière* show at Les Invalides. It's usually given in English at around 11.15 P.M. in the summer months (around 10.30 P.M. in French). Additional performances in English at 9.30 P.M. mid-April to mid-May and mid-August to mid-October. Check times locally, as they may change.

The Show's the Thing

Dinner plus floor show is one of the traditional ways of spending an evening on the town in Paris. But nightclubs are expensive and you'll usually find you're expected to drink champagne, though this doesn't stop them being full to bursting most nights. Best reserve several days ahead of time to make sure you get a good table, and don't be disappointed if your fellow guests are mostly other tourists.

Alcazar de Paris, 62 rue Mazarine, 6e. Doesn't have the same cachet as when Jean-Marie Rivière was still here, but it's still a good way of spending the evening. Dinner at 8.30, show at around 10.30.

L'Eléphant Bleu, 12 rue de Marignan, 8e. 'Exotic' dancers, a bit touristy, but quite well done. Dinner and dancing at 9, show at around 10.

Folies-Bergère, 32 rue Richer, 9e. The best-known name and it deserves its reputation. Extravagant sets, showy costumes, elaborate sound effects, spectacular semi-nude dancers. Show at around 8.45.

Lido, 116 av. des Champs-Elysées, 8e. Very lavish, full of dazzling technical tricks and sound and light effects, plus very professional entertainers. The food isn't up to much but the show's the thing, and you can dance between shows. Dinner at 8.30, shows at around 10.30 and 12.30.

Moulin Rouge, pl. Blanche, 18e. Still cashing in on the most famous name in Montmartre's night life, thanks to Toulouse-Lautrec and a whole string of famous and talented artistes; and still specializing in the one and only can-can. Very professional, but don't expect to eat well here. Dinner at 8, show at about 10.

Le Paradis Latin, 28 rue du Cardinal-Lemoine, 5e. Lively, crowded, still very 'in', thanks to the brilliant Jean-Marie Rivière, who devises and stages all the shows. A really swinging place. Dinner and show at about 8. Closed Tues.

Raspoutine, 58 rue Bassano, 8e. Russian in the grand style, with red velvet, mirrors, the lot. Maybe old-fashioned in a way, but marvelously luxurious. Dinner and show at about 9. Stays open till at least 4 A.M.

Les Girls

A lot of the shows that were once merely titillating are frankly pornographic nowadays, but these two strip shows have proved their worth and can be safely recommended:

Crazy Horse Saloon, 12 av. George-V, 8e. One of Paris's best-known names. Very well run and professional, with slick show; always crowded.

Le Milliardaire, 68 rue Pierre-Charron, 8e. Used to be called Le Sexy and is still just that. Not as stylish as the Crazy Horse, but a pretty good show for nude-lovers.

Clubs

Paris's 'private clubs' are both expensive and notoriously hard to get into, though 'club' is really a misnomer—it's a way of keeping out people they don't like the look of. It's all distinctly arbitrary and plenty of top people have been turned away, so you needn't feel you're a social failure if you share their fate. The best *entrée* is, inevitably, knowing the right people. Failing that, do your best to look interesting yet respectable, and see how you make out. If it doesn't work, never mind, Paris has thousands of other opportunities to offer.

L'Apocalypse, 40 rue du Colisée, 8e. Lively till the small hours, with restaurant open late too.

L'Aventure, 4 av. Victor-Hugo, 16e. Bright young things from Paris's most select residential areas keep coming here to see and be seen.

Cercle St-Germain-des-Pres, 15 rue Princesse, 6e. Extremely chic, and certainly the hardest to get into, unless you happen to be a friend, or a friend of a friend, of the great Jean Castel, king of Paris's night life. On three floors and very plush, with good food too, mostly enjoyed by a very young and with-it set.

Elysées-Matignon, 2 ave. Matignon, 8e. Ultra-fashionable with showbiz crowd.

Martine's, Pavillon Royal, Bois de Boulogne, 16e. Chic disco where you can dance and dine until the early hours.

Le Privilège, 3 cité Bergère, 2e. Very fashionable.

Régine's, 49 rue de Ponthieu, 8e. The rue de Ponthieu, as you'll have noticed, is *the* place for chic. And this is the most chic and luxurious of them all. Good food too.

Le Ruby's, 31 rue Dauphine, 6e. Believe it or not, this was once Madame de Pompadour's stables. Plush atmosphere, good music.

A good time was had by all

Now let's suppose you want a pleasant evening out but don't feel the urge to rub shoulders with the ultra-fashionable set, and don't want to spend a fortune on a slick show either. Here are some places that should fit the bill—pick one to suit your mood. Many close on Sun. or Mon., but this varies, so check locally.

Balalaika, 39 rue Amelot, 11e. Russian music, of course, as you'd guess from the name, and the real thing too, absolutely no imitations, in this rather out of the way spot.

La Canne à Sucre, 4 rue Sainte-Beuve, 6e; long-standing favorite for live West Indian music and rum punches.

Le Caveau des Oubliettes, 11 rue Saint-Julien-le-Pauvre, 5e. This famous medieval cellar seems to have been going for ever, but the picturesque atmosphere and the jolly French songs are as much fun as ever they were.

Chez Félix, 23 rue Mouffetard, 5e, in the picturesque Contrescarpe area. Light-hearted ambiance, where you can have a drink or a pleasant candlelit dinner and enjoy listening to music, dancing, watching the odd *chansonnier* or whoever happens to be on the bill.

Chez ma Cousine, 12 rue Norvins, 18e. Colorful Montmartre cabaret, with singers and poets and entertainers of all kinds. Reasonably genuine atmosphere, unlike some places in Montmartre. You'll enjoy dinner or late supper here too.

Don Camilo, 10 rue des Saints-Pères, 7e. Good dinner and show at reasonable prices. Comfortable and not too frenetic.

Le Lapin Agile, 22 rue des Saules, 18e. Won its reputation in the days when Montmartre's artist colony spent their nights here. But still great fun, with its wooden tables and lively atmosphere. It's perched high up above Paris and you'll enjoy sipping the traditional glass of cherries preserved in brandy and listening to the show (mostly old French songs, with a handful of newer ones). The prices are reasonable too.

La Main au Panier, 3 rue de Poissy, 5e. Dedicated to giving its customers a jolly good laugh. Dinner and show.

Peanuts, 51 rue Lucien-Sampaix, 10e, by the picturesque Saint-Martin canal. Cheerful thirties atmosphere, with songs and sketches in English as well as French. Closed in Aug.

La Rôtisserie de l'Abbaye, 22 rue Jacob, 6e. Folk songs—usually in French and English—and guitar playing make a lively accompaniment to your dinner or late-night supper. Closed Aug.

Shéhérazade, 3 rue de Liège, 9e. Another atmospheric Russian cabaret, in very plush surroundings.

Villa d'Este, 4 rue Arsène-Houssaye, 8e. Nicely varied entertainment, with singers, conjurors, sketches and plenty of dancing to a good band. You can dine well, if expensively.

The Jazz spots

Caveau de la Bolée, 25 rue de l'Hirondelle, 6e. One of the oldest and still one of the best, in a roomy cellar close to the place Saint-Michel. Modern and traditional French songs, definitely not for innocent ears.

Caveau de la Huchette, 5 rue de la Huchette, 5e. One of the earliest jazz cellars and still popular, mostly with students. Low prices.

Le Fürstenberg, 27 rue de Buci, 6e. A mixture of modern and not-so-modern. Pleasant atmosphere in a fairly spacious cellar.

Méridien-Jazz Trad, in Méridien Hotel, 81 blvd Gouvion-Saint-Cyr, 17e. A good place to enjoy a drink in the bar of this otherwise rather impersonal hotel, listening to good jazz the while.

La Paillote, 45 rue Monsieur-le-Prince, 6e. Jazz on discs, friendly. Low prices.

Le Petit Journal, 71 blvd Saint-Michel, 5e; New Orleans mostly. Closed Aug.

Le Riverbop, 65 rue Saint-André-des-Arts, 6e. For aficionados, as the bands are really good.

Slow Club, 130 rue de Rivoli, 1er. Still going strong and one of the best. Discs only in Aug., live the rest of the year. A good place for dancing.

Men (or women) only

Paris seems to be full of gay places these days, some fairly rough. Here are two of the more respectable:

Madame Arthur, 75bis rue des Martyrs, 18e. Long-established cabaret for men only.

Chez Moune, 54 rue Pigalle, 9e. Describes itself as a 'feminine cabaret.'

Discos

As you'd expect, Paris is full of discos these days and many a little bar or club that used to offer live music now throbs to the latest discs, more often than not accompanied by strobe lighting and special effects, some stylish, some frankly tasteless. The audience is mostly young. As is the way with such places, they come and go, sometimes enjoying a meteoric rise to fame then dying a quick death, sometimes carrying steadily on as fashions wax and wane. Some are chic and elegant, others are on the seedy side. The ones we list here should be still on the go by the time you read this, but don't blame us if some of them have changed their name—it seems that some places get an urge to change every few months, which makes life pretty confusing, though the décor and the ambiance often weather the changes. Discos usually open about 10 or 10.30 P.M. and stay on the boil till around dawn. Most are closed on Mondays but a fair number open Sunday afternoons; virtually all of them stay open during the summer, but check locally.

Adison Square Gardel, 23 rue du Commandant-Mouchotte, 14e. Good place for dancing, with rather respectable clientele. Also has what the French quaintly still refer to as *thés dansants* on Mon, Tues and Fri (from 4 P.M.).

Bains-Douche, 7 rue Bourg-l'Abbé, 3e. Has been described as 'opulent tacky' and that just about sums it up. Very 'in.'

Cherry Lane, 8 rue des Ciseaux, 6e; rock and new wave music.

Club 79, 79 av. des Champs-Elysées, 8e. Special disco evenings on Fri. and Sat.

L'Eléphant Blanc, 24 rue Vavin, 6e; an old favorite in Montparnasse, with pleasant ambiance; particularly recommended for a fine summer evening but closed on Sun.

La Main Jaune, pl. de la Porte-Champerret, 17e. The 'in' place for Paris's bright young things. Afternoon sessions from 3 P.M.

Navy-Club, 58 blvd de l'Hôpital, 13e. One of the few discos where you can eat well at bistro prices. But you won't get in unless you're soberly dressed.

Le Palace, 8 fbg Montmartre, 9e. People keep on saying it's not the 'in' place any more, but it still seems pretty 'in.' Not chic, but then it never has been. Strobe lighting fills this former theater and half the fun consists of watching the rest of the very mixed audience, some of them truly outrageously dressed. It's still packing in a couple of thousand people most nights, and the music's good too, if you like it loud. Puts on rock concerts at frequent intervals. Well run, so there are no unpleasant incidents.

Whisky à Gogo, 57 rue de Seine, 6e. Pleasantly old-fashioned—in spite of the inevitable use of dazzling laser beams—and somehow nostalgic. Very popular.

Zed Club, 2 rue des Anglais, 5e. Purely disco these days, with plenty of lively dancing. Closed in Aug.

Bars

You'll never be short of a place for a drink in pleasant surroundings, before or after dinner. Here are some suggestions for bars and cafés you'll enjoy lingering in.

La Calavados, 40 av. Pierre-Ier-de-Serbie, 8e. A popular spot for smart-set drinking until the early hours—or later (it stays open all night). Good pianist.

La Closerie des Lilas, 171 blvd Montparnasse, 6e. Some people say this literary and artistic spot—it's been frequented by writers and painters since the thirties—is overrated. But the pleasant bar is very popular for a late drink.

Harry's Bar, 5 rue Daunou, 2e. Opened early this century and has never looked back, even though the Hemingway era is well and truly over. Popular with Parisians as well as expatriate and visiting Americans, it stays open year-round till the wee small hours.

Piano-Club, 12 rue Sainte-Anne, 1er. Pleasant atmosphere to a background of soothing piano music, thought the street's rather seedy these days.

Rosebud, 11bis rue Delambre, 14e. Has a reputation for being an intellectuals' bar. Rather smart, though surprisingly like a London pub in some ways.

Sherwood, 3 rue Daunou, 2e. Next door to Harry's Bar. Again an English pub atmosphere, except that it's open to 5 A.M. Youngish regular crowd.

Bars with a view

Paris's skyscrapers may have altered the city's character somewhat, but at least they give you a chance to enjoy fabulous views while you sip your drinks.

Ciel de Paris, on the top of the Tour Montparnasse.

Montgolfier, 'panoramic bar' in the Sofitel-Sèvres hotel (you are whisked up there by an outside elevator, believe it or not); even has a swimming pool.

Plein-Ciel, Conforde-Lafayette hotel at the Porte Maillot; lovely views over the Bois de Boulogne.

Toit de Paris, Hilton hotel; the view isn't marvelous, but you can dance here as well as drinking.

Cafés

People-watching from a sidewalk table outside a café is a traditional Paris delight you'll never tire of. There are hundreds—probably thousands—of them all over the city, the smartest in Saint-Germain-des-Prés, on the Champs-Elysées, in Montparnasse and around the Opéra. The prices vary according to the location, but as no one will stop you lingering for hours over a single drink, you won't blow your budget even if you try out one of the top-notch ones. Here are some of the better-known:

Café de la Paix, 12 blvd des Capucines, 9e. Just by the Opéra.

Le Colisée, on the Champs-Elysées.

La Coupole, 102 blvd du Montparnasse, 14e.

Deux-Magots, 170 bld Saint-Germain, 6e. Said to have gone down since the heyday of existentialism when Sartre and Co. practically lived here, but still smart and probably the best place of all for people-watching. You even get street entertainment thrown in these days (fire eaters, acrobats and the like).

Le Dôme, 108 blvd du Montparnasse, 14e. Another well-known Montparnasse spot.

Le Flore, 172 blvd Saint-Germain, 6e. Next door to the Deux-Magots, thought it doesn't share its unbeatable corner location. Upstairs is traditionally a gay meeting place, but the pavement tables are for all comers.

Fouquet's, 99 av. des Champs-Elysées, 8e. Very smart and expensive, on the corner of the avenue George-V. Has a good bar too.

Lipp, 151 bld Saint-Germain, 6e. Officially a brasserie (see our restaurant chapter).

La Rhumerie, 166 blvd Saint-Germain, 6e. Another Saint-Germain favorite. Always crowded.

Le Sélect, 99 blvd du Montparnasse, 6e. Has kept something of the old Montparnasse atmosphere in spite of the rebuilding that has transformed this area.

SAVOIR FLAIR

Shopping in Paris

Shopping is undoubtedly one of the delights of Paris, and even if you can't afford to make many purchases you can have a great time window shopping. In spite of the recent mushrooming of supermarkets and shopping centers, the narrow little shop with a stylish window display, selling anything from the latest fashion garments to mouth-watering *charcuterie,* from gadgety gifts to pots and pans, is still very much a feature of the Paris scene. And this doesn't apply only to the expensive districts either. No doubt because the French are nothing if not individualists, each little boutique or shop seems to have its own character, and this adds greatly to the interest of a shopping expedition.

Just as medieval cities had whole streets devoted to a single trade, so modern Paris has streets specializing in one type of merchandise: shoes on the boulevard Saint-Michel in the Latin Quarter, 'in' fashion boutiques around Les Halles and the Beaubourg/Pompidou Center and in long-fashionable Saint-Germain-des-Prés, bookshops in the Latin Quarter, china and porcelain in the rue de Paradis, and so on. In this chapter we've selected some favorite shops to get you started, but you'll soon enjoy making your own discoveries. Paris is such a cosmopolitan city that you can naturally find Indian ivory bracelets, British shoes for men, gadgets made in Hongkong and what have you. But you can find them back home too, so we've restricted our suggestions to items that are typically Parisian or French, or are particularly well made or good value in Paris.

One tip: don't be put off or upset by the occasional rudeness you'll encounter from a saleswoman (or man for that matter). 'The customer's always right' isn't a motto you'll hear in France, and by the time you get to the shops you'll already have noticed that Parisians tend to be brusque with everybody, not just with foreigners. Most assistants are in fact reasonably helpful, though they may follow you about more than you're used to at home. And here you should bear in mind that Parisiennes expect the saleswoman to take an interest and produce items that are liable to please her and fit her requirements. Whereas you may prefer to browse by yourself, she'll complain if she feels she isn't getting enough attention. As we've said before, 'When in Rome, do as the Romans do' is a vital point to remember when you're in France.

Practical hints

First, **opening hours:** shops are open roughly 9 or 9.30 A.M. to about 7 P.M. Most small food shops, however, open earlier (8 or 8.30) and don't close until 7.30 or 8 P.M., but they have a long break for lunch, usually about between 1 and 4 P.M. Fashion boutiques usually stay open all day, but antique shops and some small specialist shops close between about 12.30 and 2, and sometimes don't open until 10 A.M. In the summer, when some staff are on holiday, many shops take a lunch break even if they're open non-stop the rest of the year. Supermarkets and department stores invariably stay open over the lunch hour. Many small shops close for the whole of August, when most of their customers are away on holiday. Small food shops and a surprising number of other shops are open on Sunday mornings, and even on some public holidays. Department stores are increasingly staying open on public holidays that fall on a weekday, as they find they do a roaring trade when people are free to shop.

Second, **tourist discounts:** for details of forms and so on see our Facts at Your Fingertips section at the front of this book. In practice you'll find that the easiest places to benefit from this system are the department stores, which have special staff dealing with the problem.

They will normally give you 13 per cent on 'ordinary' goods and 23 per cent on 'luxury' items, which covers perfumes, good jewelry, cameras and so on. Small boutiques are emphatically not equipped to deal efficiently with the paperwork involved and the system is liable to break down. Some stores will give you the refund on the spot, but they'll be taking a chance if they do, because if you don't hand in your form to the customs people on leaving, they'll be out of pocket. So don't count on it. And avoid paying in any other currency than French francs if you can. Many shops with frequent foreign customers will accept other currencies, but the exchange rate will be a lot lower than in the banks.

Next, **specialized delivery services.** The system whereby goods could be delivered direct to your plane or ship no longer operates, but you can have tax-free merchandise sent direct to your home—at a price. When you pay for your goods, the tax will be deducted but the freight charge will be added. Costs naturally depend on current postal and freight rates. Time for delivery is about 10 days by air, otherwise at least 4-5 weeks. Items weighing over a kilogram (maximum is 20 kilograms) will take a good 2 or 2½ months. On the whole the system is worth it only if you have bought something so heavy you'll have to pay excess baggage charges on your plane to take it with you, or if you're going to be traveling on around Europe and don't want to be too laden. The best-known firm with a well-organized discount and shipping system is:

Michel Swiss, 16 rue de la Paix, 2e; has excellent ties, scarves and perfumes.

The department stores

These are a good place to wander about and get the feel of shopping in France without feeling any obligation to buy. The most typically Parisian, both close to the Opéra, are:

Galeries Lafayette, 40 bld Haussmann, 9e; open Mon-Sat 9.30 A.M. to 6.30 P.M.; as well as the usual range of department store goods (with particularly good fashion boutiques—stores within a store), has a hairdresser and beauty parlor, two restaurants, tea room, travel and theater agency, banking service and a team of interpreters; also has a smaller branch on the ground floor of the Tour Montparnasse, which is open 9.45 A.M. to 7.15 P.M.

Le Printemps, 64 bld Haussmann, 9e; open Mon-Sat 9.35 A.M. to 6.30 P.M.; has bar, roof terrace, snackbar, multilingual hostesses; is made up of three buildings: the Magasin Havre (household goods, hobbies, gifts, perfumes and jewelry); the Nouveau Magasin next door (ladies and children's fashion, including accessories); and the Brummel, in the street behind, for men's and boys' wear. Also has two smaller branches at the place de la Nation and place d'Italie.

Smaller but very select is the elegant **Trois-Quartiers,** 17 bld de la Madeleine, 1er; open Mon-Sat 9.40 A.M. to 6.30 P.M. (note: closes on Monday in July and

August). Excellent for accessories—scarves, handbags, gloves—and swimsuits; caters mostly to an older age group than the other two.

Less popular with foreign tourists, but a good place for seeing ordinary Parisians out shopping are three rather less select stores:

Bazar de l'Hôtel de Ville, 55 rue de la Verrerie, 4e (but with entrances in the rue de Rivoli too, opposite the Hôtel de Ville or City Hall). Very good for household articles.

Au Bon Marché, 38 rue de Sèvres, 7e. Has been modernized, but still has a slightly provincial, old-fashioned feel about it; has a well-known antiques section.

La Samaritaine, 19 rue de la Monnaie, 1 er. The big attraction here for tourists is the roof terrace, from which you get a stunning view over Paris; there's a panoramic table to help you get your bearings.

Budget chain stores

The rather similar **Monoprix** and **Prisunic** are found all over town; particularly good for stylish yet relatively inexpensive fashion accessories and childrens' clothes. Prisunic's Champs-Elysées store is open to 10.30 P.M. At back-to-school time in September both chains have excellent stationery displays that may give you some gift ideas.

Shopping centers

Paris's newest shopping center is the glittering **Forum,** in Les Halles, where the old food market used to be. Has a whole floor of fashion boutiques, plus interior design stores, gift boutiques, not to mention movies, theaters, restaurants.

The **Palais des Congrès,** at the Porte Maillot, has fashion, antiques, craft boutiques, a post office, tobacconists', drugstore.

The **Tour Montparnasse** has a branch of Galeries Lafayette and dozens of other shops.

There are several shopping arcades leading off the north side of the Champs-Elysées (the Galerie Point Show, Galerie Claridge, etc.).

Drugstores

These are really mini department stores, selling newspapers and magazines from all over the world (they're your best bet for US or British papers), books, maps, stationery, sometimes records and gadgety gifts of all kinds, even take away food—at a price. Most have a chemists' counter, and all have restaurants, mostly for fast food dishes, but with good *plats du jour* too. Open and busy to around 2 A.M. every day of the week.

Drugstore des Champs-Elysées, 133 av. des Champs-Elysées, 8e (by the Arc de Triomphe).

Drugstore Matignon, 1 av. Matignon, 8e (at the Rond-Point-des-Champs-Elysées). Also has a car-hire service and a theater reservation agency.

Drugstore de Neuilly, 14 pl. du Marché, Neuilly. Smaller and quieter than the other drugstores; no chemists' counter.

Drugstore Opéra, 6 bld des Capucines, 9e; as well as the usual departments, has a convenient exchange counter open longer hours than ordinary banks (to 7.20 P.M. on weekdays, and 12 A.M. to 7.20 P.M. on Sundays).

Drugstore Saint-Germain, 149 bld Saint-Germain, 6e (diagonally opposite the church of Saint-Germain-des-Prés). Has particularly good book department in the basement.

Fashion

Few people would dispute that French fashion is stylish and desirable at all price levels and you may well want to pick an outfit to take home. It needn't be all that expensive, providing you're careful not to be carried away by some exotic trifle you'll never feel right in. Frenchwomen are so insistent on wearing the latest fashion, and on buying clothes at fixed times of the year, that the sales are a joy—knowing they'll never be able to sell summer outfits to their regular customers in September, even if it's blazing hot, boutiques slash their prices quite dramatically in late June and July before their August closure. And the same goes for winter clothes in January and February. Foreign visitors —more flexible than the French—can pick up bargains at such times.

Frankly, few people can afford *haute couture* these days. It has been estimated by the head of the haute couture designers' federation that only about two thousand women worldwide could afford to buy it regularly. So here is a list of some of the less expensive, though still chic, boutiques, all of whom do ready to wear clothes.

SAINT-GERMAIN-DES-PRÉS Anastasia, 18 rue de l'Ancienne-Comédie, 6e; mostly Indian and Peruvian fabrics, but with inventive French designs too.

Biba, 18 rue de Sèvres, 7e; fairly avant-garde, on the expensive side.

Cacharel, 30 rue de Buci, 6e; classic separates.

Chantal Thomass, 5 rue du Vieux-Colombier, 6e; avant-garde clothes for the young and slim.

Chloe, 2 and 3 rue de Gribeauval, 7e; very elegant and expensive, in tiny street near the rue du Bac; beautiful designs by Karl Lagerfeld.

Daniel Hechter, 146 blvd Saint-Germain 6e; an old favorite with lovers of classic, sporty elegance.

Dorothée Bis, 17 rue de Sèvres, 7e; long-established leader in avant-garde fashion, mostly fairly casual.

SAVOIR FLAIR

La Gaminerie, 187 blvd Saint-Germain, 6e; an old favorite for lively young styles by top avant-garde designers; good shoes too.

Mic-Mac, 13 rue de Tournon, 6e; mostly casual and elegant separates.

Sonia Rykiel, 6 rue de Grenelle, 6e; brilliantly coordinated separates, especially fetching knitwear.

Tan Giudicelli, 2 and 13 rue de Tournon, 6e; evening outfits at no. 2, more casual wear at no. 13.

Tiffany, 12 rue de Sèvres, 7e; eminently wearable clothes, many of them fairly sporty.

FAUBOURG SAINT-HONORÉ/MADELEINE/CHAMPS-ELYSÉES

Berteil, 3 pl Saint-Augustin, 8e; beautifully cut trousers in the latest styles.

Mac-Douglas, 155 fbg Saint-Honoré, 8e; divine leather and suede pants, trench coats and jackets of all kinds.

No Problem, Galerie Point Show, 66 av des Champs Elysées, 8e; up-to-the-minute styles at very reasonable prices.

Catherine Savoye, 14 rue Marbeuf, 8e; good range of the latest ready-to-wear designs.

LES HALLES **Agnès B,** 3 rue du Jour, 1er; 'in' yet wearable fashions in a very pretty boutique.

Halles Capone, 12 rue de Turbigo, 1er; the pun in the name of the shop may be terrible, but the clothes are very chic.

In the nearby place des Victoires:

France Andrévie, at no. 2; sophisticated separates with a definite style of their own.

Jungle Jap, at no. 3; gorgeous way-out designs by Kenzo, with good accessories too, mostly for the younger set.

Thierry Mugler, at no. 10; highly inventive, fairly way-out.

Victoire, at no. 12; very popular with an elegant clientele; latest styles by leading ready-to-wear designers as well as Victoire's own designs.

PASSY/VICTOR HUGO **Apostrophe,** 11 av. Victor Hugo, 16e; lovely silk outfits in jewel colors.

Franck & Fils, 80 rue de Passy, 16e; mini department store devoted mainly to ladies' fashion; closed Mon, in July and August.

Fouks, 7 av. Victor Hugo; classic separates.

Georges Rech, 23 av. Victor Hugo, 16e; very wearable clothes and good accessories.

Méredith, 14 rue de Passy, 16e; good range of well-cut styles by leading avant-garde designers.

Pierre Bruhin, 4 av. Victor Hugo, 16e; the sort of classic styles you can go on wearing for years without feeling out of date.

Swann, 17 av. Victor Hugo, 16e; very elegant, well-coordinated separates.

Zoa, 13 rue de Passy, 16e; good boutique for all kinds of outfits.

Shoes

A lot of the most beautiful shoes in Paris are, inevitably, Italian, but there are still a few genuinely French *bottiers*. The boulevard Saint-Michel in the Latin Quarter has more shoe shops than any other street in Paris, so you might well start your search there. You'll find exclusive, and therefore expensive, stores alongside the cheaper chain stores. Two of the best chains are **Raoul** and **André,** which you'll spot all over the city. Shoes there are surprisingly inexpensive, yet they always have up-to-date styles in whatever happen to be the year's fashion colors. For a wider range of colors, and for stylish models in beautiful soft leather, you'll normally have to pay quite a bit more.

Handbags and leather goods

The big stores are a good bet, especially **Galeries Lafayette, Printemps** and **Trois Quartiers.** The inexpensive **Monoprix** and **Prisunic** chains have surprisingly stylish designs in a limited range of colors. But *the* store for all kinds of leather goods (even saddles!) is the great **Hermès,** 24 fbg Saint-Honoré, 8e. It's been going for over a hundred years and is a byword for luxury, with handmade goods that virtually never wear out. Very expensive, naturally, though the salespeople will be just as polite if you treat yourself to a (relatively) inexpensive leather notebook.

The shops along the rue Saint-Honoré and the rue de Rivoli specialize in beaded and *petit-point* designs and you'll find some surprisingly attractive and good-value models in the city's street markets, especially in summer, when the food stalls are closed for the holidays.

Scarves

Paris has long been known as one of *the* places for stunning silk scarves. The best-known name is of course **Hermès,** if you can afford it. **Trois-Quartiers** has a particularly good selection, and the other department stores are good bets too. Most of the designer boutiques have a small selection of exclusive scarves, usually designed to go with their outfits. The souvenir shops along the rue de Rivoli (the Tuileries section) are the place for those corny but attractive scarves with pictures of the Eiffel Tower or the Arc de Triomphe or, nowadays, the Georges Pompidou/Beaubourg Center.

Jewelry

Your pocketbook must be your guide here. The world's top jewelers will sell you a little trifle for more than you can possibly imagine, or you can buy a little Eiffel Tower charm for a bracelet for a few francs. In between these two extremes, you'll find some good, well-designed costume jewelry too.

The big boys are conveniently grouped together on the place Vendôme in between the Opéra and the Tuileries Garden. Here you'll find **Boucheron, Chaumet** (who made Napoleon's imperial crown, orb etc) and **Van Cleef & Arpels.** Just around the corner, at no. 13 rue de la Paix, is **Cartier.**

For inventive one-off pieces at slightly lower prices, try:

Jean Dinh Van, 7 rue de la Paix, 2e.

Ilias Lalaounis, 364 rue Saint-Honoré, 1er; heavy but beautiful designs.

Jean Vendôme, 352 rue Saint-Honoré, 1er.

Fred, 6 rue Royale, 8e; popular with foreign tourists rather than Parisians.

You'll find attractive modern designs at reasonable prices at:

Aussi, 159 blvd Saint-Germain, 6e.

Fabrice, 26 rue Bonaparte, 6e (and also at nos 33 and 54 in the same street); the best bet for elegant pieces that won't date yet seem modern.

Fleurmay, 204 rue de Rivoli, 1er; particularly well-designed silver pieces.

For the latest fashions in brooches, earrings, lapel badges, what have you, try the department stores; the inexpensive **Monoprix** and **Prisunic** chains have current styles in plastic which make great presents to take back home to young friends. Otherwise, you'll have a lot of fun if you visit:

Agatha, 8 rue de la Paix, 2e, 59 rue Monge, 5e, 97 rue de Rennes, 6e, also in the Galerie des Champs, 84 av. des Champs-Elysées, 8e and in the Forum; this is *the* place for fun, up-to-the-minute bits and pieces, at prices you can afford without hesitating.

Perfumes

The best way to buy perfumes is to go where you can sniff at a wide variety at your leisure. So your best bets are the department stores, the specialist shopping house we've already mentioned, **Michel Swiss,** 16 rue de la Paix, 2e, or **Sephora,** 50 rue de Passy, 16e and in the Forum; they claim to be the world's largest perfumery store and may be right; huge selection (including beauty products) at lower prices than the tiny specialist shops.

Men's fashions

You'll soon notice that most of the best men's shops in Paris are British, or at any rate most of what they sell comes from Britain, though there's a lot of Italian menswear too. But you will find a few very Parisian places:

Arnys, 14 rue de Sèvres, 7e; classic styles.

Christian Aujard, 15 rue de Tournon, 6e; 74 av. des Champs-Elysées, 8e; separates by good ready-to-wear designers.

Berteil, 3 pl. Saint-Augustin, 8e; Parisian institution; well-cut trousers; time-honored favorite.

Cacharel Hommes, 34 rue Tronchet, 8e, 30 rue de Buci, 6e, Palais des Congrès, 17e and in the Forum; well-cut casual wear.

Pierre Cardin, 27 av. de Marigny, 8e and 59 fbg Saint-Honoré, 8e; very expensive.

Daniel Crémieux, 6 bld Malesherbes, 8e; elegant sportswear; good value.

Courrèges Hommes, 28 rue La Tremoille, 8e; not *too* expensive for this top design name.

Daniel Hechter, 146 bld Saint-Germain, 6e, 50 av. des Champs-Elysées, 8e, 12 fbg Saint-Honoré, 8e, 71 rue de Passy, 16e, and in the Forum; chic causals.

Lanvin, 15 fbg Saint-Honoré, 8e, and newer **Lanvin 2,** 2 rue Cambon, 1er classic, elegant styles at high prices.

Ted Lapidus, 52 rue Bonaparte, 6e, 37 av. Pierre-Ier-de-Serbie, 8e, 23 fbg Saint-Honoré, 8e and 6 pl. Victor-Hugo, 16e; and in the Forum. Expensive but stylish.

Renoma, 129 bis, rue de la Pompe, 16e; elegant casual styles, chic, yet they don't date easily.

Saint-Laurent, 12 pl. Saint-Sulpice, 6e and 38 fbg Saint-Honoré, 8e; expensive.

Gift boutiques

New gift shops seem to be springing up all the time in Paris. You'll find very attractive items at:

Beauté Divine, 40 rue St-Sulpice, 6e; pretty little boutique selling bathroom accessories old and new.

La Carpe, 14 rue Tronchet, 8e; lovely kitchen accessories.

Come-Bac, 21 rue du Bac, 7e and 42 rue de l'Université, 7e; attractive gifts of all kinds, some gadgety, some more practical.

Dans un Jardin, 1 rue du Marché Saint-Honoré, 1e and in the Forum; tiny green-and-white boutique selling attractively packaged toiletries, perfumes and dried flowers.

Descamps, in the Forum and all over Paris (you can't miss them); beautiful tablecloths, napkins, towels, sheets etc.

SAVOIR FLAIR

Léon, 220 rue de Rivoli, 1er. Pretty Sèvres porcelain boxes and thimbles, paperweights etc.

L'Herbier de Provence, 18 rue du Bac, 7e and in the Forum; pretty sachets of dried herbs, dried flowers, Provençal pottery, honey, candles.

Le Monde en Marche, 28 rue Dauphine, 6e; attractive wooden toys, puppets, mobiles.

Les Olivades, 27 rue Saint-Louis-en-l'Isle, 4e; Provençal boutique, with scarves, pottery, basketwork etc.

Françoise Thibault, 1 rue Jacob, 6e and 1 rue Bourbon-le-Château, 6e; an old favorite for very attractive little gifts, with some lovely handpainted boxes.

La Tuile à Loup, 35 rue Daubenton, 5e; traditional craft work from all over France.

Craft centers

Craft work of all kinds is so fashionable these days in France that you'll find new boutiques (and craft classes too) all over the place. For a good selection of individual styles try:

Les Artisans de France, Palais des Congrès, Porte Maillot, 17e; a whole gallery of craft stalls, which change over once every 2 weeks, on the lower-ground floor; good place to browse in wet weather.

A Mon Seul Désir, 26 pl. Dauphine, 1er. Really well designed craft pieces in a pleasant setting.

Prints

The Saint-Germain area is the happiest hunting ground here, but before going there stop off just the other side of the Seine, at the Chalcographic Department in the Louvre, which makes prints from old plates (they have literally thousands of them, by some of the world's best-known artists).

You'll find prints of varying quality all along the bookstalls lining the Seine, but for some specialist shops, try:

Bateau-Lavoir, 16 rue de Seine, 6e; has drawings too.

Berggruen, 70 rue de l'Université, 7e; contemporary artists.

La Hune, 14 rue de l'Abbaye, 6e; part of a famous bookshop in the boulevard Saint-Germain.

Paul Prouté, 74 rue de Seine, 6e; Paris's best-known name, with hundreds of thousands of prints, carefully categorized.

Posters

Berggruen, 70 rue de l'Université, 7e.
Galerie Documents, 53 rue de Seine, 6e; good theater posters.

Pompidou/Beaubourg Center, rue Saint-Martin, 4e; good selection on ground floor.

Postcards

You'll find a fair choice on the bookstalls along the Seine and in the flea markets. The stamp market at the **Carré Marigny** (by the Rond-Point-des-Champs-Elysées) has a good postcard section (Thurs, Sat, Sun only). Also:

Jehanno, 6 rue Bailleul, 1er.

Antiques and bric-à-brac

For dozens of little shops under one roof:

La Cour des Saints-Pères, off the street of the same name, 7e, has several small shops grouped together in an attractive courtyard.

Les Jardins Saint-Paul, again off the street of the same name, 4e, has both shops and craft workshops in a skillfully restored series of courtyards on the edge of the Marais.

Le Louvre des Antiquaires, 2 pl. du Palais-Royal, 1er; Paris's newest antique emporium and a great success; prices can be surprisingly reasonable.

Village Suisse, 52 av. de la Motte-Piquet, 15e; high-class antique dealers, rather overpriced.

Flea markets

Paris's most famous *marché aux puces* takes place between the Porte de Saint-Ouen and the Porte de Clignancourt on Sat, Sun and Mon only. There's a lot of rubbish, but it's great fun, and if you get there early, you may find a bargain.

Less well-known and therefore less expensive are:

Place d'Aligre, 12e; mornings only, except Mon; mostly fairly junky, but picturesque.

Porte de Montreuil, 20e; a lot of real tat, but if you're brave enough to wade through it this is the place where bargains really are found before the dealers snatch them up.

Auctions

Paris's major auction house, **Drouot,** moved back in 1980 to the rue Drouot, 9e, after 4½ years' very successful exile in the old Gare d'Orsay. Its new building on the old premises is dazzlingly contemporary, but you can buy some good antiques here. Check newspapers for current sales.

Books

Books in English are naturally more expensive than back home. However, you may want to buy books about France once you've arrived, so here are the best places:

Galignani, 224 rue de Rivoli, 1er; has been going since 1800.

Smith & Son, 248 rue de Rivoli, 1er; also has huge range of British newspapers and magazines.

Village Voice, rue Princesse, 6e. Lively American bookshop. Also offers health food meals, poetry readings.

For books in French you'll find the largest concentration of bookshops in the boulevard Saint-Michel. But perhaps the most convenient and pleasant in all Paris is:

La Hune, 170 bld Saint-Germain, 6e; open 10 till midnight Mon-Fri, till 7.30 P.M. on Sat; has good art book section.

Also open late is the good bookshop in the **Pompidou/Beaubourg Center** (to 10 P.M. every day but Tues); a good place for browsing. The bookstand in the **Louvre** is excellent for art books.

Food

You can find plenty of goodies in the little local *charcuteries* and *épiceries,* but if you feel like splashing out, here are some gastronomic temples:

Androuët, 41 rue d'Amsterdam, 8e; probably the world's best-known cheese specialist.

Bistro d'Hubert, 36 pl. du Marché Saint-Honoré, 1er; fine boutique next to the well-known restaurant of the same name.

Christian Constant, 26 rue du Bac, 7e; chocolates.

Comptoir Grourmand, 32 pl. de la Madeleine, 8e; the brilliant chef Michel Guérard of *cuisine minceur* fame has made a success of his shop right next to the great Fauchon.

Aux Douceurs de France, 70 blvd de Strasbourg, 10e; pretty boxes of special sweets and candies from all over France.

Fauchon, 26 pl. de la Madeleine, 8e; the greatest name of all.

Hédiard, 126 rue du Bac, 7e, 21 pl. de la Madeleine, 8e, 70 av. Paul-Doumer, 16e, 106 blvd de Courcelles, 17e and in the Forum; a *very* superior grocer's.

Maxim's de Paris, 76 fbg Saint-Honoré, 8e; another great name.

If you prefer to leave your shopping to the last minute, Orly and Roissy/Charles-de-Gaulle airports have good food boutiques.

ILE DE FRANCE

Heartland of a nation

by
GEORGIANNA POUZZNER

For visitors, the Ile de France is the most heartwarming of all the French provinces. First, there is the pleasure of imagination satisfied: there is something strangely familiar about the look of lanes bordered with silvery poplar trees, the golden haze in the air, the gray stone of a village steeple. No wonder, for scores of painters have immortalized them. Corot began with the forest of Fontainebleau and the village of Barbizon. Pissarro and Cézanne worked at Pontoise; Renoir, Monet, Sisley and Degas chose Louveciennes, now a suburb to the west of Paris. Sisley's famous riverside canvases were painted at Moret-sur-

Loing near Fontainebleau; and Monet frequently painted the river Epte at Giverny.

Just as the Ile de la Cité is the heart of Paris, so the Ile de France is the ancient heartland of France, the core from which the French kings gradually extended their power over the rest of a rebellious, individualistic nation. Architecturally and historically the Ile de France—with the exception of the Midi provinces—is all France in miniature. Here, all the great architectural styles are spread before your eyes. There is the Romanesque church at Morienval, the magnificent Gothic structures at Chartres and Beauvais. There are great feudal castles, such as Pierrefonds; 18th-century châteaux, including Compiègne and the Trianons at Versailles; the family home of the duc de Luynes at Dampierre. There are ancient forests at Rambouillet and Villers-Cotterêts. If you want to see France's progress into the 20th century, drive about a bit in the Paris suburbs. New buildings, some quite attractive, some made of 40-story-high apartment dwellings with rectilinear streets, are mushrooming along every main road.

Touring the Ile de France

One of the great beauties of the Ile de France is that none of its major monuments is more than half a day's drive from Paris. Though small, the Ile de France is so rich in treasures that a whole day of fascinating exploration may take you no more than 96 km (60 miles) from the capital. You'll not be able to enjoy all it has to offer if your pace is too swift. See it slowly, see it well. The five tours suggested detail the major points of interest and skip what's monotonous or pedantic. They have been geared to two or three days of travel.

If you have a weekend or two at your disposal, choose the trips to Versailles, Chartres, or Senlis, with Fontainebleau as a fourth alternative. And if you have only one day, make a single jumbo tour beginning with Versailles in the morning, lunch at Jouy, afternoon in Chartres, and high tea or dinner at Montfort l'Amaury on your way back to Paris. However, you'll be pretty dead-tired!

1—PARIS WEST TO VERSAILLES, CHARTRES, ST-GERMAIN

The once magnificent château of St-Cloud was destroyed by the Germans in 1871. Beautifully terraced grounds remain, however, and they are well worth a visit. On the other side of the St-Cloud park at Sèvres are the Sèvres National Porcelain Factory and the National Porcelain Museum (which is closed lunchtime). The factory has guided tours twice a month. Here there are beautiful examples of ceramic art, as well as—conveniently enough—a sale room where you can choose your own favorite pieces.

Versailles

Versailles marked the end of feudalism in France, and in its insensate glory, foreshadowed the French Revolution a century later. Psychologically, historically, Versailles may be regarded as the result of a childhood shock suffered by the young king Louis XIV. With his mother, Anne of Austria, he was forced to flee Paris, and was captured temporarily by a group of nobles, known as the *Frondeurs*. Louis conceived a hatred of Paris and of the Parisians, who had sided with the conspirators. His distaste was such that he visited his country's capital only a few times once he had come of age.

At the age of 23, just after the blow to his pride received at Vaux-le-Vicomte, where his own finance minister lived more richly than he, Louis began work on his tremendous palace at Versailles. The problems of nature did not daunt him—hills were razed, marshes were drained, and water for the magnificent fountains was channeled to Versailles from the Seine several miles away. Work on Versailles continued over a period of 50 years. Three years after the entire court was installed there, 36,000 men and 6,000 Percheron horses were still laboring away. The Orangerie, as hothouses were then called, was filled with 3,000 almond trees, laurel roses, pomegranate and orange trees. Over 150,000 flowers were planted each year and entire forests were transported to ornament the grounds.

With over 1,000 of France's greatest nobles living in the palace with him, Louis XIV began to substitute royal privileges and sinecures for local power and feudal rights. Holding the king's chemise when he dressed soon became a more important source of wealth and status than the possession of an entire county in the provinces.

The succeeding king, Louis XV, and his mistress, Madame de Pompadour, beautified the château even more, and brought a new note of intimacy and refinement into their private apartments—an inside staircase linked their two sitting-rooms. Louis XV also built the Grand Trianon, a poetic pink marble palace overlooking a small garden with a terrace facing the Grand Canal.

Louis XVI, last of the Bourbons to live in the great palace, found it a prison. He took refuge from its stifling atmosphere in the Petit Trianon, while Marie-Antoinette, his queen, disported herself in the pastoral village her husband indulgently built for her.

If you are short on time, above all visit the main palace—the guided tour (you are not allowed to wander around alone) takes about an hour and gives you at least a glimpse of the way the Bourbons lived. It also gives you a glimpse into why, more than two centuries later, the French still speak of *grandeur*. If you have a whole morning or afternoon, you can continue, even if hastily, to the Trianons, and stroll through the gardens of the main palace. The views are stupendous, but fall, when the leaves change color, is probably the most spectacular time of year to visit. If you're just passing through and would like an instructive glance, drive past the main palace to the Grand Trianon, then walk across its terrace down to the parapet overlooking the cross-shaped Grand Canal.

Before entering the château, stop for a glance at the exterior. Appropriately in the middle are the rooms in which the king lived; on his left, the queen and later Madame de Maintenon. The two wings were occupied by the royal children and the princes of the blood. The courtiers lived in the attics.

Among the major sights of your tour will be the solemn Mansart-designed chapel where king and queen attended mass daily in their gilt boxes. Of the reception rooms, the most famous and loveliest is the Galerie des Glaces where the Treaty of Versailles ending World War I was signed in 1919—and where the German Empire was proclaimed in 1871. The gallery, which had been empty for decades, is once again furnished, and on a few special occasions is still lit by the blaze of candles reflected in the shimmering mirrors.

The royal bedrooms are properly ceremonious—but far more interesting are the *petits appartements* where the king and queen actually lived in the company of their close friends and servants. The miniature opera house, built by Gabriel for Louis XV, was restored in the 1950s and is sumptuously decorated.

In recent years, many of the once sadly empty and cold state rooms have been refurnished with period furniture painstakingly collected, purchased and donated from all over France and other countries, particularly the United States. This long task of restoration and renovation reached an important stage in 1980 when President Giscard d'Estaing ceremonially opened the refurbished bedroom of Louis XIV. While there is still much work to be done, it is now possible to enjoy Versailles in something approaching its original splendor.

The grounds of Versailles

The grounds of Versailles, covering some 100 hectares (250 acres), were created by Le Nôtre and decorated with many sculptures. Parisians love the lawns, formal flowerbeds and ornamental lakes, and go there time and time again, particularly in fall. But the most breathtaking sight is the playing of the great fountains. Their operation costs a fortune in our democratic days, so they play only ten times a year (first and third Sunday each month May through September, between 4 and 5 P.M.). Also a must, if you're lucky enough to be there at the right time, are the magnificent *fêtes de nuit*, with floodlighting and fireworks, usually held at about 9 o'clock on a couple of evenings in July and September.

Starting at the main terrace of the château gardens, the best itinerary for visiting the fountains is as follows: Parterres d'Eau, which are the two large basins in front of the terrace, Fontaines de Diane and du Point-du-Jour, Bassin de Latone, the Salle de Bal, with its quiet grotto, Bassin de Bacchus, Colonnade, the Bassin d'Apollon, with its spectacular chariot rising from the water, Encelade, with its 22-meter (75-ft) cascade of water, Obélisque, Bassin de Flore, Bassin des Dômes, Bains d'Apollon, Bassin des Couronnes, Pyramide, Bain de Diane, the Allée d'Eau, which contains 22 small fountains surrounded by bronze groups of children, Bassin du Dragon, and, finally, Bassin de Neptune, which is the largest and most elaborate fountain in the gardens.

The Grand Trianon is a palace just for play, one of the loveliest in France. Only one story high with a colonnade linking its two sections, this pink marble fantasy was erected in six months by Mansart. Its very size makes it ideal for a guest house, as the roster of its famous visiting list—including Peter the Great and Madame de Pompadour—indicates.

The Petit Trianon, ordered by Louis XV and built by Gabriel, designer of the place de la Concorde in Paris, owes its fame to its last owner, ill-starred Marie-Antoinette. She came to this grey stone mansion nearly every day to flee the noxious atmosphere of the court. Close by she built the village, with dairy and mill where, dressed as shepherdesses, she and her companions lived a make-believe bucolic life and most visitors are more fascinated by the village and its setting.

There are guided tours of the old town of Versailles, which has some beautiful houses and gardens.

The Chevreuse valley and Rambouillet

About halfway between Versailles and Rambouillet is the Chevreuse valley, a small-scale version of everything you'll find in the Ile de France. Visit the château at Dampierre, home of the duc de Luynes; dating from the Middle Ages, it was rebuilt in the 17th century and has a fine library, a family collection of fine paintings, and gardens designed by Le Nôtre. Not far away is the château of Breteuil, which has been owned and lived in by the same family since it was built in the early 17th century. It has many fine pieces of furniture, the most famous of which is the 'Teschen table', a gift from Empress Maria Theresa of Austria and inlaid with jewels and precious stones. The lifesize wax figures dressed in period costume in many of the rooms (including the novelist Marcel Proust, who stayed here) bring the château's past to life in a particularly attractive way. The young marquis de Breteuil and his wife have reacted energetically to the problem of the cost of upkeep (they have won an award for their dynamism) and organize all sorts of concerts, plays and other events to attract visitors. As with many an English stately home, you will probably find them greeting visitors in person.

Nearby are the ruins of the Jansenist abbey of Port-Royal-des-Champs, where the great 17th-century dramatist Jean Racine received much of his education, with a museum close by.

Rambouillet is a small town with three impressive buildings—the town hall, the hotel diagonally across the street where Ernest Hemingway set up headquarters with advance units of the American army on its way to Paris, and the château surrounded by the river-laced forest. The 14th-century château was one of the homes of Catherine de Médicis and Henri IV, and although it is nominally reserved for the president of the Republic, you can visit it between 10 and 5 when he is not in residence. There is a good deal to see, including Marie-Antoinette's boudoir, and the room in which Napoleon spent the last night before he was sent off to his final, lonely exile on St Helena.

At the end of the attractive park is the National Sheepfold, founded by Louis XVI with a flock of 376—now 600—sheep imported from Spain.

Chartres and its cathedral

No European expedition is quite complete without a look at this pure masterpiece of medieval cathedral architecture. For Chartres, one of Christianity's great shrines, choose the A11 motorway or the N10 across the Beauce, one of the most extraordinary plains in France. As you bowl along through its opulent wheatfields, there seems no sign of life—not a house, not a village. But they are there, nevertheless, hidden in the green valleys that rivers have cut into the plateau. Just after Ablis, look across the horizon. You'll see a spire rising up from the oceans of wheat—it is Chartres, still 18 km (11 miles) distant—a most curious, but also most beautiful, visual impression. Actually, the cathedral and town cap a hill separated from the undulating Beauce plain by the budding river Eure.

Upon all who visit it, the cathedral dedicated to Our Lady of Chartres produces a most moving impression of sanctity, very pure and very old. The exquisite Gothic structure we know today is the sixth church built on the same site. After a fire in 1194, princes and paupers, barons and bourgeois gave their money and their labor to build the new cathedral. Ladies of the manor came to help monks and peasants on the scaffolding in a tremendous resurgence of religious faith that followed the Second Crusade.

The old tower on the right was built between 1145 and 1165. This simple and somber masterpiece of Romanesque architecture makes a striking contrast with the Gothic tower, built by Jehan de Beauce to replace the left spire which was destroyed by fire in 1506. Just beneath the disparate towers stands the Royal Portal showing the life and triumph of the Saviour. The stylized figures and expressive faces of the statues are among the masterpieces of French art. The glorious 12th- and 13th-century stained-glass windows hold the visitor spellbound with their jeweled splendor.

Jehan de Beauce designed the altar enclosure, which includes 200 statues depicting the life of Christ and the Virgin. The choir in Renaissance style makes a striking contrast to the Gothic sanctuary. Beneath the nave and the choir there is a vast 11th-century crypt, and a 9th-century crypt beneath the sanctuary. You can also climb the 105 meters (346 ft) to the bell tower.

Behind the cathedral are the bishopric gardens overlooking the peaceful river Eure, and in them stands the 17–18th-century episcopal palace, which now houses the Museum of Fine Arts. The exhibits include a fine collection of tapestries, 14th-century embroidery, medieval enamels and ivories, a great deal of French, Flemish and Italian painting, and a collection of arms and armor.

The district around the church is notable for its Renaissance houses. Visit especially the rue du Bourg running down to the Eure, the rue des Ecuyers and the rue St-Pierre. Walk down to the river for look at the old houses and bridges, and at the restored Romanesque church of St-André.

Maintenon and its château, Dreux, Mantes

On the way from Chartres to Dreux, take the road along the Eure towards Maintenon. The château of Maintenon, with its Renaissance façade, 17th-century wing, and vast gardens designed by Le Nôtre, is flanked on the right by a branch of the Eure, and on the left by a late Gothic chapel. Of unusual interest is the interior, completely furnished as it was in the days of its most famous occupant, Madame de Maintenon, morganatic wife of Louis XIV. Still living there are members of the de Noailles family, descendants of the niece to whom Madame de Maintenon presented the château in 1698.

Drive further along the charming Eure valley via Nogent-le-Roi until you reach the ancient town of Dreux. In its center is a belfry, whose 142 steps will give you a good opportunity to stretch your legs. The cathedral of St-Pierre on the square dates from the 13th-16th centuries and has three beautiful stained-glass windows. Stroll along the Grande-Rue for a glimpse of the unusual wooden houses dating from the 15th and 16th centuries. On a bluff northwest of town, situated in a park surrounded by the fortified walls of a ruined château, is the royal chapel of St-Louis. Built by Louis-Philippe, it contains the tombs of the dukes of Orléans.

Across the forest of Dreux on the Mantes road is the lovely château of Anet, designed by Philibert Delorme for Diane de Poiters, favorite of Henri II, and destroyed by fire during the Revolution. All that remains are the entrance gate, the exquisitely furnished left wing, and the chapel decorated with Jean Goujon's delightful bas-reliefs. It can be visited on Wednesday, Thursday, Saturday, Sunday and holidays from March through October; Sundays and holidays only for the rest of the year, though the funerary chapel is open daily (except Tuesday) all year.

The most interesting *quartier* of Mantes was demolished during World War II, but the cathedral of Notre-Dame is worth a visit. Built at the same time as its famous namesake in Paris, the two are remarkably similar in many details. The nearby château of Rosny was built in 1560 by Sully, the celebrated minister of Henri IV. The interior luxuriously furnished in the style of the period, contains many works of art, paintings, and tapestries.

From Mantes you can visit the 16th-century château of Thoiry, which has interesting manuscripts and letters as well as some fine pieces of furniture. But Thoiry is best known for its zoo and safari park in the grounds, which has over 800 animals, many of them roaming free (including giraffes, elephants, zebras and lions), and a reptile house.

Many sideshows and other forms of enterainment all help to make Thoiry very popular, especially with children.

From Mantes to St-Germain-en-Laye, the most scenic route passes through Meulan, a center for water sports, and Triel, boasting an interesting church, with Gothic nave and Renaissance south porch and choir. Then comes Poissy, whose church of Notre-Dame has two Romanesque steeples and where St Louis was baptized.

The miniature forest at St-Germain-en-Laye once stretched as far as Rambouillet. The Renaissance château in the center of town was built by François I as a royal residence, and Le Nôtre designed the long terrace, but Louis XIV preferred to live at Versailles. Mary Queen of Scots lived there until the age of 16, when she married her childhood playmate, the French dauphin. Later, James II spent the last years of his exile in the château, which today houses an extensive collection of prehistoric remains and other antiquities. After visiting the château, walk along the terrace for a fine view over the Seine to Paris. A new museum devoted to the painter Maurice Denis, a member of the Nabis group, opened here in 1981, in an old priory where he once lived.

At Maisons-Lafitte, to the north, a popular water sports and horse racing center, is the château of Maisons, Mansart's masterpiece. Marking the transition between the art of the Renaissance and the style of Louis XIV, it was once occupied by the banker Lafitte, who added his name to that of the château.

The château of Malmaison

Nearer to Paris, at Rueil, is the château of Malmaison, the country house where General Napoleon Bonaparte and his beloved Josephine lived during the early 1800s. Although Napoleon lived in later years at both Compiègne and Fontainebleau, it was here at Malmaison that he spent his happiest years. There is something enchanting yet absurd about this pretty house with its rose gardens and stone basins, making it the most moving of all the Napoleonic museums. All of the rooms are authentically furnished. Josephine's bedroom on the first floor is exactly what a *riche* young Creole would have liked in 1799, and the tent-draped ceiling must have seemed the last word to this young couple very much on their way up in the world. Fascinating also are the library, games-room, and dining-room with their handsome furnishings, as well as the display of Josephine's gowns and jewels. Here she spent her remaining years following her divorce from Napoleon.

At nearby Nanterre is one of the most modern departments of the University of Paris, as well as one of the Ile de France's most touching memorials: the fortress prison on the Mont Valérien hill, where may young Resistance fighters—even high school boys—were imprisoned and executed by the Germans during the last war. The walls are covered with their inscriptions.

At Marly-le-Roi, the pavilions of the château were designed by Mansart like signs of the zodiac around the Sun King. All that remains today is a pleasant park and the *Machine de Marly,* giant waterwheels that have pumped water from the Seine for the fountains of Versailles since the days of Louis XIV. Neighboring Bougival is one of the Ile de France's loveliest river towns, long a favorite of painters, including Corot. Georges Bizet, composer of the opera *Carmen,* also lived in the vicinity. Not far away, at Louveciennes, is the château of Madame du Barry and, at La Celle-St-Cloud, that of Madame de Pompadour.

II—PARIS SOUTH TO ETAMPES, FONTAINEBLEAU, PROVINS

Leaving Paris by the Porte d'Orléans (N20), be sure to stop off at L'Hay-les-Roses, just outside, where you will see what are probably the finest rose gardens in the world. Continuing on, you come to the magnificent park of Sceaux, designed by Le Nôtre. Nothing is left of the original château, built by Colbert and made famous by the duchesse de Maine, except the outbuildings. The interesting Museum of the Ile de France is housed in a modern château, and between mid-July and early October, France's major chamber music festival is held in the Orangerie designed by Mansart. At nearby Robinson, somewhat self-consciously rustic for the tourist trade, you may dine on an outdoor terrace with a fine view of Sceaux. South of Sceaux is Montlhéry, noted for its 13th—15th-century tower and its automobile racetrack.

Etampes enjoys a particularly attractive location along the banks of the river Chalouette, and has a wealth of lovely old buildings. In the rue Louis Moreau, the church of St-Basile has an interesting Romanesque portal, the rest of the church dating from the 12th through the 16th centuries. Behind St-Basile, the rue de la Cordonnerie leads to the Gothic church of Notre-Dame du Fort, with its 60-meter (200-ft) steeple and its southern façade reminiscent of the Royal Portal at Chartres. Nearby is the house of Diane de Poitiers, favorite of Henri II, who keeps popping up in our wanderings through the Ile de France and the neighboring valley of the Loire. Following the rue du Château Guinette brings you to the oddly shaped Guinette Tower, a royal lookout of the 12th century, a bit farther on to the Gothic church of St-Martin with its curious leaning tower of the Renaissance period.

On the way to Fontainebleau is the village of Barbizon, now a single street lined with restaurants and hotels for the visitors who come in search of the beauty found there by painters since 1830. Corot was the first Barbizon enthusiast, followed by Millet and Daubigny. If you want to get an idea of how Barbizon looked when Corot was there, stroll down the rue de Fleury with its old-fashioned-village look. The houses of Millet and Rousseau have become small museums, so has the Ancienne Auberge du Père Ganne, where the artists used to spend merry evenings.

The forest and château of Fontainebleau

The famous forest of Fontainebleau, covering some 16,200 hectares (40,000 acres), is deliciously and typically French. Wild it is, yet the roads and alleys that wind through it are marked, classified, and entered on Touring Club maps that show every meander, including short cuts. They are named, of course, and so are individual oaks and beeches noted for their age and beauty, among them the Jupiter, the Washington, and the La Fayette. Highway signs point out stag and boar crossings, and all winter long you may meet hunts with hounds and horns. The Fontainebleau rocks are celebrated, and also have names: the best known, Plutus and Gargantua, are used as training schools by the French Alpine Club. The two most interesting drives are the Hauteurs de la Solle, which cross magnificent groves and then drop down to the Seine valley, and the road from Barbizon to the Gorges d'Apremont with the best view of the rocks.

For many the château of Fontainebleau is more redolent of the spirit of France—and more aesthetic, too—than Versailles. Louis VII seems to have been responsible for beginning the castle, but it was the flamboyant François I who transformed the medieval château into a magnificent Renaissance palace, importing Primaticcio and Rosso from Italy to direct the flock of decorators, painters and mosaic and stucco experts in creating a setting suitable for his mistress, the duchesse d'Etampes. Benvenuto Cellini was installed in a studio here while he worked for François, and the 'Mona Lisa' was first brought to France because François bought it for one of his rooms. His successor, Henri II, ornamented the palace with his initial interlaced with D for Diane de Poitiers, his lady love. After his death his queen, Catherine de Médicis, continued the building work.

The gardens were designed by Le Nôtre under the patronage of Louis XIV, who also did some classical remodeling in the building itself. It remained for Napoleon to appreciate its dormant possibilities. He had the estate completed and redecorated and then used it as a prison for Pope Pius VII, who finally abdicated there. It was in the same place, in the grim spring of 1814, that Napoleon Bonaparte called together his Old Guard and bade them farewell before he was escorted to Elba. Then it was known as the Cour du Cheval-Blanc; now it is known as the Cour des Adieux.

Unlike Versailles, Fontainebleau possesses the secret of intimacy, perhaps because each successive generation of kings added a wing of his own. The guided tour will lead you through the Empire-period Red Room, scene of Napoleon's abdication, then the Council Room dating from Charles IX and Louis XV, the Throne Room, and the Queen's Bedroom—beautifully redecorated for Marie-Antoinette. In the royal apartments you'll see the famous Gobelin tapestries and a magnificent mantelpiece by Primaticcio. The Oval Court, which you reach after descending the King's Staircase, occupies the site of the original *château-fort*. During great stag hunts, this courtyard was the setting for the *curée,* a ceremony in which the dead stag, still warm and steaming from the chase, was thrown to the ravenous dogs to the accompaniment of ancient calls played on hunting horns.

When the classic tour is ended, ask to be shown the small apartments of Napoleon and Josephine and the Galerie des Cerfs. In the latter, Queen Christina of Sweden, a guest at the château, ordered the assassination of her favorite courtier Monaldeschi. You can see his coat-of-mail hanging there.

Nearby, on the shores of the Loing, nestles the charming village of Moret, now a favorite weekend haunt of Parisians, who convert old mills in the area. Moret was immortalized by the painter Sisley, who lived there for 20 years. The local people stage a magnificent show on summer evenings, a mixture of *son et lumière* and pageant, with spectacular costumes and special effects, illustrating the history of their ancient town.

Provins, city of roses

From Moret continue to Montereau, then through Montigny to Provins. This is one of the most interesting cities in the whole Paris area. It grew up on the site of a Roman camp, and under the influence of the counts of Champagne became the economic capital of that province. Famous for rose-growing ever since the time of the Crusades, Provins was the third most important city in France, after Paris and Rouen, during the Middle Ages. In the 13th century the red rose of Provins was introduced into the arms of the House of Lancaster by a member of that house who was by marriage a count of Provins.

You will want to visit Caesar's Tower, a magnificent keep of the early 12th century, the Grange aux Dîmes, or Tithe Barn, housing an interesting collection of precious stones, and the church of St-Quiriace. In the lower city, walk along the ramparts, and stop for a look at the 12th-century abbey church of St-Ayoul.

Not far from Provins is Rampillon, whose remarkable 13th-century church is well worth a visit. On its portal are superbly carved figures depicting Christ and the Apostles, the labors of the 12 months, and the Last Judgement. From Provins, take the N19 and N36 for Vaux-le-Vicomte.

Fouquet's magnificent château

Vaux-le-Vicomte is one of the great monuments of 17th-century architecture, built by Le Vau for the famous Fouquet. When the château was finished, its owner decided to give a party in honor of his king, young Louis XIV. There were 80 tables, 30 buffets, 6,400 pieces of solid gold plate, a dinner by Vatel, and a new play by Molière set in a garden rustling with 1,200 fountains and cascades. The king, wild with rage at being outshone, banished Fouquet and confiscated his wealth.

The approach to the château is rather grim—two huge stone gods stand guard over the gate, and the façade set between two outbuildings is stern and imposing. The gardens, designed by Le Nôtre, forecast his brilliant achievements at Versailles, with its Grand Canal, its terraces, cascades and alleys of carefully trimmed trees.

A number of delights reward the traveler returning from this southern tour. First stop is the town of Brie-Comte-Robert, with its Gothic church and arcades, the latter in the rue des Halles. Next, the 16th-century château of Gros-Bois, which belonged at one time to the count of Provence, the future Louis XVIII. Now a state museum, Gros-Bois contains a fine collection of furniture and works of art of the First Empire.

Nearby, at Condé-en-Brie, is a 17th-18th-century château that once belonged to the prince de Condé. Sumptuously furnished, with many of the pieces originally designed for the Condés, it now belongs to the Sade family, who possess a great many unpublished manuscripts written by the present marquis's great-great-great-grandfather, the original marquis de Sade.

A short detour to the right brings us to the charming château of Ormesson, encircled by a mirror of water and beautiful grounds designed by—you guessed it—Le Nôtre. It is supposed to have been built by Henri IV for Gabrielle de Santény. Then two delightful spots—Chennevières-sur-Marne, with a fine panoramic view of the countryside, and St-Maur, delightfully situated on the isthmus of a peninsula formed by the sinuously twisting Marne. Near the church of St-

ILE DE FRANCE

Agnes-de-Gravelle, route D123 joins the autoroute that follows the right bank of the Marne and returns you to Paris in jig-time.

III—PARIS EAST ALONG THE MARNE

This tour combines famous battlefields and small châteaux. The battlefields date from Caesar to 1914, the châteaux from the 14th to the 18th century. The journey begins with the Ourcq valley, through groves of willows and poplar trees to the site of the first of the Marne battles that saved France in 1914. The most dramatic moment came on September 7 after Joffre had explained to his troops: 'Advance, and if you cannot, hold your positions and be killed'. To support the British entrenched in the Grand Morin valley, the French brought 6,000 troops from Paris in 600 Paris taxis, each of which made the perilous trip twice.

At Meaux, about 43 km (27 miles) from Paris on the N3, an interesting 13th-century cathedral makes the trip worth while if only to climb its 60 meter (200-ft) tower for the wonderful view of the valley. Inside is the tomb of its illustrious bishop and confessor to Louis XIV, Bossuet, the 'Eagle of Meaux'.

Château-Thierry, virtually in the Champagne area (see chapter on Champagne), has an ancient castle built by Charles Martel in 720. The town has always been the cynosure of invaders' eyes. American troops covered themselves with glory there on Hill 204 and at Belleau Wood in World War I. For the French, Château-Thierry is chiefly celebrated as the birthplace of witty fabulist La Fontaine, whose 16th-century mansion, appropriately located at 12 rue Jean de la Fontaine, is open to visitors.

Three notable châteaux

From Château-Thierry, drive back to Jouarre and south to Coulommiers, then follow N34 towards Paris, branching off at Lagny for a brief visit to the first two châteaux. (Another interesting château near by, Jossigny, is undergoing restoration work and will not reopen to the public in the foreseeable future.) The first is Guermantes, with park and charming 17th-century interior, which was opened to the public in 1954. Its name so appealed to Marcel Proust that he borrowed it for his great multi-volume novel. The second is Champs, which may be used by the French president or premier as a summer residence. Built in the early 18th century, its most celebrated tenant was the marquise de Pompadour. Champs is a model of comfortâble living in the old style. Each suite was equipped with its own dressing-room and bath, a novelty for the times, as was the basement kitchen, moved there from a separate hut where it was usually placed. The garden with its perspectives and ponds is unusually attractive; so are Madame de Pompadour's bedroom and the sitting-room decorated with *chinoiseries* by Huët.

At the gates of Paris are the woods and château of Vincennes. The château, a magnificent edifice of the 14th and 17th centuries, occupies the site of a hunting lodge maintained by the kings of France since the 12th century. Dominating the entrance is a tower 51 meters (168 ft) high; even taller is the *donjon*, or keep, splendidly preserved, the most beautiful in France. A visit to the interior of this palace-fortress is well worthwhile. It was used as a military stronghold as late as 1814, when one of Napoleon's generals, the doughty one-legged Daumesnil, refused to surrender it to the Coalition armies.

IV—PARIS NORTHEAST TO SENLIS AND COMPIÈGNE

By the direct N17 route from Paris, Senlis is only 45 km (28 miles) away (or you can take the A1 motorway). A detour of about 12 km (8 miles), however, allows us to visit Mortefontaine, Ermenonville, and Chaâlis. Just outside Mortefontaine is the parc de Valliéra, which inspired many of Corot's paintings, notably *Souvenir de Mortefontaine*, and may have been the inspiration as well for Watteau's *Embarquement pour Cythère*. A short distance beyond are the 18th-century château and park of Ermenonville. The latter, designed by the marquis de Girardin, was one of the first examples in France of the informal country garden *à l'anglaise*. To help nature along, fake ruins were added and rocks were inscribed with philosophical quotations. Jean-Jacques Rousseau, who died while a guest of the marquis de Girardin at Ermenonville, was formerly buried on the tiny Island of Poplars. The old grave is still marked, although his remains were later moved to the Panthéon in Paris. In town there is an interesting 16th-century church with 13th-century choir.

The 18th-century abbey at Chaâlis—the work of Jean Aubert, architect of the stables at Chantilly and the Rodin Museum in Paris—is notable for the simplicity of its design and perfect proportions. Beyond the abbey gate stretches the strange *Mer de Sable*, a 'Sea of Sand' whose glistening whiteness is in startling contrast with the lush of green

ILE DE FRANCE

surrounding it. Here, children will enjoy a visit to the amusement park, where camels carry them across the dunes and Indians attack the mail train, and to Jean Richard's small zoo, complete with US-trained dolphins. Meanwhile, adults can take in the cultural sights.

Across the twin forest of Chantilly and Ermenonville lies one of the brightest stars in the Ile de France firmament, Senlis. Surrounded by a splendid beech forest, Senlis has a Gothic cathedral older than those of Paris and Chartres. Nearby stand the remains of the royal palace that housed French rulers from the time of Charlemagne to Henri IV. In an 18th-century addition to this château you will find a hunting museum. Fragments of the Gallo-Roman walls of Senlis can still be seen. West of the town are remains of a Roman arena that once seated over 10,000 spectators. We strongly recommend a conducted tour of the old town.

Continuing on the same road, you come to the stunning castle of Pierrefonds perched on a promontory, with fairytale towers soaring to the sky. The original edifice was dismantled by Louis XIII, so the present château is merely a 19th-century facsimile. As painstakingly restored by Viollet-le-Duc, however, it gives a wonderful impression of a great 17th-century fortress. Quite near Pierrefonds is one of the most fascinating Roman remains in France, an army camp located on the old main road from Senlis to Soissons. The excavations have never been completed and you have the pleasant impression of discovering the camp for yourself. Most striking is an outdoor theater, or coliseum, holding 4,000 spectators. Nearby are the baths and a temple dedicated to Apollo. One km (½ mile) away are the ruins of a small 12th-century Romanesque church rebuilt by the Franks upon Roman foundations. The area has been inhabited since the Stone Age and bears many traces of Druid sacrifices.

Historic Compiègne

A beautiful drive along Route Eugénie through the majestic oak and beech forest of Compiègne leads to the town of Compiègne, whose history, dating from Charlemagne, has offered moments of great drama. Joan of Arc was imprisoned here before she went to the stake, and Corsica was ceded to France in a treaty that was signed here. Louis XV built the château, impressive but rather lifeless, which ranks after Versailles and Fontainebleau as one of the great palaces of the French monarchs. Napoleon married Marie-Louise here. Eugénie and her Bonaparte husband made it the scene of some of their greatest weekend parties. The château houses one of the richest collections of First Empire furniture and a series of paintings illustrating 'The History of

Don Quixote'. In another building in the grounds is the Vehicle Museum, with carriages, bicycles and automobiles of all periods.

The beautiful 16th-century Hôtel de Ville was built by Louis XII; in its bell-tower the quarter-hours are noted by carved wooden figures moving into view and then disappearing unostentatiously. It houses two museums that specialists will find exciting: the Musée Vivenel displaying a fine collection of Greek vases, and the Musée de la Figurine Historique, with 85,000 lead, tin and wooden soldiers from Vercingetorix to de Gaulle. Visit also the 13th-century churches of St-Jacques and St-Antoine, the abbey built by Charles the Bald, and the 12th-century tower from which Joan of Arc is alleged to have set out before her capture by the Burgundian and English armies.

A short distance from Compiègne, near Rethondes, is the Clairière de l'Armistice, where a railway coach was run out on a spur line specially for the occasion. In it the Armistice of 1918, marking the Allied victory, and the French surrender of 1940 were signed—the latter accompanied by Hitler's jig for joy.

In 1978 a moving ceremony commemorating the 60th anniversary of the Armistice was performed here by the French President and by representatives of the armies of all the Allied nations. There are two other interesting visits to be made in the vicinity. One is to the Museum of Franco-American Cooperation at Blérancourt. Housed in two wings of the château, the collections tell the story of Franco-American friendship from the days of the American Revolution to the present. At Chiry-Ourscamp are the remains of a Cistercian abbey, begun during the 12th century. Most remarkable is the infirmary, dating from the middle of the 13th century, whose interior is one of the finest examples of Cistercian architecture.

Noyon and Soissons

Farther northeast along the river Oise is Noyon, an ancient village which, in spite of damage in both world wars, still proudly displays treasures of the Middle Ages. The cathedral was built in the late 12th century and the early part of the 13th. Its transitional character, combining the simplicity and strength of the Romanesque with the grace and daring of the Gothic, makes the cathedral one of the most interesting in this region. South of it is the war memorial rotunda, and the 16th—17th-century bishopric contains the municipal museum. The Hôtel de Ville, built during the same era, was largely destroyed in World War I, but it, as well as the birthplace of John Calvin, has been restored.

Its geographical location has made Soissons, east from Compiègne, a predestined battleground. Both the town and its handsome 13th-century cathedral of St-Gervais suffered heavy damage during World War I. The latter lost one of its towers and its nave was split in two, but has since been restored. At the end of the choir may be seen Rubens' 'Adoration of the Shepherds'. Also worth seeing are the 13th-century church of St-Léger, the beautiful façade of the abbey of St-Jean-des-Vignes, the abbey of St-Médard and its 9th-century crypt, and in the rue de la Bannière, the memorial to the British soldiers who fell during the 1914—18 battles of the Aisne and the Marne.

On the road from Villers-Cotterêts

A short detour after leaving Soissons permits a visit to the château of Villers-Cotterêts, begun by François I, decorated by Philibert Delorme, and enlarged to include a park by Le Nôtre. The vast forest of Villers-Cotterêts which you cross on your return to Paris consists of over 12,000 hectares (30,000 acres). It was a royal hunting ground until 1789, and stag hunts are still held there. In the town you may be interested in looking up 54 rue d'Alexandre Dumas, père, where the elder Dumas was born. There is also a museum dedicated to father and son Dumas. At La Ferté Milon is the birthplace of Jean Racine, the great classic dramatist. From Villers-Cotterêts, the N2 brings you back to Paris.

V—PARIS NORTH TO ENGHIEN, ECOUEN, BEAUVAIS AND CHANTILLY

The exits and entrances to most modern cities are ugly, and Paris is no exception. St-Denis is an industrial suburb 6 km (4 miles) distant, along the northerly loop of the Seine. Driving towards it, you see looming up on the right the basilica of St-Denis. The first sanctuary was built in 475, to be replaced in 630 and again in 775, but the present basilica was begun in 1140. Here French monarchs were crowned and here also, since Dagobert in 638, they were buried. Inside are the celebrated *gisants*, tombs bearing carved images of such illustrious personages as François I, Catherine de Médicis and Henri II. St-Denis also has an interesting and attractively arranged art and history museum in a newly restored Carmelite monastery.

Beyond St-Denis is Enghien, noted not only for its casino and racetrack, but for a small lake and thermal springs with sulphurous water. A short detour brings us to Montmorency, a 12th-century town 13 km

(8 miles) from Paris. This was the family seat of the Condés, of which Louis II was a member. There is an ancient and enormous forest of about 3,250 hectares (8,000 acres) and the town and its surroundings were used by Jean-Jacques Rousseau as background for some of his best writing. The famous site of the mill at Sannois, 152 meters (500 ft) above the town, affords a magnificent panorama of Paris and the Seine valley.

North of both St-Denis and Enghien is the beautiful 16th-century château of Ecouen, which has recently been transformed into the very interesting new Museum of the Renaissance.

To the northwest of Pontoise, and some 32 km (20 miles) from Paris, is L'Isle-Adam, a small village situated on the Oise at the edge of a fine forest. This is a wonderful weekend spot, with numerous overnight hostelries and good restaurants, all near a popular river beach. You can see the remains of the Bourbon castle and the Renaissance church of St-Martin. However, before reaching L'Isle-Adam, we shall pass through a number of picturesque little towns, such as Auvers-sur-Oise and Valmondois, favorite haunts of La Fontaine, Corot and Van Gogh, among others, before reaching Beaumont, where the road leads on to Beauvais.

Beauvais' unfinished cathedral

Beauvais is crowned with the tallest, as well as one of the most beautiful, cathedrals in Christendom. The cathedral of St-Pierre, still unfinished, is well worth a trip from Paris, even though the town that surrounds it was ravaged by the bombings of June 1940.

After the usual early history of destruction by fire, the Beauvais religious authorities decided in 1225 to build the largest and highest cathedral in the world. Their ambitions were inflated—the height of the vaulted roof (43 meters/141 feet) is higher than that of Notre Dame in Paris. From then on, Beauvais' history was an unfortunate sequence of faith, miscalculation and collapse. Forty years of labor were required to prevent the choir from falling down. Then, after finishing the transept, the bold Beauvasians unwisely topped it with a steeple. Inadequately buttressed, it crashed to the ground in 1573, and with it the last hope that the cathedral could ever be completed.

Even in its present state, the cathedral is fascinating. The pillars that swoop to the sky give a marvelous impression of lightness and are a thrilling sight, as are the Beauvais and Flemish tapestries and the stained-glass windows dating from the 13th, 14th and 16th centuries. The cathedral also contains a famous astronomical clock.

Chantilly

South from Beauvais and through Clermont is Chantilly, celebrated for cream, lace, horseraces, a forest and a château. Thunder and lightning, if you can arrange them, are the best setting for this supremely romantic Renaissance château built on two islands in the midst of a small lake. Chantilly's real story begins in the 16th century with the connétable de Montmorency, who held power under six successive kings. Even Catherine de Médicis liked him—he found the cure for her sterility. To kill him off at the age of 75 in the battle of St-Denis, the opposing Protestants found that it required five sword thrusts, two pike blows, and a cannonball in the spine.

As you come up to the château gate, gaze over to the left at the 18th-century stone stables built by the duc de Condé to house 240 horses and 420 dogs for stag and boar hunts in the nearby forest. The stables, with their indoor and outdoor paddocks, are still used today, and the nearby parc de Sylvie is the site of a rather spectacular cross-country competition in the early fall. In the park, designed by Le Nôtre, are the *maison de Sylvie* and the *hameau,* Chantilly's version of a Marie-Antoinette village for play. The nearby racetrack is one of the prettiest in Europe.

The château itself actually consists of two edifices, the 16th-century Petit-Château and the 19th-century Grand-Château, harmoniously joined together and mirrored in the ponds that surround it. Housed inside is the Musée Condé containing magnificent paintings and tapestries hung in paneled halls, as well as one of France's great 15th-century illuminated manuscripts, the *Très Riches Heures du Duc de Berry,* depicting the 12 months of the year. The collection of miniatures by the first great French painter, Fouquet, is outstanding, and it alone is worth the trip from Paris. In the Jewel Room is the enormous pink diamond known as *Le Grand Condé.* When Chantilly was bequeathed to the French Academy by the duc d'Aumale, one of the conditions was that the masterpieces were never to be loaned to any exhibition.

Nearby is one of the Ile de France's architectural treasures, the Gothic abbey of Royaumont. The dormitory, chapter hall and library are now occupied by the International Center of Culture. Concerts are held here in the summer months.

PRACTICAL INFORMATION

WHEN TO GO. Weather should certainly not be the determining factor in making your trip through the Ile de France—it rains on and off nearly every day. But gray-blue cathedrals and castles and shimmering green countryside look their very best in a misty setting and it's never very cold even in the depths of Jan. and Feb. (but bear in mind that many of the region's châteaux are closed in the winter months). If you can, make your trips on weekdays. On Sun., all Paris takes to the road for a mid-day meal in the country. The *Festival de l'Ile de France* runs from early May to mid-Nov, with a gap in Aug and the first half of Sept. Concerts are held in the châteaux, abbeys and the town halls, including Royaumont Abbey, and the Châteaux of Sceaux, Vincennes, Ecouen and Fontainebleau.

April Blessing of the horses at the tiny 12th-cent. Lamorlaye church the next to last Sat. **May** Archery festivals at Chambly, Creil and Mareuil-sur-Oise; Lily of the Valley festivals in Compiègne and Rambouillet; ten-day festival of French music in the Parc de Sceaux; festival of opera and theater at Versailles; playing of the great fountains at set intervals in Versailles (see below); major religious pilgrimage to Chartres at the end of the month (Paris students make the 96-km/60-mile journey on foot), with further pilgrimages on Aug. 15 and Dec. 8. **June** Pardon of Anne de Bretagne at Montfort l'Amaury early in the month; elegant flat horse races (*Prix du Jockey* and *Prix de Diane*), at Chantilly; Boatmen's Pardon at Conflans-St-Honorine (last Sat.); Festival at St-Germain-en-Laye (concerts and exhibitions); in **July** and **August** St-Germain-en-Laye has its huge *Fête des Loges* in the woods. **September** Bean Fair at Arpajon (mid-month); Bee Fair in Houdan (following week).

WHAT TO SEE. First, naturally, is Versailles with its fabulous palace, its restored 18th-cent. opera house, the two Trianons, and the gardens and fountains. The grounds are open daily, dawn to dusk; the château is closed Mon.; for details of opening times of the various buildings see page 130. The fountains play at 4 and 5 P.M. on the first and third Sun. of the month, May through Sept.; floodlit and fireworks displays occasionally, for which reserved tickets are necessary (known as *Fêtes de Nuit*). Inquire at theater agents or Paris tourist office.

Then the cathedral at Chartres with its spires pointing above golden fields of wheat; Fontainebleau, the forest and castle; Beauvais cathedral; the cathedral and champagne cellars at Rheims, the châteaux of Vaux-le-Vicomte, Breteuil, Condé-en-Brie and Thoiry, still lived in by their owners. Also the castles at Chantilly and Compiègne and the forests that surround them; the heavily re-

ILE DE FRANCE

stored but interesting Royaumont abbey; the medieval town of Senlis; the Renaissance Museum at Ecouen. Children will enjoy a visit to the Jean Richard zoo and amusement park at the Mer de Sable, Ermenonville. Versailles's Summer University has good classes and lectures plus educational and cultural excursions.

HOW TO GET ABOUT. The average tourist takes in the Ile de France on one or several day-long trips out of Paris; there are excellent guided tours in luxury buses to Versailles, Chantilly, Compiègne, Fontainebleau and Chartres. French-speaking visitors will enjoy excursions to lesser-known châteaux and churches, run by the *Régie Autonome des Transports Parisiens* (tickets at pl. de la Madeleine or 53 quai des Grands Augustins, Paris). A company called *Paris et son Histoire* also organizes guided coach tours with experts, often enabling you to visit places not normally open to the public. Other companies running tours are: *Cityrama:* Chantilly, Senlis, Saint-Denis, Thoiry; *Europe Autocar:* day trip by coach to Chartres; Chantilly, Compiègne and Pierrefonds; Thoiry; Versailles and Port-Royal, Malmaison; Vaux-le-Vicomte and Moret-sur-Loing (including *son-et-lumière*). On Nov 11 (Armistice Day), *Europe Autocar* has a day coach excursion to Compiègne for the moving ceremony in the *Clairière de l'Armistice*.

By train. The fastest way to reach four of the Ile de France's sights, Versailles, Fontainebleau, Chantilly and Chartres, is by train. Services to Versailles operate from Gare des Invalides, Gare de Lyon and Montparnasse. The most frequent and the fastest (15 mins) are from the last named. The RER (express metro) now goes out to Versailles, too (line C). For Fontainebleau use the Gare de Lyon, several services daily taking 35 mins. For Chartres use the Gare Montparnasse, about ten services daily in each direction taking around 50–55 mins for the 88-km (55-mile) journey. There are regular trains from the Gare du Nord to Chantilly and Beauvais.

By river boat. One of the pleasant ways to see the Ile de France is to float along the Marne and Yonne rivers, taking in the vineyards and cellars of Champagne, the châteaux and cathedrals en route.

By bike. Many RER stations, such as St-Germain-en-Laye and St-Rémy, now hire out bikes on weekends.

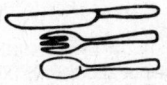

REGIONAL FOOD AND DRINK. Ile de France cuisine has no particular style of its own. It resembles Paris cooking, which is compounded of the best regional specialties. During the hunting season there are all kinds of game dishes. *Crêpes suzettes* are an Ile de France specialty. These paper-thin pancakes are usually flavored with jam, rum, kirsch or Grand Marnier.

THE FACE OF FRANCE

HOTELS AND RESTAURANTS. Accommodations in the Ile de France are rarely outstanding—perhaps because thousands of Paris families have purchased little farms, peasant houses, manors and châteaux in the area and rarely spend their weekends in inns. With prices in Paris getting higher all the time and parking problems increasing, more and more foreign tourists are preferring to stay outside the city. Malmaison, St-Germain-en-Laye, St-Rémy-les-Chevreuse are now easily reached by the express Métro (RER), so it's quite possible to enjoy the peace (and the lower prices) away from Paris.

Many of the hotels listed have excellent restaurants; some restaurants have a few rooms, which they will let to patrons who dine there. All distances given are from Paris. Restaurants and hotels are designated *E, M* or *I*, for expensive, moderate, inexpensive. Remember that hotels usually close for a period during the year, usually around Nov. when there is little business. Restaurants close at least one day a week, often Mon. or Tues.

BARBIZON. 58 km (36 miles). *Bas-Bréau*, with attractive gardens, excellent *nouvelle cuisine*, tennis courts (E). *Alouettes* (I). *Clé d'Or* (I).
Restaurants. *Grand Veneur* (E), handsome, on main road to Fontainebleau (avoid on Sun.). *Charmettes* (M), garden, has some rooms. *Relais*, pleasant, unpretentious (M).

BEAUVAIS. 75 km (47 miles). Best hotel is *Chenal* (E), no restaurant. *Mercure* (M), on road to Paris, has pool and restaurant.
Restaurants. *Côtelette* (M), good place for regional specialties. *Crémaillière* (I).

BLÉRANCOURT. 104 km (65 miles). *Hostellerie le Griffon* inn (I), overlooking château grounds. Good restaurant (M).

BOUGIVAL. 18 km (11 miles). *Forest Hill* (E), attractive, modern, with openair pool set in inner patio, buffet-type restaurant (M), pleasantly sited next to Bougival park and overlooking river.
Restaurants. *Le Coq Hardi* (E), magnificent gardens, famous, rather overpriced. *Camélia* (E), rated among France's best, *nouvelle cuisine*.

BRIE-COMTE-ROBERT. 29 km (18 miles). **Restaurant.** *A la Grâce de Dieu* (I), charming, good cuisine.

CHANTILLY. 48 km (30 miles). *Campanile* (M), peaceful. In **Lys Chantilly**, a lovely woody area, try the *Hostellerie du Lys* (M), a peaceful and comfortable inn without restaurant. The best rooms are to be found in the new wing.
Restaurants. *Tipperary*, pleasant, if unimaginative, and *Relais Condé*, in an old chapel, both (M). The modest *Petit Vatel* (I) is good for unpretentious meals, carefully cooked, at budget prices; always crowded, with a sprinkling of jockeys

ILE DE FRANCE

and their families on racing days. *Relais du Coq Chantant* (M) is on the road to Creil; now serves *nouvelle cuisine*.

CHARTRES. 88 km (55 miles). *Grand Monarque* (M), very comfortable, good classical cuisine. *Jehan de Beauce* (I), convenient for station.
   Restaurants. Well known *Henri IV* (E), with both classical and 'new' dishes. *Buisson Ardent* (M), good value *nouvelle cuisine* in attractive old building. *Vieille Maison* (E), another attractive building, new cuisine.

CHAUMONTEL. 30 km (19 miles). The Prince de Condé's hunting lodge is now the *Château-Hotel de Chaumontel*, peaceful, lovely gardens; expensive (closed mid-July to end Aug. and Christmas).

CHENNEVIÈRES-SUR-MARNE. 18 km (11 miles). **Restaurant.** *Ecu de France* (M), good, pleasantly situated on the Marne.

CHEVREUSE. Restaurant. *Auberge du Mouline* (M), attractive, good service. *Puszta* (M), well-known Hungarian restaurant. Lots of atmosphere.

COIGNIÈRES. 40 km (25 miles). **Restaurants.** *Capucin Gourmand* (E), excellent and a charming setting. *Auberge d'Angèle* (E), very attractive, excellent *nouvelle cuisine*.

COMPIÈGNE. 82 km (51 miles). Best hotels are *Résidence de la Fôret* (M), slightly old fashioned but lots of charm. *Harlay* (M), no restaurant.
   Restaurant. *Royal-Lieu* (M), nice atmosphere; also has some rooms. At **St-Jean-aux-Bois,** 11 km (6 miles) away, *Bonne Idée* (M), pleasant inn with excellent, mostly classical cuisine. Also has some delightful rooms.

CONFLANS-STE-HONORINE. Restaurant. *Au Bord de l'Eau*, charmingly situated, as its name suggests, at the water's edge, serves straightforward grills and good fish dishes (M). Dinner on Fri. and Sat. only, but this is a good spot for lunch.

COYE-LA-FORÊT. 38 km (24 miles). **Restaurant.** *Etangs* (M), classical French cuisine. No longer has rooms.

CRÉPY-EN-VALOIS. 70 km (43 miles). *Trois Pigeons* (I), small, with pleasant restaurant.

DAMPIERRE. 37 km (23 miles). *Auberge du Château* (I), 15 rooms, restaurant (M). **Restaurant.** *Au Tout Va Bien* (I), cheerful, unpretentious, family-type.

DREUX. 82 km (51 miles). 4.5 km away at Montreuil, *Gué des Grues*, good, 5 lovely rooms overlooking fields and river (M). Good *nouvelle cuisine* (M). *Auberge Normande* (M), also good, classical cuisine.

ENGHIEN-LES-BAINS. 16 km (10 miles). *Bains* (E), good restaurant.
Restaurants. *Duc d'Enghien* (E), in casino and attached to *Bains* hotel, now serves *nouvelle cuisine*. *Carpe d'Or* (M).

ERMENONVILLE. 43 km (27 miles). *Croix d'Or*, inexpensive, modest.

ESBLY. 43 km (27 miles). **Restaurant.** *Vallée de la Marne* (M), closed in Aug. Outdoor meals in fine weather.

ÉTAMPES. 51 km (32 miles). **Inn** *Auberge de Courpain* (M), 9 km (5½ miles) away at **Fontaine-la-Rivière**, very peaceful and friendly, big garden, pleasant restaurant.
Restaurant. *Grand Monarque* (I), pleasant surroundings. Good value.

FERTÉ-SOUS-JOUARRE. 64 km (40 miles). **Restaurants.** *Auberge de Condé* (E), good classical, rich cuisine; *Relais*, annexe to the above (I), good.

FONTAINEBLEAU. 66 km (41 miles). *Aigle Noir* (E), very grand; excellent restaurant. *Toulouse* (M), attractive, good service, no restaurant. At nearby **Ury**, modern *Novotel* (M), with pool and tennis courts. At **Recloses**, *Casa del Sol* (I), peaceful Relais du Silence, reader-recommended.
Restaurants. *Filet de Sole* (I), *Chez Arrighi* (M), good. *Dauphin* (M), reader-recommended.

L'ISLE-ADAM. 38 km (24 miles). *Cabouillet* (M), attractive, beside river, goodish restaurant.
Restaurants. *Métairie* (M), good; *Auberge de Jouy* (M), just outside town, also good. *Relais Fleuri* (I).

LOUVECIENNES. 24 km (15 miles). **Restaurant.** *Auberge les Tilleuls* (M), with delightful leafy terrace overlooking the Seine, on the N13 road.

MAISONS-LAFFITTE. **Restaurant.** *Vieille Fontaine* (E), famous for *nouvelle cuisine*.

MALMAISON. 14 km (9 miles). **Restaurants.** *El Chiquito*, pretty garden, specialty is fish (E); *Relais de St-Cucufa* (M), attractive; some regional dishes.

MARLY-LE-ROI. 24 km (15 miles). *Roy Soleil* (E). New and classical cuisine served in what was once Louis XIV's laundry; lovely garden for summer meals.

ILE DE FRANCE

MASSY-PALAISEAU. (near Orly airport) *Novotel,* moderate, 151 rooms, pool, grill room, carpark; makes a good base for exploring the region combined with visits to Paris (easily reached by RER too).

MEAUX. 43 km (27 miles). *Sirène* (M), charming 18th-cent. mansion, excellent food.
Restaurants. *Relais St-Etienne* (M), good classical dishes. *Marée Bleue* (M), good, fresh fish.

LES MESNULS. Restaurant. *Toque Blanche,* inventive cuisine (M). Closed Aug.

MEULAN. 24 km (15 miles). **Restaurant.** *Grande Pinte* (M), overlooking Seine. Also has 10 rooms.

MILLY-LA-FORÊT. *Lion d'Or* (M). **Restaurant.** *Moustier* (M), magnificent 12th-century setting; inventive cuisine.

MORET-SUR-LOING. 69 km (43 miles). **Restaurant.** *Auberge Terrasse* (M), closed mid-Dec through mid-March. Also has some (I) rooms.

OZOIR-LA-FERRIÈRE. 48 km (30 miles). **Restaurant.** *Le Relais* (I), good, closed most of Aug.

POISSY. 29 km (18 miles). **Restaurants.** *Esturgeon* (E), excellent classical cuisine; terrace overlooking the Seine. Closed Aug. *Bon Vivant* (M), again overlooking river.

PONTCHARTRAIN. 40 km (25 miles). **Restaurants.** *Aubergade* (E), beautiful garden, pleasant interior with fireplace. *Chez Sam* (M), whose food is excellent. A couple of miles south is *Auberge de la Dauberie,* delightful thatched building in pretty garden (E). Also has 9 rooms.

PROVINS. 85 km (53 miles). *Fontaine* (I); plus good restaurant with mostly Burgundian cuisine.
Restaurants. *Chalet* (M), *Berri,* good, rather rich cuisine (I). *Vieux Remparts* (I), attractive, good value.

RAMBOUILLET. 51 km (32 miles). *Saint-Charles,* moderate, no restaurant.

ST-GERMAIN-EN-LAYE. 22 km (14 miles). *Forestière* (E), attractive, quiet, good restaurant (see below). *Cèdre,* moderate, quiet, 30 rooms. **Restaurants.** *Cazaudehore* (E), in the Forestière hotel, in the midst of the St-Germain woods; rustic interior, lovely garden. *Pavillon Henri IV* (E), reopened 1982 on edge of

Grande Terrasse; very grand and chic. *Petite Auberge,* charming, reservation essential (M).

ST-RÉMY-LES-CHÈVREUSE. 29 km (18 miles). **Restaurant.** *La Cressonnière,* good 'new' cuisine (E). Very pleasant location, and many interesting walks in the vicinity.

SAMOIS-SUR-SEINE. 58 km (36 miles). **Restaurant.** *Auberge de L'Ile Chez Fernand* (I), good home cooking, family atmosphere.

SENLIS. 42 km (26 miles). *Saint-Eloi,* a typical French provincial hotel, no restaurant, moderate.
 Restaurants. *Rotisserie Formanoir,* in converted 16th-century monastery, is a delightful place to eat (M); the unpretentions little *Chatel,* on same street, is amazing value (I).

SENLISSE. Restaurant. *L'Auberge du Pont Hardi,* in peaceful little village near Dampierre, has good, rather rich cuisine and an excellent wine list (E). Also has a few attractive rooms (M).

SOISSONS. 96 km (60 miles). **Restaurant.** *Grenadin* (I), closed Aug.

THOIRY. 51 km (32 miles). **Restaurant.** *Chez Irma* (I) at **Goussonville,** nearby, pleasant. The original Irma is now, sadly, dead, but her restaurant is as welcoming as ever.

VARENNES-JARCY. 32 km (20 miles). **Restaurants.** *Hostellerie de Varennes* (M), a converted château set in a large garden. *Moulin de Jarcy,* charming old mill, fishing, adequate restaurant, with rooms (I).

VERSAILLES. 22 km (14 miles). *Trianon Palace,* deluxe, on the edge of Trianon Park; first-class service, good food. Compares with any of the Paris luxury hotels. *Bellevue* (M), *Versailles* (M); both close to Château. *St-Louis* (I), modest, charming, in historic St-Louis area.
 At nearby **St-Cyr-l'Ecole,** far from the madding crowd, is the restful, modern little *Aérotel* (M), no restaurant.
 Restaurants. *Les Trois Marches* (E), 3 rue Colbert, in a delightful 18th-cent. mansion opposite the château; fine *nouvelle cuisine. Boule d'Or* (M), 25 rue du Maréchal-Foch; boasts of being the oldest inn in Versailles (not surprising when it dates from 1696). A new touch here is the decision to revive dishes cooked by the all-time greats of French cuisine, ranging from the 14th to the 18th

century. *Potager du Roy* (I), 1 rue du Maréchal-Joffre, newish cuisine at reasonable prices.

VILLE D'AVRAY. 16 km (10 miles). **Restaurant.** *Père Auto* (M), delightful setting, good home-style cooking. Closed in August.

BRITTANY

Land's end with Celtic folklore

by
JOHN ARDAGH

Except perhaps for Alsace, no other mainland province is more different from the rest of France, or at any rate feels itself to be more different, than Brittany. This is because, alone among Frenchmen, the Bretons are of Celtic origin. Their land was colonised in the 5th and 6th centuries by Celtic emigrés from Britain, and to this day Bretons have more in common in some ways with the Welsh, Irish or Scots than with other Frenchmen. Like the Irish, they are passionate, whimsical, witty and high-spirited; but they are also tenacious and hard-working, like the Scots. And they have a truly Celtic sense of mystery and love of legend. Their vast windswept granite peninsula is still haunted by distant echoes of a magical past, of Tristan and Isolde, of Merlin and King Arthur.

Brittany was not annexed to the French crown till 1532, and today most of its people still feel a sense of Breton nationhood. Few desire secession from France, but they do want more autonomy and are keen to keep alive the old Breton culture. It is true that the Breton language, akin to Welsh, is dying out as a vehicle of daily speech except among some older people in remoter areas; but some eager young patriots are now seeking to revive it. The young have also led a renaissance of Breton folklore, music and dance. Alas, the picturesque old Breton costumes are no longer a part of daily wear: but they are readily brought out of mothballs for the numerous summer festivals in towns and villages, and for the typically Breton religious ceremonies known as *pardons,* when costumed villagers parade through the streets, carrying banners, statues and candles, to pay homage to their local saint (Brittany has hundreds of its own saints, few of them recognized by Rome). It is then that you will see women wearing the famous Breton *coiffes*—white lace head-dresses whose style varies from area to area.

Bretons today may be losing some of their old piety, but they remain more devoutly Catholic than most other French people. In the 16th century they developed their own special religious architecture, which survives today around the churches of some villages—stone crucifixes and ossuaries (sarcophagi) with elaborate carvings depicting local saints, the life of Christ and the Passion. Some of them stand alone by the sea where drowned sailors are commemorated. Indeed, Breton piety was in the past closely linked with the sea, for many sons of this seafaring race lost their lives in storms off these treacherous coasts. Today, with Europe's fishing industries declining, only some 10,000 Bretons are fishermen: but many others still man France's Navy and merchant fleets, and the sea continues to play a big part in Breton life—above all through tourism.

The 2,000-mile coastline is heavily indented and richly varied: awesome rocky headlands, where the waves burst into spray, alternate with secretive sandy coves or wide pristine beaches, and idyllic forest-lined creeks and estuaries. This is ideal territory for a family seaside holiday or for sight-seeing. All along the coast and just inland are scores of handsome abbeys and tall churches, ancient shrines, turreted castles, and towns enclosed by medieval ramparts. Nearly all the buildings are in grey local granite, which gives then an austere beauty different from the styles of much of the rest of France.

Culturally, the province is divided into two parts: Upper Brittany to the east, around the capital Rennes; and, to the west, Lower Brittany *(la Bretagne bretonnante),* the more interesting and typically Breton of the two. Here traditions and the Breton language survive more strongly than in the eastern area, which has long been more exposed to French influences. The dividing line is roughly from St-Brieuc in the north to a point east of Vannes in the south. Scenically, however, the contrasts in Brittany are less between east and west than between north and south, between the coast and the interior. The north and west coasts are more rugged and grandiose, the south is more open and gentle, and warmer. But even in the north there are fertile plains close to the sea where farming is rich. The coastal area is quite thickly populated, while the interior is emptier, poorer and more desolate.

This chapter first follows the coast from St-Malo round to Nantes, then strikes inland.

St-Malo and the rugged north coast

A journey anti-clockwise round the coast begins in the northeast corner, across the Norman border from the abbey of Mont-St-Michel. The first Breton town you come to is Dol, with a 13th-century granite cathedral. For a good view of the area, drive to the top of nearby Mont-Dol, where St. Michael is said to have done battle with Satan. Round the bay is the pretty fishing-port of Cancale, and just beyond it the rugged rocky headland of the Pointe du Grouin. To the west, at Rothéneuf, do not miss the bizarre sculptures carved on the rocks by Abbé Fouré—a good example of *l'art brut*.

St-Malo is one of the best-loved of Breton towns. The ancient walled city stands on a peninsula within massive 13th-century ramparts; there is a broad walk along the top, with fine views of the coast. The old city was badly bombed during the Allied siege of this Nazi redoubt in August 1944, but has been carefully restored and is still very picturesque. The castle is worth a visit, also the Quic-en-Groigne wax-works museum of local history and—just offshore—the tomb of Chateaubriand on the islet of Le Grand Bé. Two miles up the Rance estuary is the world's first tidal powered hydro-electric dam. There are four tides a day here, instead of the usual two. The dam is open to visits.

Further up the Rance, the charming old town of Dinan also has fine ramparts, as well as half-timbered houses and an old castle with a towering keep. Dinard, on a headland facing St-Malo, is a large, sedate family resort, not as fashionable as in pre-war days. Westwards from here there stretches a magnificent succession of craggy capes and sandy beaches backed by pine-forests. Of the many lively bathing-resorts, St-Cast, Sables-d'Or and Le Val-André are the best. The fortress of La Latte stands majestically on a headland, while Cap Fréhel has grandiose scenery of red and black cliffs.

Inland from here, east of the pleasant market town of Lamballe, are the massive ruins of the 13th-century castle of La Hunaudaie. Going west, you pass through the cathedral city of St-Brieuc, capital of this part of Brittany. You then enter the wild country of Goëlo, where l'Arouest is another wild and lovely headland, facing the rocky, romantic island of Bréhat (accessible by boat-trip). The fishing-port of Paimpol was the setting of Pierre Loti's novel *Pêcheur d'Islande;* Tréguier is noted for its glorious Gothic cathedral, with a fine cloister and Renaissance choir-stalls.

Perros-Guirec, a lively place on a promontory, is Brittany's largest resort after Dinard and La Baule. West of here there stretches the strange and lovely Coast of Pink Granite, noted for its profusion of pink, bizarrely-shaped rocks. At the resort of Trégastel they stand scattered on the beach as well as spilling out over the sea in a myriad of tiny islands. This area is ideal for children who like climbing, shrimping and playing in rock lagoons. The more scientifically-minded can go just inland, to Pleumeur-Bodou, to visit France's leading space-communications center with its big white balloon-like dome. History-lovers can go beyond Lannion to explore the ruins of the hilltop castle of Tonquédec. So many contrasts, so close together!

The romantic west, around Brest and Quimper

At Morlaix you enter Finistère, the most typical and truly Breton part of Brittany. Morlaix is the capital of a rich market-gardening region that exports artichokes and cauliflowers. To its southwest are two villages with some of the finest religious stone sculptures in Brittany, dating from the 16th and 17th centuries— St-Thégonnec with its triumphal arch, ossuary, richly-carved crucifixion, and ornate pulpit in the church; and Guimiliau where the baptistry in the church vies in splendor with the vivid sculptures of its crucifixion.

To the north is the modern port of Roscoff, where the ferries sail for England, and nearby is the market town of St-Pol-de-Léon whose old streets are dominated by the tower of its 13th-century cathedral and the 250-foot steeple of the mighty Kreisker chapel, prototype of the many tall churches in this part of Brittany: another, as fine, is at Le Folgoët, to the west. Further on lies the mysterious open landscape of the Pays de Leon, stretching to the 'Coast of Legends' by the Atlantic, where lush pastures slope to lovely fjords known as *'abers':* Aber-Wrac'h, a fashionable yachting center, is the most typical. From the port of Le Conquet, or from Brest, you can take a two-hour boattrip to the island of Ouessant where the waves dash against jagged rocks and thousands of migrating birds nest in the ledges of the cliffs.

Brest, the leading French naval base on the Atlantic coast, stands on the north side of a huge and magnificent natural harbor. The town was heavily bombed in the war, and has been rebuilt in an ugly rectangular style; what's more, the heyday of its naval glory is past, though it is still a major repair center for tankers and other big ships. You can visit the dockyards, or get a good view of them from the Cours Dajot. To the east, the village of Plougastel-Daoulas has a remarkable crucifixion. It is also the center of a strawberry-growing district.

The Crozon peninsula, south of Brest harbor, has several attractive fishing-ports, such as Camaret whose ladies misbehaved in France's best-known lewd drinking-song. For a good view of the whole area, you should drive to the summit of the Menez-Hom hill. Then go south to Ste-Anne-la-Palud, venue for one of Brittany's most famous *pardons;* then on to the picturesque village of Locronan, with a fine church and Renaissance houses round a square.

Douarnenez, France's leading sardine-fishing port, has not much of interest. To the west, the Cap Sizun peninsula points a long finger into the Atlantic, ending in the Pointe du Raz, the most westerly tip of France. On this towering headland you can scramble amid the rocks—preferably led by a local guide—and watch the waves lashing the rocks far below. Cap Sizun has a bird sanctuary, best visited in the spring. The nearby village of Plogoff was the notorious scene of violent local demonstrations in 1980 against plans to build a nuclear power station. Some 8 km (5 miles) out at sea is the bleak Ile de Sein whose 600 inhabitants, mostly fisherfolk, live in tiny houses furnished partly from shipwrecks. The island is an hour's boat trip from Audierne. It covered itself in glory in June 1940 when the entire male population sailed to England to fight with the Free French.

Southwest of Quimper, around Pont l'Abbé, is the Pays Bigouden, where Breton traditions survive most strongly: here on special days women still wear their tall distinctive white *coifs,* and here Per-Jakez Hélias set his famous best-selling study of Breton rural life, *The Horse of Pride* (1975). Worth a visit are the Eckmühl lighthouse, the prehistory museum at St-Guénolé, and the crucifixion by the lonely seaside chapel of Notre-Dame-de-Trenoën. Next you will come to Quimper, a graceful city with quaint old streets, a fine cathedral, and a good picture museum. From here a delightful boat-trip can be made down the lovely river Odet to the sea at Benodet.

Concarneau to Nantes: the gentle south coast

South Brittany has a gentle, open coast of wide sandy beaches backed by dunes and pinewoods. It is less rugged than the north or west and the climate is warmer. Benodet and Beg-Meil, south of Quimper, are two smart and lively bathing-resorts with echoes of the Riviera. Going east, you come to the big tunny-fishing port of Concarneau whose walled island citadel in the harbor, the Ville Close, is highly picturesque. You can wander in its old streets and visit its museum of fishing.

East again is Pont-Aven, a pretty little town which the Post-Impressionist painters loved: Gauguin was one of those who lived and worked there. Nearby are the lovely wooded estuaries of the Aven and Belon, the latter famous for its oysters. At Quimperlé, the apse of the 12th-century church of Ste-Croix is Brittany's finest Romanesque building. Lorient, a naval base and major fishing port, was the main German submarine base on the Atlantic during the war and was subsequently badly damaged. It has since been rebuilt in spacious rectangular style. The huge submarine base is visitable by French citizens only.

The Carnac/Vannes sector of the south coast is of exceptional and varied interest. The resort of Carnac draws archeologists from the world over because of its strange druidical and pre-druidical remains— notably the thousands of stone menhirs (standing stones) and megaliths in long straight rows, and the big Tumulus of St-Michel with its funeral chambers. There is a good archeological museum. You should visit, too, the curious church of St-Cornély (local patron saint of horned cattle!). On its facade are figures of the saint and two bulls. At the nearby abbeys of St-Michel and Ste-Anne you can hear superb Gregorian plainsong.

The big resort of Quiberon stands on a peninsula south of Carnac, wild and rocky on its west side. Here at the Hotel de la Plage, St-Pierre, Jacques Tati shot parts of *M Hulot's Holiday*. Offshore, easily reached by boat, is the lovely Belle-Ile, with many coves and grottes and a fine rugged coastline. Back on the mainland, just east of Carnac, you come to La Trinité, training center for ocean-going yachtsmen, and then to Locmariaquer which has more megaliths. The village faces onto the Gulf of Morbihan, an inland sea of great beauty, studded with small islands and rich in birdlife. On one islet is the remarkable Tumulus of Gavrinis, probably the ancient tomb of a Celtic king. On the Rhuys peninsula south of the gulf, the village of St-Gildas used to contain a monastery where Abelard nursed his grief after parting from Héloise. To the east is the 13th-century castle of Suscinio, formerly a ruin, now partially restored.

Vannes is a graceful old town of character, with massive ramparts, a fine 13th-century cathedral and quaint gabled houses. Auray is also attractive, while Ste-Anne d'Auray is Brittany's leading pilgrimage center, with a big annual *pardon*. Southeast from here you come to the marshy salt lagoons of the Guérande peninsula, between the lively fishing-port of Le Croisic and the large and more sophisticated resort of La Baule. There is little of interest at St-Nazaire, a shipbuilding town that has seen better days; but just inland lies the strange marshy lagoon of La Grande Brière, with a bird sanctuary and an outdoor museum of rural life.

Finally to Nantes, which is not typically Breton nor today officially part of Brittany, but has historic associations with the province nonetheless. Today it is a large, busy industrial city and port, with much also to interest the lover of art and history—notably the massive ducal palace, the Gothic cathedral (superb interior), and a number of museums, including one devoted to regional folk arts. At Nantes in 1598 Henri IV signed the Edict giving protection to France's Protestants.

Rennes and the wild interior

Brittany's interior may be less exciting than its coast, but has much to offer the discerning traveler. To the east, around Rennes, it is undulating pastoral country; to the west it is more wild and remote, a region of forests and rock-strewn moorlands where many farms and villages have scarcely yet been touched by modern prosperity.

Rennes, Brittany's capital, is a dignified, friendly town with two universities. The main sights are the cathedral (fine altar-piece), the Palaise de Justice, and the Musée des Beaux-Arts. There are quaint medieval streets round the cathedral. Combourg, to the north, is a charming old town by a lake with a feudal castle that was the home of the writer Chateaubriand. Fougères, to the east, has an even more splendid castle, with towers and massive ramparts: Balzac set his novel *Les Chouans* in this area. The little town of Vitré has preserved its medieval character almost intact and also boasts a romantic many-turreted castle.

The forest of Paimpont, west of Rennes, lies at the heart of Celtic legend, for this was the original 'Brocéliande', the home of Merlin the Enchanter according to the Arthurian tales. Today the forest's character is somewhat different: Coëtquidan, on its southern fringe, is the site of France's leading military academy, St-Cyr, recently transferred from Versailles. The lovely town of Josselin, to the west, has a majestic towered chateau that rivals Fougeres' as one of the two finest in Brittany. It stands by a river, with old houses stretching up the hill to the basilica of Notre-Dame-du-Roncier, site of a major *pardon.*

A beauty spot of the western hinterland is the long, curving lake of Guerlédan, created artificially and used as a reservoir and for sailing. The village of Kernascléden has an old church with remarkable 15th-century frescos (restored), while at Pleyben is the most impressive of all Breton crucifixes. Pleyben is at the heart of a strange, austere upland region where great rocks stand as lonely sentinels on hilltops. To its east lies the Montagne Noire, and to its north the Monts d'Arrée, where

BRITTANY

on a fine day the Roc Trévezel offers a stunning panorama over northwest Brittany as far as the coast at Brest and at Roscoff.

PRACTICAL INFORMATION

WHEN TO GO. For the coast, June through Sept. are the best months. Most of the important religious festivals (*pardons*) and folklore events also occur during this season. These attractions draw huge crowds, so if you want a little elbow-room try for late spring or fall.

In **February** the great Pardon of Terre-Neuve takes place at St-Malo, and in **March** Nantes celebrates with a pre-Lenten carnival procession. Throughout **April**, fairs and horseraces in Nantes, Rennes and Vannes invite the off-season tourist. Turf events continue through **May** in Nantes, Rennes and St-Malo, the folk festival of Bleun-Brug is held each year in a different town, and at Etel there is the festival of the tuna fishermen. On May 19 there is the notable Pardon of St-Yves, patron saint of lawyers, at Tréguier. Another of the great *pardons* takes place at Rumengol on Trinity Sunday, at the end of May or early **June.**

June is also the month of the Feast of John the Baptist, honored by the ceremonial *Feux de la St-Jean* (on 24 June or the nearest weekend), at Locronan and Nantes, and by a week-long festival and fair at Lannion. **July** offers three important festivals: Lorient's Triumph of the Duchess of Armorica (ancient name for Brittany), Quimper's *Fêtes de Cornouaille,* France's major folklore event, and St-Cast's international amateur film festival. Early in the month Rennes has its *Tombées de la Nuit* celebrations, lasting about a week and with the accent on typically Breton crafts, cuisine, music, theater, etc. Among the *pardons* are those at Locronan on the second Sun. in July and at Ste-Anne-d'Auray on the 26th. The Cowes-Dinard yacht race is the top event in a sports calendar that includes horseracing at Le Val-André, Rennes and Combourg, and regattas at Morlaix and Cancale. The château of Combourg offers its *son-et-lumière* show.

Of outstanding interest among the **August** offerings are: Concarneau's Festival of the Blue Nets, Pont Aven's Festival of the Golden Gorse, Lorient's Celtic Festival, which includes performances by dancers and musicians from Ireland, Scotland and other Celtic lands, and Carnac's Festival of the Menhirs. In the early part of August there is the international bagpipe festival at Brest. Two of the most important *pardons* take place on the 15th at Perros-Guirec and on the last Sun. of the month at Ste-Anne-la-Palud. La Baule and Dinard present that typically French spectacle, the *Concours d'Elégance Automobile,* as well as regattas, ballet, and bridge tournaments. In the middle of the month, an international horse show is held in Dinard. From Belle-Ile are held the top sports events, international yacht races to Plymouth, England, and Santander, Spain. *Pardons* again are a feature during **September,** the principal one on the 18th, at Le Folgoët.

THE FACE OF FRANCE

HOW TO GET ABOUT. By train All rail services from Paris to Brittany leave from the Gare Montparnasse. The route lies west to Le Mans and then splits. One route then goes via Rennes (3¼–4 hrs) where it again splits: the northern section runs via St-Brieuc and Morlaix to Brest (6–7 hrs from Paris) with branches serving several coastal and inland towns; the southern route from Rennes goes via Redon and Lorient to Quimper (8–9½ hrs from Paris). From Rennes there is also a service to both St-Malo and Dinard connecting with Paris trains. The second route from Le Mans goes southwest through Angers to Nantes (4 hrs) and then La Baule (5 hrs).

By air. *Air France* flies London-Dinard-La Baule several times a week, July till mid-Sept.; *Touraine Air Transport (TAT)* flies London (Gatwick)—Dinard from late June to early Sept., functions only. *Brit Air* flies London-Gatwick to Morlaix, Quimper and Rennes, and Cork-Rennes. *Intra Airways* flies Jersey—Dinard daily year-round and St-Brieuc—Jersey three times a week in summer, once a week mid-Sept. to mid-June. *TAT* flies Cork (Ireland)—Rennes, late June to early Sept., weekends only again. *Airwales* also flies Cardiff—Dinard. All these flights use small planes, so reserve early. From Paris, *Air Inter* flies to Dinard and Brest. Various other air links between towns in Brittany and French centers such as Lyon are worth looking into if you're trying to see as much of the country as possible in a short space of time.

By boat. For travelers from Britain, there are regular car-ferry services (passengers without cars, too), the most direct being from Plymouth to Roscoff and to St-Malo, Portsmouth to St-Malo, Newhaven to Dieppe, Southampton to Le Havre and Cherbourg, Rosslare (Ireland) to Roscoff. In season, there are air and hovercraft day excursions from Jersey and Guernsey to St-Malo.

Leisurely Breton vacations can be had by moving slowly along Brittany's many canals. *Touring Club de France*, 65 av. de la Grande-Armée, 75016 Paris, will furnish maps and rules. *Blakes International*, Wroxham, Norwich, England offer inclusive two-week cruises. *Brittany Ferries* do packages with accommodation in splendid Relais et Châteaux hotels.

By bus. Brittany is served by a fairly good network of regular and excursion buses. *Europabus* has a seven-day guided coach tour of Brittany leaving Paris every Sun. from mid-May to mid-Sept. Inexpensive coach tours are offered from Britain by *Townsend Thoresen* Car Ferries and other operators. *French Travel Service* also have a coach tour of Brittany from Britain. Many other British firms offering package deals in France (including *AA Travel*) provide hotel or self-catering stays in Brittany.

By bike. Inspired by France's cycling champion, Bernard Hinault, who hails from Brittany, most towns and many villages now have a bike-rent service.

DISABLED VISITORS. An excellent guide full of useful hints about getting about in Brittany is available from 68B Castlebar Rd, Ealing, London W5 called *Access in Brittany;* no charge, but payment to cover postage will be appreciated.

BRITTANY 247

MOTORING. Motorists touring the Loire valley may conveniently reach Brittany by taking the N23 at Angers, then the N165. The D751 along the southern bank of the Loire is slower but more picturesque. From Normandy and Mont-St-Michel, take the N175 from Rennes, then the N24 from Pontorson.

From Paris, take either the A10 to St-Arnoulf and then the A11 to Rennes, or, if you prefer to avoid the motorways, the N10 to Chartres and the N23 to Le Mans. You may also take the N157 to Rennes and the N12 to St-Brieuc, and on to the D786 for Perros-Guirec. The N12 continues via Guingamp and Morlaix to Brest. From Rennes the N24 goes to Lorient via Josselin. From Lorient take the N165 to Quimper. Branch off on to the N23 at Le Mans for Nantes.

EXCURSIONS. By boat. The offshore islands provide an outstanding attraction. The Ile de Bréhat may be reached from the Pointe de l'Arcouest (half-hourly in summer, 15 mins); Ile d'Ouessant from Brest or Le Conquet (twice weekly, about 4 hrs); Ile de Sein from Audierne or Pointe du Raz (thrice weekly in winter, daily in summer, 1½ hrs); Ile de Groix from Lorient (six times weekly, about 1 hr); Houat and Hoedic (three times weekly), and Belle-Ile (three times daily in summer, 45 mins, also by air), all from Quiberon. Glénans, with France's most famous sailing school—and possibly one of the best in the world—can be reached daily from Concarneau on the tuna fishing boat *Espoir*.

Not to be missed are the trips on the river Rance from Dinan to Dinard and St-Malo (about 2 hrs); on the river Odet from Quimper to Bénodet or Loctudy (about 1½ hrs); across the gulf of Morbihan from Vannes to Port-Navalo (two or three times daily, about 2 hrs.).

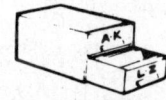

USEFUL ADDRESSES. For information on the various regions, the *tourist offices* at (Mont-St Michel—St-Cast area) 5 rue du Maréchal-Leclerc, Dinard; (Finistère area) rue du Roi-Gradlon, Quimper; (Morbihan area) 29 rue Thiers, Vannes. *Welcome Information* offices for Côte d'Armor, pl. de l'Hotel-de-Ville, 22700 Perros-Guirec and at pl. du Change, Nantes, and (for the Côte d'Amour) at 8 pl. de la Victoire, La Baule.

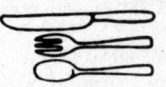

REGIONAL FOOD AND DRINK. Surrounded on three sides by water, Brittany is superb for fish and shellfish. This is the domain of *homard à l'armoricaine* (lobster with cream sauce), not to be confused with 'Américaine'! The word derives from the ancient name for Bretons—Armorici. In addition, there are plentiful supplies of oysters, cod, turbot and eels. The last are usually roasted and eaten with a very spicy and distinctive sauce. Other specialties are *andouille* (chitterling sausage), *galettes de sarrasin* (buckwheat pancakes), hearth-smoked bacon, butter and cider. For dessert, the province is justly renowned for its *crêpes dentelles* (pancakes) and its macaroons.

THE FACE OF FRANCE

HOTELS AND RESTAURANTS. During high season (July–Aug.) prices rise by about 20%; plus you must also reserve ahead for these months, especially if bringing a family. Rooms in chic resorts (Dinard, La Baule) are about 25% less than in Paris, while tiny ports or resorts may be 50% cheaper or more, but hotels here can be spartan and old-fashioned.

AUDIERNE. *Le Goyen* (M), pleasant, facing harbor; excellent restaurant (M–E), with 'new' cooking.

BATZ-SUR-MER. Restaurant. *Lucullus* (I–M), comfortable, good value.

LA BAULE. *Hermitage* (L), large, spacious and chic, facing beach. *Castel Marie-Louise* (L–E), small, quiet, fine cuisine (E). *Bellevue-Plage* (E), facing sea. *Royal* (E), large, fashionable, near beach. *Christina* (M); *Helios* (M); *Les Pléiades* (M), all without restaurants; *Bretagne* (I–M).
Restaurants. *L'Espadon* (E), elegant, with fine inventive cooking; *Henri* (I–M).

BEG-MEIL. *Thalamot* (I–M), simple; goodish food.

BELLE-ILE. Island off Quiberon. At **Port-Goulphar:** *Castel Clara* (E,L), smallish, beautiful; heated pool; good food. *Manoir de Goulphar* (M), quiet. At **Sauzon:** *Le Cardinal* (M), modern, quiet, idyllic setting, garden.

BENODET. *Gwel-Kaër* (E), modern, near beach. *Ker Moor* (M) and *Kastel Moor* (M), near beach; twin hotels with pool and tennis.

BILLIERS-PENLAN. *Château de Rochevilaine* (M–E), romantic Renaissance manor by the sea.

BLAIN. Restaurant. *Le Port* (I–M), bistrot by the canal, good value.

BREST. *Continental* (M), sedate, central. *Le Voyageurs* (M), with excellent restaurant. *Vauban* (I). 6 km (4 miles) to north is *Novotel* (M,E), with snack/grill.
Restaurants. *Frère Jacques* (M), inventive cooking; *Le Poulbot* (M).

BRIGNOGAN-PLAGE. *Castel Régis* (M), small, quiet, informal, near the sea; pool; splendid restaurant (M–E).

CANCALE. *Continental* (M), by port; *Phare* (I).
Restaurants. *Bricourt* (M), luxurious, in a lovely old house, with good inventive cooking. *Le Cancalais* (M), with some rooms.

BRITTANY

CARANTEC. *La Falaise* (I), small family hotel with good food (I).

CARHAIX. Restaurant. *Auberge du Poher* (I–M), good value.

CARNAC. *Diana* (E), facing beach. *Novotel Tal Ar Mor* (E), by habor, with pool, next to salt-water cure center. *Alignements* (M), inland, in town, friendly.
Restaurant. *Lann Roz* (M–E), good, with some rooms (M).

CHATEAULIN. Restaurant. *Auberge des Ducs de Lin* (I–M), good value; some rooms (M).

COMBOURG. *Château et Voyageurs* (M), central.

CONCARNEAU. *Belle Etoile* (E), 5 km (3 miles) south, by Le Cabellou beach; small, elegant. *Grand* (M), by harbor, no restaurant. *Sables Blancs* (M), quiet, by beach.
Restaurants. *Galion* (M–E), *Douane* (M), *Coquille* (M), all good, notably for fish.

LE CROISIC. Restaurants. *Bretagne* (M), overlooks port. *Océan* (M), at nearby Port-Lin, good seafood; some rooms (M).

DINAN. *D'Avagour* (M), elegant, facing ramparts and garden; excellent 'new' cooking. *Remparts* (M), no restaurant.
Restaurants. *Caravelle* (E), superb 'new' cooking. *Mère Pourcel* (M).

DINARD. *Reine Hortense* (L), small, luxurious, no restaurant. *Grand* (E), palatial, facing sea; good food (M). *Bains* (M), *Balmoral* (M), *Dunes* (M). *Altair* (I), with good food (I–M).

DOL-DE-BRETAGNE. *Logis de la Bresche d'Arthur* (I), simple; good food (I–M).

DOUARNENEZ. *Bretagne* (I), good value; meals in summer only. *Auberge de Kerveoc'h* (I–M), converted farm, friendly ambience, is 5 km (3 miles) out on Quimper road.

ERDEVEN. *Château de Keravéon* (E), elegant, spacious and peaceful.

LE FAOU. *La Vieille Renommée* (M), simple but modernized.

LA FORET-FOUESNANT. *Manoir du Stang* (E), graceful 16th-century manor in a park, with lakes. *Espérance* (I).

FOUGÈRES. *Voyageurs* (M), no restaurant; *Mainotel* (I), modernized, good value; tennis.

GOUAREC. *Blavet* (M), with good local *cuisine* (I–M).

LA GOUESNIÈRE. *Gare* (I), poorly sited by a railway, but comfortable, with distinguished cooking (M).

GUIDEL. *La Châtaigneraie* (E), quiet, secluded, with hyper-elegance bordering on pretentiousness; no restaurant.

GUINGAMP. Restaurant. *Relais du Roy* (M), stylish, in an old house; good for fish; some rooms (M).

HÉDÉ. Restaurant. *La Vieille Auberge* (M), rustic decor and garden; good value.

HENNEBONT. *Château de Locguénolé* (E), stately and seigneurial, in a big garden by a river; best cuisine in Brittany (E), mainly 'new'.

JOSSELIN. *Château* (I–M), with view of castle.

LÉZARDRIEUX. *Relais Brenner* (E), smart modern mansion in a park above a river; good food (E).

LIFFRÉ. Restaurant. *Hôtellerie du Lion d'Or* (E), elegant, with lovely garden and outstanding 'new' cooking; its annexe, *Le Jardin* (I), is good value, also with garden.

LOCMARIA. Restaurant. *Auberge de la Truite* (M–E), rustic decor, good Breton cooking; some rooms (I).

LOCRONAN. *Manoir de Moëllien* (M), secluded, just outside village, folksy atmosphere.

LORIENT. *Richelieu* (E), no restaurant. *Bretagne* (M), with good food (M). At **Lanester,** 5 km (3 miles) out, *Novotel* (M), with pool.
Restaurants. *Le Poisson d'Or* (I–M), *Les Arcades* (I–M). *Pic Assiett* (I), lively bistrot, good value.

MOËLAN-SUR-MER. *Les Moulins du Duc* (E), luxuriously converted millhouse in charming rural setting, with brilliant inventive cooking by Japanese chef (E).

BRITTANY

MORLAIX. *Europe* (M), central, excellent food (I–M). *Minimote* (M), no restaurant.

MUR-DE-BRETAGNE. *Auberge Grand Maison* (M), comfortable, with very good cooking, mostly 'new' (I–M).

NANTES. *Frantel* (E), *Sofitel* (E), both with good restaurants (E–M). *Astoria* (M), no restaurant; *Central* (M); *Colonies* (M), no restaurant; *France* (M). *Atlantique* (I), no restaurant. Just out of town, *Novotel* (E), with pool; light meals only.

At **Orvault**, *Domaine d'Orvault* (E), smart, in large garden, with excellent 'new' cooking (E).

Restaurants. Among the many good ones in town: *Les Maraîchers* (M–E) for 'new' cooking; *La Sirène* (M); *La Cigogne* (M), tiny bistrot; *Le Nantais* (I–M), bustling place with home-style cooking. At **Bellevue:** *Delphin* (E), distinguished mainly 'new' cooking.

PAIMPOL. *Repaire de Kerroc'h* (E), handsome 18th-century house overlooking harbor; good food, notably fish (M).

PERROS-GUIREC. *Grand Hotel de Trestraou* (M), with good restaurant, *Homard Bleu* (I–E); *Levant* (M), facing harbor; *Morgane* (M), with garden and pool; *Printania* (M), with garden and view of sea. *St-Yves* (I).
Restaurant. *Sphinx* (M), with 11 rooms (M).

PLÉHÉDEL. *Château de Coatguelen* (E), quiet, comfortable 19th-century château in big park; tennis, pool; good 'new' cooking (E).

PLENEUF-VAL-ANDRÉ. Restaurant. *La Cotriade* (M–E), superb fish.

PLÉVEN. *Manoir de Vaumadeuc* (E), 15th-century manor, sumptuously converted by its aristocratic owners; large garden.

PLOUDALMÉZEAU. *Voyageurs* (I), simple inn with good inexpensive food.

PLOUGASTEL. Restaurant. *Chevalier de l'Auberlac'h* (M), inventive cooking, good value.

PLOUNÉRIN. Restaurant. *Relais de Bon Voyage* (M), excellent.

PLOUMANAC'H. *Parc* (I), no lunches.
Restaurant. *Les Rochers* (M–E), good for fish; some rooms (M).

POINTE DU RAZ. *Baie des Trespassés* (I), 3 km (2 miles) on D784; secluded, good view.

PONT-AVEN. Restaurants. *Moulin de Rosmadec* (M), an old mill, with antique furniture, by a stream; excellent food. *La Taupinière* (M), 4 km (2½ miles away) on Concarneau road; very good inventive cooking.

PONT-L' ABBÉ. Restaurant. *Relais Ty-Boutic* (I–M), 3 km (2 miles) away on Plomeur road; superb value.

PONTS-NEUFS. Restaurant. *Lorand-Barre* (E), fine old Breton décor; superb classical cooking.

PORNICHET. *Sud Bretagne* (M–E), with pool. *Les Charmettes* (M), family hotel with garden.

QUESTEMBERT. Restaurant. *Bretagne* (E), luxurious, with distinguished 'new' cooking.

QUIBERON. *Sofitel* (L), sumptuous, peaceful, facing sea; excellent restaurant, *Thalassa* (M–E). *Ker Noyal* (E), very attractive. *Beau Rivage* (M); *Hoche* (M); *Petite Sirène* (M), modern, with good food (I–M). *Gulf Stream* (I), no restaurant.

QUIMPER. *Griffon* (E), 3 km (2 miles) on Bénodet road. *Tour d'Auvergne* (M). *Terminus* (I), no restaurant.
Restaurant. *Les Tritons* (I), good value.

QUIMPERLÉ. *Hermitage* (M), 2 km (1½ miles) on D 49, attractive, with pool and garden. *Auberge de Toulfoën,* (I), 3 km (2 miles) on D 49, small, with good food (M).

RAGUENÈS-PLAGE. *Chez Pierre* (M), delightful family-run place, peaceful; excellent cooking (I–M).

RENNES. *Frantel* (E). *Novotel* (E), by S ring motorway, with pool; snack menu only. *Cheval d'Or* (M). *Du Guesclin* (M). *Président* (M), no restaurant. *Astrid* (I).
Restaurants. Many good ones, notably *Escu de Runfäo* (M–E); *Coq-Gadby* (M); *Corsaire* (M); *L'Ouvrée* (M), 'new' cooking; *Pastourelle* (M); *Ti Coz* (M), very old house with period decor; *Palais* (I–M), good value.

RIEC-SUR-BELON. Restaurants. *Chez Mélanie* (M), good for fish; some rooms (M). *Kerland* (M–E), 4 km (2½ miles) on D 24, attractive inn with good view, ambitious 'new' cooking.

ROSCOFF. *Gulf Stream* (M), quiet, modern; good food (M). *Bellevue* (I–M), good view indeed.

BRITTANY

ROSPORDEN. *Arvor* (I), comfortable; meals very good value (I–M).

STE-ANNE-D'AURAY. *L'Auberge* (I), with good food (I).

STE-ANNE-LA-PALUD. *La Plage* (E), lovely, luxurious inn, secluded by the beach; superb cooking (M–E).

ST-BRIEUC. *Le Griffon* (M), at airport. *Alexandre I* (M); *Pignon Pointu* (I–M); neither with restaurant.
 Restaurant. *La Vieille Tour* (M), excellent, notably for fish.

ST-CAST. *Ar Vro* (M), by beach, among pines, good food (M–E). *Pins* (M), at **Pen-Guen**, peaceful, amid pines above sea; good food (M). *Angleterre et Panorama* (I).

ST-GUÉNOLÉ. *La Mer* (M), with restaurant, noted for its fish (M–E).

ST-JACUT. *Vieux Moulin* (I), honest family hotel, good value, good cooking (I).

ST-JOACHIM. Restaurant. *Auberge du Parc* (M), excellent local cooking.

ST-MALO. *Central* (M–E), inside old town; first-class food (M).
 At **Paramé**: *Thermes* (M), by spa centre; *Chateaubriand* (I–M), no restaurant.
 At **St-Servan**: *Valmarin* (E), 18th-century house, no restaurant. *Servannais* (I).
 Restaurants. *La Métairie de Beauregard* (E), excellent; at St-Servan. *La Porte St-Pierre* (I–M).

ST-NAZAIRE. *Berry* (M). *Europe* (M), no restaurant.
 Restaurants. *Bon Accueil* (I–M), very good; has rooms (I). *Parisien* (I), good value.

TRÉBEURDEN. *Manoir de Lan-Kerellec* (E), handsome manor in its own park; first-rate food (M–E). *Ti al-Lannec* (M), very attractive and peaceful; excellent cooking (M). *Family* (I–M), *Ker-an-Nod* (I–M).

TRÉBOUL. *Arcades* (I), with pleasant restaurant (I–M).

TRÉGASTEL. *Belle Vue* (M), peaceful, with garden. *Mer et Plage* (M). *Greve Blanche* (I) has lovely sea view.

TRÉGUIER. *Estuaire* (I).

TREGUNC. *Le Menhir* (I–M), lively, with good food (M).

TREMBLAY. *Roc Land* (M), in big garden, tennis, very good food (M).

TREVOU-TRESTEL. *Le Charma* (I), yes, a charmer, but very simple.

VANNES. *Manche-Ocean* (M), no restaurant. *La Marébaudière* (M), friendly, with good restaurant, *La Marée Bleue* (I–M). *L'Image de Ste-Anne* (I), with good restaurant (I–M). At **Conleau** *Le Roof* (M), with good food (M).
Restaurant. *Richemont* (I–M), comfortable, fine cooking.

VITRÉ. *Chêne Vert* (I), *Petit-Billot* (I).

NORMANDY

Beach-heads and Abbeys

by
VIVIENNE MENKES

William the Conqueror and Joan of Arc, the Bayeux Tapestry and Norman architecture, the Canadian Jubilee raid and the D-Day landings—Normandy probably has more associations for English-speaking visitors than any other part of France. Easily reached from Paris and Britain, it offers varied scenery ranging from the wild granite cliffs in the west to the long sandy beaches along the Channel coast, from the wooded valleys of the south to the lush green meadows and apple orchards in its heart. Its rich butter, cheese and cream, cider and calvados have also made it one of the finest gastronomic regions of a country famed for fine eating. It contains many historic cities and a wealth of fine buildings and museums. And there is Mont St-Michel, the glorious Gothic abbey perched on a rocky mound in the sea and one of the country's most dramatic and wonderful sights.

For many people today, though, Normandy is chiefly remembered for the key role it played in World War II. Here, on the long Channel beaches, the D-Day landings took place in June 1944, beginning the long process that led to the final victory of the Allies. Normandy payed a terrible price in the war, suffering twice over—first when the Germans invaded in 1940 and again during the Battle of Normandy in 1944. But restoration and reconstruction followed soon afterwards and the region today is prosperous and hard working. It is ideal for either short one- or two-day visits or for longer vacations.

Rouen—old and new

Rouen was the former capital of Normandy. In 1979, the ancient city acquired its very latest 'monument', a fitting symbol of the invigorating blend of old and new in this attractive and important city. This is the dazzling modern church and monument dedicated to France's patron saint, Joan of Arc, in the place du Vieux-Marché, the ancient market place where she met her death. The stylish new buildings are a conscious attempt to ensure that the 20th century will leave as lasting an architectural memorial in Rouen as previous centuries. Everywhere you see the contrast of old and new—the glass and concrete conference center beside the Gothic cathedral, the traditional Théâtre des Arts and the ultra-modern Espace Duchamp-Villon and, set in the windows of the brand-new Joan of Arc church, are gorgeous 16th-century stained-glass panels thankfully removed from a nearby church before it was destroyed in the devastation of 1944.

Other sights you won't want to miss include the great cathedral of Notre Dame. Its richly carved façade is flanked by the early Gothic St-Romain Tower on the left and the Butter Tower on the right, so called because it was built with money donated by wealthy citizens for the privilege of eating butter during Lent. Inside, the beautiful 13th-century choir has an ambulatory enriched by the tombs of the earliest dukes of Normandy. Much superb restoration has been accomplished, as it also has at the nearby church of Saint-Maclou, which has an extraordinary façade with five gables. Its lacy intricacy will soon make clear why this type of late Gothic architecture is known as Flamboyant. Parts of the church are still closed for restoration, but the abbey church of St-Ouen has now been reopened after a long program of restoration. Both churches are used for concerts and recitals.

One historic building that survived the bombing unscathed is the strange Aître St-Maclou. It was once a cemetery for people who had died of the plague and is said to have inspired the French composer St-Saëns's *Danse Macabre*. Its timber-frame buildings are carved with skulls, bones and gravediggers' implements, though they are now set around a pretty flower-filled courtyard.

Rouen's liveliest street is the rue du Gros-Horloge, bridged by a Renaissance clock house containing an ornate clock once located in the adjoining belfry. Near here are the early Renaissance law courts with a stunningly intricate façade. Beneath the courtyard is a mysterious Romanesque building with Jewish inscriptions that has excited and puzzled scholars the world over. It is undoubtedly the earliest surviving Jewish building in France and is now open to the public. Harder to find, as it is now part of a bank, is the Hôtel de Bourgthéroulde, an elaborate Gothic and Renaissance mansion with a carved frieze depicting the meeting of the French and English kings on the Field of the Cloth of Gold. In the city center, you'll also find the Tour Jeanne d'Arc, where the Maid was threatened with torture. Near here, watch out for the pretty chapel of St-Louis and the Lycée Corneille, where the great 17th-century dramatist studied.

In many ways, the whole of old Rouen is a museum, but before leaving try to visit at least two of the city's museums. The Fine Arts Museum has some magnificent paintings plus a wonderful ceramics collection. Almost next door is the Secq-des-Tournelles Museum, which has the world's finest collection of wrought iron. The city is a major cultural center, so you may like to round off your day by attending a concert in the Théâtre des Arts, the fine new music academy or one of the ancient churches.

The Seine valley and its abbeys

Between Rouen and the English Channel, the meandering Seine valley is full of interest. Among its sights are the soaring ruins of the abbey of Jumièges, the imposing church at St-Martin-de-Boscherville and the no less monumental Pont de Brotonne, a new toll bridge spanning the Seine just upriver from Caudebec-en-Caux. This dramatic modern structure sounded the death knell for a couple of little ferries that used to cross the river, but there are a few other car ferries still in business that add color to a leisurely exploration of the broad river.

Due west of Rouen at St-Martin-de-Boscherville is the mighty Romanesque abbey church of St-Georges. Amazingly, this huge building never served more than 35 to 40 monks in its heyday. Beyond the little town of Duclair, you come first to Jumièges, consecrated in the year after the Battle of Hastings in the presence of William the Conqueror. Allow plenty of time to wander among the highly romantic ruins. A few miles further on, the abbey of St-Wandrille, founded in the 7th century, still houses a community of Benedictine monks. The conducted tour by one of the monks includes the ruined Gothic church, the cloisters and the splendid 'new' church, erected in 1969. Actually it's a huge 13th-century tithe barn brought here from southern Normandy.

Nearby is Caudebec, rebuilt after extensive damage in World War II, though the fine Gothic church, which Henri IV believed the most beautiful in his kingdom, escaped destruction. The little resort of Villequier is further on. It is chiefly known for the Victor Hugo Museum, opened because the author's favorite daughter was drowned here while boating with her husband only six months after their wedding. The cause of the tragedy was the *mascaret,* a dramatic tidal wave that used to be one of the sights of Caudebec and Villequier before damming work lessened its effect.

Before heading for the coast, cross the river and take a look at the imposing ruins of the castle of Robert le Diable and at another abbey, Bec-Hellouin near Brionne. It is set in a pretty, rather English-looking village with an interesting church. One of its abbots, Lanfranc, became adviser to William the Conqueror and Archbishop of Canterbury, an office later held by his successor at Bec-Hellouin, St Anselm. A community of Benedictine monks took over the abbey again in 1948 and the 15th-century St Nicholas tower, the cloisters and other monastic buildings can all be visited. Next to the abbey is a popular vintage automobile museum.

Other historic buildings in this area are the château of Harcourt, with its tree museum, and the château of Champ-de-Bataille, the seat of the Harcourts, one of France's most famous families. This is the département of the Eure, the capital of which is Evreux. This too was a war casualty, but nonetheless still has several buildings worth visiting, notably the belfry, the bishops' palace and the beautifully restored cathedral with its marvelous stained glass.

The Alabaster Coast and Dieppe

At the mouth of the Seine, beyond Lillebonne with its Roman ruins, lies the busy port of Le Havre, much of which was flattened in World War II. Today it is a thriving port and has been extensively rebuilt in what is generally agreed to be a not very inspired style. But it does have an excellent modern museum with paintings by Dufy, Boudin, Monet and Pissarro.

East of Le Havre, the coast is best known for its spectacular white cliffs (hence the name Alabaster Coast). The most famous spot is the resort of Etretat, where you can admire the extraordinary shapes into which the sea has carved the chalk. Beyond Etretat is Fécamp, a fishing port and yacht harbor with a fine abbey church that for centuries was a major pilgrimage center. The pilgrims were drawn by a priceless relic; a lead vessel allegedly containing a few drops of Christ's blood. Pilgrimages are still made here, but many tourists prefer to visit the distillery producing Benedictine liqueur.

A string of modest resorts follows, such as Saint-Valéry-en-Caux and Veulette-sur-Mer. The biggest town on this coast is Dieppe, a pleasing mixture of seaside resort—it has a casino, good hotels and the usual amenities—and busy fishing and trading port. On Saturdays, there is a colorful market beside the church. Towering over the eastern end of the shingle beach, beyond the memorials to the many Canadians who died here during the Jubilee raid in 1942, is the massive bulk of Dieppe castle. It contains a marvelous collection of ivories and some good paintings, including a group by the British painter Walter Sickert, who lived and worked here.

Inland from Dieppe you can make many pleasant excursions to the delightful Norman countryside, full of green fields, half-timbered barns and orchards. You may like to visit the château of Miromesnil or the little spa town of Forges-les-Eaux, well known to Parisian gamblers as the nearest spot where they can indulge their passion for roulette. Under an old law, this allegedly wicked game cannot be played within 100km of the capital and Forges is just outside that limit.

Other trips from Dieppe include the new War Museum on the road to Pourville, and leafy Varengeville, where there is a tiny church perched on the cliff top and surrounded by a graveyard where Georges Braque is buried. He lived here and designed some of the stained glass in the church. Another attraction here, from Easter through October, is the enchanting Moutiers garden surrounding a house built by the British archtitect Sir Edwin Lutyens in 1898. Also worth a visit is the Manoir d'Ango, once the country house of Jean Ango, a 16th-century shipping magnate whose profiteering (with royal approval) resulted in the sinking and capture of over three hundred Portuguese ships.

The Côte Fleurie and the Pays d'Auge

To learn more about the colorful Ango, you should visit Honfleur, one of Normandy's most picturesque harbors on the other side of the Seine from Le Havre. In the Ethnographic Museum there are many exhibits connected with Ango and other Norman seafarers, including those who founded Quebec in the 17th century. Although long a haunt of painters, Honfleur is still a busy working harbor, which explains why the attractive waterfront with its tall slate-hung houses is relatively untouristy. Don't miss the wooden church of Ste-Catherine and the little Eugène Boudin Museum. He was born in Honfleur and later worked here with Monet. Just outside the town is the Ferme St-Siméon, now a chic hotel and restaurant, but visited by Monet and other painters when it was still a farm. Above the town you can visit the chapel on the Côte de Grace where a special sailor's mass is said on Whit Monday.

Following the coast westward, we come to Trouville, the first of the resorts on the Côte Fleurie, or Flowery Coast. Originally a tiny fishing village, Trouville is the oldest seaside resort in France, having started to become fashionable during the Second Empire. This smart bathing place has a long sandy beach, many hotels, a huge swimming pool and an aquarium. There is also a casino which is now enlivened by backgammon king Omar Sharif, one of the organizers of the galas and other attractions staged here. In spite of this sophistication, Trouville still has a fishing harbor, while its grander neighbor and rival, aristocratic Deauville, is and always has been nothing but a pleasure ground for the rich who flock here during the short summer season and on weekends all year round. Deauville's life centers around its glittering white summer casino (the winter casino is smaller and less opulent), its two race courses and its fine sandy beach dotted with brightly colored tents and sun umbrellas. The beach is bordered by the famous *planques,* wooden walkways along which anybody who is anybody parades up and down to see and be seen.

West of Deauville, the resorts are more modest. Cabourg, with its curious fan-shaped pattern of streets and avenues radiating out from the casino, was one inspiration for Marcel Proust's imaginary resort of Balbec in his novel *Remembrance of Things Past.* It is taking on a new lease of life these days, and its sedate turn-of-the-century aura is disappearing. It has a new yacht harbor and several swinging discos, including a branch of Paris's ultra-fashionable Le Palace.

Other pleasant resorts beckon, such as Houlgate and Villers-sur-Mer, but don't neglect the delightful inland area known as the Pays d'Auge. This is cheese, cider and calvados country. It is from here that Camembert, among the most famous cheeses in the world, comes. Another cheese, Pont l'Evêque, is named after a pleasant little town that still has a few old timbered houses in spite of wartime bombing, as does Lisieux, larger and further inland. But Lisieux is best known as a place of pilgrimage. It was here in the Carmelite convent that St Teresa of Lisieux lived and died at the end of the 19th century. The vast basilica dedicated to her in 1954 is such a notable Catholic pilgrimage center that it was the only place outside Paris visited by the Pope during his visit to France in 1980. Lisieux also has an elegant 12th-century cathedral.

Caen, Bayeux and the landing beaches

West of Lisieux is the important town of Caen. It suffered appallingly during the war, but has been very successfully rebuilt and is now a lively modern city with an active cultural life. Ironically, the war damage was a good thing in one sense: William the Conqueror's castle, surrounded by buildings and virtually invisible before the war, can now be seen to full advantage perched on its low hill in the city center behind the richly-carved Gothic church of St-Pierre. Within its ramparts are an excellent modern museum containing fine paintings and the interesting Normandy Museum, devoted to regional crafts and traditions.

You should also visit the twin abbeys, the Abbaye aux Hommes and Abbaye aux Dames, built by William and his wife Matilda of Flanders as a condition of the pope's raising the excommunication he had served on them—they were cousins and needed papal dispensation before marrying. The church of St-Etienne in the Abbaye aux Hommes is the finest building in Caen, a magnificently austere Romanesque building with Gothic additions.

From Caen you can visit the charming little Romanesque church of Thaon, set in an idyllic valley, and the Renaissance château of Fontaine-Henry. And it is only a short journey to Bayeux, the first town in France to be liberated by the Allies. Its most famous possession is the Bayeux Tapestry (in fact an embroidered scroll), which illustrates the Norman Conquest. This miraculous survival from the Middle Ages is now housed in a converted 18th-century seminary near the cathedral, where you can first watch a good audiovisual introduction to its history and then study the tapestry itself, with cassette mini-guides to help you spot the details. Both introduction and cassettes are available in English. Do also visit the fine cathedral, a harmonious blend of Romanesque and Gothic.

But the main goal for visitors to this part of Normandy is the D-Day landing beaches, a few miles away on the coast. To obtain a graphic impression of those dramatic days in June 1944, you must visit the excellent museum on the seafront at Arromanches. It is impressive even when it is swarming with visitors. To the east lie Gold, Juno and Sword Beaches, where the British landed, and the pleasant little resorts of Courseulles (known for its oysters), Ouistreham and Riva-Bella. Inland from Ouistreham you can visit Pegasus Bridge, taken by British parachutists on the night of 5/6 June. West of Arromanches, beyond the little fishing port of Port-en-Bessin, is the enormously impressive American Cemetery. Its moving rows of white marble crosses and stars of David stretch never-endingly toward the cliff edge overlooking Omaha Beach, where so many young Americans lost their lives.

The Cotentin Peninsula and Mont St-Michel

The coast continues to the Pointe du Hoc, which offers splendid views of the Cotentin Peninsula, the curious finger of land thrusting out into the sea at the northwestern tip of Normandy. The east coast, where much of the American force was concentrated during the Normandy landings—Utah Beach is here—is one long stretch of sand. The west coast is wilder and more varied with small resorts such as Barneville-Carteret and Granville, a picturesque old town dominated by its fortress. This part of the coast is known as 'The Coast with the Big Tides' and the tides are indeed spectacular, especially at Mont St-Michel. But the wild northwest coast is also worth visiting for its magnificent scenery, particularly the granite promontory of the Nez de Jobourg and the Cap de la Hague.

The port of Cherbourg on the north coast has an important naval dockyard where France's atomic submarines are built, an art gallery and a museum devoted to World War II in general and the liberation of France in particular. Inland is Valognes, sometimes referred to as Normandy's Versailles because of the fashionable life it enjoyed in the 18th century and which still has many fine mansions in spite of wartime damage. Further south, Coutances has one of the country's purest Gothic cathedrals. Other places worth visiting are Villedieu-les-Poëles, famous for its beautiful wrought copper articles, and the nearby abbey of Hambye.

Most of the peninsula is relatively undeveloped and is a good place for a holiday if you like to be off the beaten track. But when you come right down to the south, near the border with Brittany, you are back in tourist territory. From Avranches, where the US forces achieved a major breakthrough in 1944 (the town has a memorial to General Patton), you have a magnificent view of Mont St-Michel, which, except for Paris and Versailles, attracts more visitors than any other place in France.

It has been called the *Merveille de l'Occident,* the Wonder of the West, and truly it is wonderful. You may have seen dozens of pictures of this strange granite offshore mount, surmounted by a Gothic abbey with a tall spire, but nothing can prepare you for the breathtaking sight and you'll never grow tired of gazing at it.

Don't be put off by the hordes of tourists and souvenir sellers. The Mount has been a popular pilgrimage center since the first chapel was built in the eighth century and medieval pilgrims were as eager for souvenirs as today's tourists. And only about a quarter of the people who visit the Mount climb up the many steps to visit the marvelous Gothic abbey, so you shouldn't find it too crowded. Conducted tours of the abbey in English take place at frequent intervals and include the pre-Romanesque and Romanesque churches as well as the Gothic abbey with its many rooms and chambers and airy cloisters. Don't miss walking round the ramparts and visiting the terraced gardens with their glorious view of the abbey and the bay. But be careful if you walk round the Mount—the tide comes in at a dangerous speed, especially at the equinoxes, and there are nasty patches of quicksand. The bay itself is silting up and conditions are changing rapidly. It would be wise to pay close attention to any advice available locally.

Southern Normandy—spas, woods and horses

East of Mont St-Michel, the southern stretch of Normandy has many pleasant towns, such as Mortain, Domfront and Normandy's main spa, pretty Bagnoles-de-l'Orne. Further east lies Alençon, a lacemaking center (you can visit the lacemaking academy and museum) with a dazzling Flamboyant Gothic church. This delightfully wooded area is now known as the Normandie-Maine nature reserve. North of Alençon, try to visit the Haras du Pin, France's national stud founded in the early 18th century. South-east of here, the Perche region is also renowned for its horses, while to the west lies the area described rather misleadingly as Norman Switzerland. Its wooded river valleys make it ideal walking country. A good center is Falaise, which boasts the huge château in which William the Conqueror was born.

The miracle of Giverny

Before we leave Normandy, there is one last pilgrimage to be made, not to an abbey this time but to view the results of a miraculous rescue operation completed in 1980. In the little village of Giverny near Vernon, on the south-east edge of the region, you can now visit the house where Impressionist painter Claude Monet lived and worked. And better still, you can wander in the beautiful gardens he captured so brilliantly on canvas. All has been lovingly restored and the waterlilies now bloom on the lily pond again.

PRACTICAL INFORMATION

WHEN TO GO. The main tourist season is July to Aug.—the best time to enjoy the beach resorts—but early summer and fall are best for seeing the region's historic sights; the crowds are thinner and the weather usually pleasant. For Normandy's famous apple blossom, pick mid-April through May. For Mont St-Michel, try to come when the tides are at their most dramatic (about Mar. 21 and Sept. 23); the local tourist office can supply tide tables. For cultural events, spring and early summer are best, though concerts in abbeys and churches are often performed during high summer. The spa season in Bagnoles-de-l'Orne runs May-Sept.

Special events include the Boudin (Blood Sausage) Fair in Mortagne-au-Perche in **March;** in **May,** there are regattas and sailing events in Cherbourg and Rouen, where the Joan of Arc celebrations are also held (Sunday nearest to May 30) and a traditional folk festival in Etretat; also, Sailors' Pilgrimage in Honfleur and St Theresa Pilgrimage in Lisieux (both Whit Sunday). In **June,** there are celebrations commemorating the D-Day Landings along the Landing Beaches, and Fécamp has a major pilgrimage celebrating the Precious Blood. **July** sees the pilgrimage across the sands to the Mont St-Michel and the Mount's Music Festival; Deauville has horse racing and polo; on the last Sunday of the month, Granville has its Pardon des Corporations de la Mer, with open-air masses, processions; and, towards the end of the month, the stud farms at St-Lô and the Haras du Pin stage riding events.

August's best-known event is the Yearlings' Sale in Deauville. August 15 (Assumption Day) sees processions and fairs in many places; seaside resorts stage carnivals and sports competitions throughout the month. In **September,** the Haras du Pin has more equestrian events and towards the end of the month (usually the last week) there is the festival of the Archangel Michael at Mont St-Michel, the solemn pilgrimage to St Theresa in Lisieux and, on a more worldly plane, Caudebec-en-Caux's colorful Cider Festival. In **October,** Rouen has its antiques fair and in **November** there are more yearling sales in Deauville.

HOW TO GET ABOUT. By air. From Britain, *Brit-Air* flies London-Gatwick to Caen and Le Havre; *Brymon Airways* from Plymouth and Southampton to Cherbourg; *Aurigny Air Services* from Channel Islands to Cherbourg; *Haywards Aviation* from Shoreham—Dieppe.

By sea. *Normandy Ferries* and *Townsend Thoresen* sail between Southampton and Le Havre and Portsmouth and Cherbourg; *Sealink* between Weymouth and Cherbourg and Newhaven—Dieppe; *Irish Continental Line* have a Rosslare to Cherbourg and Le Havre service.

NORMANDY

By train. Trains from Paris to Normandy leave from the Gare St-Lazare and there are fast turbotrains every day. Trains to Rouen take just over an hour on non-stop services, while the coastal resorts of Deauville and Trouville can be reached in 1 hr 40 mins. The electrified line to Rouen continues to Le Havre (about 2 hrs). The two other main lines are to Evreux (about 1 hr), Caen (about 2 hrs) and Cherbourg (about 3¼ hrs), and to Granville (about 3½ hrs). Special rates on direct trains in summer to Carteret, and cheap day returns on summer Sundays to Deauville-Trouville, Dieppe and some other resorts. French Railways run a number of bus services connecting with trains. They offer special winter weekend rates to various resorts from Paris.

By bus. *Europabus* have 2-day tours to much of Normandy, including Honfleur, Bayeux, Omaha Beach, Deauville and Mont St-Michel and then on to St Malo in Brittany, and a 4-day tour which also covers the Loire Valley. The first two days of *Cityrama's* 'Magnificent France' tour (see Facts at your Fingertips) are devoted to Normandy and they also have a 2-day trip similar to Europabus's and a 3- or 4-day Normandy, Brittany and Loire Valley tour. *Paris Vision* have a 2-day Normandy tour and 2- and 3-day tours covering both Normandy and the Loire. Day trips to the Mont St-Michel are run by *Paris Vision* and *Cityrama,* and to Giverny and Rouen by *Cityrama* and *Paris Vision*. The *RATP* (Paris Transport Service) have day trips at weekends to Mont St-Michel, the Seine Valley, Rouen, Arromanches, Bayeux, Etretat, Honfleur, Deauville, Cabourg, Alençon and some abbeys and châteaux.

MOTORING. The fastest route from Paris is the A13 (*Autoroute de Normandie*) to Rouen, Pont l'Evêque and Caen, with turn-offs to Deauville, Honfleur and other resorts. For a more leisurely drive, take the N13 and N13B along the Seine Valley to Rouen and Le Havre. The N13 goes through to Cherbourg via Lisieux and Caen. For Mont St-Michel, take either the motorway as far as Caen, then branch off on to the N175, or take the slower N12 due west which runs through the Perche region and Alençon, Domfront and (with a slight detour) Bagnoles-de-l'Orne. For Giverny, take the A13 and then the D181 to Vernon, followed by the D55 (watch out for signposts when you're by the river in Vernon).

WHAT TO DO. Perhaps Normandy's special delight is its abbeys, many of which have been restored and are now open to the public. Ask at tourist offices for their special leaflets. The easiest way to visit most abbeys is by car, though plan trips to fit in with opening hours as most close for 2 hours at lunch and evening closing times vary greatly. If you do not have a car, see the *How to get about* section for details of bus trips from Paris and check on local buses. But be prepared to walk a mile or so from the bus stop to the abbey. One of Normandy's main attractions is sampling its gastronomic delights. The Calvados *département* has several interesting routes for *gourmets* (the Cider Route, the Cheese Route, the Calvados Route), with signposted roads; special leaflets available from tourist offices. Specially marked farms will allow you to taste and buy their produce. A similar route is organized in the Normandie-Maine nature reserve for tasting pear cider (the Route du Poiré).

You may like to include a **cookery course** in your holiday. The *Dieppe Cookery Course* offers classes in English, Tues. through Fri., with rates based on half-board in one of three good hotels from Mon. evening to Sat. morning. Classes take place late Sept. through April, and prices start around 1000 frs. Write Dieppe Cookery Course, Secretariat, 18 bld de Verdun, 76200 Dieppe. The *Marie-Blanche de Broglie* cookery school in Paris runs 1-week *Cuisine au Château* classes in a château near Rouen. Accommodations in refurbished little houses in the château grounds. (See Facts at your Fingertips at the beginning of this book.)

Salt water cures are held at Trouville's Cures Marines center; cures last for a weekend, a week or longer. Or rejuvenate at the attractive Château Diane near Etretat. Write Château de Diane, Ecrainville, 76110 Goderville. Slimming and health courses of all kinds.

Normandy is excellent for **horse riding**, and many riding holidays are available. Alternatively, sit *behind* the horse in a caravan meandering through the Pays d'Auge. Write *Les Roulottes du Valdoré*, Route de Manerbe, Le Pré d'Auge, 14340 Cambremer. **Trout fishing** is also good in Normandy, though you'll need a national and local permit. **Sea fishing** trips are available in Trouville, but bear in mind that the trips last a full 12 hours, because you depend on the tides.

Deauville is the best-known **yachting** center, but you can sail from most resorts. **Windsurfing** is also popular, and the long sandy beaches are ideal for **sand sailing**. **Cycling** is a good way of getting about. The Seine-Maritime has a signposted cyclotouring circuit covering about 60 km. **Swimming** in the sea can be cold, but many resorts and some towns have heated pools. **Tennis** courts are found in most seaside places; Cabourg runs special tennis classes.

USEFUL ADDRESSES. The *Commission Régionale de Tourisme pour la Normandie* is at 35 rue Joséphine, 27000 Evreux. *Welcome Information offices* for Normandy are at pl. de l'Hotel-de-Ville, 76059 Le Havre; pl. St-Pierre, 14300 Caen; and 25 pl. de la Cathédrale, 76008 Rouen. Write to them for free brochures and tourist literature. They will also reserve hotel rooms, but not more than 5 days in advance. The *tourist offices* are at the same addresses. In Paris, the *Maison de Normandie*, 342 rue St-Honoré, 1er, is a useful source of information.

American Express, 57 quai George-V, Le Havre.

Car hire. *Avis*, 45 rue de Paris, Alençon; 44 pl. de la Gare, Caen; 1 bld Maritime, Cherbourg; 180 route d'Orléans, Evreux; 37 av. du Général Archinard, Le Havre; 24 rue Malouet, Rouen. *Europcar*, 27 pl. Patton, Avranches; 43 quai de Juillet, Caen; quai de l'Ancien Arsenal, Cherbourg; 33 rue Thiers, Dieppe; av. des Vendéens, Granville; 25 cours de la République, Le Havre. *Hertz*, 34 pl. de la Gare, Caen; 43 rue du Val-de-Saire, Cherbourg; pl. de la Gare and 27 cours de la Republique, Le Havre.

NORMANDY

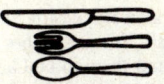

REGIONAL FOOD AND DRINK. Normandy is the land of cream, cheese and *calvados,* a powerful apple brandy. In the old days, on festive occasions, the Normans set a table that included 24 courses. Between the *entrée* and the main meat dish, there was a *trou* (hole), often lasting several hours, during which it was the custom to drink calvados; hence the expression *'le trou normand'*. Many dishes are cooked with rich cream sauces; in fact the description *à la normande* usually means 'with a cream sauce'. Local dishes include *canard à la Rouennaise* (duck), *tripe à la mode de Caen* (tripe), salt-marsh lamb, and *sole dieppoise* (sole poached in a sauce with cream and mussels). With a Norman meal, it is sacrilegious to forget to eat cheese and you may like to try drinking a dry cider (*cidre brut* is the best) instead of the usual wine. Among the 20-odd types of cheeses produced are *Camembert, Livarot* and *Pont-l'Evêque.* The huge apple produce allows for several varieties of cider and calvados.

Camping and gîtes. Write tourist offices for lists of campsites, *gîtes ruraux* and farms willing to take in guests for bed and breakfast. Rooms in private houses (even in châteaux occasionally!) can often be found by inquiring at tourist offices on the spot. Watch out too for farm inns *(fermes auberges),* where you can eat and stay (or camp) for very low prices.

HOTELS AND RESTAURANTS. There are accommodations to suit every taste in Normandy. Even in the plush resort of Deauville, it is possible to find delightful and inexpensive little hotels. Both Honfleur and Pont-Audemer hotels are crowded most weekends, with an influx of Paris weekenders and the British yachting set, on top of the usual holiday makers. In the beach resorts the season is very short, July-Aug. only, but weekends are busy for much of the year; in June and Sept., accommodations are usually available at short notice. But dates vary, as with closing days and months for restaurants, so best check in advance. Hotels and restaurants listed *E, M* or *I* are expensive, moderate or inexpensive.

ALENÇON. *Grand Cerf,* 32 rooms, *Gare,* 22 rooms, are moderate. *France,* 31 rooms, inexpensive, rather noisy.
   Restaurants. Best is *Petit Vatel* (M), good mixture of new and classical dishes.

ARGENTAN. *Renaissance* (M), with good restaurant. *Donjon* (I).

ARROMANCHES. *Normandie; Marine* (M), pleasant, nice views, with restaurant.

AVRANCHES. *Auberge St-Michel,* (M), good restaurant. *Croix d'Or* (M), with rustic décor, garden, restaurant. *Normandie* (I).

BAGNOLES-DE-L'ORNE. Nicest is *Bois Joli* (E), attractive, typically Norman architecture and décor, with pretty garden and rich Norman dishes in restaurant (M). *Lutétia-Reine Astrid* (M), close to park and thermal building, with (E) restaurant. *Gayot* (M), right by the station, with restaurant. *Camélias* (M), a bit further out, but pretty setting near park, with (I) restaurant. *Ermitage* (M), no restaurant. *Nancy* (I), near casino, with restaurant. *Terrasse* (I), just by station, no restaurant.

At **Tesse-la-Madeleine** on outskirts: *Celtic* (M), best known for good restaurant. *Tesse* (M), attractive setting, with some (I) singles. 5 km (3 miles) away at **Antoigny**, *Vallée de la Cour* (E), peaceful, lovely setting in the woods, nice atmosphere, with adequate restaurant.

Restaurants. Most visitors eat in the hotels, but for a change try *Café de Paris* (M), overlooking lake, mostly Italian specialties.

BARNEVILLE-CARTERET. *Marine* (M), delightful; *Angleterre* (M), *Plage et du Cap* (M). All with restaurants, but the Plage's is open summer only.

BAYEUX. *Lion d'Or*, comfortable, moderate, 30 rooms, good restaurant.
Restaurant. *Ma Normandie* (I), 41 rue St-Patrice.

LE BEC-HELLOUIN. *Auberge de l'Abbaye* (M), 8 quiet and comfortable rooms, well-known for its restaurant (E).
Restaurant. *Tour* (I) is much easier on the purse.

BEUVRON-EN-AUGE. Restaurant. *Pavé d'Auge* (M), attractive and delightful spot on village square, with genuine regional cuisine.

CABOURG. Best is the *Grand* (E), 70 rooms, now owned by PLM chain, then *Chat Botté*, 30 rooms, expensive; *Au Caneton*, 20 rooms, moderate; *Paris*, 23 rooms, no restaurant, moderate. Inexpensive: *Castel Fleuri* and *L'Oie qui fume*.

Restaurants. *Balbec* in Grand Hotel, (E), good and smart. *Caneton* (in hotel) just as good but less expensive. *Potinière* (I), good value, friendly, unpretentious.

On road to **Gonneville**, 7km southwest, *Hostellerie du Moulin du Pré*, peaceful, pretty and good food (M); also has 10 rooms.

CAEN. Nicest is *Relais des Gourmets* (M), 15 rue Geôle, well run hotel overlooking William the Conqueror's castle, with, as its name suggests, good restaurant. *Moderne* (M), again as its name suggests, is modern and functional, central yet quiet (pedestrian streets all around), with good restaurant. *Malherbe* (M), pl. Foch, quite near station, but not so convenient for sightseeing, no restaurant. *Univers* (I), liked by readers, is near yacht basin. *France* (I), just by station, no restaurant.

Restaurants. *Dauphin* (M), 29 rue Gémare (also has rooms), *Echevins* (M), 36 rue Ecuyère, mixture of classical and new cuisine, rather chic. *Pomme d'Api* (I), 127 rue St-Jean, upstairs, an old favorite, good value. At nearby **Benouville**,

NORMANDY

the charming *Manoir d'Hastings* (E), *nouvelle cuisine*, in converted 17th-century priory.

CARENTAN. *Commerce et Gare* (I), 16 rooms, home-like atmosphere.
Restaurant. *Auberge Normande* (M), very attractive, regional dishes in *nouvelle cuisine* style. Also has some (I) rooms.

CAUDEBEC-EN-CAUX. *Manoir de Rétival* (E), overlooking the Seine Valley, is pleasant, quiet, but has no restaurant. *Marine* (M), beside river, good restaurant. Small *Normandie* (I), also beside river, has good-value restaurant.

CHERBOURG. *Mercure* (E), at Gare Maritime, with restaurant. *Sofitel* (E), at the Gare Maritime, with view of port; restaurant (M); *Louvre*, moderate, and *Moderna*, comfortable, inexpensive, both without restaurant.
Restaurant. *Vauban*, quai Caligny, good value (M); has fashionable dining room upstairs too (E).

COURSEULLES-SUR-MER. *Paris* (I), just behind beach with good seafood restaurant. *Crémaillère* (M), with another good restaurant.
Restaurants. Apart from the hotels, *Pêcherie* (M) and *Cursella* (M), latter with a few rooms.

COUTAINVILLE. *Hardy* (M), family-run provincial inn with imaginative cuisine. *Neptune*, small, no restaurant, moderate.

COUTANCES. *Grand* (M), by station, *Moderne* (I), no restaurant.
Restaurant. *Verte Campagne* (I), at **Trelly**, 12km (7 miles) south, peaceful farmhouse with walled garden; also has a few rooms (M).

DEAUVILLE. Deluxe are *Normandy*, near the casino and facing sea; *Royal*, by the beach; and for those who prefer the peaceful countryside, *Golf*, 3km (2 miles) south on D278, facing the golf course. These three famous hotels retain that traditional charm and service that is sometimes lacking today. New *PLM Port Deauville* (E), no restaurant, is in stylish new marina. *Fresnaye* (E), *Résidence* (M). Neither has restaurant. Inexpensive: *Paradis*, 12 rooms, and *Patio*, 11 rooms, latter has no restaurant.
Restaurants. *Ambassadeurs* (E), in the casino, and *Ciro's* (E), prom. Planche (lunch only) are chic, very good. *Augusto*, 27 rue D.-le-Hoc (E), also chic. *Saratoga* (M), 1 av. Général-de-Gaulle, good for fish. Also has a few rooms. *Joyeuse* (I), 172 av. de la République. Cheerful and central. *Trois Canards* (I), 11 rue Victor Hugo, modest and far from chic, but good value.

DIEPPE. *Présidence* (E) tops the list; *Univers* (E), a bit old fashioned, but pleasant; *Windsor* (M); *Aguado* (E). All are on bld Verdun, facing sea, and have some rooms for the disabled. All but Aguado have restaurant. *Ibis* (M), recent arrival on the outskirts at **Val Druel,** modern and functional; useful if you are traveling by car.

Restaurants. *Horizon* (M), at the casino, is good. *Marmite Dieppoise* (M), 8 rue St-Jean. An old favorite, popular with British visitors. *Sully* (M), 97 quai Henri-IV, arguably the best of the quayside restaurants. A rival is *Armorique* (M), 17 quai Henri-IV. *Normandy,* by Aguado Hotel, is very good value (I). *Grisch,* in pedestrian precinct, is a good spot for light lunches and for tea (I). *Victoire,* on harbor, is a very typical little café restaurant, friendly, unpretentious, good seafood (I).

Ten km (6 miles) away at **Ste-Marguerite-sur-Mer** is the peaceful *Sapins,* with 25 rooms, attractive garden and good restaurant (I).

DIVES-sur-MER. Restaurant. *Guillaume le Conquérant* (M), delightful 16th-cent. coaching inn.

DOMFRONT. Hotel-restaurant: *Poste,* comfortable, 28 rooms, good cooking (M).

DUCLAIR. *Poste* (I), 19 rooms with good value restaurant overlooking the Seine.

Restaurants. *Parc* (M), very pleasant, also overlooking river. *Canard* (M), attractive 16th-century dining room.

ETRETAT. *Dormy House* (E), attractive location near golf links, view of beach cliffs, quiet, with restaurant (M). *Angleterre* (I). *Falaises,* moderate, no restaurant.

Restaurants. *Aiguille Creuse* (M), pl. Gen.-de-Gaulle. *Roches Blanches* (I), rue Abbé-Cochet.

EVREUX. *Grand Cerf* (E), just by cathedral, renowned for its restaurant. *France* (M), very attractive rooms, inventive cuisine. *Normandy* (M), good restaurant. *Orme,* (M), no restaurant.

Restaurant. *Vieille-Gabelle* (M), noted for apple tarts.

FÉCAMP. *Angleterre* (M), no restaurant; *Poste,* moderate.

Restaurant. At **La Rouge,** 1.5 km (1 mile) south via D925, is *Auberge de la Rouge* (M).

FORGES-LES-EAUX. *Continental* (I), with good restaurant *(Cardinal)* in casino building (M).

Restaurants. *Paix* (M), good value. *Paris* (I), unpretentious café-restaurant on market square.

GRANVILLE. Best is *Bains* (M), 59 rooms; also *Michelet* (I), 19 rooms, no restaurant. *Gourmets,* 19 rooms, is inexpensive.

NORMANDY

Restaurants. The *Normandy Chaumière* (M), 20 rue P. Poirier, is good.

LE HAVRE. *Mercure* (M) in World Trade Center, 96 rooms and all modern amenities. Opposite yacht harbor is the comfortable *Bordeaux* (E), no restaurant. *Marly* (M), no restaurant. *Monaco* (M), best known for its restaurant. *St Louis* and *Celtic* are (I), neither with restaurant.

Restaurants. *Monaco* (M) (see above). *Mon Auberge* (M), 35 rue General-Sarrail, best to reserve. The *Buffet Gare* (I) is good too.

HONFLEUR. *Ferme St-Siméon* (E), delightful converted 17th-century farmhouse, now has additional rooms in nearby manorhouse; Relais et Châteaux member, with local dishes cooked with a light touch in the excellent restaurant. *Lechat* (M), just behind harbor in pretty square, good service, a bit stuffy. *Cheval Blanc* (M), overlooking the *avant-port*, a bit old-fashioned, but good value, with adequate restaurant. *Tour* (M), modern, no restaurant.

Restaurants. Many around picturesque harbor, including: *Ancrage* (M), excellent seafood. *Gars Normands* (M), attractive old building, always crowded. *Chez Laurette* (I), popular cafe-restaurant, conveniently serves seafood platters all day, not just at usual mealtimes.

HOULGATE. *Ferme du Lieu Marot*, outside town (D24), set among apple trees, moderate. Pleasant restaurant.

Restaurant. *Hostellerie Normande* (M), with a few rooms.

JULLOUVILLE. *Casino*, (M), quiet, with restaurant.

JUMIÈGES. *Auberge des Ruines* (I), modest, friendly, full of character.

LÉRY. Restaurant. *Beauséjour* (E), fine cuisine and friendly service; fixed-price menu is good value.

LISIEUX. *Espérance*, 100 rooms, moderate with fine restaurant (M). *Place* (E), by cathedral, comfortable, with restaurant. *Grand Hotel Normandie*, with restaurant (M). *Coupe d'Or* (M), good home cooking.

Restaurants. *Acacias*, 13 rue Résistance (M), *Auberge du Pêcheur* (M), near the basilica.

MESNIL-VAL. 30 km from Dieppe. *Hostellerie de la Vieille Ferme*, an old, converted Norman house, moderate with restaurant, tennis courts.

MONT-ST-MICHEL. *Mère Poulard* (E), 28 rooms, has comfortable well-decorated rooms and unexpectedly good restaurant for such a touristy spot; mixture of regional and 'new' cuisine (E) but good value *menus* too. Closed Oct. through March. Half-board compulsory in summer. *Guesclin*, with good restaurant (M) and terrace overlooking the sea, and *Digue* (M), just off the island.

Also, 1.5km on D976, the *K Motel*, 60 rooms, moderate, and *Motel Vert* (I), 30 rooms. 4km south via D976 is the modest *Desfeux* (I), with restaurant.

Restaurants. *Mère Poulard* (see above). *Terrasses Poulard* (I), lovely view, friendly, good value.

NEUFCHATEL-EN-BRAY. *Lisieux* (I), small hotel-restaurant, reader-recommended.

ORBEC. *France,* small and moderate with restaurant.
Restaurant. *Au Caneton* (E), rue Grande, book ahead. Attractive 17th-cent. building and good Norman cuisine.

OUISTREHAM. Hotel-restaurants. *Broche d'Argent* (M), by yacht harbor, serves good fish dishes. *Normandie* (I), nice Logis de France, good restaurant.

PONT AUDEMER. Restaurants. *Le Petit Coq aux Champs* (E), 5km south via D810 and D29, a charming inn, superb cuisine; also has 11 attractive rooms; Relais et Châteaux member. *Auberge Vieux Puits* (E), an old Norman house, with beamed ceilings, shining copper pots and pans. Also has a few (M) rooms.

ROUEN. Best are modern *Frantel* (E), rue Croix de Fer, by cathedral, underground garage, good restaurant; and *Dieppe,* pl. B-Tissot, by station, excellent restaurant (M). Modern *Arcade,* close to free multistory carpark, moderate. At **Rouen-Sud,** the expensive *Novotel,* 135 rooms. Also outside town, *Mercure,* (M), *Cathédrale,* (M), 12 rue St-Romain, in pedestrian street near cathedral, a bit shabby but full of charm, no restaurant. Inexpensive: *Solférino,* 51 rue Thiers, 16 rooms, no restaurant. *PLM Vaudreuil* (E), by motorway at **Vaudreuil.**
Restaurants. *Couronne,* 31 pl. Vieux-Marché, said to be the oldest inn in France (1345) (E); *Le Beffroy,* 15 rue Beffroy, attractive old building, good cuisine (M). *Ecu de France* (M), 1 rue de la Pie, *Marée* (M), 20 pl. Vieux-Marché. *Petits Parapluies* (M), 46 rue du Bourg-L'Abbé has interesting new cooking. *Vieux Marché* (I), in *place* of the same name, is a bustling bistro with tables outside in summer. *Le Roi d'Ys* (I), 92 rue République, very friendly service, near cathedral.

ST LÔ. Restaurant. *La Crémaillère* (M), pl. Préfecture, excellent, crowded on Sundays. Also has 12 rooms.

ST VAAST-LA-HOUGUE. *France et Fuschias* (M), charming, family run, coaching inn, goodish restaurant (M).

SEES. Restaurant. *Cheval Blanc* (I), reader-recommended. Also has a few rooms.

NORMANDY

THURY-HARCOURT. Restaurant. *Relais de la Poste* (E), on the Caen road, excellent; has a few rooms.

VERNON. *Evreux* (M), 20 rooms, with good restaurant. *Roussel* (I).
Restaurants. *Beau Rivage,* 13 av. Mar.-Leclerc, and *Les Fleurs,* 71 rue Carnot, both (I). At **Port-Villez,** 4km out, *La Gueulardière* (M), attractive.

VEULES-LES-ROSES. Restaurant. *Galets* (M), delicious cuisine, lovely service. Popular with British visitors arriving at Dieppe or Le Havre.

VILLEDIEU-les-POÊLES. *St-Pierre et St-Michel* (I), with good value restaurant.

VILLEQUIER. *Domaine de Villequier* (E), converted 18th century château, with lovely views and good restaurant, (E).

VILLERVILLE. Plain but comfortable is *Bellevue* (M), on the road to Honfleur, nice views, quiet.

VIRE. *Voyageurs* (I), near station with surprisingly good restaurant.
Restaurant. *Cheval Blanc* (M), attractive setting, very good cuisine; also has some rooms.

VIRONVAY. *Saisons,* (E), with attractive garden, tennis court, and restaurant. A pleasant stop between Paris and the Normandy coast.

CASINOS. When in Dieppe, Deauville, Trouville and Bagnoles-de-l'Orne, you may try your luck at boule, roulette, baccara, blackjack and 30-et-40 from about noon on. You will need your passport to enter.

THE LOIRE VALLEY

Château country

by
VIVIENNE MENKES

The Loire Valley region southwest of Paris, with its broad meandering rivers—the Cher, the Indre and the Vienne, as well as the Loire itself—its lush green meadows, acres of vineyards, pearly skies and pleasantly mild climate is known to Frenchmen as the Garden of France, but foreign tourists rightly think of it as 'Château Country'. Here you'll find no fewer than a thousand châteaux gracing every town and village, ranging from imposing feudal castles to intricately decorated pleasure palaces and tiny manorhouses.

Of those thousand lovely buildings, around thirty regularly attract large numbers of visitors and we refer to the finest of them in the following pages. But this is a part of France that repays leisurely exploration, and wherever you go you'll find lesser-known châteaux that anywhere else in the world would be star attractions.

You may like to follow one of the tourist routes planned by the local tourist authorities: you can concentrate on the Ladies of Touraine—Eleanor of Aquitaine, Agnès Sorel, Diane de Poitiers, Marguerite of Navarre—or revive memories of your schooldays by retracing the careers of the turbulent Plantagenet dynasty; or follow in the footsteps of Rabelais, Ronsard or King Louis XI. You may prefer to take the well-planned excursions in comfortable buses and then pick your favorite châteaux for a more extended visit. But whichever way you choose to explore the region, you'll have the added delight of sampling the deliciously light and fruity local wines, tasting the plump fish from the region's many rivers and reveling in the wonderfully fresh produce of the fields and farms in this exceptionally fertile valley.

Perhaps because of the mild climate, the local people, who incidentally are said to speak the purest French anywhere in France, are friendly and helpful.

Tours and the Touraine châteaux

The pleasant and lively city of Tours, only two hours by train or road from Paris, makes a good base from which to start out on a voyage of discovery in the rich and fertile region bordering the majestic river. Although many tourists hurry off every day to visit the châteaux and attractive towns nearby, Tours itself deserves an extended visit. It has been a prosperous city down the centuries, yet has managed, in spite of postwar expansion, to retain the charm of a peaceful provincial center. An imaginative development and restoration scheme has left the heart of the old city intact, banishing tower blocks and industrial buildings to the outskirts or the suburbs, so that as you wander the picturesque streets of the Old Town, le Vieux Tours, or the elegant district around the cathedral where the clergy once lived, you'll find it hard to remember that you're in one of France's major cities.

Everything of interest in Tours is conveniently within walking distance of the center and you should allow time to ramble at leisure. The splendid St-Gatien cathedral makes a good starting-point, its soaring west front illustrating Late Gothic craftsmanship at its finest. The view of the east end from the attractive place Grégoire de Tours is particularly fine. Inside you'll find some magnificent early stained glass, some dating from the thirteenth century, and miraculously still intact in spite of wartime bombing. The area behind the cathedral has been restored and is most picturesque; this was once the heart of a Roman town, and the semicircular street leading off from the south-eastern corner of the cathedral follows the line of the long-vanished amphitheater. Beside the cathedral, the former bishop's palace, a graceful building with a lovely garden, is now the Fine Arts Museum.

The rue Colbert, a narrow and attractive street with some picturesque old houses, including one on the site of a slightly earlier shop where Joan of Arc bought her suit of armor before setting out for Orléans in April 1429, leads to the Old Town. On the way you'll come to one of Tour's most interesting museums: the small Wine Museum, devoted to the craft of wine making through the ages, in the cellars of a now-vanished abbey. Behind it you can see two wine presses, one dating from the Gallo-Roman period, the other from the Middle Ages. Almost next door is the Musée du Compagnonnage, which offers a fascinating picture of craftsmanship illustrated by extraordinarily intricate 'master pieces' made by members of an association of *compagnons*, a sort of alternative guild or trade union movement which started as early as the fifteenth century. The Old Town nearby suffered badly from wartime bombing and subsequent neglect, but has now come into its own again after patient restoration. Most of the narrow streets are banned to cars and are ideal territory for lovers of old buildings.

Places of interest close to Tours include the Grange de Meslay, a medieval tithe barn which makes a superb setting for summer concerts, and also offers an audiovisual presentation of local history; the wine village of Vouvray and the priory at Saint-Cosme, where the poet Ronsard lived and died. But most tourists head for Touraine's splendid châteaux, all of which are in easy reach of Tours.

Amboise's château first became a royal residence in the Gothic period, but the dominant feature now is the Renaissance wing built by François I. Don't miss the graceful St-Hubert chapel built for Anne of Brittany by her first husband Charles VIII. An interesting 'Renaissance Show' called 'At the Court of King François' is held here on summer evenings, with 16th-century music, hundreds of actors, fireworks, light effects and marvelous costumes. As you watch this entirely local show, planned and staged by the inhabitants of Amboise, you'll find it hard to believe that the château was the setting in 1560 of a hideous massacre in which over 1000 Protestant Huguenots who had been involved in a plot to abduct the young François I and his queen Mary Stuart, later Mary Queen of Scots, were strung up from every available hook, pole and balcony—including what is now known as the Conspirators' Balcony on the Logis du Roi. Before leaving Amboise don't miss the attractive manorhouse of Clos Lucé, where Leonardo da Vinci spent the last few years of his life under the patronage of the young François I. The museum in the basement is filled with models, made by the IBM company, to detailed plans by Leonardo for the inventions that prove he was centuries ahead of his own age.

Whereas the château of Amboise is perched up above the Loire, lovely Chenonceau, only a few miles away, sits astride this region's other major river, the peaceful Cher. With its formal gardens, its beautiful gallery spanning the river and filled with the sparkling reflections of sunlight on water, and its associations with two remarkable women, it is one of the few major châteaux to have enjoyed a relatively peaceful history. Henri II presented it to Diane de Poitiers, his mistress, on his accession, but his queen, Catherine de Médicis, had her revenge in due course—when Henri died she confiscated Chenonceau (which was after all royal property) and offered Diane the much less attractive Chaumont instead. Chenonceau is one of very few châteaux in which you are allowed to ramble at will without a guide, so leave yourself plenty of time to enjoy it and to admire the lovely gardens. The *son-et-lumière* show staged here is also planned to let you roam through the grounds, rather than sitting on reserved seats—a magical experience as well-known actors declaim poetry and prose connected with the château and the major periods in its history and the woods are filled with birdsong and music.

South of Chenonceau are the châteaux of Montpoupon and Montrésor, both well worth a visit, but the major attraction here is the delightful town of Loches, set peacefully by the meandering river Indre. Much of it has changed little since the Middle Ages and to step inside the citadel perched above the town is to step back many centuries in time. This impression will be heightened if you can be there over the July weekend when Loches stages its Peasant Market, with local craftsmen and shopkeepers dressed in early peasant costume as they demonstrate their skills or cry their wares. But at any time of year you'll be enchanted by the picturesque streets (most of them now restored), the interesting little Folklore Museum in the Porte Royale, the curious St-Ours church crowned by twin pyramids, and by the château, part castle and part Renaissance pleasure palace. In one of the rooms you can see the recumbent statue of Agnès Sorel, Charles VII's beautiful favorite, who lived here in the 16th century. Far gloomier are the barred cells you will be shown in the massive keep, parts of which date from the 11th century.

The Forest of Loches offers many interesting excursions and the peaceful Indre Valley is a good place for a restful picnic when you need a break from château-visiting.

Azay-le-Rideau, Ussé and Chinon

Fairy-tale châteaux mirrored in still waters will be one of the abiding memories you take back with you from this beautiful part of France, and none seems more magical than Azay-le-Rideau, a jewel-like

Renaissance structure built partly over the Indre downstream from Loches. There is little of interest inside, apart from a famous portrait of Henri IV's striking mistress Gabrielle d'Estrées, but the outside seems sheer perfection, with its corner turrets and its four-storied Great Staircase.

Nearby Ussé has an even truer claim to the description of 'fairy-tale château', for Charles Perrault, who gave us many of our best-loved tales, is said to have been inspired by it for the setting of *The Sleeping Beauty*. Its shimmering whitish blocks of stone and romantic turrets set against the dark trees of the Forest of Chinon certainly fit the legend perfectly. A lovely Gothic chapel with Renaissance decorative details can also be visited in the grounds, but its major treasure—a series of magnificent Aubusson tapestries depicting the life of Joan of Arc—was stolen in 1975 and has never been recovered.

The city of Chinon is reflected in yet another river, this time the Vienne, which flows into the Loire at nearby Candes. Like Loches, Chinon still has a maze of narrow medieval streets, with overhanging houses that are gradually being restored. During its famous Medieval Market in August you can see tumblers and acrobats performing in medieval dress, listen to concerts of medieval music and even gorge yourself on a medieval banquet with the local citizens dressed as serving wenches or jesters. You will of course drink the red wine of Chinon, one of this region's two famous red wines (the other comes from nearby Bourgeuil on the other side of the Loire). Chinon's château is a real castle for once, but little of the original fortress is left now. It was at Chinon that Joan of Arc first recognized the Dauphin as he lurked among his courtiers and the city's *son-et-lumière* show is appropriately devoted to her.

A few miles from Chinon you can visit La Devinière, the house where François Rabelais was born and lived as a child, describing it in his rumbustious novel *Gargantua*.

Fontevraud and Saumur

Near Chinon—for one of the delights of this region is that distances are not great—is the abbey of Fontevraud, a must for English-speaking visitors because it contains the recumbent statues of four English kings and queens: Richard the Lionheart, Henry II, Eleanor of Aquitaine, and Isabel of Angoulême, wife of King John. They were all buried here too, along with other members of the Plantagenet dynasty, but their tombs were broken open and their bones scattered during the French Revolution. The fine Romanesque abbey seems a little stark now, perhaps because the monastery buildings were used as a prison from the early 19th century right down to 1963. But the huge aisleless nave, with

THE LOIRE VALLEY

finely carved capitals, and the exceptionally light-filled choir are most impressive and make a splendid setting for concerts staged by the Cultural Center that is now housed here. You will also be shown a most unexpected building—the octagonal kitchens, topped by a series of conical turrets disguising the chimneys. The strange appearance of this Romanesque building was caused by an over-zealous 19th-century restorer who believed it to be a chapel; it was a British visitor, originally dismissed as a lunatic by the French authorities, who proved that it was designed as a purely functional building used chiefly for smoking meat and fish.

Further downriver lies the pleasant town of Saumur, the home of France's best-known cavalry school. It was once a major Huguenot center and it has never entirely recovered from the revocation of the Edict of Nantes in 1685, which caused a very large number of its inhabitants to flee into exile. Nearer our own time it was the scene of a heroic stand by a group of officers and cadets from the cavalry school, who managed to hold up the German advance in 1940 for a few days, though many of them died in the attempt.

The château is said to have inspired one of the miniatures in the famous Book of Hours painted for the Duc de Berry, with its high walls and many-turreted silhouette. It now houses a Horse Museum and a Decorative Arts Museum with a particularly fine ceramics collection; but do allow time to gaze at the wonderful view of the Loire rolling towards the sea. If you're in the area in late July, try to get tickets for the famous 'Black Squadron' (*Cadre Noir*) cavalry display and military tattoo. Apart from horses, the other specialties of the Saumur area are mushrooms, most of them grown in cliff caves that were originally quarries (you can visit an interesting Mushroom Museum in just such a cave in Chênehutte-les-Tuffeaux near Saumur), and the famous sparkling white wine known as *Saumur champenoise*—a great deal cheaper than champagne, but many think it just as good. Champagne cellars can often be visited (inquire at the tourist office in Saumur).

Angers

Further west still is the town of Angers, once a busy port but now better known as the center of production for the celebrated Anjou wines. Its mighty château is very much a fortress, with its curtain wall, massive towers and drawbridge. It was originally put up by the violent Foulques Nerra, one of the Counts of Anjou, but was rebuilt by Saint Louis (Louis IX) in the 13th century, and is a splendid example of feudal architecture. The finest exhibit inside the château is the magnificent *Apocalypse* tapestry, displayed in a specially built gallery. It was made in the 14th century for Louis I of Anjou and was originally nearly

170 metres long; as so often in France it suffered at the hands of the Revolutionaries, but 107 metres were recovered during a 19th-century reconstruction.

Other splendid tapestries can be seen in the Governor's Lodge (Logis du Gouverneur) and the Logis Royal, but be sure to visit Anger's beautiful Saint-Maurice cathedral too. With its Romanesque façade, the original stained glass windows and wonderfully carved doorway it is perhaps the finest cathedral in this part of France. The former St-Jean Hospital—an interesting illustration of medieval health care—houses another remarkable set of tapestries, dating this time from the mid-20th century and known as *Le Chant du Monde.*

East of Tours—Blois, Chambord and Cheverny

The attractive little town of Blois, like Tours, is a good center for visiting more of the region's châteaux, and also for excursions into the strange Sologne area to the south, with its wild and sometimes desolate landscapes favored as a haunt of game by shooting enthusiasts.

Blois itself is dominated by its château, much of it built by François I, including the superb Renaissance staircase. You are allowed to wander freely, though if you choose the guided tour you'll be regaled by details of the bloodiest deed committed here—the assassination of the powerful Duc de Guise in 1588 by men in the pay of Henri III. For lovers of architecture Blois is a right royal feast, with its three separate wings dating from the late Middle Ages, the Renaissance and the classical period under Gaston d'Orléans.

The church of St-Nicolas is the most interesting of Blois's many churches; once part of a Benedictine abbey, it is just below the château and close to the Loire. The old streets of the area round the rue Haute and the cathedral of St-Louis are gradually being restored and are well worth exploring.

The best-known château near Blois is huge Chambord, standing in vast grounds that are said to be as large as Paris. This somewhat forbidding royal palace was a favorite residence of François I, who loved hunting in the woods surrounding Chambord. There is little to see inside Chambord, but Cheverny, with its beautiful furnishings, is more like a stately home—it is still lived in in fact. It also houses an interesting Hunting Museum and you can even see hunts setting out from here with packs of hounds; on some summer evenings splendid shows using hunting horns and fireworks are staged here. The other major château near Blois, Chaumont, is another feudal castle with towers and battlements, but on a less massive scale than Chambord.

THE LOIRE VALLEY

Orléans

Further east still and only an hour's train ride from Paris is the city of Orléans, which suffered badly from wartime bombing but has now been extensively restored. Orléans's heroine is Joan of Arc, who saved the city from the besieging English and Burgundian armies in 1429. On 7 and 8 May every year she is celebrated in the brilliant Joan of Arc Festival. Unfortunately the wartime devastation has left little of major interest to see in Orléans, but the cathedral of Ste-Croix, a majestic building built at intervals over the centuries (it was begun in the late 13th century), should certainly be visited. The wonderfully carved choir stalls are perhaps its greatest treasure; they were designed by no less a trio than Mansart, Gabriel and Lebrun and date from the early 18th century.

The city also has a good Fine Arts Museum, a graceful Renaissance town hall and many interesting old streets, though many of the buildings are inevitably reconstructions. Ask for a map at the Tourist Office and explore in the best possible way—on foot.

Upstream from Orléans undoubtedly the finest building is the Benedictine abbey at St-Benoît-sur-Loire, one of the most beautiful pieces of Romanesque architecture in the whole of France and a fit resting place for the saintly founder of the Benedictine order. St Benedict had originally been buried in the monastery at Monte Cassino in Italy in the 6th century, but an enterprising abbot decided during the following century that his remains, and those of his sister St Scholastica, must be brought back to France. He sent a raiding party of monks to Italy and, their mission successfully accomplished, renamed the abbey Saint-Benoît (it had originally been known as Fleury). To attend a mass when the Gregorian chant is being sung is a most moving experience.

Beyond the Loire region—Bourges, Le Mans and Vendôme

Although they are some way from the Loire, the towns of Bourges, Le Mans and Vendôme are often visited from one of the Loire centers. Bourges still has many medieval houses and cobbled streets, and a particularly fine cathedral, St-Etienne, with lovely stained glass said by some to be a worthy rival to Chartres's. Because of its excellent acoustics, frequent organ recitals and concerts are given here.

Bourges had its moment of glory in the 15th century, when Charles VII had to flee from the invading English armies and made the city the temporary capital of his kingdom. The most dashing figure in Bourges at that period was Jacques Coeur, a wealthy merchant who traded with the Levant and became Charles's treasurer. His sumptuous Renaissance palace is still standing and you'll find that his name is always cropping up in Bourges; even the city's finest restaurant is named for him. A good way of exploring this area right in the center of France is to follow the *Route Jacques Coeur* (maps and brochures from tourist offices), which includes splendid châteaux and abbeys set in rolling countryside and was organized by the château owners themselves. One of its highlights is the pretty town of Gien with its International Hunting Museum in the château: even if hunting normally leaves you cold, you're bound to be fascinated by this well-planned museum, with its wonderful paintings of 'the chase', still-lives, hunting trophies, weapons and tapestries.

Le Mans's pride is its cathedral of St-Julien with its wonderful Gothic east end supported by soaring flying buttresses and a superbly sculpted Romanesque porch. Inside you can see some fine Renaissance tombs, Romanesque stained glass and 16th-century tapestries. The most interesting building in the Old Town, the Vieux Mans, is the Maison de la Reine Bérangère, dating from the early 16th century and now housing a small museum devoted to the history and ethnography of Le Mans and the whole of the Sarthe region. Incidentally Queen Bérengère was Richard the Lionheart's wife in the 13th century and has nothing to do with the house named for her, though she did found a convent close to Le Mans. The Old Town, surrounded by the city's Gallo-Roman ramparts, is a pleasant place for strolling.

The high point of life in Le Mans is of course the famous '24 Hours' motor race, which draws huge crowds.

Vendôme, attractively set on the river Loir (not to be confused with the Loire with an 'e'), seems to be surrounded on all sides by water, and you'll find that you're constantly crossing little bridges over canals and streams as you stroll through its pleasant streets. The view of the beautiful Gothic abbey church from the old heart of the city (known as the Quartier Ancien) is particularly fine. Vendôme also has a picturesque ruined château.

Nighttime magic

No visit to the Loire Valley and its châteaux would be complete without at least one *son-et-lumière* performance, so if you're there in the summer months do try to plan accordingly. The most splendid of all is undoubtedly the show at Le Lude in the Sarthe, a feudal castle converted into a pleasure palace which makes a perfect setting for the over 300 beautifully costumed local actors and actresses who illustrate five centuries of history accompanied by dazzling light and sound effects and marvelous fireworks. Special coaches leave from Tours bus station to take you to the show and bring you back when the last magic

THE LOIRE VALLEY

sound has faded. Other coaches go to Amboise, which again has hundreds of local actors, and to Azay-le-Rideau, which looks particularly fairylike at night.

Son-et-lumière performances are also given in Chinon, illustrating the life of Joan of Arc; in Chenonceau, where you are free to wander at leisure; and in the little known village of Ste-Catherine-de-Fierbois near Ste-Maure-de-Touraine, which stages a delightful show called 'The Pilgrims' Halt'.

Word of warning: it tends to get chilly at night in this well-watered part of France, so do dress warmly.

PRACTICAL INFORMATION

WHEN TO GO. The Loire valley's temperate climate gives the countryside a gentle, limpid quality seen at its best from May to October. These are the best months for visiting the châteaux when the great *son-et-lumière* performances are given, as well as for enjoying a camping or river vacation. Late spring and early fall are particularly attractive in this area.

Wine fairs are held in **January** (Angers, Vouvray, Tours); **February** (Saumur, Montlouis, Azay-le-Rideau), and **March** (Chinon, Bourgeuil, Amboises, Loches). In **May,** on the 7th and 8th, Orléans celebrates its brilliant annual festival of Joan of Arc. In **June,** dramatic festivals are held in Beaugency and in Le Mans the famous 24 Heures motoring Grand Prix. Blois holds a music festival in **July, August** and **September,** and in and around Tours a series of concerts are given during the Semains Musicales in **July.** The festival of Anjou, held in **June** and **July,** has dance, music and drama, including a festival of French tragedy. Loches has its famous peasant market, with craftsmen demonstrating their skills, in **July.** Later in the month a highlight in the calendar is the magnificent Cadre Noir cavalry display and military tattoo at Saumur. On 26 July Tours still holds the centuries-old Garlic and Basil Fair.

In **August** the streets of Old Chinon are the appropriate setting for a picturesque medieval market. On the first Sun. in the month, Savonnières holds its famous Donkey Fair. The grapes that make the region's fine light wines are harvested in the fall. St-Hubert, the patron saint of hunters is honored by the town of Sully-sur-Loire in **October,** while Orléans honors its patron saint, St Aignan, with a pilgrimage and fair at the end of **November.**

WHAT TO DO. The major attraction in this lovely part of France is, of course, the famous châteaux, most of which are open year-round, though many close during the lunch hour. Concerts, sometimes followed or preceded by a dinner, are often held in the various châteaux.

An official *Guide-Lecturers* service enables you to visit the châteaux privately (individually or in groups) with English-speaking guides. For information and reservations contact *Service de Tourisme,* 16 rue de Buffon, 37032 Tours cedex, or ask at one of the main tourist offices. Other tours set out from Blois, Loches, etc. Guided tours of various cities take place in summer (e.g. Tours, Amboise, Chinon, Loches).

For a different angle—the Loire châteaux can be seen from the sky; circuits in small planes for two or three people can be arranged by Blois-le-Breuil aerodrome, 41330 La Chapelle-Vendômoise, tel. (54) 79–17–68. This is a year-round service but normally operates weekends only; advance reservations advisable.

Riding is particularly good here, especially in the countryside around Tours, and in the vast forests at Loches and Teillay, between Chinon and Azay-le-Rideau. In winter you can go **hunting** with one of the region's many packs of foxhounds (usually on Tues. or Sat.). **Canoeing** is popular nowadays, on the Loire itself, and also on the Cher, the Vienne and part of the Creuse. **Fishing** is also good, but you will need a permit from one of the local associations (inquire at the nearest tourist office).

Walkers can follow the clearly marked paths GR3, GR32, GR36 and GR13, while **cyclists** will have no trouble hiring a bicycle as this is a popular way of getting about in this mostly flattish area. There are three major **golf** courses (9 hole at Orléans and 18 hole at Sully and Tours) and many tennis courts. **Sailing, parachuting** and **swimming** are found everywhere.

An enterprising organization dedicated to preserving **steam trains** runs an excursion between Ligré (near Chinon) and Richelieu. The delightful old train travels weekends mid-May to mid-September plus a few extra days with opportunities for **wine tasting** and sampling local cheeses at stations en route. Details from *Trains à Vapeur de Touraine,* 41 rue Godot-de-Mauroy, 75009 Paris, or local tourist offices, or from Richelieu station on the days when the train is running.

The Institute de Touraine, 1 rue de la Grandière, 37000 Tours, is a good place for **learning French** where it is allegedly at its purest; lodging with families or in modest hotels.

HOW TO GET ABOUT. By train. Every day an average of 15 *rapide* or express trains link this whole area with Paris. Best services are: Paris (Gare d'Austerlitz) to Orléans (1 hr); to Blois (1½ hrs); to Tours (2 hrs). Trains also go from here to Bourges and Châteauroux. From the Gare Montparnasse there is another route serving Angers taking around 2½ hrs for the 305 km (190 mile) journey via Chartres and Le Mans.

Note. Most of the fast trains to Orléans and Tours do not go right in to the cities; you have to change at Les Aubrais (for Orléans) and St-Pierre-des-Corps (for Tours). A shuttle service takes you into the main city station in about 5 minutes, so there is no delay, but do beware of this, as signboards misleadingly

THE LOIRE VALLEY

refer to them as "non-stop" services (though the timetable makes the change clear).

By bus. *Europabus* and *Thomas Cook* run coach tours of the Loire valley châteaux from Paris during the summer, usually of two-four days duration. *Cityrama* has 1-day and 2-day trips year-round on Sun, and daily Apr.-Oct. *Paris Vision* also has 1-day and 2-day trips, and another combined with Mont St-Michel. *Europe Autocar* has a 2-day châteaux trip in June. Local bus tours of the major châteaux leave daily during summer from Tours, Blois, Angers, Orléans, Saumur etc. and the SNCF runs coach tours from Tours station. Regular bus services give you more time to visit individual châteaux, but are infrequent, so you need to plan carefully. Inquire at the *Gare Routière* (bus station), usually next to the railway station; detailed timetables are normally posted up. Special buses leave Tours station on summer evenings for the major *son-et-lumière* shows.

By air. *Air France* offers fly and drive rates London–Nantes. *TAT* has daily flights Lyon–Tours, which may come in handy.

MOTORING. From Paris, the most direct route is the A10 motorway to Orléans, Blois and Tours. If this is crowded, try the N20 via Etampes and Orleans. Longer and more scenic is Paris-Tours via the N10, passing through Versailles, Rambouillet, Chartres, Châteaudun and Vendôme. A somewhat more roundabout, but delightful tour would branch off onto N23 at Chartres for Le Mans and Angers. From Chartres a number of attractive small roads lead to the Loire, such as D921, D935; or from Etampes on D97 or D921.

There is a weekend motor-rail service Toulouse-Orléans in summer.

DISABLED VISITORS. A very useful booklet, *Access in the Loire,* covering the main towns from Nantes to Orléans and 20 of the major châteaux, gives invaluable information. Available free of charge from 68B Castlebar Road, Ealing, London W5 but a donation to cover postage will be appreciated.

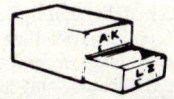

USEFUL ADDRESSES. The main *Office du Tourisme* for the region is in Tours, pl. Mar.-Leclerc. It includes a *Welcome Information* office. Other *Welcome Information* offices are pl. Albert-ler, 45000 Orléans and 3 av. Jean-Laigret, 41000 Blois. *Touring Club de France,* 25 rue des Déportés, 37000 Tours. *Automobile Club de l'Ouest,* 4 pl. Jean-Jaurès, Tours.

Car hire. *Europcar,* 26 bld du Gén.-de-Gaulle, Angers; 29 av. Jean-Jaurès, Bourges; 72 rue de Chanzy, Le Mans; *Centre Commercial les Trois Fontaines,* Orléans; 6 rue George-Sand, Tours; *Avis,* 13 rue Max Richard, Angers; 23 av. Henri-Laudier, Bourges; 14 av. du Gén.-Leclerc, Chaumont; 8–12 rte Nationale, Le Mans; 76 fbg Madeleine, Orléans; 5 rue de Rouen, Saumur; 39 bis bld Heurteloup, Tours.

CHATEAU ACCOMMODATIONS. An association called *Château-Accueil* (c/o Château de Thaumiers, Thaumiers, 18210 Charenton-du-Cher) publishes a brochure giving details of châteaux where you can stay, be sure of a friendly welcome and learn about the history, architecture, culture and cuisine of the region.

WINE TASTING. The *Comité Interprofessionnel des Vins de Touraine,* 19 sq. Prosper-Mérimée, 37000 Tours (behind the Wine Museum), will provide lists of wine cellars that can be visited for tasting and buying, and information on all Touriane wines.

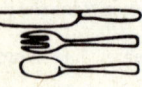

REGIONAL FOOD AND DRINK. Some of the specialties of the Loire valley are: Orléans and Blois; *pâté de Paques* (Easter pie made of veal and pork); *andouillettes* (chitterlings), *saucisses* (sausages); *volailles du Gatinais* (poultry); *canard à la Solognotte* (duck); *civet de lièvre de Sologne* (jugged hare); *gâteau d'amande* (almond cake) and *cotignac* (quince spread).

Tours and Angers; *rillettes de Tours* (pork or goose minced, seasoned, cooked, and served in earthenware dishes); *coques* (black pudding spiced with herbs); *boudins blancs* (white pudding of pork etc.); fried Loire fish; *sandre* or *brochet au beurre blanc* (perch or pike with white butter sauce); *saumon de la Loire* (salmon); *aloses farcies* (stuffed shad); *truit au Vouvray* (trout with a wine sauce); *pêche au Chinon* (fat peaches poached in red wine); and *tarte aux pruneaux* (prune tart).

The local wines are mostly white, including the delicious sparkling Saumur champenoise, best in its very dry (brut) version. Others you will come across are Touraine Sauvignon (very grapey), Vouvray and the famous light and dry Muscadet. Two very fine red wines are Chinon and Bourgueil (the wines of Rabelais); and the sweetish rosé d'Anjou is well known. Touraine has some dry rosé wines, and the sweetish local rosés make a popular chilled apéritif.

Specialties to take home as gifts include pretty boxes of marzipan, stuffed prunes *(pruneaux fourres),* and barley sugar *(sucre d'orge).*

HOTELS AND RESTAURANTS. Lodging and dining places in this region are known for comfort, friendliness and atmosphere rather than for *grand luxe.* Several of the hotels were formerly historic residences, and are often set in large gardens outside the towns. Modest hotels in towns do not usually have a restaurant, but in the countryside almost every one will, often serving excellent food. The letters *E, M, I* indicate expensive, moderate, inexpensive.

AMBOISE. *Château de Pray* (M), just outside town; attractive small château in own grounds. *Lion d'Or* (M), 17 quai Guinot, just by château and overlooking river; comfortable, with home style cooking. Modern *Novotel* (M), outside town.

THE LOIRE VALLEY

France et Cheval Blanc (I), on quai Général-de-Gaulle overlooking river, reader-recommended for value, efficiency and good cuisine.

Restaurants. *Auberge du Mail* (M), 32 Gén.-de-Gaulle, good classical cuisine and excellent regional wines. Also has some rooms. *Epicerie* (I), opposite château, friendly bistro, straightforward cooking.

ANGERS. *Concorde* (E), 18 bld Foch, modern, central, with brasserie. *Anjou* (M), also in bld Foch, very comfortable, good restaurant. *France* (M), pl. de la Gare, goodish restaurant. *Croix de Guerre* (I), central, good value, no restaurant. *Boule d'Or* (I), 27 bld Carnot, with restaurant, a bit further out.

Restaurants. *Quéré* (M), 9 pl. du Ralliement, good *nouvelle cuisine*. *Vert d'Eau* (M), 9 bld Dumesnil, good regional dishes; and the excellent *Toussaint* (M), 7 rue Toussaint, for *nouvelle cuisine* versions of regional specialties.

AZAY-LE-RIDEAU. *Grand Monarque* (M), restaurant (E) has tables outside in delightful courtyard-cum-garden in summer. *Muscadin* (M), tiny, good service, nice atmosphere. *Salamandre* (I), convenient for quick grills, teas or soft drinks.

BEAUGENCY. *Ecu de Bretagne* (M), pl. du Martroi, comfortable, good regional cooking in restaurant. 2 miles away at **Tavers**, *Tonnellerie* (M), peaceful and delightful, pool, good restaurant.

LES BÉZARDS. Restaurant. *Auberge des Templiers* (E), one of best in area, good mixture of classical and new cuisine. Is also a deluxe hotel.

BLOIS. *Château* (M) and *Gare et Terminus* (M), with restaurant, are behind the château. *Grand Cerf* (M), across the river. On the edge of town, *Novotel* (M), with pool, and *Ibis* (M). *Gerbe d'Or* (M), reader-recommended for good value. Popular with locals. *Anne de Bretagne,* (no restaurant), *Etoile d'Or*, (no restaurant), *Monarque, Vendôme,* are all Logis de France. (I).

Restaurants. *Hostellerie Loire* (M), 8 rue Maréchal-de-Lattre-de-Tassigny. Also has 17 rooms. *Péniche* (M), converted barge moored on river, good service. *Mangeoire* (I), 9 rue Haute, tiny, good for light meals.

BOURGES. *Angleterre* (M), *Olympia* (I), no restaurant.
Restaurant. *Jacques Coeur* (E), 3 pl. Jacques-Coeur, good classical cuisine.

BRACIEUX. Restaurant. *Relais* (E), good *nouvelle cuisine,* attractive setting. Also has rooms.

CHAMBORD. *St-Michel* (M), comfortable, opposite château, with restaurant.

CHÂTEAUDUN. Best is the peaceful *Beauce* (I), 50 rue Jallans, no restaurant. *St Louis* (I), 41 rue de la République, with restaurant, garage, across town from château.
  Restaurant. *Caveau des Fouleurs* (M), 33 rue des Fouleries, good value and attractive setting, closed second half Aug.

CHAUMONT-SUR-THARONNE. *Hôtel de la Croix-Blanche* (E), attractive, excellent local specialties, plus some from southwestern France.

CHENONCEAUX. *Bon Laboureur et Château* (M), on main Tours road, has good restaurant. *Hostel du Roy* (I), again on main road. Rooms fine, though restaurant is unexciting. At **Chisseaux**, *Clair Cottage* (I), pleasant Logis de France.
  Restaurant. *Gâteau Breton* (I), rue Nationale, cheerful atmosphere. There is also a good self-service restaurant (I) in the château grounds.

CHINON. *Boule d'Or* (M), river view. *France* (M), typical French hotel overlooking leafy square; no restaurant. 4 miles away at **Marçay** is the *Château de Marçay* (E), dating from the 15th-cent. Comfortable, good restaurant.
  Restaurants. *Ste-Maxime* (M), excellent. *Auberge St-Jean* (I), also has a few rooms. *Années Trente* (I) in picturesque street in Old Town. *Lion d'Or* (I), small and friendly; also has rooms. 3 km away on road to **Marçay** is *Caveaux Rabelaisiens* (M), in converted wine cellars with lots of atmosphere.

COULLONS. *Don Quichotte* (M), comfortable, peaceful, pleasant restaurant.

COUR-CHEVERNY. *Trois Marchands* (M), good restaurant. *St-Hubert* (I), also has restaurant.

FONTEVRAUD. Restaurants. *Abbaye* (I), at bottom of hill. *Croix Blanche* (I), opposite abbey, also has rooms. *Petit St-Michel* (I), opposite abbey, good for pancakes and salads.

GIENS. Restaurant. *Lion d'Or* (I), modest little place in village beside Loire.

GRAND-PRESSIGNY. Restaurant. *Espérance* (M), good *nouvelle cuisine* versions of regional cooking; charming atmosphere. Good value *menus.*

LANGEAIS. *Duchesse Anne* (M), small with restaurant. *Hosten* (M), 2 rue Gambetta, small, no restaurant.
  Restaurant. *Pont-Levis* (I), cheerful little place opposite château.

LOCHES. *Château* (M), 18 rue du Château, small, no restaurant. *George Sand* (M), Logis de France. *France* (I), good value accommodations and cuisine. Pretty courtyard for summer meals.

LUYNES. Genuine antiques surround you at *Domaine de Beauvois* (E), a 15–16th-cent. château in wooded grounds; excellent restaurant. A Relais et Châteaux member. Has pool, tennis courts, angling, riding.

LE MANS. *Concorde-Le Mans* (E), 16 av. Gén.-Leclerc, central, good restaurant. *Central* (M), 5 bld Levasseur, no restaurant. *Moderne* (M), 14 rue Bourg-Belé, good restaurant.
Restaurant. *Calandre* (M), 94 rue Gambetta, lunch only.

MONTBAZON. *Château d'Artigny* (E), built in early 20th-cent. in Louis XV style. Rather grand atmosphere, rooms like ballrooms; classical cuisine, elegantly served. Holds delightful 'musical weekends' Oct. to March, with all-in rates. Across the valley is the *Domaine de la Tortinière* (E), with pool. *Chancelière* (I), delightful, imaginative versions of regional dishes.

MONTRICHARD. *Bellevue* (M), overlooking river Cher, good restaurant. *Tete Noire* (M), comfortable, with restaurant.
Restaurant. *Grill du Passeur* (M), tiny old building picturesquely built on bridge serving delicious food cooked over an open fire.

MONTSOREAU. Restaurant. *Diane de Méridor* (M), delicious local fish and wines; good value *menus*. Is also hotel (called *Le Bussy*).

MUR-DE-SOLOGNE. Restaurant. *Croix Blanche* (I), well run, busy restaurant, specializing in game; also has rooms and private stretch of river for anglers.

ONZAIN. *Domaine des Hauts de Loire* (E), beautifully restored manor house set in 150 acre grounds, with excellent food, tennis courts, angling; Relais et Châteaux member.

ORLEANS. Modern *Sofitel* (E), 44 quai Barentin, with restaurant. *Orléans* (M), 6 rue A.-Crespin, no restaurant. *St-Aignan* (M), 3 pl. Gambetta, no restaurant. *Terminus* (M), central, by station, no restaurant. *St-Jean* (I), 19 rue Porte St-Jean, no restaurant. *Touring* (I), 142 bld Châteaudun, no restaurant. One mile from town, on the Blois road, is the attractive *Auberge de la Montespan* (M), 10 rooms, garden, restaurant, garage. *Ibis* at **Fleury-les-Aubrais,** new, rather impersonal. *Novotel* (M), 7 miles south of town. *Reine Blanche* (E), 4 km (2½ miles) away at **Olivet;** modern, well run, quiet, with grill room; belongs to Frantel chain. *Rivage* (M), again in Olivet, pleasant setting overlooking river, with good restaurant.
Restaurants. *Crémaillère,* best for *nouvelle cuisine* (E). *Porte Barentin,* pretty, classical cuisine (E); *Antiquaires* (M), *nouvelle cuisine; Poutrière* (M), again *nouvelle cuisine. Etoile d'Or* (I), 25 pl. du Vieux-Marché; also has a few rooms.

LES ROSIERS. *Restaurant. Jeanne de Laval* (E), one of the best in the region for classical cuisine. Also has a few rooms.

SAUMUR. *Budan* (M), 3 quai Carnot, overlooking river, with restaurant. *La Gare,* 12 rooms (I). 5 miles from Saumur at **Chenehutte-les-Tuffeaux,** is the elegant *Prieuré* (E), 36 rooms in a Renaissance manor house, plus 12 bungalow rooms. Set in enormous grounds overlooking the Loire, with pool and miniature golf. Very good cuisine (E).
Restaurants. Gambetta (I), 12 rue Gambetta, good for regional cuisine. *Auberge St-Pierre* (I), pl. St-Pierre, good value family restaurant.

TOURS. *Méridien* (E), 292 av. de Grammont, airconditioned rooms, with pool, tennis courts, disco, car-hire service; a bit far out. *Univers* (E), 5 bld Heurteloup, central, good restaurant. *Bordeaux* (M), 3 pl. du Maréchal-Leclerc, by station, modernized with good restaurant.
Armor (M), Logis de France, near station, no restaurant. *Central* (M), 21 rue Berthelot, in quiet street near station and Loire, garden, no restaurant. *Châteaux* (M), 21 rue Gambetta, small and friendly, comfortable rooms in central but quiet street, no restaurant. *Grand* (M), by station, spacious, soundproofed rooms; good old fashioned service; no restaurant.
Akilène (I), 22 rue du Grand Marché; attractive, in Old Town, no restaurant. *Colbert* (I), 78 rue Colbert, small, tiny garden, friendly service, convenient for town center, no restaurant.
On the outskirts: *Campanile* (M), on Chinon road, modern motel-type, with grillroom. *Climat de France* (M), in **St Avertin** suburb. *Fontaines* (M), in **Rochecorbon,** well-decorated rooms, beside river.
Restaurants. Best known is *Barrier* (E), av. de la Tranchée, excellent classical cuisine. *Buré* (M), 1 pl. de la Résistance, good classical cuisine. *Tuffeaux* (E), 19 rue Lavoisier, a find near the cathedral, with local fish cooked in interesting ways. *Rôtisserie Tourangelle* (M), 23 rue du Commerce, carefully cooked local specialties. *Rûche* (I), 105 rue Colbert, remarkable value, and *Renaissance* at no. 64. *Bidoche* (I), 18 rue de la Longue-Echelle, good grilled meat. *Chouette Colbert* (I), 41 rue Lavoisier, excellent value. *Os à Moelle* (I), 6 rue de la Rôtisserie. *Poivrière* (I), 13 rue de Change. Many (I) brasseries in the central av. de Grammont.

VALENÇAY. *Espagne* (E), small, delightful Relais et Chateaux member.

VEIGNE. *Moulin Fleuri* (I), attractive converted mill, with pleasant restaurant.

VENDÔME. *St-George* (M), 14 rue de la Poterie, good restaurant. *Vendôme* (M), 15 fbg Chartrain, good restaurant.

VÉRETZ. *Restaurant. St-Honoré* (I), pleasant Logis de France (also has rooms), overlooking river Cher.

VILLANDRY. *Cheval Rouge,* with good restaurant (M). Right next to château. *Doulce Terrasse* (I), good for teas or drinks, is a bar-cum-brasserie.

VOUVRAY. Restaurant. *Auberge du Grand Vatel* (M), elegant dining room, adequate food. Also has a few rooms.

THE NORTH

Ferry-boats and Flanders' fields

by
JOHN ARDAGH

The northern regions, Picardy and Nord-Pas-de-Calais, are the gateway to France for hordes of visitors on their way to Paris and the south. They seldom linger long in these industrial lowlands, which at first sight may not seem promising tourist country but in fact are full of interest—mighty cathedrals (such as Amiens), famous battlefields (the Somme), historic ports (Calais), elegant resorts (Le Touquet), and much besides.

Skies are often gray, and the landscape is mainly flat, broken here and there by isolated hills and giant slag heaps. From Valenciennes via Lille to the coast at Dunkerque, the sector beside the Belgian border remains one of the major industrial areas of France, but its pattern is changing as traditional industries decline (coal, textiles, steel) and new ones arrive (automobiles, electronics, petrochemicals). The government has been making a special effort to help this change-over by providing new infrastructure—hence the area has a better network of new motorways and wide canals than any other part of France.

A crossroads of invasions across the centuries, the north abounds with battle memorials, from Crécy where England defeated France in 1346, to Vimy where the Canadians fought so heroically in 1917, and Dunkerque with its epic souvenirs of 1940. Used to visitors of all kinds—armed or unarmed—the people of the north are warm-hearted and open-minded, and they compensate for their tough industrial slog by a social and club life of unusual variety. Carnivals and parades fill the calendar, while the passion for unusual sports and hobbies (archery, darts, puppetry, pigeon fancying) seems more English than French. An even closer affinity is with Belgium, for the district around Lille forms the French part of Flanders: the towns with their giant belfries and stepped house façades are strikingly similar to Belgium's Flemish cities.

The Channel ports: Dunkerque, Calais, Boulogne

Dunkerque, an old fortified seaport, was in the 17th century a stronghold of pirates, led by Jean Bart. They destroyed or captured 3,000 ships and took 30,000 prisoners. But the town's finest hour, as the world knows, came in May/June 1940, when an impromptu armada of little boats of every kind set out from England and rescued 350,000 men, two-thirds of them British, from the encircling *Wehrmacht*. The town was 80 percent destroyed in the war. But it has since expanded into a major industrial center with a population of 84,000, big refineries, chemical plants and steelworks (which can be visited). Its commercial port is the foremost in France in terms of tonnage handled.

Calais, to the west, is France's most important passenger port, handling a large part of the traffic with Britain (Dover is a mere 32 km/20 miles away). Small wonder that the town's history has long been bound up with the English, who owned it from 1347 to 1558 (Queen Mary Tudor said, 'When I am dead and opened, you shall find "Calais" lying in my heart'). The local places of interest are mostly connected with England: near the town hall is Rodin's famous sculpture, 'The Burghers of Calais', the six citizens who offered themselves as hostages to save the city from the English in 1347; and 5 km (3 miles) away are the preliminary earthworks for the Channel Tunnel—the on-again-off-again project that has been marked by endless delays. New enthusiasm on the part of President Mitterrand may mark a new phase in its history.

Calais was rebuilt after massive World War II destruction. Today it has a variety of industries, notably chemicals and fabrics. The traditional lace manufacture is in decline.

Boulogne, to the southwest, is Calais' rival for the cross Channel traffic with Britain. It is also the leading fishing port of the Common Market, and a major cold-storage center. Boulogne was a town in Roman days, starting-point both of Caesar's successful invasion of Britain in 54 BC and of Bonaparte's abortive bid in 1803. The main feature of interest today is the old part of the town on a hilltop *(la ville haute)*, girt by a great medieval wall.

Le Touquet and other beach resorts

Along the coast from Cap Gris Nez to the Somme estuary, the sandy beaches are among the best in France. Hardelot-Plage, just south of Boulogne, has recently become *à la mode*, and its pine forests are filling up with the modern weekend villas of the well-to-do. South again lies Le Touquet-Paris-Plage, a shining name in the history of tourism. Its golden age of chic was in the railroad's heyday, when the rich and smart from Paris and London found it so relatively accessible. Today, such people prefer to jet away to the sunnier south, and Le Touquet has moved a bit down market. But it still fills to bursting in summer with holidaymakers of all kinds, attracted by its varied facilities—long beaches of fine sand, a racetrack, riding and yachting, tennis and golf, nightclubs, concerts, two casinos, and the Palais de l'Europe for congresses and festivals.

Further south is another noted beach resort, Berck-Plage, frequented year-round because it is also a medical center for the treatment of bone illnesses. And inland from the beaches, two towns are especially worth a visit: Montreuil, with a 16th-century fortress, and ramparts dating from the 12th century; and St-Omer, southeast of Calais, where the magnificent 13th-century cathedral of Notre-Dame has a range of beautiful sculptures and carvings.

The battlefields of 1914–18

Many of the fiercest battles of that long, cruel war of the trenches were fought in the Artois district, north of Arras, and in the rolling country above the Somme valley, northeast of Amiens. These areas are dotted with poignant war memorials, and with scores of Allied and German cemeteries, still neatly tended and carefully signposted. To visit them is a sobering, instructive kind of tourism—arguably worth any number of visits to castles or casinos.

The most majestic memorial is a Vimy Ridge, dominating the valley north of Arras—two mighty stelae of stone, flanked by sculptures of weeping, pensive women, 'erected by the people of Canada, in memory of its 60,000 dead'. The Canadian army seized this ridge in April 1917. Close by, the Canadian trenches and dug-outs have been preserved and can be visited. Just to the north is the French military mausoleum of Notre-Dame-de-Lorette, with a small war museum.

Much further south, the terrible casualties of the Somme battles of 1916 are commemorated by the giant British monument at Thiepval, the nearby Ulster Tower, and the Newfoundland Division's memorial park of Beaumont-Hamel, where the trenches are still clearly visible. Of likely interest to American visitors is the cenotaph at Bellicourt, just off the Cambrai-St-Quentin road, paying tribute to the US army's attack on the Hindenburg Line in 1918.

Industrial decay, as well as the sound of shellfire long silenced, haunts the plain of Artois around Lens and Béthune. Here the landscape is pitted with scores of conical coal tips, memorials to an industry that is fast dying. This was formerly one of the major coalmining regions of Europe, but the mines are nearing exhaustion and most have now closed. Flat landscapes, gray skies, decaying mines, long-buried soldiers—this is possibly the most melancholy part of France, but with its own sad beauty, like the war poems of Wilfred Owen.

The inland cities: Lille, Arras, St-Quentin, Amiens

The metropolis of Lille is capital of the north, hub of a conurbation of over a million souls that includes the textile town of Roubaix, and Armentières where a Limey veteran today would be unlikely to find many girls unkissed for 40 years. Despite its dour exterior, Lille is a vibrant place, full of culture and night life, and a major center of commerce and industry, notably textiles, metalwork, brewing and food-processing—as well as a brand-new subway system with easy access for the handicapped.

The Belgian frontier is on the back doorstep, and the architecture and ambience are so Flemish—cobbled streets, stepped façades, wood-paneled cafés—that a visitor may feel he is in Belgium. Among Lille's many noted buildings, the art museum stands first: it is one of the richest in France, with works by Rubens, Van Dyck, Goya, Delacroix, Dufy and many other European masters. The old Bourse is a fine example of 17th-century Flemish architecture, while the church of Ste-Catherine contains the beautiful 'Martyrdom of St Catherine' by Rubens. You should also visit the Paris Gate and the 15th-century Hospice Comtesse with its museum of popular art. In the old part of the town, the rue de la Monnaie is lined with graceful Flemish houses, which have recently been restored: through their windows you may be able to glimpse the delicacy of the brickwork.

At Hem, in the suburbs near Roubaix, the chapel of La Sainte-Face is adorned with outstanding stained-glass murals by the modern artist Gustave Manessier. Arras, 48 km (30 miles) southwest of Lille, is also well worth a visit. Despite wartime damage, its picturesque 17th-century Flemish architecture stands intact, notably in the Grand'-Place and the place des Héros, two impressive squares enclosed by brick houses with gables and arcades. The city hall with its belfry and the ancient abbey of St-Vaast with its museum are other glories of Arras.

St-Quentin, to the southeast, was the scene of a famous battle in 1557 when Philip II of Spain defeated the French. Today the town is worth a halt chiefly for its Lecuyer Museum, with a fine collection of 18th-century portraits by Quentin de la Tour, and its Gothic basilica, with stained-glass windows and sculptures of the 13th and 14th centuries. Valenciennes, a big town to the north, brings us back with a jolt into the late 20th century—here in 1979 there were violent riots against the planned closure of the local steelworks at Denain.

Finally to Amiens, capital of Picardy. Its great Gothic cathedral, begun in 1220, is one of the finest in France. Note especially the four-sided reliefs on the lower half of the west front, symbolizing the virtues and vices, local arts and crafts, and some fables; and the rich carvings of the 16th-century choir stalls. The 113-meter (373-ft) steeple and the large rose window also date from the 16th century.

The Picardy Museum has an eclectic wealth of paintings by everyone, or almost, from Frans Hals to Fragonard, from Tiepolo to Renoir and Dali. And talking of Dali, modern culture in Amiens is also represented by the palatial Maison de la Culture, one of the largest of the chain of new arts centers foisted on France in the 1960s by de Gaulle's culture minister, author André Malraux. It survives to prove that even a white elephant can sometimes house interesting exhibitions, concerts, plays and film shows. Lastly, on a fine day in spring or summer it might be worth taking a look at the curious *hortillonnages* in the eastern suburbs—a network of small canals enclosing market gardens. Till recently, this was a real market-on-the-water, with growers selling their wares from small barges, as in Bangkok. But the boats have now been replaced by unromantic trucks on *terra firma*. Such is progress.

THE NORTH

PRACTICAL INFORMATION

WHEN TO GO. For the Channel beach resorts June through Sept. are the best months for a visit. The spring and fall are especially pleasant for those who wish to visit the cathedral cities, when roads and accommodations are less crowded. The region's principal events take place during the spring and summer.

Carnival time gets under way in **February** and **March.** Bailleul has its procession of the giant Gargantua, Dunkirk celebrates its Three Festive Days, in Lille there is the procession of the giants Lidéric and Phinaert. Festivities continue through **April,** when the procession of the giants 'Reuze Papa' and 'Reuze Maman' highlights Cassel's carnival (Easter Monday), and during the last two weeks Amiens holds its combined exhibition and fair. At the end of April there is the great international fair at Lille, which originated during the Middle Ages.

A leading religious event is the procession of the Mysteries of Notre-Dame at Albert. 'Papa Reuze' appears on the scene again in **June** as the star of Dunkirk's Follies. St-Omer opens its *son-et-lumière* show, which runs until October. **July's** calendar is full and varied. Boulogne has its Fish Fair and Maubeuge its Beer Festival. The Le Touquet season begins with an international horse show and other social events. There is a summer carnival at Bailleul, and at Douai the procession of the giant Gayant, a festival dating from the 15th cent. Arras celebrates the lifting of the siege of the town by the Spaniards in 1654 with a great five-day festival during the month of **August.** This is also the month of Boulogne's traditional procession of Notre-Dame de Boulogne, and of Hardelot's Jazz Festival. On the first Mon. in **September** Lille has its *'Grande Braderie',* a vast sale that lasts till midnight, with the whole town transformed into one gigantic flea market. Lille's music and drama festival is in **November.**

WHAT TO DO. Swimming of course, with over 128 km (80 miles) of wide sandy beaches, and **sailing. Fishing,** too, is excellent, both at sea (day fishing trips in groups from Dunkirk and Boulogne) and in the rivers (carp, trout, pike, and crayfish are plentiful). **Riding** weekends are offered at Le Touquet and other places, and Le Touquet also has 23 **tennis** courts and 2 **golf** courses. **Archery** is a favorite sport in Picardy. **Hikers** will enjoy using the GR121 marked path, which runs for 250 km (156 miles) from the Belgian border. The SNCF offers special rates (30% off) for hikers setting out for the 2000 km of marked paths in Picardy; ask for *'train et randonnée'* leaflet at rail stations in Paris or in the Picardy region. **Sand-sailing** is popular on the long sandy beaches, and so is **wind-surfing** (though the Channel can be rough).

Nature-lovers will want to visit the bird sanctuary and nature reserve at St-Armand-Raismes. And for those in search of peace and quiet, what better than a **barge** holiday along one of the northern canals? Alas, the barge elevator at Fontinettes near St-Omer is no longer in use, but you can still make the trip to see it.

The famous thalasso-therapy (**saltwater and sea air cure**) center at Le Touquet has special rates for 'relaxation weekends' or for longer visits (with free access to tennis courts, riding center and golf course if you are taking the waters). St-Armand-les-Eaux is a spa offering all-in rates either in a 3-star hotel or staying in a private home.

Lille has excellent **theater** and the tourist office has organized special theater weekends: package covers good seat for the performance of your choice, plus 3-star hotel and breakfast, country-style buffet or gastronomic meal, with opportunities for conducted tours of Old Lille and shopping expeditions.

Not to be missed if you like studying **local customs** is the traditional Sun. evening hop at Herzeele, where you dance to music played by two huge barrel organs, just as in Breughel's day. And **cockfighting,** though you may need a strong stomach for it, is another tradition in this part of the world—ask at tourist offices for dates.

Local tourist offices will provide maps and leaflets describing two interesting tourist routes: **The Hop Road** and **The Standing Stone Road** (Route des Menhirs)—a must for anyone interested in prehistoric times.

HOW TO GET ABOUT. By air. Frequent flights Paris–Lille, with less frequent service from Bordeaux, Lyon, Metz, Nantes, Strasbourg and Toulouse. For many British tourists in particular, the North is the gateway to the Continent. There are twice-daily flights by *Air France* from London to Lille. Year-round; 45 minutes flight. The British travel firm *Time Off* has all-in rates for Boulogne and Le Touquet, with travel by plane, hovercraft or boat.

By boat. Boulogne and Calais are easily reached by hovercraft or ferry from Dover or Folkestone; Dunkirk by ferry from Dover.

By rail. From Calais, Boulogne or Etaples you can use the rail services to see much of the area. From Calais and Boulogne there are frequent services to Abbeville, Amiens, Arras and Lille. From Calais several services daily to St-Omer, Lille, Valenciennes and Hirson. From Paris (Gare du Nord) there are fast and frequent services to Amiens, Arras, Douai, Lille and also to Etaples (for Le Touquet). Special weekend trips to Lille, including visits to the old town, are organized from Paris. Details from Lille tourist office or Maison Nord-Pas-de-Calais in Paris (see addresses section).

MOTORING. If you're coming from Belgium, Lille is only an hour by motorway from Brussels. The main Calais–Paris motor route is the N43 to St. Omer, then the A26 to Arras and the A1 *(Autoroute du Nord)*. The *Route Sang et Or* (N1) goes via Boulogne, Abbeville, Amiens and Beauvais.

THE NORTH

From Dunkirk, take the A25 to Lille, where you join the *Autoroute du Nord* (A1).

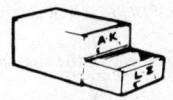

USEFUL ADDRESSES. *Welcome Information office* (Accueil de France) at Palais Rihour, B.P. 205 pl. Rihour, Lille. *Comité Régional de Tourisme,* rue Faidherbe, 59000 Lille. *Comité Departemental de Tourisme* for the Somme, 21 rue Ernest-Cauvin, 80000 Amiens; for the Nord, 14 sq. Foch, 59800 Lille; for the Pas-de-Calais, 44 Grande-Rue, 62200 Boulogne-sur-Mer. *Touring-Club de France,* 56 bis bld Liberté, Lille. *Automobile-Club du Nord de la France,* 12 rue Maréchal Foch, Roubaix. *Office du Tourisme* in all main centers. In Paris: *Maison du Nord-Pas-de-Calais,* 18 bld. Haussmann, 9e.

Car hire. *Avis,* 153 rue J.-Barni, Amiens; 36 pl. d'Armes, Calais; 9 rue Belle-Vue, Dunkerque; 1 rue St-Sauveur, Lille, and at airport. *Europcar,* 13 rue Ste-Catherine, Abbeville; 104 rue J.-Barni, Amiens; 58 av. St-Exupéry and ferry port, Calais; 15 pl. Jeanne-d'Arc, Dunkerque; 155 rue du Molinel, Lille, and airport. *Hertz,* 58 bld Alsace-Lorraine, Amiens; 38 pl. d'Armes, Calais; 8 av. Guynemer, Dunkerque; 41 rue Gustave-Delory, and airport, Lille.

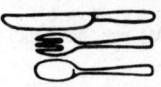

REGIONAL FOOD AND DRINK. Fish and shellfish are the star features in the menus of the region. North Sea herrings and oysters, *moules* (mussels), *coques* (cockles), *crevettes* (shrimps) are particularly succulent. Flanders has its own local dish, the *hochepot* (hotpot), as well as *veau* (veal) *à la Flamande. Pâté de bécasse* (woodcock pâté) and *carbonnade,* beef braised in beer. In Picardy, duck pâtés and *ficelle picarde* (a ham and mushroom pancake) are popular. The region does not produce any wine, but brews and drinks beer in large quantities; cider is also made here. *Genlèvre* is a juniper flavored fine-grain spirit.

The North is not so well known for its cheeses— *Maroilles, Mont des Cats* and *Goyère* —as for its pastries and confectionery. Among the latter are such delicacies as the *gaufres fourrées* (layered wafers) of Lille and Douai, *beignets* (fritters) of St-Quentin, *chiques* (caramels) of Berck-sur-Mer, and macaroons of Amiens.

HOTELS AND RESTAURANTS. Some resort hotels are open only Easter and summer, so check in advance. You will find that the regional specialties in even the most modest hotel restaurant are good, often excellent. Hotel restaurants with outstanding cuisine are listed with the selected restaurants, which are labeled *E, M* or *I,* for expensive, moderate, inexpensive.

ABBEVILLE. *France,* 76 rooms, garage, restaurant, moderate.
Restaurants. *Condé* (I), also has rooms, good value. *Etoile du Nord* (I), 14th-century inn serving grills and regional dishes.

AMIENS. *Carlton-Belfort,* 40 rooms; *Nord-Sud,* 26 rooms, good cooking; *Univers,* 41 rooms, no restaurant. All moderate. *Paix* (I), no restaurant. At **Boves,** 6.5 km (4 miles) out, the 92-room *Novotel,* expensive, with pool.

Restaurants. *Bois de Boulogne* (I), 505 chaussée J.-Ferry. *Joséphine* (I), 20 rue Sire-Firmin-Leroux.

At **Dury,** 4.5 km (3 miles) out, *La Bonne Auberge* is the best in the region. *L'Aubergade,* also good. Both (M).

ARDRES. *Grand Hôtel Clément* (M), suitable hotel for this historic town.

ARRAS. *Univers* (M), in an old monastery. Comfortable, quiet. *Moderne,* (M), no restaurant.

Restaurants. *Le Chanzy* (M), 8 rue Chanzy, liable to be crowded. Also has rooms. *Ambassadeur,* at the station, has very good classical cooking (M).

AUVILLERS-LES-FORGES. *Hostellerie Lenoir* (M), a country inn in the Meuse valley. Excellent restaurant (E), with *nouvelle cuisine.*

BERCK-PLAGE. Beach resort. *Terrasse et Terminus* (M), near bus depot, no restaurant. *Florida* (M). *Renaissance* (I), close to casino.

BOULOGNE. Important cross-Channel and fishing port. *Faidherbe,* 35 rooms, *Métropole,* 28 rooms, none with restaurant; newish *Ibis* does have restaurant. All moderate. *Monsigny, Mirador,* inexpensive.

Restaurants. *Matelote* (M), just by beach and casino, good *nouvelle cuisine,* popular with British food lovers. *Charlotte* (M), 11 rue Doyen, tiny and pretty, newish cuisine. *Plage* (I), 125 bld Ste-Beuve, also has rooms. *Hamiot,* 1 rue Faidherbe (I).

CALAIS. Cross-Channel port. *Meurice* (M), best with restaurant (called *Diligence*), comfortable. *Sauvage,* 36 rooms, moderate. *Victoria* (M), 15 rooms, no restaurant.

Restaurants. *Channel* (M), bld Résistance, very popular, on seafront. *Moulin à Poivre* (M), rue Neuve, art nouveau decor, friendly atmosphere. *Sole Meunière,* bld de la Resistance (M). *Feuillandine* (I), pl. d'Armes, good basic cooking. *Dune* (M), 1.5 km (1 mile) away at **Blériot-Plage,** is good and has a few rooms.

LE CROTOY. Seaside resort. **Restaurant.** *Baie* (M), an old favorite overlooking the sea.

DOUAI. *Terrasse* (I), has good restaurant. **Restaurant.** *Air Acceuil* (M) is an excellent medium-priced restaurant on the Arras road, at airport.

THE NORTH

DUNKIRK (DUNKERQUE). *Frantel* (E), no restaurant. *Europ Hotel* (M). *Borel* (M), 30 rooms, well-run family hotel, no restaurant. Inexpensive, near rail station, *Hôtel-Restaurant Félix,* with good seafood.

Restaurants. *Richelieu* (M), at station, and *Métropole* (M), 28 rue Thiers. At **Teteghem,** 6 km away, is delightful *Meunerie* (E), in a converted mill.

FUMAY. *Roches* (M), small, comfortable, nice views from most rooms, with (I) restaurant.

HARDELOT-PLAGE. Bathing resort. *Ecusson,* 20 comfortable rooms, with terrace restaurant, is (M). So is attractive new *Régina,* 40 rooms. *Pré Catalan* (I), small and peaceful. All have restaurants, the latter specializing in trout.

Restaurant. *Du Golf* (M) is good.

HESDIN. Hotel-restaurant *Rôtisserie des Flandres* (M).

LILLE. Best are the 106-room *Royal Concorde,* the 70-room *Carlton* and 80-room *Bellevue,* all without restaurants, and expensive. Near the station: comfortable *Chagnot* (M), with grillroom. *St-Nicolas* (I), no restaurant, central.

Near the airport, *Holiday Inn* (E) and *Novotel* (E), both with pool.

At **Englos,** about 6.5 km (4 miles) out, another *Novotel* (E), with pool, and nearby on N352, *Mercure* (M), with pool.

At **Marcq-en-Baroeul,** just north of town, *Holiday Inn* (E), with grill, cafeteria, pool.

Restaurants. Lille is, surprisingly enough, despite its stolid exterior, one of France's better gastronomic cities. Best is *La Devinière,* 61 bld Louis XIV (E), marvelously inventive, digestible cuisine, closely followed by *Le Paris,* 52 bis rue Esquermoise (E); *Le Flambard,* 79 rue d'Angleterre (E). Also fine are the old *Huitrière* (M), 3 rue des Chats Bossus; *Compostelle* (M), 4 rue St-Etienne, good regional specialties; and the *Queen Victoria* (M), 10 rue du Pas, which, in spite of its name and gimmicky pub décor, serves authentic French cuisine. Upstairs in same building, *Belle Epoque* (E), chic. All these have *nouvelle cuisine.*

Lille has several good bistros, such as: *Verdière* (M), 25 rue du Plat; *Le Club* (E), 16 rue du Pas, an old favorite.

At **Prémesques,** 10 km (6 miles) away, is *Armorial* (E), in a delightful chateau; good newish cuisine, popular with the English.

MALO-LES-BAINS. Seaside resort next to Dunkirk. Near the beach is the *Hirondelle,* with 33 rooms, inexpensive. Also near the beach are the 13-room *Trianon,* no restaurant, inexpensive, and *Rivage* (I), with restaurant.

MAUBEUGE. *Grand* (M), 31 rooms with excellent restaurant. *Mercure* (M), 59 rooms, on N2. Pool.

Restaurant. *Langouste* (M), has good seafood.

MERLIMONT. Restaurant. *Hostellerie Georges,* with excellent fish dishes (E).

MONTREUIL-SUR-MER. *Château de Montreuil* with grounds and pool, 14 rooms, good cuisine. Now belongs to the Roux brothers, who are well known to London gastronomes. A Relais et Châteaux hotel. *Central,* (I), 10 rooms.
Restaurants. At **La Madeleine-sous-Montreuil,** 3 km (2 miles) north on D139: *Grenouillère* (E), rambling riverside inn, delicious cooking.

POIX. *Poste* (I), with good value restaurant.
Restaurant. 6.4 km (4 miles) west, at **Caulières,** is *Auberge de la Forge* (M).

ROUBAIX. *PLM Grand Hôtel,* moderate, comfortable rooms in modernized building in town center. No restaurant.
Restaurants. *Caribou* (E), mostly classical cuisine. *Charly* (M), cheerful atmosphere, home-style cooking. Open for lunch only.

ST-OMER. *Bretagne* (M), best known for its restaurant. 6 km (4 miles) away, at **Tilques,** *Vert Mesnil* (E), a quiet manor house with nice grounds, tennis courts and good food.

ST-QUENTIN. *Grand* (M), with good restaurant. *Paix et Albert I* (M), good restaurant. *St Jacques* (I), no restaurant. Plain.
Restaurants. *Petit Chef* (M), 31 rue Emile-Zola, unpretentious, good. Also good is *Café Riche,* 10 rue des Toiles (M). At **Neuville-St-Amand,** 3 km (2 miles) southeast via D12, *Château* (E), deservedly popular.

LE TOUQUET-PARIS-PLAGE. *Westminster* (E), is quite palatial, 145 rooms, very comfortable, quiet, pleasant view, but no restaurant. Closed Nov. to Easter. Also expensive is the modern *Thalamer,* a member of the Novotel chain, right on the sea, with 104 rooms. Next to the thalassotherapy (salt-water cure) center. A bit less expensive, *Côte d'Opale,* 28 rooms. Moderate: *Nouvel Hôtel,* 20 rooms, no restaurant; *White Star,* 14 rooms; *Windsor,* 27 rooms. Inexpensive: *Hirondelles, Le Caddy.*
At the golf links, 3 km (2 miles) south of Le Touquet: *Manoir* (E), attractively situated, quiet, comfortable, 47 rooms.
Restaurants. For particularly fine food, there is the smart *Flavio-Club de la Forêt* (E), 1 av. Verger. *Chalut* (M); close to beach. 1.5 km (1 mile) east, at the airport, *L'Escale* (M). *Chez Pérard* (M), busy, bustling, crowded, but friendly atmosphere; good seafood. *Diamant Rose,* pleasant, family-type (I).

TOURCOING. *Novotel* (E), with pool and snack bar, at nearby **Neuville-en-Ferrain.** Cheaper is *Ibis* (M), in town.
Restaurants. *Au P'tit Bedon* (M), inventive dishes. *Saucière* (M), pleasant atmosphere, good *nouvelle cuisine.*

THE NORTH

VALENCIENNES. *Mapotel Grand Hôtel* (M), by station. *Notre Dame* (M), no restaurant. 5 km (3½ miles) out, on N30, *Novotel* (E), with pool.
   Restaurant. *Buffet de la Gare* (M), in the rail station; rather somber but a great gastronomic stop.

WIMEREUX. Seaside resort. *Aramis,* 1 rue Romain, 16 rooms, is moderate but has no restaurant. *Hôtel du Centre,* 18 rooms, comfortable, inexpensive, with good restaurant. *Atlantic* (M), 10 rooms, popular with British visitors; best known for its good restaurant (M).

WISSANT. Seaside resort. *Bellevue* (I). *Normandy* (M), with pool.

CASINOS. Much of Le Touquet's resort life revolves around its two casinos, one of which is open year-round, the other Easter to end Sept. only. There you may enjoy the facilities of restaurant, bar, cabaret and other entertainment as well as trying your hand at the gambling tables. To gain admittance to the latter, bring your passport. Boulogne's casino is open year-round nowadays; you can play boule, baccara and roulette here.

CHAMPAGNE

Sparkle from the chalk

Champagne, a place name that has come to be a universal synonym for joy and festivity, is a word of humble origin. Like Campagna, its Italian counterpart, it is derived from the Latin *campus,* which means nothing more than an open field. In French, *campus* became *champ.* The old language extended it to *champaign,* meaning battlefield, and *champaine,* a district of plains.

Both 'battlefield' and 'plains' accurately describe the province. Lying between the Ile de France and Lorraine, with Belgium above it and Burgundy below it, Champagne is criss-crossed by Roman roads along which defenders and invaders have clashed for two millennia. In our own time, the history of World War I is dotted with names of its towns and localities, such as Rheims (Reims), Verdun, Soissons and the Chemin des Dames; more recently, the tiny village of Colombey-les-Deux-

CHAMPAGNE

Eglises, home of Charles de Gaulle, has become a mecca; his house, La Boisserie, is now open to the public. The landscape of the area is sufficiently varied to include forests and flowers, hills and valleys, rivers and streams, and even several caves. But a great part of it consists of monotonous chalk plains, which Stendhal, who preferred mountains, called 'the atrocious flat wretchedness of Champagne'.

There is little flat wretchedness to be seen in the heartland of Champagne, where the grapes that go into its wine are grown. On the contrary, the 10,940 hectares (27,000 acres) of vineyards are scattered over a beautiful countryside of rolling hills and valleys. The principal grape-producing districts are three: the Montagne de Rheims, lying like a lopsided horseshoe a few miles south of Rheims; the lovely east-west Vallée de la Marne, a little farther south, and the picturesque Côte des Blancs, running due south from Epernay.

If you are visiting the region in the autumn, plan to drive along the Champagne Road through vineyards golden in the harvest sun. The views are enchanting and the prospect of one of France's storehouses of wealth is a pleasing sight for eyes and mind.

The chalk deposits (610 meters/2,000 ft deep in some places) left by a prehistoric inland sea may not embellish the topography, but they are the principal source of Champagne's glory. From blocks cut out of them, the great cathedral of Rheims was built. The chalky subsoil is what makes Champagne grapes healthy and gives them their distinctive taste. Burrowing through solid chalk 30 meters (100 ft) beneath Rheims and Epernay are 193 km (120 miles) of cellars where the sparkling wine is stored at an unvarying 10°C (50°F), exactly the temperature required to keep it continually at his best.

Just across the Marne lie the 'hors classe' vineyards of Ay. About 5 km uphill (3 miles) to the west is the hilltop village of Hautvillers and the fine old Benedictine abbey where, in the 17th century, the learned Dom Pérignon discovered how to make champagne a blended sparkling wine, instead of the unblended still wine the abbey had produced up to that time.

The panorama from the abbey gardens is superb, but you will perhaps find the hilly region between Hautvillers and Ay even more visually satisfactory. Ten minutes from Epernay on the Rheims bus will take you to a high point appropriately named Bellevue. From here, the view over miles of vine-covered hills and valleys along the Marne is spectacular. And if you walk back downhill for about 3 km (2 miles) to the village of Dizy, you will find that the beauty of the constantly changing view never diminishes.

The cathedral city of Rheims

Rheims and its incomparable cathedral deserve a place high on any tourist's itinerary. In 1918, after four years of pounding by German artillery, about all that remained of the beautiful old city were some hundred houses, a few churches and public buildings, and the battered cathedral. Present-day Rheims is a new city, with wide, straight streets and modern buildings. Salvaged from its past are, besides the cathedral, the 3rd-century Porte de Mars; the church of St-Rémi, which, with its curious mixture of Gothic and Romanesque styles, is of particular interest to students of architecture; and the dignified place Royale, which has been restored to look as it did when built under Louis XV. The Fine Arts Museum contains many fine tapestries and paintings, including the work of Delacroix, David, Daumier and Corot. The city itself, sharing the spotlight with Epernay, is the home of some well-known champagne firms.

World War II bequeathed Rheims a brand-new historical monument in the form of the room in the Modern and Technical College, where the German capitulation was signed on May 7, 1945. The room, its walls covered by the operational maps of General Eisenhower's headquarters, has been kept exactly as it was when the German army and navy chiefs sat down at its bar table to admit their defeat to the Allied conquerors. Rheims now also has a new university, a *maison de culture* and a *théâtre populaire*.

But the essential pride and glory of Rheims is its cathedral, one of the greatest Gothic structures in existence. It was here that France's kings were consecrated. Planned by Jean d'Orbais, the cathedral was begun in 1211 but not finished until a century later; its twin towers were completed at the end of the 15th century. Although work on it was not continuous, the entire cathedral is a marvel of unity and harmony. The western façade, with its three-pointed portals, its enormous rose window, its gallery of kings and its two unfinished towers, is a bewildering cascade of statuary and carved stone whose overall effect is one of unbelievable richness, grace and beauty. The interior is so simple it would be austere were it not for the majesty of its perfect proprotions. The high vaulted nave and single chapel aisles on either side gain immeasurably in impressiveness through the total absence of the all-too-familiar paintings and modern religious statuary. In one of the side chapels are six splendid stained glass windows by Russian-Jewish artist Chagall, a moving link between the centuries and the differing religions of mankind.

After 700 years, Notre-Dame of Rheims rises as an inspiring symbol of its city and province. As fragile and airy as a glass of champagne when seen from the distance, the noble pile is in reality as solid as the deep chalk deposits from whose blocks its walls were built. Defaced during the French Revolution, shattered and burned during World War I, the cathedral stands today restored and almost as it was on the day in 1429 when Joan of Arc led Charles VII through its portals for his consecration.

An area of particular natural beauty and interest lies southeast of Rheims. This is Les Faux de Verzy, a woodland of mutated beeches characterized by their peculiar umbrella-shaped tops. Some of them are over 500 years old, and they were first mentioned in the records of the abbey of St-Basles in the 6th century.

The Champagne region, without its sparkling wine and its cathedral, would doubtless still be, as far as the tourist is concerned, what its name originally implied—just a plain and a battlefield. As things turned out, these two products of its chalky soil make it a region of France that no visitor should miss.

The Ardennes

Almost forgotten by the tourist, the Ardennes region of France lies mostly in Champagne, partly in Lorraine, yet it resembles neither. A land of water and forest, it is ideal for the fisherman, the camper or naturalist, or just for lazy motoring across its pleasant terrain. This is one of the few regions in France where boar and deer still roam naturally. The Ardennes forest is still somber, and the villages are often perched starkly between cliff and river.

The land of Rimbaud, it also inspired Victor Hugo, George Sand and Théophile Gautier, all of whom lived here and wrote of the Ardennes' beauty. Essentially a plateau, it is bisected by the Meuse, in and around whose wide valley you find its chief tourist attractions: Charleville-Mezières, home of Rimbaud and boasting an impressive place Ducale; Sedan, with the largest castle in Europe (about 3 hectares/8 acres in area) and the château of Bellevue, where Napoleon III surrendered on September 2, 1870, to the Germans; and the Ardennes forest, filled with natural delights.

If you have time, try also to see the little town of Revin, originally Spanish; the church of St-Hilaire in Givet; the star-shaped town of Rocroi; and Monthermé, with its fortified church of St-Léger (15th century).

PRACTICAL INFORMATION

WHEN TO GO. Spring through fall is the best time for touring. Although the champagne cellars are open year-round and visitors are always welcome, a visit in the fall during the grape harvest is of particular interest. Champagne has fewer folklore events and *fêtes* than most other regions in France.

Verdun's heroic role during 1914–18 is observed by a solemn pilgrimage of veterans and a memorial service during **February**. In **March** there is the Spring Fair at Bar-le-Duc, and in **May**, horseraces at Rheims. May is again a month of commemorative services at Verdun, including the celebration of Memorial Day at the American cemetery of Romagne. Also in May, festivities in Rheims in honor of Joan of Arc. Three important events in **June** are the anniversary of the great 1916 battle of Verdun, Château-Thierry's La Fontaine Festival, and Rheims' fortnight-long exhibition and fair. Towards the end of **July**, the battles of the Argonne are recalled at Verdun. For the Sedan Fair, come in **September**. During **October** Verdun celebrates the recapture of the Fort of Douaumont, and Rheims presents its exhibitions of furniture and decorative arts. Bar-le-Duc winds up the season with an Autumn Fair.

WHAT TO SEE. Rheims, the regional capital, is the number one goal of most tourists coming to the Champagne. Its star attraction is, of course, the glorious Gothic cathedral, severely damaged during World War I, and still in the process of restoration. Rheims has many Roman remains, the abbey of St-Rémi, where Clovis was baptized in 496, and an outstanding Museum of Fine Arts, with incomparable collections of tapestries and paintings including portraits of German princes by the 16th-cent. painters Lucas Cranach the Elder and the Younger. The city is the center for excursions to the World War I battlefields of Château-Thierry, Belleau Wood, Hill 204, and the famed Montagne de Rheims grape-growing area.

In Châlons-sur-Marne the beautifully carved 12th-century cloister of Notre-Dame-en-Vaux, discovered by accident during restoration work, has been skillfully reconstructed and is well worth a visit.

Troyes now has a splendid new Modern Art Museum, opened in 1982 in the former bishop's palace, which has been skillfully converted to house a generously donated collection including works by Picasso and Braque.

The valley of the Meuse provides interesting and scenic excursions, both by car and by boat (by bus to Joigny), from Charleville-Mezières, to the peaks called the Quatre Fils-Aymon, the town of Monthermé and Laifour, and the rocky wall known as the Dames de Meuse.

CHAMPAGNE

The Comité Régional de Tourisme Champagne-Ardenne offers a wide range of all-in holidays with the emphasis on some leisure activity such as fishing, shooting, riding, golf, cultural excursions, wine-tasting. For addresses see below.

Champagne route. This route actually comprises three circuits through the main vine-growing districts, each circuit clearly marked in a distinctive color. The *Green Circuit* starts from Epernay and circles the Côte des Blancs vineyards, famed for their white grapes, via D40 and D10. The *Red Circuit* follows the valley of the Marne, from Tours-sur-Marne to Dormans via Hautvillers. The *Blue Circuit* starts from Rheims and circles the celebrated Montagne de Rheims district via N31, D26, and N44. You may want to visit at least one of the *caves,* or cellars, along the route, some of which are over 24 km (15 miles) long and date from Roman days. The leading champagne companies are happy to show you around on certain days. A full list is published by the *Comité Interprofessionnel du Vin de Champagne,* 5 rue Henri-Martin, 51200 Epernay. English-speaking hostesses are normally available to take groups or individuals around.

The Aube *département* now has its own Champagne Route which starts and finishes in Bar-sur-Aube.

The Sacred Way. From Bar-le-Duc to Verdun, the *Voie Sacrée* (Sacred Way) crosses World War I battlefields; those at Verdun—the scene of desperate struggles, when the rallying cry was 'They shall not pass'—may be visited in the course of three separate tours. The nearby village of Colombey-les-Deux-Eglises, where Général de Gaulle lived and died, is an attraction for his admirers who cover the simple cross in the cemetery with flowers and tributes. De Gaulle's home, *La Boisserie,* has been open to the public since 1979. A tall Cross of Lorraine on a hilltop and a small memorial museum are moving tributes to France's hero of the 20th century.

Battlefields. From Rheims it is a short drive to Dormans, site of both 1914–18 battles of the Marne to Château-Thierry, and nearby Hill 204 (4 km, 2½ miles) and Belleau Wood (9.5 km, 6 miles). The Battle of Verdun was fought in the heights surrounding that city. A complete tour includes three circuits; the first two are served by buses. The first circuit (about 29 km, 18 miles) is particularly recommended, for it includes visits to the forts of Vaux and Douaumont, and the Trench of Bayonets, where an entire infantry battalion was buried alive rather than surrender. The second circuit (about 85 km, 53 miles) tours the Argonne, visiting Mort-Homme, the Butte de Montfaucon with its American memorial, the American cemetery at Romagne-sous-Montfaucon, and Varennes-en-Argonne. The third circuit (about 104 km, 65 miles) follows the banks of the Meuse to the crater of the Eparges, Hattonchâtel, Apremont and St-Michel.

HOW TO GET ABOUT. By train From Paris (Gare de l'Est) there is a good service every day to Rheims. The fastest expresses travel via Epernay, the majority stopping there en route both ways. The 173 km (108 miles) by this route takes about 1½ hrs, a few minutes longer when there is a stop at

Epernay. There is another route, bypassing Epernay, served also from Gare de l'Est. Although 16 km (10 miles) shorter it takes some 20 mins or so more.

By bus. The SNCF have a day coach trip to Rheims including a visit to a champagne cellar, a candlelit gastronomic lunch and a tour of the cathedral. Cost includes half a bottle of champagne, but as this trip operates rather infrequently, inquire at one of the tourist bureaux in the main Paris rail stations, at the Châtelet (the coaches start from there) or at 127 av. des Champs-Elysées, 8e. They also offer a more frequent trip to Troyes and Colombey-les-Deux-Eglises, always on a Sun. Cost includes lunch (but no drink this time!). *Cityrama* have a day coach trip twice a week; visits Rheims, Epernay and Château-Thierry, plus champagne cellar. Cost includes lunch. *Paris-Vision* has a tour twice a week covering World War I battlefields, Rheims, Epernay and a visit to a champagne cellar and tasting.

By boat. Opportunities for hiring boats or joining river cruises increase every year; ask at tourist offices for their *Tourisme Fluvial* and *Navigation de Plaisance* brochures.

MOTORING. From Paris, motorists may reach Rheims by the A4 motorway *(Autoroute de l'Est)*. If you prefer to avoid the motorway, you can drive by way of Soissons (via N2 and N31), more directly by way of Meaux and Château-Thierry (via N3 and RD380), or a bit more deviously by way of Epernay (N3 and N51). Rheims is now also linked to Paris by the Paris-Metz-Germany autoroute. From the north, the best route to Rheims is via Arras, St-Quentin, and Laon. For Verdun take the A4 all the way from Paris or the RD31 from Rheims. For Troyes and southern Champagne, take N19.

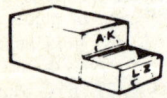

USEFUL ADDRESSES. The *Welcome Information office* for the Champagne region is at 3 bld de la Paix, 51000 Reims. *Comité Régional de Tourisme Champagne-Ardenne,* 2 bis bld Vaubécourt, 51000 Châlons-sur-Marne. *Offices de Tourisme* and *Syndicats d'Initiative:* 16 bld Carnot, Troyes; pl. Godart, Châlons-sur-Marne; pl. Thiers, Epernay; 3 bld de la Paix, Reims. *Touring-Club de Reims,* 26 rue Jean-Jacques-Rousseau. *Touring-Club de Troyes,* 16 bld Carnot.

Car hire. *Avis,* 9 av. de la Gare, Châlons-sur-Marne; 14 bld Joffre, Rheims; 4 av. Pierre Brossolette, Troyes; *Europcar,* 7 quai de la Villa, Epernay; 4 rue Thiers, Reims; 2 rue Voltaire, Troyes. *Hertz:* 7 av. de la Gare, Chalons-sur-Marne; 26 bld Joffre, Reims; 31 rue Voltaire, Troyes.

Write to the Comité Régional for their *Guide des Campings* leaflet, which also gives details of all-in holidays, farm holidays, youth hostels, sporting activities.

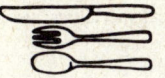

REGIONAL FOOD AND DRINK. There are the hams of Rheims and the Ardennes, *andouillettes* and *langues fourrées* of Troyes, *pâtés de pigeon, de grives* (thrush) and *de sanglier* (wild boar), and the celebrated *pieds de porc* (pig's trotters) of Ste-Ménehould. Among the fish specialties are those concocted with *écrevisses* (crayfish) from the Meuse, *brochets* (pike) from the Aisne, and *truites* (trout) from Montmirail and the Argonne. Sample one of the chicken dishes, *poulet au champagne* and *coq au vin de Bouzy*, and also one of the succulent cheeses of Brie, Coulommiers or Maroille.

The wines from the Montagne de Rheims district are firm and delicate *(Verenay, Verzy)* or full-bodied and fully-flavored *(Bouzy* and *Ambonnay)*. Those from the Vallée de la Marne, made from black grapes, are well-balanced and fragrant, while the Côtes des Blancs wines are very subtle and elegant. With champagne, the amount of *liqueur* (a solution of sugar and older, non-sparkling champagne) added to each bottle determines its taste: *sec* (2–3%), *brut* (5%), or *demi-sec* (5–8%). Champagne is usually thought of as a dessert wine, but it is an excellent aperitif, and is the only wine that can be served throughout an entire meal, starting with the younger, lighter, and drier wines, and progressing gradually to the older, sweeter ones. Champagne should be served cool, but not iced, as icing tends to weaken its bouquet, or flavor.

HOTELS AND RESTAURANTS. There is nothing fancy about the hotels of the Champagne country, but they are generally comfortable. Many are fairly new, owing to postwar rebuilding of large segments of towns. Most hotels close for a period during the year, as do restaurants, which also close at least one day a week, so check in advance. Restaurants are listed *E, M* or *I* for expensive, moderate or inexpensive.

AMBONNAY. *Auberge St-Vincent* (I), small Logis de France with restaurant (M).

BAR-SUR-AUBE. *Pomme d'Or,* comfortable, moderate, 30 rooms. *Commerce,* comfortable, 16 rooms. Good cuisine (M).

CHAMPILLON. *Le Royal Champagne,* an 18th-cent. stagecoach inn with a splendid view of the vineyard. Expensive. Good restaurant (E). Belongs to Relais et Châteaux association.

CHARLEVILLE-MÉZIÈRES. *Relais du Square* (M), by the station and near the old town; pleasant modern building with restaurant. *Modern'Hôtel* (I), with restaurant. *Paris* (I), no restaurant.

On the Charleville-Sedan road (N43), at **Villers-Semeuse**, is the modern *Mercure* (M), with pool and restaurant.

CHESNE. *Restaurant. Charrue d'Or* (I), with good local specialties; also has rooms.

COLOMBEY-LES-DEUX-ÉGLISES. *Mapotel Dhuits,* moderate, 30 rooms, very modern and comfortable. With restaurant.
Restaurant. St-Eloi, moderate, also has a few rooms. *Montagne* (I), good value, also has rooms.

EPERNAY. Best is *Champagne* (M), 30 rooms with bath, no restaurant. *Europe* (I), in old postal relay station, a bit run down, but pleasant. Good restaurant, with mostly regional dishes.
At **Vinay**, 6 km (4 miles) east, *Briqueterie* (E), quiet, modern, very pleasant. Fairly good restaurant (E).
Restaurant. Chapon Fin (M), pleasant atmosphere.

FÈRE-EN-TARDENOIS. *Hostellerie du Château* (E), 20 rooms and 7 suites, just north of town. A handsome 16th-cent. manor house. Excellent restaurant (E). Relais et Châteaux member.

GIVET. *Univers,* moderate, beside station, with good restaurant (M). *Deux-Avenues* (I), by station.
Restaurant. Baudouin (M), near river.

JOINVILLE. *Poste,* (I), good restaurant (M). *Grand Pont,* rue Aristide Briand, moderate. *Le Petit Vatel,* friendly, inexpensive, has good restaurant (I).

LAON. *Bannière de France* (M), with good restaurant. *Commerce* (I), no restaurant.
Restaurant. Châteaubriand (I), good for regional dishes. At **Etouvelles** is an excellent restaurant, *Bon Acceuil* (I), quiet, very popular.

MONTMIRAIL. *Auberge de la Tour d'Auvergne,* tiny (7 rooms), reader-recommended for its excellent yet inexpensive restaurant. Closed Jan. and Wed. (except July and Aug.). *Vert Galant* (I), with pleasant restaurant.

RHEIMS (REIMS). *Frantel* (E), bld Paul-Doumer, near motorway, modern and exceptionally comfortable, with good and rather elegant restaurant (M), called *Ombrages*. *Paix* (M), 9 rue Buirette, well run and excellent value, with pool and good restaurant (M) called *Drouet;* fairly central (near canal). *Bristol* (M), 76 pl. Drouet-d'Erlon, central, comfortable, good old-fashioned service, no restaurant. *Nord* (M), 75 pl. Drouet-d'Erlon, central, no restaurant. *Gambetta* (I), 13 rue Gambetta, near Cathedral, no restaurant.
On the outskirts: *Mercure Reims Est* (M), route de Châlons, Les Essillards, modern, efficient, with pool. *Novotel* (M), route de Soissons, with pool and snack bar. *Campanile* (M), av. Georges-Pompidou in Val de Marigny, with grill room.

CHAMPAGNE

Restaurants. *Boyer* (E), bld Vasnier, Rheim's best known restaurant, and one of the best in France, with deliciously imaginative cuisine. Moved in 1983 to splendid 19th-century mansion with huge garden in center of town. Will also be a hotel in 1984. *Florence* (M), 43 bld Foch, good value *menus,* very popular with the locals. *Foch* (M), 37 bld Foch, is another good bet. *Colbert* (I), 64 pl. Drouet-d'Erlon, good home-style cooking.

Eight km (5 miles) northwest, at **Châlons-sur-Vesle**, is the fine *Assiette Champenoise* (E), excellent, with 'new' French cuisine.

Eleven km (6 miles) south at **Montchenot,** *Auberge du Grand Cerf* (M), good value and attractive, with inventive cuisine. Also has 10 rooms.

SEDAN. *Strasbourg* (M), 31 rooms. *Univers* (M), near station. *Europe* (M), 25 rooms, are best. *Croix Blanche,* 13 rooms, inexpensive.
Restaurants. *Au Bon Vieux Temps* (E), pl. de la Halle, good cooking. *Chariot d'Or* (M), pl. de Torcy.

SEPT-SAULX. *Cheval Blanc* (M), very pleasant and peaceful Relais du Silence, with garden, tennis courts and excellent restaurant (E) with local specialties.

SÉZANNE. *France* (I), with good restaurant.

TOURS-SUR-MARNE. Hotel-restaurant. *Touraine Champenoise* (I), good value Logis de France, family atmosphere.

TROYES. *Grand* (M), 100 rooms, with restaurant (M) and brasserie (I). *Royal* (M), 40 rooms, beside station, also has restaurant, as does *France* (M), near cathedral. *Thiers,* 38 rooms, and *Champenois,* 20 rooms, are inexpensive. Neither has restaurant.

Near the airport, on N19, is the *Novotel* (M), 84 rooms and pool.
Restaurants. *Le Bourgogne* (M), 40 rue Gén.-de-Gaulle, is very good. *Butat* (I). *St-Vincent* (I), at station.

At **Pont Ste-Marie,** 3 km (2 miles) north, *Hostellerie Pont-Ste-Marie* (M), a hotel with good 'new' cuisine in the restaurant.

VERDUN. *Coq Hardi* (E), 8 av. de la Victorie, near river, with good restaurant *(nouvelle cuisine). Bellevue* (M), rond-point Maréchal-de-Lattre-de-Tassigny, no restaurant. *St-Paul* (I), 12 pl. Saint-Paul, best known for its restaurant. *Montaulbain* (I), 4 rue Vieille-Prison, small and quiet, near Cathedral, no restaurant.

VERTUS. *Hostellerie de la Reine Blanche* (M), peaceful, with restaurant. *Commerce* (I), modest little place with popular restaurant.

ALSACE AND LORRAINE

The Marseillaise and Joan of Arc

Only the Rhine separates Germany from Alsace-Lorraine, a region that often looks German and even sounds German. But its heart—just to prove how deceptive appearances can be—is passionately French. One has only to recall that Strasbourg was the birthplace of the *Marseillaise,* and that the region was for 48 years under German domination, to appreciate why Alsace and Lorraine are the most intensely pro-French of all France's provinces. In 1940–44 the Germans tried to annex Alsace.

Although primarily agricultural, the region is also one of great industrial activity, and its soil is rich in healing mineral waters that draw many to its world-renowned spas. Scenically, the Alsace-Lorraine-Vosges region has much to attract the visitor, for the countryside is a procession of colorful towns and villages.

ALSACE AND LORRAINE

An old Alsatian song tells in ironic fashion the story of 'Hans in Schnokeloch' (John and the Mosquitoes) who 'has everything he can desire, but does not want what he has got, and has not got what he wants.' To some extent this is true of the Alsatian. Living in a land of incomparable beauty and richness, he has been thwarted by unceasing wars, and he and his sons have been forced throughout the long years of history to abandon the plough and the vineyard for the destructive arts of war. And this has, not unnaturally, produced a character that often seems contradictory and unpredictable. For he is at once good-natured yet easily provoked to expenditure. He is also hard-working, perhaps because of the German example close at hand, perhaps because history has taught him not to rely on others. Productivity figures are high, and Alsace is the leading French region in terms of export value per head of the population.

Strasbourg, capital of Alsace

One of France's largest cities (400,000 inhabitants), Strasbourg has greatly increased its importance since the war, as the home first of the Council of Europe and now also of the EEC's European Parliament. The first direct elections to this Parliament, which took place in June 1979, boosted Strasbourg's role still further. The Strasbourgeois have prevented a plan put forward by member-states of the Common Market to move Parliament to a single house in Brussels. The city is dominated by its rose-colored Gothic cathedral, with a 143-meter (470-ft) spire. Go just before noon, for then the famous astronomical clock displays its ingenious complications. The hour is struck by a figure representing Death, while the Apostles receive the blessing of Christ, and the cock crows in memory of Peter's denial.

Strasbourg is full of interest: medieval streets with carved timbered houses; the impressive château des Rohan (housing the museums of archeology, fine arts, and decorative arts), built in the 18th century for the cardinal, friend of Cagliostro, whose dissolute life shocked Marie-Thérèse; the placid beauty of the district known as La Petite France, and the Bainaux-Plantes, dominated by its four massive 14th-century square towers, with old gabled houses reflected in the canals that serve as streets; the charming little square, delightfully named Marché-aux-Cochons-de-Lait (the Suckling Pigs Market), in which there is a beautiful 17th-century house ornamented outside by carved timber galleries.

At the end of the rue du Vieux-Marché-des-Poissons, where the old fish market used to stand, is the grimly named Pont du Corbeau—the Bridge of the Crow—for here it was, in medieval days, that malefactors were executed and their bodies exposed to the voracity of the crows. If you find this too grisly a spot in which to linger, go to the Alsatian

Museum just on the right, at 23 quai St-Nicholas, where a beautiful collection of old Alsatian dresses, furniture and popular art will show you the lighter side of life in old Alsace.

The place Kléber is the liveliest spot in Strasbourg, and it is a pleasant place in which to sit with a cool tankard of Alsatian beer. In the nearby place Gutenberg is a statue to the inventor of movable type, Johann Gutenberg, who completed his great work here from 1434 to 1444. Not far distant is place Broglie, where, on the site of the present Bank of France, Rouget de Lisle composed the words and music of the *Marseillaise* in a fever of patriotic excitement following a public dinner in 1792. It is interesting to note that the song was first called *Chant de guerre de l'armée du Rhin* ('War Song of the Army of the Rhine'), but received its present title when it was adopted by the Provençal volunteers taking part in the storming of the Tuileries in Paris. The port of Strasbourg is one of the most important in France. You can visit it and also take boat trips from there on the Rhine.

Lying between Saverne, in the valley of the Zorn, and Strasbourg is the well-known region of Dabo-Wangenbourg, which separates Alsace from Lorraine. Here is superb and picturesque country with forests, mountains, valleys, waterfalls, rocky promontories; in fact a replica in miniature of all the natural beauties of both Alsace and Lorraine. Dabo and Wangenbourg, set high in the Vosges Mountains, will delight the traveler who seeks rest and tranquility. From either you can tour the district by car, see the lovely waterfalls of Nideck and the tree-covered valley of the Zorn, climb the rock of Dabo and see the majestic panorama from the summit of its chapel dedicated to St-Léon, or spend peaceful days fishing in the rivers of the Zorn.

Colmar

With its painted and carved old houses, and its Venetian Quarter crossed by the river Lauch, Colmar is one of the loveliest towns in Alsace. The Maison Pfister at the corner of the rue Mercière is a particularly beautiful house. In the church of St-Martin is the exquisite *Virgin and the Rosebush* by Martin Schongauer, the 15th-century painter and engraver who was born and lived here; his house can be visited. You will be entranced by the serenity of the 13th-century cloisters in the Unterlinden Museum, a former convent that is now one of the showplaces of Colmar, with a famous altarpiece by Mathias Grünewald. And do not miss the Maison des Têtes (so called because of the variety of carved heads that ornament its façade).

It is difficult to believe that this picturesque old town could have been the birthplace of Baron Haussmann, the energetic genius who demolished the old roads of Paris to make way for his magnificent boulevards.

It is perhaps fortunate that he transferred his activities to Paris and left the wayward charm of Colmar intact.

At the beginning of 1945 the Germans launched a large-scale offensive to retake Alsace, and succeeded in forming the 'pocket of Colmar', about halfway between Strasbourg and Colmar. The French General de Lattre de Tassigny, supported by several American divisions, reacted vigorously to this danger and forced the Germans to abandon their positions.

Mulhouse and the Crest Road

Mulhouse is a serious and industrial town. Although it can trace its origins to the 13th century, even its Hôtel de Ville, with its magnificent coffered ceiling and stained-glass windows, offers little competition with the splendors of Colmar and Strasbourg.

Mulhouse is renowned for its weaving and spinning factories, which give a striking picture of the wealth of Alsace as their enormous chimneys belch forth the smoke that darkens the buildings. The richest deposits of potash in the region lie nearby.

For all this industrial activity, Mulhouse is surprisingly neat and tidy. Well-groomed parks and newly painted window boxes bursting with geraniums might be called the city's trademarks. One of the interesting features of its postwar housing developments is the circular apartment house. Mulhouse was once allied to the Swiss cantons, became an independent republic, and in 1798 voted to ally itself with France. Today it shares an airport with the Swiss city of Basel, and is connected by the Rhône–Rhine canal with Strasbourg, in northern Alsace. It now has an interesting Motor Museum (Musée de l'Automobile) too, as well as the National Rail Museum.

From Mulhouse you can make a magnificent excursion up the superb Crest Road, or Route des Crêtes (built along the front in 1914), from Thann to the Col de la Schlucht. Far removed from the industrial preoccupations of Mulhouse, this road, as its name indicates, links up some of the highest mountains in the Vosges. Two, at least, are worth a visit, the Hohneck and the Grand Ballon. Both are accessible by mountain paths reaching to their summits, and the view is truly breathtaking. From the Grand Ballon you can see the Black Forest, and, on a clear day, as far as the Bernese Alps. And, a few miles beyond the Col de la Schlucht, the Lac Vert, glowing in splendor like an emerald in its lonely mountain setting.

Markstein, near the Grand Ballon, is an excellent and popular winter sports resort. Kaysersberg, on the banks of the river Weiss, charming with its medieval houses, is the birthplace of Albert Schweitzer. The town has a museum commemorating the great humanitarian.

Along the Wine Road

Ribeauvillé, at the foot of the Vosges Mountains, has three ruined castles and vineyards that produce those most delectable of Alsatian wines, Riesling and Traminer. Nests of storks perch on its high towers, and during its delightful annual festival in September with music and dancing a procession proceeds to the place de l'Hôtel de Ville, and wine, flowing from the Fontaine du Vin, is served free.

Obernai, along with Riquewihr and Eguisheim, is very picturesque. Despite the usual summer invasion of tourists, it manages to retain a *gemütlich* charm. Ste-Odile, patron saint of Alsace, was born here. The convent of Ste-Odile is a place of pilgrimage as well as one of the most beautifully situated places in the whole of Alsace. The nuns of the convent have installed a guesthouse where visitors may stay as in an ordinary hotel, and this makes an ideal spot from which to visit the region. The tree-covered mountain, encircled by its Pagan Wall (9 km/6 miles long), whose mysterious purpose and origins baffle archeologists, is indeed a fitting setting for the saint of Alsace.

Picturesquely perched on a peak over 760 meters (2,500 ft) high is the castle of Haut-Koenigsbourg. Dating from the end of the 15th century—with a 13th-century keep from which there is a magnificent view—it was somewhat over-conscientiously restored by Kaiser Wilhelm II between 1900 and 1908. Nearby Riquewihr is one of the most curious little towns in Alsace, with its ancient houses and medieval walls. The surrounding vineyards produce the famed Riesling wine.

Art cities of Lorraine

The plateau of Lorraine, with its gentle undulating country watered by the Moselle and the Meurthe, offers a striking contrast to the wild scenery along the Route des Crêtes. But Lorraine has its own charm, and Nancy, its southern capital, typically French in its harmoniously constructed squares and buildings, has the quiet elegance that one always associates with the best in French architecture.

Curiously enough it was a Pole, and not a Frenchman, who was responsible for much of what is beautiful in Nancy. Stanislas Leszczynski, whose daughter Marie was married to Louis XV, through whom he was elected King of Poland, had to renounce the throne in 1737. As compensation he received the duchies of Lorraine and Bar, which at his death were to devolve on France. Stanislas settled in Nancy, and devoted himself to the embellishment of the city.

The place Stanislas, with its beautiful wrought-iron railings, its perfectly proportioned square with its fountains, will almost certainly remind you of Versailles. On one side of it is the Hôtel de Ville, with its magnificent staircase leading to the Salle des Fêtes from whose windows the full beauty of the place Stanislas may be appreciated. Opposite is the Arc de Triomphe erected by Stanislas to the glory of his son-in-law, Louis XV. See the ducal palace, built in the 13th century but unhappily much mutilated subsequently by wars and fire. Intelligent reconstruction has saved most of its beauty, and it now houses the fine Lorraine Museum.

The church of the Cordeliers was the traditional burial place of the dukes of Lorraine, and here the pomp and power of these feudal princes, once among the greatest in Europe, are evident in magnificently sculpted tombs in the old church. The tomb of the Duchess Philippa de Gueldre, with its realistic sculpture, is one of the most impressive in France.

From the place Stanislas, the Arc de Triomphe opens on to the superb place de la Carrière, lined with trees and elegant 18th-century houses leading to the Palais du Gouverneur, once the official residence of the governors of Lorraine; to the right is the enormous Pépinière, with its zoo and rose garden.

Lunéville, too, is reminiscent of Versailles. Here it was that Duke Léopold, at the beginning of the 18th century, built a small-scale replica of the château of Versailles, where he imitated, also on a more modest scale, the magnificence of the French court. But here again we see the hand of Stanislas, for, finding Lunéville an admirable resort, he sought to embellish it, much as he had done Nancy. The château and the beautiful Parc des Bosquets, with its gardens and fountains, owe much to this genial prince, who was so sensitive to the spirit of 18th-century France. This spirit is evoked in the *son-et-lumière* show presented during the summer season.

The northern capital of Lorraine is Metz, a city not much visited by tourists, but worth attention nevertheless. Its location, at the junction of the Seille and the Moselle, in which there are several islands, is pleasant. And there are many interesting buildings, especially the churches that antedate the Roman conquest of Gaul. Metz became, successively, a great Roman city, the cradle and center of the Carolingian Empire, and an independent republic, before finally joining with France.

Of particular interest are the 7th-century church of St-Pierreaux-Nonnains, the oldest in France, the 13th–15th-century Porte des Allemands, and the medieval Hôtel St-Livier and city granary. The Gothic cathedral of St-Etienne has been described as the 'apotheosis of light'. The nave, one of the masterpieces of Gothic art, and the stained-glass windows are especially worth studying.

From the 18th century, when Metz became an important citadel, date the impressive buildings of the place d'Armes, the Porte Serpenoise, and the Esplanade, with its delightful walks along the banks of the Moselle. In the Museum of Fine Arts, part of which is in the Ancient Bath-house, are important Gallo-Roman collections, paintings by 17th-century Dutch masters, and by artists of the French School.

For the past century the region between Metz and Longwy, to the northwest, has been the principal center of the French steel industry. But in recent years it has suffered increasingly from the world steel recession, and in the winding valleys the great blazing steel furnaces are closing down one after the other. Longwy, an austere, grimy town that lives entirely by steel, leapt into the world's headlines in 1979 when plans were announced for the closure of its main steelworks, and the workers replied with rioting that went on for weeks. New motor factories are arriving in northern Lorraine, but they are not enough to offset the very high unemployment levels in this depressed corner of France where the down-at-heel townlets have the look of having known better days.

Joan of Arc country

Lorraine is the country of France's patron saint, Joan of Arc. Follow the D164 road that winds between Contrexéville and Void, and you will be on Joan's native soil. At Neufchâteau, then a fortified town guarding the region, the inhabitants of Domrémy sought refuge in 1428 from the English armies that threatened their village. It was in Domrémy that Joan was born in 1411 or a year later. There you may visit her birthplace, and recall that it was in the garden that she heard her voices for the first time, at the age of 13. A single tower remains of the church in which she was baptized. A *son-et-lumière* performance based on many of these events is presented in Domrémy during the summer.

Near Coussey Joan of Arc danced with the other children at country fairs attended by Pierre de Bourlémont, the local *seigneur*, and his wife Béatrice—the château of Bourlémont may still be seen. Associated with Coussey and Brixey are St-Mihiel and Ste-Catherine, who, with the Archangel St Michael, appeared to Joan. In the chapel of Notre-Dame at Bermont, where Joan vowed to save France, are the statues that existed in her time.

The small town of Vaucouleurs recalls Joan's arrival on May 13, 1428 to ask the help of the governor, Robert de Baudricourt. On February 23, 1429, clad in page's garb and her hair cut short, Joan of Arc rode out through the Porte de France to meet her destiny. Here you may visit the ruined château of Baudricourt, the church where Joan often worshipped and the house where she stayed.

ALSACE AND LORRAINE

PRACTICAL INFORMATION

WHEN TO GO. This region has something to offer the visitor at almost any time of year. Summer, when the wine fairs are held, and fall, when the festive grape harvests occur, are both delightful seasons for touring. Although Luxeuil-les-Bains is open year-round, most of the other spas, including Vittel, Contrexéville, Plombières and Bains-les-Bains, are open during the summer months only.

International ski competitions are held at Markstein in **February.** Carnivals, masked balls, and confetti battles are held before and after Lent at Mulhouse, Sélestat, Metz and Nancy. Épinal celebrates the return of spring on Maundy Thursday. **April** is greeted with a Daffodil Festival in Gérardmer, when the snow disappears from the mountainsides and the flowers that replace it are plucked to decorate the city. In **May** there are horseraces and a tremendous folk festival in Wissembourg, and festivals honoring Joan of Arc in Domrémy and Nancy. At Geispolsheim on the second Sun. after Whitsunday, houses are gaily decorated, and costumed villagers join in a great procession.

Every other year, in **June,** Saverne holds a Rose Festival. Strasbourg's important Music Festival and Colmar's weeklong celebration of its medieval past also take place during the month. Other traditional events are the Feux de la St-Jean at Bussang and Metz, the living tableaux enacted by the children of Épinal and the curious Burning of the Three Pine Trees at Thann, recalling the miraculous origin of the city. **July** sees the celebrations honoring Ste-Odile at Mont-Ste-Odile, the fairs of Nancy and Mulhouse, and the opening of the polo season at Vittel.

August is the time for the Wine Fairs of Sélestat and Colmar. Among popular folk festivals are the dance festival of Engwiller, the Corso Fleuri of Sélestat, the Beer Festival of Schiltigheim, and the Fêtes de la Mirabelle at Lunéville, Metz and Nancy.

September is crowded with fairs—Strasbourg's great European Fair and the International Fair at Metz—pilgrimages, at Ronchamp and Sion-Vaudemont, and Colmar's month-long (into Oct.) Sauerkraut Festival. One of the region's most popular folk festivals is Ribeauvillé's 'Pfiffertag' held on the first Sun. in Sept. Dating from the medieval celebrations in honor of the musicians' patron saint, Notre-Dame-de-Dusenbach, the festival today features choral singing, fanfares, wine flowing in fountains, and country dancing. From the end of the month through **October,** grape-harvest festivals are held in the towns along the Wine Road, notably in Turckheim, Riquewihr, Guebwiller, Barr, Obernai and Dambach. In **December** there are festivals of Ste-Odile at Mont-Ste-Odile, and of Ste Barbara at Metz, the latter celebrated with processions of soldiers and miners. December 6 is St Nicholas Day in Lorraine, when the children of

Épinal, Metz and Nancy place their shoes near the fireplace for the good saint to fill with toys and sweets. Nancy has a drama and music festival.

WHAT TO SEE. There is a marked contrast between Alsace and Lorraine. In Alsace, the architecture, gastronomy and language are influenced by Germany. This is particularly apparent in the picturesque villages, with their spires and gabled houses, where some villagers wear the traditional costumes during the many regional festivals.

Lorraine is a province of battles, industry, iron, spas, and art. Metz is ringed with the Franco-Prussian War battlefields of 1870, and marks the terminus of the *Voie de la Liberté*, the route followed by the American armies from the Atlantic coast during the liberation of France in 1944. The iron deposits of its sub-soil are among the richest in the world. And nature also has been lavish with healing mineral waters, attracting many to Vittel, Contrexéville and Plombières (for digestive ailments) and to Luxeuil-les-Bains and Bussang (for circulatory disorders). Famed the world over is the crystal of Baccarat—in the town itself there is a stunning modern church in which the stained-glass windows have been made of crystal.

Among the many art treasures in both provinces are the magnificent cathedral of St-Etienne in Metz, and the 7th-cent. church of St-Pierreaux-Nonnains, the oldest in France; medieval artist Martin Schongauer's painting 'The Virgin and the Rosebush' in Colmar's church of St-Martin; Grünewald's Isenheim Altar in the former Dominican convent of Unterlinden; the Gothic buildings and 17th-cent. ramparts of Toul; the gracious city of Nancy, with its outstanding Musée Lorrain and Fine Arts Museum; nearby Chartreuse de Bosserville (open to visitors during Aug. and Sept.) and Épinal's Musée de l'Imagerie and Musée des Vosges. Between Contrexéville and Void (N164), in the valley of the Meuse, lies the country of Joan of Arc, almost unchanged since the Middle Ages. *Son-et-lumière* shows are staged in Domrémy on weekends and holidays during the summer.

A picturesque route (N410) through pine forests to northern Alsace brings you to the town of St-Dié, which has a certain amount of interest for Americans: in 1507 a geographical treatise was published here that for the first time proposed the name of America for the continent, whose discovery was then credited to Amerigo Vespucci.

Strasbourg is a fascinating combination of old and new. In its central quarter, ringed by the river Ill (from which was derived the province's original name, Illsass), are covered bridges and ancient buildings; in the modern sections are a magnificent park and a busy port. In addition to its splendid museums, including the unusually interesting Maison de l'Oeuvre Notre-Dame, are the 18th-cent château des Rohan and a cathedral with a remarkable west façade. Mulhouse and Belfort are centers of industrial activity, while in Colmar, the Middle Ages mingle gracefully with the Renaissance. The Maison Pfister, Maison des Têtes, and Hôtel des Chevaliers de St-Jean are some of the most notable old houses.

ALSACE AND LORRAINE

At Kintzheim, 3 km (2 miles) from Sélestat, nature-lovers will enjoy the *Volerie des aigles* (Eagle Eyrie), in the grounds of the ruined 14th-cent. château, where more than 50 large birds of prey live in complete freedom (9–12; 2–7). At nearby Monkey Mountain, under the shadow of the famous Haut-Koenigsbourg château, over 100 monkeys live freely among the trees (10–12, 2–6).

HOW TO GET ABOUT. By train. All rail services from Paris leave from the Gare de L'Est and are both very fast and frequent. Two TEE trains per day serve Strasbourg taking about 4 hrs for the 506-km (315-mile) journey stopping en route at Nancy. Other fast routes are Paris to Metz (about 3 hrs), Paris to Colmar, Belfort and Mulhouse (all about 4 hrs). There are through trains from Ostend and Brussels to Metz, Strasbourg, Nancy and Mulhouse. The Brussels–Zurich trains stop at Metz, Strasbourg and Mulhouse.

There are a number of local routes operating within this area serving Vittel, Epinal and Ronchamp. Local buses connect with trains.

The SNCF has several 3-day trips a year to Alsace and the Vosges; all-in rates for meals and accommodations, with drinks and museum fees extra.

By air. Strasbourg is 55 mins from Paris; flying time to Mulhouse is about 1 hour; both operated by *Air Inter. Air France* flies London–Strasbourg direct.

By bus. *Europabus* has a day tour following the Wine Road *(Route du Vin)* in Alsace. This coach tour starts from Strasbourg on Wednesday in July and August only, stopping for lunch (with wine of course!). Cost (transport only) is about 100 frs. There is also a Villages in Alsace tour. *Europe Autocar* have a weekend coach trip from Paris to Alsace and Lorraine and a 5-day Alsace and Black Forest tour that takes you into Germany as well.

By boat. Traveling by boat is becoming increasingly popular with visitors to Lorraine who want to enjoy a restful pace; ask at tourist offices for their *tourisme fluvial* documentation.

MOTORING. The main road from Paris to the east is the Paris–Metz–Germany A4 autoroute, with branches to Nancy (A31) and Strasbourg (A34). Alternate routes are N3 to Metz via Châlons-sur-Marne and Verdun and N19 to Belfort and Mulhouse via Troyes, Chaumont and Vesoul.

The roads are satisfactory, but usually full of trucks; the best time for motoring, unless you take the autoroute, is during the early morning or lunch.

WINE ROAD. The cool, comfortable, and scenic *Route du Vin* between Mulhouse and Strasbourg was devised by wine producers and civic leaders to introduce tourists to the province's attractions. The main towns are floodlit from May through Oct. (for a map of the route, inquire at the tourist office in Strasbourg, Colmar or Mulhouse). There is a topnotch restaurant in Ammerschwihr, and picturesque Ribeauvillé makes a convenient stopover.

THE FACE OF FRANCE

USEFUL ADDRESSES. *Welcome Information offices* at Palais des Congrès, 67002 Strasbourg (for mail), with additional offices at 10 pl. Gutenberg, pl. de la Gare and pont de l'Europe; at Porte Serpenoise, 57000 Metz; and at 14 pl. Stanislas, 54000 Nancy. *Tourist offices* at the same addresses and in other main centers. *Departmental Tourist Committee* for Bas-Rhin is at 47 rue du Marechal-Foch, 67000 Strasbourg; for Haut-Rhin at Prefecture, 68020 Colmar; and for Vosges at BP 332, 88008 Epinal. In Paris, the *Maison de l'Alsace* is at 39 av. des Champs-Elysées, 8e.

Care hire. *Hertz,* 12 av. General-de-Gaulle, Epinal; pl. Thiers, Nancy; 26 rue de Bâle, Mulhouse; 14 rue Deserte, and airport, Strasbourg. *Avis,* 21 pl. des Vosges, Nancy; 68 rue Nordfeld, Mulhouse; 33 bld de Nancy, Strasbourg.

The *Maison des Jeunes et de la Culture,* 27 pl. de la République, Nancy, is a useful source of youth information, and the *Touring Club de France's* office at 9 rue des Carmes, Nancy, is invaluable.

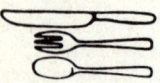

REGIONAL FOOD AND DRINK. Alsace and Lorraine are the lands of good white wines and sauerkraut: as made in this area, it is the main ingredient of the dish and is garnished with breaded veal cutlets or sausages. Other regional treats are *kugelhof*—oven-baked buns, and Strasbourg apple tarts, smothered with cream.

The thing to drink with *choucroute* (sauerkraut) is, of course, beer, and it is in Alsace that the best beer in France is brewed. But it would be a mistake to neglect the excellent fruity white wines, particularly delicious in warm weather. Unlike other French wines, Alsatian wines take their names from the type of grape used in making them—Riesling, Traminer, Sylvaner, etc. The ordinary grades are sold under this name alone; the finer wines bear in addition the name of the locality from which they come—Riesling de Ribeauvillé for instance. The best come from Ribeauvillé, Barr, Riquewihr, Ammerschwihr and Turckheim.

Alsace also produces some of the finest liqueurs made from fruit to be found in France—*kirsch, quetsch, mirabelle, pruneau,* etc., and the delicate *framboise,* distilled from raspberries. Unfortunately, they are rather expensive these days.

Currant preserve *(confiture de Groseilles)* is a specialty in Bar-le-Duc. Don't miss the fabulous local dessert, *Duchesse-le-Duc,* consisting of vanilla ice-cream with currant preserve in generous quantities, topped with whipped cream and decorated with sugared violets.

HOTELS AND RESTAURANTS. Alsace-Lorraine is well supplied with good accommodations in all categories, and this region is one of the less expensive in France, though the city of Strasbourg is a major exception to this rule—thanks to the number of Eurocrats visiting the European Parliament, it is one of the most expensive in all France. Hotels are usually open year-round. Restaurants listed *E, M* or *I* are expensive, moderate or inexpensive. Restaurants close one day a week, and often July or Aug.

ALSACE AND LORRAINE

AMMERSCHWIHR. Restaurant *Aux Armes de France* (E). One of the best in Alsace, well worth a visit. Serves both classical and *nouvelle* cuisine. Also has 8 rooms.

BAINS-LES-BAINS. Spa (season, May–Sept.). *Poste* (I). *Sources* (I), very modest. Both have (I) restaurants.

BALLON D'ALSACE. Winter sports center. **Restaurant.** 1.5 km (1 mile) out of town is *Chaumière* (I).

BAR-LE-DUC. *Metz et Commerce,* 53 rooms, good restaurant, inexpensive. *Exelmans* (I), modest, no restaurant.
Restaurant. *Meuse Gourmande* (I), near station, good for regional specialties.

LE BONHOMME. (Col de Bonhomme). *Poste,* nice view, moderate, and *Lion d'Or,* simple, inexpensive, the former with good restaurant (M). Both are Logis de France.

BUSSANG. Spa and winter sports resort (seasons, Easter, Christmas, mid-June–mid-Sept.) *Des Sources,* 2.5 km (1½ miles) southeast, peaceful, with garden, is moderate. *Deux Clefs,* also moderate, with restaurant (I).

COL DU DONON. *Hôtel du Donon,* 20 rooms with kitchenette; fishing stream and restaurant; Logis de France.

COLMAR. *Terminus-Bristol* (E), 7 pl. de la Gare, central and near station, with good restaurant (see below); generally well-run, though one reader complained of poor service. *Champ-de-Mars* (M), 2 av. de la Marne, modern, surrounded by greenery but a bit impersonal; with two restaurants. *Park* (M), 52 av. de la République, near station, with restaurant. *Turenne* (I), 10 route de Bâle, friendly Logis de France; no restaurant. At **Wettolsheim,** 4½ km (2½ miles) away, *Auberge Père Florand* (M), friendly Relais du Silence with excellent restaurant.
Restaurants. *Schillinger* (E), 16 rue Stanislas, an old favorite, one of the best in Alsace, newish cuisine. *Rendez-vous de chasse* (E), in Terminus-Bristol hotel, again newish cuisine, smiling service. *Feu Rouge* (E), 52 Grande-Rue, imaginative dishes. *Meistermann* (M), 2 av. République, long standing, good value. *Trois Poissons* (M), 15 quai Poissonerie, specializes, as its name suggests, in fish dishes. *Unterlinden* (I), 2 rue Unterlinden, opposite museum and deservedly popular for its good value regional cuisine served in generous portions.

CONTREXÉVILLE. Spa (season, May–mid-Sept.). *Cosmos,* moderate, is very comfortable and quiet in own grounds. *Etablissement* (M), comfortable, well modernized old-style hotel just by spa building, with grill room-cum-restaurant. *Souveraine* (M), nearby in the park and under same management, shares the Etablissement's restaurant. *Sources* (M), near spa building and station, with restaurant. *Parc* (I), with good value restaurant.

Restaurant. *Aubergade* (E), rue du 11 Septembre, excellent.

DABO. *Rocher* (I), about 1.5 km (1 mile) southeast of town, at foot of Rocher de Dabo. Modest, with restaurant.

ÉPINAL. *Cadet Roussel* (M), with restaurant (called *Mouton Blanc*). *Azur* (I), no restaurant.

Restaurant. *Relais des Ducs de Lorraine* (M), well-known for classical cuisine; also has rooms.

GÉRARDMER. *Bragard* (E), quiet, with good old-fashioned service, pool and good restaurant (M), called *Grand Cerf*. *Paix* (I), facing lake; nice Logis de France. *Progrès* (I), central, with restaurant. *Chalet du Lac* (I), is 1 km (½ mile) away with views over lake and (M) restaurant.

At **Saut des Cuves,** 3 km (2 miles) east on road to Col de la Schlucht: *Saut des Cuves,* moderate, 27 rooms.

At **Col de Martimpré,** 5 km (3 miles) east on D8: Hotel-restaurant *La Bonne Auberge* (I), simple nice view, 12 rooms, moderate.

At **Bas-Rupts,** 4 km south west, *Bas Rupts,* moderate, chalet-style but elegant; good *nouvelle cuisine* in restaurant (E). A Relais du Silence.

LE GRAND BALLON. Winter sports center. *Grand Ballon* in out-of-the-way spot with lovely view, inexpensive. Pleasant Relais du Silence with restaurant.

GUEBWILLER. Outside this little industrial town are a few charming inns: *Hostellerie St-Barnabé* (M) **(Murbach)**, closed Jan through Mar.; *Ferme de Thierenbach* **(Jungholtz)**, where all the products used in cooking come from the home farm; *Biebler* (I) (Jungholtz-Thierenbach road), with lovely little rooms and good value meals. Also in Jungholtz, *Residence des Violettes* (M), a Relais du Silence, with flower-filled garden and good restaurant.

HAUT-KOENIGSBOURG. In the nearby villages are several unpretentious *winstubs,* where you can try typical Alsatian country fare for fairly modest prices: *Gilg* (M) at **Mittelbergheim**, with some (I) rooms; *Arnold* (M) at **Itterswiller.**

HOHRODBERG. In the Vosges, *Roess* (I) and *Panorama* (I) are Logis de France and have magnificent views of mountain and valley. Both have restaurants.

LE HOHWALD. *Grand* (M), beautiful surroundings with restaurant. *Marchal* (I), peaceful and friendly Logis de France, with (M) restaurant.

ALSACE AND LORRAINE

ILLHAUSERN. Restaurant. *Auberge de l'Ill* (E). One of France's greatest restaurants beautifully situated on the banks of the river Ill. Traditional regional dishes cooked in *nouvelle cuisine* style.

KAYSERBERG. Near Colmar. *Chambard* (E), opened 1981, small and very pleasant with very good *nouvelle cuisine* restaurant. *Château* (I) and *Remparts* (M), no restaurant, both small.
Restaurants. *Chambard* (E), in hotel. *Arbre Vert* (M), has 24 rooms.

LANDERSHEIM. Restaurant. *L'Auberge du Kochersberg*, in the clubhouse run by Adidas, the sports equipment firm, a surprising setting perhaps for a first-rate restaurant with excellent 'new' cooking (the chef was trained under Paul Bocuse, among others), but cheaper *menus* too.

LEMBACH. *Cheval Blanc* (M), 18th-century inn with excellent food and a few rooms.

LUNÉVILLE. *Pages* (M), good value, no restaurant.

METZ. Newest are *Sofitel*, 115 rooms, with pool and, near the station, *Frantel*, 112 rooms. Both have good restaurants. Also, *Royal-Concorde*, 76 rooms, some accessible to the handicapped, restaurant, with regional specialties. All expensive. *Foch* and *La Pergola* are comfortable, inexpensive; neither has restaurant.
At **Maizières-lès-Metz**, 10 km away, is the 129-room *Novotel* (M), with pool.
Restaurants. *Dinanderie* (M), best in the area. *Ville de Lyon* (M), a favorite with the locals.

MOLSHEIM. *Diana* (M), quiet and comfortable Logis de France, with good restaurant.
Restaurant. *Auberge du Cheval Blanc* (M). A wide choice of Alsatian specialties and wines. Also has some (I) rooms.

MULHOUSE. *Frantel* (E) with good restaurant, opposite rail station. *Bourse* (E), quiet and comfortable, no restaurant. *Europe* (M), near canal. *Bâle*, inexpensive, no restaurant.
At **Sausheim** (6 km/4 miles), the expensive *Sofitel* and moderate *Novotel* and *Mercure*, both with restaurant, pool.
Restaurants. *Relais de la Tour* (M), on 31st floor and revolving, with magnificent views over Mulhouse and the countryside. *Vieux Paris* (M), attractive art nouveau decor and inventive cuisine. *Bûcherie*, interesting menus (M). *Guillaume Tell* (M), attractive building, regional specialties, with some (I) rooms.
At **Steinbrunn-le-Bas**, a few miles south, superb *Moulin du Kaegy* (E), in 16th-cent. mill, but with distinctly 'new' cuisine.

At **Riedisheim,** 2 km (1 mile) east, *Poste* (M), old-established, good, classical cuisine with a few inventive touches.

NANCY.
Grand Hôtel Concorde (E), good classical restaurant, beautifully sited in 18th-cent. building in the pl. Stanislas. *Frantel* (M), restaurant with *nouvelle cuisine* and also a brasserie. *Europe,* 81 rooms, no restaurant, moderate; *Cigogne* (M), pleasant, no restaurant. *Astoria et Albert 1er* (M), 3 rue de l'Armee-Patton, twin hotels in city center, but quiet as all rooms overlook garden or courtyard; no restaurant. *Choley,* in 18th-cent. house, is delightful yet inexpensive.

At **Heillecourt,** just south, *Novotel Nancy-Sud* (M), pool and pleasant garden. Four km/2 miles west on road to Paris, *Mercure* (M), with restaurant. *Novotel Nancy-Ouest* (M) with pool and snackbar.

Restaurants. Best are *Le Gastrolâtre,* superb regional cooking, plus excellent 'new' dishes (E); *Capucin Gourmand* (E), *nouvelle cuisine* and good value menus, and *Gentilhommière* (M-E), elegantly furnished. Also more than adequate: *Les Nouveaux Abattoirs,* specializing in meats (M); *La Chaumière* (M); *Café de Foy* (I). *St-Georges* (I), 79 rue St-Georges, good value brasserie.

One of the best in the region is *Les Vannes* (E), 16 km (10 miles) northeast at **Liverdun,** overlooking the river Moselle. Also has 5 (M) rooms.

NIEDERBRONN-LES-BAINS.
Spa (season, Mar.–Oct.). *Grand* (E), quiet, comfortable, close to spa buildings, good restaurant. *Cully* (M), Logis de France with goodish restaurant. **Restaurant** *Parc* (M), pl. des Thermes.

NIEDERSTEINBACH.
Cheval Blanc (I), quiet former coaching inn, good value restaurant.

OBERNAI.
Duc d'Alsace (M), friendly. Restaurant serves dinner only. *Parc* (M), with restaurant, peaceful Relais du Silence.

Nearby at **Ottrott,** *Beau Site,* moderate, is an old Alsatian house, with good cuisine. *Hostellerie des Châteaux* (M), delightful Relais du Silence on edge of forest, with good restaurant.

ORBEY.
Vosges resort. *Le Saut de la Truite* (M) with lovely view; secluded.

At **Pairis,** 1.5 km (1 mile) southwest, is the *Pairis* (I), with nice view. Logis de France.

PLOMBIÈRES-LES-BAINS.
Spa (season, May–Sept.). *Grand* (M), 110 rooms; *Alsace* (I), 60 rooms, *Abbesses* (I), with good restaurant *(Des Capucins).* A mile or so southwest, *Fontaine Stanislas,* is delightfully secluded in the middle of a forest, with a lovely garden, moderate, comfortable. Restaurant.

REMIREMONT.
Les Chanoinesses, 16 rooms, moderate, good cuisine.

ALSACE AND LORRAINE

At **St-Nabord** 3 km (2 miles) on N57, *Hostellerie Claire-Fontaine* (E) is a *Relais et Châteaux* hotel, with beautiful antique furniture and pool. Restaurant is (M).

RIBEAUVILLÉ. *Pépinière*, just out of town, in woods, moderate, with good terrace-restaurant (M). *Vosges* is inexpensive, with a good restaurant (M). *Tour* (M), delightful converted *winstub*, no restaurant.
Restaurant. *Clos St-Vincent* (E), good, classical dishes, has a few deluxe rooms.

RIQUEWIHR. Restaurant. *Auberge du Schoenenbourg* (M), surrounded by vineyards. *Nouvelle cuisine* versions of regional specialties.

STE-MARIE-AUX-MINES. *Cromer* (M), comfortable, restaurant, Logis de France.

ST-HIPPOLYTE. *Ducs de Lorraine* (M), with vineyards. 40 comfortable rooms, good and rather grand restaurant.

SAVERNE. Hotel-restaurant, *Geiswiller* (M), on N4 road to Paris, with very good restaurant, and *Boeuf Noir*, good cuisine, also moderate.
Restaurant. *Chez Jean* (M), nice atmosphere. Good value *menus*.

SCHLUCHT, COL DE LA. Winter sports center. *Chalet*, simple but satisfactory, inexpensive.

STRASBOURG. *Sofitel*, pl. St-Pierre-le-Jeune, 180 rooms, is deluxe. So is *Terminus-Gruber*, pl. de la Gare, 78 rooms. *Hilton* (E), av. Herrenschmidt, very comfortable, in lovely leafy setting near congress center, with good restaurant (E), called *Maison du Boeuf*, and a second restaurant for light meals (M), called *Jardin*. *Novotel Centre Halles* (E), modern, well-run, with snack bar. *Monopole-Métropole* (E), rue Kuhn. *Holiday Inn* (E), pl. de Bordeaux, indoor pool. *Rohan* (I), has more charm than most of the others. The *National*, pl. de la Gare, 87 rooms, comfortable, is moderate, with snackbar. *Lutétia* (I), 2 rue Général-Rapp, 43 rooms, and *Rhin* (I), pl. de la Gare, 63 rooms, neither with restaurant.

On the outskirts: *Novotel*, 76 rooms, close to the A35 at Illkirch; at Ostwald is the *Mercure*, 97 rooms. Both expensive. Motel: *PLM Pont de l'Europe*, 100 rooms, at the Rhine bridge.

Restaurants. *Buerehiesel* (E), 17th-century building in lovely Orangerie park, has delicious *nouvelle cuisine*. *Crocodile*, 10 rue de l'Outre, elegant, an ideal place to sample Alsatian cuisine and wines, with many 'new' dishes (E); *Valentin-Sorg* (E), 6 pl. Homme-de-Fer, excellent classical cuisine. Also excellent *Maison Kammerzell* (E), in beautiful 16th-cent. house on pl. de la Cathédrale. The best *choucroute* is supposed to be at *Maison des Tanneurs* (M), in interesting setting at 42 rue Bain-aux-Plantes. *Zimmer* (M), 8 rue du Temple-Neuf. *Wladimir* (E), 14 av. Marseillaise, small, new cuisine, well worth a visit.

Try some typical Alsatian wine taverns: *Gourmet sans chique* (M), 15 rue Ste-Barbe, typical Alsatian decor, popular. *Strissel* (I), pl. de la Grande-Boucherie, long-standing and fun. *S'Burjerstuewel* (M), 10 rue du Sanglier. *St-Sépulchre* (I), 15 rue des Orfèvres. *Buffet de la Gare* (I), is also good.

At **La Wantzenau**, 13 km (8 miles) north: *Moulin* (M) on Strasbourg road, charming converted mill; also has rooms; Relais du Silence. *Zimmer* (M), 18 rue des Héros, also good.

THIONVILLE. Restaurant. *Concorde,* atop skyscraper, excellent food (E).

LES TROIS EPIS. Vosges resort. *Mapotel Grand* (E), pool, lovely mountain view. *Mon Repos,* garden, inexpensive.

Restaurants. *Marchal,* with lovely views over forest, serves classical dishes (M); it is also a hotel. *Hohlandsbourg* (E), in Grand Hotel, good for nouvelle cuisine. *L'Auberge* (M), local specialties, also in Grand Hotel.

TURCKHEIM. Restaurant. *Auberge du Brand* (I) has good regional specialties. Also has 7 (I) rooms.

VITTEL. Spa (season, May–Sept.). *Angleterre* (M), near station, with restaurant. *Bellevue* (M), quiet, overlooking park, with restaurant. *Castel Fleuri* (M), quiet with garden and good restaurant (M). *Chalet* (I), 11 rooms.

A little out of town is the *Orée du Bois* inn (M), 33 rooms, nicely furnished, moderate, with good restaurant (M).

WANGENBOURG. *Parc* (I), with restaurant, indoor pool and tennis courts.

WISSEMBOURG. Hotel-restaurant *Ange,* moderate, 10 rooms; excellent regional cuisine (M) in a 16th-century building.

THE JURA AND FRANCHE-COMTÉ

Forested mountains, eastern bastion

The Jura Mountains, that huge natural barrier some 240 km (150 miles) long and 40 to 80 km (25–50 miles) wide, which throws its curved length between France and Switzerland, was known to Caesar, who referred to it in his Commentaries as the Mons Jura. Jura is derived from *Juria,* which means a forest, and no more fitting phrase could be found to describe this region than that of 'the forested mountains'. It is the name by which the region of the Franche-Comté—the 'free country'—is generally known to foreign visitors.

Approached from the French side, the Jura-Franche-Comté rises in a series of slopes from the valleys of the Saône and the Doubs to the sparkling, vineyard-covered slopes of which Arbois is the capital, and finally to the Jura Mountains. These fall away abruptly on the Swiss side as they descend to the lakes of Neuchâtel and Geneva.

A land where winter lingers long, where the mountain roads make motoring hazardous, where the peasants spend the long months until spring grouped round their firesides making wooden toys, clocks and pipes to supplement their meager earnings, this land is enchanting and diverse in what it has to offer. Turbulent mountain streams abounding with trout; lakes poised in lonely, tranquil beauty; cool, green valleys; solitary, winding mountain roads whose sides sometimes drop away abruptly into sheer vertiginous precipices: all these you will find in the Jura as you journey from one unpretentious, picturesque little town to the next. Do not miss St-Claude, world famous for its pipes (and with a Pipe Museum), lying amid its wild rugged mountains; Ornans, where the river Loue flows between old houses built on piles; the solitary splendor of the source of the river Lison; the magnificent Cascades du Hérisson in the Jura lake district; the deep Gorges de la Langouette crossed, high up, by a slender bridge; the unforgettable beauty of the valley of the Loue. Altogether, the region is ideal for a budget-priced quiet vacation.

Besançon, watchmaking capital

At Besançon the river Doubs forms a large loop, somewhat in the shape of a pear, completely encircling the old town. The narrow end of the loop is filled by an enormous rock, 120 meters (400 ft) high, on which towers the ancient citadel. From its summit you can see the town and the river down below, as did, centuries ago, the sentries in the citadel as they paced the heights. See the ancient Roman Grande-Rue, which cuts right through the town, from the cathedral of St-Jean, at the foot of the rock, to the Pont de Battant, at the other end. Nearly everything worth seeing in Besançon lies along or near this road.

Besançon has a curious mixture of architectural styles, for in addition to the native forms there are, as in other towns in this district, traces of the Spanish occupation. Some of the old houses have beautiful wrought-iron grilles in front of the windows. The 12th-century cathedral of St-Jean, with its 13th-century Gothic nave, and the subsequent additions and alterations made during the 15th, 16th and 18th centuries, houses a superb 'Virgin with the Saints', by Fra Bartolomeo. Opposite is the Porte Noire, a 2nd-century Roman triumphal archway, through which you pass into the Grande-Rue.

Here you will find the Palais Granvelle, a magnificent Renaissance building with a delightful cloistered courtyard. Further on, in the place de la République, is the luxuriantly carved façade of the town hall, while not far away, in the place de la Révolution, is the Musée des

Beaux-Arts, where you may see a fine collection of French, Dutch, Italian, Spanish and English paintings, and an archeological section with Egyptian, Greek and Gallo-Roman remains. There is also an Apothecary Museum, founded in 1640 by an apothecary who had a magnificent collection of ancient jars and pharmaceutical implements. The entire pharmacy, as it was in 1640, is in the Hospital St-Jacques. Victor Hugo was born in this old street, as were the brothers Lumière, who invented the cinema.

But Besançon is not just a collection of antiquities. It is a busy town, with industries ranging from plastics and cheese processing to the making of the celebrated aperitif, *Pernod.* Far and away the most important, however, is the watch industry, established in 1893 by Swiss immigrants, though now in financial trouble. Besançon is also a lively town, and rich in the varied beauties of the surrounding countryside. Waterfalls, caves with fantastic grottoes, lakes and wooded hills, can be found within a short distance of the town.

It also has an interesting museum devoted to the Resistance movement in France during World War II and to the tragic deportation by the Germans of Jews and others.

South of Besançon

Nearby is the spa of Besançon-la-Mouillière, with its hotels, restaurants, casino, and thermal baths for the treatment of bone and circulatory diseases. The salt springs of the region contain an unusually large percentage of iodine, sulphur and iron.

Dôle, the birthplace of Pasteur, is an entrancing little town, halfway between Besançon and Dijon. The old town, with its houses clustered around the ancient church of Notre-Dame, its narrow, twisting, climbing streets, the charming place aux Fleurs (with a picturesque flower market), is essentially a place in which you must *flâner*—stroll idly about. As in Besançon, you will find the wrought-iron work reminiscent of Spain.

Arbois, a little town noted for its wine, has a Pasteur Museum in what was once the family home; among other things you will be shown the vine on which he conducted experiments into spontaneous generation. It also has a Wine Museum. The whole area round about is noted for its strange, yellow-tinged wine *(vin jaune)* and for the local 'straw wines' (known as such because the grapes are dried on straw)—pause when you sample one of them to remember that Pasteur's discovery of bacteria was helped along by the unusual wines made here!

Lons-le-Saunier, where Rouget de Lisle, author of the *Marseillaise,* was born, is a typical Jura community. A short distance away is Montaigu, a little village famous for the view it affords of the immense plain.

Not far away are the extraordinary grottoes of Baume-les-Messieurs, enormous caves with their grotesque, petrified rocks.

Nantua, set by the side of its lake, with mountains sheltering it to the north and south, is charmingly situated, and you can make delightful excursions in its neighborhood. Motorboats tour the lake, while the restaurants are reputed for their food. (*Sauce Nantua*, a delectable pale pink sauce made with crayfish, is a local specialty that rates as one of the finest in classical French cuisine—don't miss it.)

In the extreme southern corner and right on the border of Switzerland, only 13 km (8 miles) from Geneva, is Divonne-les-Bains, a thermal spa. Probably best known for its casino, it also holds an international music festival each year between June and July in the Divonne theater. The sleepy town is very international these days; gaming rules are even printed in Japanese. Roulette is still strong; black jack is most popular, and *banque à tout va* is for the real gamblers. Then, for sportsmen, there is a fine 18-hole golf course, a swimming pool and tennis courts.

Winter sports centers

Morez is the kind of resort you find only in the Jura. A long narrow town consisting virtually of only one street, stretching for over a mile in the deep valley of the Bienne, with mountains towering above on each side, it is an ideal winter sports center for those who really want exercise, or merely a rest. This and other Jura centers are family winter resorts par excellence, with plenty of inexpensive accommodations.

The combined facilities of Morez and Les Rousses comprise the Jura's leading winter sports center. Situated only about a mile from the Swiss frontier, it occupies a vast sunny plateau, interlaced with pine forest and dominated by La Dôle, one of the highest peaks in the Jura chain.

Pontarlier, while less spectacular in its setting, is still a splendid spot for winter sports and is becoming more popular yearly. Only 17 km (11 miles) away is another of the important Jura centers: the Jougne-Les Hôpitaux-Neufs-Métabief-Mont d'Or group of resorts, situated on a rolling plateau, with sunny slopes and a magnificent view of the Mont d'Or range.

Belfort is not strictly in the Jura for it stands by the Trouée de Belfort, which separates the Jura from the Vosges. It is now a modernized industrial city of over 40,000 inhabitants, having grown from a small fortified town of 8,000 souls in 1870. Its chief interest for the visitor lies in the superb statue of the Lion of Belfort—22 meters (72 ft) long and 10 meters (35 ft) high—dramatically placed at the foot of the 60-meter (200-ft) rock on which the ancient citadel stands. Carved

THE JURA AND FRANCHE-COMTÉ

by Bartholdi, who also made the Statue of Liberty in New York Harbor, it symbolizes the heroic resistance of the town to the German siege in 1870, when, after much suffering, it surrendered on the orders of the French government.

Some 19 km (12 miles) west of Belfort, on the N19, is one of Europe's great examples of modern architecture, built after another and later war. During the offensive to recapture Alsace in 1945 the chapel of Notre-Dame du Haut in the little town of Ronchamp was destroyed. To replace it, Swiss-born French architect Le Corbusier designed an astonishing and now famous chapel. With its rolled-back roof and 'sun-breaker' windows, it resembles a ship.

PRACTICAL INFORMATION

WHEN TO GO. This region is a great favorite with sportsmen and nature lovers all year round, but particularly in late spring and early fall. This is also the season for taking the waters at one of the region's numerous and well-equipped spas, such as Salins-les-Bains, Divonne-les-Bains, and Lons-le-Saunier, whose waters are effective for nervous, digestive, and circulatory disorders. For touring, summer is the time to come, and for the winter sports fan, Dec. to March.

This part of France has few internationally known festivals but you will find that local festivals occur frequently and give a good picture of how people really live and work here, without the artificial folklore element that colors far too many tourist events elsewhere. Here are a few dates that may help you plan your trip: **March** Daffodil Festival in Montagney, carnival in St-Claude; **May** Besançon Festival; **June** and **July:** International Chamber Music Festival in Divonne-les-Bains; **July** special 'summer night' performances at Belfort's château; Cherry Fair in Fougerolles; **September** International Music Festival in Besançon (with special competition for young conductors); Beer Festival in Luxeuil.

WHAT TO DO. Although this region of France is generally thought of as offering more natural attractions than man-made ones, the 300th anniversary of Franche-Comté's becoming French was celebrated in 1978 with the Year of Châteaux and Villages in Franche-Comté. Lovers of **architecture** will find that most of the arrangements made then to ensure that the area's architectural beauties are better known have had a lasting effect. Châteaux open to the public include those of Filain, Sorans, Moncley, Belvoir, Cléron, while picturesque villages, such as Syam, are found everywhere. Another feature of this region is the interesting examples of industrial architecture it offers, the best-known being the salt works at Arc-et-Senans. In the summer many of these architectural masterpieces are floodlit and some of them provide the setting for cultural events of all kinds, with the emphasis on regional history.

But this is only one aspect of tourism hereabouts. A quick glance at the Regional Chamber of Commerce's suggestions for all-in holidays will give you an idea of the variety on offer. They include **cross-country skiing** for beginners *(ski de fond)*, **fishing, cycling, pot-holing, regional gastronomy, riding,** a week in a horse-drawn carriage, discovering regional products (including visits to vineyards). For these and other suggestions write to the Service Régional de Réservation Hôtelière, 7 rue Charles-Nodier, 25042 Besançon.

THE JURA AND FRANCHE-COMTÉ

Fishing is particularly good in this area of France, with the lake of St-Point and many rivers (the Saône, the Doubs, the Loue, etc.) full of fish, and permits easy to obtain.

Rapids racing through narrow gorges (and many famous waterfalls, including no fewer than 28 in the Hérisson valley) mean that this is ideal country for **canoeing** and **kayaking**, while with 42 water sports centers and many indoor and outdoor pools enthusiastic **swimmers** and **sailors** will be able to indulge to their hearts' content.

The very varied scenery and the relatively peaceful roads offer opportunities for **touring** of all kinds—by car of course, but also by bicycle, on horseback, and on foot. There are many unspoilt stretches where you will have the place entirely to yourself. The *Route des Sapins* is a particularly pleasant and attractive itinerary covering 128 km (80 miles) of fir forest between Levier and Champagnole.

Hiking and **walking** are also ideal here, with special signposted footpaths organized by the nationwide Grande Randonnée organization, the best-known being GR5 (via Gromagny, Montbéliard, St-Hippolyte, Les Rousses and along the Swiss border) and the GR59 (which covers all the four *départements* that make up the Franche-Comté region).

The GR5 is also used for the famous *Traversée du Jura*, a cross-country **skiing** track running for 250 km (155 miles), though this is only one of the many opportunities for skiing in the Jura. The ski resorts tend to be used by local people rather than visitors from other parts of France or abroad, but they are well equipped and because they are less fashionable they are much better value than many centers in the Alps or Pyrenees (though they tend to be short on sun). The best-known ski resorts are Métabief-Mont d'Or, Les Rousses and Gex, but there are plenty more.

If you prefer a less active type of holiday you may like to look into the many possibilities for **craft** classes, which include wood-carving, weaving, stone-carving, pottery and wrought-iron work. New courses of instruction in these and many other crafts are being devised all the time, so contact the local tourist offices for details.

HOW TO GET ABOUT. By air. Frequent flights by *British Airways/Swissair* from London to Mulhouse/Bâle and by *British Airways* or *Air France* to Lyon. Flights by *British Airways* and *Swissair* to Geneva are also convenient for parts of the region. From Paris *Air Inter* has several flights a day (fewer at weekends and in July and August) to Mulhouse/Bâle. *TAT* flies from Corsica (Ajaccio and Bastia), Lille, Lyon, Metz and Nice to Mulhouse/Bâle.

By car. If you're driving you've got various possibilities, the fastest of which involve using the new A36 Beaune–Mulhouse motorway, which passes close to Dôle, Besançon, Montbéliard and Belfort. It links up with the A6 (Paris–Lyon) at Beaune. From Britain and Dunkirk you can take the A25 to Lille and on to Paris on the A1, then the A6 and A36 as above. (From Calais you start with the N43, then the A26 and join the A1 at Arras.) The alternative, if you prefer to avoid the expensive motorways, is to take the N43 to Cambrai, then the N44 via St-Quentin, Laon, Rheims and Châlon-sur-Marne, and the N77 to Troyes. You then take the N19 via Chaumont, Langres and Vésoul to Belfort, or the N71 to Dijon and the N5 to Dôle, or on to Besançon via the N73. More restfully, the car-couchette journey from Paris to Evian-les-Bains takes you close to the southern part of the Jura.

By train. The fastest train from Paris to Belfort takes under 4 hrs. The TGV (high-speed train) now operates in this part of France; the Besançon line is via Dijon and Dôle. Paris–Besançon takes 2½–3 hrs, while from Strasbourg it's under 1½ hrs to Belfort and 2 hrs 40 mins to Besançon. The SNCF has occasional weekend tours of the Jura, including a 'gastronomic dinner' in Champagnole and a visit to a wine cellar.

By bus. Useful if you're coming from Switzerland, as many tourists visiting this part of France do, are the *Europabus* routes Geneva–Besançon and Lausanne–Besançon. But both run July and Aug. only, twice a week in each case, taking 3 hrs and 2 hrs 20 mins respectively. There are plenty of local bus routes from main centers.

USEFUL ADDRESSES *Welcome Information office* for the Franche-Comté region is in the pl. de la 1ère Armée Française, 25000 Besançon; the Departmental Tourist Bureau for the Doubs is at the same address, and so is the city's own tourist pavilion. The Tourist Committee for the Haute-Saône *département* is at 12 pl. de la Gare, 70000 Vésoul; and for the Jura at the Préfecture, 31000 Lons-le-Saunier. The Departmental Tourist Association for the Territoire de Belfort is at 3 rue de la République, 90000 Belfort. Departmental Tourist Committee for the Ain: 2 rue Guichenon, 01002 Bourg-en-Bresse. In Paris, Maison de la Franche-Comté, 10 rue du Colisée, 8e.

Car hire. *Avis,* 7 pl. Flore, Besançon; 13 av. Wilson, Belfort; and at airport. *Hertz,* 3 pl. Flore, Besançon; 17 rue Aristide-Briand, Belfort; bus station, Dôle; 13 av. Aristide-Briand, Lons-le-Saunier. *Europcar,* 10 rue de Belfort, Besançon.

The *Club Alpin Français* is at 14 rue Luc-Breton, 25000 Besançon; Le Château, 25200 Montbéliard; 63 rue de la République, 25300 Pontarlier; and 1 av. de Belfort, 39200 St-Claude.

For riding holidays, *Association Départementale pour le Tourisme Equestre,* 12 pl. de la Gare, 70000 Vésoul (they organize special riding weekends for groups of not less than four experienced riders).

For canoeing and kayaks, *Canoë-Kayak du Haut-Doubs,* 25470 Goumois. For fishing permits apply to the local tourist office.

For pot-holing contact one of the following: Monsieur R. Mauer, 10 rue Moncey, 25000 Besançon, or Monsieur P. Petrequin, rue Mégevand, 25000 Besançon.

For flying and all types of related sports: *Aéroclub du Doubs,* Thise, 25000 Besançon.

THE JURA AND FRANCHE-COMTÉ

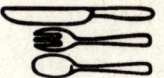 **REGIONAL FOOD AND DRINK.** The finest local dishes make use of fish and shellfish from the region's lakes and streams, especially trout and crayfish, the game that can be shot in the local forests and mountains and, perhaps best of all, the amazing variety of edible fungi found everywhere in this part of France. *Morilles* are particularly delicious mushrooms. Trout are often served with some sort of cream sauce *(truite à la crème)* and watch out for the beautiful pale pink *Sauce Nantua,* made from crayfish, which can be served with various dishes, including *quenelles de brochet* (a sort of paste or mousse of pounded pike with cream and so on, formed into sausage shapes). A similar dish of pike mousse with crayfish sauce will probably appear on the menu as *soufflé de brochet à la bisque d'écrevisses.* Poultry and pork products are also good, with special local sausages and a famous *pâté-en-croute* made in Besançon. The local wine is used for several specialties, such as hare *(chaudronnée de lièvre au vin d'Arbois)* or chicken *(coq au vin jaune).*

Cheeses are widely eaten here, with *fondue* a popular dish. Local cheeses you're likely to come across include *Comté* and *Cancoillotte* (but you may find the latter too strong for your taste).

The best-known wines are *Arbois, Château-Chalon, Etoile, Pupillin* and *Ménétru,* as well as the yellow wine *(vin jaune)* and straw wine *(vin de paille)* we've already referred to. Like most mountainous districts in France, Franche-Comté and the Jura produce some interesting fruit brandies or liqueurs. You'll find that the local plum and sloe brandies, kirsch and the unusual *gentiane,* distilled from gentians, will make a memorable end to a meal.

And if you're looking for something gastronomic, remember that the Jura area is known for its truffles.

 **HOTELS AND RESTAURANTS.** Hotels are normally clean and comfortable but tend to be in the modest range, with few deluxe establishments. The local tourist offices or the Fédération Nationale des Logis de France (see 'Facts at your Fingertips' section) will let you have a list of *Logis de France* and *Auberges de France* in Franche-Comté. Hotels and restaurants listed *E, M* or *I* are expensive, moderate or inexpensive. Restaurants are normally closed at least one day a week and many of them, like the region's hotels, close for part of the year, so check first.

ARBOIS. *Messageries* (I), no restaurant. *Paris* (M) small, has very good restaurant (E) with some *nouvelle cuisine* dishes and intelligent use of local produce (especially mushrooms).

BAUME-LES-DAMES. *Hostellerie du Château d'As,* recently redecorated, has 10 inexpensive rooms and an excellent restaurant (E) with classical cuisine. Also two small and inexpensive hotels: *Parc* and *Central.*

At **Pont-les-Moulins,** 6 km (4 miles) away, *Levant* (M), with restaurant serving rich local specialties.

BAUME-LES-MESSIEURS. Restaurant. *Grottes et Roches* (I), 3 km (2 miles) south, lunches only.

BELFORT. Best is *Grand Hôtel du Lion* (M), with good restaurant (called *Le Vauban*). *Hostellerie du Château Servin* (closed Aug.) is a small and expensive hotel with excellent restaurant. *Paris,* moderate, and *Thiers,* inexpensive.
 At **Danjoutin** (3 km/2 miles away), *Mercure* (M), with pool and restaurant; good restaurant *Le Pot d'Etain* (M), closed July.

BESANÇON. *Frantel,* 96 rooms, modern, expensive, with good restaurant. *Mercure,* in pleasant garden setting. *Novotel* (E), close to station, but quiet, with pool. *Nord* (I) and *Paris,* moderate, neither with restaurant.
 Restaurants. *Le Vesontio* (in Frantel hotel), is good with some unusual dishes (M). *La Tour de la Pelote* (M) is in a 16th-cent. tower. *Poker d'As,* in attractive square is (M).

CHAMPAGNOLE. *Ripotot,* moderate, very quiet, attractive patio, good cuisine. *Vouivre,* small, peaceful, moderate, set in grounds slightly outside town, with tennis courts and fishing but no restaurant; *Parc,* modest, inexpensive.
 At **Ardon,** 5 km (3 miles) north, is the *Pont de Gratteroche,* inexpensive, with restaurant (I).

CHARQUEMONT. *Poste* (M), good value, with restaurant.

DIVONNE-LES-BAINS. Spa (season, Easter–Oct.). Best here is *Golf et Grand* (E), with pool, tennis courts, and casino, thermal baths, theater and golf course nearby. Lively, international. *Château de Divonne* (E), is attractively situated, comfortable, with fine views and extensive grounds. *Alpes* (M), with attractive gardens. *Bellevue* (I), 18 rooms, good restaurant. *Coccinelles* (I), quiet, also 18 rooms, but no restaurant.
 Restaurant. *Marquis* (in Bellevue hotel) (M), very good, with particularly good trout.

DÔLE. *Grand Hôtel Chandioux* (E), good restaurant (M). *Chaumière, Nouvel,* moderate. *Pomme d'Or, Abréal* (I). All have restaurants.

FAUCILLE, COL DE LA. Winter sports center. *La Mainaz,* less than 1 km (½ mile) south, chalet-style, lovely location with magnificent view, moderate; with restaurant (M). *Petite Chaumière* (M), with good restaurant. *Couronne* (I), peaceful Logis de France, lovely views. Restaurant.

GEX. *Parc,* moderate. *Roseraie* (I), pleasant, with restaurant. At **Echenevex,** 3 km (2 miles) south, is the excellent restaurant *Auberge des Chausseurs* (M), with a few moderately priced rooms.

THE JURA AND FRANCHE-COMTÉ

GOUMOIS. *Taillard* (M), small and attractive (chalet-style) Relais du Silence, with good restaurant. *Moulin du Plain* (I), lovely leafy setting by river Doubs, just on Swiss border, with restaurant.

LES HÔPITAUX-NEUFS. Winter sports resort. *Chamois* and *Robbe*, both inexpensive, both with restaurants.

JOUGNE. Winter sports resort. *Deux Saisons, Bonjour, Col des Enchaux, Poste,* all small, adequate, inexpensive, with restaurants (I).

LELEX. Winter sports resort. *Crêt de la Neige* (M), small, with tennis courts and restaurant. *Mont-Jura* (I), tiny and modest, with restaurant.

LONS-LE-SAUNIER. Spa (season, mid-May–mid-Sept). *Grand Hôtel de Genève* (M), comfortable; *Cheval Rouge,* moderate and comfortable, with good restaurant (E). *Nouvel* and *Excelsior,* inexpensive, no restaurant.

LUXEUIL-LES-BAINS. Spa (season, Apr.–Oct.). *Beau Site* (M), secluded, is best, near casino and very close to the thermal baths, lovely garden, good restaurant. *Thermes* (M), 21 rooms; no restaurant. Also moderate are *Métropole* and *France,* former without restaurant.
Restaurant. *Thermes* (I), good value.

MAICHE. *Panorama* (M), perched on hilltop with lovely views.

MALBUISSON. *Le Lac,* very comfortable, moderate, with good restaurant (M). Half-board only in season. *Les Terrasses,* moderate, *La Fuvelle,* inexpensive, no restaurant.
At **Granges-Ste-Marie,** 2 km (1 mile) south on D437, is the *Pont* (I), with restaurant.

MÉTABIEF. Winter sports center. *Etoile des Neiges* (I), small, with restaurant.

MONTBÉLIARD. *Bristol,* moderate, with restaurant, is best but is closed in Aug. Small *France* is moderate, has no restaurant. *Ibis* (M), pleasant member of the well-run chain, with snackbar.
Restaurant. *La Tour Henriette* is good (M), but is closed for most of Aug.

MOREZ. Winter sports center. *Europa,* inexpensive, 30 rooms. *Poste* (I), 45 rooms, comfortable. *Deux Gares,* nice view, very inexpensive. Also modest is the *Commerce.*

NANTUA. *France* (M), comfortable, with good classical cuisine (M). *Lyon* and *Lac* are small, inexpensive. A little way out, near lake, is the moderate *Embarcadère*. All have restaurants.

ORCHAMPS-VENNES. *Barrey* (M), modern Logis de France in small town, with good walks in nearby pine forests; good restaurant.

POLIGNY. *Paris* (I), with pool. *Vallée Heureuse* (I), with pool, restaurant and big garden, on Geneva road.
At **Monts de Vaux,** 4 km (2½ miles) east on Geneva road, is the charming *Hostellerie Monts de Vaux* (E), with 9 rooms. Half-board only in summer. Relais et Châteaux member. At **Passenans-Sellières,** 11 km (7 miles) west, peaceful *Revermont* (M), Relais du Silence with restaurant.

PONTARLIER. Winter sports center. *Grand Hôtel de la Poste* (M), more modest *Bon Gîte* and *Commerce* (M), well run Logis de France. Inexpensive are *France* and *Terrasse*. Both have restaurants. At **Montbenoît,** 14 km (8½ miles) away, popular *Bon Repos* (M), delightful Relais du Silence with pretty garden and good restaurant serving local specialties (but open May through Sept. only).

RONCHAMP. *Ronchamp* (I), close to Le Corbusier's chapel, reader-recommended for good value and helpful service. No restaurant.

LES ROUSSES. Winter sports resort. *France* (M), with good restaurant. *Redoute, Risoux,* moderate, *Rousses,* inexpensive.
Restaurants. *Relais des Gentianes* (M), good, also has rooms. About 3 km (2 miles) out, at **La Cure,** is the *Arbez* (M).

ST-AMOUR. *Commerce* and *Alliance* (in a 17th-cent. building, with garden), both inexpensive, with good food.

ST-CLAUDE. *Poste* and *Jura* are modest, inexpensive. Neither has restaurant. *St-Hubert* (M), no restaurant. Three km (2 miles) south is hotel-restaurant *Joly* (I), good cuisine.

SALINS-LES-BAINS. Spa. *Ermitage,* quiet, moderate. *Messageries,* inexpensive, near the casino.

SEYSSEL. *Rhône* (M), has a good restaurant. *Beau Rivage* (I), lovely views.

VALDAHON. *Relais de Franche-Comté* (M), rather stark modern building, but quiet and friendly, with regional cuisine.

WINTER SPORTS. The Jura are not as high as the Alps or Pyrenees, which accounts for their shorter season, but there are good snow conditions from Dec.–Mar. The slopes are less abrupt than the higher ranges elsewhere in France, and the centers are well equipped and comparatively inexpensive. The leading centers are Les Rousses-sur-Morez and Métabief-Mont d'Or. Gex-La Faucille, Giron and Pontarlier are popular, and there are small resorts with more limited facilities. None is higher than 1,220 m (4,000 ft). Near Morteau the Doubs forms a natural skating rink nearly 5 km (3 miles) long.

BURGUNDY

The treasure house of history

Famous vineyards drenched with sunshine; undulating country with billowing wooded hills; hospitable people who have perfected all that is best in eating and drinking; old towns and villages, rich in history and artistic treasures; and all along the roads from Dijon, the names of world-famous wines greet us, for all this is Burgundy.

Evidence that man has lived in this region since prehistoric times has been found near Beaune, at Solutré, which has given its name to an archeological period, and in the grottos of Arcy-sur-Cure near Auxerre. Just off the A6 motorway south of Beaune, the *Archéodrome* is an imaginative reconstruction illustrating a thousand centuries of life in Burgundy, with reproductions of huts, temples and fortifications built when Caesar ruled Alesia. The remarkable Treasure of Vix, in the museum of Châtillon-sur-Seine, includes objects that decorated the tomb of a Celtic princess buried more than 2,500 years ago in a nearby village.

Frenchmen in a hurry to reach Lyon or Geneva usually hurtle down the A6 (branching off at Pouilly-en-Auxois or Tournus for Geneva), pausing only for a quick cup of coffee. However, is you are in no hurry, along the N5 and N6 (what is today the N5 was built after Caesar's decisive victory over the Gauls at Alesia) lie towns that are fascinating and beautiful.

Sens and its cathedral

Sens, about 112 km (70 miles) south of Paris, was for centuries the ecclesiastical center of France. The cathedral of St-Etienne, a model for England's Canterbury Cathedral, is one of the oldest Gothic cathedrals in France. But it is its treasury, one of the richest in France, that is of particular interest. For here can be found the robes of Thomas à Becket, who fled from England to escape the wrath of Henry II. He returned to England only to find himself again differing with the king, this time regarding the legal rights of priests, and was murdered in his own cathedral of Canterbury in 1170. Also in the treasury are the richly woven gold and silver robes of the archbishops of Sens and the 15th-century tapestry presented to the cathedral by Louis de Bourbon.

If you visit the 15th-century château of Saint-Fargeau, where la Grande Demoiselle, Louis XIV's cousin, was exiled as a result of her activities during the Fronde rebellion, you'll have, on top of the interest presented by the château itself with its six huge towers, its horse museum and its beautiful furniture, the extra pleasure of knowing that you're helping to save it from ruin. It was bought in 1979 by two energetic young brothers and they have already restored one whole wing and the roof, doing most of the work themselves. To raise the money needed to complete the restoration they run a summer festival of dance and drama that attracts some big names, and welcome visitors every day from April 1 to the first weekend in November. There's *son-et-lumière* here too.

The abbey of Fontenay

About 6 km (4 miles) from Montbard is the abbey of Fontenay. Founded in 1118 by Bernard, Abbot of Clairvaux, it was built by a group of Cistercian monks in a remote spot, for it had been decreed that their monasteries could not be established anywhere near 'cities, feudal manors, or villages'.

By the end of the 12th century, the church and other buildings comprising the monastery were finished. Membership in the order at

Fontenay grew steadily until, at the beginning of the 14th century, the abbey had some 300 monks or converts. Under powerful protection the monastery prospered mightily.

The 16th century marked the beginning of the fall of Fontenay. The religious wars were partly responsible for the deterioration, but a more important cause was in the administration of the abbey itself. During this period, abbots were selected by the king with little regard for ecclesiastical capabilities. Exercising their rights as abbots, they dissipated the wealth that had made Fontenay powerful.

The French Revolution spelled the end of Fontenay as a monastery. It was sold for 78,000 francs to a buyer who transformed the monastery buildings into a paper factory. Fontenay served in this industrial capacity until 1906. During this time great care was taken not to damage the historic buildings. After the paper concern relinquished control, restoration of the abbey was undertaken by its new owner, Edouard Aynard. Using ancient plans, he accomplished the remarkable task of returning the church and all of the buildings to their original 12th-century condition.

Along the road to Dijon

The château of Bussy-Rabutin, south of Montbard, was built in the middle of the 17th century by Roger de Bussy-Rabutin, satirist and wit at the court of Louis XIV. The king enjoyed the young man's clever sallies directed at various members of the court, for Bussy-Rabutin made a point of studying minutely the private and public lives of all the noblemen and court hangers-on. But he wrote a book entitled *L'Histoire Amoureuse des Gaules,* a thinly disguised account of the love-life of Louis XIV. The enraged king had the impudent Bussy-Rabutin exiled from Paris. Selecting land near Les Laumes, he built a château. As a further insult to Louis, he personally designed the gardens of his château, taking meticulous care to copy the gardens of Versailles. Bussy-Rabutin's ribald personality persists to this day within the confines of the château, particularly in the Mistress Hall, which contains portraits of all of his mistresses.

Alise-Ste-Reine, known as Alesia a century before the birth of Christ, was in its day one of the most important towns in Gaul. Well-fortified, and perched on the summit of a hill, it was considered impregnable. Yet it was at this city that Julius Caesar completed the conquest of Gaul, defeating the youthful Vercingetorix.

Although the fortifications built by Caesar at Les Laumes have now been covered over, Alesia is in an excellent state of preservation. Roman occupation forces took over the city, engineers and builders were brought in and the city took on a Roman aspect. A theater, forum

BURGUNDY

and Roman district were built, and a central heating system was installed to heat all the Roman houses. Although the Romans destroyed part of the Celts' homes to build their own, a sizable Celtic or Gallic district remains. In it is a dolmen, or Celtic stone altar. A visit to Alesia provides the traveler with an example of how the Celts lived prior to, and just after, the Roman conquest of Gaul, the conquest that marked the beginning of the cultural birth of France. Nearby is the Merovingian church of Ste-Reine.

The two little medieval towns of Avallon and Vézelay, lying on the northern tip of the great Burgundian vineyards, are not only charming but are also excellent centers from which to explore the northern part of the nearby Morvan forest. Avallon, perched on a high rocky promontory and surrounded by ancient ramparts, gives a magnificent view over the striking valley of the Cousin. Vézelay, which was in the Middle Ages one of the most important places of pilgrimage in the Christian world, boasts one of the largest and most beautiful Romanesque churches in France, the basilica of Ste-Madeleine (restored by Viollet-le-Duc in the 19th century), with its rightly famous central tympanum carved by an unknown 12th-century sculptor, and rivaled only by the tympanum of the cathedral of St-Lazare at Autun.

Burgundy's capital

Dijon is not only the capital of the province and the historical center of all Burgundy, but it is also one of the renowned gastronomic capitals of France. Its streets are literally crammed with restaurants and pastry-shops, each vying with the others to offer you the best of Burgundian fare.

There is plenty to see in Dijon. The 13th-century cathedral of St-Bénigne, and the equally ancient Gothic church of Notre-Dame with its stained-glass windows; the 16th-century church of St-Michel with its famous Renaissance façade; the 15th-century Hôtel Chambellan, in the picturesque rue des Forges, which contains the beautiful 16th-century Hôtel Maillard; the Chartreuse de Champmol, founded in the 14th century by Philippe le Hardi: its magnificent doorway and the Well of Moses were the work of the 14th-century sculptor Claus Sluter.

The Museum of Fine Arts, which is housed in the old palace of the dukes of Burgundy, is famous for the wealth and variety of its collections. The tombs of Philippe le Hardi (Claus Sluter's masterpiece) and of Jean sans Peur are celebrated examples of Burgundian art at its finest, while the picture galleries, which cover all periods of French painting, and the section devoted to Renaissance furniture and medieval *objets d'art* leave no doubt of the claim that this museum is one of the best in France. The magnificent new Granville Donation, the modern art section, is housed and excitingly arranged in what used to be the attics.

Passing southwards through strips of well-tended vineyards, we come to places whose names have made Burgundy famous. Stop for a moment at the little village of Chenôve, for here are probably the oldest wine-making installations in France. Built by Alix de Vergy in 1238, it still has the original winepress with its enormous stone block weighing no less than 26 tons, and it is still in use.

The wine district

At Gevrey-Chambertin you may taste the famous Chambertin wine, renowned among connoisseurs and prized by Napoleon above all wines. Clos-Vougeot, with its 16th-century Renaissance château dominating the enormous vineyards that were planted by the monks of the Abbey of Cîteaux, is the place where the members of the Confrérie des Chevaliers du Tastevin ('brotherhood of the knights of winetasting') meet some 12 times a year with their guests to dine in Rabelaisian sumptuousness. Nuits-St-Georges, where wine was made in Roman times, produces a wine that Fagon, the royal physician, prescribed in much later days to Louis XIV on account of its 'dry, tonic, and generous qualities'. And again journeying southward we pass vineyard after vineyard, until at last we come to Beaune, capital of the great region known as the Côte de Beaune, which includes such famous vineyards as Pommard, Volnay, Aloxe-Corton and others.

The Hôtel-Dieu, or Hospital of Beaune, is one of the most curious in the world. Built in 1450 by Nicolas Rolin, chancellor of Burgundy, it carried on its activities without interruption until 1971, the nurses still wearing the curious medieval dress they wore when the hospital admitted its first patient in the 15th century; you may still see, in the Hospital Musuem, some of the strange instruments used by doctors in those early days. The museum also possesses the polyptych of the *Last Judgement* by Rogier van der Weyden, together with a fine collection of tapestries. Nor should art lovers miss Beaune's beautiful 12th-century basilica.

But the Hospital of Beaune has another claim to distinction. It is so wealthy that it has no need to ask for aid either from the state or from individuals. Under the name of Hospices de Beaune, it is the proud owner of some of the finest vineyards in the region—notably Pommard and Volnay. These are farmed out on a profit-sharing basis, and each year there is a sale, attended by connoisseurs and wine dealers from all over the world.

In the Hôtel des Ducs de Bourgogne is the Wine Museum, where the entire history of winemaking is traced, together with the step-by-step process. The mansion housing the museum is itself of great interest. Built in the 15th and 16th centuries, it has been well restored, and is now much as it must have been in the days when it was the country seat of the dukes of Burgundy.

Autun is one of the most interesting old towns in Burgundy. Caesar called it 'the sister and rival of Rome itself', and you may still see traces of the Roman occupation in the Temple of Janus and the fine gates of St-André and Arrouz. Parts of the Roman wall surrounding the town remain and give a fair indication of its size in those days. Near Autun, the curious Pierre de Couhard, a pyramidlike Roman construction, has so far baffled archeologists, who are undecided as to its significance. But the 12th-century cathedral of St-Lazare, with its tympanum of the Last Judgement and its capitals carved by the famous sculptor Gislebertus around 1130, is one of the finest examples of medieval art in all France. The Rolin Museum, with its collection of Burgundian sculpture (including Gislebertus's masterpiece, *Eve*, formerly in the cathedral) and its painting of the *Nativity* by the Maître de Moulins, make Autun one of the most richly endowed *villes d'art* in Burgundy.

The abbey of Cluny, founded near the beginning of the 10th century and set in lovely rolling country was, in its day, famous throughout the Christian world; though little of the original buildings survive, the remains of the church, and the sculpture exhibit, are well worth a visit. The little town of Cluny itself is rich in medieval and Renaissance buildings, including a number of interesting Romanesque houses.

South of Beaune lies the district of Meursault, where two of the great white wines of Burgundy, Meursault and Montrachet, are produced. If you are lucky enough to be there at the time of the grape harvest, when the *Paulée de Meursault* takes place, you will need a strong constitution to digest all the rich Burgundian fare that is provided at this annual feast.

Tournus and its Romanesque abbey

At the beginning of the 11th century, after years of invasions and internal dissension, peace and order were established for a while in Burgundy. The countryside flowered with great churches and abbeys built in a new style, known as Romanesque. The most spectacular and best preserved of these is the abbey of St-Philibert at Tournus. Although massively built, the interior is spacious and light. Unadorned cylindrical pillars, over 1 meter (4 ft) thick, support the curved arches of the nave. Designed purely as a place of prayer, no attempt was made to decorate or embellish it. The sole attempt at frivolity is the use of red and white stones arranged alternately in the round arches of the nave.

The town itself retains much of the charm of the Middle Ages and the Renaissance, for most of the houses were built during these periods: all historic buildings are well marked with signs. The antique collector will be delighted with Tournus, for the narrow, winding cobblestone streets abound with antique shops. Tournus is also a good base for visiting Brancion, Cluny and Mâcon.

As far as Mâcon, on the southward journey, the vines grow on limestone soil typical of the great Burgundian vineyards, but from Mâcon almost to the gates of Lyon the land changes and covers a hard granite base that nevertheless produces a number of high-quality wines such as Juliénas, Fleurie, Morgon, Brouilly, Moulin-à-Vent and Pouilly-Fuissé, a fine dry wine that seems to have been produced expressly to bring out the succulent flavor of oysters, while leaving untouched their subtle delicacy.

Mâcon, an old, sleepy town with wide quays along the banks of the Saône, is dominated by the two octagonal towers of the ruins of its medieval cathedral of St-Vincent. It was the birthplace of the great poet Lamartine. In the place aux Herbes is a wooden house of the 16th century still in an excellent state of preservation.

BURGUNDY

PRACTICAL INFORMATION

 **WHEN TO GO.** Burgundy looks its best in Sept. and Oct., the time of the grape harvests, and these are good months for visiting, though spring is also a delightful time to tour the region. Interesting events and celebrations are held during most of the year, many of them in honor of gastronomy.

On the last Sat. in **January**, the Knights of Tastevin pay homage to St Vincent, patron saint of winegrowers, with a festival held in a leading wine city. Up to Shrove Tuesday, Chalon-sur-Saône holds a Mardi Gras carnival. Two traditional **May** events are the Ring Race at Sémur-en-Auxois, a horse-race dating back to the 17th cent., and Mâcon's Wine Fair and National Wine Exhibit, attended by buyers from all over the world. On weekends from May through Sept., there are concerts, art exhibitions, plays and floodlighting of monuments as part of the Night Festivals of Burgundy, and Vézelay's *son-et-lumière* show should be seen.

June starts off with Beaune's Wine Fair, and the ceremonial blessing of the vines of France; about mid-month comes the Feast of the Sacred Heart at Paray-le-Monial, where Ste-Marguerite-Marie Alacoque had her revelation in 1675. One of the important religious ceremonies takes place at Vézelay on **July 22**, the Feast of St Mary Magdalen, whose relics were enshrined there during the 10th cent. Also in July is Autun's music festival, and the *'Côte Illuminée'* circuits of the Vintage Road start. Then comes Vézelay's music festival in **August**.

At Dijon's **September** Wine Festival, the new wine flows in the Bareuzai fountain, and during the **November** International Fair, gourmets can sample French regional as well as exotic foreign fare. The *Trois Glorieuses* wine events are held in **November**: on the third Sat., enthronement of the Tastevins at Clos-Vougeot; third Sun., wine auction at the Hospices de Beaune, which sets prices the world over; third Mon., the Feast of the Paulée at Meursault. Beaune has a particularly beautiful midnight mass in Notre-Dame basilica on **Christmas Eve**.

 **WHAT TO DO.** Burgundy offers the tourist a wide variety of things to do and see. The **gourmet** may embark on a tour of its great restaurants and vineyards (for details, see below under 'Vineyards' and 'Hotels and restaurants'). **Art lovers** may visit the Romanesque centers of Vézelay, Cluny, Autun, the Cistercian abbeys of Fontenay, Cîteaux and Tournus and the medieval and Renaissance treasures of Dijon, Beaune, Avallon, Noyers-sur-Serein and Sémur-en-Auxois, to name but a few. **Archeology** fiends should not miss the Treasure of Vix in the small but fascinating archeological museum of Châtil-

lon-sur-Seine, and the Gallo-Roman ruins of Alesia, Autun and Fontaines-Salées. **Music lovers** will find concerts throughout the summer at Avallon, Tonnerre, Sémur-en-Auxois, Dijon, Joigny, Vézelay, Sens, St-Florentin and Pontigny. Burgundy has more than 100 **châteaux,** such as La Rochepot, Châteauneuf, Tanlay, Ancy-le-Franc, Bussy-Rabutin, Bazoches, Vougeot (now headquarters of the Chevaliers du Tastevin), many still family-inhabited. **Nature lovers** will explore the granite range of the Morvan, with its hills, rivers, lakes (Settons, Pannecière, Chaumeçon, Crescent) and grottoes (Arcy-sur-Cure). Details of **horse-riding** excursions or holidays may be obtained from the tourist offices in Dijon, Saulieu or Château-Chinon.

There are 3,500 km (2,175 miles) of navigable waterways in Burgundy, and the canals and rivers are almost free from commercial traffic. **Boating** or **canoeing** in the gentle Burgundian countryside is one of the best ways of discovering this infinitely varied region. You may hire a boat from one of over 30 companies in Burgundy (see 'Useful addresses', or ask any local tourist office or *Syndicat d'initiative),* or stay in one of the barge-hotels which sail up and down the canals and rivers. **Fishing** enthusiasts will not be disappointed. The rivers Saône, Doubs, Yonne, Grosne, Arconce, Ternin, Loire, Canche, Selle, Serein, Cure, Cousin, Seille and Cozanne abound in trout, bream, carp, gudgeon, perch and pike, and crayfish may be found in many of the smaller streams.

VINEYARDS. The great vineyards of the Côte d'Or are situated between Dijon and Chalon-sur-Saône. The northern ones are known as the Côtes de Nuits, the central ones as the Côtes de Beaune, and the southernmost as the Côtes de Chalon. At Vougeot you can visit the château and see the enormous wine presses used by the Cistercian monks. The abbey of Cîteaux is nearby.

For routes to follow, addresses for wine-tasting, contact the *Comité Interprofessionel des Vins de Bourgogne,* 21200 Beaune, and the *Comité Interprofessionel des Vins de Bourgogne et de Mâcon,* BP 113, 71000 Mâcon, or the local tourist offices.

Travel organizations in both the US and the UK arrange tours of vineyards from time to time, with tasting, sightseeing and gastronomic elements well to the fore. The National Tourist Offices will have details of trips available.

HOW TO GET ABOUT. By train. As Burgundy is on the main Paris–Riviera, Switzerland and Italy routes it has an excellent service of fast trains. Dijon is the hub through which all these trains go and almost all stop. The TGV (high speed train) now serves Dijon taking under 2 hrs from Paris. There are good frequent local services, and by changing in Besançon you can get there from Strasbourg quite quickly.

By coach. *Europabus's* run from Antwerp and Brussels to Nice and Menton stops overnight in Dijon. The *SNCF* runs combined rail-motorcoach tours from

BURGUNDY

Paris (among them several weekend tours of the region's art cities), as well as motorcoach excursions to the Morvan section from Auxerre.

By boat. French Leave/CIT have holidays involving one night in Paris and six or seven nights on board the hotel-barges *Palinurus* or *La Guêpe Buissonnière,* with all meals (including unlimited wine), and even the use of bicycles during your peaceful cruise on Burgundy's rivers and canals (Apr. through Oct.). Latest recruit to the barge stakes is the luxurious *Janine,* on which you can have a leisurely 1-week cruise from Dijon to Lyon and back again, with gastronomic meals and more comfortable accommodations than on most barges, for which you naturally pay higher prices (contact M. Streat, 59 High Street, Braunston, Daventry, Northants, England).

MOTORING. The fastest way down from Paris is the A6, which easily links up with the A1 (if you're coming direct from Britain) via the *boulevard périphérique* round Paris, though don't try to use it during the rush hours. You branch off at Pouilly-en-Auxois if you want to get to Dijon (about half an hour on the link road), or carry on to Beaune, Châlon-sur-Saône, Tournus, Mâcon, all of which are on the autoroute. For Nuits-St-Georges you branch off just before Beaune on the A37. If you don't feel like motorway driving, you can take the N6 via Fontainebleau, Sens, Auxerre, Avallon and Saulieu to Châlon-sur-Saône. Suggested variations of itinerary: from Sens, continue on D905 via Montbard and the abbey of Fontenay to Dijon, thence south to Beaune, connecting with N6 at Chagny; from Avallon, detour on D957 to Vézelay; below Avallon, branch off on N70 for Dijon route; from Saulieu, take D980 to Autun, thence via N80 to Le Creusot and D980 to Cluny, N79 to Mâcon.

USEFUL ADDRESSES. The *Welcome Information office* for Burgundy and Dijon's own tourist office is in the Pavillon du Tourisme, pl. Darcy, 21000 Dijon. There are tourist offices or *syndicats d'initiative* in all towns of a reasonable size, which will give information on cultural and leisure activities. *Regional Tourist Committee,* Hôtel du Département, 21041 Dijon.

Car hire. *Avis,* 135 bis route de Dijon, Beaune; 49 av. de Paris, Châlon-sur-Saône; 5 av. du Maréchal-Foch, Dijon; 23 av. Edouard-Herriot, Mâcon. *Europcar,* 9 av. Gambetta, Auxerre; 78 rte de Pommard, Beaune; 31 rue du 11-Novembre, Châlon-sur-Saône; 47 rue Guillaume-Tell, Dijon; 35 rue Lacretelle, Mâcon. *Hertz,* 4 rue Maréchal-de-Lattre-de-Tassigny, Châlon-sur-Saône; 18 bis av. Foch, Dijon; 77 rue Victor-Hugo, Mâcon.

Boat hire. *Locaboat Plaisance,* quai du Port-aux-Bois, 89300 Joigny; *Nautic-Voyage,* 8 rue du Milan, 75009 Paris, and Verdun-sur-le-Doubs; *Croisière Bourgogne,* Le Beugon, 89650 Arcy-sur-Cure.

Riding. *Association départementale de Tourisme Equestre,* Nièvre Tourisme, Préfecture, Nevers; *Association Régionale de Tourisme Equestre Bourgogne-Morvan,* 9 grande-rue, Charny.

THE FACE OF FRANCE

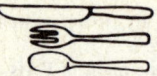

REGIONAL FOOD AND DRINK. Famous regional dishes are *boeuf bourguignonne* (beef cooked slowly in wine with glazed onions, button mushrooms and bacon), *oeufs en meurette* (eggs poached and served in a rich red wine sauce), *pochouse* (freshwater fish stewed with herbs, onions and wine), *jambon persillé* (terrine of ham with parsley and garlic), *coq au chambertin* and jugged hare. Burgundy's large snails are famous, and Dijon is for many people synonymous with mustard (which you can buy in pretty jars to take home as attractive presents). Mustard is often used in dressings for salads, while *saupiquet montbardois* is a local spicy sauce. Gingerbread is also well known here, and so are little boiled sweets flavored with blackcurrant.

Casssis, a blackcurrant liqueur, is another local specialty. It is used to make the delicious *kir*, an apéritif of white wine with *cassis*, or, for special occasions, the even more delicious *champagne kir*.

Regional cheeses include Chaource, Epoisses, St-Florentin, Soumaintrain, Crottin de Chavignon and other small goat cheeses, and *pourri*, a very strong cheese in which cow's and goat's milk are combined and mixed with olive oil, white wine and *marc* (a spirit made from grape skins after they have been pressed to make wine and also used to make the excellent *marc de Bourgogne* brandy).

The wines of Burgundy are of course world-famous—burgundies and bordeaux (clarets) are the two great groups of French wines. Each separate region produces its own distinctive wines: dry, light wines *(Chablis)*, rich, full-bodied reds from the Côte du Nuits, the best-known of which are *Nuits-Saint-Georges, Gevrey-Chambertin* (which was apparently Napoleon's favorite wine!), *Chambolle-Musigny* and *Vosne-Romanée*. The Côte de Beaune also produces some of France's finest red wines, such as *Pommard, Volnay* and *Savigny-les-Beaune*, as well as magnificent white wines *(Meursault, Puligny-Montrachet)*. Further north, the Yonne region produces the interesting *Pouilly-Fumé*, while the other well-known name beginning with Pouilly, *Pouilly-Fuissé*, is an excellent white wine from the Mâcon region.

HOTELS AND RESTAURANTS. Burgundy has many comfortable and attractive hotels and inns, usually offering excellent food served in generous portions (the Burgundians have a reputation for large appetites to go with their full-bodied wines). Small country restaurants usually provide splendid meals, and meals can be found all over the region for reasonable prices on the whole, except in the really top-class gourmet restaurants. In country districts you usually have a choice of two or three fixed-price meals (often there is no *carte* at all), but even the cheaper ones may easily consist of a starter, an *entrée*, a main course, cheese and fruit or a dessert. Eating is an important part of life in Burgundy, so don't try to persuade restaurateurs to prepare you a quick snack—meals generally last some time, so that you have plenty of opportunity to savor the splendid wines. Hotels in this area do not usually close for part of the year, but it's always advisable to check just in case. But restaurants are

BURGUNDY

normally closed at least one day a week, often Mon. Most close on Sun. evening. The letters *E, M* and *I* in the following list stand for expensive, moderate and inexpensive.

ARNAY-LE-DUC. *Poste* (I) and *Terminus* (I), both small; the latter has a good restaurant, with regional specialties (M).
Restaurants. *Relais St-Jacques* (I), also has 10 rooms. *Chez Camille* (M), attractive 16th-century building with delightful covered courtyard for serving delicious meals.

AUTUN. *St-Louis* (M), very comfortable, with restaurant (M) and garden. *Tête Noire,* comfortable, with restaurant (M). *Hostellerie du Vieux Moulin,* near the Porte d'Arroux, with restaurant (M), very attractive.
Restaurants. *Chalet Bleu* (I), excellent value, but a bit far out (in St-Pantaléon suburb).

AUXERRE. *Maxime* (E), comfortable, with a good restaurant (M). *Cygne* (M), quiet and comfortable, no restaurant, and *Fontaine,* no restaurant (M). *Sainte-Nitasse,* on the Chablis road, with restaurant (I).
Restaurant. *Grilladerie* (M), good grilled meat; friendly.

AVALLON. *Hostellerie de la Poste,* expensive, in charming 18th-cent. posthouse with garden and one of the best restaurants in Burgundy (E). Napoleon is even said to have slept here. *Hostellerie du Moulin des Ruats,* in the Vallée du Cousin, very comfortable old mill-house with garden and restaurant with regional specialties (E). *Moulin des Templiers* (M), another old mill-house in the same valley; no restaurant. *Le Relais Fleuri,* quiet and comfortable, with restaurant (M). Modern, near motorway, yet quiet.
Restaurant. *Le Morvan,* on the Paris road, good, inventive cuisine (M).

BEAUNE. *La Poste* (E), first class but noisy. Now modernized. Restaurant with good cooking, superb wines (E). Smaller and quieter *Cep* (E) in a charming old house. Just outside town, on the Autun road, is *Closerie* (M), modern, comfortable and quiet, with a garden and pool; no restaurant. The 120-room *Bourgogne* (M) and 62-room *Samotel* (E) (on Autun road) also modern, both with swimming pools and restaurants. The 150-room *Motel PLM* (M), on the A6 motorway is quiet and convenient if driving. Restaurants nearby, on motorway.
Restaurants. *Poste* (E, in hotel), *Auberge Bourguignonne* (M) (also has rooms) and *Rôtisserie de la Paix* (M). *Auberge St-Vincent* (M), attractive, friendly, newish cuisine. Just outside town on Dijon road, *Raisin de Bourgogne* (M), refreshingly light cuisine, with good value *menus;* also has a few rooms. At **Chorey-lès-Beaune,** *Ermitage de Corton* (E), elegant, interesting cuisine.

BOUILLAND. Near Savigny-lès-Beaune. *Hostellerie du Vieux Moulin* (M), a pleasant, quiet country hotel with excellent riverside restaurant, inventive cuisine, local trout and crayfish (M).

CHABLIS. *Etoile* (I), small, with good cuisine (M).

CHAGNY. *Lameloise* (E), an old Burgundy house, elegantly furnished, with one of the best restaurants in France for *nouvelle cuisine* (E). A Relais et Châteaux member. *Poste* (M), no restaurant. *Hostellerie du Château de Bellecroix* with restaurant (M).
Restaurants. *Lameloise* (see above). At **Chassey-le-Camp,** is the *Auberge du Camp Romain* (I), with a good view and a few (M) rooms.

CHALON-SUR-SAÔNE. *Mapotel Royal* (M), modernized and comfortable, with *Trois Faisans* restaurant (M), very good. *St-Georges* (M), and *Mapotel St-Régis,* both (M) with good restaurants (M). *Nouvel Hôtel* (I), no restaurant.
Restaurants. *Le Provençal* (M); *Le Bourgogne* (M) in an 18th-cent. house.

CHÂTEAU-CHINON. *Vieux Morvan* (I), with good restaurant (M). A Logis de France. Made famous by President Mitterrand who often comes here (this used to be his constituency).

CHÂTILLON-SUR-SEINE. *Côte d'Or* (M), pleasant hotel with garden and a very good restaurant (E).

CLUNY. *Bourgogne* and *Moderne,* both moderate with good restaurants (M).

DIGOIN Restaurants. *Gare* (M), excellent *nouvelle cuisine.* Has some (M) rooms. *Diligences et Commerce* (M), an old favorite for classical cuisine; also has some (I) rooms.

DIJON. *Cloche* (E), reopened 1982 after extensive modernization; very comfortable, well furnished and central. with good restaurant in the fabulous old cellars. *Frantel* (E), modern on the edge of town by exhibition center, good restaurant. *Chapeau-Rouge,* also expensive, with good classical cuisine and a lovely old building. *Central* (M), now belongs to Ibis chain; pleasant restaurant. *Nord* (M), close to station, central, good restaurant. At **Marsannay-la-Côte** (8 km/5 miles), *Novotel* (E), with pool, modern and moderate. At **Val-Suzon** (14 km/9 miles), in a charming woody valley, is the *Hostellerie du Val-Suzon* (M), quiet, comfortable with good classical cuisine, served in pretty setting.
Restaurants. *Pré aux Clercs et Trois Faisans* (M), now back on form. *Chouette* (M), in an attractive old street, and *Vinarium* (M), the latter with a good selection of wines. *Rallye* (M), with mostly *nouvelle cuisine.* *Thibert* (M) has inventive regional dishes. At **Marsannay,** *Gourmets* (M), attractive, with tiny garden; judicious blend of classical and new cuisine.

BURGUNDY

FIXIN. Well-known **restaurant** *Chez Jeannette* (M) has rich Burgundian dishes. Also has some peaceful rooms (I).

FLEUREY-sur-OUCHE (near Dijon). **Restaurant.** *Le Sanglier* has good local cuisine, elegant dining room (M).

GEVREY-CHAMBERTIN. *Grands Crus* (M), modern and comfortable, without restaurant. *Les Terroirs,* quiet and moderate, and *Aux Vendanges de Bourgogne,* unpretentious and inexpensive, with restaurant (I).
Restaurant. *Rôtisserie du Chambertin* (E), pleasantly located, good service, wonderful wines and excellent cooking—some say the best in Burgundy, yet prices aren't high for the quality. Serves both classical Burgundian cuisine and more inventive dishes. Must reserve.

JOIGNY. *Côte St-Jacques* (E), chic little hotel with pool and good *nouvelle cuisine* and fine wines (E). *Mapotel Modern' Hôtel,* moderate, with good restaurant (E). Again mostly *nouvelle cuisine*. *Paris-Nice* (I), pleasant Logis de France.

MÂCON. *Bellevue* (E), comfortable, good classical cuisine. *Frantel* (E), comfortable, good restaurant with regional specialties (M). *Genève* is moderate, with restaurant (M), and *Nord,* simple and inexpensive, without restaurant. At nearby **Crèches-sur-Saône,** the *Château de la Barge,* comfortable, in an old house with a large garden and vineyards; restaurant (M). *Sofitel* (E), beside A6 motorway, with pool and restaurant; peaceful (rooms are soundproofed). *Novotel* (M), again close to A6. 4.5 km (3 miles) away on Bourg road, *Huchette* (E), chic, with pool, pleasant grounds and restaurant. *Motel Vieille Ferme* (M), with garden pool and restaurant, is 4 km (2½ miles) away on N6 road.
Restaurants. *Auberge Bressane,* good regional dishes (M). *Rocher de Cancale* (M), good fish dishes. *Pierre* (I), pleasant atmosphere and reasonable cooking (I).

MERCUREY. Restaurant. *Val d'Or* (M), also has 12 rooms.

NEVERS. *PLM Loire,* moderate, 60 rooms, modern, beside river with restaurant. *Molière* (I), peaceful but away from center. *Château de la Rocherie* (M), 5 km outside town, quiet and pleasant, with pool and big garden; has good restaurant too.
Restaurant. *Porte du Croux* (M), also has a few rooms.

NOLAY. The pleasant little *Ste-Marie* restaurant (I), also has some rooms.

NUITS-ST-GEORGES. *Ibis* (M), in town, modern and efficient, with snack bar for light meals. *Gentilhommière* (M), small, comfortable, is 1 km (½ mile) northwest; good restaurant with fine wine list. **Restaurant.** *Côte d'Or* (E), also has 10 rooms. Mixture of classical and new cuisine. Marvelous wines.

POUILLY-SUR-LOIRE. *Bouteille d'Or* (I). *Relais Fleuri* (I), attractive.
Restaurants. *Espérance,* good regional cooking (E), *Coq Hardi* (M), in Relais Fleuri hotel.

QUARRÉ-LES-TOMBES (in the Morvan) *Auberge des Brizards* (M), with good local dishes (I).

LA ROCHEPOT. *Relais du Chateau* (M), with restaurant.

SAULIEU. *Côte d'Or,* (M), newly decorated rooms, well-known for its superb restaurant, one of the best in France (E). Now has good-value fixed-price menu too. *Poste* (M), a delightful 17th-century posting house, no restaurant. *Quatrevents* (I), modest, with restaurant.
Restaurant. *Borne Impériale* (M), has a few rooms. Good classical cuisine and smiling service.

SÉMUR-EN-AUXOIS. *Lac* (I), 3 km (2 miles) outside town, near the dam. Good restaurant.
Restaurants. *Auberge des Quinconces,* regional specialties (I). *Cambuse* (M), good value, newish cuisine. *Gourmets* (I), modest little place with popular restaurant.

SENS. *Paris et Poste,* expensive; now run by same family as excellent *Modern* in Joigny and successfully modernized. Good mixture of classical and new cuisine. *Hôtel-Résidence R. Binet* (I).
Restaurants. Best is in *Paris et Poste* hotel (E). *Palais* (I), good traditional dishes and *Auberge de la Vanne* (I).

TONNERRE. *Abbaye St-Michel* (E), delightful converted abbey, comfortable, pleasant view, with good restaurant (E).

TOURNUS. *Rempart* (E), near station, modern, good restaurant. *Sauvage* (M), with good restaurant. *Clos Mouron* (I), a motel, functional but pleasant.
Restaurant. *Greuze* (E), one of best in France for classical dishes. Rather grand atmosphere.

VERDUN-SUR-LE-DOUBS. *Hostellerie Bourguignonne* (M), old country inn overlooking the river, fine imaginative cuisine (E).

VÉZELAY. *Poste et Lion d'Or,* expensive, comfortable, with good restaurant. *Cheval Blanc* (I), with garden and restaurant.
Restaurant. *L'Espérance* (E), at **St-Père** (3 km/2 miles), has excellent 'new' cuisine, plus some rooms (including a few in an attractive converted mill). Must reserve.

THE RHÔNE VALLEY

Gastronomy, gorges and craftmanship

Even though Lyon is France's second largest city, this part of the country is surprisingly little known to foreign tourists, who tend to hurtle through it on their way down south to the Côte d'Azur or to Italy, maybe stopping off for a gastronomic meal (probably at astronomic prices too), but rarely exploring the regions on either side of the mighty river.

Yet the Rhône valley certainly doesn't deserve this neglect. It is full of interest, with a long history stretching back to the Romans, hundreds of churches, châteaux and abbeys, magnificent scenery, fine wines, unspoilt villages—and many small restaurants serving excellent local dishes at only a fraction of the prices charged in the better-known centers. To the west of the Rhône (and the motorway) lies the Ardèche, poised between the verdant valley and the rough mountainous Cévennes, and increasingly attracting holidaymakers who want to see the unspoilt countryside and the traditional way of life in rural France before it disappears for ever. To the east, between the Rhône and the Alps, is the lavender-scented Drôme, full of delightful little towns offering a foretaste of sunny Provence. To the north is the Beaujolais wine-producing district, which is in a way a continuation of the great Burgundy vineyards.

And right in the center of course is busy, bustling Lyon, which makes a good starting-point for your journey.

Lyon—silk and industry

Center of the French mechanical industry, with its many bridges spanning the mighty Rhône and Saône rivers, its massive stone houses, its prosperous, perpetually hurrying inhabitants, Lyon is far removed from the old Burgundian towns you may have driven through before reaching this great metropolis, second only to Paris in size and population. Although it can trace its history back to Roman Lugdunum, it is essentially a modern city, surrounded by motorways. Its traditional silk industry is today somewhat in decline, but it has numerous large mechanical and chemical firms and is also recovering something of its former role as a capital of banking and international commerce. It has a new civic and commercial complex (La Part-Dieu) and a handsome new university campus in the suburbs. Since 1978 it also has its own Métro (subway) and its main street has recently been banned to traffic, in keeping with the new 'quality of life' vogue. Thousands of people attend its annual International Fair, held in early April in special buildings along the Rhône, and throng to the great summer festival of Lyon-Charbonnières. Lyon also has the country's leading provincial theater: Roger Planchon's remarkable Théâtre National Populaire, in the suburb of Villeurbanne, specializing in radical and experimental plays.

Many people have drawn parallels between Lyon and the northern English manufacturing towns so well described by Arnold Bennett, mainly because the Lyonnais is traditionally taciturn and difficult to get to know. His life still revolves largely around his family, and strangers are rarely invited into his home. But though you may be disappointed at not being invited for dinner to sample the region's magnificent cuisine as cooked for an ordinary family, Lyon is so full of restaurants that you won't know how to choose one.

The 18th-century place Bellecour is the lively heart of this bustling city, and here you'll find a whole host of restaurants and cafés (the Lyonnais are fond of café life). Not far from here are the city's major museums. The interesting Musée Historique des Tissus (the Textile

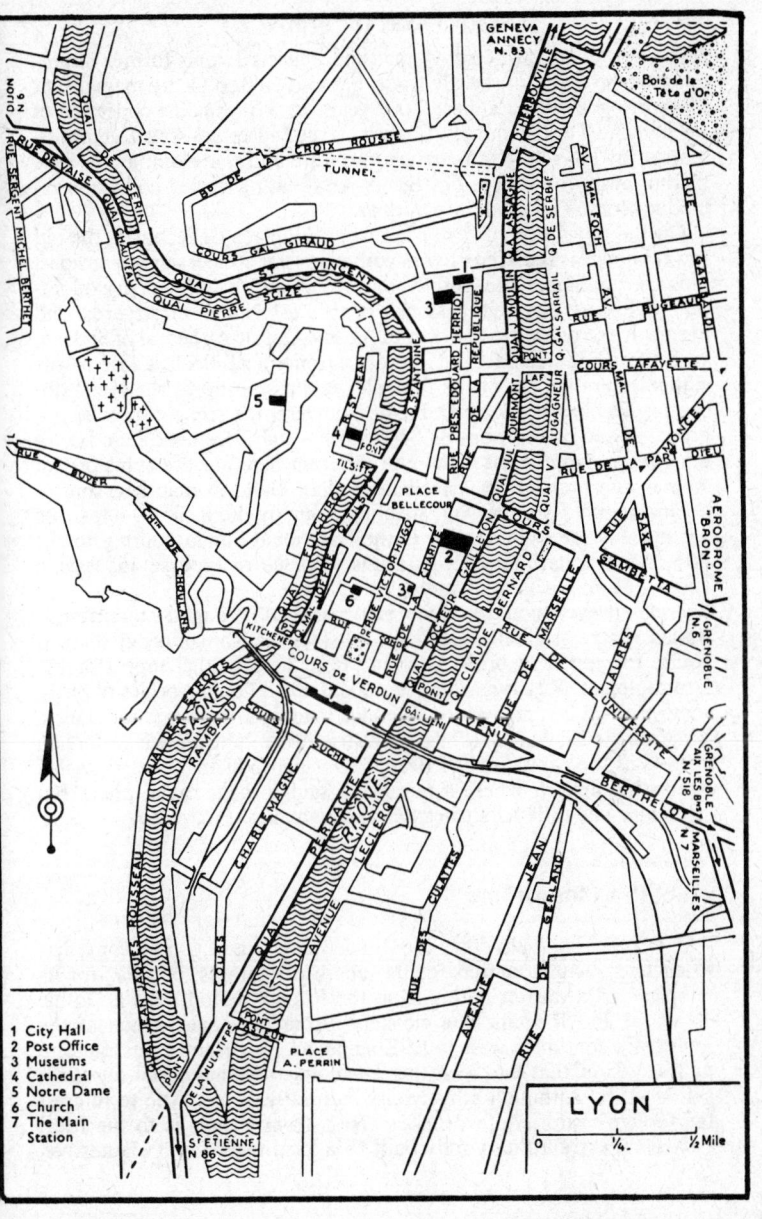

Museum), in an 18th-century mansion, reflects Lyon's former importance as the center of the silk trade, but also on display are magnificent tapestries going back almost 2,000 years, as well as a fine collection of Persian and Turkish fabrics. Close by is the Musée des Arts Décoratifs, a must for lovers of 18th-century furniture and porcelain, and a little further away the Musée des Beaux-Arts, with a varied collection including some fine modern paintings.

On the other side of the Saône from the place Bellecour is the old town, known as the Vieux Lyon, with many fine Renaissance mansions, plus a sprinkling of late Gothic houses. This area is well worth exploration, with its covered passages *(traboules),* inner courtyards and decorative wrought ironwork, and the fine Gothic cathedral of St-Jean, with beautiful stained glass and an astronomical clock. Close to the cathedral is the base of the funicular taking you up to the late 19th-century basilica of Notre-Dame-de-Fouvière, the scene of special pilgrimages and celebrations on September 8 and December 8, and commanding a magnificent view. Not far from here are the ruins of two Roman theaters and the excellent modern Gallo-Roman Museum.

Don't leave Lyon without strolling along by the Rhône—a favorite pastime for the Lyonnais, as is the traditional Sunday outing to the little spa of Charbonnières-les-Bains, with its racecourse and casino and, in March, a famous motor rally.

A classic excursion from Lyon is to medieval Pérouges, a picturesque walled village originally dating from before the Roman occupation. If you're interested in birds, continue from here to the huge Dombes Ornithological Reserve, which has about 400 different species of birds, some of them extremely rare. A minor road from Pérouges takes us to Villefranche-sur-Saône, a busy industrial town best known to foreign visitors as the capital of the Beaujolais wineproducing area. It has an interesting church where a miracle is said to have taken place, but otherwise has little to attract the holidaymaker.

South to the Drôme

If we continue south down the Rhône valley from Lyon we come first to ancient Vienne, famous for its superb restaurants, but also for its temples and a theater dating from the Roman period, plus a Gothic cathedral and Romanesque cloisters. From here one branch of the motorway continues west to St-Etienne, an important industrial and mining center that has been the scene of serious industrial unrest in recent years. Although a lively city culturally, it has little to interest the foreign visitor. A favorite excursion from Vienne is to the Ideal Palace, an extraordinary folly built by a local postman in Hauterives, but check that it is still open to the public as it has been suffering from too many sightseers.

South of Vienne lie Tain-l'Hermitage and Tournon, where the celebrated L'Hermitage wine is made, and then Valence, the capital of the Drôme, a busy industrial and market town with a university once attended by François Rabelais. Its 16th-century Maison des Têtes, in the Grande-Rue, is known for its richly carved façade. Further south still is Montélimar, famous throughout France as the center of nougat production (you can even visit a nougat factory if you feel like it, but anyway you're sure to want to take home a prettily packed box of this great delicacy). But the chief interest of Montélimar is as a center for excursions into the unspoilt Drôme, a region of lavender-scented hills and peaceful little towns unknown, fortunately, to the developers. One attractive road from here leads to the busy little town of Crest, with delightful gardens and a 12th-century keep; another to tiny Grignan, where the great marquise de Sévigné is buried (she used to stay with her daughter, the countess of Grignan, in the 16th-century château, which can be visited, and wrote many of her celebrated letters in the countryside around here).

From here we can continue to Nyons, an ancient town with medieval houses and ramparts, popular with summer visitors, passing on the way through Valréas and the 'Enclave of the Popes', which was part of the papal dominions from the 14th to the 16th centuries. A different road takes us to Dieulefit, a center of craftsmanship where many of the traditional crafts (especially glass-blowing) are being revived, and to Le Poët-Laval, with the ruins of a fortress built by the Knights of Malta and a Protestant Museum. The whole of this unspoilt area is an ideal hunting ground for those who like exploring off the beaten tourist track.

The Ardèche

On the other side of the Rhône, the Ardèche, too, is mostly off the tourist map, even though the warmth and welcome of the Vivarais district are legendary. This part of France offers extraordinarily varied scenery, with vivid contrasts from one valley to the next, plus picturesque hill villages and dramatic river gorges. Its best-known natural feature is the broad and beautiful river Ardèche itself, rushing down from the heights of the Massif Central—shooting the rapids in a canoe is becoming a major tourist attraction nowadays, but the river is also good for swimming and picknicking along its narrow beaches. The whole length of the Gorges de l'Ardèche, from Vallon-Pont-d'Arc to Pont-St-Esprit, with a magnificent new road winding above the valley, is a feast for lovers of natural grandeur.

Most holidaymakers approach the Ardèche from the Rhône valley, via Privas or Aubenas. Privas is a charming and bustling market town and the capital of the Ardèche *département*. From here the road climbs spectacularly over the Col de l'Escrinet, at an altitude of 760 meters (2,500 ft). Pause here to gaze at the Ardèche spread out at your feet, its gray and golden mountains stretching to the distant horizon. The splendid road down to Aubenas passes through the village of Vessau, where you may well be dazzled by its multicolored church spire glinting in the sunlight. Before reaching Aubenas turn west to gracious Vals-les-Bains, an attractive spa town producing millions of bottles of mineral water every year and a magnet for those suffering from liver and stomach complaints. Lace is produced here too. A picturesque road winds through peaceful villages to Antraigues, a typical hill village with narrow streets that has become a mecca for young people eager to revive local crafts.

Beyond Antraigues is the Gerbier de Jonc, a wild and curiously shaped mountain over 1,520 meters (5,000 ft) high commanding spectacular views. Near the summit is the source of the great river Loire. The Mézenc, higher at over 1,675 meters (5,500 ft), is volcanic.

After this side trip you should return to Aubenas, perched high on a hill with a fine view, once the capital of the silk-weaving industry in the Ardèche (which has many mulberry trees on which the silk worms fed), and now known for its attractive little boxes of *marrons glacés*. It makes a good center for excursions, first to neighboring Largentière, formerly, as its name suggests, a silver-mining town, but then left as empty as the ghost towns of the Wild West; it too is experiencing a revival of local crafts and you will find crowds of hippie-type youngsters in the summer selling enamel objects and wood carvings. Your road winds on amid lovely scenery to the little summer resort of Valgorge—notice as you drive along two typical features of the Ardèche: houses with arched balconies once used for drying the silk that was the region's major source of income, and the chestnut trees that still bring it prosperity. Beyond Valgorge are two cols—the Col de la Croix de Bauzon and the Col de Meyrand—both of them offering breathtaking views.

If you are continuing on south from Aubenas to Provence, stop briefly at Joyeuse, a tiny walled town with an imposing castle and a history dominated in the 16th and 17th centuries by the exploits of the lively and versatile Joyeuse brothers, who included a marshal of France, a cardinal and a capuchin friar. From here you can make many delightful excursions into the wild and rugged scenery on the edge of the Cévennes.

THE RHÔNE VALLEY

PRACTICAL INFORMATION

WHEN TO GO. As this is not an area geared to mass tourism there is no real tourist season, though there are more opportunities in the summer months for outdoor sports such as canoeing in the Ardèche. Lyon is a busy, bustling city year-round, but many of its famous restaurants are closed in Aug. and there are more cultural events in the spring and autumn than in the summer. On the other hand guided tours of old Lyon and the other historic towns usually take place only from May to Sept. From the weather point of view, Aug. can be too hot and the winter months are harsh in the Ardèche; best time is late spring and early summer, or in Sept.

Early **March** is the time for the Lyon-Charbonnières motor rally and a month later, in early **April,** comes Lyon's International Fair, which was revived in 1916 but dates back to the 15th cent. On Ascension Day in **May** horse racing fans travel miles to watch Lyon's steeplechase; this month also sees the start of Vienne's Festival of Religious Music, which lasts into June and July. In **June,** Vienne's summer festival begins (music, drama, dance) lasting into August. On the Sun. after June 16 Lalouvesc stages its picturesque pilgrimage in honor of St François Régis. As elsewhere in France, the Feast of John the Baptist on **June 24** (or the nearest weekend) is celebrated with fireworks and traditional bonfires, especially in Villefranche-sur-Saône. In **July** Valence has its summer fair in the old part of the town, plus chamber music recitals, and Lyon has an international music and drama festival. On **July 14** the National Holiday is celebrated with jousting on the Rhône, at Condrieu and also at Tournon. Saint-Donat's Bach Festival starts at the end of July. Condrieu has more water tournaments in early **August** and this month also sees regattas in other places. Craft fairs are held in the Ardèche at this time, too, and St-Donat organizes an international Bach festival. Lyon's puppet festival comes in **September. October** and **November** are the months for wine fairs in the vine-growing district. On **December 8,** the Feast of the Immaculate Conception, the people of Lyonnais light many-colored lanterns in their windows and parade through the streets, and on **December 24** another lantern procession in Pérouges leads to a picturesque midnight mass.

WHAT TO DO. This is a good area for those wanting to learn a new **craft,** with opportunities for watching local craftsmen at work all over the Drôme and the Ardèche. For instance weaving classes are held at the Etablissements Berliet, 49 montée de Grande-Côte, Lyon, and woodcarving, enameling and silk-painting are taught in the Ardèche, which is becoming one of *the* centers for reviving traditional crafts (the craft fair held here in Aug. is particularly interesting, though inevitably crowded). **Cookery** classes are also a specialty in the Ardèche, where they are held year-round. For information on these and many other classes, contact the local and regional tourist offices, or an organization called *Art Paysan de l'Ardèche,* pl. du Marché, 07140 Les Vans.

Lyon, like most big towns in France, offers the opportunity to learn French in a class, but it is also an important cultural center, with many concerts and plays staged throughout the year. Further north Beaujolais-lovers will be able to enjoy **wine-tasting**, while in Lyon itself, with its proud tradition of good eating, you can study the art of classical *cuisine.*

You can sample the delights of **riding**, especially in the Ardèche, while the region is well equipped for **water sports** of all kinds (**canoeing** and **kayaking** are becoming increasingly popular in the Ardèche, with the famous gorges offering an exciting opportunity to travel from Pont-d'Arc to St-Martin by canoe, which includes a number of rapids). **Cycling** and **walking** are both good here, though you may find it difficult in smaller places to find a bike to hire. The Ardèche's rivers are cold, but are usually beautifully clear for **swimming** and **angling**.

HOW TO GET ABOUT. By air. *British Airways* and *Air France* have daily flights from London-Heathrow to Lyon-Satolas airport, which also has direct flights from the United States and many European countries. *Air Inter* has several flights daily between Paris and Lyon, as well as Marseille–Lyon. Also *TAT* between Tours and Lyon.

By train. Lyon is on the main Paris–Riviera route and is well served by good trains, including the new TGV (high speed train) which now takes only 2 hours Paris–Lyon. There are also through routes from Calais for British visitors. There are several cross-country lines passing through Lyon, which are useful if you want to combine visits to various different areas. Here are a few examples: Strasbourg–Lyon (about 7½ hrs), Bordeaux–Lyon (about 7 hrs), Nantes–Lyon (about 6 hrs), Metz–Lyon (about 5 hrs). There are fairly frequent local services between Lyon and the main centers in this region, and most of the fast trains between Paris and the Riviera also stop in Valence. Some of the good trains from Lyon to Clermont-Ferrand stop at St-Etienne. In the Ardèche, the 22-mile scenic railway between Tournon and Lamastre is a joy.

The *SNCF* has a '*Lyon à la Carte*' package covering rail fare, hotel and breakfast for as many nights as you please.

By coach. *Europabus's* run to Nice and Menton stops in Lyon, but otherwise there are few coach tours of this region. The *SNCF* has a combined coach and rail tour called 'Discovering the Ardèche'; it lasts over a long weekend, but unfortunately it runs only a few times a year.

MOTORING. The quickest way to get to Lyon from Paris is the A6 motorway (which you can join after leaving the A1 from Calais and travelling round Paris on the *boulevard périphérique*). From there the A7 continues the *Autoroute du Soleil,* passing close to Vienne, Tournon, Valence and

Montélimar. If you prefer to avoid the motorway, take either the N7 or the N6 (see Burgundy chapter) to Lyon.

For the Ardèche, you can leave the A7 motorway at either Loriol or Montélimar-Nord: from Loriol you take the N104 to Privas and Aubenas, which involves crossing the spectacular Col de l'Escrinet; from Montélimar-Nord take the easier N102 at Le Teil to Aubenas. For Crest and Die leave the A7 at Valence and take the D538A and the D93. For Grignan and Nyons, leave the A7 at Montélimar-Sud and take the little D541 and D94. There are many attractive little roads in the lavender-filled area west of Montélimar, with little heavy traffic.

You can also take a day-long excursion along the Rhône from Lyon to Avignon, or a three-day trip to Arles and the Camargue (address: Marcel Couly, Pont La Feuillée, Lyon, or Blake's International, Wroxham, Norwich, England). On the first one you stop at Vienne, Tournon, Valence, Montélimar and the great Donzère dam. The second excursion takes you to the art cities of Avignon, Beaucaire and Arles, and back to Lyon by train.

USEFUL ADDRESSES. The *Welcome Information office* for the Rhône valley is in the pl. Bellecour, 69223 Lyon cedex 1. The city's own *tourist* office is also here, with other subsidiary offices at the Centre d'Echange de Perrache, 69002 Lyon, and esplanade des Invalides, 69006 Lyon, in the new Part-Dieu district. *Comité Régional du Tourisme Vallée du Rhone,* 5 pl. de la Baleine, 69005 Lyon. The *Departmental Tourist Committee* for the Ardèche is at 8 cours du Palais, BP 221, 07002 Privas, for the Ain at 2 rue Guichenon, BP78, 01002 Bourg-en-Bresse, and for the Drôme at 1 av. de Romans, 26000 Valence. In Paris, the *Maison de la Drôme* is at 14 bld Haussmann, 75009 Paris.

American Express, 48 cours de la Liberté, Lyon.

Car hire. *Avis,* 32 rue Danton, Perrache rail station, cours de Verdun, all in Lyon; 27 av. Denfert-Rochereau, St-Etienne. *Europcar,* 7 rue Duhamel and 16 pl. Jules-Ferry, Lyon; 8 av. Denfert-Rochereau, St-Etienne. *Hertz,* Perrache station and 211 rue de Gerland in Lyon; 4 pl. Fourneyron, St-Etienne. All three companies also have offices at Lyon's Satolas airport.

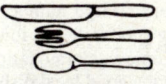

REGIONAL FOOD AND DRINK. Lyon is generally reckoned to be the heartland of French cuisine and there must be more good restaurants to the square mile here than anywhere else in France. But don't think that Lyonnais cooking is elaborate—it is often rich and great trouble goes into its preparation, but it is at heart based simply on excellent ingredients carefully cooked. Hence its high reputation. *Quenelles de brochet* (pounded pike formed into sausage shapes and usually served with a rich crayfish sauce) are a specialty often found here, while more simple fare includes the famous *saucisson de Lyon,* generally served hot with boiled and sliced potatoes. *Poularde demi-deuil* is another well-known dish, consisting of a plump chicken with slivers of truffles slipped beneath its skin, then boiled in stock. Poultry is in fact particularly good here, another specialty being chicken with a cream sauce *(poulet à la crème)*. Eel and trout from the local rivers are often served, and a *ragout* of crayfish *(écrevisses)* is not to be missed if you see it on a menu. *Gras-double à la lyonnaise* is a feast for tripe lovers.

The Ardèche is the main area for *marrons glacés* in France, so don't be surprised to find chestnuts from the region's magnificent trees in a number of dishes; they are particularly good with goose. You will also find many traditional country dishes, with fine game birds in season (partridge, quail and even thrush), generally braised slowly rather than roast. Walnut oil is often used for dressing salads here, giving them a distinctive and interesting flavor. The Ardèche is also known for its *charcuterie* (particularly a type of sausage surprisingly called a *'Jesus'*) and its goat's cheeses.

If the Ardèche is known for *marrons glacés,* Montélimar is even better known for nougat, which has been made here since the late 16th cent. (Packed in pretty boxes it makes a good present to take home.) The cuisine in this part of the Rhône region is otherwise fairly close to Provençal cooking, though some Alpine specialties can be found here too, the mountain influence being specially obvious in the number of potato dishes.

The long tradition of gastronomy in this part of France is, not surprisingly, accompanied by an equally long tradition of wine production. Beaujolais, produced in the north of the region, is a light wine tasting of the grape and is often drunk as a refreshing drink outside ordinary mealtimes. The famous *Beaujolais nouveau,* drunk in Nov. almost as soon as it has been bottled, is particularly popular. Lower down the Rhône valley you will come across the Côtes-du-Rhône wines, made from wines grown in the vineyards on both sides of the river. Particularly well known are the excellent *Condrieu* and *Château-Grillet*, both white and drunk very cold, and the slightly sparkling *Clairette de Die,* while the Hermitage wines, from the area round Tain and Tournon, are unusually fruity.

HOTELS AND RESTAURANTS This part of France is known for its cuisine and has many fine restaurants. Because of the wide choice of eating places we recommend that you should not eat in your hotel (which anyway may well not have a restaurant) but sample the delicious food in the local restaurants. Lyon is an important business center and has a large number of hotels in all categories, but you won't have trouble finding good hotels in towns elsewhere. In the wilder parts of the Ardèche and the Drôme accommodations are scarcer, but there are pleasant country inns, often serving good local dishes.

ANNONAY. *Midi,* (M), comfortable Logis de France, no restaurant.
Restaurants. *Café du Château* (M), good value (with some (I) *menus*), interesting cooking by a woman chef. *Célerien* (I), opposite the station.

ANTRAIGUES. Restaurant *Lo Podello* (E), furnished with antiques, has delicious Ardèche specialties, including the excellent local *charcuterie* and *pâtés.*

THE RHÔNE VALLEY

AUBENAS. *Pinède* (M), quiet, just outside town with beautiful view and restaurant.

Restaurant. About 1.5 km (1 mile) on the way to Alès is the attractive *Directoire* (E).

BAIX. *Cardinale*, a 17th-century manor house in attractive large grounds, with annex. 3 km (2 miles) away: *Résidence*, 10 rooms and pool. Has fine restaurant (E).

BOURG-EN-BRESSE. Best is *Logis de Brou* (E), no restaurant, or *France* (M) more central, with (I) restaurant. *Mail* (I), good restaurant with local specialties and nice garden.

Restaurant. *Auberge Bressane* (E), in suburb of Brou, with regional specialties.

CHARBONNIÈRES-LES-BAINS. *Parc* (M) peaceful, good restaurant, *Mercure* (M), modern. *Beaulieu* (I), no restaurant. *Euromotel* (M) on main road to Paris (N7), with pool.

Restaurants. *Sangria* (E), in the casino, open for dinner only. *Gigandon* (M), pleasant.

COLLONGES-AU-MONT-D'OR. Near Lyon. **Restaurant** *Paul Bocuse au Pont de Collonges* (E), one of the world's most brilliant and ambitious restaurants, run by Paul Bocuse, France's most famous restaurateur, and most vocal champion of cuisine based on ultra-fresh ingredients (not necessarily *nouvelle cuisine*, which he now tends to deride). Magnificent cooking, opulent décor, prices to match, though now offers fixed-price meals too, at considerably lower prices.

GRIGNAN. *Sévigné* (I), small, no restaurant.

LAMASTRE. *Midi* (E), with fine restaurant. *Commerce* (I), good Logis de France. *Château d'Urbilhac* (M), 2 km (1 mile) away via D2, peaceful and attractive, with lovely grounds and views; dates from 16th century and opened as hotel in 1983.

LYON. Has many hotels and restaurants in its main districts: central (between the Saône and the Rhône); east of the Rhône; and on the outskirts.

Central. Deluxe: *Sofitel*, 20 quai Gailleton, with the *Trois Dômes* (E) restaurant, terrace overlooking the Rhône. Expensive: *Royal*, 20 pl. Bellecour; *Grand Hotel Concorde*, 11 rue Grôlée; *PLM Terminus*, 12 cours Verdun, near Perrache rail station; *Carlton*, 4 rue Jussieu; *Alfotel-Tourinter*, 23 cours Charlemagne, 122 rooms, restaurant, primarily for businessmen. (M) hotels include: *Bristol*, 28 cours Verdun; *Beaux-Arts*, 75 rue Prés. Herriot. (I) hotels include: *Bordeaux et Parc*, 24 cours Verdun; *Axotel*, near cours Verdun; *Continental*, 17 pl. Carnot;

Azur, 64 rue Victor-Hugo; *Normandie,* 3 rue Bélier; *Moderne,* 15 rue Dubois; *Simplon,* 11 rue Duhamel.

East. (E) hotels include: *Frantel,* 129 rue Servient, with good view and two restaurants. *Roosevelt,* 25 rue Bossuet. *PLM-Park,* 4 rue du Professeur-Calmette, functional and sensible, nice grill. (M) hotels include: *Piolat et Lutétia,* 114 bld des Belges, good. *Terminus-Brotteaux* (I), 97 bld des Belges. *Lyon-Bron* (M), no restaurant.

Outskirts. At **Bron airport,** 196 rooms, *Novotel* (E), with pool and restaurant. At **Satolas airport,** *Méridien.* At **Porte de Lyon** (9.5 km/6 miles north), *Holiday Inn,* 204 rooms; *Novotel,* 107 rooms; *Mercure.* All (E), with restaurants, pools. New *Campanile,* rather spartan, moderate, American-type motel, one of a chain. At **Crépieux-la-Pape** (6.5 km/4 miles north), *Larivoire* (M). Old favorite overlooking Rhône, now serves newish cuisine, good service.

Restaurants.

Central. *Nandron* (E), 26 quai J.-Moulin, outstanding, modern décor. *Mère Brazier* (M), 12 rue Royale, excellent cuisine and cellar; *Vettard* (E), 7 pl. Bellecour, good value; *Léon de Lyon* (E), 1 rue Pleney, very good, Lyonnaise ambiance; *Tour Rose,* 16 rue du Boeuf, fashionable (E); *Nord* (E), 18 rue Neuve, a favorite, good; *Orsi,* 3 pl. Kléber, very promising (M); *Bourillot* (M), 8 pl. des Célestins, with both classic and 'new' dishes. *Voute* (M), 11 pl. Antonin-Gourju, an old favorite, loads of atmosphere. *Chevallier* (I), 40 rue du Sergent-Blandan, high quality, many regional specialties and cheeses; *Tante Alice,* 33 rue Remparts-d'Ainay, small, good home cooking, pleasantly served (I).

MAISONNEUVE. *Relais de la Vignasse* (M), attractive Logis de France, perched up on hill with lovely views, restaurant.

MIONNAY. Restaurant. *Alain Chapel* is run by one of France's most brilliant chefs and is one of the country's top restaurants; superb 'new' cooking, well worth the high prices (E); also has 13 expensive rooms, for which you must reserve well ahead.

MONTBRISON. *Hostellerie Lion d'Or,* moderate, attractive, with good restaurant (M).

MONTÉLIMAR. *Relais de l'Empereur* (E), delightful, good service; restaurant is a bit of a disappointment. *Dauphiné-Provence* (I). Near the A7, north of town, is the *Logiroute* motel (M), with pool but no restaurant. **Restaurant** 4 km (2½ miles) north at **L'Homme d'Armes,** *Bastide* (M), delightful 15th century building, regional cuisine.

PÉROUGES. *Ostellerie Vieux Pérouges* (E), (with a few less expensive rooms in an annex) with well-known restaurant; picturesque atmosphere in a 13th-century half-timbered building. Also a favorite spot for 'afternoon teas' consisting of *galettes* and cider.

THE RHÔNE VALLEY

POËT-LAVAL (near Dieulefit). *Hospitaliers* (E), medieval building in lovely old village with glorious views, pool and good restaurant (E).

PONT-DE-VAUX. Restaurants. Good value are *Commerce* (M), *Reconnaissance* (M) and *Raisin* (I); all with a few rooms.

PRIVAS. *Chaumette* (M), peaceful, friendly with good restaurant (I). At the **Col de l'Escrinet**, 13 km (8 miles) away, is the modern *Escrinet*, with spectacular views, pool, and a balcony to every room, yet only moderate prices.

ROANNE. *Grand* (M), with restaurant, in town. *Ibis* (M), outside town, just off N7. **Restaurant.** *Frères Troisgros* (E), pl. de la Gare, one of France's best, with exquisite 'new' cuisine, not to be missed. Also has 24 rooms. Belongs to Relais et Châteaux association.

ST-ANDRÉ-DE-CORSY. Restaurant. *Bérard* (E), interesting cuisine in this attractive half-timbered building.

ST-ETIENNE. *Frantel* (E), modern, with excellent restaurant (*Ribaudière*), on outskirts beside Parc de l'Europe. Comfortable *Grand* (E), more central, again with good restaurant (*Gillet*).
At **Andrézieux** (16 km/10 miles), *Novotel* (M), with pool.
Restaurants. *Pierre Gagnaire* (M), brilliantly inventive cuisine at reasonable prices.
At **St-Priest-en-Jarez** (4 km/2½ miles), *Clos Fleuri* (M) is good, a favorite with local businessmen.

TAIN L'HERMITAGE. *Deux Côteaux* (M), no restaurant. *Commerce*, with pleasant restaurant (M).
Restaurants. *Grappe d'Or* (I), pleasantly situated.

TARARE. *Gît'otel* (M), modern, opened 1981, well run with restaurant.

THOISSEY. *Chapon Fin* (E), elegant, pleasant, good restaurant (E). A Relais et Châteaux hotel.

TOURNON. Across the Rhône from Tain l'Hermitage. *Paris* (M). **Restaurant.** *Château* (M), good cooking and attentive service. Has 7 rooms.

VALGORGE. *Le Tanargue (Chez Coste)* (M), chalet-type family hotel with a garden, set in a narrow valley; good food in restaurant (especially locally picked mushrooms) but get there early as it is often very busy.

VALS-LES-BAINS. A spa town (May–Sept.) *Grand Hôtel des Bains* (E), is best, with excellent service and delightful flower-filled balcony, set in attractive grounds. *L'Europe,* moderate, has good restaurant with classical cooking; half-board is compulsory here in season.

LES VANS. *Cévennes* (I), pleasant little hotel-restaurant, very good value. *Château le Scipionnet* (E), 3 km (2 miles) northeast via D104A, on Joyeuse road, very peaceful and well run, in lovely wooded setting, with pool and tennis courts and (M) restaurant.

VIENNE. *Résidence de la Pyramide* (M), charming, but near autoroute. No restaurant.
At **Chasse-sur-Rhône,** *Mercure Lyon-Sud* (M), modern, efficiently run. At **Pont-Evêque,** *Hôtel du Midi* (M), set in lovely garden, friendly service, reader-recommended. No restaurant.
Restaurants. *Pyramide* (E), bld F.-Point, famous, excellent classical cuisine (now back on form), garden dining: Reserve, as space is limited. *Chez René* (E), across the river, and *Magnard* (M), 45 cours Brillier, good for regional dishes, are good runners-up. *Bec Fin* (M) is close to cathedral and serves *Lyonnais* specialties.

VONNAS. *Georges Blanc,* one of the best restaurants in France for *nouvelle cuisine* (E). Now has some very attractive rooms and suites too, plus pool and tennis courts.

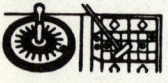

CASINOS. Charbonnières-les-Bains (near Lyon) has a casino open year-round. You can play boule, baccara, roulette, blackjack and American roulette here, as well as dining, dancing and what have you.
At little **Vals-les-Bains** in the Ardèche you can only play boule, but the casino there is now open all year too.

THE FRENCH ALPS

One area, two countries

Along the southeastern border of France rises a mighty barrier of mountains that provides some of the most spectacular scenery in Europe—the French Alps, soaring to their climax in Europe's highest peak, Mont Blanc, 4,805 snowy meters (15,772 ft), into the air. Its chief divisions, north to south, are—the Mont Blanc country; Savoie, lying along the Italian border; the Dauphiné, of which Grenoble is the capital; the Hautes-Alpes, centered about Briançon; and the Alpes-de-Haute-Provence and Alpes Maritimes, that extend down to the lemon and the orange trees, the palms and the bougainvillaea, and the warm blue waters of the Mediterranean.

The northern part of the French Alps, the Mont Blanc area and the Savoie, is double-treat playground country—lakes for summer vacationists, mountains for both summer and winter. The lakes, north to south, are those of Geneva, Annecy and Bourget; the great mountain is Mont Blanc, which dominates the scenery for miles around.

Of the lake resorts, the best known is undoubtedly Aix-les-Bains. On Lake Bourget, more than 4,450 hectares (11,000 acres) in area, this resort has all the machinery of the European spa. This might sound expensive, and it can be, but Aix-les-Bains is large enough for hotels to exist at all levels. The lake becomes rather polluted in high summer, and bathing is inadvisable (a new purification plant is easing this problem), but you can sail, fish, and, around the shores, play golf and tennis.

Annecy, on the lake of the same name, is dominated by the four towers of its 12th-century castle. Arcaded lanes alternate with quiet canals in the old quarter round the lovely 16th-century Palais de l'Isle, and the relics of the monastery of the Visitation are widely venerated. The lake is marvelously clean, and is a paradise for all water sports.

Evian, on Lake Geneva, is smaller, but no less pleasant, and it has the resources of Europe's largest lake to draw upon. A noted spa, its still, tasteless water is bottled and may be bought anywhere in the country. It shares its lakeside position with Thonon, also a spa, and a comparatively inexpensive one.

Chambéry, which lies only a few miles south of Aix-les-Bains, is a delightful old city, with the château of the dukes of Savoy rising above the arcades of its picturesque old streets, while the surrounding countryside produces raspberries and strawberries whose flavor is matchless.

Mont Blanc region

On one side of Mont Blanc lies Chamonix, the oldest and biggest of French winter sports resorts. Site of the first Winter Olympic Games in 1924, it still challenges experts to get down the Brévent run used on that occasion. Now cablecars carry skiers to runs which, though less difficult, begin 1,066 meters (3,500 ft) higher. A lift deposits them only 548 meters (1,800 ft) below the summit of Mont Blanc, whence they can make a run of 28 km (17½ miles) with a drop of 3,350 meters (11,000 ft).

In summer, Chamonix is a center for mountain climbers interested in scaling Mont Blanc—and for the less experienced and adventurous, there are some relatively easy routes, requiring no ropes or special equipment. Chamonix is also the starting point for spectacular cable-car rides across the glaciers to Courmayeur, in Italy. For truly energetic skiers, there is the famous six-day Chamonix-Zermatt trip: for this you need to be a good skier *and* a trained athlete.

Avoriaz, reached by cablecar from the old resort of Morzine, has most attractive architecture, and a chic clientele. The absence of automobiles makes the atmosphere particularly restful. Flaine, designed by Marcel Breuer, seems rather stark and chilly for many. Deliberately designed to be the intellectual's ski resort, it provides avantgarde art galleries, double-dome seminars, farout films as well as particularly well-organized skiing.

In the next valley is the smartest of the Mont Blanc region resorts: Megève—which is consequently also one of the most expensive. It has a lively non-skiing life, like Chamonix. Indeed, perhaps the after-ski amusements tend to submerge the skiing, for in general the slopes here are comparatively easy, and skiers of only modest ability will find Megève more to their liking than Chamonix. It also has attendant resorts, which can be reached easily—St-Gervais, and the smaller Praz-sur-Arly, Combloux and Col de Voza-Prarion. St-Gervais is a winter sports resort that is also popular in the summer, and is also quietly famous for its sulfuric thermal springs, used with success to treat very bad burn cases.

Lesser resorts are Les Contamines tucked away in the mountains between Chamonix and Megève; La Clusaz (conveniently reached from Annecy by bus); Samoëns and Les Gets, near Morzine.

Resorts in Savoie

In Savoie, the leading winter resorts are the high-altitude Val d'Isère and its twin, Lac de Tignes, just over the mountain tops. Courchevel, with its twin Méribel just over the ridge, is connected by ski lift with St-Martin-de-Belleville, Les Menuires and Val Thorens, all of which make for a vast skiing area. Tignes is one of the fastest-growing and largest resorts in the area with an enormous complex of lifts which connect it not only with Val d'Isère, but also with the smaller resorts of La Daille, Les Boisses and Les Brevières. Tignes and Val are very sporty, and there is little nightlife, since everyone skis all day long, every day. Courchevel is the smartest of the Savoie resorts, with lots of nightlife. Méribel, just over the mountain, is a rather strung-out place, where the smart set go in for villas.

La Plagne, not far from Tignes, is attractive and well-organized. Les Arcs, a budding resort reached by cable car (or road) from Bourg St-Maurice, is for those who like a tranquil early-to-bed life after a day on the slopes. Tignes offers a 9-hole golf course, sailing on its lake, swimming, and excursions to the Vannoise National Park during the summer months; Les Arcs also has a golf course and special crash courses for beginners.

This is lovely summer vacation country, too; you can stay at Courchevel itself, or seek a vacation spot more associated with summer holidays than winter ones—say Bourg St-Maurice, to the northeast, set in a basin of meadows and orchards. Bourg St-Maurice is a junction of valleys and roads, and also a rail terminus, and from here you can make a magnificent trip which is possible only in summer: through Val d'Isère and beyond it over the summer road through the Alps.

This trip will offer you some unparalleled high-altitude mountain scenery. You pass along the highest mountain highway in Europe and approach its culminating point—the Iseran Pass, 2767 meters (9084 ft) up; and if the air is clear, you might stop at the inn right on the pass and drink in, among other things, the unbeatable view over the Tarentaise mountain range and the glacier-streaked peaks of Albaron and de Charbonel. The latest date at which you can expect to make this trip is the end of September. By October the pass is usually choked with snow, and it stays that way until the end of June.

Dauphiné and Grenoble

Grenoble, capital of the Dauphiné, has grown faster since World War II than any other French city—the population has risen from 80,000 to a huge 360,000 (including suburbs). 'France's little Chicago in the Alps', this boom city has been called, for its rows of new skyscrapers fill a narrow plain with mountains on all sides. In this striking setting, ultra-modern industries specialize in electronics and engineering, while nuclear research flourishes, and the large universities attract thousands of foreign students. Grenoble, the venue for the 1968 Winter Olympics, prides itself on being a pace-setter in France for all kinds of new developments, social and cultural as well as industrial. Its Socialist mayor, regarded as the most dynamic in France, has been trying to pioneer a new, open style of civic participation.

Modernistic and cosmopolitan, Grenoble has an air of self-assertiveness that some may find more American than European. Yet it is also well rooted in French culture and tradition. Its art museum is a fine one, with works by Rubens, Cranach, Watteau and other old masters, and a fine modern collection including Gauguin, Matisse, Rouault, Utrillo and Picasso. It has notable architecture as well—the church of St-Laurent, with a 6th-century crypt; the early Renaissance Palace of Justice; and the 12th-century cathedral, in the district where Stendhal, author of *Le Rouge et le Noir* and *La Chartreuse de Parme,* was born. Canalized between stone banks, the river Isère rushes swiftly through the city, and over it swings the *téléférique,* which takes you up to Guy Pape park, on the hill beyond the river, for a remarkable view over the city and the surrounding countryside.

The famous monastery of the Grande Chartreuse is in a setting that is both austere and serene, enclosed by wooded heights and limestone crags. Situated about a mile from the main road, the vast agglomeration

THE FRENCH ALPS 377

of buildings covers almost 5 hectares (12 acres). Here originated the distinctive style of hermitages and communal institutions followed by 24 charterhouses throughout the world. Founded by St Bruno in 1084, the monastery was destroyed many times by fire, and rebuilt. During the Revolution, it was stripped of its possessions and the monks were expelled. Permitted to return a few years later, they began the manufacture of the Chartreuse liqueurs that provided their main source of income. Expelled again in 1903, they finally returned in 1940. The Grande Chartreuse itself cannot be visited, but the Correrie, about 3 km (2 miles) from the main road, presents an excellent picture of the contemplative life.

To the south is the pleasant little spa of Uriage-les-Bains, and then Vizille, where the first rebellion against royalty occurred in 1788 when the deputies of Dauphiné demanded the convocation of the States General. They had last met in 1614, and their return to activity set in action the chain of events that led to the French Revolution. A little farther south is the lake of Laffrey, where the royal troops sent to arrest Napoleon caught up with their man—and promptly joined his army. A splendid statue, isolated in lonely grandeur on a wind-swept plateau, commemorates this *volte-face*. Be very careful driving around here, the roads are very steep and full of sharp turns; at Vizille there have been some terrifying accidents.

Hautes-Alpes and Briançon

The eastern part of what was once the old province of Dauphiné is now the modern department of the Hautes-Alpes, and its heart is Briançon, a city of much more than passing interest. If you visit it in the summer, you would do well to take the high-altitude Route des Grandes Alpes, for its scenery is magnificent. From the north you would come from Val d'Isère over the Iseran Pass, and then through Bonneval and Lanslebourg where the road joins the N6 west through Modane, the frontier point for train travel into Italy. In July, the famous Tour de France bicycle race passes over this gruelling route. At St-Michel it turns south, again over a road that demands a little effort from the driver but repays him by the scenery of the Col du Télégraphe and the Galibier Pass, 2,642 meters (8,675 ft) up, before reaching Briançon.

Briançon is old and intriguing, and prides itself on being the highest city (as distinguished from towns or villages) in Europe—its altitude is 1,325 meters (4,350 ft). Fortified by Vauban, the military architect of Louis XIV, it still has its old ramparts into which the cathedral snugly fits. The citadel is crowned by Bourdelle's statue of France, presiding over a superb alpine panorama. Outside the walls, spread out along slopes that descend towards the resort, is the new town, called Briançon-Ste-Catherine. Briançon is a wonderful center from which to set out on hikes into the mountains, and it is also a starting point for bus excursions in all directions—for instance into the charming rustic beauty of the Var and Queyras valleys.

If you visit Briançon for winter sports, you will not be able to take the routes suggested above. Whether you come from north or south, you will have to travel by way of Gap, the only road left open after the snow begins to pile up in the passes. Close by are two leading winter sports resorts, Serre-Chevalier and Montgenèvre, the latter with one of the most famous ski jumps in France.

A few minutes' drive from Chorges, the old capital of the Cartigues, the vast 3,040-hectare (7,500-acre) lake formed by the Serre-Ponçon dam provides a whole new pleasure-ground for water sports. A little farther down the valley, the small lake at Le Lauzet does the same on a miniature scale.

Alpes-de-Haute-Provence and Alpes Maritimes

South of Briançon and Gap (which is becoming rather built-up and terribly noisy) are the Alpes-de-Haute-Provence. The mountains are less majestic, and the tall pines give way to a drier, stubbier kind of vegetation. The scent of lavender and thyme wafts from the fields, the skies are bluer (we are approaching the Mediterranean) and the atmosphere is less austere. There are a number of small, picturesque towns to visit, and the little village of Seyne-les-Alpes is a good center for exploration.

Among the hill towns worth visiting are Sisteron, with its fortress rising sheer from the great cliff that springs from the river bed; and Digne, with its old cathedral and basilica, Notre-Dame-du-Bourg, one of the finest Romanesque churches in France. Castellane is the starting point for one of the most popular excursions in this area, into the Grand Canyon of the Verdon. Sometimes called, with great exaggeration, the European Colorado, it is usually visited from the Riviera (bus excursions from Cannes and Nice). Although no true Grand Canyon, the gorges are lovely for hiking, canoeing, driving. Late spring is probably the best time to make this excursion: the weather is warm, but the crowds have not yet descended.

These towns are all threaded on the Route Napoléon, lined by imperial eagle milestones, the route the emperor followed in March 1815, after his return to France. Through scenic limestone mountains, the road arrives at Gap, and then plunges through the broad and majestic valley of the Durance to Sisteron. Here you know you are at last in the south—the Midi. The olive has appeared, with rippling silvery-green

THE FRENCH ALPS

leaves, the earth is red, the orchards rise in terraces on the slope. Now you pass the spectacular row of rocks, the Pénitents des Mées, which mark the junction of the Durance and the Bléone, and follow the valley of the latter to Digne.

South of Digne, the Route Napoléon dives down to Castellane and Grasse, the perfume-making town, whose surrounding slopes will be covered with fragrant lavender in midsummer. And another road from Digne will take you down to Nice in a couple of hours (or take the scenic Chemin-de-Fer de Provence, a narrow-gauge railroad using the valleys of the Var and the Verdon) via picturesque Entrevaux and Puget-Théniers.

On the eastern side of the Alpes-de-Haute-Provence, on the Route des Grandes Alpes, the chief town is pleasant, rather sleepy Barcelonnette, which in winter is a minor sports center. The two modern resorts nearby, Sauze and Super-Sauze, are fairly lively. If you have a good head for heights and steady nerves on the hairpin bends, a spectacular day's tour from Barcelonnette twists up through the mountains to the 2,250-meter (7,385-ft) Col d'Allos, then down through the fortified town of Colmars and across a luxuriant valley to Digne. Between Barcelonnette and the coast, there are a few ski resorts reached from the Riviera: Auron, Valberg or Beuil. Surprisingly, sometimes there is more snow and it is colder at Auron or Valberg than in the northern Alpine resorts. The new ski resort of Isola 2000, close to the Italian border, has become popular.

PRACTICAL INFORMATION

WHEN TO GO. Visitors make use of this spectacular region at two distinct periods—the winter sports enthusiasts from about mid-Dec. to mid-Apr. (into May in the high altitudes); the general tourists, hikers, climbers and spa attenders from June-Sept. Therefore, the special attractions are grouped around these two seasons.

Winter. By late Dec., resorts above 900 m (3,000 ft) usually have sufficient snow; Jan. is usually the coldest and least popular month. Fanatics can ski on the high glaciers above Tignes and Val d'Isère even in July and Aug.

During the International Mont Blanc Week in **January**, Megève, Les Contamines and St-Gervais participate, with varied skiing events, including the Emile Allais Cup races. National ice hockey and curling championships, and the triple-threat skiing event, the Grand Prix International de la Vallée de Chamonix, are features of Chamonix's Grande Semaine de Glace. January is the best month for spectacular events at Auron and Montgenèvre, while **February** is the time for Barcelonnette, Serre-Chavalier, and Villard-de-Lans. The ski instructors have a chance to prove their mettle in the Journée des Moniteurs at Chamonix. The French championships are held early in **March**; check with any tourist office for the location, which changes from year to year. Chamonix stages its Derby des Citadins (City Dwellers' Derby), and Méribel-les-Allues, Tignes and Val d'Isère have various Spring International Grand Prix slalom events. As late as **May** one of the year's top races, the Courses des Améthystes, is scheduled for the high altitude slopes above Chamonix. The winter season opens again in **December** with international ski-jumping contests at Chamonix.

Summer. June through Sept. is the season for the important spas—Aix-les-Bains, Brides-les-Bains, Evian-les-Bains, St-Gervais-les-Bains, Thonon-les-Bains—whose therapeutic mineral waters aid in the treatment of nervous, circulatory and nutritional disorders.

Evian and Aix-les-Bains stage music festivals in **June** and **July**. Each of the spas and resorts offers a varied program of concerts, plays, festivals, and sporting events. The **August** calendar of events ranges from the Semaine d'Evian to the international festival of Alpine guides at Chamonix, and the Bacchu-Ber, a traditional sword-dance performed Aug. 16 at Pont-de-Cervières.

WHAT TO SEE. Scenically, the French Alps constitute one of the spectacular regions in Europe. Every visitor will want to see Mont Blanc, and to take a trip on the cog-wheel railway up to the Mer de Glace. It is also possible to take a series of cable-car rides across Mont Blanc from Chamonix

THE FRENCH ALPS

to Courmayeur, with stupendous views of the great white mountains and glaciers.

There are numerous other scenic attractions in the French Alps: the beautiful lakes of Geneva, Annecy, and Bourget; Mont Pourri (3,780 m/12,409 ft) and the curious Mont Aiguille (Needle Rock), whose 2,000-m (6,562-ft) heights were first scaled in 1492, the first recorded ascent in mountaineering annals; the Col de la Croix-Haute and Col d'Izoard, where you pass from green Alpine pastures to Mediterranean vegetation; the mountain plateau of the Vercors, gallantly defended by a handful of Resistance fighters during 1944; the Col de l'Iseran (2,768 m/9,085 ft), the highest pass in Europe accessible to automobiles; the Col du Galibier (2,643 m/8,675 ft) and the Col du Lauteret, from which there is a superb view of the wild Pelvoux region dominated by the glaciers of La Meije (3,980 m/13,068 ft) and the Barre des Ecrins (4,099 m/13,454 ft). In contrast to these heights are the spectacular gorges of Verdon, Cians and Romanche.

The National Park of the Vannoise is a paradise for nature lovers. Photo safaris to photograph the shy ibex and chamois are organized. Contact the tourist office in Val d'Isère for information.

Visit the abbey of Hautecombe, burial place of the princes of the House of Savoie; remains of Roman baths at Aix-les-Bains; the castle of the dukes of Savoie at Chambéry, and nearby Les Charmettes, country residence of philosopher Jean-Jacques Rousseau's patron Madame de Warens; the secluded monastery of the Grande Chartreuse, original home of the world-famed liqueur; the 17th-cent. château of Vizille, a residence of the president of the French Republic; Grenoble, with its 16th-cent. law courts, outstanding art museum—one of the richest in France—and museum devoted to novelist Stendhal; the 13th-16th-cent. château of Menthon-St-Bernard; the city of Briançon, with its ramparts by Vauban and statue of France by Antoine Bourdelle, and nearby Château Queyras, with its medieval watchtower and fortifications; the modern (1950) church at Assy, designed by Novarina and decorated with paintings and sculptures by Matisse, Léger, Bonnard, Rouault, Braque, and others; the Romanesque cathedral at Embrun; picturesque villages, such as Pont-en-Royans, Queyras, Bourget, Colmars, Tout, Flumet, and Conflans; the 13th-15th-cent. Château Bayard, near Pontcharra, birthplace of Chevalier Bayard, the knight without fear and without reproach; the impressive cathedral of St-Pierre at Moutiers, with its rich treasure of medieval ivories and enameled ware; the curious fortified little stronghold of Mont-Dauphin.

Rivaling the other Alpine wonders are such engineering achievements as: the 460-km (287-mile) Rte Napoléon–Rte des Alpes, which takes the motorist from Cannes via Grenoble to St-Julien, and the 670-km (416-mile) Rte des Grandes Alpes from Nice to Evian; the dam of La Girotte, built under the glacier; the dam of Tignes, highest in Europe; the *téléférique* (cable-car) of l'Aiguille du Midi (3,839 m/12,600 ft), and of Serre-Chevalier (about 3 km/2 miles). Latest is the 12-km (7½ mile) tunnel under Mont Blanc from Chamonix to Entrèves, just over the Italian border, near Courmayeur. This epic engineering feat, built by the French and the Italians, each starting from their side of the border, took almost seven years to complete. It shortens the distance between Chamonix and Turin considerably and functions even when the passes are blocked.

HOW TO GET ABOUT. By train. Trains from Paris to this area leave from the Gare de Lyon or Gare d'Austerlitz. The TGV has cut times dramatically; by 1984 Paris-Grenoble (with change at Lyon) will take only 3¼ hours. *TGV* service to Chambery (via Aix) takes around 4 hours. As Aix-les-Bains and Chambéry are on one of the main routes to Italy (via Mont Cenis) they are served by international expresses. Paris to Aix-les-Bains takes about 5½-6 hrs. Sleeping and couchette cars run to various stations at or close to skiing centers such as Bourg St-Maurice, St-Jean-de-Maurienne, Moutiers.

There is also a very beautiful route by rail from Marseille via Aix-en-Provence and St-Aubin to Grenoble and Briançon. Another route is Geneva to Grenoble via Aix-les-Bains. The TEE (Geneva–Barcelona) uses this route. From Nice there is a spectacular route through Digne and St-Aubin to Grenoble. The *Rome Express* stops at both Aix-les-Bains and Chambéry. The *Alpazur,* one of the SNCF's popular tourist trains, travels Nice-Geneva through the mountains, via Digue and Grenoble.

The SNCF has a week's package involving train ride to Chamonix and half-board, from various French towns. Inquire at one of the tourist bureaux at the main rail stations in Paris.

This is an area where one has to plan rail travel carefully. From Dec. to Mar. there are snowtrain through coaches from Calais to Bourg St-Maurice and to St-Gervais every weekend.

By air. Quicker are the *British Airways* and *Swissair* London–Geneva flights and *Air France's* Paris–Geneva run; buses carry passengers to resorts in the Mont Blanc region. Skis are carried on the planes without extra charge if not in excess of free weight allowance. These flights connect with a number of international air services from North America and Great Britain.

TAT flies Paris–Annecy and Paris–Chambéry; also Paris–Courchevel in winter. *TAT* also has a regular *navette des neiges* (snow shuttle) service in winter between Chambéry and various ski resorts, such as Bourg-St-Maurice, Tignes, La Plagne, Val d'Isère, Moutiers. *Air Inter* has a Paris–Grenoble service. A small company called *Air Savoie* (BP 33, 73120 Courcheval; tel. (79) 08–0049) runs an air-taxi service between Courchevel and Geneva, Grenoble, Chambéry, Lyon and Nice. Doesn't work out too expensive if there are three or more of you (most planes are three- to six-seater). They can also take you right to the *pistes* in Alpe d'Huez and Megève, weather and snow conditions permitting. Service runs approx. 20 December to 15 April. If you want to make inquiries outside this period, write *Air Savoie,* Aérodrome de Périgny, 03120 Lapalisse.

From Chambéry it is an easy bus ride to the various resorts of the Mont-Blanc area. Buses at Courchevel and Méribel connect with St-Gervais, Megève, Les Houches, Chamonix, Les Gets, Morzine and Val d'Isère.

By bus. Regular service between Geneva airport and most of the top ski resorts. *Europabus* has coaches with a guide traveling once a week from Paris

THE FRENCH ALPS

via Grenoble, Sisteron and Digne, so you can get off at any of these places. Europabus also runs one-day tour of Verdon Gorges (a 300-km. trip) from Cannes twice a week April through Sept. They also have a one-day Mont Blanc Tour, leaving Chamonix or Megève three times weekly in season, and a one-day Valais Circuit (daily in season). A network of local buses provides regional services and circular tours from Annecy, Megève, Grenoble, Chamonix, Aix-les-Bains, Briançon, Mont Dauphin, Moutiers and Bourg ST-Maurice.

MOTORING. Most winter visitors will use one of the other services rather than come by road, as driving conditions on the mountain highways are hazardous and the passes are often blocked. The summer motorist has several routes.

From Paris, take the A6 motorway to Lyon, then the A43 to Chambéry. From here the N90 and N212 go to Megève and St-Gervais and the Mont Blanc region. The A41 motorway takes you from Chambéry to Aix-les-Bains and Annecy. For Grenoble, branch off the A43 (Lyon–Chambéry) after Bourgoin-Jallieu on to the A48. The A41 between Grenoble and Chambéry and on to Aix and Annecy is also useful.

If you don't like motorways, take the N6 to Lyon and the N6/N49I on to Chambéry and Aix, but it'll take you a lot longer. From Britain and Calais you can avoid Paris altogether by traveling via Laon, Rheims, Câlons-sur-Marne, Chaumont, Besançon and on down toward Geneva. Much better save valuable time by taking the car-sleeper train from Paris to Grenoble or St-Gervais (Sept. to May only).

Hautes-Alpes, Alpes-de-Haute-Provence and *Alpes Maritimes:* to visit the western slopes, take the Rte Napoléon (N85) from Grenoble via Gap, Sisteron, Digne and Castellane. You must be prepared for a great deal of turning and doubling around hairpin bends.

To visit the eastern slopes, take the Rte des Grandes Alpes (D902), one of the most sensational mountain roads in Europe, that links Briançon with points in the Alpes-de-Haute-Provence and Alpes Maritimes as well as in the Mont Blanc region. It traverses the highest passes and deepest gorges in France, but from Nov. to June large sections of it are blocked by snow. The majority of Alpes Maritimes ski resorts may be reached via the southern section of this route from Nice, and in addition, the gorges of Vésubie, Cians and Daluis.

Both roads are spectacular, and the best way to become acquainted with this part of France is to go down one and come back the other, if the time of year permits. The north–south direction is the only practical one for visiting the Alps thoroughly. East–west, a crossing can be effected from the Rhône valley by taking either D93 and D993 via Die or D94 and D994 via Nyons to Gap and then across the artificial lake of Serre-Ponçon to Briançon, or by D900 to Barcelonnette and on to Italy. Another possibility is the route from Grenoble to Briançon (N91), following the Gorges of the Romanche and crossing the Col du Lautaret.

USEFUL ADDRESSES. *Welcome Information offices* at pl. Maurice-Mollard, 73100 Aix-les-Bains (for Savoie); pl. d'Allinges, 74501 Evian (for Haute-Savoie); and 14 rue de la République, 38019 Grenoble (for the Dauphiné). *Tourist offices* (and *thermal office* for Aix-les-Bains) are at the same addresses.

In Paris the *Maison des Hautes-Alpes* is at 4 av. de l'Opéra, 1er; the *Maison des Alpes-Dauphiné* (particularly helpful hostesses) at 2 pl. André-Malraux, 1 er; and the *Maison de Savoie* at 16 bld Haussmann, 9e.

Car Hire. *Europcar,* 2 av. de Verdun, Aix-les-Bains; 3 quater, av. des Chevennes, Annecy; 94 cours Jean-Jaurès, Grenoble. *Avis,* 49 av. Wilson, Aix-les-Bains; 14 av. de Genève, Annecy; 22 cours Jean-Jaurès, and 55 av. de Vigny, and airport, Grenoble. *Hertz,* 37 pl. de la Gare, Aix-les-Bains; 15 bis rue de la Gare, and airport, Annecy; 89 rue Mallifaud, 55 av. Léon-Blum, and airport, Grenoble.

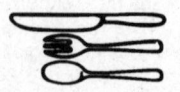

REGIONAL FOOD AND DRINK. The Alpine region is famed for the breeding of dairy cattle that produce high quality butter and cheese, so many specialties feature these products. A special favorite is *fondue,* a cheese dish made with kirsch. Then there are the cheeses themselves, made of both goat's and cow's milk, among them *Tomme, Reblochon, Persillé, Sassenage* and *St-Marcellin.* Delicious fish dishes are made from local trout and *omble chevalier* (char). The raspberries and the mushrooms here have an excellent flavor.

Pastry and confectionery specialties include *Gâteau de Savoie* (light sponge cake), and the delectable chocolate-covered liqueurs known as *Roseaux d'Annecy.*

This is not a region of great wines, but the slopes do produce a few wines of superior quality, notably *Crépy, Ayse, Chignin, Montmélian,* and the *Roussettes* of Frangy and Seyssel. And sample the justly famed liqueur of the Grande Chartreuse and the potent *framboise* made from local raspberries. *Génépi* is an unusual liqueur made from an aromatic local plant.

HOTELS AND RESTAURANTS. Accommodations range from the luxurious in the larger cities and resort centers to modest ones for the budget-minded. Most hotels open only seasonally (for Easter, the summer and winter sports seasons) so always check in advance. Many insist on at least half-board terms.

Restaurants, listed *E, M* or *I,* indicating expensive, moderate or inexpensive, close one day a week, and for a period during the year.

AIX-LES BAINS. All (E): *Iles Britanniques,* with garden, quiet; *International Rivollier,* with excellent restaurant (M); *Bristol,* near casino; *Thermal.* All (M): *Manoir,* pleasantly sited, with good restaurant (M). *Cloche, Dauphinois,* garden, nice restaurant. *Campanile,* new; *Paix; Metropole.* Both (I) are: *Nice-Savoie,* quiet, near park, no restaurant; *Gallia-Beauséjour.*

Restaurants. At **Grand Port** (3 km/2 miles north), *Lille,* on lake, and *Davat,* nearby, rustic, with small zoo; both (M) and have a few rooms.

ALBERTVILLE. *Million* (M), old-established, elegant, imaginative cuisine in restaurant (E).

Restaurant. *Uginet* (E), excellent *nouvelle cuisine.*

ALLEVARD. Spa. *Parc* and *Ermitage,* near casino, moderate. *Les Pervenches* and *Nouvel,* both small, inexpensive. At **Pinsot,** 7 km (4 miles) south *Belle Etoile* (I), quiet, attractive, with big garden, tennis courts and restaurant.

ALPE D'HUEZ. *Ours Blanc* (E), *Belle Aurore* (M) and *Grandes Rousses* (E), with pool. All have fine views. *Christina* (M), and *Chamois d'Or* (M), open mid-Dec through April only, with excellent restaurant (M).

ANNECY. *Trésoms et de la Forêt* is expensive, with marvelous views. *Carlton* (M), no restaurant. *Abbaye* (M), in old town. *Allobroges* (M), *Belvédère* (M). *Coin Fleuri* (M). *Crystal* (I). On outskirts, *Campanile* (M), near lake, with restaurant, modern but not impersonal. *Ibis* (M), near lake and river, a member of the well run chain, with restaurant.

At **Albigny,** 1.5 km (1 mile) east, the moderate *Faisan Doré;* inexpensive *Muses.*

Restaurants. *Auberge de Savoie* (E), 1 pl. St-François, *Belvédère* (M), route du Semnoz.

At **Chavoires,** 5 km (3 miles) east on N509, *Pavillon Ermitage* (E) is renowned, has floral garden by lake. Also has a few rooms.

LES ARCS. *La Cachette* (E); *Golf* (M); *Winston* (M), with pool; all quiet, with restaurants.

ARGENTIÈRE. *Bellevue* (M), with pool and good restaurant; *Becs Rouge* (M), just outside town; restaurant is open summer only. *Dahu* (M), with good restaurant.

AURON. *Pilon* (E), comfortable, quiet, with pool; *Savoie* (M). *Las Donnas* (M). All have restaurants (M).

AUTRANS. *La Buffe* (M), restaurant. *Poste* (I). *Terrasse,* budget; good value full-board rates.

AVORIAZ. *Les Dromonts,* with avantgarde décor, and *Hauts Forts* (no restaurant), attractive, are expensive. *Snow* (I), studios with kitchenettes.

BARCELONNETTE. *Grande Epervière* (M) is best, no restaurant. *Alpes,* (M), no restaurant. *Grand, Cheval Blanc,* inexpensive.

At **Le Sauze,** 5 km (3 miles) east: *Alp Hôtel,* (M), with attractive garden and restaurant; a Relais du Silence. *Séolanes* (I), small and quiet.

At **Super Sauze,** 10 km (6½ miles) south, *Ourson* (M), modern, comfortable, pleasant restaurant. *Op Traken* (M), with restaurant and huge sunny balcony. *Pyjama* (M), comfortable but no restaurant.

BEUIL. The small *Bellevue* and *Edelweiss,* simple, are (I).

BONNATRAIT. Near Thonon. *Château de Coudrée* (E), medieval, with garden and pool, good restaurant (M).

BONNEVAL-SUR-ARC. *La Bergerie* (I).

LE BOURGET-DU-LAC. Best, with stunning views, is *Ombremont* (E), Relais et Châteaux member in attractive grounds 2 km (1 mile) outside town, with restaurant (E). *Beaurivage* (I), beside lake, good restaurant. 4 km (2½ miles) out at **Bourdeau,** *Terrasse* (I), Logis de France.

BOURG ST-MAURICE. *Hostellerie Petit St-Bernard* (I); *Petite Auberge* (M), nice country hotel.

BRIANÇON. *Vauban* (M), friendly, good service, with restaurant. *Edelweiss* (M), no restaurant but large garden.

CASTELLANE. *Ma Petite Auberge* (M).

CHAMBÉRY. *Ducs de Savoie,* expensive, good restaurant (M–E). *Lion d'Or* (no restaurant), moderate. *Pervenches* (I), a mile south.

Restaurants. *Roubatcheff* (E), 6 rue Théâtre, well-known, but cuisine can be variable. *Chaumière* (M), 14 rue D.-Rochereau, good value. *Tonneau,* 2 rue St-Antoine (I).

CHAMONIX-MONT-BLANC. *PLM Chamois Blanc* (E), central, just by *téléférique* up to Aiguille du Midi. *Mont-Blanc* and *Albert I et Milan,* each with pool and excellent restaurant (M), and *Sapinière,* are expensive. So is *Auberge du Bois Prin,* at **Moussoux,** small, very peaceful. Moderate: *Hermitage et Paccard* (*pension* only); and *Richemond.* Inexpensive: *Bon Coin* (no restaurant); *Marronniers,* family-type, no restaurant; *Arve; Arveyron.*

At nearby **Bossons,** *Aiguille du Midi,* moderate, and *Novotel* (E), with pool.

At **Lavancher,** *Les Gentianes,* with pleasant garden, very quiet, moderate.

At **Praz-de-Chamonix,** 3 km (2 miles) north: *Rhododendrons* (full board only), *Simond et Golf,* moderate.

THE FRENCH ALPS

CHATEL. *Fleur de Neige* (E), with nice garden and restaurant. *La Savoyarde* (I).

LA CLUSAZ. *Vieux Chalet* (M), tiny, delightful; good restaurant. (M) are *Christiania, Aravis 1500*, with pool, *Nouvel, Floralp* (I).

COMBLOUX. *Ducs de Savoie* (E), modern (chalet-style) and comfortable, with good views of Mont-Blanc, pool and restaurant. *Idéal Mont-Blanc* (M), quiet and attractive Relais du Silence with good home-style cooking. *Coeur des Prés* (M), again good views of Mont-Blanc, quiet and friendly, with restaurant. *Aiguilles de Warens* (M), another good bet, with restaurant. At **Haut-Combloux** (M), small, well run, quiet, with (I) restaurant. At **Gemoën,** 2 km (1 mile) away, nice little *Caprice des Neiges* (I).

LES CONTAMINES-MONTJOIE. *Chamois* (M), *Dômes* (M), both with restaurant.

COURCHEVEL. At **1850:** *Bellecote* (E), full-board only; *Carlina* (E), attractively sited; *Ducs de Savoie* (E), garden; *Lana* (E), full-board only; *des Neiges* (E), pension only; *Rond-Point des Pistes* (E). *l'Albaron* (M), no restaurant; *Dahu* (M); *Pomme de Pin* (M), good views. At **1650:** *Zenith* (E), excellent value. *Portetta* (M), full-board only. At **1550:** *Lamay* (E), with restaurant, quiet, good views.
Restaurant. *Yaca* (E), at **1300,** chic. *Bateau Ivre* (E), in *Pomme de Pin* hotel. *Bergerie* (E), a converted sheepfold, adequate Savoyard specialties, a place to be seen.

DIGNE. *Grand Paris* (E) with excellent restaurant (M). *Hostellerie Aiglon* (I). *Central* (I), well run, no restaurant. On road to Nice, *Ermitage Napoléon* (E), beautifully restored, comfortable.

EVIAN-LES-BAINS. Above town, *Royal,* near funicular, rooms and apartments at super-deluxe rates; and nearby *La Verniaz et ses chalets,* exclusive, isolated. Both have good restaurants (E). Expensive: 1.5 km (1 mile) east, on lake, *Lumina,* with garden and pool, very attractive. About 8 km (5 miles) east on Thollon road, *Les Prés Fleuris,* with good restaurant (E). (M): *Régence,* with restaurant. *Paris* (no restaurant). (I) are: *Palmiers Cygnes,* by lake; *Flots Bleus* (no restaurant); last two on outskirts.
Restaurant. *Bourgogne* (M), 73 rue Nationale. Also has rooms.

FLAINE. *Totem* (E), (a Relais et Châteaux member) and *Gradins Gris* (E). *Aujon* (M). All very comfortable, with restaurants.

GAP. *La Grille,* moderate, with good restaurant (I). The *Paix* (no restaurant), *Michelet* and *Le Clos* are inexpensive.

LES GETS. *Marmotte* (E), full-board only, with pool. *Ours Blanc* (M), small and quiet, full-board only. (I) are: *Maroussia*, comfortable; *Alpina*, convenient for skiers.

GRENOBLE. *Sofitel*, with pool, and *Park*, both expensive, latter with excellent restaurant (E). Moderate: modern *Mercure Alpotel*, good, with restaurant; *Terminus*, *Angleterre* and modern *Gallia*, none with restaurant. Inexpensive: *Paris–Nice*, *Lux*, neither with restaurant. *Alpes*, friendly, no restaurant.

At **Corenc-Montfleury**, 3 km (2 miles), *Trois Roses* (M), no restaurant.

At **Claix**, 9.5 km (6 miles) on D269, *Les Oiseaux*, moderate, with pool. Relais du Silence (and headquarters of that excellent association).

Restaurants. In town, *Auberge Bressane* (M), 38ter impasse Beaublache, excellent regional specialties. *Poularde Bressane* (M), 12 pl. Mistral, interesting cuisine. *Grillade* (M). At **Bresson**, 8 km (5 miles) via D264, *Chavant* (E), excellent; also a hotel.

At **Varces**, 13 km (8 miles) south, *Escale* (E) is good. Also has rooms. At **Chevallon**, 11 km (7 miles) northwest, *La Petite Auberge* (E) specializes in fish. *Pique-Pierre* at **St-Martin-le-Vinoux**, under 1 km (½ mile) north, and *Les Mésanges* at **Montbonnot**, 6.5 km (4 miles) on N90, are both (M) and excellent.

GRÉSY-SUR-ISERE. *Tour de Pacoret* (M), attractive Relais du Silence with lovely views and restaurant.

LES HOUCHES. *Novotel* (E), with pool and restaurant. *Piste Bleue* (M). *Roches*, *St-Antoine* are (I). At **Bellevue** the *téléférique* landing. *La Hutte* (I), with restaurant.

ISOLA. *Le Chastillon*, and *Druos*, both expensive and peaceful.

MEGÈVE. Deluxe are the *Mont-d'Arbois*, exclusive, isolated; *Mont-Blanc*, elegant, sophisticated; *Résidence*, all with pool. Expensive: *Triolet*, tiny Relais et Châteaux members; very comfortable and attractive, with restaurant. *Mont-Joly*, with good restaurant (M); *Coeur de Megève*. Moderate: *Fleur des Alpes*, *Estellan*. All small. Inexpensive: *Rond-Pont d'Arbois*.

Restaurants. The chic place to be seen is *Les Enfants Terribles*, in Mont-Blanc hotel. Very good food too (E). *Capucin Gourmand* (E), Rte Crêt-du-Midi.

LES MENUIRES. *PLM Menuires* (E), some suites, *Skilt* (E).

MÉRIBEL-LES-ALLUES. *Grand Coeur* (E), comfortable and peaceful, with pool. *Belvédère* (M), full-board only. *Orée du Bois* (M), with pool. *Chaudanne* (M), with kitchenettes.

MONTGENÈVRE. *Rois Mages* (M). *Alpet* (M). *Chalet des Sports* (I).

MORZINE. *Carlina* (M), classical comfort. *Dahu* (M), particularly pleasant service and ambiance. *Savoie* (M), *Champs Fleuris* (M), near *téléférique; Tremplin* (E). Inexpensive are *Igloo,* no restaurant, *Alpina; Ours Blanc; L'Aubergade; Beau Regard.*

LA PLAGNE. *Christina* (E), good restaurant. *Graciosa* (M), restaurant good but a bit over priced (E).

PRA-LOUP. *Airelles* (M), no restaurant. *Prieuré* (I), at Les Molanès; restaurant open evening only.

PRAZ-SUR-ARLY. *Les Quatre As,* comfortable, moderate. *Mt Charvin* (M). *Val d'Arly,* small, inexpensive.

RUFFIEUX. *Château de Collonges* (E), attractive Relais du Silence, near Lac du Bourget, well furnished, with lovely grounds and restaurant.

ST-GERVAIS-LES-BAINES. *Carlina, Hostellerie du Nerey,* both (M) with pool. *Splendid* (M), and *Adret* (M); neither has restaurant.
At **Bettex**, intermediate resort on *téléférique,* comfortable *Arbois-Bettex,* moderate, with pool, good restaurant (M).

SALLANCHES. *Sorbiers* (M), pleasant Logis de France, with restaurant.

SAMOËNS. (M) are: *Neige et Roc* and *Glaciers,* both with pool; *Eteski* (I), very peaceful, with splendid mountain views. All have restaurants.

SERRE-CHEVALIER. At **Chantemerle**, *Grand* (M), restaurant.
At **Villeneuve-la-Salle**, attractive *Vieille Ferme* (E), in old house. *Serre Chavelier* (M), restaurant is closed in summer months. *Lièvre Blanc* (M), with pool, restaurant.
At **Monetier-les-Bains**, *Auberge du Coucas* (E), delightful and friendly Relais du Silence, with good restaurant (M). *Europe* (M), quiet with restaurant.

SEYNE-LES-ALPES. *Vieux Tilleul* (M), with small pool; plus family-run restaurant (I) in 16th-cent. farmhouse with modern comforts.

SISTERON. *Hôtel du Cours* (M) and *Sélect* (I), neither with restaurant. *Tivoli* (I).

TALLOIRES. *Abbaye,* deluxe, has garden, lake view and good restaurant (E). *Le Cottage,* on lakeshore, expensive, also has outstanding cuisine (E). *Hermitage* (E), comfortable and peaceful Relais du Silence, with lovely views, pool, tennis courts and restaurant, plus open air grill service. *Lac* (E) and *Beau-Site,* moderate.

Restaurant. *Auberge du Père Bise* (E), on lake shore. Excellent classical cuisine, but prices need some swallowing. Also has a few rooms, expensive.

THONON-LES-BAINS. *Savoie et Léman*, pleasantly located, expensive. *Clos Savoyard*, moderate, 2 km (1 mile) southwest on N5, attractive restaurant. *France*, moderate. Inexpensive are: *L'Ombre des Marronniers*, *Terminus*, by station, no restaurant. *Victoria*, with good restaurant. At **Sciez**, 10 km (6 miles) southwest, *Château de Coudrée* (E), converted medieval castle, charming and comfortable, good restaurant, pool.
Restaurants. *Comte Rouge*, with rooms, 10 bld du Canal, and *La Grillandière*, 11 av. de Genève, both quite good (M).

TIGNES. Moderate: *Aiguille Percée; Campanules*, modern, cheerful; *Neige et Soleil; Pramecou*, no restaurant. *Lo Terrachu* (I), full-board only.
At **Val Claret**, *Ski d'Or* (M), charming, cozy, Relais et Châteaux member, with good (E) restaurant. *Curling* (E), no restaurant. *Vanoise*, with restaurant, is moderate.

URIAGE-LES-BAINS. *Grand* (M), indoor pool and tennis courts. *Manoir* (M).
At **St-Martin d'Uriage**, above town, *Belvédère* (I), good views.

VALBERG. Best is *Adrech de Lagas*, moderate. *Chalet Suisse*, also moderate. *Clé des Champs* is inexpensive.

VAL D'ISÈRE. Deluxe: *Sofitel Val d'Isère*, with pool. (E) are: *Christiania*, (full board only), fine view, quiet; *Grand Paradis*. *Savoyarde* (E), with good restaurant. Moderate: *Glaciers*, with good restaurant (M); *Galise*. *Kandahar* (M), Alsatian cuisine in restaurant (no lunches).

VALLOIRE. *Valloire et Galibier* (M), full-board only. *Sétaz*, moderate, with pool. *Centre* (I), *Gentianes* (I), full-board only.

VAL THORENS. *Novotel* (E) with pool, *Corotel* (M), small and pleasant, with lovely views.

VARS-LES-CLAUX. *Hôtel-Club Olympic*, moderate with discotheque, boutique, gymnastics room and its own *crêperie*.

VILLARD-DE-LANS. *Christiania* (M) and *Eterlou* (E), each with pool, good restaurant (M); *Paris* (M), in lovely grounds. Inexpensive: *Les Bruyères*. *Villa Primerose*, family type, has good food.

THE FRENCH ALPS

WINTER SPORTS. French ski resorts have been expanding fast. Most centers used to grow up around an existing village, but the newer ones (Courchevel, Avoriaz, Flaine, La Plagne, Belleville, Super-Tignes, La Daille, Les Menuires, Les Arcs, Corbières, Val Thorens, Isola 2000) were built by developers whose idea was to put the village where the snow is: they arose from the architects' drawing boards complete with supermarkets, nightclubs, boutiques, underground galleries, assembly-line ski schools, etc. Some, such as Avoriaz and Flaine, are extraordinary architectural achievements, others look like ordinary modern suburbs.

The development of new trails and lifts from year to year is also enormous. You can now ski, in a day, from Val d'Isère to Tignes to Les Brevières and back without following the same slopes; from Tignes or Val d'Isère to La Plagne; from Courchevel to Méribel to Les Menuires to Val Thorens. Or you can hire a helicopter to fly you to the top of a glacier and ski dizzily down, making tracks in virgin snow (only for good skiers).

You can also turn international: eight French resorts, including Les Gets, Morzine and Avoriaz, and four Swiss (including Champéry and Morgins) have abolished frontiers. Result: 480 km (300 miles) of ski territory, 154 lifts, innumerable ski schools, restaurants, etc. With tickets bought in one place, you can ski all over—if you don't collapse from exhaustion first. Note, however, that in this area, aside from Avoriaz, the resorts are fairly old-fashioned, which means, at times, rather limited comfort. However, they are more authentic than the new creations.

All 11 winter sports in the Mont Blanc region have formed an association to make holidays more enjoyable: the inclusive Ski-Pass allows unlimited use of 134 ski lifts, local transportation, ski classes. Other all-inclusive cover tickets for lifts, inter-hotel and restaurant meal checks, and sometimes weekly hotel rates which include ski lessons and lifts. Nine new resorts have grouped in the SNO Association, a similar setup.

There are numerous children's ski classes and some 'snow kindergartens' (nurseries) at Chamonix, Clusaz, Combloux, Megève, Courchevel, Notre Dame de Bellecombe, Valloire, Val d'Isère, Tignes, La Plagne, and St-Gervais, among others.

The French ski schools are excellent and offer a standardized system of instruction. This has advantages for those who wish to begin a course in one center and continue in succeeding seasons elsewhere in France. Ski-school and lift-tickets are valid in every resort, as well as from one year to the next.

Ski packages. All the main winter resorts offer special all-inclusive plans, providing for complete vacations at reduced rates (highest from early Feb.–early May, Easter week; lowest in Jan. and late Mar.). Nearly all major hotels, and their restaurants, subscribe to the plan, with various types of accommodation.

Flaine also has a package for the truly serious skier: a week of skiing in a small group, 9 to 5, with the same instructor. Twickenham Travel, 378 Richmond Rd, East Twickenham, England, offers good skiing holidays in Flaine, Isola 200 and Les Arcs.

Several American ski clubs and agencies offer value-priced two or three week charter trips which take in several resorts: Zermatt or Verbier in Switzerland, followed by Val d'Isère or Courchevel in France, for instance. Consult your travel agent. Many of the resorts now offer *ski de fond* (cross-country skiing) packages too, especially in the Dauphiné.

At the skiing centers described below, all have ample facilities in the way of ski lifts, *téléfériques*, jumps, rinks, etc. Chamrousse is the center for the new, rather dangerous sport of delta-planing, which you can also try at Tignes. The season is Dec.–Apr., unless otherwise stated.

Many ski resorts now have crèches for small children. If this is an important factor for you, write the *Association des Maires des Stations Françaises de Sports d'Hiver,* 61 bld Haussmann, Paris 8e, for list and details.

Alpes Maritimes

AURON 1,607 m (5,275 ft). Smartest of this region's resorts. Lots of winter sun, thanks to Mediterranean climate. Slopes face north, so retain their excellent powdery snow. Regional clientele. *Téléférique* ascends 700 m (2,300 ft) to Las Donnas, to fine series of slopes of all grades of difficulty. Season: Dec.–May.

BEUIL 1,480 m (4,858 ft). Near Valberg. At Les Launes, slopes of Perce-Neige offer admirable skiing area.

ISOLA 2000 2,437 m (8,000 ft). Has easy skiing, plenty of sun.

SUPERDÉVOLUY 1,614 m (5,300 ft). A new and growing resort. Young crowd.

VALBERG 1,698 m (5,576 ft). A chic resort popular with the people of Nice. Sunny. Easy slopes, also some of average difficulty.

Dauphiné

L'ALPE D'HUEZ 1,858 m (6,100 ft). Large, fashionable. Good for all types of skiers. Great place to mix cocktails and skiing. Exceptional sunshine, fine beginners' slopes. Lac Blanc *téléférique* reaches snowfields over 2,437 m (8,000 ft). Season: Nov.–May. Also has 30 km of footpaths for those who prefer to stick to their own two feet.

AUTRANS 1,096 m (3,600 ft). Center for long distance skiing.

CHAMROUSSE 1,614 m (5,300 ft). Used for the 1968 Winter Olympics, so has excellent facilities. *Téléférique* of Croix de Chamrousse tops slopes over 2,132 m (7,000 ft), permitting late spring skiing.

THE FRENCH ALPS

LES DEUX ALPES 1,797 m (5,900 ft). Very sporty, good place to practise the long-distance *ski de fond* so popular throughout Europe nowadays.

VILLARD-DE-LANS 1,049 m (3,444 ft). Family resort. Easy trails. Highly recommended for children and beginners. *The* place for cross-country skiing. Has now spread upwards to Balcon de Villard.

Hautes-Alpes and Alpes-de-Haute-Provence

BRIANÇON 1,310 m (4,300 ft). A popular resort, and the highest city in Europe.

FOUX D'ALLOS 1,828 m (6,000 ft). Skiing with a Provençal accent. Close to Col d'Allos and good for walkers too.

MONTGENÈVRE 1,828 m (6,000 ft). Almost on Italian frontier, between Italian resort of Sestrières and Serre-Chevalier, with which there are bus connections. Gaining rapidly in size and popularity owing to its excellent snow conditions and brilliant sunshine. Season: Nov.–May.

PRA-LOUP. Run by a former trainer for the French Olympic ski team. Varied slopes, splendid views.

LE SAUZE-SUR-BARCELONNETTE 1,370 m (4,500 ft). Dry climate permits snow to remain powdery despite brilliance of southern sunshine. A family resort. Higher up, at 1700 m is the newer **Super-Sauze.**

SERRE CHEVALIER 1,349 m (4,428 ft). Group of villages (St-Chaffrey, Chantemerle, Villard-Laté, Les Panaches, Villeneuve, Le Bez) at foot of immense snowfields. Good training ground for experts, and excellent for long-distance flat skiing. A favorite with many Americans. Season: Nov.–May.

VALLEYS OF VARS AND QUEYRAS. A number of small centers offer good skiing conditions. Altitudes range from 1,614–2.132 m (5,300–7,000 ft). The valley has series of 21 lifts providing closed circuit and a number of marked trails. Centres are Vars-Ste-Marie, Vars-St-Marcellin, Col de Vars; Valley of Queyras centers are Aiguilles, Arvieux, St-Véran.

Mont Blanc Region

ARGENTIÈRE 1,252 m (4,110 ft). Very sunny. Good trails for all skiers from beginner to expert. For those who take their skiing seriously.

AVORIAZ 1,370 m (4,500 ft). Above Morzine, and reached *only* by cable car; particularly attractive due to its architecture. Well-organized skiing, lively and chic social life. Favored by the movie set. Trails not difficult. Connected by ski to seven other French and five Swiss resorts. Good cross-country skiing too. Has a well-run Children's Village ski school.

BONNEVAL 1,005 m (3,301 ft). Picturesque small resort, moderate facilities.

CHAMONIX 1,847 m (3,444 ft). Oldest and biggest of winter resorts. A busy place for serious skiers—the classic trails are *not* for beginners—but plenty of entertainment for the whole family, and a casino. Season: Dec–June, spring skiing at high altitudes. Cross-mountain ski jaunts from Chamonix to Zermatt from Mar. 28 to May 31, six days. Cable lifts go high into Mont Blanc chain: Aiguille du Midi, 3,838 m (12,600 ft); Brévent, 2,437 m (8,000 ft); Croix de Logan, 1,963 m (6,445 ft); Grands Montets, 3,294 m (10,814 ft); Aiguille du Goûter, 4,356 m (14,300 ft). La Flégère, at Super-Chamonix, gives access to runs suitable for less experienced skiers and novices.

CHÂTEL 1,188 m (3,900 ft). In valley of Abondance, a bit isolated. Slopes for experts and beginners.

LA CLUSAZ 1,039 m (3,411 ft). Small, for those who prefer to do their skiing in peace and quiet. Crêt du Loup trails used in international competition. Snow conditions on Combes des Aravis permit skiing into May.

LES CONTAMINES 1,142 m (3,750 ft). Season Dec. into May, while Trélatête glacier stretches the season to the beginning of summer.

FLAINE 1,828–2,437 m (6–8,000 ft). Very modern architecture; concerts, art shows, etc. Good, well organized.

LES GETS 1,142 m (3,750 ft). Developed to complete ski terrain near Morzine. Sunny, with a variety of slopes.

LES HOUCHES 1,009 m (3,313 ft). Sunny slopes, mainly for the expert. Run from Bellevue *téléférique* used in international competitions. More suitable for the less experienced are slopes served by Col de Voza-Prarion and Le Tourchet lifts.

MEGÈVE 1,112 m (3,650 ft). Very social, elegant, expensive: casino, nightclubs. Sunny slopes, linked with Chamonix, Les Houches, and St-Gervais by chain of *téléfériques*. Helicopter service to other resorts and high-altitude slopes.

MORZINE 1,000 m (3,280 ft). A family resort. Open terrain for beginners.

ST-GERVAIS 907 m (2,978 ft). Ski trails not too well placed, but slopes are good. Fine for beginners. Not too sunny. More popular with local people than with tourists. Cog-wheel railway reaches Col de Voza where tow continues to Prarion and where *téléférique* connects with Les Houches snowfields.

SAMOENS 822 m (2,700 ft). Rather isolated. Good snow conditions. Fine, open slopes.

Savoie

LES ARCS 1,584 m (5,200 ft). Recent, right above the bustling village of Bourg St-Maurice and in the Val d'Isère–Tignes region. Range of off-trail powder-snow skiing.

LE CORBIER 2,437 m (8,000 ft), near La Toussuire. Rather limited skiing.

COURCHEVEL 1,848 m (6,068 ft). Very chic. Sunny, open country; magnificently equipped. Enough variety to suit the expert yet not neglect the beginner. Also excellent *ski de fond*. Lively and varied nightlife. Group of resorts includes Moriond, Le Praz, St-Bon, Courchevel 1550 and Courchevel 1850 (the smartest).

LA DAILLE Suburb of Val d'Isère, but now a resort in its own right.

MÉRIBEL-LES-ALLUES 1,653 m (5,428 ft). Another chic resort, although less nightclubby than Courchevel, now very residential. On the other side of the mountain from Courchevel. You can ski down to Courchevel from the top of the lift. Sunny. Trails not too easy, scattered. Proximity to Péclet-Polset chain makes skiing possible into May.

LA PLAGNE 2,010 m (6,600 ft). Built by private developers on virgin slopes, all in same modern style of light pine and glass. All shops, restaurants, nightclubs and even the church are connected by underground gallery. Known as the *polytechniciens* resort, since many graduates of France's famous Ecole Polytechnique have bought bedsitters and apartments here. Season lasts into May.

PRALOGNAN-LA-VANOISE 1,377 m (4,520 ft). Good slopes near hotels, fine for beginners. *Téléférique* serves snow fields of Bochor, over 2,132 m (7,000 ft).

ST-MARTIN-DE-BELLEVILLE–LES MENUIRES. These twin resorts connect with Courchevel and Méribel, forming one of the largest ski areas. Popular French family resorts.

TIGNES 2,111 m (6,930 ft), highest of the Savoie resorts. Top-notch and varied skiing from Nov. on. Excellent spring skiing on the glaciers of the Grande Motte (3,960 m/13,000 ft) as well as the wide-open slopes surrounding this almost treeless resort. Cross-country skiing in Apr. and May; summer skiing on top of the Grande Motte through July and Aug. A few slopes for beginners, but this is above all a place for serious and energetic skiers. With Val d'Isère, Tignes forms the largest skiable area in France at present. Has well-organized summer program too, including "photo safaris" in nearby Vanoise national park and all-in holidays centered around instruction in the exciting sport of ski acrobatics.

VAL D'ISÈRE 1,848 m (6,068 ft). One of best equipped of all European resorts, very popular with British and German skiers. Basically for the experienced, but beginners can take the *téléférique* to the top of Solaise for easy, wide glacier slopes. Year-round skiing on glaciers; lots of off-trail skiing.

VALLOIRE 1,428 m (4,690 ft). Extensive tree-free slopes. Excellent snow conditions, wide variety of slopes, a family spot.

VAL-THORENS 2,102 m (6,900 ft). Excellent for long-distance skiing. Connects with St-Martin-Méribel-Courchevel to make one vast white area.

THE RIVIERA

High life with a suntan

A kind of mental Garden of Eden exists in the mind of everyone, a place painted in the vivid colors of imagination where someday you can go before leaving this earth—a place where you can bask in the warm sunshine every day of the year, or swim in a placid sea of incredible blue that is so clear you can see your shadow moving over the firm smooth sand bottom 6 meters (20 ft) below.

This is the dream we seek as we plunge into what is one of the most famous stretches of coast in the world—the Côte d'Azur, which stretches from Marseille to Menton. Unfortunately, the once lovely coastline is being covered by a wall of cement; skyscrapers abound, while marinas jut into a sea that is often polluted in high summer, and housing developments crowd the shoreline. But the regional administration has encouraged the preservation of the remaining little coves and beaches, while trying to restore the balance between the overcrowded coast and the deserted hills, where the tranquil traditional world of old Provence is threatened not by immigration but emigration. Thanks to increasing amenities, we suggest that, unless you come off-season, you abandon the coast for one of the hill villages. This way you can swim in the morning and retire later to the hills, rather than fight the crowds and heat all day.

The Côte d'Azur ranges from opulent ostentation to plebian crowding (especially in the huge, dusty roadside campsites, a nightmare in August); from the elegant and sophisticated to the picturesque and colorful. The most interesting spots are described in the following pages, beginning in the west with the ancient city of Marseille, which gave its name to France's national anthem.

Marseille, ancient port

Marseille, the third largest city in France after Paris and Lyon, with nearly one million inhabitants, has been a dominant port in the Mediterranean for almost 2,600 years, since the arrival of the first Greek settlers in the splendid natural harbor of what is today called the Old Port. The remains of the first port can still be seen nearby. But today, the main shipping traffic is from modern and rather depressing docks. In 1943 the Germans blew up the port area, with its narrow streets, its subterranean passages, and its houses of ill fame. The district extending from the port to the cathedral of La Major, the original church built on the foundations of a Roman temple, is frankly uninspiring; this is even true of Marseille's landmark, Notre-Dame de la Garde, consecrated in 1864 high upon a hill above the opposite side of the port, and topped by a gilded statue of the Virgin. But the view from its terrace is stunning: huge skyscrapers, spreading to Le Corbusier's 'Cité Radieuse', an architectural wonder of the 1930s, rise from the vast conglomeration hemmed in by barren hills and the sea. An ancient monument is the 5th-century St-Nicolas, a base for the Foreign Legion just near the ancient Greek port, where officers in tropical uniform and *képis* still saunter about, while the most modern, the Mediterranean Center of International Commerce, was completed in 1980. In 1981 an attractive new theater, the Criée, opened overlooking the Old Harbor in the old fish auction building.

One of the few remaining old houses is the *Maison Diamantée,* now the Museum of Old Marseille. There are early-Christian crypts under the abbey of Ste-Victorie, and a Marine Museum on the Canebière, but more interesting is the Canebière itself, shaded by lovely old plane trees leading to the center of the town from the quai des Belges, where the balconies of the famous fish restaurants overlook the fishing craft in the

Old Port. The interesting Roman Docks Museum contains just that—they were discovered when the Old Port was being rebuilt, together with remains of boats, amphoras, pottery and so on.

But Marseille is quite different from what it was ten years ago, mainly due to the North African immigrant population, which is creating a situation similar to that in New York and Chicago: city streets are no longer safe after dark, and it is wiser not to wander into the 'picturesque' Algerian areas, where hostility towards the outsider is not dissimilar to that found in Harlem.

The whole region round Marseille has changed considerably in recent years. It is now the second largest harbor complex in Europe, with many huge industrial installations—oil refineries, petrochemical plants and the like—as well as ship and aeroplane building. Since 1977 Marseille has had its own Métro.

A recent survey carried out by the news magazine *Le Point* placed Marseille at the bottom of its chart of major French towns graded according to their 'ecological' purity. But, as many people pointed out, life is a lot more fun here than in some of the cleaner cities! Anyway, things started improving in 1981, as the government agreed to produce funds to build a purification plant in the Calanques area.

Take a boat to the island of Château d'If, from which Dumas's Count of Monte Cristo made his famous excape. The guide will solemnly show you the hole through which this imaginary character made his way to freedom.

Accessible from Marseille by car is Martigues, once a delightful fishing port on the Besse basin but very different since a series of oil refineries (which incidentally you can visit) were built near here. A vast fly-over bridge was completed in 1972, crossing the Caronte Canal.

From Marseille to Toulon

Some 19 km (12 miles) east of Marseille lies Cassis, on the coast road that climbs steeply, until, at the Vaufrège Pass, it affords a magnificent view of the bay of Marseille and the islands of Calseraigne and Riou. Cassis is a small sheltered fishing port with three beaches surrounded by rocks and beautiful scenery, beneath Europe's highest cliff, the vertiginous Cap Canaille (365 meters/1,200 ft). It attracted many artists in search of the unspoiled until it became too fashionable.

The *calanques* of Cassis, the most celebrated in the Mediterranean, are long creeks between steep rocks that often reach a height of 146 to 198 meters (480–650 ft); the deep clear water, exposed only to the sky, takes on an intense blue, that contrasts dramatically with the whiteness of the rocks. An excursion along these twisting, fiord-like waterways lasts about two hours, and is generally made in boats hired in Cassis.

Other *calanques* abound along the coast between Marseille and Toulon, and are best visited by boat, though some can be reached by scrambling down the cliffs.

La Ciotat, in ancient times called Citherista, has long been a ship-building center. Its bay, 6 km (4 miles) wide, with exceptionally deep waters, and its favored situation have contributed largely to the importance it has enjoyed since the 16th century.

Bandol and Toulon

Bandol, pleasant both in winter and summer, has two sandy beaches and a casino. The promenade along the quai du Port is flanked by acacias and palm trees. In summer a carnival atmosphere prevails on the nearby Ile de Bendor with its beaches, zoo, Provençal village, theater and wine museum.

Sanary, a fishing port of some 3,000 inhabitants, sheltered by wooded hills that keep the *mistral,* a violent wind, at bay, is a perfect winter resort; in summer, fresh breezes cool the Mediterranean sun. With its little port crowded with fishing boats and yachts, Sanary fully deserves its success.

Like Marseille, Toulon, the capital of the Var *département,* has managed to retain most of its Mediterranean atmosphere in spite of its importance as a naval base and as a center for the munitions industry. Yet here too much has changed, especially in the picturesque quarter adjoining the Old Port. Reconstruction may have given a new face to parts of Toulon but the modern buildings blend with the older surroundings. The rectangular basin of the Old Port, crowded with yachts and fishing boats, is wisely barred to motor traffic.

On the Corniche de Tamaris, leading west to La Seyne-sur-Mer, George Sand wrote her most famous novel, *Tamaris,* and though well into her 60s received her lover, who rowed over all the way from Toulon. Nearby is the Naval Museum on the Fort de Balaguer, and from the heights above Captain Napoleon Bonaparte drove an English garrison in 1793. Below are the long gray walls behind which, until recently, condemned men awaited deportation to Guyana.

Hyères to St-Tropez

Hyères-les-Palmiers (of the Palm Trees), as it is sometimes called because of the luxuriant palm trees that line its wide roads, is the oldest of the Mediterranean winter resorts with luxurious villas for those who favor quiet and comfort. When bathing became fashionable in the 1920's, it established the beach of Almanarre in the Golfe de Giens, to which Europe's largest municipal camping ground, La Capte, was later added; Port de Hyères provides anchorage for 1,600 pleasure craft. This combination resulted in such great pollution that in 1972 bathing had to be prohibited. Thanks to the establishment of a purification plant and of floating buffers to protect the Salt Route along the promontory, all the 22 km (14 miles) of beach were declared safe again in 1978. Hyères is, moreover, the horticulture center of the western Côte d'Azur.

The tree-covered Ile d'Hyères makes a charming excursion easily accessible by boat (frequent services), though the actual point of embarkation is difficult to find. Although there are four islands in the group, Porquerolles, Port-Cros, Ile du Levant and Bagau, it is the first two that are usually visited. The crossing is made from Toulon, Hyères, Le Lavandou, or the tiny port of La Tour Fondue at the tip of the promontory of Giens. Although short, at some seasons of the year it can be uncomfortably rough.

Porquerolles, largest of the islands, was bought by the State in 1971. It has many sandy beaches bordered by pine and briar, luxuriant vegetation, a riot of gaily colored wild flowers, and a climate that although cooler in summer and warmer in winter than on the mainland, is marred occasionally by violent storms.

Port-Cros, more rugged and hilly than Porquerolles, is almost entirely wooded. Pine and eucalyptus perfume the air, while in the thick undergrowth myrtle, briar, lavender and a variety of subtropical vegetation make exploration frequently impossible. Although the island may be visited, it is private property and there is a ban on camping, lighting fires—and even smoking. It is officially classified as a national park, so all wild life is under protection (including plants).

The Ile du Levant is noted throughout France for a special reason. It contains a nudist colony, Heliopolis. In recent years, however, the nudists have had to share their Eden with a French naval base.

Traveling eastward along the coastline, beaches are superseded by salt marshes, and it is not until you reach the tiny town of Cabasson that you find good bathing again. Crescent-shaped and dominated by the brooding fortress of Bregançon, its charming beach slopes gently into the sea, reached by a road from the foot of the hill leading to Bormes.

Although now some distance from the beach, the ancient town of Bormes-les-Mimosas was originally by the sea, but Saracen invaders forced the townsfolk to settle on the steep hillside in 730. Here there is so little level ground that the houses have alleys and streets tunneled through their ground floors. Winding streets abruptly change to stairways as they wander through the town. Often you will be convinced that you have blundered on to someone's private walk as the street emerges into a lovely garden, only to plunge into another tunnel that opens on yet another cobbled street. Bormes' beautiful gardens, its old houses and the breathtaking view of the sea and the Iles d'Hyères more than outweigh the minor disadvantage of its distance (3 km/2 miles) from the sea. During the season, buses make regular trips to the beach from place Gambetta.

The old castle of Fos above the town is now private property. Built between the 11th and 13th centuries, it appears to be a ruin, but the inside has been rebuilt.

Behind the sandy beach of Le Lavandou has arisen a crowded, busy town, full of cheerless concrete buildings, cars and fumes, surrounded by the tent cities erected by campers. The little fishing port, the lovely bay, and the view looking across to the islands remain, however.

Lavandou is reputed to have derived its name from the wild lavender that grows in profusion on the neighboring hills. The liveliest spot is the place Ernest-Reyer, where locals and visitors alike assemble to watch the fishermen dragging their boats on to the beach, or mending their nets in the brilliant sunshine. Its sheltered climate attracts visitors all year round.

St-Tropez and Ste-Maxime

These two towns, less than 14 km (9 miles) apart, are very different. St-Tropez lost the charm of the original fishing village, but was not fashionable long enough with the international set to consolidate an unshakable eminence as did the older resorts further east. Its fading reputation as an in-place still attracts quantity, but quality has largely departed. In contrast, Ste-Maxime is a family-type resort.

St-Tropez came by its name in a curious way, according to legend. In AD 68, when Nero was emperor of Rome, a Christian named Torpes refused to give up his religion. Nero had him beheaded and his body set adrift in an open boat. The boat came ashore at what became St-Torpes and, eventually, St-Tropez.

St-Tropez first came gently into the limelight when it was discovered by painters like Signac and Segonzac, closely followed by the writers Colette, Kessel, and others. But it was in 1956, when Roger Vadim and Brigitte Bardot shot *And God created woman . . .* here, that St-Tropez suddenly acquired the blazing notoriety that has never left it since. *You should avoid St-Tropez from early July to early September unless you like crowds, noise and high prices.* Yet if you sit at a café terrace before luncheon or between 5 and 8 P.M., and watch the world go by, or walk along the still lovely port and admire the fabulous yachts (and their complement of pretty girls), you will understand the attraction it still exerts, and why its habitués remain faithful, in spite of the influx of mass tourism and all that entails.

THE RIVIERA

Across the place de l'Hôtel de Ville is a low-arched gateway leading to the Vieux Port. This is the really old part of St-Tropez. Here are twisting narrow streets designed to break the impact of the *mistral*, tiny squares with fountains, and old houses with curious doorways. If you keep climbing, you will ultimately reach the citadel, a fortress overlooking the vast panorama of the gulf of St-Tropez. It was built over the remains of a Greek temple—for St-Tropez was originally settled by the Greeks in about 470 BC.

There are two *fêtes* in St-Tropez, called *'bravades'*, which take place in May and June. The most important is the one in May honoring St Tropez, the patron saint. For two days the town is alive with banners and flowers and the air is filled with the music of fife and drum. A bust of St Tropez is hoisted to the shoulders of sturdy Tropéziens, traditionally dressed, and paraded to the quayside where sailors fire a salute. Amid pealing bells the saint is returned to the church and the entire population swarms to the old port, where street dancing lasts until dawn.

There are no beaches in St-Tropez proper, so you really need a car—or at least a bicycle. Outside town, the beaches are wide and sandy, and often quite expensive, once you have rented umbrella, mattress, etc. The most popular are probably Pampelone and Tahiti, where the topless fad began and still continues.

St-Tropez is an excellent base from which to visit a fascinating group of hilltop villages. Just off N559 is Gassin, where the houses are huddled together high above the Mediterranean. Behind the ramparts of the town, fishermen and farmers retreated to wait out the raids of the Saracen hordes. From the church the view is superb over the gulf of St-Tropez and to the south all the way to the Iles d'Hyères. On a clear day you can even see the snowcapped Alps. The neighboring town of Ramatuelle is another example of a typical old Provençal town. A climb up to the three abandoned windmills is worth the effort for the rewarding view of the coastline.

Less attractive than either Gassin or Ramatuelle, Cogolin does offer two visits of great interest. The first is the rug-weavers establishment called Tapis et Tissus de Cogolin. The management is happy to show visitors through every stage of the process. The second industry in Cogolin is that of pipemaking. Several craftsmen in hole-in-the-wall workshops carve pipes in strange and delightful shapes.

Down the coast again, be sure to visit Port Grimaud, a true operetta village, a totally man-made pastiche of an Italian fishing village, very fashionable.

Ste-Maxime, on the north of the gulf of St-Tropez, is hardly less popular than St-Tropez, though it attracts a rather different set. Better provided with hotels, it makes an excellent place in which to stay, and is a typical bourgeois seaside town. Grand villas testify to the financial stability of its inhabitants, who are mostly business people, or members of the professions. Here all is orderly and well regulated, and the noise and bustle of St-Tropez are regarded with well-bred disapproval. Ste-Maxime has one very solid advantage over St-Tropez. It is sheltered from the *mistral* that often rages over the latter town, and so its season lasts year round.

In July and August the road between St-Tropez and Ste-Maxime is a nightmare of jammed traffic. We suggest you take the hill road, though longer, or travel by one of the *navettes* (ferries) across the bay.

In 1930 the little town of Garonette, a short distance from Ste-Maxime, decided to participate in the tourist industry of the Riviera. Today it has become a center of aquatic sports and is called Val d'Esquières.

Fréjus, founded by Julius Caesar in 49 BC, became the thriving Roman naval base where Octavius built the ships that defeated Antony and Cleopatra at the Battle of Actium and to which he brought back their captured galleys. The town's extensive Roman ruins, including an amphitheater still used for bullfights, have earned it the name of the 'Pompeii of Provence'. Equally impressive is the cathedral with its beautiful 13th-century cloister and its superb baptistry dating from the 5th century. Among the nearby attractions are an Indo-Chinese pagoda, a Sudanese mosque, a full-scale safari park, the wide beach of Fréjus Plage, and orchards that produce Fréjus peaches, renowned throughout Europe. In recent years a great deal of building has been done on the outskirts of the town, mainly holiday flats and villas, and Fréjus is now a thriving tourist center.

St-Raphaël and the Esterel coast

St-Raphaël is outshone by the attractions of St-Tropez and Ste-Maxime, but it is still a favorite resort of many families who swarm over its beaches and in the streets of the little town. Holiday camps abound in the region, offering inexpensive vacations.

St-Raphaël likes to be designated as the town where the Côte d'Azur begins, and with its palm-lined boulevards, sun-splashed port, its life concentrated in the narrow streets and on the beach, it is the prototype that many British and American visitors imagine when they plan their trip to the south of France.

Between St-Raphaël and Cannes there is a cluster of little resorts set in the bays and creeks along the Corniche de l'Esterel. This twisting, narrow road should be treated with all due care by motorists, but the surface is excellent along the whole 40 km (25 miles) of its length. As the road turns and swoops, the full beauty of this rugged coast can be appreciated. Agay, with its delightful little bay dominated by the jagged red rock of the Rastel d'Agay, is often used as a place of refuge in the occasional rough weather that can transform this usually placid coast into a sailor's nightmare. Le Trayas possesses innumerable creeks and *calanques* where you may often come across deserted little beaches, protected by the rocks from the wind. Many of these are more accessible by boat than from the coast road. (The red rock formation is characteristic of this region and affords a dramatic contrast with the deep blue of the sea.) Théoule and La Napoule, with their small pebble beaches and heavy traffic, are not the best places to bathe, but they are good places to eat. The twin marinas in La Rague and La Napoule are filled with yachts, and a little outside Théoule is a handsome modern ensemble of small apartment buildings, plus a club, hotel, restaurants, pools, called La Résidence de Port-la-Galère. Between Le Trayas and Théoule is the Pointe de l'Esquillon, where the French landed during the operations of August, 1944.

Cannes and its islands

Three names—Cannes, Nice, Monte Carlo—are to be found postered on the walls of every travel agency in the world, conjuring up the sunshine, the blue Mediterranean, and the best-known playgrounds of Europe. Of these three, Cannes is lively, in a dignified chic way; Nice is big, sprawling, grown beyond the limits that permit the collective but intimate fun elsewhere, but with the advantage of big-city attractions such as numerous movie-houses and concerts. Monte Carlo indolently allows its devotees to do what they please, provided they do it elegantly, although here, too, the development of mass tourism is changing the character of this tiny nation.

Cannes is in many ways the infant prodigy of the Côte d'Azur. Although its origins lie deep in the past—it was a center of defense in the 10th century against the Saracens—it was a small fishing port until a chance visit by Lord Brougham, the British Lord Chancellor, nearly 150 years ago. He was on his way to Nice when an outbreak of cholera prevented him from continuing his journey, and he decided to stay in Cannes. He found the place delightful, and built himself a house there. Thenceforth, from 1834, when he first arrived, until his death in 1868, he never failed to spend the winter in Cannes. His example was soon followed by others, and Cannes quickly grew into a winter resort for the aristocracy seeking refuge from the rigors of the English winter. King Edward VII was a devoted visitor.

Today Cannes welcomes its guests almost year round, and has a wide variety of entertainment. The old Municipal Casino has been demolished but a second Palais des Festivals, including a brand-new casino, is being built on the same site, and the glamorous Palm Beach Casino is now open all year. Sun-worshippers and bathers literally rub elbows on the long sandy beach, while frequent excursion boats make trips to the nearby Iles de Lérins. The Old Port has disappeared in an artificial extension of the beach westward to La Napoule, yet the overcrowding in season is hardly relieved. The picturesque boats of the few remaining local fishermen are lost among the luxury yachts in the marina.

The Promenade of the Croisette started brilliantly as the haunt of café society and was taken over by the jet set. No film star or financial magnate would dream of staying elsewhere than in one of its great hotels. At the gala nights in the Palm Beach Casino, open to anyone who can afford a ticket, it is a 'must' to be seen. Parallel to the Croisette runs the rue d'Antibes, whose shops can supply the visitor with everything his heart desires—and his purse can stand. In recent years, many of Cannes' most luxurious villas and apartments have been bought by oil-rich Arabs and Iranians, who also gamble heavily in the casinos. Cannes also has a splendid new 'Palace of Festivals'—a huge complex overlooking the harbor and housing a convention center, theater, casino, nightclub, boutiques and much else besides.

A funicular runs up to Super-Cannes—climb the observation tower for a magnificent panorama. If you prefer more picturesque surroundings go up to Mougins, an ancient Roman village. From the top of its monastery tower you will get an unparalleled view of the whole Riviera coastline. Valbonne, about 11 km (7 miles) above Cannes, has an excellent golf course and swimming pool.

Just off the coast of Cannes two islands are silhouetted against the horizon. They are the Ile Ste-Marguerite and the Ile St-Honorat, known collectively as the Iles de Lérins. The fort in the Ile Ste-Marguerite is famous, for it was here that the 'Man in the Iron Mask' was imprisoned in 1687 and kept in solitary confinement by order of Louis XIV. This is one of the episodes enacted during the light-and-sound performance (weekends only, June to mid-September). Crossings, by frequent boat service from Cannes, take 15 minutes to Ste-Marguerite and half an hour to St-Honorat. During the summer season thousands of holidaymakers visit the islands to picnic and spend the day in the cool pine woods.

From Cannes to Nice

Juan-les-Pins, still technically a suburb of Antibes, is today one of the flashiest places on the Riviera. The sand is better than the artificial beaches of Cannes, but Juan is better known for the quality—or quantity, if you will—of its nightlife rather than its daylife. It goes in for the big and brassy attitude—lots of noise-making. Not elegant, but very popular and expensive. If you *must* visit in July or August, book well in advance.

About midway between Cannes and Nice lies the picturesque old town of Antibes. Although flower-growing (principally roses) for perfume and Europe's flower markets is the mainstay of Antibes, it has not forgotten the visiting tourist. There are beaches and a casino, and visitors wander thorough the streets every summer to visit the market place, stacked with exotic fruit and flowers, and to visit the Musée Grimaldi in the ancestral castle of the Grimaldi family, built on a terrace overlooking the sea. It is an excellent small museum of modern painting and ceramics, dominated by Picasso, open daily except Tuesday (and the whole of November) and well worth a visit.

From the bustling market place the street in front of the town hall descends sharply to the old port. The life there has a timeless Mediterranean charm and the fishermen with their weather-beaten faces, lounging beside their tiny craft, might well belong to any other century than the 20th, despite the backdrop of enough uninspiring apartment buildings to prompt one visitor to remark that Antibes had certainly beaten the record for instant building permits. A popular excursion from Antibes is to Marineland, an amusement park with dolphins, a whale, seals and so on.

Midway between Antibes and Nice is Cagnes, actually two towns: Haut-de-Cagnes, vine-covered and artist-inhabited, made famous by Renoir, who spent the last years of his life nearby (his house has been turned into an attractive small museum); and the beach town about a mile away, Cros-de-Cagnes. At Haut-de-Cagnes is a Grimaldi château, now housing a museum. From its tower there is a good view of the old town below and the countryside around.

Here too is the huge new Côte d'Azur racecourse (the racing runs from December to March, and then again in August and September).

Nice, queen of the Riviera

And so to Nice, the undisputed capital of the Riviera and for many people almost synonymous with it. Superbly set along the lovely Baie des Anges against a backcloth of hills and mountains, it has attracted visitors for well over 100 years. With their palatial hotels lining the Promenade des Anglais and reflected in the deep-blue waters of the Mediterranean, the Niçois have long been accustomed to receiving foreign visitors—once the English aristocracy and American millionaires, now more often sheiks from the oil-rich Middle East.

If you have known Nice in the past you'll find that it has changed a great deal in recent years. It still of course has the attractions of sun and sea and flowers, casino and carnival, glittering boutiques and gourmet restaurants, but with changing patterns in holidaymaking the dynamic Niçois have been rethinking their whole approach to tourism, on which much of the town's prosperity is based. Once a mecca for rich foreigners (and the French) seeking refuge from the rigors of the northern winter, this large city—it has nearly 350,000 inhabitants—is now increasingly attracting summer visitors from a less rarefied income bracket. To make up for the loss of much of the winter tourist trade a determined effort is being made to attract congresses and conferences and by the mid-1980s Nice will have a huge and attractive congress center running from the old place Masséna and stretching eastwards, with hotels and restaurants, many smart boutiques and a new casino (the old municipal casino closed some time ago), the whole complex adorned with paved patios and flower-decked gardens. Already traffic has been banned from much of the town center, an enormous bonus for visitors, who can now stroll and window-shop without fear of being mown down by the happy-go-lucky Mediterranean drivers. Soon the picturesque old town with its winding alleyways, Italianate churches and famous flower market is now mostly traffic-free too. The busy old harbor to the east, from which the huge car ferries sail to Corsica, is soon to lose the pleasure craft now moored there—by the end of the eighties they will have a new berth to the west, where land has been reclaimed from the sea to build a marina and to extend the busy Nice–Côte d'Azur airport, France's second largest.

All this means that Nice is taking on a new lease of life. Don't believe those who tell you it's a staid town—except at carnival time—more suited for rich retired people than for the young at heart. In fact it has a great deal to offer tourists in every age and income bracket, with hotels ranging from the super-deluxe to the modest family-run establishment, luxury restaurants and inexpensive pizzerias, events of all kinds, both traditional (the carnival and the 'flower battles') and cultural (ballet, theater and concerts are staged here throughout the year).

Nice's best-known event is its fantastic Mardi Gras carnival, the only winter one these days to pack the city till it almost bursts at the seams. The place Masséna and the surrounding streets and squares are lavishly decorated and lit and His Majesty King Carnival makes his ceremonial entry while processions of flower-decked floats parade along the Promenade des Anglais. But if you come at other times of year you won't be disappointed—sports of all kinds are catered for (including winter sports in the ski resorts up in the nearby mountains), while nightclubs and concerts take care of your evenings. Gamblers should head for the luxurious Casino Ruhl, on the site of the old Ruhl Hotel, Nice's only casino for the time being (the famous Palais de la Méditerranée has been demolished, and the new casino won't open until the mid-1980s).

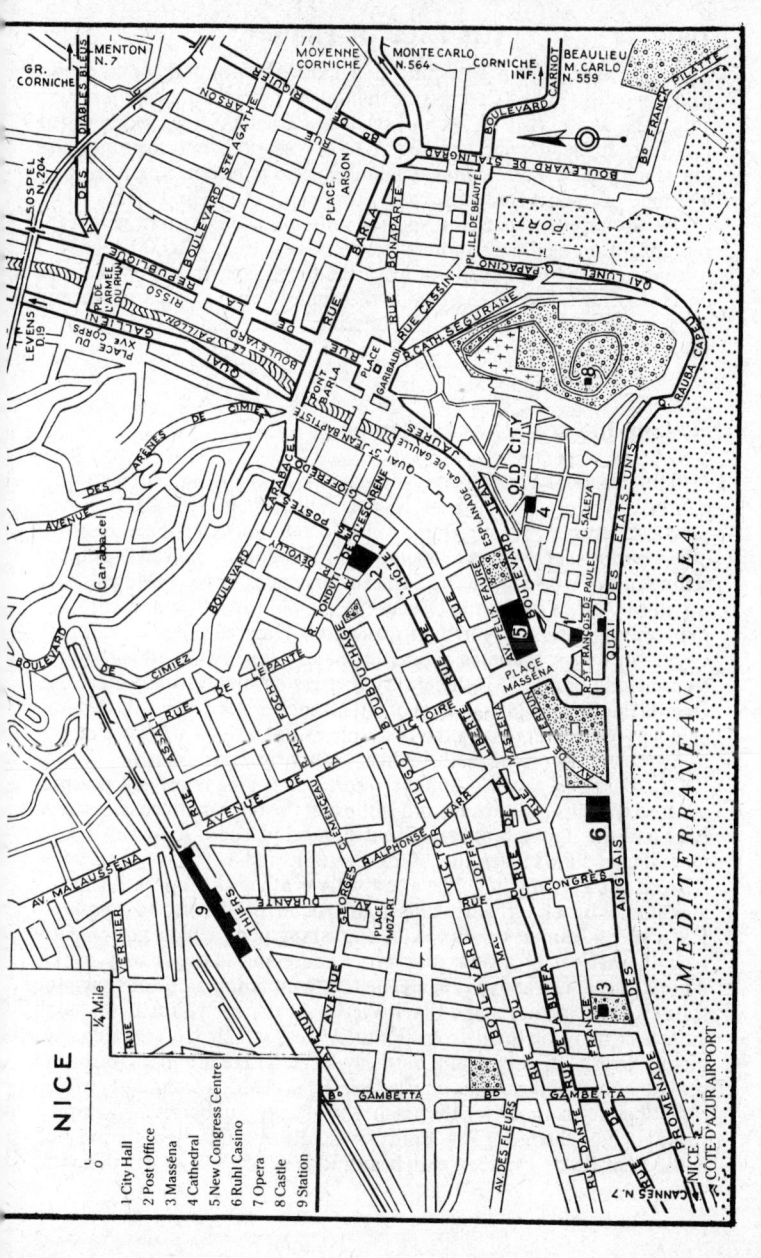

In the daytime we recommend a guided tour of the Old Town (inquire at the Palais Lascaris or the tourist office) with its interesting churches, and a visit to Nice's excellent museums. For details of the city's art museums see our 'What to do' section, but we must also mention the new Terra Amata paleontological museum, which recently won one of the coveted European Museum of the Year awards. Close to the old harbor, this well-displayed museum is on the spot where the remains of an elephant hunters' camp no less than 400,000 years old were discovered during site preparation for an apartment block. Also on the eastern side of the city is the ruined 'castle', with a peaceful garden perched on a high mound offering breathtaking views along the coast.

Along the corniches to Menton

Going eastward from Nice, you encounter one delightful spot after another. Almost a suburb of Nice is Villefranche, whose deep bay, pinched between Mount Boron on one side and Cap Ferrat on the other, permits large ships to anchor. Villefranche has played host to the sailors of the world since the Saracens first came here. Their influence is still to be seen in the rue Obscure in the old town, a tunnel recalling the covered streets of North African *souks*. Huge ships from the Mediterranean fleet sometimes appear in the bay for a while, dwarfing the local fishing boats. A 16th-century fortress dominates the waterfront. One of the greatest attractions of Villefranche, apart from its fashionable fish restaurants along the quayside, is the little fishermen's chapel of St-Pierre, decorated with biblical scenes by Jean Cocteau.

Cap Ferrat is a world-famous resort but is still relatively peaceful because it forms a peninsula and is thus off the busy main road between Nice and the Italian border. It is a delightful place for long walks, with magnificent views over the Mediterranean and as far as the Italian Riviera in clear weather. The finest walk is along the footpath starting at Paloma Beach, which winds right round the beautiful Pointe St-Hospice. St-Jean, at the tip, is an old fishing port, which has recently seen the arrival of a new marina to house the many luxury yachts moored here. Up above it is a cemetery containing a curious gigantic statue known locally as the Black Virgin. At the zoo you may see small animals (many of them from South Africa, which has a similar climate), lizards, insects, and a butterfly farm. There are many beautiful private homes and gardens on Cap Ferrat, probably second only to Cap d'Antibes as an abode for the wealthy, but they can barely be glimpsed through high hedges. The Ephrussi de Rothschild Foundation and Musée de l'Ile-de-France, set in beautiful grounds, is well worth a visit.

It has fine porcelain and furniture collections, and is also the setting for concerts in the summer months.

The next resort, Beaulieu-sur-Mer, is more modern; it has a big casino and boasts several attractive hotels. It is preferred by those who are less fond of the worldly whirl of nearby Monte Carlo. Beyond it is Eze-sur-Mer, but at Beaulieu you should leave the coast road and go up to the Moyenne Corniche to visit Eze-Village, perched like an eagle's nest on its crag. Seen from afar, the village looks much as it did in the Middle Ages except that its former château is now a ruin surrounded by a garden of exotic plants and flowers.

For this same easterly trip from Nice you can also take the Grande Corniche, the high road along the crests of the mountains, with a plunging view down towards the sea. Don't gaze fascinated seaward during the whole trip, or you'll miss a point where there's a break in the mountains, through which in clear weather with no heat haze you can look northward into a region of ever higher peaks until those in the distance glitter with snow in the Mediterranean sun.

On this route you will pass through La Turbie, where a few columns perched curiously on a rock above the town are all that remain of the Trophy of the Alps, built by Augustus in 5 BC to commemorate Rome's subjection of the Ligurians. But the chief attraction of La Turbie is the view from its terrace—the panorama of Monaco lying far below, spread out like a map against the sea, below the massive gray mountain known, from its shape, as the Tête de Chien—the Dog's Head.

On the way down from La Turbie to Monte Carlo (see following chapter), you pass Roquebrune, another hill town and one well worth visiting with its feudal château hewn directly out of the rock. The curious religious procession held there on August 5 commemorates a happy deliverance that took place in the town during the Middle Ages, when an epidemic of cholera was miraculously stopped.

Menton

At the extreme tip of the Riviera, with the Italian frontier only a few hundred yards away, stands Menton, which was until recently two distinct and quite separate towns. The eastern side, which lies nearer to the Italian frontier, is still inhabited by fishermen living in tall, typically Mediterranean old buildings with narrow little streets, while the much larger western side, devoted entirely to pensioners and tourists has spacious avenues, modern first-class hotels, a casino and a beach that is thronged in summer by the countless devotees of sea and sunshine. But there is now a yacht marina and a new wide sandy beach (Les Sablettes) to the east, both of which have added a youthful attraction to this old town, which is a haven for the retired. So the old division between east and west is no longer so striking.

Menton has a picturesque Lemon Fair in February (lemon trees flourish all year here, in what is traditionally the warmest spot on the whole Côte d'Azur) and an internationally known chamber music festival in August, with some of the concerts held in the attractive Italianate churches in the old town. They are well worth a visit, as is the Cocteau Museum down by the harbor. Cocteau also painted the famous frescoes in the Salle des Mariages in Menton's town hall. Menton is also one of the best centers on the Riviera from which to make excursions. A few minutes' walk and you are across the frontier into Italy, where you can take a bus to San Remo or (a favorite with tourists) to the Friday flower market in Ventimiglia (called Vintimille in French). Don't forget your passport. Or you can leave the hot sunshine of the beach and go up into the hills to visit such picturesque villages as Ste-Agnès, Castellar or Gorbio.

Haute Provence

The hills behind the Côte d'Azur are full of towns and villages built for protection against invasion, whether from the sea by fierce Saracens or from the land by marauding mercenaries in the Middle Ages. They were dominated by the lord's fortress behind its thick walls where, when the church bells rang the danger signal, all could take refuge.

Today, invaded as they often are by fake antique shops, quasi-artists and multilingual tourists, they still afford a glimpse of what life was like in the early Middle Ages in Provence, and despite these modern incursions they still retain a certain charm and picturesqueness. Many famous artists, actors, writers (Chagall, Vasarely and, earlier, Picasso) chose to retreat to these villages with their magnificent views.

Vence is sophisticated and international, a tourist mecca, but still full of color: visit the market and the old walled quarter. St-Paul-de-Vence, home of the Maeght Foundation, an indoor-outdoor museum of modern art, climbs up the hill and is full of charm, except in August. Tourrette and Tourtour are more off the beaten track.

Relatively untouched are the ancient villages of Peillon, above Cap d'Ail; Sospel, above Menton in the high valley of the Roya; St-Martin de Vésubie, a small resort popular with climbers, almost on the Italian border; and little Peïra-Cava, a ski resort also popular with hikers in summer, and famous for the many different types of edible fungi found locally. All are reached by breathtakingly beautiful winding roads, where you cannot drive faster than 50 km (30 miles) an hour. The Vallée des Merveilles near the Italian border, with over 4000 prehistoric rock carvings, is a magnificent summer excursion for seasoned walkers (guide recommended).

Gréolières is in stony, windswept countryside where almost the only sound is the bleating of sheep. Then there are Brignoles; Flayosc; Salernes, the sleepy *sous-préfecture* of Draguignan; Fayence, nestling high in the hills; Ste-Agnès; Gattières. In all of these you will find the true flavor of the Midi. Another impressive and largely unspoilt area is the Grand Canyon du Verdon, in a wild part of Provence north of Draguignan. The cliffs are up to 457 meters (1,500 ft) high, and the road winds dramatically around. You can also walk (hard) on the bottom of the canyon, even take a dip in the pure icy water. There is a Touring Club mountain refuge at La Maline, but most people prefer to stay at attractive Moustiers Ste-Marie, where famous pottery has been made for centuries.

PRACTICAL INFORMATION

WHEN TO GO. Here, more than any other spot in Europe, it is worth your while to visit out-of-season. Throughout July and Aug. accommodations are difficult to obtain, prices are higher, the beaches and roads jammed. From mid-May through June, and during Sept., you can generally count on good swimming and sunbathing weather and uncrowded beaches. In Oct., the icy *mistral* tends to blow from the north, and in Nov. and Dec. it rains a good deal, but from Jan. through Apr., there is often mild weather for which a topcoat is needed only in the evening.

Warning: In the early '80s an invasion of back-packers, mostly from northern Europe, followed inevitably by drug pushers, pickpockets and other hangers-on, caused havoc in the coastal resorts in July and August, driving many traditional tourists away. The Interior Ministry reacted by enforcing local by-laws about sleeping on the beach, vagrancy and so on, and bringing in new legislation too; but the problem is still there, so we advise you to be careful during these high-summer months.

In **January** there are horseraces and equestrian competitions, automobile rallies, battles of flowers, golf and tennis matches, yachting events, concerts, and ballets. In **February** are the Mimosa Festival (Cannes) and the Lemon Festival (Menton). On Easter Sunday at Vence, the Feast of St Mark, patron saint of Provençal winegrowers, is celebrated with folksongs and dances. The fantastic Nice carnival, originating in ancient ceremonies celebrating the return of spring, lasts for about two weeks preceding Ash Wednesday.

From mid-**March** to early **April,** Cannes holds its International Music Week, and in **May,** its famous Film Festival. The Nice Corn Festival held in the Roman arena of Cimiez, and the fête of the patron saint of St-Tropez are also in May. **June** is the month of the Toulon Fair and the St-Tropez bravade. The popular Antibes jazz festival is usually in **July,** as is the open-air jazz festival in Nice's Cimiez area and Hyères' film festival. And in this month there is the Folklore Festival in Nice and Nice's 'Battle of Flowers'. Menton's Chamber Music Festival and the medieval religious procession at Roquebrune are in **August.** Throughout summer until mid-**September,** the Iles de Lérins have their *son-et-lumière* performance. In September Cannes also holds an International Amateur Film Festival, and Marseille stages its fair. Wine harvest festivals are staged by villages in the hills of Provence above the Côte d'Azur.

THE RIVIERA

WHAT TO DO. The most obvious attractions of the Côte d'Azur—the opportunities it offers for **sunbathing, swimming, sailing, waterskiing, walking** (and even **skiing**) in the hills of Haute Provence, plus the many fashionable events that take place here—need little description here. Information about them can be obtained from the area's exceptionally dynamic and helpful tourist offices. Nice has some good all-in **tennis** and **golf** holidays.

But when you have had enough of these well-known pursuits, there are many other things to see and do. We have mentioned some of them in the preceding pages, but too few foreign tourists know that the Riviera has its own **Modern Art Road**—a pilgrimage way for all those interested in the art of the 20th cent. Here are some of the highlights: Picasso's moving War and Peace frescoes in a tunnel-shaped medieval chapel in Vallauris; the Chapelle du Rosaire in Vence, decorated by Matisse; Renoir's house and studio in Haut-de-Cagnes; the Léger Museum in Biot, which is exceptionally well lit and arranged; the excellent Maeght Foundation in St-Paul, with important temporary shows and an outstanding permanent collection, including some lovely Giacometti sculptures strikingly displayed in an open air courtyard; the magnificent biblical paintings, sketches, engravings, tapestries, mosaics and sculptures that form Chagall's 'Biblical Message', displayed in the Chagall Museum in Nice; the Matisse Museum in Nice; the Picassos in the Musée Grimaldi in Antibes; the Cocteau frescoes in Villefranche and Menton; further west, the excellent Annonciade Museum in St-Tropez (a former chapel) has a well-displayed collection of modern paintings. Nice now has a museum devoted to **Naïve Art,** which opened in 1982.

If your taste in art lies further back in time, you can make a study of the 'School of Nice', 16th–17th-cent. painters whose work can be seen in Nice (Musée Masséna), the best-known being Louis Bréa. Many of the hill villages have beautiful murals and altarpieces dating from this same period, though unfortunately because of the danger of theft it is not always easy to find someone to unlock the little churches and chapels where they can be seen.

Alternatively you may prefer **craftsmanship**, both traditional and modern. If so, you will be in your element here. The local pottery is particularly interesting and varied, much of it made to traditional designs and much sought-after. Vallauris, Biot, Vence and many other hill villages are full of workshops where pottery is still being made, though the influx of tourists has sadly led to the arrival of quite a lot of tasteless modern designs alongside the beautiful, and far simpler, traditional ones. Inquire at the local tourist offices for opportunities to take classes in pottery and other crafts, such as weaving, painting on silk, basket-making. Many of these classes are held in the picturesque villages in the hills behind the coast, and you may be able to arrange accommodation in one of the local farmhouses. For glass lovers, the place to go is the island of Bendor, which specializes in glass blowing and has some beautiful examples on display.

If you're a **music-lover,** you'll find much to attract you. There's Menton's famous chamber music festival in Aug., and its Young Pianists' Week in early July, while Antibes and Juan-les-Pins have their Young Soloists' Festival from

April to June. Antibes also has an International Jazz Festival in July, which is also the month for Nice's Cimiez openair jazz festival. Concerts are held in Nice throughout the year.

HOW TO GET ABOUT. By air. There are several daily flights between London and Nice (takes about 1½ hrs), run by *Air France* and *British Airways*. In summer *Air France* uses the gigantic Airbus on the London–Nice run. There are also daily flights direct from New York, as well as many flights from Paris (*Air Inter*). From Lyon, Bordeaux, Clermont-Ferrand, Lille, Nantes, Strasbourg and many other places in France *Air Inter* fly to Nice for most of the year. *TAT* flies to Nice from various French cities such as Metz, Mulhouse, Nancy, Vichy and Figari in Corsica (some flights are seasonal only). There are also flights from most of the world's capitals, so there's no need to start out from Paris. Luckily Nice airport is being enlarged and modernized. *Air France* and *British Airways* operate a multi-tier fare structure (similar to the London-Paris rates) for their Paris-Nice run. *Air Inter* offer good-value Nice packages (see Facts at Your Fingertips).

You can also fly from Paris and London to Marseille, Nice airport can be used by private planes, and Cannes's Mandelieu airport charters helicopters, as well as running a helicopter service on the Riviera. *TAT* flies between Marseille and Clermont-Ferrand, Figari in Corsica, Nantes and Toulouse; and from Lille to Toulon.

Getting to town from the airport. There's an efficient coach service between Nice airport and the town center, and to many resorts along the Riviera. Also a helicopter service to Monaco, which is extremely useful. Marseille's Marignane airport has a bus service to the Gare-St-Charles in the town center.

By train. Trains from Paris leave from the Gare de Lyon. By 1984 the TGV service will have cut travel time to Marseille to under 5 hrs. Fastest ordinary service: Marseille taking under 7 hrs; to Toulon, 7½ hrs and to Nice, 9½ hrs. Most of the trains to Nice stop at Cannes and Antibes. There are also frequent services along the coast, between Nice and Marseille, Menton and so on; good trains run between Strasbourg and Marseille and Nice via Lyon. With only one change you can make such journeys as Quimper (in Brittany) to Marseille, and if you've started off in the southwest there's a fast line from Toulouse and Montpellier to Nice via Marseille. The overnight sleeping-car train from Paris to Ventimiglia is a little slower than some, but is a good way to travel as you waste no potential sunbathing time! It stops at all the main resorts on the coast. The luxurious *Azur 2000* travels between Paris and Menton once a week, leaving Paris on Fri. evening and Menton on Sun. evening. Has cinema car, restaurants, bars. There are car-couchette trains between Rheims and Nice on weekends. Paris-Nice trains now have special coaches with access for the handicapped.

The *SNCF* has special package fares for Nice and Cannes, covering train fare, hotel and breakfast, with optional car hire.

A good train running along the whole coast is *Le Ligure*, which takes just over 3 hrs from Avignon to Nice, then continues on to Milan in Italy.

THE RIVIERA

If you're coming from Britain, the best train is the *Flandre–Riviera Express,* with through sleeping and couchette carriages from Calais right through to San Remo in Italy. Otherwise you have to change in Paris between the Gare du Nord and the Gare de Lyon for one of the many trains down via Dijon and Lyon.

Going inland from Nice to Digne there is the local Provençal rail which operates one-class cars several times daily in each direction, calling at all stations; the 150-km (93-mile) journey takes about 3¼ hrs. The *Alpazur,* one of the SNCF's new tourist trains, is another leisurely delight.

By bus. *Europabus* have comfortable coaches with hostess (usually English-speaking) on board, between Paris and Nice. There are two itineraries: via the Rte des Alpes on Fri. and via the Rhône valley on Mon. You can either pay just for the bus or take a package deal covering hotel in Lyon, breakfast and other meals. There are reductions for senior citizens, and special rates if you do the complete bus journey Paris–Nice, then return by rail. About mid-June to mid-Sept., but be sure to check dates. *European Express* has coach services from Apr. to Oct. from London to Antibes, Cannes, Fréjus, Nice and St-Tropez. *Europe Autocar* has a week-long coach trip from Paris to Nice Carnival.

Europabus has a tour four times a week all year except Nov., Dec. and Jan. The trip Nice–Menton and back via the Grande Corniche includes a visit to Monte Carlo. Another trip goes twice a week Feb. through Oct. from Nice to Saint-Paul, Vence and Grasse. Or you can go from Cannes four times a week year-round to the Italian border via the Grande Corniche and back via the Corniche Inférieure, with lunch in Monte Carlo. From Cannes you can go in the other direction to Ste-Maxime, St-Tropez, Port Grimaud, St-Raphaël, La Napoule; twice a week year-round.

MOTORING. Car sleeper express trains operate in summer from Boulogne via Paris to St-Raphaël and Nice, also from Boulogne to Avignon. From Avignon you take the A7 (which you can also reach from Paris by driving on the A6 to Lyon). At Aix it branches and becomes the A9 to Marseille and points west; A8 to the easterly Riviera resorts and Italy. You can also take N7 (Rte Bleue), from Lyon down the Rhône valley, or N86 (very winding) on the opposite side of the Rhône. Pretty and less traveled are the N100, N96 and N85, which go from Remoulins. From Paris, there are several routes. The fastest, of course, is the A6/A7 to Marseille or Nice, but you can also follow N7 via Nevers, Moulins, Lyon, Valence, Avignon; on N6 via Sens, Auxerre, Avallon and Saulieu to Lyon. From Lyon you can head for Grenoble, and the Rte Napoléon (N85) via Gap, Sisteron and Digne.

SNCF has car-couchette services from Paris to St-Raphaël and Nice year-round. Also Rheims-Nice on weekends and Boulogne–Avignon in summer months.

For motorists from the Channel ports, the best route to follow is the *Autoroute du Nord* (A1), which you join from A25 out of Dunkirk or from Calais or Boulogne, or on A26 at St. Omer. You can now bypass Paris completely (follow the signs showing A6 or Orly-Fontainebleau to avoid getting sucked back into city traffic).

The A8 from Marseille to Nice, with turnouts at Antibes, Mougins and Mandelieu, avoids the mountainous Estérel or the often crowded coast road. From Nice to Menton you have a choice of four roads, according to your mood: the autoroute makes it possible to drive all the way from Calais to Palermo by motorway; the *Shoreline Corniche,* through Beaulieu and Monaco, often curving around high rocky promontories, but with the Mediterranean always at your side; the *Middle* or *Moyenne Corniche,* darting inland to Eze and thence down to Monaco; and the *Grande Corniche,* with its splendid mountain panoramas and hairpin bends amid the Alpine heights.

EXCURSIONS. *Europabus* has coach excursions from various centers, such as Avignon to Arles and Les Baux, Cannes to St-Tropez and Port Grimaud; some are accompanied by guides. From Marseille, Cannes, Nice, Monaco and Menton, frequent bus services run circular tours along the coast and to the hinterland.

BICYCLES. You can hire bikes in many resorts, from about 50 frs a day. Scooters are about 70 frs daily, unlimited mileage. You'll have to show your passport and leave a fairly large deposit.

BEACHES. You might expect to find the best beaches near Cannes, Nice, Monte Carlo and Menton: actually, except for Cannes and Menton, they are rather poor. At Cannes, the once-narrow sandy beach was widened with sand brought from Fréjus, and is now a respectable size. From Nice to the Italian border, the beaches are of gravel or rock. Between Cannes and St-Raphaël rise the magnificent red rocks of the Corniche, which, although breathtaking in their beauty, provide little in the way of places to swim. The most elegant beaches, all tiny, expensive, exclusive, are those on Cap d'Antibes.

The best beaches are along the more than 96 km (60 miles) of coast from St-Raphaël to Hyères—at Cabasson, Le Lavandou, St-Clair, Cavalière, Tahiti, Pampelone, Salins, ranging from tiny crescent beaches to dazzling ones that sweep for over 5 km (3 miles) along the sea. They are all fine, white-sand beaches that slope gently into the sea, quite clean off season.

Unfortunately, the water off the more crowded resorts such as Nice, Cagnes, St-Raphaël and Ste-Maxime, although not exactly polluted, is rather dirty. But a new water-purification plant in St-Raphaël is helping to solve the problem.

At most beaches, except the public ones (always very crowded), it is almost obligatory to rent cabin, umbrella, mattress or chairs. Prices vary, but are often rather high. Meals on these private beaches are usually expensive.

THE RIVIERA

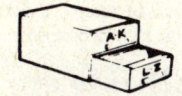

USEFUL ADDRESSES. *Welcome Information offices* for the Riviera–Côte d'Azur region are at the main rail stations in Cannes and at av. Thiers, 06000 Nice; 4 La Canebière, 13001 Marseille and 8 av. Colbert, 83100 Toulon. *Tourist offices* at the same addresses, plus another office on the bld de la Croisette in Cannes and at 13 pl. Masséna in Nice. Other major tourist offices in Menton, Juan-les-Pins, Antibes, Grasse and so on.

US Consulate, 9 rue Armeny, 13000 Marseille. *GB Consulate,* 24 av. du Prado, 13000 Marseille.

In New York, the dynamic *Niçois* have opened a City of Nice Promotion office at 683 Fifth Ave.

If you want to know about Nice's many festivals, parades and galas, write to the *Comité des Fêtes de la Ville de Nice,* 5 promenade des Anglais, 06000 Nice.

Promovar, the information service of the Conseil Général du Var, 1 bld Foch, 83300 Draguignan, is a very useful source of guidance, as it publishes maps, lists of hotels, campsites, vacation villages, museums, festivals, craftsmen, rural fairs, markets, cycle routes, and much else besides. It also has two offices on the A8 motorway, at the Aire de Brignoles-Cambarette and the Aire de Vidauban-Sud.

Car hire. *Hertz,* 147 rue d'Antibes, Cannes; 129 bld Wilson, Juan-les-Pins; Nice airport; Hôtel Terminus, pl. de la Gare, Antibes; bld du Maréchal-Juin, Cagnes-sur-Mer; 22 av. de Toulon, and airport, Hyères; 7 av. des Commandots d'Afrique, Le Lavandou; 16 bld Ch.-Nédelec, Marseille, and Marignane airport; 12 av. de Suède, Hôtel Hyatt Regency, 223 promenade des Anglais, and airport, Nice; 60 av. F.-Cuzin, Toulon. *Avis,* 69 La Croisette, Cannes; 32 bld Albert-ler, Antibes; 44 av. Gambetta, Hyères; 38 bld Ch.-Nédelec, Marseille, and Marignane airport; 9 rue Victor-Hugo, Menton; pl. Massena, Nice, and airport; 175 bld Maréchal-Joffre and 14 bld Maréchal-Foch, Toulon. *Europcar,* 26 bld Foch, Antibes; 3 rue du Commandant-Vidal, Cannes; on RN7, Golfe-Juan; 4 bld Victor-Hugo, Grasse; 7 bld Maurice-Bourdet, Marseille, 93 av. du Prado, and Marignane airport; rond-point de Bir-Hakeim, Toulon.

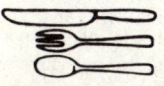

REGIONAL FOOD AND DRINK. Riviera cooking is related to the Italian (you will find the best-known Italian dishes done well here) but there are also a considerable number of interesting local specialties. Any dish labeled 'Provençale' will be rich in garlic, like *tomates provençale* or *coquille St-Jacques provençale* (scallops lightly fried with garlic and breadcrumbs).

The great contribution of Marseille is *bouillabaisse,* a fish stew, sometimes with the inclusion of lobsters, though purists frown on this. What they do insist on is *rascasse,* a Mediterranean fish. The small fish are strained to make the liquid part of the soup, the large fish cooked in it, but served in a special dish. The soul of *bouillabaisse* is the saffron that gives it its orange color. In the depths of the liquid are slices of bread liberally dosed with garlic.

Farther east, towards St-Tropez, *soupe de poissons* (fish soup), or *bourride,* is more favored. You can order a *rouille* to go along with it—a local sauce made with hot red pepper incorporated in a garlic mayonnaise. In many Riviera restaurants you can order *soupe au pistou,* a filling vegetable soup whose secret is the basil flavoring.

Nice has many specialties. *Salade niçoise* is a refreshing hot weather prelude to a meal—tomatoes, peppers, celery, ripe olives, tunafish, anchovies: a sandwich variant of it, very pleasant to eat on the beach, is *pan bagna,* the same ingredients between the two slices of a round bun moistened with olive oil. *Poulpe à la niçoise* is octopus with tomato sauce, while *supions* are squid. *Pissaladière* is an onion tart, sometimes with anchovies on top, sometimes tomato sauce. *Ratatouille* is eggplant (aubergine) tomatoes and zucchini (courgettes) stewed in oil with lots of garlic, until it is a homogeneous mass.

Fish play an important part in Riviera menus, though oddly enough two of the most popular fish dishes are made from salt fish from other countries. *Morue provençale* is salt cod, tomatoes, garlic and parsley cooked into a creamy sauce-like substance. Cod is also the basis for the famous *brandade,* a mixture of cod, garlic and olive oil, traditionally eaten on Good Friday.

Fresher products of the sea include *rouget,* the delectable red mullet of the Mediterranean; *loup,* generally considered the noblest fish of these waters, often grilled over a fire of fennel branches; and *chapon,* not always easy to find, which connoisseurs rate above the more widely known *loup. Oursins* (sea urchins) are becoming increasingly rare and expensive, but you may come across sea urchin sauce with fish dishes.

Except for the white wines of Cassis, the region's wines are not great, but they are pleasant. Most of them are *rosés,* pinkish in tint, pleasant in hot weather, light to the palate, but don't be deceived—they can be heady. The traditional drink in this part of France is the aniseed-flavored *pastis,* drunk as an apéritif—or at any other time for that matter.

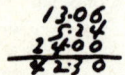

WHAT IT WILL COST. Generally speaking, the Côte d'Azur, and the inland region immediately behind it, are the most expensive areas in France for hotels, restaurants, beach charges and food, especially in season. There are some inexpensive spots, but you do not come here for a budget vacation. Prices may be as much as 30% more than in equivalent hotel and restaurant categories in surrounding areas such as the hill towns, where there are budget accommodations and restaurants.

The promotion and publicity departments of the City Hall and Tourist Office in Nice are always devising new schemes to attract visitors, most of them offering substantial reductions in, say, shops, theaters and museums. Ask your travel agent to check what possibilities are available.

The Baies du Soleil hotel chain, with hotels of all categories between Cassis and Hyères, offers various reductions and special services between Oct. and June. Riviera-Hotels (1- and 2-star) have seven-day all-in packages. Check with your travel agent. Air France's *Jet-Tours* subsidiary also does a fairly expensive package of airfare plus hotel in Nice, Cannes (and also Monaco), for a long weekend or a full week.

Small hotels may close for a period during the year, as do some restaurants, which also close one day a week. In hotel and restaurant listings, *L, E, M* or *I* denote deluxe, expensive, moderate or inexpensive.

Marseille–Toulon

HOTELS AND RESTAURANTS. The unpretentious little resorts along this strip of coast attract a predominantly French clientele. At approaches to Bandol, Le Lavandou, Sanary, see illuminated hotel indicators for current vacancies. Many hotels are closed Nov. through Feb.

BANDOL. *PLM Ile Rousse,* deluxe, with pool, private beach, restaurant and snack bar. *Provençal* (M). *Ker Mocotte* (M).
On **Bendor Island** *Delos,* deluxe, with annex *Le Palais; Soukana* (E), shares restaurant with Delos. Both with pool and under same management.
Restaurants. *Auberge du Port* (E), allées J.-Moulin; *La Réserve* (M), on Sanary road, with a few rooms; *La Grotte Provençale* (I), rue Dr L.-Marcin.

LE BEAUSSET. *Auberge Gruppi* (I), small Logis de France, with pleasant restaurant.

CASSIS. *Roches Blanches* (E), with private beach, lovely site, quiet; *Plage* (M), on Bestouan beach about 1.5 km (1 mile) south, comfortable, has good restaurant (called *Bestouan*). Less than 1 km (½ mile) inland is the *Jardins du Campanile,* with pool; no restaurant, quiet.
Restaurants. *Presqu'ile* (E), very attractive, with interesting 'new' versions of regional dishes. *Chez Gilbert* (E); *Nino* (M), with an airy terrace, facing the port.

CASTELLET. Medieval village. **Restaurant.** *Castel Lumière* (M), lovely setting, also has a few rooms.

LA CIOTAT. *Lavandes* (M), *Rotonde* (M), both in town, no restaurant. At **Ciotat-Plage,** *Provence-Plage* (M), with restaurant. At **Liouquet,** 6 km away on Bandol road, *Ciotel,* modern, expensive.

FOS. *Frantel,* pleasant; *Novotel.* Each with pool, (E).

GEMENOS. *Relais Magdeleine* (E), very attractive, with pool and restaurant.

LES LECQUES. *Grand* (E), *Chanteplage* (M). They offer bathing, seclusion, and a fine view.

MARSEILLE. Deluxe and central are the *Concorde-Prado, Grand Hôtel Noailles, Concorde-Palm-Beach* (with pool) and *Frantel.*

On the Corniche is *Le Petit Nice et Marina Maldormé,* with lovely garden, good restaurant (E). Moderate: *Résidence Bompard,* with kitchenettes, overlooking the Corniche. Moderate: *Dieudé, Deux Mondes, Pilote* and tiny *Capricorne.* Inexpensive: *Estérel,* well decorated, good value, no restaurant; *Martini,* no restaurant.

On the Vieux Port, *Sofitel-Vieux-Port,* deluxe, harbor view; pool; *PLM-Beauvau, PLM Astoria* (E), 60 modern rooms and period furniture in lounges; no restaurant.

Near the airport, 27 km (17 miles) northwest at **Marignane,** *Novotel Marseille Aéroport,* expensive; also the more luxurious *Frantel* and *Sofitel* and the cheaper *Mercure. PLM Terminus,* impersonal, but conveniently situated on A7 motorway.

At **St-Menet,** 9.5 km (6 miles) east, *Novotel Marseille Est,* expensive.

Restaurants. *Chez Maurice Brun* (E), 18 quai Rive Neuve, top cuisine in quality and quantity. *New York Vieux-Port* (E), 7 quai des Belges, elegant. *Oursinade* (E), in Frantel hotel. *Mavro* (E), quai des Belges, first-floor restaurant, opened 1983, excellent for fish. *Michel-Brasserie des Catalans* (M), 6 rue Catalans, famous for *bouillabaisse* with lobster (limited seating, so reserve), as is *Calypso* (M), at no.3, same street. All round the old port. In the same area, all (M) are: *Miramar,* 12 quai Port; *Chez Caruso,* at no. 158; *Chez Arnould,* 38 cours d'Estienne d'Ores; *Au Pescadou,* 19 pl. Castellane, and *Au Jambon de Parme* (Italian), 67 rue de la Palud, excellent. Good pizzeria, *Antoine* (I), 35 rue du Musée.

On the Corniche, *Chez Fonfon* (M), excellent seafood.

SANARY. *Hôtel de la Tour* (M); *Grand Hôtel des Bains* (I); *Primavera* (M), comfortable.

TOULON. *Frantel La Tour Blanche,* deluxe, has bungalows, pool, splendid view. *Grand,* no restaurant, bay view, expensive, and *Maritima* (I) (no restaurant). *Résidence* (I), no restaurant. *Novotel* (M), at **La Seyne** 7.5 km (4 miles) away near motorway, with pool.

Restaurants. *La Calanque* (I), excellent *bouillabaisse. Le Dauphin* (I), very good value, is best in town. *Madeleine* (I), good value *menu. Lutrin* (E), attractive, a bit over priced, but good cuisine.

At **Les Sablettes,** about 11 km (7 miles) south, *Provence-Plage,* moderate. Good restaurant is *La Jetée* (M) at St-Elme.

Hyères-Cannes

HOTELS AND RESTAURANTS. Prices here in the smaller and quieter towns are often less expensive than around Cannes and Nice, but don't think you're going to get away for nothing. Several of the big hotels are pricey; the smaller ones are upping their prices too. In St-Tropez, Port Grimaud and other fashionable spots you're paying deluxe prices.

THE RIVIERA

AGAY. *Baumette* (E), superb setting overlooking sea. *Sol e Mar* (M). Both have pools.

AIGUEBELLE. *Roches Fleuries,* expensive, private beach. *Résidence Soleil* (M), no restaurant.

BORMES. *Safari,* very comfortable, pool, serves dinner only. *Belle Vue* (I). **Restaurant.** *Tonnelle des Délices* (M), very pretty, dinner only except weekends.

CAVALAIRE. *Calanque* (E), with pool and sea views; half or full board only. *Alizés* (M), on promenade. *Pergola,* and *Bonne Auberge,* both moderate. All have restaurants (M).

CAVALIÈRE. *Le Club,* on the beach, deluxe, with excellent restaurant (E); *Surplage* (E), comfortable. *Cap Nègre,* moderate.

FRÉJUS. *Les Résidences du Colombier,* expensive, 3 km (2 miles) away on the road to Banyuls, is delightfully set in a pine forest; has a good grill. **Restaurant.** *Vieux Four* (M), very friendly and attractive. Also has a few rooms. Dinner only in summer.

GASSIN. Lovely hilltop village with ruined château. **Restaurants.** *Bello Visto* (M), also has rooms, and *Auberge Verdoyante* (M).

GRIMAUD. Restaurants. *Les Santons, Bretonnière* (E); *Café de France* (M). *Gacharel* (M), local specialties.

HYÈRES. At the beach, *Pins d'Argent,* high moderate. About 13 km (8 miles) south, at **Giens,** *Provençal,* 50 rooms, pool, expensive, and *Relais du Bon Accueil,* 10 rooms, fine view, moderate.
Restaurants. *Tison d'Or* (M); *Marius* (I). *Vieux Puits* (I) is at **La Bayorre,** 3 km (1¾ miles) east.

ILE DE PORQUEROLLES. *Relais de la Poste* (E) (all-meals only), *Mas du Langoustier,* (E). *Ste-Anne,* comfortable; full board only, moderate.
Restaurants. *Auberge de l'Arche de Noé* (I), fine cooking. Some (M) rooms.

ILE DE PORT CROS. *Manoir,* full board only, very pretty site, moderate.

LES ISSAMBRES. Restaurant. *La Réserve* (M), an old favorite. Has 6 rooms.

LE LAVANDOU. *Résidence Beach* (restaurant does not serve lunches), and *Auberge La Calanque,* with garden, are expensive, *Beau Rivage* (E), (half board only) and *Belle Vue* (E), have nice view, the latter at **St-Clair**, 3 km (1¾ miles) on St-Tropez road.

Restaurants. *Vieux Port* (E), excellent fish and shell fish; *Calanque* (in hotel) (M); *Bouée* (M).

MIRAMAR. *St-Christophe*, lovely garden, private beach, deluxe. Attractive *Tour de l'Esquillon* (E), cable car down to beach. Restaurant is (M).

Restaurant. *Père Pascal* (M), with good value *menu*.

LA NAPOULE. *Ermitage du Riou*, deluxe. Has good restaurant (E) and pool. *Rocamare*, inexpensive.

Restaurant. *Oasis* (E), one of France's finest, excellent for seafood cooked in *nouvelle cuisine* style. *Auberge du Port*, good fish dishes (M).

PORT GRIMAUD. *Giraglia*, very expensive, with private beach and port, good restaurant (M).

Restaurants. *Marine* (M), *Amphitrite* (E) (in Hôtel Giraglia).

RAMATUELLE. *Baou*, expensive. Ultra-modern with marvelous view over the coast.

Restaurant. *Chez Camille*, beside beach, good *bouillabaisse* (M).

STE-MAXIME. *Belle Aurore*, expensive, good restaurant, terrace overlooking sea. *Résidence Brutus*, expensive, no restaurant. *Croisette Résidence*, moderate, no restaurant, on St-Tropez road. *Ensoleillé*, inexpensive.

At **Beauvallon**, 4½ km (2½ miles) west, *Golf*, expensive, lovely views and attractive grounds.

At **Plan-de-la-Tour**, about 10 km (6 miles) away up in the hills, tiny, charming *Ponte Romano*, expensive, with good restaurant (E) and pool.

Restaurants. *Esquinade* (M), by harbor. *Réserve* (I), on pl. Victor-Hugo. *Gruppi* (E), excellent fish dishes.

ST-RAPHAËL. *Excelsior* (M), with a pleasant view; *Beau Séjour*, moderate. *Select* (M), small, reader-recommended, no restaurant.

At **Boulouris** is *Potinière* (E), with apartments as well as rooms. Has pool and tennis courts.

Restaurants. *La Voile d'Or* (M), very special Provençal cooking. Family run *Pastorel* (M), friendly, good value. *Maison de Provence* (M), friendly. *Templiers* (I), reader-recommended.

ST-TROPEZ. *Byblos*, with pool, great view, beautifully furnished, *Résidence de la Pinède*, next to beach and in a pine wood; both deluxe and very expensive. *Mandarine*, beautifully quiet, like a small provincial village, *Résidence des Lices*, without restaurant, with pool, expensive; slightly less expensive *Ponche*, pic-

THE RIVIERA

turesque. Moderate: *Lou Troupelen, Ermitage,* neither with restaurant. *Motel St-Tropez* (M), pool, no restaurant, 3.5 km (2 miles) away.

Restaurants. *Leï Mouscardins* (E), highly recommended for seafood. *Auberge des Maures* (E) is charming and smart. Less expensive are *Palmyre, Fifine, Escale, Frégate.* For snacks, *Chez Sénéquier* and *Suffren Bar,* both also for aperitifs. At *Ramade* (M), you eat fish caught by the chef!

SEILLANS. *Hôtel des Deux Rocs,* moderate, small, beautifully decorated country inn. *France,* with pool, good restaurant (M).

THÉOULE. *Adrienne,* small, inexpensive hotel, has good value restaurant.
At **La Galère,** 1.5 km (1 mile) south: *Guerguy* is deluxe; delightful, recently redecorated rooms; lovely gardens and views. Excellent restaurant with friendly service (E).

Cannes-Menton

HOTELS AND RESTAURANTS. This is the older luxurious and cosmopolitan Riviera. Here you will find the highest prices and the most deluxe accommodations, but there are less expensive places, too.

ANTIBES. *Mapotel Tananarive* (E), with good restaurant. *Royal* (M), quiet, private beach. *Mas Djoliba* (M), with huge garden. At **Sophia-Antipolis** on the road to Grasse and rather hard to find, *Novotel Sophia Antipolis* (M), with pool, very secluded in the middle of a pine forest.

Restaurants. About 5 km (3 miles) north on N7 at **La Brague,** *La Bonne Auberge* (E), Provençal dining-room and terrace. Now owned by Jo Rostang, and one of the Riviera's top spots. *Marguerite* (E), elegant, with good value *menus. Vieux Murs* (E), chic but overpriced. *L'Auberge Provençale* (M) is better value, still rather smart. On the same square (pl. Nationale) is *Le Caméo* (M), busy, with tables outside beneath the trees. *Chez Juliette* (I) is just off the pl. Nationale and near the market, also has pizzas. *Oursin* (I), good value seafood.

BARGEMON. Restaurant. *Blanc,* friendly, rustic inn (M) though lunch only in July and Aug.

BEAULIEU-SUR-MER. *Réserve* (L), extremely luxurious interior, wonderful view, good restaurant with fine chef; *Métropole* (L), vast terrace over sea, pool, excellent food and service. Modern *Don Grégorio,* expensive, no restaurant. *Havre Bleu* and *Flora* are inexpensive. *Sélect* (I), small, reader-recommended, no restaurant.

Restaurants. *Agaves* (M), popular with readers; *La Pignatelle* (I), good for local specialties.

BIOT. Restaurants. *Café de la Poste* (M), on village square, attractive, good regional cuisine and wines. *Café des Arcades* (M), very attractive.

CAGNES. *Le Cagnard,* Provençal atmosphere, at **Haut-de-Cagnes,** expensive. *Tiercé,* moderate, no restaurant.

Restaurants. *Grimaldi,* pl. du Château, and *Douchka,* with Russian specialties. Both (M).

At **Cros-de-Cagnes,** *Auberge du Port* (I), good for fish; a few rooms.

At **Haut-de-Cagnes,** *Peintres* (I), good value, and cute *Josy-Jo* (M).

CANNES. Deluxe are the *Majestic,* with new chef; *Carlton,* 288 rooms; *Martinez-Concorde; Grand,* large rooms with balcony; *Sofitel-Méditerranée.* All are magnificently sited along the beach. *Gray d'Albion,* just behind promenade, with good *nouvelle cuisine;* ultra modern, very comfortable. *Montfleury Intercontinental* (L), with 2 pools, 10 tennis courts, ice-rink.

Expensive: *Canberra-Victoria,* twin hotels, airconditioned, no restaurant; *Savoy; Fouquet's,* very pretty, no restaurant; *Splendid; Belle Plage; Mondial; Orangers.*

Moderate: *Cheval Blanc,* older *Amirauté,* and *Wagram,* comfortable, as are *Roches Fleuries* and *Etrangers.* Modern *Campanile* (M), out by airport. Inexpensive: *Mimont,* near station, *Poste.*

Restaurants. *Mère Besson* (M), *Gaston-Gastounette* (M), the famous and always fashionable *Félix* (M), *Blue Bar* (M). *Bec Fin, Rescator* (M), *nouvelle cuisine* at reasonable prices. *Mal Assis, Coq Hardi,* all (M). *Coquille, Monaco, Poivre Vert, Pompon Blanche, Caveau Provencal,* beside Vieux Port, all (I).

10 km (6 miles) away, at **Mouans-Sartoux,** is the delicious little *Palais des Coqs* (M), and *Auberge Mourrachonne,* beautifully situated (E). On the road to **Pegomas,** *Oriental* (E) for North African specialties.

CAP D'AIL. *Normandy,* inexpensive. **Restaurant** *Balkans* (M).

CAP D'ANTIBES. *Cap Eden-Roc,* admirably situated, beautifully renovated; *Résidence du Cap,* both deluxe. *La Garoupe,* comfortable, moderate.

Restaurants. *Cap* (E), famous, exclusive, in hotel. *Cabestan* (M), delicious seafood. *Gardiole* (M), *Garoupe* (I), no lunches, both also in hotels.

COLLE-SUR-LOUP. *Marc Hély,* moderate, very quiet and comfortable, with garden but no restaurant.

Restaurants. *La Belle Epoque* is very good, particularly for delicious fish dishes (E). *Strega* (M), unpretentious, friendly.

EZE-BORD-DE-MER. *Cap Estel,* deluxe, formerly private residence, beautifully situated on point of land jutting out into sea, private beach and pool, very expensive. *Cap Roux,* with kitchenettes, no restaurant; *La Bananerie,* moderate.

EZE-VILLAGE. *Mimosa Cottage,* inexpensive.
  Restaurant. *La Chèvre d'Or* (E), worth a visit, also has rooms. *Couletta* (E), delicious 'new cuisine'. *Bergerie* (M), local dishes. *Nid d'Aigle* (M), good value *menus.*

FAYENCE. *Moulin de la Camandoule,* on the Draguignan road, in lovely leafy setting, pool, civilized attention (M), with restaurant (April through Sept. only).

GOLFE JUAN. *Jasmins* (E), on N7, 37 rooms, with pool. *Golf Motel,* also with pool, and *Golfe* are (M). *Beau Soleil,* in quiet cul-de-sac, is also moderate.
  Restaurants. *Tétou* (E) specializes in bouillabaisse. *Bistrot du Port* (M). *Chez Claude* (I), friendly atmosphere.

GRASSE. Best is *Régent,* expensive, on Nice road 3½ km (2½ miles) away, with pool and lovely views. *Bellevue,* moderate. *Oasis,* inexpensive, no restaurant.
  Restaurants. *Chez Pierre* (I). At **Opio**, 7 km east, *Mas des Géraniums* (I), friendly, also has rooms. At **Spéracédes**, *Soleillade* (I), local dishes.

JUAN-LES-PINS. Deluxe: *Juana,* with excellent restaurant, peaceful and chic, with private beach, very expensive; *Belles Rives,* less fashionable but very comfortable; *Hélios,* not quite as expensive as the other two. Expensive: *Beauséjour.* Moderate: *Pré Catalan,* nicely located, quiet, *Régence* and *Manon, Mimosas,* with garden; *Eden, Mexicana, Idéal, Midi. Admiral* (M), friendly.
  Restaurants. Best is *Terrasse* (E), in Juana Hotel, *Perroquet* (M), good. *Bijou-Plage* (M), seafood specialties. *Lou Capitole* (I).

MENTON. Newest is *Europ'Hôtel* (E), no restaurant. *Napoléon* and *Viking* (E), with pool and restaurant; *Chambord* (E), no restaurant, and *Parc* (E). Moderate: *Princess et Richmond* (no restaurant). *Carlton* (M) is comfortable: *Pin Doré, Céline-Rose.*
  Restaurants. *Francine* (E), good for seafood. *Hacienda,* on road to Gorbio, (M). *Le Nautic,* close to harbor, has good local dishes (I).

MOUGINS. *Mas Candille* (E), with pool and very good restaurant. *France* (M), good restaurant. *Vaste Horizon* (E).
  Restaurants. *Ferme de Mougins* (E), *Bistrot* (I), fine Provençal cooking.
  At **Notre-Dame-de-Vie**, 3 km (2 miles) southeast on D3: *Clos des Boyères* (E). One of France's top restaurants, for *nouvelle cuisine; Moulin de Mougins* (E). Also has 6 rooms.

MOUSTIERS-STE-MARIE. *Relais,* inexpensive.

THE FACE OF FRANCE

NICE. Deluxe: *Méridien-Nice, Hyatt-Regency,* on the promenade des Anglais but quite near the airport, *Sofitel-Splendid,* modern, with pool, solarium, bar; airconditioned. Old-established favorites: *Négresco,* elegant; *Westminster-Concorde; Plaza,* overlooking gardens and the sea; *Frantel.* A bit less expensive: *Atlantic, Pérouse, Park, Victoria, Napoléon.*

Comfortable, moderate: *Magnan, Savoie, Georges, Petit Palais, Windsor,* older *Vendôme, Little Palace* and *Des Etrangers,* in the center of town, *Résidence Azur-Etats Unis,* with studio rooms and frigidaires. *Bruxelles,* 17 rue de Belgique, is comfortable, if a little impersonal, and convenient for the main rail station and the post office. *Darcy* near railroad station, *Oasis,* quiet, *Helvétique, Flots d'Azur,* near the sea, are all inexpensive. *Petit Louvre* (I), 10 rue Emma-Tiranty, reader-recommended.

Near the airport, 105-room *Novotel* (E), recent. Some readers report this is better value for money than the older, grander hotels. Also, if you're traveling by car you're better off here as it's almost impossible to park in the center, where some roads are closed to traffic.

Restaurants. Best are *Chantecler* (E) in the Negresco Hotel, one of the very best in France for *nouvelle cuisine; Petit Brouant* (M), 4 bis rue Deloye, *Poularde* (E), across the street; *Madrigal* (M), av. Georges-Clemençeau; *L'Ane Rouge,* 7 quai Deux-Emmanuel (E).

Cassole (M), *Chez Rolando,* fashionable (M); *Rotonde* (M), although it's in the deluxe Hôtel Négresco, is surprisingly reasonable—misleadingly called a coffee shop, it in fact offers good home-style cooking in a magnificent Art Nouveau setting.

Rive Gauche, full of pretty youngsters (I), *Cave Niçoise* (I), in the pedestrian area, has been going for years and is still good value (I). *Tramway* (I), 11 rue Lamartin, rather chic with young Niçois, good value.

In the Old Town are: *Merenda* (M), 4 rue de la Terrasse; *Madrague* (I), at no. 13b is on the other side of the market, has good fish dishes, friendly service; *Chez les Pêcheurs* (M), full of atmosphere. *Safari* (I), with genuine Niçois cooking, popular with the young crowd. *Fernand la Moule* and *Taca d'Oli* are (I). A bit far out, beyond harbor, but lovely setting overlooking bay: *Coco Beach* (E), 2 av. J. Lorrain, seafood only. *Saetone* (I), 8 rue Alsace-Lorraine.

A good place to try if you're tired of seafood is *La Nissarda* (I), 17 rue Gubernatis, or *Florian,* specializing in Alsatian dishes.

Henri Auer, 7 rue St-François-de-Paule, is a splendid tearoom with 19th-cent. décor and delicious preserved fruit to take away.

PÉGOMAS. *Bosquet* (I), quiet, attractive, with pool and garden, no restaurant.

PEILLON. Lovely village. **Restaurant.** *Auberge de la Madone* (M).

ROQUEBRUNE-CAP MARTIN. *Vistaëro,* deluxe, on Grande Corniche, fabulous view, with good restaurant (E). Attractively located *Alexandra* and *Victoria* are expensive. Moderate: *Princessias, Westminster.*

Restaurants. *Roquebrune* (E), lovely views and good cuisine, mostly fish. *Lucioles* (M), lovely view over the old town. *Grand Inquisiteur* (I), in picturesque little street, good value.

ST-JEAN-CAP-FERRAT.
Grand Hotel du Cap Ferrat, isolated, exclusive, fine cuisine; *Voile d'Or,* in magnificent situation overlooking the harbor. Both deluxe. *Panoramic,* no restaurant, expensive. *Brise Marine* (M), small, modest. Restaurant open evenings only. *Clair Logis* (M), away from beach, but set in pretty grounds and very peaceful; no restaurant.

Restaurants. *Cappa* (M), av. J. Mermoz; *Petit Trianon* (M), bld Gén.-de-Gaulle. *Les Hirondelles* (E), av. J. Mermoz. There are several new restaurants beside the new marina such as *Le Sloop* (M).

ST-PAUL-DE-VENCE.
Auberge Colombe d'Or (E), charming décor and pleasant service. Pool. Paintings by Picasso, Miró and Leger. *Remparts,* moderate. Overlooking the village is the elegant, deluxe *Mas d'Artigny:* bungalows, each with its own mini-pool; also large pool, tennis. *Orangers* (E), attractive, no restaurant.

Restaurants. *Aubergo dou Souleu* (M), regional specialties. Also has rooms. *Morateur,* good home style cooking (M), also has rooms. About 1.5 km (1 mile) on D7 is *Oliviers* (E), good cuisine; garden.

TOURTOUR.
Lovely *La Bastide de Tourtour,* expensive, in a pine wood with pool, excellent restaurant (M), and the moderate *Auberge St-Pierre,* also with pool, good restaurant.

Restaurant. *Chênes Verts,* good local specialties (E). *Chez Francine* (M), good.

TURINI.
Trois-Vallées (M), with restaurant.

VALBONNE.
Restaurant. *St-Bernadin* (I), very popular, must reserve.

VENCE.
Château du Domaine St-Martin, about 3 km (2 miles) north, deluxe, with pool, wonderful views, and excellent restaurant (E). The *Diana,* in town, is moderate. No restaurant.

Restaurants. *Auberge des Seigneurs* (M), is a Provençal inn serving excellent regional specialties. *Farigoule* (I); *Portiques* (M). At **Tourette-sur-Loup** 6 km away, *Belles Terrasses* (I), very attractive. Logis de France.

VILLEFRANCHE-SUR-MER.
Versailles, expensive, with pool. *Provençal* (M), interesting paintings; *Welcome* (E), at the port, with good restaurant; *Darse* (M), no restaurant.

Restaurants. *La Mère Germaine* (E), best of waterside places. *Frégate* (M). *Campanette* (M), attractive, in picturesque street in Old Town above harbor; regional dishes cooked in *nouvelle cuisine* style. Open evenings only.

VILLENEUVE-LOUBET. Modern motels: *Baie des Anges* (M), with restaurant. Some rooms with kitchenettes. *Méditerranée, Palerme,* and *Pesage.* All moderate, no restaurants.

Restaurant. *Singe Nu* (M), Chemin Batterie, excellent.

RENTING A VILLA. If you plan to stay for a month or over, and particularly if you have children, it can work out cheaper to rent a villa or apartment. Write *France-Accueil* office, 32 rue de l'Hôtel des Postes, 06000 Nice, for a list of rental agents in Nice, or the tourist office of the town where you want to rent. There are multitudes of villa specialists, particularly in London: contact the French National Tourist Office for a complete list. Most of the good villas are taken by Apr. or May—some as early as Jan., so don't count on getting one at the last moment. Renting sight-unseen can be risky; it's best to try to visit the area yourself ahead of time, or get a friend to do so. Most villas are completely furnished, except for linen, and maids are occasionally available. For rentals in the hinterlands, try the *Gîtes Ruraux* (see 'Facts at your Fingertips').

CASINOS. This is casino-land par excellence, with Cannes, Nice, Juan-les-Pins, Antibes and Monte Carlo offering any number of opportunities to toy with the dream of 'breaking the bank'. Cannes's glamorous Palm Beach Casino is now open year-round and a chic new municipal casino opened in 1982. Nice's Ruhl Casino, ultra-modern, with a grand cabaret where a floor show in the style of the Paris Lido is staged every night, was having financial and other problems at our presstime. Nice's new congress center, due to open in the pl. Masséna in 1984, will include a new municipal casino. Beaulieu's less frenetic casino has a discotheque every night and is unusual in offering open-air *boule* tables in summer, as well as roulette, chemin-de-fer and blackjack.

NIGHTCLUBS. There are altogether five nightclub centers on the Riviera—St-Tropez, Cannes, Juan-les-Pins, Nice and Monte Carlo (see next chapter). St-Tropez in June, the beginning of July, and Sept. caters to an eclectic combination of very rich European society, the French movie crowd (Brigitte Bardot owns a villa in nearby, secluded Madrague), refugees from St-Germain-des-Prés and nice young things from Paris's wealthy neighborhoods. In Aug. St-Trop is invaded by people from all over France and Europe, is crowded, smelly, noisy and not even very French. Cannes is still elegant; international café society has made its casinos and nightclubs a name-dropper's paradise. Juan-les-Pins is the honky-tonk Riviera. It blazes with gaudy nightclubs and bars on the lines of Paris's Pigalle. Nice has the Ruhl and an additional batch of nightclubs, most of which have floorshows. There are hundreds of discos along the coast these days.

THE RIVIERA

CANNES. *Palm Beach Casino* is also stylish and exclusive, one of the elegant places in Cannes. *Whisky-à-Gogo,* 115 av. de Lérins. Discotheque, relaxed atmosphere.

Other discotheques are *Lord Club,* sq. Brougham; *Le Privé de la Chunga,* 72 La Croisette (opposite Hôtel Martinez), open until dawn; *Cyrano,* 26 rue Meynadier (closed Sun.). The décor at *Le Charleston* nightclub, 5 rue Lafontaine, includes a fascinating collection of turn-of-the-century posters. *Blue Moon,* Port Canto, has a panoramic view over the harbor. *Play Girl Club,* av. de Lérins, and *Roxy Club-La Chimère,* 10 rue Teisseire, specialize in entertainment by the third sex.

At **Valbonne,** 12 km (7½ miles) from Cannes in the mountains, are the two most fashionable nightclubs of the area: the *Val de Cuberte,* with its swimming pool where all the best people end up fully-clothed (it's part of the legend, like Ethel Kennedy's pool at Hickory Hill), and the exotically decorated, but comfortable discotheque, *Akou-Akou,* which also has a pool; you can spend your entire day here, as well as most of the night.

JUAN-LES-PINS. Nightlife in Juan these days is very much for the young crowd. If you're close to 20 and like a lot of noise try *Cha in Cha* or *Jackie O* (with restaurant and private yacht harbor)—otherwise we recommend you stick to the *Siesta* at Antibes (see below).

ANTIBES. *La Siesta,* a beach club-cum-nightclub that holds 3,000 people and has every gimmick you could want down to a restaurant for dogs, boutiques, open-air bars with dance-floors, illuminated waterfalls, flaming torches, corners for flirting, eating, dancing. Also karting, bowling, casino. Fun all day and all night.

NICE. Nice has a much more ambitious nightlife than Cannes. The show at the Ruhl Casino rivals those in Las Vegas or the Paris Lido (but check that it has reopened after extended closure in the early 80s). A favorite with the *Niçois* is *La Pignata,* 242 chemin de Fabron, dinner and comic show; best to know French. There's even a mini-*corrida* in summer! *Au Pizzaiolo,* 4 bis rue du Pont-Vieux, has a crazy madcap show, includes singing waiters, imitations, etc.

Among discotheques are: *La Chunga,* 6 rue Masséna; *Cha-Cha,* at no. 19 in same pedestrians-only street. Other lively places are *O'Samba,* pl. Vieille in Old Town; *Chat Noir,* 24 Cours Saleya (by flower market).

ST-TROPEZ. The in place is *Les Caves du Roy,* in the Byblos hotel. Next, the *Papagayo.* Also *Krak du Chevalier* in the Byblos, and *L'Esquinade.*

MONACO

Glittering principality

A sunlit paradise of mountain, seas and vegetation, Monaco is one of the tiniest countries in the world. Its shores are swept by the Mediterranean, its back is shielded by the Alps, and its frontiers are controlled by France. With 33 sq km (13 sq miles) of fun and flowers, its population normally at 27,000 may swell fourfold during the tourist peak.

In 1982, this tiny nation was the sad focus of world attention when the beautiful American princess, formerly Grace Kelly, died after a road accident. She had helped to create a vibrant social and cultural life for the principality and was sincerely mourned.

Legends about Monaco are legion, and one of the most firmly entrenched is that the people pay no personal income taxes because all government expenses are financed through the proceeds of the world's most famous casino. While it is true that the citizens of Monaco, the Monégasques, are less burdened by taxes than most of the rest of us, the actual fact is that the casino provides only between 2 and 4 percent of the annual budget. And if you dream of becoming Monégasque to save on income tax, you'd better give up the idea right now. Monégasque citizenship is one of the hardest in the world to obtain, and is not given automatically even to everyone born and raised in the principality. There are only 4,000 Monégasque citizens, and 1,500 of them are employed by the Government, another 500 by the Societé des Bains de Mer, which operates the casino, the Monte Carlo Golf Club, Jimmy'z nightclub, the Country Club, the leading hotels, to mention but a few. The remainder of the population is basically French or Italian, some of whom have been settled here for generations.

The principality, until recently, consisted of three towns: the ancient community of Monaco, built on a rock with the cathedral, the prince's palace, and its famous Oceanographic Museum; La Condamine, where business thrives and the Monégasques live; Monte Carlo, where stuccoed mansions are being replaced by high-rise hotels and apartment buildings. On land reclaimed from the sea, Monaco's fourth town, Fontvielle, is a rising industrial area.

New ports have been built to house a growing flotilla of pleasure craft; almost 22 hectares (55 acres) of land have been reclaimed from the sea in an effort to provide more space for Monégasques, and, more particularly, beaches for tourists. In fact, over the past 20 years, Monaco has beaten all world records for peaceful territorial expansion, increasing its area by 20 percent. The skyline which a few years ago knew nothing but palm trees and the delicately colored villas of the wealthy, now bristles with tall new buildings, and the important new conference and congress center opened here in 1979 is adding considerably to the already active business life of what people wrongly believe to be nothing but a sun-drenched playground. Inevitably, traffic congestion can occur at times.

Miraculously enough Monaco has still retained something of the operetta-like charm that made it internationally famous for years. The principality's palm-lined avenue still teems with sleek sports cars, but the clientele no longer consists exclusively of the rich and the famous. Monaco has become more democratic, and therefore less glamorous, though Prince Rainier and his family still live in the royal palace on the promontory jutting out to sea, and the port is still filled with gigantic luxury cruisers and slim sailboats from all over the world, often crewed by one-time British or German naval personnel.

Monaco's royal family

Despite its minuscule army renowned for tall shakos and fancy dress, Monaco maintains firm representation abroad with 95 chancelleries and consultates. She flaunts all the attributes of a grown-up state plus the pomp and circumstance that accompany royalty. Her history can be traced back to the seafaring Phoenicians; later from this port, Caesar sailed with his legions to meet Pompey. Monaco has been a sovereign, independent state since its restoration to Prince Honoré V of the ancient Grimaldi family (originally from Genoa) by the victorious Allies in 1815, after the Napoleonic Wars.

Prince Albert I of Monaco, who died in 1925, was world-famous for his oceanographic researches (the cabin of his ship, with the scientific instruments invented by him, may be seen in the Musée Océanographique, which includes the world's largest aquarium); he found time also to endow his country, in 1911, with a democratic constitution, and at the same time to increase its prosperity in a spectacular fashion.

The present ruler, Rainier III, the 30th descendant of the Grimaldi dynasty, which has ruled Monaco since the early Middle Ages, is one of the world's most titled monarchs, with 24 official titles. In fact, the Grimaldi are Europe's oldest reigning dynasty.

Welcome to Monaco

Monaco is the easiest state to visit in all the world today. No customs officers burrow into your carefully packed valises, and no police subject your passport to suspicious scrutiny as you cross, without stopping, the frontier between this extraordinary little country and France. Near the Monte Carlo post office, the frontier plunges through town without anything to mark it. The only hardship that a Monégasque may encounter is that he is forbidden entry to the casino's gambling rooms. However, he can attend its theater, a tiny Second Empire masterpiece designed by the architect of the Paris opera house, which has been the scene of many notable premières, including a number of those presented by Diaghilev when Nijinski was the star of the Ballets Russes.

Everything about Monaco gives an impression of contrasts, real and unreal, old and modern. Most picturesque is the medieval neighborhood, Le Rocher, just a block from the palace.

Climb up (you must always climb up or down in Monaco) to the prince's palace. If you arrive at noon you will see the changing of the guard in its toy-like setting under the crenelated tower which dominates the courtyard ringed by small cannons, each with its heap of well-piled cannon balls. This setting and the ceremony conducted by

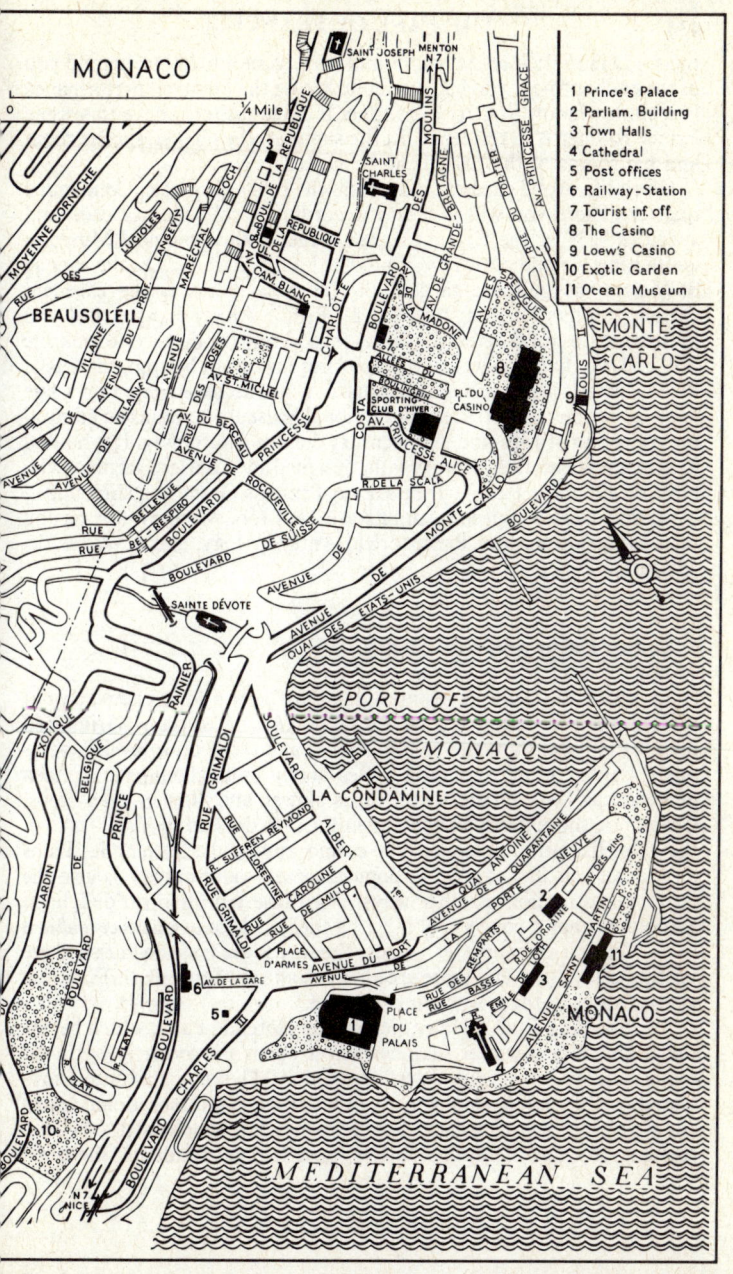

the soldiers in their *opéra bouffe* uniforms cannot help but remind you of the enchantment you had as a child seeing the identical performance in a store window at Christmas time. If a flag flutters above this scene Prince Rainier is in residence. In the summer, the chapel, throne room and ballrooms of the palace can be visited.

Go to the exotic gardens laid out on the rocks above the Condamine quarter. There you will find an extraordinary collection of cacti and succulents. Near the Exotic Garden is the Anthropological Museum, containing Roman antiquities found at La Condamine. On the avenue St-Martin, beyond the gardens of the same name, is the excellent Oceanographic Museum founded by Prince Albert I, a learned and industrious natural scientist. Here, in addition to displays of marine life, you will find apparatus for exploring the ocean bottom, models of fishing vessels and the famous aquarium in the basement. For a fine view, go to the roof-terrace. The National Museum contains an admirable collection of 18th-and 19th-century dolls and automata. It is housed in a magnificent 19th-century villa designed by Charles Garnier (who built the Opera in Paris) on the avenue Princess Grace and surrounded by a rose garden. Special exhibits are held too. Monaco also has an interesting Museum of Prehistorical Anthropology, and a Waxworks Museum.

Monte Carlo and the casino

To break the bank at Monte Carlo has been a long-cherished but seldom-realized dream. *'Faites vos jeux. Rien ne va plus.'* Grimfaced men watch intently while young lovelies and older once-lovelies nervously tighten mink and satin stoles about their shoulders. A hush descends as the roulette wheel turns slower and slower, then stops. Croupiers, those deadpan gentlemen for ever dressed in black, rake in the chips like autumn leaves. The casino, run by the Société des Bains de Mer (it was first formed to popularize sea-water cures!), is also the center of attraction in other ways. For those who find no delight in gambling it has a concert-room and a theater: Monte Carlo can afford to pay for first-class artistes. Across the way is the Café de Paris, where visiting celebrities (and there are always some at Monte Carlo) sip their aperitif or take their after-dinner coffee.

The Sporting Club d'Hiver, next to the Hôtel de Paris, which begins the Monte Carlo winter season when it opens its doors, is world famous, and jealously guards its reputation. The smart Monte Carlo Country Club holds, among many other events, an international tennis championship, which attracts the big names and which used to be won regularly by one of Monte Carlo's most famous residents, the great

MONACO

Bjorn Borg. And other important sports events are held here throughout the year.

August is the season if you want to see the rich at play, though nowadays they're more likely to be industrial magnates or oil millionaires than princes and filmstars. Come along the avenue Princess Grace to the Monte Carlo Beach—in French territory—where the bathing costumes are sometimes too fragile or too costly to be exposed even to the mild rigors of the Mediterranean. The beach, where the casino crowd suns away the day, is entirely manmade. Workmen must continuously replace its fine imported white sand. About the luxurious pool, multicolored parasols tilt their cheerful heads as the world's most pampered citizens bake or soak in the warm, filtered waters. Later they may saunter to the restaurant for a bite or amble down to one of the tiny luxury bungalows, coveted for holding private beach parties. Between noon and two, yachts from Cannes or San Remo anchor in the small harbor while their moneyed masters cocktail ashore at La Pointe.

At the Cinema d'Eté, each day for two months, a newly released film is shown to an indolent public, comfortably seated on an open-air terrace. Sometimes there is a dazzling ball, when outstanding artists are heard while a dance orchestra plays beneath the stars beside a twinkling ocean.

Beyond the casino, between port and beach, a complex of new hotels, restaurants, apartment blocks, swimming pools and a marina has been built. All this is changing Monaco's character, making it a modern tourist center, rather than the domain of the nobility.

A thrill for spectators is provided by Monaco's Grand Prix for formula one cars, which is held in May and counts towards the Championship. The world famous and spectacular Monte Carlo Rally is held each January.

Despite its carefree atmosphere, a great deal of very serious business is carried on in Monaco. But it is kept discreetly in the background. To all appearances, the tourist is king, and this tiny yet sophisticated toyland exists but to amuse itself and its guests.

Word of warning: Monaco has its own postage stamps, so don't try using French ones, even if you don't feel you've crossed a frontier!

PRACTICAL INFORMATION

WHEN TO GO. Winter and spring have traditionally been the smart seasons, but with the increase in the numbers of less wealthy tourists, the seasons extend to both winter and summer. The winter season is marked by fancy dress balls and sporting events. Excellent opera, concerts, theater and ballet are offered in the casino theater and the opera house. **January** features yachting regattas, and the procession and symbolic burning of a wooden ship honoring the patron Ste Dévote (27 Jan.). The renowned Monte Carlo Rally is held in this month, though Monaco is only the finishing point for the rally.

February to end **April:** many golf tournaments and the International Monte Carlo Tennis Championships, and the pre-Lenten Carnival. On Good Friday, bracketed torches flare along the narrow streets as white-robed figures beat black-draped drums, and there is a procession from the pl. de la Mairie. **Easter:** International Open Tennis Tournament. The big event of **May** is the Monaco motoring Grand Prix, but there are also many concerts and other events; and an international Bridge Tournament is staged in **June.** In **July** and **August** there are concerts in the palace courtyard (tickets available from the Opera House). **November 19** is the national holiday. Sports events held throughout fall culminate in Christmas tennis and golf tournaments. **December:** International Circus Festival. This month also sees the start of the Monte Carlo International Arts Festival, with ballet, theater and concerts continuing right through to April.

HOW TO GET ABOUT. By air. An efficient helicopter service links Monaco with Nice airport in only 6 minutes. There is also a regular bus service. **By train.** For rail services to Monaco see the previous chapter on the Riviera. The principality has one station, called Monaco–Monte Carlo. In summer the Métrazur rail service has trains running between Cannes and Menton every half-hour.

By bus. *Europabus* has a service Antwerp – Brussels – Rheims – Dijon – Lyon – Avignon – Cannes – Nice – Menton stopping at Monte Carlo, which is useful for those trying to combine visits to several centers in France or Europe. *Europabus* also has an excursion four times weekly from Cannes via the Grande Corniche and La Turbie to the Italian border; stops for lunch and sightseeing tour of Monte Carlo/Monaco. Regular bus service along the coast between Nice and Menton.

By car. The best approach to Monaco by road is via one of the Corniche drives (Shoreline or Middle) from Nice (for routes to Nice from the north, consult the chapter on the Riviera).

MONACO

USEFUL ADDRESSES. *Direction du Tourisme et des Congrès,* 2a bld des Moulins, Monte Carlo. In Paris the *Office de Tourisme de la Principauté de Monaco* is at 9 rue de la Paix, 2e.

American Express: 35 bld Princesse Chalotte (exchange office); also at 3–5 av. de Monte Carlo. The Crédit Foncier de Monaco has an exchange office in the place du Casino, open daily, including Sun. and public holidays, 10 A.M. to midnight. *Wagon-Lits Cook,* 2 av. des Spélugues. *Consulates:* see the Riviera chapter for addresses in Marseille; **Car hire** *Avis,* 9 av. d'Ostende. *Hertz,* 57 rue Grimaldi.

The *Société des Bains de Mer* is a good source for information about events sporting and cultural and just plain fun. Write to them in Monaco (no address needed) or in Paris: 24 rue Marbeuf, 75008 Paris. They publish a list of events twice a year. Hotel reservations for the SBM hotels are handled in London by David Adams, Society Hotels, Sherwood St., Piccadilly, London W.1 (tel. 01-439 9751) and in the US by SBM at 505 Park Avenue, New York, NY 10022 (tel. (212)-688-98-90).

In the US: *Monaco Government Tourist and Convention Bureau,* 20 East 49th Street, New York, NY 10017. In Britain: *Monaco Government Tourist Office and Convention Office,* 34 Sackville St, London W1X 1DB.

HOTELS AND RESTAURANTS. Most hotels and restaurants in Monaco are, needless to say, the last word in luxury. But it is possible to find relatively inexpensive accommodations and you can eat well for surprisingly little, especially at lunchtime, when many restaurants have moderately priced set menus. Most locals seek restaurants with tables outside at lunchtime, so make sure you get there before 1 to be sure of a table. The range is wide, from simple family meals in bistrots and cafés to exquisitely served meals under the frescoed ceilings of the Rococo Hôtel de Paris. Hotels and restaurants listed *L, E, M, I,* are deluxe, expensive, moderate and inexpensive.

Hotels. The *Hôtel de Paris* (L), is incomparable, not only the best in Monaco but one of the best in all Europe. Next on the list comes *Hermitage* (L), just behind it. Both are near the Casino. Also (L), but modern and without the grandeur of the first two, are *Loew's,* built on stilts below the old casino, with good restaurant (called *Foie Gras*), *Mirabeau* and *Beach Plaza*. *Balmoral* (E) isn't chic, but old-fashioned and pleasant.

Poste (I), in an old alley below the casino, is quiet, with particularly good-value rates in winter. Also quiet and (I) is *Cosmopolite,* in rue de la Turbie behind the station. *France* (I) is on same street.

Restaurants. The best food in the principality is undoubtedly found at *P'tit Bec* (E), 11 av. de Grande-Bretagne. *Bec Rouge* (E) is under same management. The chic local residents flock to *Salle Empire* (E) in the Hôtel de Paris, one of the world's most elegant eating places. On the eighth floor of the same hotel is the famous *Grill* (E), with a sliding roof and a large charcoal fire. Across the road is the *Café de Paris* (M), where people go to be seen and often eat very little, sometimes just a hamburger with a carafe of local wine. *Restaurant du Port* (M), with Italian cuisine, is very popular, with tables outside even in winter. Another place to be seen is *Pinnochio* (E), up on the Rock; immensely chic, if somewhat cramped and overpriced. *Monte-Carlo Beach Club* (E), actually on French territory, is a truly glamorous place for lunch and a swim; perhaps best for a drink, as tourists can feel like outsiders.

For delicious food in an unpretentious atmosphere, old-fashioned *Costa Rica* (M). *Maison du Caviar* (M) has an atmosphere of days long gone and an excellent set lunch menu. Again thought highly of by local people is *Salon du Privé* (M) in the casino (dinner only), where you can watch the roulette players and the sea below. *Rampoldi* (M), av. Spélugues, is another favorite.

On the Rock and around the marketplace is a whole series of pleasant and excellent-value places. Or you may be tempted by the marvelous morning markets on pl. d'Armes and behind St Charles's church into organizing a picnic on the rocks beyond the exclusive Yacht Club by the harbor.

GAMBLING. The famed Monte Carlo Casino is operated by the Société des Bains de Mer, which pays the Monaco government for the right to operate its gambling monopoly. In addition to Monégasques, inhabitants of neighboring French districts, minors, soldiers, and certain public officials are forbidden entrance. Admission to the public gaming rooms (open 10 A.M. to 2 A.M.) is about 30 frs. Entrance to the private rooms *(Salles Privées)* costs considerably more. They do not open until 4 P.M. Indicated at each table is the minimum stake *(unité de mise)*, which may vary from about 10 frs up. Stakes or bets are placed with counters or chips of different colors that represent various sums in French frs. These are sold and redeemed in the gaming rooms. Roulette, baccara, chemin-de-fer, trente-et-quarante, boule, craps and blackjack are played. In fact, the main room has been christened the *Salle des Amériques* and has two crap tables, two or three blackjack tables and two American-style roulette tables (American-style roulette is played with fewer people and each person has different-colored chips). Slot machines (made in Chicago) are scattered about here and there.

The gaming rooms in Loew's Casino are open daily at 1 P.M. Entrance is free.

NIGHTLIFE. The place to be seen (if you can afford it) is the elegant *Monte-Carlo Sporting Club,* a restaurant and nightclub complex by the sea which includes a gaming room, the *Maona* restaurant, *Jimmy'z, Chez Regine,* nightclub queen Régine's spot (open May-Sept.), pool, and the *Salle des Etoiles* for dancing and big shows. *Jimmy'z d'hiver* is the winter version of the disco in the Casino.

During the winter season, the *Sporting d'Hiver* and the *Cabaret du Casino* (open Dec.-June), provide dancing and spectacular shows. The casino theater offers excellent opera, concerts, theater and ballet.

Popular nightspots are: *Parady'z; Living Room; Tiffany's* (disco); *Boccaccio* and *Gregory's . . . after dark,* both on av. Princess Grace and open year-round. *Folie Russe,* in Loew's hotel.

Out of town, on av. Winston Churchill (rte du Littoral), Robert Viale's *Pirate* and *Les Frères de la Côte* attract the young from both Italy and France.

PROVENCE AND THE CAMARGUE

Rome away from Rome

No other region of France is so steeped in history as Provence, so blessed by nature, so full of beautiful things to see. The Romans called it *provincia*—the province—for it was the first part of Gaul they occupied and needed no further name. Then, from the 9th to the 15th centuries it was an independent realm, ruled by kings and counts, and right up to the Revolution it retained some of this autonomy. Today Provence Cote d'Azur is just one among the 22 administrative regions of France. But it has kept alive its traditions and folklore and is justly proud of its glorious past, of the Romans and troubadours, Popes and princes that forged its history, and of its beautiful old Provençal language.

PROVENCE AND THE CAMARGUE

It is a land on which history lies in thick layers. The Romans have left their finest remains outside Italy here—there is Nîmes and the Pont du Gard, Arles and St-Rémy, Orange and Vaison. Superb medieval abbeys and churches are everywhere, many of them in purest Romanesque style. And there are sophisticated modern cities too, for places like Aix and Avignon are anything but dead museum-towns: they possess a vibrant life of their own.

It is a land of clear, dazzling light and pure Mediterranean landscapes, of fertile plains and dry limestone hills. Slender cypresses stand beside red-roofed farmsteads, and the air is heavy with the scent of lavender or alive with the whirr of cicada. These are the harsh, brightly-colored landscapes that inspired Van Gogh and Cezanne and that pulsate through many of their finest paintings.

This chapter covers western and central Provence (the previous one dealt with the Provençal coast to the east, from Marseille to Menton, known as the Côte d'Azur or Riviera).

Nîmes, Uzès and the Pont du Gard

At the western gateway to Provence, on the border of Languedoc, stands the city of Nîmes. It was for long a center of defiance against Paris and played a leading role in the 16th- and 17th-century Protestant revolts. Today, it is an industrial center (fruit-canning, shoes and textiles) but also has the typically sleepy feel of the Midi. It calls itself 'the Rome of France'—an exaggeration, though it does contain two of the finest Roman remains in Europe. One is the majestic Arena, well preserved, which held 21,000 spectators. The other is the graceful Maison Carrée ('square house'), built by Agrippa as a temple in Hellenic style. It has delicate carvings above its fluted Ionic columns, while its interior is a museum of Gallo-Roman art (note the statue of Apollo and the Venus of Nîmes).

In addition, next to the ornate 18th-century Garden of the Fountain, are the ruins of a temple of Diana, all that remains of the big thermal center the Romans built beside a gushing spring. From here a path leads up to the Tour Magne, a massive tower on a hilltop that the Romans put up probably as a watchtower (fine views from its summit). In town, the old quarter of Nîmes north of the Arena has some attractive Renaissance houses. The Musée des Beaux Arts contains a splendid Roman mosaic.

North of Nîmes, a road winds over dry scrub-covered hills, known as *la garrigue,* to the enchanting little medieval town of Uzès, seat of a great ducal family that can be traced back to Charlemagne. They still live in their romantic-looking castle above the town, built in a mixture of styles from early feudal via Renaissance to 19th century. Uzès has many fascinating old streets and buildings: notably, the arcaded Place aux Herbes, and the Tour Fenestrelle, a curious circular six-story bell-tower, of a kind common in north Italy but in France unique to Uzès.

South of here is the famous Pont du Gard, one of the grandest and most elegant of Roman monuments. It was built in 19 B.C. as an aqueduct to carry water to Nîmes. Very much later, Napoleon, the modern Emperor, repaired it. It is 900-ft long and consists of three tiers (you can walk along the top, so long as you're not afraid of heights). The stones weigh up to 6 tons each, and engineers today still find the whole construction a marvel.

South of Nîmes, the small town of St-Gilles is worth visiting for its 12th-century abbey church, with marvelously vivid sculptures on its Romanesque facade. In the crypt is the tomb of St-Gilles, a 7th-century hermit who, according to legend, sailed from Greece to Provence on a raft. Little remains now of the great medieval monastery that flourished here. However, you can still inspect Le Vis, a curious spiral staircase with roofed-over steps, giving a funnel effect.

Amid the lagoons and marshes of the coast southwest of Nîmes is the imposing walled medieval city of Aigues-Mortes, a kind of maritime Carcassonne. Here St-Louis set sail for the Seventh Crusade in 1248; here today 4,000 people still live within the ramparts. At one corner is the Tower of Constance, once used as political prison: on some walls you can still read the brave and poignant graffiti of the prisoners.

The Camargue: horses, bulls and flamingoes

These 300-square-miles of lagoons and marshy plains in the Rhône delta are a haunting region like none other in France. Birds and animals in rich variety here lead their special life; herds of half-wild white horses roam the marshes; and at dusk a flock of pink flamingoes may soar up from the reeds. The northern part of the Camargue near Arles, desalinated after the war, is now France's main rice-growing area. To the south is the large lake of Vaccarès, now the center of a Nature Reserve with many unusual wild plants and flowers: special permission is needed to enter, but even from outside you can often see flamingoes and other birds by driving along the lake's east side to the Gacholle lighthouse.

The Camargue is divided into 30 private ranches, each with its own herd *(manade)* of bulls and horses, cohabiting happily. The bulls are not bred to die in the local corridas, but for the more harmless sport of *courses à la cocarde* (see Arles, below). The famous white horses are sturdy, hardy animals with short legs, yet nimble and amenable; they

PROVENCE AND THE CAMARGUE

are not put in stables but left out free at night. They are hired out to tourists—this is a great place for a riding holiday—and you can gallop alone across the marshes, or go in a group with one of the local *gardians* who look after the herds. Known as 'the aristocrats of the Camargue,' these tough, gipsy-like men and women live out on the marshes in remote thatched cottages. One of their annual rituals is the *ferade* (branding of yearlings), which takes place amid much drinking and jollity and has become a popular tourist spectacle. There are museums of Camargue history, traditions and wildlife at the Pont de Rousty on N570 and at Les Saintes-Maries-de-la-Mer.

There are still some true gipsies in the Camargue, though today their caravans are all motorized. Every May gipsies from many lands gather at Les Saintes-Maries for their famous and colorful festival. This little town by the sand-dunes is partly an unkempt bathing-resort, partly a center of strange legend: Mary Magdalene and two other holy Marys are said to have arrived here in a boat without sails, together with Sarah, their African servant, who today is the gipsies' patron saint. Her shrine is in the crypt of the town's curious tall fortified church, built in the 11th century as a defence against the Saracens.

Arles, from Rome to Van Gogh; Les Baux and Tarascon

Arles breathes history in its every stone. In Roman days it was a major trade center and key port on the lower Rhône, rivaling Marseille. The Romans made it capital of Provence and then of the 'three Gauls' (France, Spain, Britain). Later it became a powerhouse of early Christianity (St. Augustine was here consecrated first bishop of Canterbury). In the 10th century it was the capital of a sizeable kingdom, but then it fell into decline. Today, a sleepy town of 50,000 people, it contains an astonishing wealth of monuments and museums that tell of Roman and medieval glories.

Chronologically, they are as follows: the Arena (46 B.C.) was one of the largest in the Roman world, holding 25,000 spectators, and is still in good condition. It was used for gladiatorial contests and fights with wild beasts. Today, this gory tradition continues with bullfights in the summer. But it is also the scene of the gentler sport of *courses à la cocarde*, when young men compete to pluck cockades from the horns of young bulls.

The Roman Theater, begun under Augustus, is today a ruin, though its two surviving columns are impressive. A drama and music festival is held here in July. By the Rhône, the vast baths of Constantine are all that remain of the palace built by that emperor. Nearby, the Museum of Pagan Art offers a rich display of Greek and Roman works, found locally, including statues of Venus and Augustus and Greek sarcophagi.

Early Christian sarcophagi, richly carved, are in the Museum of Christian Art, formerly a Jesuit chapel. From here, steps lead down to the huge basement gallery that the Romans built below their Forum and used as a granary. In the southeast suburbs, yet more sarcophagi are to be seen at Les Alyscamps, a wide tree-lined avenue that was one of the most fashionable cemeteries of early Christendom. Back in town, the ex-cathedral of St-Trophîme is famous for the rich carvings on its 12th-century Romanesque portal, a contrast with the interior's cool simplicity. The adjacent cloister is probably the loveliest in Provence: note the graceful marble pillars, the vivid carvings on the capitals, and the tapestries in a side-chapel.

The Réattu Museum, in a former priory of the Knights of Malta, brings a leap forward in time: its eclectic art displays include some Brussels tapestries bizarrely depicting the Wonders of the World; works by Léger and other modern masters; and a set of satirical colored cartoons by Picasso. After this, another abrupt change of mood is needed for a visit to the Muséon Arlaten, by far the best folklore museum in Provence, lovingly assembled by the great Provençal poet Frédéric Mistral (1830–1914). Here you'll find a fascinating array of costumes, coiffures, puppets, mascots, tableaux of rural life, and much else. Alas, the famed Arlésienne beauties no longer use the lovely local costumes for daily wear, only for special festivals.

Northeast of Arles you should visit Montmajour, Les Baux, St-Rémy and Tarascon. Built on a low hill, the former Benedictine abbey of Montmajour dates from the 10th century and was once a wealthy and powerful religious center. Today it is partly ruined, but still worth seeing for its lofty donjon (inner tower), its Romanesque church and crypt and charming cloister. The nearby chapel of Ste-Croix is another Romanesque gem. Further east, on a hill outside Fontvieille, is the windmill that inspired Alphonse Daudet's stories, *Lettres de mon Moulin:* the mill can be visited, and contains a small Daudet museum.

A little further on, the mysterious ghost-village of Les Baux perches on a spur of the craggy Alpilles hills. The ruined castle here was the home of one of the great feudal families of medieval France. First it was a center of the 'Courts of Love,' where troubadours sang. Then it was the stronghold of a cruel despot who kidnapped local people in order that they might amuse him by jumping to their deaths from the clifftop. Les Baux then fell into decay and today is largely deserted. You can walk up past the village's souvenir shops to the gaunt castle above, with its fine view over the valley. A visit by moonlight is a haunting experience.

PROVENCE AND THE CAMARGUE

Just south of St-Rémy is ancient Glanum, where you can see the remains of Greek houses and of Roman baths and temples; there is also a small, well-preserved Roman triumphal arch and a cenotaph honouring two grandsons of Augustus. Close by, the former priory of St-Paul-de-Mausole (lovely Romanesque chapel and cloister) is now a mental home: Vincent Van Gogh was a patient here after cutting off his ear in Arles. In St-Rémy is a museum of Greek and Gallo-Roman finds from Glanum.

Westwards a road leads to Maillane, where Mistral lived: his house is now a museum. Further on is Tarascon, where King René's splendid medieval turreted castle stands above the Rhône. Inside, there is an elegant inner court with a minstrels' gallery, and a spacious banqueting-hall. The castle was subsequently used as a prison: on one wall are the pathetic graffiti of English seamen captured in the 18th century. Tarascon is famous also as the setting of Daudet's *Tartarin* novels, and for the weird ancient legend of St Martha and the Tarasque. The saint, so the tale goes, found the town terrorized by a child-devouring dragon whom no knight could defeat. But St Martha did so, with the sign of the Cross. She is venerated in the lovely Gothic church that bears her name; and the dragon, the Tarasque, is the subject of a quaint annual pageant.

Across the river lies Beaucaire, with its half-ruined hilltop castle (fine views). From the 13th to 19th centuries the town was the site of Europe's greatest annual trade fair.

Avignon and the Palace of the Popes

Though 14th-century ramparts, (much restored 500 years later) ring the noble city of Avignon, the city itself is dominated by the giant fortress-like hulk of the Palace of the Popes, often called Europe's greatest medieval building. Finding Rome too corrupt and disorderly, the Papacy moved here in 1307 and set about building their palace. The popes ruled in it till 1377, then officially moved back to Rome. However, a number of cardinals contested the return. They stayed in Avignon and elected an Antipope, thereby precipitating the Great Schism of the West which was to last till 1449.

The palace is in two contrasting parts, the result of having been built in two phases by two very different popes. Benedict XII's 'old palace' reflects his own austerity (he had been a Cistercian monk); the 'new palace,' on the other hand, is far more ornate. It was built by Clement VI who loved the arts and high living. In his day, Avignon was a city of luxury, pomp and loose morals—to the fury of some puritans at court such as the poet Petrarch who called it 'a sink of vice.' The guided tour (not to be missed, despite dense crowds in summer) will enable you to see the very worldly decor in Clement's bedroom and study, clear evidence of his less than entirely spiritual tastes. There is much else to admire too—frescos, tapestries, portraits—in this vast labyrinth of corridors, halls and chapels. The palace is also the focal point of Avignon's famous drama festival in July.

Close by, the 12th-century cathedral contains the tomb of Pope John XXII in flamboyant Gothic. From here it is a short walk to the hilltop garden of the Rocher des Doms, with a fine view. Below, on the Rhône, is the half-ruined 12th-century bridge of St-Bénézet, the 'pont d'Avignon' of the well-known song. The best museums in town are the Petit Palais (splendid French and Italian paintings of the 13th to 15th centuries) and Calvet (variable French 16th- to 20th-century works). It is also worth strolling in the narrow streets of the old town south of the palace. You will quickly note that Avignon today is an unusually sophisticated and lively town, with an air of youthful *joie de vivre*—a place that even Parisians admit to be fashionable.

Just across the Rhône is Villeneuve-lès-Avignon, formerly a fortress town: hence its two major military buildings, the Tower of Philippe le Bel and the Fort St-André. Also worth seeing are the enormous Charterhouse and two exquisite art works—de Quarton's *Coronation of the Virgin* (1453) in the municipal museum, and the curved ivory statuette of the Virgin and Child in the church of Notre-Dame. Climb, too, to the terrace of the St-André fort for a glorious view of the Papal Palace in the setting sun.

From Orange to the Lubéron hills

Orange was a thriving city in Roman days, with baths and a big stadium. These are now gone: but there remain two of the finest Roman buildings in Europe—the Triumphal Arch, built by Julius Caesar to mark his victories over local Gauls; and the vast Theater, well preserved, with a big statue of Augustus in the central niche of its stage. The theater is best seen from the hill of St-Eutrope to the south, and preferably by moonlight. At the music and opera festival here in July, the audience sits on the rows of stone seats, just like Roman nobles of old.

The Romans called the town Arausio—hence 'Orange', which has nothing to do with the fruit (that name comes from the Arabic *narandji*). Orange was a tiny principality in the 13th to 17th centuries. It was acquired by the Dutch prince, William of Nassau, who liked it so much that he called his dynasty the House of Orange, a title that his descendants, the Dutch royal family, carry to this day. The Protestant 'Orange' movement in Ulster gets its name from the same connection.

PROVENCE AND THE CAMARGUE 449

South of Orange, the famous vineyards of Châteauneuf-du-Pape once belonged to the Avignon popes (hence the name); the village has a small wine museum. To the east, the old city of Carpentras has much of interest—a 15th-century cathedral rich in works of art, several good museums, a small Roman arch with bas-reliefs of captives, and France's oldest synagogue (the town was once a major Jewish center). Venasque, nearby, has a 7th-century Merovingian baptistry.

Memorials of Roman grandeur survive also at Vaison-la-Romaine which the Romans built as a wealthy residential town with patrician villas. Excavations have revealed shops, hanging gardens, salons, baths, even latrines and kitchens—a whole way of life, in fact, as at Pompeii. Do not miss the museum of local Roman art, the Romanesque cathedral, and the medieval quarter across the river. Southward rises the lofty pyramid-shaped Mont Ventoux, 'windy mount' (6,260 ft high), with a good road leading to its summit; also the dramatic limestone crags of the Dentelles de Montmirail.

South of Mont Ventoux is the interesting hilly region of the Plateau de Vaucluse and the Lubéron. Fontaine de Vaucluse is so called because here the river Sorgue surges out of a cavern to form a dramatic cascade of spray in the wet season or when snows are melting (in dry weather it is much duller). The Italian poet Petrarch spent 16 years here, 1337-53, pining for his Laura, and it inspired some of his work.

Eastward is the lovely hilltop village of Gordes, whose château is now a museum of the works of Vasarély (see Aix, below). In this area are scores of strange primitive stone huts, beehive-shaped, known as *bories:* the *village des bories* is a museum of rural life. Just north of Gordes, the beautiful 12th-century Cistercian abbey of Sénanque stands majestically alone in a wild valley: it is well preserved, and among much else it houses—oddly—a museum of the Sahara.

East again is the hill-village of Roussillon, popular with artists. Its houses of local stone are all shades of orange, red and pink, for this is ochre country where quarrying has slashed the cliffs into bizarre shapes. Going southeast you come to Apt, whose cathedral contains remarkable treasures relating to the local cult of St-Anne, mother of the Virgin.

Southwards there rises the long range of the Lubéron hills, part of it wild and craggy, part a lush plateau covered with vines and lavender. Here you should visit Bonnieux, to see the impressive 15th-century German paintings in its basilica; and, high on a rocky spur, the medieval village of Oppède-le-Vieux which, having fallen into ruin, is now being carefully restored by local artists and others. South again, on your way to Aix, do not miss another lovely Cistercian abbey: Silvacane.

Aix-en-Provence, a brilliant ex-capital

Aix-en-Provence is a 'must.' Of all French cities, it could most readily be mentioned in the same breath as Florence or Oxford—a proud, patrician place whose modern student life is enacted against an elegant backdrop of classical buildings and historic monuments.

From the 12th to 18th centuries it was Provence's dazzling capital. Then it became overshadowed by the rise of Marseille. But today it is still a lively town of 114,000 people, with a major university and busy cultural activity.

Since Roman days it has been a spa town ('Aix' comes from the Latin *aquae,* 'water'). Its golden age was in the 15th century under 'Good King René,' count of Provence, a jovial and beneficent ruler, intellectual and patron of the arts, who is still venerated by Aixois today. After his death Provence was united with France, but it retained some autonomy and Aix was the seat of its parliament. Its many graceful 17th- and 18th-century mansions were built by wealthy local dignitaries.

The main avenue is the famous Cours Mirabeau, named after the Revolution's orator, Count Mirabeau, who lived here. It is shaded with plane trees and has four fountains, plus a statue of King René. Nearby, the Musée Granet holds works by Ingres and other French painters, and a striking collection of Celto-Ligurian sculptures, excavated locally.

The heart of 'Vieil Aix' is a fascinating network of narrow traffic-free streets and picturesque little squares, notably the Place Albertus. Here there is much to explore. The cathedral of St-Sauveur is built in an odd mix of styles, from its 5th-century Gallo-Roman baptistry to the 16th-century Gothic facade. The sacristan will unlock for you the ornate wood-carvings on the door-panels and Froment's superb triptych, *The Burning Bush.* The famous Brussels tapestries are no longer on view, alas: but in the adjacent Archbishop's Palace you can see some fine Beauvais tapestries, including a set depicting the life of Don Quixote. The courtyard of this palace is the main venue for Aix' celebrated music and opera festival in summer.

Nearby, the Vieil Aix museum of folklore has a large collection of Provençal *santons* (dolls and puppets), while the 17th-century church of Ste-Marie-Madeleine contains a remarkable 15th-century painting of the *Annunciation.* Out in the suburbs, it is worth visiting the Pavilion Vendôme, former home of a cardinal; and the Fondation Vasarély, a big ultra-modern museum full of the highly-colored murals, mosaics and glass sculptures by that provocative Hungarian-born artist.

Aix was the home of a greater aritst, Paul Cézanne, who is buried in the town cemetery. You can visit his rather austere studio on a hillside above the town, near to the spot where in varying lights and hues he would obsessively paint and repaint Mont Ste-Victoire, the high conical limestone ridge that looms above Aix.

The market town of Salon-de-Provence, northwest of Aix, was the home of the astrologist Nostradamus. His tomb is in the 14th-century church of St-Laurent, and the house where he lived is now a museum devoted to him. Another museum, this one of military history, is in the 10th-century Château de l'Empéri on a rock above the town. Finally, 16km (10 miles) west of Aix is the impressive 19th-century aqueduct of Roquefavour, much larger than the Pont du Gard.

The hinterland: abbeys, museums, gorges

The sprawling hinterland of central Provence between Aix and Fréjus, though less well known than the coast or the Rhône valley area, holds much of interest. East of Aix, at St-Maximin-la-Ste-Baume, the beautiful 13th- to 16th-century basilica is the noblest Gothic building in Provence; it also has sarcophagi dating from the 4th century. Just south of here, the craggy limestone massif of La Ste-Baume is both very scenic and is also a place of legend and mystery, for near its summit is a cave where St Mary-Magdalene is said to have spent her final years, in solitude; it is now a shrine, and a center of pilgrimage.

A spiritual atmosphere also infuses the lovely 12th-century Romanesque abbey of Thoronet, built by Cistercian monks in a secluded valley northeast of Brignoles. With its charming cloister and chapter-house, it forms an ensemble of rare purity and harmony. Try to attend vespers in the chapel on a fine evening, when the stone glows gold in the setting sun. Or go north for a total change of mood to the château at Entrecasteaux, now turned into the most bizarre museum in Provence by the late Ian McGarvie-Munn, surrealist painter and Scottish nationalist, and sometime soldier, adventurer and art-fancier.

North again, you come to the Grand Canyon of the Verdon, a winding gorge 13 miles long and 2,000 ft deep, the most spectacular in France. Its bed is impassable, but good roads dizzily follow the cliff-top on either side, while for hardy and experienced hikers there are footpaths zigzagging down the cliff towards the rushing river Verdon. Just to the west, the pottery village of Moustiers-Ste-Marie is worth a visit for its faience (decorated earthernware) museum and its setting at the foot of a ravine, while the tiny ancient town of Riez has a 5th-century Christian baptistry *and* the remains of a Roman temple—yet another surprise of the delightful Provençal hinterland.

PRACTICAL INFORMATION

WHEN TO GO. The best time to visit this part of France is May or June, or Sept. and Oct., since July and Aug. are hot, dusty and crowded. The dreaded *mistral*, an icy wind sweeping down the Rhône Valley, blows mostly in the fall and winter. The Camargue has now been cleared of most of the mosquitoes that used to make it torture for summer and fall visitors, but you can still get bitten there (even though most hotels have mosquito nets), so visit it in the spring or early summer if you can.

Most of the major regional festivals are staged during the summer months, the first one being the *Féria Pascale* in Arles. At the end of **April** Arles has its *Fête des Gardians*, with ceremonies surrounding the legendary Camargue 'cowboys' and traditional blessing of their horses. On **May** 24/5 comes the Gypsies' Pilgrimage to Les Stes-Maries-de-la-Mer, accompanied by fairs and folklore events of all kinds. **Whitsun** is the time for Nîmes *Féria de la Pentecôte*, with bullfights in the Roman arena. Tarascon celebrates its legendary deliverance from the monster Tarasque by St Martha and a handful of heroic citizens on the last Sun. in **June** with processions through the town.

In **July** Arles stages dramatic performances in its Roman theater. **July** is also the month for the start of the famous Avignon Festival (theater, music, dance); for Vaison-la-Romaine's drama festival in the Roman theater; for Orange's *Chorégies* (concerts and plays, again in the Roman theater); and for Aix-en-Provence's celebrated music festival. On July 14 Tarascon stages a special ceremony for the arrival of the bulls, and on July 21/2 La-Ste-Baume has the *Fête de la Madeleine* with a midnight mass. Carpentras's *Fête de Notre-Dame-de-Santé* also comes in July.

Throughout July and **August** there are bullfights and 'games' with bulls in the arena at Arles and Nîmes. Many of the music and drama festivals also continue into this month (check dates, as they vary from year to year). Arles has a special bullfight in mid-**September** to celebrate the grape harvest and on a Sun. towards the end of **October** Les Stes-Maries-de-la-Mer has another procession. **December** is the month for *foires aux santons* (fairs where little clay or wooden figures for the Christmas crib are sold) in various places; and on **Christmas Eve** itself special Provençal midnight masses are held, the most picturesque being at Les Baux, where local shepherds bring their lambs.

HOW TO GET ABOUT. By train. From Paris (Gare de Lyon) frequent service to Avignon, Aix and Arles. Now that the TGV is in service, you can reach Avignon in under 3 hours and Nîmes in 4¼ hours from Paris (1983 times). For deluxe travel, use the TEE trains. Some through trains to Arles from

PROVENCE AND THE CAMARGUE

Paris, otherwise change at Avignon. The main cities are also served by a few trains from Calais and Boulogne.

By bus. A fairly good network of regional train and bus services reaches points of interest from such centers as Avignon, Arles, and Aix. Day excursions are offered by *American Express* from Marseille. From Avignon the *SNCF* has a bus program called *Circuits Touristiques de Provence*.

By boat. For something a little different, motor launches or barges, if you really have time, carry passengers on the Rhône from Lyon (pont Galliéni, cours de Verdun) to Donzère (8½ hrs), and Avignon (12 hrs), from Apr. 15 to Sept. 15. Reduced return fares by rail are available (for details write La Déscente du Rhône, 142 cours Lafayette, 69003 Lyon).

Another interesting boat trip idea is to take one from Saintes-Maries-de-la-Mer, which lasts about 1½ hrs and shows you 'a typical part of the Camargue'.

The *Compagnie Générale Transméditerranéenne* has package holidays with a week in Aix, Arles, Marseille, etc. Write Groupement des Agences de Voyages, 2 rue Beaurau, 13001 Marseille.

By gipsy caravan. For a really leisurely holiday, contact Le Domaine St-Saveur, 84320 Entraigues (tel: (90) 83–16–26).

MOTORING. Motorists from Britain can take the car-sleeper express from Boulogne or Paris, to Avignon, or the day car-carrier to Lyon. The fastest road route into this region is the A6 Paris-Lyon, then the A7 (take the A1 Calais–Paris).

At Orange, take the A9 to Nîmes and the N113 from there to Arles. The A7 continues to Marseille, but you can branch off on the A8 for Aix-en-Provence. You can, of course, follow the N7 from Lyon via the east bank of the Rhône through Vienne, Valence, Montélimar, Orange and Avignon, but traffic is apt to be heavy. A much slower route, passing through a number of small, picturesque towns, follows the west bank. At Avignon, you may choose to branch off to Remoulins (for Pont du Gard) and Nîmes (N86), or to follow N570 to Tarascon and Arles; continuing on N7 brings you to Aix-en-Provence, where you should try to avoid the rush hours when the narrow streets are clogged with cars. For Les Stes-Maries-de-la-Mer continue on the N570 from Arles.

USEFUL ADDRESSES. *Welcome Information office* is at 41 cours Jean-Jaurès, 84000 Avignon. The city's *tourist office* is at the same address, with an additional *maison du tourisme* at 3 pl. des Arènes. In Aix-en-Provence the tourist office is at 2 pl. Général-de-Gaulle; in Arles, at 35 pl. de la République. The *Compagnie des Autocars de Provence* can be contacted via the tourist office in Arles.

Car hire. *Avis:* 16 bld St-Dominique, Avignon; 12 bis av. Victor-Hugo, Arles; 4 av. des Belges, Aix-en-Provence; 1 bis rue de la République, Nîmes. *Hertz:* 2 bld St-Michel, Avignon; 39 bld Gambetta, Nîmes; 11 bld E.-Daladier, Orange.

Europcar: 55 bld de la République, Aix-en-Provence; 16 bld G.-Clemenceau, Arles; 12 bld St-Michel, Avignon; pl. de la Libération, Nîmes.

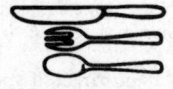

REGIONAL FOOD AND DRINK. This is a remarkable gastronomic region, with a varied and spicy cuisine, relying heavily on garlic and local herbs, and olive oil (which generally replaces butter in cooking). Many of the dishes, especially the fish ones, are the same as on the Riviera (see preceding chapter). As there, a meal may well start with a buffet of cold *hors d'oeuvres,* or with a basket of raw vegetables *(crudités)* served with French dressing. Try *aioli,* a garlic mayonnaise with boiled cod and vegetables. The range of meat stews includes *boeuf en daube* or (in the Camargue area) *boeuf gardian, civet de lièvre* (jugged hare) and *lapin à la moutarde* (rabbit in a mustard sauce). *Agneau de Sisteron* is local lamb whose aromatic flavour comes from its having grazed on wild herbs.

Vegetables and fruit grow in abundance and are succulent—artichokes, eggplants, asparagus and tomatoes, as well as (in season) strawberries and sweet pink Cavaillon melons. The region has few cheeses of note; but the sweet-toothed will enjoy the candied fruit of Apt and the almond *calissons* of Aix.

Native to the region are the Côte du Rhone wines (*Châteauneuf du Pape, Tavel* and *Gigondas* are the best), the red and *rosé* wines of the Costières du Gard; the *rosés* of Var and the Provençal coast.

HOTELS AND RESTAURANTS. Accommodations are not expensive, apart from a few luxurious country inns and modern hotels in cities. Many *auberges* and country hotels provide really good cooking. In our listings, establishments are graded L, E, M or I for luxury, expensive, moderate or inexpensive.

AIGUES-MORTES. *Remparts* (E), in atmospheric old building; *St-Louis* (M); both with good restaurants.

Restaurant. *La Camargue* (M), trendy, crowded, amusing; flamenco music and candles at dinner; copious food; must book.

AIX-EN-PROVENCE. *PLM Le Pigonnet* (E), ave. du Pigonnet, with romantic garden and fine cuisine. *Paul Cézanne* (E), 40 ave. Victor-Hugo, with rooms in different period styles but no restaurant. *Thermes Sextius* (M), 55 cours Sextius, central; has restaurant. *Nègre Coste* (M), 33 cours Mirabeau, also central, no restaurant. *Caravelle* (I), 29 blvd du Roi-René, and *St-Christophe* (I), 2 ave. Victor-Hugo, are central; neither has restaurants.

Just southeast of the town, by the motorway, are the *Novotels Aix Sud* (M-E) and *Aix-Est* (M-E); both with pool and snack-bar.

Restaurants. *Charvet* (M), 9 rue de Lacépède, has the best food in town, closely followed by *Les Caves Henri IV* (E-M), 32 rue Espariat. *Le Clam's* (M), 22 cours Sextius, and *Abbaye des Cordeliers* (I), 21 rue Lieutaud, garden setting,

PROVENCE AND THE CAMARGUE

both also recommended. *Les Augustins* (I), 59 rue Espariat, is a noisy and lively pizzeria.

APT. *Le Ventoux* (I), hotel with good medium-priced restaurant.

ARLES. *Jules César* (E), blvd des Lices, spacious, comfortable, with splendid inventive cuisine. *D'Arlatan* (M), 26 rue du Sauvage, in a lovely 15th-century house, with garden; enchanting atmosphere, but no restaurant. *Mireille* (M), 2 place St-Pierre, with restaurant and pool, and *Le Cloître* (I), 16 rue du Cloître, no restaurant, are more functional.
Restaurants. Best is *Le Vaccarès* (M), place du Forum; local cuisine. *Les Arènes* (I), 62 rue Refuge, and *Le Tambourin* (I), 65 rue Amadée-Pichot, are inexpensive and friendly.

AVIGNON. *Europe* (E), place Crillon, a 16th-century house where Napoleon once stayed; luxurious period decor, romantic outdoor dining. *Cité des Papes* (M), 1 rue Jean-Vilar, *Bristol-Terminus* (M), 44 cours Jean-Jaurès, and *Angleterre* (I), 29 blvd Raspail, are more utilitarian, without restaurants.
North by the A7 motorway is *Sofitel* (E), with restaurant. East at **Montfavet** is *Les Frênes* (E), with lovely decor, garden, and good food (E).
Restaurants. *Hiély-Lucullus* (E), 5 rue de la République, a sober, classic place with superb Provençal cuisine. Also good, with a 'newer' style of cooking, are *Brunel* (E), 40 rue de la Balance, and *Le Vernet* (M), 58 rue Joseph-Vernet, the latter with a charming garden. Hiély's other restaurant, *La Fourchette* (I), 7 rue Racine, is always packed out, stylish, and great value. Or try *Les Trois Clefs* (I-M), 26 rue des Trois Faucons, or *La Férigoulo* (I-M), 30 rue Joseph-Vernet.
Just west on the Nîmes road, at **Les Angles**, is the outstanding *Ermitage Meissonnier* (E), with 'new' cuisine, a pretty garden, and some luxurious bedrooms (M).

LES BAUX. Below the village, in elegant grounds with pool, the deluxe *Oustaù de Baumanière* (L), noted for its restaurant, one of France's best and very pricey. Nearby, same ownership, *La Cabro d'Or* (E), slightly cheaper; very good food too. *La Benvengudo* (M-E), delightful small rustic hotel; dining in a pretty patio. *Hostellerie de la Reine Jeanne* (I) is up in the village; dining with view over valley.
Restaurant. *La Riboto de Taven* (E), at foot of the rocks, with attractive terrace, first-rate food.

BEAUCAIRE. *Robinson* (I), on the Pont du Gard road, a simple place with good cheap food.

BONNIEUX, Luberon. *L'Aiguebrun* (M), 4 miles to southeast; secluded, idyllic, with good inventive cuisine.

BRIGNOLES. *Mas de la Cascade* (M), attractive and peaceful, with good restaurant (M) overlooking waterfall.

CARPENTRAS. *Univers* (I), central, well run, good food.

CHATEAU-ARNOUX. *La Bonne Etape* (E), 17th-century coaching-inn, stylish and friendly; plus brilliant, inventive cooking (E).

COMPS-SUR-ARTUBY. *Grand Hotel Bain* (I), modest, very friendly; plus good local cooking (I).

FLASSANS-SUR-ISSOLE. *La Grillade au Feu de Bois* (M), a converted farmhouse, secluded in the woods, run in unusual personal style; no restaurant.

FONTAINE DE VAUCLUSE. *Le Parc* (M); has a terrace-restaurant (I-M) beside the river.

FONTVIEILLE. *La Régalido* (E), luxurious and welcoming, with a lovely garden, also has excellent food (E). *Valmajour* (M), on Arles road, modern, no restaurant.

GORDES. *La Mayanelle* (M), gracefully converted 17th-century mansion; fine views, good local cooking (M).
Restaurant. *Les Bories* (E), 1.5 km (1 mile) away, picturesquely converted from ancient stone huts *(bories),* excellent food; 2 bedrooms.

LAMBESC. Restaurant. *Moulin de Tante Yvonne* (E), a lovely 15th-century mill, with good Provençal cooking.

MANOSQUE. *François Premier* (I), simple, central. *Hostellerie de la Fuste* (E), 6.5 km (4 miles) east, a luxuriously converted 17th-century coaching-inn, with garden; distinguished 'new' cooking (E).

MAUSSANE. *L'Oustaloun* (M), friendly little auberge with sound local cooking (I).

MENERBES. Restaurant. *Pascal* (I), a large, lively and crowded auberge with a garden and copious country food.

MEYRARGUES. *Château de Meyrargues* (M), an imposing 12th-century hilltop château, very baronial and romantic, super views; goodish food (E).

NÎMES. *Imperator* (E), quai de la Fontaine, imposing, with garden and good food (M). Also central are the *Louvre* (M), 2 sq. Couronne, and *Michel* (I), 14 blvd Amiral-Courbet, the latter with no restaurant, while by the motorway on

PROVENCE AND THE CAMARGUE

the southern outskirts are the *Sofitel* (E) and *Novotel* (M); both latter with restaurants (M).

Restaurants. Nothing much in town, but try *La Louve* (I), 1 rue de la République, a busy bistro. By the **airport,** 8 km (5 miles) south, is *Alexandre* (E), formally elegant, with excellent food; some bedrooms (E).

NOVES. *Auberge de Noves* (E), a luxurious converted manor, with big garden and pool, in lovely open country; superb, imaginative cuisine, mostly 'new' (E).

ORANGE. *Arène* (M), place Langes, and *Louvre et Terminus* (M), 89 avenue Frédéric-Mistral, neither with restaurant. *Euromotel* (M), just outside the town, near motorway, with pool, and restaurant (M).

Restaurant. *Le Pigraillet* (M), chemin de la Colline St-Eutrope, on a hill above the town.

PONT-DU-GARD. *Vieux Moulin* (M), by the river, good view of the great bridge; restaurant (I-M).

PORT-CAMARGUE. *Spinaker* (M), very modern floating restaurant in the yacht harbor; good food (E).

ROCHEGUDE. Near Orange. *Château de Rochegude* (E), elegant, with pool; restaurant (E).

ROUSSILLON. *Résidence des Ocres* (M), small, neat and modern; no restaurant.

Restaurant. *David* (M), smart, fine view, classic food.

ST-RÉMY-DE-PROVENCE. *Château de Roussan* (E), just out of town on Tarascon road: elegant château with rambling, romantic garden, run in personal style by its charming, cultured owners; no restaurant. *Le Castelet des Alpilles* (M), sedate, and *Les Arts* (I), lively and bohemian, both with good restaurants (I-M).

SAINTES-MARIES-DE-LA-MER. In town, the hotels are mostly dull - but try *Le Galoubet* (M), no restaurant. To the north, on or near N570, are a dozen or so modern ranch-hotels, good for riding and other sports (many hire horses, with or without guides): among the best, *Mas de la Fouque* (E), *L'Etrier Camarguais* (M-E), *Pont des Bannes et Mas Ste-Hélène* (E), all with pools and restaurants (M).

Restaurant. *Pont de Gau* (I-M), 5 km (3 miles) north of town; good value; some bedrooms (I).

SALON-DE-PROVENCE. In town: *Vendôme* (I), 34 rue Maréchal-Joffre; *Sélect* (I), 35 rue de Suffren, neither with restaurant. 5 km (3 miles) northeast via D16 is the secluded *Abbaye Ste-Croix* (E), a smartly converted 12th-century abbey, with pool and excellent restaurant (E) serving classic and 'new' dishes.

SEGURET. *La Table du Comtat* (M), a 15th-century house, perched high up, with sweeping views; pool, and very good restaurant, fairly priced (M).

TARASCON. *Terminus* (I), simple, serviceable, with restaurant (I).

TOURTOUR. *La Bastide de Tourtour* (E), rather grand and baronial, built recently in local style; pool, and vaulted restaurant with good cooking both 'new' and classic. *Auberge St-Pierre* (M-E), a graceful 18th-century manor, run in unusual style by lovers of animals and local traditions; solar-heated pool, home farm, Provençal cooking (M).
Restaurant. *Les Chênes Verts* (E): high-quality 'new' cooking in a secluded rustic setting.

UZÈS. *Entraigues* (M), 15th-century town mansion, tastefully and soberly converted; light snacks only. Same owners run the *Hôtel d'Agoult, Château d'Arpaillargues* (E), 4.5 km (3 miles) to west, a finely-furnished 18th-century manor in a big park; sophisticated ambiance, pool; goodish food (M).

VAISON-LA-ROMAINE. *Le Beffroi* (M-I), quaint 16th-century mansion with antique furniture, in old part of town; terrace with view; restaurant (M).

VILLENEUVE-LÈS-AVIGNON. *Le Prieuré* (E), gracious and sophisticated, a converted priory, with pool, tennis and lovely garden; notable cooking, though a bit overpriced (E). *La Magnaneraie* (M-E); lovely 15th-century house on a hill, elegant decor, good food (M).

CASINOS. The casino at Aix-en-Provence, formal and sedate, is open all year. There's dining, dancing, cabaret on offer, plus boules, baccara, roulette and 30/40.

LANGUEDOC AND ROUSSILLON

Modern resorts and ancient fortresses

by
JOHN ARDAGH

The region that today bears this name borders the Mediterranean from the Pyrenees to the Rhône delta, and is in two halves. First, the lower Languedoc, around Montpellier, eastern part of that vast historic province where the people spoke 'the tongue of *oc*' ('yes' for them was *oc*, not *oil* or *oui* as in the north). This sun-baked land of vine-clad plains and dry, stony hills has been a crossroads of many civilizations since pre-Roman days. Before the Cathar massacres, it saw the flowering of the gentle, courteous age of troubadours with their courts of love. That glory is now lost, but the local people retain an assertive sense of regional identity, and a mistrust of all that comes from Paris.

For miles on all sides stretch the vineyards. This area produces most of France's cheap wine, but so cheap is it that many growers claim they cannot make a living, and in recent years they have repeatedly been in revolt, blocking the roads with tractors and even attacking the police. They have made common cause with the local separatist movement of young hotheads who dream vaguely of a free Occitania (the historic name for southern France) and daub walls with their 'OC' symbol. Politically, their real influence is slight.

This is France's deep south, where under the dazzling sun the pace of life is easy; a land of cypress and cicada, where small red-roofed towns lie sleepily beneath the walls of mighty old fortresses, such as Carcassonne. Yet, without losing its charm, Languedoc is now facing modern change. Huge modern seaside resorts line the coast; new factories and new irrigation schemes are arriving. Quiet, aristocratic Montpellier, the regional capital, has mushroomed into a big commercial metropolis.

Even further south is the small province of Roussillon sometimes known as French Catalonia. It is prosperous, thanks to farming and tourism: spas and ski resorts in the Pyrenees vie with the beaches of the Vermilion Coast, while the fertile plain around the capital, Perpignan, has some of the richest farms in France, producing fruit and early vegetables. Like Brittany and the Basque country, Roussillon is a corner of France that feels different: its flavor is Spanish (not surprisingly, for Roussillon belonged to Spain till 1659), and the people here are Catalans, brothers to their neighbors in the much larger Spanish Catalonia around Barcelona. Today, local cultural self-expression is all the rage: the Catalan language is being revived, folk festivals multiply, and the red-and-yellow Catalan flag flies defiantly over Perpignan. A minority—but only a small minority—want to politicize this trend, to detach Roussillon from France and federate it with Spanish Catalonia.

From the Cerdagne to Prades

Southeast of Andorra, the Toulouse-Barcelona main road leads to the frontier town of Bourg-Madame. Here the Spanish townlet of Llivia forms an enclave inside France, the result of a concession won by Spain when she ceded Roussillon in 1659. We are now in the Cerdagne, an upland plain of meadows and pine forests, backed by snowy mountains. Its altitude is 1,066 meters (3,500 ft), yet it seems like a pastoral valley, and its sunshine level is the highest in France. Hence its choice as the main site of French experiments with solar energy. Europe's largest solar furnace, at Odeillo near Font-Romeu, is a massive square building where 62 swiveling mirrors reflect the sun on to one giant concave mirror; some of the scientists live in strange little houses with ugly glass façades, heated by solar energy. A much larger solar furnace is now being built a few miles away.

The sun brings skiers as well as scientists to the Cerdagne—Font-Romeu is a superbly equipped resort where Olympic champions often train. From here it is a mile's walk through the forest to the Hermitage, shrine of the strange Vierge de l'Invention. This austere Romanesque madonna is black with age, and through having been buried during the Arab invasions, like many sculptures of that time. The name 'Invention' (discovery) comes from the local legend whereby this Virgin was accidentally unearthed, centuries later, by a bull scratching at the ground. Each year, on September 8, the statue is solemnly carried to the church at Odeillo, then back to the shrine on Trinity Sunday.

From the Cerdagne, the road to Perpignan skirts the fortress of Mont-Louis (built by Vauban as a defense against the Spaniards), then descends a steep and winding valley. Just off this road is Vernet-les-Bains, an elegantly laid-out but now fading spa, once much colonized by the British, like Pau. The classic excursion from here is to the remote mountain abbey of St-Martin-du-Canigou, accessible only by jeep or—preferably—a 30-minute walk up a steep path. Built just after AD 1000, the abbey fell into ruins after the Revolution, but has been carefully restored during this century and is now used for retreats by laity and priests alike. Austerely beautiful, it lies lost to view in the folds of Mount Canigou, highest Pyrenean peak of Roussillon.

Further down the valley is the town of Prades, center of a rich district of peach, cherry and apricot orchards. The cellist Pablo Casals lived here for many years before his death, and an annual music festival is held in his honor. Just to the south stands the beautiful abbey of St-Michel-de-Cuxa, in the 11th century the leading church of Roussillon. During the Revolution it was abandoned and later pillaged, but in 1913 an American sculptor managed to collect many of the missing bits of the cloisters, which today have been reassembled at Fort Tryon Park, Manhattan. The abbey itself is now restored: its cloister, though incomplete, is of rare grace. The place is occupied by Catalan Benedictines, who use it as a center for the propagation of Catalan culture. The Casals Festival concerts are also held in the abbey.

Perpignan, sardañas, and the Côte Vermeille

Perpignan, capital of the so-called 'kingdom of Mallorca' in the 13th century, is today the largest Catalan town, with a population of 120,000, after Barcelona. Legend claims it takes its name from a cowherd, Père Pinya, who was magically guided to found a city on the most fertile spot in the valley. It is a pleasant southerly town, with promenades lined with planes and palm trees. Its most interesting building is the Castillet (citadel), an old brick fortress housing a museum of local arts and traditions. Worth a visit too are the 14th-century cathedral of St-Jean; the palace of the kings of Mallorca; and the elegant Loge de Mer, built in 1397 and then for centuries used as a trade center where maritime disputes were handled.

In the little square beside the Loge, the locals dance the *sardaña*, national dance of all Catalonia on summer evenings. If you want to see more spontaneous *sardañas*, go to almost any local village square on a summer weekend, or to the festivals at Arles-sur-Tech or Amélie-les-Bains (or, better still, to Barcelona). Oddly, this is not a traditional dance but a fairly recent invention.

East of Perpignan the coast is flat, and resorts such as Argelès have wide sandy beaches backed by pine woods. A few miles south, where the Pyrenees stumble into the sea, is the Côte Vermeille (Vermilion Coast), named after its reddish rocks and hills. Banyuls is a pleasant if cluttered resort, whose vines on their steep slopes produce the famous sweet Banyuls wine (you can visit the old wine cellars, and get a free tasting). The prettiest resort is Collioure, which has kept much of its charm despite the tourist hordes who descend on this picture-postcard fishing village, once lived in (and painted so often), by Matisse, Dufy and others. The village with its narrow cobbled streets lies below a vast 12th-century castle, right on the sea; there are fishing boats drawn up along the pebbly beach, their bows holding the great globes of the special lamps the fishermen use to lure their fish at night.

Places to visit inland from here are Elne, with its superb cathedral cloister, and the delightful old town of Céret, where Picasso worked for some years. Its museum has canvases by him and other painters of his period. North of Perpignan is the fortress of Salses, built by the Spaniards in the 15th century. Alas, work on a quarry near here may mean that this important fortress will be closed to the public, though as important prehistoric remains have been excavated here there is a good chance of a reprieve.

Narbonne and Carcassonne

North of Salses we cross into Languedoc and are soon in Narbonne, today a quietish little town but in Roman times a major city, capital of the province of Gallia Narbonensis. Its port, today silted up, was then the busiest in the western Mediterranean. Narbonne's chief glory, and its oddity, is the cathedral of St-Just, begun in 1272 but never completed: when the choir had been built, the local Consuls refused to

LANGUEDOC AND ROUSSILLON

let the nave be added—and so it remains today. It is one of the tallest Gothic cathedrals in France, little lower than Beauvais. The cloister leads to the massive fortified Palace of the Archbishops, housing museums of art and ancient history. Visit, too, the lapidary museum (in a deconsecrated church). An elegant 16th-century building, the Maison des Trois Nourrices (House of the Three Wet-Nurses) is so named because the cornice of its fine Renaissance window is supported by Raquel Welch-like caryatids!

Southwest of Narbonne is the superb 11th-century Cistercian abbey of Fontfroide, with a noble cloister and a peaceful garden lined with cypresses. Westward range the strange, wild limestone hills of the Corbières, which give their name to the best wine of Languedoc, produced here. Further west is Limoux, a town producing a popular champagne-type wine (the cellars can be visited).

And so to fabulous Carcassonne, Europe's largest medieval fortress and one of the most complete. If you can, see it first at night, from a distance, when the mighty circle of towers and battlements, aloft on their hilltop, are brilliantly floodlit. The newer town, on the plain, is unexciting. Our concern is with La Cité, the walled city, and its epic history. Parts of its walls were first built by the Romans, then the Visigoths enlarged it into a great fortress in the 5th century (the present line of the towers is theirs). Charlemagne laid siege to the place for five years in the 9th century, cutting off all supplies—and thereby hangs a tale. According to an anecdote cooked up later by the troubadours, a certain Dame Carcas broke the siege by ringing the tocsin, then stuffing a pig with the last grain remaining in the city, in full view of the besiegers. She threw the pig off the battlements: it burst, scattering grain. Carlemagne was thus convinced that the city must have plenty to waste, and called off the siege. So the place, in her honor, was called 'Carcas Sonne' (Carcas rings). We need not believe this punning joke: the Romans had long previously known it as Carcaso.

In the 13th century, the fortress fell to the anti-Cathar crusaders, and Simon de Montfort took it as a command post for his routine massacres. St Louis and his son Philip the Bold then strengthened the fortifications, giving the place the appearance it has today. It was by now self-contained enough to withstand any siege: a wheat-grinding mill was built, smiths forged hinges and armour, a mint coined money, and in the great Narbonne Tower was a cistern able to hold six months' supply of fresh water. The cathedral of St-Nazaire was built, as well as an open air theater which is still used today.

After the annexation of Roussillon in 1659 the fortress lost much of its military importance and slowly fell into ruin. Finally, in 1844, Viollet-le-Duc was commissioned to rebuild the battlements, towers and cathedral—the world's first restoration on such a scale. This great architect has been much criticized for doing too good a touch-up job; at close quarters much of his detail looks artificial, like a Hollywood cardboard set. But time is finally mellowing his work, which now blends less uneasily with the original elements. And at least he restored the original skyline of towers and turrets, to provide full romantic effect from a distance.

You can take a guide around the city, or wander at leisure, admiring the intricate fortifications of the two castellated walls, one inside the other, about a mile in circumference. The views from the battlements towards the Pyrenees are stunning. Visit the cathedral, over-restored in places, but remarkable for its stained-glass rose windows, fine statues, elegant Romanesque nave and Gothic transepts. The city still has 500 permanent inhabitants, mostly poorer people—and its quaint medieval streets are lined, inevitably, with scores of cheapjack souvenir shops, plus a few more elegant craft boutiques.

The new resorts: pyramids and nudists

Does this region share something of America's mania for building 'the biggest'? Carcassonne, Europe's biggest fortress—and now, in modern times, the 193-km (120-mile) Languedoc-Roussillon coastline is the scene of the biggest planned tourist development in European history.

This coast has wide sandy beaches, backed by saltwater lagoons, but till recently the mosquito reigned supreme and bathers were few. Then in 1963 the Gaullist government set about creating eight new resorts as an overspill for the near-saturated Riviera. The lagoons were dredged, the mosquitoes wiped out, and new marinas and a new road network built. When the project is finished, in the late 1980s, some 280,000 new tourist beds will have been provided (at present it is just past the halfway stage). The futuristic design of resorts such as La Grande Motte may not appeal to lovers of old-world charm. But at least the project is proving a success with hundreds of thousands of foreign tourists, as well as French. And it has given a shot-in-the-arm to the economy of an area still too vulnerably dependent on its badly organized wine industry.

The northerly resorts, near Montpellier, are on the whole more attractive and popular than the southerly ones, near Perpignan, where the architecture is not so inspired and the winds too strong for comfort. From south to north, this is the picture:

St-Cyprien has a pleasant new country club with golf course; at Port-Barcarès a Japanese-owned converted Greek passenger boat, the *Lydia,* has been towed on to the beach to serve as a nightclub, casino and restaurant; at Port-Leucate, the nudist village of Aphrodite is run by the British—of all people! Cap d'Agde, much further north, is in many ways the pleasantest of the resorts, a pastiche of a traditional fishing village, with pretty buildings in pastel shades. Next to it is the showpiece of tourism's fastest growth-sector: nudism. The nudist holiday town here, Europe's largest, has casinos, supermarkets, nightclubs, the lot, and accommodations for 20,000 lovely (or unlovely) bodies.

La Grande Motte, most sophisticated and highly publicized of the resorts, is Brasilia-on-Sea, a Le Corbusier vision with motor yachts and beach parasols added. Its ranks of ten-story ziggurat pyramids contain smart holiday flats, boutiques and discothèques. Some of the newest blocks are in weird shapes and colors (one resembles a giant fairground wheel). Not everyone may want to spend a holiday in these surrealistic pop-art surroundings, however jolly the colors and lavish the amenities (superb restaurants, large marina), but La Grande Motte signals unmistakeably the face of the new France, and provides an intriguing contrast with the sleepy, classical hinterland. Nearby Port-Camargue is more exclusive, attracting a well-heeled yachting set.

Along the coast, a few old ports and fishing villages manage to survive the Brave New World. One of the quaintest is Gruissan, built in a circular shape and dominated by a ruined tower. But here too a new resort has sprung up, harmonizing quite well with the old village. It is a good place to set out for walking or riding excursions in the Clape chain of hills just behind the coast. Sète, further east, a lively, fair-sized town, is France's leading Mediterranean port after Marseille. The outdoor fish restaurants along the main canal are a delight. The poet Paul Valéry was born and lived in Sète, and a museum is devoted to him: beside it, on a hillside facing the sea, is the romantic cemetery where he was inspired to write his greatest poem, *Le cimetière marin*.

Montpellier, and the surprises of the hinterland

The regional capital has grown since World War II from dozy provincial town to commercial metropolis (population, 300,000). Its large university is one of France's largest (Rabelais was a student here) and is noted for medicine and chemistry. Off the central square with its pleasant paved piazza is a snazzy new commercial and shopping center, the Polygone. Yet Montpellier has not lost its old seigneurial charm. The narrow streets of the older quarter, on a low hill, are lined with elegant residences of the 17th and 18th centuries. Here too is one of France's best provincial museums, the Musée Fabre, and a handsome formal garden, the Peyrou.

The hinterland, where the mountains of the Cévennes and the Massif Central meet the plain, offers many fascinating surprises. This is *garrigue* country of stony hills covered with scrub and bush, opening to far horizons. The Pic de St-Loup is a conical limestone peak rising up from the plain, with a ruined white castle on its ridge. Further north are the Grottes des Demoiselles, among the loveliest caves in France, containing enormous stalactites in many bizarre forms, one of them known as the Virgin and Child because of its shape. Southwest from here, St-Guilhem-le-Désert is a remote and picturesque village, built in a ravine of the Hérault gorge. Its fine 10th-century abbey church has been shorn of its cloister—sold to the Metropolitan Museum in New York!

On the road from Montpellier to Béziers, take a look at Pézenas, a little town that was once the capital of lower Languedoc and today preserves intact its impressive ensemble of 15th- to 17-century houses. The great dramatist Molière and his company gave many performances here and a festival is held annually in his honor. Béziers, a big modern city with one of France's best rugby teams, has a Museum of the History of Wine. Just to the west is the remarkable early Celtic settlement of Ensérune, unearthed on a hilltop. It dates back to at least 600 BC and had 8,000 inhabitants in the 3rd century BC. The museum has an interesting collection of Celtic domestic objects.

Finally, on westwards to Minerve, an old village on a limestone cliff, dominating the vineyards below. Its now ruined castle was once a Cathar stronghold, besieged and captured by Simon de Montfort. He and his crusaders then burned 140 Cathars alive, watching the fires 'with great joy', according to an eyewitness account. The villagers tell you this story today with seething indignation, as if it happened last year. After 750 years, at Montségur and Minerve, the martyrs' blood is not yet dry.

LANGUEDOC AND ROUSSILLON

PRACTICAL INFORMATION

WHEN TO COME. Early summer and fall are probably the best seasons to visit this area, as the heat and glare in midsummer can be tiring, and beaches, hotels and campsites are crowded. The five *départements* that make up the official Languedoc–Roussillon administrative region boast of having 2,750 sunshine hours per year, so you don't need to stick to the main summer months. Sports activities continue throughout the year in many resorts, though *son-et-lumière* performances (in Carcassonne's walled city, for instance) generally run about May–Sept. only. You're likely to encounter strong winds throughout the year, particularly on the coast near the Spanish border.

February is the month for carnivals in Limoux, Amélie-les-Bains, Perpignan and other centers, and for Perpignan's cinema festival. **March** sees processions of black-robed penitents in various places in Roussillon, and Perpignan's rather Spanish-seeming 'Sanch Procession' in the old town. **Easter** is the occasion of many colorful religious ceremonies, with more processions of penitents and 'processions of the risen Christ' in Arles-sur-Tech, Céret and Collioure, while **April** sees Béziers in festive mood with its procession and *Danse des Treilles* to celebrate the feast day of St Aphrodise on the 28th. In **May** Fontfroide Abbey stages its Musical Week and Gignac has its traditional 'donkey dance', accompanied by a procession and all sorts of fun and games. **June** sees the traditional bonfires, dancing in the streets and other festivities throughout the region on Midsummer Day, the feast of John the Baptist (June 24), or the nearest weekend, and Perpignan starts staging traditional local dance displays, which continue right through the summer. Gruissan has a Fisherman's Fair on June 29, St Peter's Day, and similar celebrations take place in Sète and sometimes in Palavas-les-Flots. In **July** the Hérault region has more traditional ceremonies, including bull-branding and jousting, Font-Romeu has its International Festival of the *Sardane,* Carcassonne a drama festival, La Grande Motte has a jazz festival and a windsurfer festival, Palavas its *Fête de la Mer,* with a boat-blessing ceremony, fireworks and jousts at sea. In both July and **August** there are local festivals and celebrations throughout the region, including Bézier's *Grande Féria,* and August also sees an International Folklore Festival in Amélie-les-Bains. Prades's famous Casals Festival is usually held in August too, though it sometimes starts at the end of July. Gruissan has a tuna-fishing festival. **September** is the month for wine festivals and, on the 8th, for the procession of Notre-Dame de l'Invention in Odeillo. **October** has an international wine fair in Montpellier and a Bach Festival in St-Pons, while Perpignan celebrates the feast of St Martin at the beginning of **November. Christmas Eve** brings picturesque ceremonies centered round the midnight mass—shepherds bring their lambs, traditional singing and dancing.

WHAT TO DO. **Swimming**, **sailing** and **water sports** of all kinds can be practised in ideal conditions in the well-equipped resorts with their magnificent sandy beaches.

Windsurfing is probably the most popular activity at the moment, and you can hire your *planche à voile* for around 40 frs per hour. In La Grande Motte they are free. Port Barcares and Saint-Cyprien have good sailing schools, but all the new resorts offer tuition in sailing, windsurfing and other water sports. Cap d'Agde's **tennis** village, presided over by French champion Pierre Barthès, offers well-organized all-in tuition at all levels and you'll find courts at all the new resorts too. St-Cyprien has two **golf** courses (18-hole and 9-hole) and offers all-in golfing holidays.

Sunbathing is obviously no problem in this sundrenched area, but if you're a naturist you'll have to make for the two naturist villages at Cap d'Agde and Leucate. There's a naturist camp beautifully set by the river near Méjannes-le-Clap.

Riding is better in the inland regions (inquire at the tourist office in Montpellier or at the Chambre d'Agriculture, pl. Chaptal) but **cycling** is easy on the coast, as you can hire bicycles; ask at the tourist offices in Palavas, Port-Barcarès, Port-Leucate and La Grande-Motte, and in many other resorts too. In 1980 St-Cyprien started running cycling holidays presided over by ace French cyclist Raymond Poulidor. **Walkers** can find out about Languedoc's many footpaths from the *syndicat d'initiative* in Lézignan-Corbières, and **fishing** is excellent in the mountainous region to the north. You may also find that fishermen in Palavas or one of the other small fishing ports will take you out for sea fishing. Tunny or tuna fishing (known as *pêche au tout gros*) is becoming a specialty here, especially in the new resort of Gruissan.

One particularly good center for excursions, and for taking part in the many sports opportunities offered by this region, is the château of the ducs de Joyeuse, in Cathar country 40 km (25 miles) from Carcassonne. The 16th-cent. château has been turned into a center offering tennis, riding, hiking, shooting, fishing, canoeing and even rugby, plus excursions throughout the region, and special-interest holidays (themes include rural living, regional cuisine, local wines, pottery, weaving). Write to the Château des Ducs de Joyeuse, 11190 Couiza, France for detailed information: usually only groups (20 people upwards) are accepted, but you may be able to join in with others.

Another way of getting to know more about the Cathars is to take a three-day organized tour including a conducted tour of Carcassonne, excursions throughout the region (including the Hunting Museum in Nébias) and talks and audio-visual presentations about the Cathar heresy, plus full board and lodging (including wine at meals). Obviously you'll get more out of it if you speak French, though English-speaking lecturers are sometimes available. Write to *Fédération Audoise des Oeuvres Laïques*, 22 rue Antoine-Marty, 11001 Carcassonne. No tours in July and Aug.

If you're in need of a cure for your liver after all those rich meals, Le Boulou is a little **spa** on the river Tech, 20 km (12½ miles) from Carcassonne, with mineral waters thought to be good for liver complaints, but there are plenty of

LANGUEDOC AND ROUSSILLON

other opportunities for leisure activities there too. If, on the other hand, your liver is still in good shape, try visiting some of the Corbières wine producers to find out more about the little-known wines of this region. A *Wine Road* has been mapped out (ask at tourist offices for the leaflet), and the new resort of Gruissan runs a course of introductory lessons in 'wine connoisseurship'.

HOW TO GET ABOUT. By air *Dan Air* flies 6 times a week to Montpellier and 3 times a week in summer to Perpignan, from London (Gatwick). Alternatively you can fly with *Air France* to Nîmes, which is in the official Languedoc–Roussillon region and is close to the centers we refer to. There are many different possibilities if you're coming from Paris: *Air Inter* flies to Carcassonne, Montpellier and Perpignan (and also to Nîmes); *TAT* to Béziers.

By rail. From Paris you have two alternative routes: via Toulouse or via Avignon. Thanks to the TGV the service Paris-Montpellier takes only around 4½ hours; there are at least four runs daily. You can save time by taking overnight trains to Montpellier, Sète, Agde, Béziers, Narbonne, Perpignan or Carcassonne. The Cévenol route, Paris-Lyon-Nîmes, is so attractive as to be worth changing in Nîmes even if you are not planning to visit Provence. Ordinary trains from Paris via Lyon take about 7 hrs to Montpellier, 7½ hrs to Sète, 8 hrs to Béziers, 8½ hrs to Narbonne. The Paris (Austerlitz)-Barcelona service via Toulouse takes about 9 hrs to Narbonne and another hour to Perpignan. The excellent Barcelona Talgo runs at night, stopping at Montpellier, Béziers, Narbonne and Perpignan. The overnight Paris-Carcassonne service is a good timesaver (it travels via Toulouse). Good trains link Marseille and Nice with Perpignan on the Barcelona line, and with Montpellier, Béziers, Narbonne and Carcassonne. You can also travel from Hendaye to Montpellier direct, and from Bordeaux to Montpellier. There is also a very good car-couchette service for drivers from Paris to Narbonne and from Boulogne to Narbonne.

By coach. The *SNCF* has a combined five-day coach and train tour called *Soleil en Roussillon* from Paris a few times a year, and a more frequent *Circuit Cathare*, again five days, which goes also from Toulouse, not just from Paris.

By canal. Cruising on the region's canals is a delightful way of getting about. The British company *Blue Line Cruisers*, based at Castelnaudary on the Canal du Midi with a branch line at Marseillan at the eastern end of the Thau lagoon, hires boats on which you can travel between these two centers. You can also continue on from Marseillan to Sète (a total of 118 miles). Alternatively, you can explore the lagoons around Marseillan or go up to the Camargue. Plenty of expert advice and information is available, so beginners need have no worries.

MOTORING. From Paris the best way is to take the A6 motorway to Lyon and then the A7 via Valence to Orange. From here you move on to the A9 (known as *La Languedocienne*) and drive via Nîmes to Montpellier, Béziers, Narbonne and Perpignan. For Perpignan you can also leave the A9 at Narbonne and join the new A61 *(Autoroute des Deux Mers)* to Carcassonne. To get to La Grande Motte, Palavas and the other coastal resorts you leave the A9 at Montpellier and take the D62. For Sète you must take the N112 from Montpellier. If you don't want to take the motorways, take the N7 from Paris to Bollène, then the D994 to Pont-St-Esprit, where you cross the Rhône and join the N86 to Nîmes; here you take the N113, which goes right through to Carcassonne via Montpellier, Béziers, Narbonne. Another alternative is to take the N7/N9 via Moulins, Clermont-Ferrand, St-Flour and Clermont l'Hérault and down to Narbonne. A good coast road connects the new resorts with Marseille and thence with the Côte d'Azur.

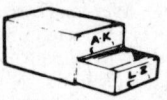

USEFUL ADDRESSES. The Languedoc–Roussillon administrative region has a *Welcome Information office* at quai de Lattre-de-Tassigny, 66005 Perpignan and another at 6 rue Auguste, 30000 Nîmes. The *Comité Régional de Tourisme* is at 12 rue Foch, 34000 Montpellier, as is the *Union des Offices de Tourisme et Syndicats d'Initiative de l'Hérault* and the city's own *tourist office* (also pl. de la Comédie, but the Welcome Information office here has been closed). The Aude's tourist committee is at 14 rue du 4-Septembre, 11000 Carcassonne, and for the Pyrénées–Orientales *département* write to the *Régie du Tourisme,* Palais Consulaire, 66200 Perpignan. The Gard tourist committee is at 3 pl. des Arènes, 30000 Nîmes (see Provence chapter).

There are five tourist offices on the motorways known as *La Languedocienne* (A9) and *La Catalane* (B9) which provide a very useful last-minute hotel reservation service. And all towns of any size have their own tourist office or *syndicat d'initiative.*

Car hire. *Avis,* 52 rue Antoine-Marty, Carcassonne; 49 rue Frédéric-Basille and airport, Montpellier; and 13 bld du Conflent and airport, Perpignan; *Europcar,* 30 rue Antoine-Marty, Carcassonne; 6 rue Jules-Ferry, Montpellier; and 2 bis av. du Général-de-Gaulle (also at no. 21 ter) and airport, Perpignan; *Hertz,* 18 rue Jules-Ferry, Montpellier; and 9 bis cours Escarqual, Perpignan.

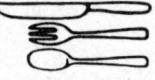

REGIONAL FOOD AND DRINK. All along the coast the fish and shellfish are excellent, and here you find the glorious garlicky fish dishes of the French Mediterranean—among them *bouillabaisse* (maybe not quite as good as in its Marseille homeland), *bourride* (another variety of rich fish stew) and *brandade de morue* (salt-cod mousse). The local oysters can be eaten all the year round, unlike in other parts of France. Sète is famous for its mussels, and has special fish dishes of its own, such as *rouille de seiche* (cuttlefish in a garlicky sauce).

In Roussillon, the Catalan cooking is generally better than in Spain. Olive oil here reigns supreme, and a local maxim has it, 'The fish must die in oil, as it is born in water.' *Civet de Langouste* (lobster stew) is a specialty of Banyuls, while Collioure is noted for its anchovies and fresh sardines. A Catalan national dish is *ouillade,* a soup of beans and cabbage, each cooked separately and mixed

LANGUEDOC AND ROUSSILLON

just before serving. Try also *perdreau à la catalane* (partridge with bitter oranges).

Around Carcassonne the great dish is *cassoulet* (see Pyrenees chapter). The Languedoc hinterland is a country of game dishes (in season) and of unusual peasant soups: *oulade* is a soup of cabbage, potatoes and mushrooms, with a little salt pork; *mourtaîrol* is a chicken bouillon with saffron; and *aigo bouillido*, in the Cévennes, is a soup of garlic, eggs and herbs. *Alicuit* is a stew made by simmering the giblets of duck and goose, then adding *cèpes* (a kind of mushroom) and chestnuts. The remarkable *saucisse à la languedocienne* consists of skewered sausages, sautéed in goose fat and served with spiced tomato purée.

Languedoc produces vast quantities of cheapish table wine, much of it thin and mediocre, but some of fair quality. Best are the full-bodied reds of Corbières and Fitou, from the area southwest of Narbonne, or the gentler Minervois. Around Montpellier, the most drinkable wines tend to be the *Clairettes-du-Languedoc* and the *Coteaux-du-Languedoc*. *Blanquette de Limoux*, from the town of that name, is a sparkling wine made by the champagne method. Roussillon produces some very pleasant reds, and two well-known natural sweet wines, *Rivesaltes* and *Banyuls*, usually drunk on their own before or after meals.

HOTELS AND RESTAURANTS. So many vacationers prefer to rent or camp these days, that the new resorts tend to be short on hotel accommodations, though steps are being taken to remedy this. Towns such as Montpellier, Narbonne, Perpignan, and Carcassonne, however, are plentifully supplied with hotels; inland, you'll find a fair number of pleasant if modest hotels and inns. The resort hotels may close between late October and April. Many offer discounts in May and October. Restaurants usually close one day a week. Hotels and restaurants are classified E, M, I, for Expensive, Moderate and Inexpensive.

AGDE. *Arraur* (I), no restaurant. *Tamarissière*, moderate, 4 km southwest, has good restaurant with *nouvelle cuisine*. See also Cap d'Agde.

AMÉLIE-LES-BAINS (Spa). *Grand Hôtel Reine Amélie* (M). *Castel Emeraude* (M), lovely garden on the banks of the clear Tech river.

At **Arles-sur-Tech** is *Les Glycines*, inexpensive little hotel with carefully cooked meals.

ARGELÈS-SUR-MER. *Plage des Pins* (M), by the beach at Argelès-Plage, modern and pleasant. Also at beach: *Marbella* (M). In town: *Golfe* (M), no restaurant.

Restaurant. *Lido* (M), by the beach; also has (M) rooms.

BANYULS-SUR-MER beach and winter resort. *Catalan*, (E), with pool by the beach. *Elmes* (M). *Cap Doune* (I).

Restaurant. Pleasant *Pergola* (I) has a few (M) rooms.

BÉZIERS. *Imperator* (M), no restaurant, *Compagnie du Midi* (M), *Europe* (M), all open all year, as is *Castelet* (I), 15 rooms, while *Midi La Rascasse* (M), with good restaurant, is closed part of Nov.

Restaurants. Best is *L'Olivier* (E), *nouvelle cuisine*. *Trou Normand*, 13 allées Paul-Riquet, and *Cigale*, same street, are both good and (M).

LE BOULOU. *Centre* (I), modest little hotel-restaurant, has been serving food for decades.

CANET-EN-ROUSSILLON. Beach resort near Perpignan. *Mar I Cel* (M), *Aquarius* (M), with pool. *Sables* (M), with pool but no restaurant.

CAP D'AGDE. Pleasant *St-Clair* (M), with pool, deserves more than its two-star rating; *Voile d'Or* (M), *Ibis* (M). All these are modern. *Grande Conque* (M), on rocky promontory, dates back to the time before the new resort was built; pleasant, but it no longer has a restaurant.

Apartment hotels: *Tourotel, Agathéa.*

Restaurants: *Brasero* (M), good fish; *Boucanier* (M).

CAPENDU. Hotel-restaurant *Top du Roulier* (I).

CARCASSONNE. *Cité* (E), spacious, comfortable, rather grand; no restaurant. *Donjon,* moderate, no restaurant, comfortable. Both these are within the city walls, rather difficult to reach by car. Outside the citadel are the nicely furnished *Montségur* and *Terminus,* no restaurant; both (M). *Aragon* (M), pleasant, is at foot of Cité; no restaurant.

About 4 km southeast, at **Auriac,** is the pleasant *Domaine d'Auriac* (E), in own grounds. Near the airport is the *Motel Salvaza* (M).

Restaurants. Best is *Logis de Trencavel* (M), 286 av. Gen.-Leclerc, which also has 12 rooms. Others are *Auberge du Pont Levis* (M), overlooking the old town, with a cheaper grill room downstairs (I). Friendly *Sénéchal* (I), in attractive building inside the walls, has good-value fixed-priced meals with local specialties like *cassoulet*. *Crémade* (I) is conveniently near St-Nazaire basilica.

CERET. *Terrasse au Soleil* (E), attractive, peaceful, with pool and interesting cuisine (M).

COLLIOURE. Best are *Méditerranée* (no restaurant), *Madeloc* (no restaurant) and *Hostellerie des Templiers,* all (M). Out of town on Port Vendres road: *Caranques* (M), small but exclusive. *Villa Basque, Casa Pairal,* moderate, *Boramar,* inexpensive.

Restaurants. *Templiers* (M), brimming with atmosphere and paintings; good fish. *Frégate* (E), good *nouvelle cuisine*. *Bodega* specializes in seafood (M). *Chiberta* (I), reader-recommended, good value. *Puits* (I), in small street near harbor.

LANGUEDOC AND ROUSSILLON

CUCUGNAN. Restaurant. *Auberge de Cucugnan* (I), delicious local recipes.

FONT-ROMEU. *Soleil d'Or,* with restaurant and separate grill room, moderate. *Clair Soleil,* moderate, has good views of the mountains. The quiet *Y Sem Bé* (M). *Romarin* (I) at **Odeillo**, 3 km away.

LA GRANDE MOTTE. *Frantel* (E), Moorish style, with good restaurant (E). *Alexandre,* good restaurant (see below), *Méditerranée* (E), with pool, no restaurant. *Quetzal* (M). Also apartment-hotels: *Garden Motel* and *Bernard de Ventadour,* bungalows. Several vacation villages.
Restaurant. *Amirauté* (E), part of the Alexandre hotel, excellent *nouvelle cuisine,* good service, lovely views, probably the best restaurant in the area.

GRUISSAN. *Corail* (M), pleasant with restaurant. *Plage* (I), no restaurant. *Motel de la Clape* (M). *Vacation Village* 5 km away, on beach.
Restaurant. *Le Chébek* (M), by harbor, good for fish dishes.

LIMOUX. *Moderne et Pigeon* (I), with restaurant.

MÉJANNES-LE-CLAP. *Dolmen,* moderate, open only April-Nov. *Méjannes,* inexpensive, is open all year. Vacation village, *Val.*

MOLITG-LES-BAINS. *Château de Riell,* expensive, romantic and deluxe, private beach on lake, sauna. Excellent *nouvelle cuisine* restaurant (E). Relais et Châteaux member.

MONTPELLIER. *Sofitel, Métropole* (E). *Frantel* (E), *George V* (M), no restaurant. Lovely *Demeure des Brousses* in a tranquil garden 4½ km east; has an arrangement with good restaurant nearby called *Mas.* (I) hotels include *Noailles* (M), *Paris* (I) and *Arceaux* (I). (None has restaurant).
At **Pérols**, 7 km on Carnon road, is the modern *PLM Fréjorgues,* moderate, with pool and restaurant and close to airport and beaches.
Restaurants. Best is *Les Frères Runel* (E), 27 rue Maguelone, excellent classical cuisine. *Nice* (M), 14 rue Boussairolles. *Rimbaud* (E), av. de Saint-Maur, outdoor dining. *Table de la Reine* (M) and *Petit Jardin* (I).

NARBONNE. Best is *Résidence* (M), furnished with antiques. No restaurant. Also recommended are *Mapotel du Languedoc* (M) with (I) restaurant and *Novotel* (M), with pool and restaurant. *Midi* (I) and *France* (I), are both in town, as is *Régina* (I). *Caravelle* (I) is at **Narbonne-Plage**.
Restaurants. *Réverbère* (M), best in town, with *nouvelle cuisine* versions of regional dishes. *Alsace* (M), 2 av. P-Semard; *Floride* (M), 66 bld F.-Mistral.

PALAVAS-LES-FLOTS. *Amérique* (M) and *Hippocampe* (M) are best. *Mar y Sol, Languedoc* and *France* are all inexpensive. Of all these, only France has restaurant.
Restaurants. *Sphinx* (M). *Oustal de la Mer* (M). *Maison de l'Huître* (M) has good shellfish.

PERPIGNAN. *Catalogne* (M) and *Park* (M), with a good restaurant (M), are best. *Christina* (M), no restaurant. *Pyrénées* is inexpensive. No restaurant.
Restaurants. *François-Villon,* rue de Four St-Jean, has new versions of Catalan recipes (M). *Bourgogne* (M), 63 av. Gén.-Leclerc. *Lyonnais* (M), 95 blvd Aristide-Briand, has mixture of classical and new cuisine. *Apéro* (M), chic, good value *nouvelle cuisine. Relais St-Jean* (I), 1 cité Bartissol.
At **L'Ecluse** on N9 to Spain is the *Auberge de l'Ecluse* (M-E), an old and beautifully sited Catalan house with 21 rooms and pool.

PEYRIAC MINERVOIS. *Château de Violet* (M), lovely rooms with antique furniture and some suites. Restaurant.

PORT-BARCARÉS. *PLM Lydia-Playa,* expensive, 192 rooms, restaurant, pool; closed Nov. to May. *Motel Suisse et Bordeaux,* moderate, near the main road. *Front-de-Mer,* more central, inexpensive, as is modest *Mer.* Several vacation villages. Residence Hotel: *Coudalère* (M).

PORT CAMARGUE. *Spinaker,* moderate, small, by harbor, with pool, and with good restaurant. The much larger *Chabian,* again with pool, is moderate.

PORT-LEUCATE. *Corail,* inexpensive.

PORTÉ-PUYMORENS. *Col,* modest, inexpensive.

PORT VENDRES. Beach resort near Spanish border, north of Banyuls. *Tamarins* is moderate and *St-Elme* is inexpensive.
Restaurant. *Costa-Brava* (I); also has a few rooms.

PRADES. *Les Glycines,* modest and inexpensive.

QUILLAN. *Chaumière* (M), with good restaurant.

RIVESALTES. *Novotel,* with pool, expensive. *Debèze* (I), small, in center of old town, with good regional cuisine.

SAILLAGOUSSE. *Planotel* (M), reader-recommended, quiet.

ST-CYPRIEN. *Glycines* (I), with pleasant restaurant (M). *Mar y Sol,* inexpensive. Both are close to the beach. Beside the golf course is *Mas d'Huston,*

LANGUEDOC AND ROUSSILLON

expensive, with pool, tennis courts, two restaurants, pleasant country club atmosphere. Also has apartment annex, (M).

ST-PONS. *Château de Pondérach* (E), charming Relais et Châteaux member on road to Narbonne, with good restaurant (E).

SALSES. On N9, 1.3 km from town, *Relais Roussillon,* moderate.

SÈTE. *Grand* (M) and *Impérial* (E) (2 km, 1 mile outside town), are best. Others include *Paris* (I), *Régina* (M) and *Brise-Lames* (M) at the old port, no restaurant. On N108, 2 km (1 mile) to the south, is the unpretentious *Floride,* moderate. At **Bouzigues,** 16 km to the west and overlooking the Thau lagoon, is the *Motel de la Côte Bleue* (E), with pool.
   Restaurants. *Madrague* (I), *Palangrotte* (M), excellent; *Marine* (M), popular. All by old harbor (*Vieux Port*).

VALRAS-PLAGE. *Mira-Mar* (M) is best. *Plage* (M) and *Moderne* (M) are smaller.

VERNET-LES-BAINS. (Spa) Best are *Résidence des Baüs* (M) and *Mas Fleuri* (M), beautiful private grounds and mountain views; comfortable. *Moderne* (I) and *Eden* (I).

CASINOS. There are casinos at Alet-les-Bains, near Limoux, Amélie-les-Bains, Le Boulou, and Vernet-les-Bains. Vernet-les-Bains, Amélie-les-Bains and Le Boulou are open year-round, Alet in the summer season only. You can play boule at all of them; Amélie also has baccara, roulette and blackjack, while Le Boulou has all these plus 30/40. Of the new resorts, La Grande Motte has a casino and Port Barcarès has a casino once again in the liner Lydia beached on the sands.

SPAS. All the above places, except La Grande Motte, are also spas, treating complaints ranging from respiratory problems to rheumatism. Further information from the regional tourist office.

WINTER SPORTS. Most of the Pyrenees skiing centers are covered in our next chapter, but Font-Romeu, at 1,798 m (5,904 ft), is in this region. Rates are lower in the Pyrenees than in the Alps, mainly because the accent is on ski rather than *après-ski,* and you also have the advantage of sunnier and warmer weather on the whole. Font-Romeu is in fact one of the smartest of the Pyrenees resorts, and it does go in for quite a bit of social life. It is also well organized to receive children and beginners. It gets a great deal of sunshine and the climate is generally mild. The season runs from approximately Dec. to Apr., both here and in the various smaller resorts in this region such as Porté-Puymorens.

TOULOUSE AND THE CENTRAL PYRENEES

Tradition as rugged as the mountains

By
JOHN ARDAGH

The high Pyrenees, separating France from Spain, form one of Europe's great natural frontiers. They are a prime cause of Spain's centuries-old sense of isolation, and to the whole region on the French side of the border they have given the feeling of being in a cul-de-sac. From Paris you drive south for nearly 800 km (500 miles) across plains and low hills, then are stopped short by a seemingly impenetrable range of snowy peaks, glowing pink in the early sun or glistening white at noon.

This is still a largely unspoilt region of swift mountain streams, lush valleys, mysterious caves, red-brick Romanesque churches and medieval hilltop castles, and from its long and turbulent history it retains today a sense of being different. In the 13th century it nurtured the famous Albigensian or Cathar heresy, and tribal memories linger of Paris's brutal suppression of those martyrs. Toulouse, the regional capital, known since medieval days as 'the counter-Paris', is still the most sullenly hostile to Paris of the larger French towns. And in Pau, to the west, the lords of lower Navarre ruled in independence from France until as late as 1620.

Even within today's centralized State, the spirit of independence persists throughout the region. People are proud, looking on Parisians as a remote and inferior breed. They speak with the twangy accent of the Midi (the general term for all southern France) and they like to live at an easy pace, even though the rhythm of the factory-belt is today impinging on that of the slow game of *boules* played in some dusty square. People are excitable and contentious, but though quarrels flare up suddenly they as quickly subside, and are buried over a friendly glass or two (or three) of *pastis* in a café. *Boules* (an early version of bowls, played with clinking metal balls) and the drinking of *pastis* (an anisette-based aperitif) are two traditions that strongly survive, and another—notably around Toulouse—is the eating of *cassoulet*, a splendid rich stew of preserved goose, pork, spicy sausage and beans. Try it, but not at lunch unless you plan to take a siesta afterwards. A newer tradition is rugby football, imported from England in the last century and today a cult practised more fervently here than anywhere in the British Isles. Most of the rest of France prefers association football, but the southwest plays rugby—just to be different!

The Pyrenees, rising to 3,200 meters (10,500 ft), are Western Europe's highest chain after the Alps. The Romans loved these mountains with their healing springs and fine climate, but during the Middle Ages they were largely forgotten. Only in the 18th century did geologists begin to examine them properly, and the work was continued in Victorian days by such pioneers as Lord Henry Russell, a Franco-Irish peer who staged a romantic ten-year retreat in a grotto.

A state reforestation program is today under way, to make good the damage done by many years of tree-felling and subsequent soil erosion. Other measures too are dispelling some of the old solitude of the mountains. Hydro-electric power has been developed in the upper valleys, and modern roads into Spain have been built over passes or through tunnels. Modern tourism has been making psychological

TOULOUSE AND THE CENTRAL PYRENEES 479

fissures in that historic mountain barrier too; and if and when Spain joins the EEC, the breaches may well grow wider.

The region is known and loved by countless visitors of many kinds, from climbers to painters, from trout or salmon fishermen to prehistorians. It has spas and ski-slopes, and is served by a modern tourist highway engineered in the best French manner—the Route des Pyrénées. Most of the hotels have been modernized too. No longer, Miranda, will you be asked to remember the fleas that tease, or the spreading of straw for a bedding. A plus for comfort, if not for romance.

Toulouse: rose-pink palaces and supersonic Concorde

The northern gateway to the Pyrenees is the ebullient city of Toulouse, one-time capital of Languedoc, today France's fourth largest town with a population of 500,000. Sprawling astride the river Garonne on a wide plain, it has grown since the war from a quiet market town to a noisy, dusty, traffic-packed industrial metropolis, animated, cosmopolitan, rich in contrasts between old and new. Like some huge Neapolitan ice-cream, it is pink in the middle, white outside: the old inner city, with its elegant Renaissance palaces and Romanesque churches, is mellow rose-pink brick, while around it lies the modern Toulouse of Le Corbusier-inspired housing estates, aircraft factories, student campuses and science centers, gleaming white under the Midi sun. This is France's aviation capital, where the Caravelle and Concorde were built, and today Airbus; it is an electronics center too, and one of the leading French university towns, with 40,000 students and a special emphasis on modern technology. Toulouse lives late: the downtown sidewalks and outdoor cafés are busy way past midnight with an international throng—Spaniards, Algerians, executives and scientists from Paris, local peasant emigrants, plus a few Germans and British at work on Airbus.

Historic Toulouse has a wealth of interest. The basilica of St-Sernin is the finest and largest Romanesque church in the Midi, and the richest in relics: its crypt holds the remains of more than 100 saints. The cathedral of St-Etienne, a strange asymmetrical building, was begun in the 11th century and never completed; other remarkable early churches are the Jacobins and the Dalbade. The leading museum, the Augustins, is noted for its antique sculptures; also worth visits are the Paul Dupuy and St-Raymond museums, the latter with the best collection of imperial Roman busts outside Italy.

In the narrow streets of the old city are great gateways opening on to courtyards, round which stand imposing Renaissance mansions (finest is the Hôtel Assezat); many are still lived in by their aristocratic owners, and some are topped by the red-bricked towers of the 'Capitouls', former consular rulers of the city. On the main square, the town hall, the Capitole, is a stately 18th-century brick palace, home also of one of the best French opera companies. Toulouse prides itself on being a musical center, and all summer concerts are held in enchantingly floodlit old courtyards or on the banks of the Garonne. Try also to see the Ballets Occitans, a polished and lively local folk-dance group.

Armagnac country; Montauban, Albi, Castres

The open rolling country round Toulouse offers much of interest. To the west is the former county of Armagnac, today producing the brandy of that name which, for many connoisseurs, rivals the best cognacs (to ask for a cognac, rather than an armagnac, can be taken as an insult in this area). North of Toulouse, the market town of Montauban on the river Tarn was a key Protestant citadel in the 16th century: it has pink brick arcades, a graceful 14th-century bridge, and a notable museum devoted chiefly to the works of the town's most famous son, the painter Ingres.

Further upstream, also on the Tarn, is the remarkable city of Albi, dominated by the towering red walls of its famous cathedral. This was formerly fortified, and is an odd mixture of Romanesque and Gothic: don't miss its intricately carved rood screen. The former episcopal palace close by was also once fortified. Today it houses a museum with the world's best collection of works by Toulouse-Lautrec, the painter of Montmartre life who was born in Albi. You can also visit his birthplace, in the street that now bears his name.

Northwest of Albi is a delightful curiosity—the tiny walled medieval town of Cordes, on a high hilltop eyrie above the valley. And to the south is Castres, still a cloth-weaving town as it was in the Middle Ages. Overhanging the river, and reflected in it, are some picturesque old balconied houses. The local museum, surprisingly, has a fine collection of Spanish art, notably Goya. Nearby is the strange plateau of Sidobre, strewn with thousands of smooth rocks in all shapes, providing granite for the local stone-carving workshops.

Pau: French nobility and English colonists

This busy and sophisticated city of 125,000 people is a good center for excursions into the Western Pyrenean area: its boulevard des Pyrénées offers beautiful views of the snowy peaks. Pau is the capital of the highly individual region known as Béarn, and it has a royal past, best studied by visiting its great château where the lords of Béarn, Foix and Navarre held sway over a large slice of France in the centuries before 1620. The inscription over the entrance, *'Touches-y si tu l'oses'* ('Touch this if you dare'), was that of the golden-haired Gaston 'Phoebus', flamboyant and volatile count of Foix in the 14th century. He murdered his brother and his only son, but was also a poet and kept open court to writers and troubadours (all this part of France was troubadour country).

Marguerite of Angoulême, a 16th-century *châtelaine,* remodeled the castle in the style of her age, the Renaissance, and its fine furnishings and Gobelin tapestries reflect her taste. This beautiful woman of parts held brilliant balls and banquets, her pastorales were performed in the castle gardens, and she wrote the *Heptaméron,* a collection of 72 tales modeled on Boccaccio. It was said of her, 'She has the body of a woman, the heart of a man, the head of an angel', but her virago daughter, Jeanne d'Albret, earned the remark, 'She has nothing of woman but the sex.' Yet it was Jeanne who gave the world the future Henri IV, amorist, life-lover, benefactor of the common people and one of France's favorite kings—'Our Henry', he is still called in Béarn.

The area round Pau breathes *douceur de vivre:* the countryside is green and gentle, the winters are mild, and it was these qualities that drew thousands of Britons to settle here, after Wellington's officers discovered the place around 1815 on their return from Spain. By the 1860s about a third of Pau's population of 9,000 was British; indeed it was the largest British colony outside the Empire, with its own shops, tea parties, balls and fox hunts. Today Pau is one of the smartest towns in France, mixing civilized elegance with industrial boom. Large deposits of natural gas were discovered in the 1950s at Lacq, and a functional new town was built close by at Mourenx to house the workers.

The Pau district offers much of cultural and geological interest. Nearby are the grottoes of Bétharram, with spectacular stalactites; the cathedral of Lescar; and fine old churches at Morlaas and Monein. In the Ossau valley, south of Pau, are the pleasant little spas of Eaux-Bonnes and Eaux-Chaudes, whose sulfurous waters are used to treat rheumatism and chest troubles. At Laruns, on some feast days, the women parade in their elaborate traditional costumes.

Northeast of Pau—take the long straight road from Lannemezan— lies Auch, standing proudly on its hill above the well-farmed plains. The home town of d'Artagnan, of Musketeer fame, Auch is an attractive, busy spot, especially on market days. The cathedral has some magnificent 16th-century stained glass and huge carved-oak choir stalls, thronged with figures.

Lourdes: the pilgrimage industry

East of Pau is the industrial town of Tarbes, whose airport receives a non-stop airlift of large jets, to and from such places as Rome, Dublin and Brussels. Why? This is also the airport for Lourdes, and in southwest France there's no growth industry like the pilgrimage industry. Lourdes has more hotel space (400 hotels) than any town in France save Paris. It claims three million pilgrims a year, drawn here by the story of Bernadette, the great churches built near the site of her visions, and the miraculous cures attributed to the spring waters.

In February 1858, Bernadette Soubirous, aged 14, daughter of a local miller, claimed that the Virgin Mary had appeared to her near the Massabielle grotto. A subsequent vision (there were 18 in all) was accompanied by the miraculous gushing of water where no known spring existed. Pilgrims flocked there, drawn by reports of the water's healing powers, and four years later the Church accepted the miracle's authenticity. Bernadette was canonized in 1933.

Of the six annual pilgrimages today, the main one is on August 15, when huge crowds attend daylight and torchlight processions. It is hard not to be impressed by the long winding columns of pilgrims bearing lighted torches, chanting 'Ave Maria', and by the fervent faces of poor and rich who have come from the five continents. But some visitors may be distressed by the sight of the armies of cripples hopefully crawling up the wide flight of steps to the Church of the Rosary; or they may be sickened by the town's blatant commercialization, where hundreds of shops sell souvenirs of the saint in every shape and form—a carnival of holy kitsch.

In 1958, the centenary of the first vision, the world's largest underground church, the basilica of Pope Pius X, was completed, able to hold 20,000 people. Through clever use of reinforced concrete, it has one single unsupported vault. You should see also the house where Bernadette was born, and the museum that shows a film of her life. Dominating the town, the fortified château is a fine specimen of medieval military architecture. It has impressive *son et lumière* shows in summer, and also houses the Pyrenean Museum, one of the best of French provincial museums, with a notable collection of peasant costumes, pottery, stuffed animals, and scenes of local life.

The high Pyrenees: spas and ski resorts

From Laruns all the way to Luchon, the Route des Pyrénées takes the motorist up through spectacular mountain scenery, under the brow of the mighty Pic du Midi de Bigorre (2,894 meters/9,500 ft) and over the Tourmalet pass (1,980 meters/6,500 ft). Here we are no longer in Béarn but in neighboring Bigorre, and the valleys are dotted with little spas and ski resorts where the athletic and the rheumatic make common cause. Cauterets, south of Lourdes, is one such ski/spa center: since Roman times its thermal springs have been thought to benefit sterile women. Is is a coincidence that Cauterets is also fertile in literary romance? Victor Hugo womanized here, George Sand discovered the thrills of adultery, Chateaubriand sighed for his 'inaccessible Occitan girl'.

From Cauterets there are two classic excursions to two of the best-known beauty spots of the central Pyrenees. One is via the Pont d'Espagne to the lake of Gaube. You drive up a steep winding road, then either climb on foot or go by chair-lift to the plateau at the end of which is the famous bright-blue 16-hectare (40-acre) lake. From here, a sturdy walker with a guide can cut over the mountains to the even more famous Cirque de Gavarnie, more easily reached by car from Luz. The road climbs up a narrow valley into rugged country and ends at the village of Gavarnie, at the foot of the Cirque (circus). This is a giant natural amphitheater, set in a ring of mountains: from its cliffs, nearly a mile high in places, plunge numerous waterfalls when the upper snows are melting. The Cirque is one of the world's most remarkable examples of glacial erosion, and has long had an appeal for mountain climbers (in the village is a statue to one of them, Lord Russell).

Barèges, to the north, is in country with streams full of trout and mountains full of partridge. Northeast again, Bagnères-de-Bigorre is both an industrial town and a health resort, and was favored in the past by Montaigne, Rossini and others. It is a good walking center, but the high mountains are not close. Some 64 km (40 miles) to the east lies the largest and most fashionable of Pyrenean spas, Bagnères-de-Luchon (usually known as Luchon). It has a golf course and luxury shops, and attracts opera singers, barristers, politicians and other windbags (its thermal specialty is treatment of the vocal chords!). The town lies at the head of a lush valley, below the highest of all the Pyrenean peaks, and it is worth driving up the 17 km (11 miles) of scenic road to Superbagnères, a ski resort perched on a plateau 1,218 meters (4,000 ft) above Luchon with marvelous views of the Maladeta range.

St-Bertrand-de-Comminges, 32 km (20 miles) north of Luchon, is also worth a visit. This was an important Roman center (Herod and Herodias were banished here), but in the 6th century the city was wiped out by plague, and its Roman forum, baths, temple and theater were silted over. Now they are being excavated. Nearby is the 9th-century church of St-Just-de-Valcabrère, half-hidden by cypresses, a marvel of early Romanesque. And a mile away, crowning a tiny walled medieval city, is the 12th-century cathedral built by Bertrand, bishop of Comminges. Its Romanesque cloister, with finely proportioned arches, looks serenely over the valley below; within there are brilliantly carved Renaissance choir stalls.

Prehistoric caves and Cathar ruins

The area between Luchon and Foix is rich in prehistory. Some 8 km (5 miles) from St-Bertrand is the grotto of Gargas, known as 'the cave of cut hands,' for its vault is covered with the imprints of mutilated hands, suggesting barbaric rituals during the Aurignacian Age. Perhaps the most remarkable of Pyrenean caves is the Mas-d'Azil, north of St-Girons. It is a natural tunnel 800 meters (2,640 ft) long, formed by the river Arize, and in its caves Magdalenian man has left rock engravings of bison, reindeer, horses and cats, as well as the bones and teeth of the prehistoric animals he ate. Early Christians in the 3rd century, Cathars in the 13th, Huguenots in the 17th, all sought refuge in these caverns, which are so vast that they were even used as aircraft factories in World War II.

Near Foix is the underground river of Labouiche, where waters have tunneled for 5 km (3 miles) through the limestone cliffs: you can take a 90-minute boat-ride, and admire the cleverly floodlit stalactites. Farther south, in the Vicdessos valley beyond Tarascon, the superb Niaux grotto is comparable to Spain's Altamira because of its well-preserved Magdalenian rock paintings, dating to about 20,000 BC. Scores of horses, deer and bison, simply but elegantly drawn, line a natural gallery just under 1 km (½ mile) from the entrance. Now that Lascaux is closed, this is the finest ensemble of prehistoric art in France open to the public; but the constant stream of tourists is damaging these paintings too, and Niaux in its turn may soon have to be closed, unless there is a strict limit on visits.

The capital of this district is the appealing little town of Foix, crowned by its 11th-century castle perched high on a rock above the town center. The castle with its three tall towers has a children's picturebook quality. It was ferociously besieged during the anti-Cathar crusade; today it houses a museum of prehistoric and medieval art. In early September the château is floodlit and colorful folkdancing takes place in the streets below.

Thirty-two km (20 miles) to the southeast are the ruins of the famous castle of Montségur, scene of the final tragic martyrdom of the Cathars in 1244. All this part of France, from Foix and Toulouse to as far east as Montpellier, was the country of the Cathars (or Albigensians) and the memory of that terrifying episode is still alive in local hearts and minds. Imported from the Middle East and the Balkans, the Albigensian 'heresy' flourished in Languedoc in the early 13th century, where

TOULOUSE AND THE CENTRAL PYRENEES

it took its name from Albi, one of its main centers. Its believers preached a doctrine of ascetic purity, rejecting earthly life as evil; and its spiritual leaders were known as 'the pure ones', *'Les Cathares'*. They implicitly criticized the worldly ways of the Church. So Pope Innocent III ordered a crusade against them, finding willing executives in the Capetian rulers of France, who identified Catharism with Languedoc nationalism and its rejection of Parisian hegemony. The crusade, under Simon de Montfort, was of appalling severity. Soldiers marched down from the north, burning towns, massacring whole populations whether practising Cathars or not: 'Kill them all, God will then recognise his own', was one commander's order-of-the-day.

Toulouse and other centers were subjugated, and the last remaining 200 'pure ones' took refuge in Montségur, where they were besieged, captured and burned alive in March 1244. The castle, today in ruins, stands in lonely splendor on a hilltop amid glorious wooded country, and is worth a visit. In the tiny village nearby is a Cathar museum, and a 'spiritualist library' of assorted religions and philosophies, run by ardent local bohemians—for Montségur today is a leading center of the new cult of interest in Catharism. This is linked with political opposition to Paris—the people of this area resent Paris's 'colonization' almost as much as their ancestors did, and so they cherish the memory of the Cathar martyrs.

Andorra, the last feudal state

High in the Pyrenees on the southward side of the passes, Andorra is one of Europe's tiniest independent states, with 21,000 inhabitants. It is also Europe's last surviving feudal protectorate: a treaty of 1278 placed it under the joint tutelage of the bishop of nearby Seo d'Urgel in Spain, and of the count of Foix, and this remains in force, save that the count's role has now passed to the president of France. The protectors rarely intervene and Andorra is in practice independent, with her own little army, her own laws and ruling council, but no separate currency: francs and pesetas are both used. Catalan is the official language.

The country's remoteness kept it from being swallowed up by its neighbors. There is still no airport or railroad, and the main road from France follows a series of dizzy hairpin bends over the highest of the Pyrenean passes, the Elvira (2,406 meters/7,900 ft). This road is closed in winter, but all through the season it is jammed with tourist traffic, and Andorra's once-primitive villages are now a concrete jungle of banks, hotels, snack bars and duty-free supermarkets. For this is a tax-free paradise, where gasoline, liquor, cameras, watches and much else can be bought at little more than half French prices. This draws trippers from France in thousands. Smuggling, too, is an organized industry.

In the side valleys, away from the main road, are a few hamlets where livestock breeding is still practised and the traditional Andorran way of life has not been totally swamped by the tourist boom. In the capital, Andorra-la-Vella, the House of the Valley where the 'parliament' meets is an interesting 16th-century building. But apart from this, the country has little to attract the visitor in search of more than cut-price goods. Even the shrine of the curious Notre-Dame de Meritxell, worshipped by Andorrans as their patroness, was destroyed by fire in 1972. Divine vengeance, maybe.

PRACTICAL INFORMATION

WHEN TO GO. Although spring in this part of France can be rainy, it is also the time when the Pyrenean flowers are at their best. June and Sept. are pleasantly uncrowded and you're virtually sure to get good weather, whereas in July and Aug. all places, especially the spas, are packed with holidaymakers and it's also very hot. Lourdes is almost unbearably crowded during the mid-Aug. pilgrimage. Fall and winter are best for trout and salmon fishing in the mountain streams. Officially the winter sports season in the Pyrenees runs from Dec. to April, but snow conditions this far south can be tricky until well into Feb. or March. Jan. is the best month if you're on a budget, since most ski resorts offer bargain-rate accommodation at this time.

Late **March** is the time for Albi's carnival, while the first major pilgrimage in Lourdes (the 'military pilgrimage') comes in early **May** or at **Easter**, with week-long celebrations. **June** sees the lively Grand Fénétra fair in Toulouse, with traditional folklore events and much dancing and singing; and the Gascony Festival in Auch. **July** is a busy month, with the Occitania Festival in Montauban; an International Guitar Festival in Castres; the Comminges Organ Festival in St-Bertrand-de-Comminges; the Theater Festival in Albi. Running through **July and August** are the Music Festival in Cordes and another one in Albi. August 13–16 is the peak time in Lourdes, with the National Pilgrimage centered round the Feast of the Assumption of the Virgin Mary on August 15 (which is also a national holiday). Barèges usually has a Mountain Fair in mid-August, while **September** is the time for the Bach Festival in Mazamet and Foix's Festival. The Rosary Pilgrimage in Lourdes normally takes place in early **October.**

WHAT TO DO. Skiing is a major attraction in the Pyrenees, and so is **climbing** (for both of these see our special sections below), but for those who like an active holiday there are plenty of other opportunities in this very varied region.

Walking holidays are particularly enjoyable here, with hundreds of miles of signposted footpaths, including some running through the Pyrenees National Park. The tourist offices will provide you with maps.

Canoeing is good in the Ariège *département* around Foix, and several organizations offer lessons in canoeing and **kayaking**, including some for young people (about 14–17). **Cycling** is also popular, you can get in some practise at hill climbs; Foix has a Cyclotouring Center and the *Comité de Cyclisme des Pyrénées* is based in Toulouse. **Riding** is good too, with riding clubs and associations in all towns of any size and many riding centers where you can have an all-in weekend or week; if you prefer to see the horse do most of the work you can have a peaceful week or so in a horse-drawn caravan, or even a little carriage.

Another peaceful way of visiting the region is to drift down the Canal du Midi on a **barge** (information from the Toulouse tourist office or from Blue Line Cruisers in Castelnaudary—see addresses section). If you want to go **fishing** in the region's mountain streams or lakes, you'll need a permit from the local fishing association (inquire at tourist office); trout and salmon are plentiful in the mountains, and you may find perch and pike in the lower-lying areas.

The **Pyrenees National Park** is a paradise for nature lovers, not least because it contains some rare specimens of fauna that are not found elsewhere in France (including 30 or so bears); the mountain flowers are beautiful too. For information write to the *Direction du Parc National des Pyrénées*, BP 300, 65013 Tarbes-Ibos, France.

Craft workshops are particularly common here, and you can learn such activities as making mosaics, lithography, painting on silk, weaving and ironwork. If you prefer more intellectual pursuits you can visit the Cathar châteaux, most of which are open May–Sept. or trace the prehistory of the region by visiting the many caves (they too are normally open in the summer only, and you usually need a guide).

Golf enthusiasts have a choice of five courses, at Lannemezan, Luchon, Mazamet and Vieille-Toulouse (all 9 holes) and at Buzet-sur-Tarn (18 holes).

Gastronomy is well catered for, not only in the region's restaurants, but in the number of opportunities for cooking lessons and classes introducing visitors to the local cuisine. The Gers *département* is particularly active in organizing such courses (write to the *Comité Départemental de Tourisme et des Loisirs* in Auch), but you can also have a week-long gastronomic tour starting from Lourdes and staying in 3-star hotels (write to *GREP Tours La Minaudière*, Poueyferré, 65100 Lourdes, France). Local tourist offices will give you details of opportunities to learn how to cook regional specialties.

HOW TO GET ABOUT. By air. *Air France* flies direct to Toulouse from London–Heathrow every day except Sat. and Sun. in winter, with additional flights in summer. *Air Inter* has frequent flights between Paris and Toulouse, and also flies Paris to Pua, while services between Toulouse and Bordeaux, Lille, Lyon, Nice and Strasbourg may help you cut traveling time. There are also frequent flights to Tarbes (for Lourdes) from Paris. *Aer Lingus* has summer flights Dublin–Tarbes. *Dan Air* flies London (Gatwick) to Toulouse. *TAT* flies to Toulouse from Ajaccio, Bastia, Clermont Ferrand, Figari, Lille, Marseille and Nantes; and to Albi from Paris.

By train. The fastest rail route is the excellent *Le Capitole*, which covers the distance between Paris (Gare d'Austerlitz) and Toulouse in only 6 hrs, also stopping at Montauban (5½ hrs). Paris–Pau via Bordeaux takes about 7½ hrs. There are several trains a day between Toulouse and Pau via Tarbes. There are also services from Toulouse to Luchon and Foix, and various picturesque local

TOULOUSE AND THE CENTRAL PYRENEES

lines passing through magnificent scenery. Car-couchette service is available between Paris and Tarbes (seasonal) and between Paris and Toulouse.

By bus. Unfortunately all the companies who used to run coach tours of the Pyrenees from Paris no longer operate, due mainly to the spread of air travel. The *SNCF* does have a combined coach and train weekend to Lourdes and the Lac d'Artouste, with excursions, but this takes place only two or three times a year. *Europabus's* Barcelona–Toulouse run may be useful if you're combining your visit with a trip to Spain. Locally, a good bus network runs circular tours to points of interest from such centers as Luchon (including an excursion into Andorra and Spain), Lourdes, Laruns, Foix, Perpignan and the Côte Vermeille (including trips to Andorra and Spain's Costa Brava). During July and August, the *SNCF* has reduced-price combined railway-bus excursions between Perpignan, Prades, or Villefranche-Vernet-les-Bains, and Mont-Louis.

MOTORING. From Paris the fastest route is the A10 *(L'Aquitaine)* motorway via Orléans, Blois, Tours to Poitiers, then the N170 to Limoges and the N20 to Toulouse via Brive-la-Gaillarde, Cahors and Montauban. For Pau you can either go to Toulouse and take the N117, or take the A10 to Poitiers, then the N10 to Angoulême and Bordeaux and the A61 (the new *Autoroute des Deux-Mers*) to Langon, then the D932 to Roquefort, D934 to Aire-sur-l'Adour and lastly the N134. For Lourdes you take the N117 from Toulouse to Tarbes and the N21 to Lourdes. Bordeaux-Toulouse now takes only 2 hrs on the A61 motorway.

Andorra can be reached in summer from France via the Pas de la Case (2,087 m/6,851 ft), and via the Envalira Pass (2,405m/7,897 ft), over a narrow twisting road (N20b branches off the N20 between Ax-les-Thermes and Bourg-Madame). No car papers beyond those needed in France or Spain are required. Fill up with the cheapest gasoline in Europe.

Within the region, a small stretch of motorway (the new A64) is open, bypassing Orthez and this continues to shortly before Tarbes.

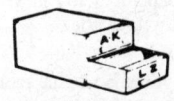

USEFUL ADDRESSES. Toulouse's *Office de Tourisme,* with *Welcome Information office,* youth information bureau, English-speaking hostesses and guides, is at Donjon du Capitole, sq. Charles-de-Gaulle. There is another office at Matabiau rail station. *Regional Tourist Committee* (for Midi–Pyrénées region) is at 3 rue de l'Esquile, 31000 Toulouse and will send you details of activities and events in the region, as well as making hotel reservations. All other main centers have tourist offices, or, in smaller places, *syndicats d'initiative.* The Midi-Pyrénées administrative region now has several reservation centers for *gîtes,* which provide popular and inexpensive holidays; inquire at tourist offices or the French Government Tourist Office. *Tourist Committee* for the Pyrénées-Atlantiques is at Parlement de Navarre, 64000 Pau.

Also in Toulouse is the *Service Départemental Jeunesse et Sports,* bld Armand-Duportal, for information about youth events and organizations and about sport. For information on accommodations, restaurants, sports leisure activities in Gascony, contact *Découverte de la Gascogne,* Maison de l'Agriculture, route de Mirande, 13200 Auch. In Paris: *Maison du Gers et de l'Armagnac,* 16 blvd Haussmann, 1er; *Maison des Pyrénées,* 24 rue du 4-Septembre, 2e; *Maison du Tarn,* 34 av. de Villiers, 17e.

Car hire. *Avis.* 3 rue Gabriel Pech, Albi; 12 bis av. du Général-Sarrail, Montauban; 66 rue d'Etigny, Pau; 14 cours de Reffye and airport, Tarbes; 26 bld Matabiau and airport, Toulouse. *Europcar,* 179 av. Gambetta, Albi; route de Toulouse, Auch; 8 pl. Clémenceau and airport, Pau; 50 bis av. Maréchal-Joffre and airport, Tarbes; 15 bld Bon-Repos and airport, Toulouse. *Hertz,* 15 bis blvd Bonrepos, Castres; 20 av. Gaston-Lacoste and airport, Pau; 24 rue du 4-Septembre, Tarbes; 16 rue Lafon and airport, Toulouse.

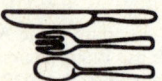

REGIONAL FOOD AND DRINK. The cuisine of the region is varied, rich, strongly seasoned, with plentiful use of garlic. The most famous dish is *cassoulet* (a succulent stew of preserved goose, spicy sausage, pork and beans), found in a number of local variations around Toulouse and Carcassonne. Like the rest of southwestern France, this is also the land of expensive *foie gras* (pâté of goose liver), most delicious when served hot with grapes. A cheaper specialty is *garbure,* an aromatic cabbage soup so thick that the spoon should stand upright in it unsupported.

In the western Pyrenees you find *magret de canard,* sliced steak of duck, cooked rare. Béarn, around Pau, is great eating country: try its richly marinaded stews, either of wood-pigeon *(civet de palombe)* or of wild goat *(civet d'isard).* The famous *sauce béarnaise* is not local, despite its name, but a Parisian invention.

This is not a region especially noted for its wines. But those of Béarn are pleasant enough, principally the white *Jurançon,* the red *Madiran,* and the *rosés.* East of Toulouse, the best wine is *Gaillac.* To the west of the city lies *Armagnac* country, producing brandy to rival the best cognacs.

In Andorra the cuisine is mainly Catalan, and usually cheaper than in France. The shops and bars sell Spanish wines and brandies at very low prices.

HOTELS AND RESTAURANTS. This is not an area for luxury hotels, but you'll find plenty of accommodations in all categories. Except in Toulouse and other major towns, and in ski resorts, hotels are often closed in winter, and so are restaurants in many cases. In the large towns prices are about 25% cheaper than in Paris, and about 40% cheaper in mountain villages and the small spa towns. Hotels and restaurants (many of which close one day a week too) are labeled *E, M* and *I* for expensive, moderate, inexpensive.

ALBI. Best is *Hostellerie St-Antoine,* expensive. *Chiffre* (M), quiet, good dining-room, is reader-recommended; *Moderne Pujol* (M). About 3 km (2 miles)

TOULOUSE AND THE CENTRAL PYRENEES

on D600, is the *Réserve*, in grounds by river, with pool, expensive, beautifully quiet.

At **Marssac**, 10 km (6½ miles) west, *Francis Cardaillac* (M), with pool, big garden and very good restaurant.

ANDORRA. At **Andorra-la-Vella:** *Président*, expensive, with pool. *Eden Roc* (E), *Flora*, moderate, no restaurant. *Consul*, inexpensive. At **Santa Coloma:** *La Cerqueda*, moderate, with (I) restaurant.

At **Les Escaldes:** *Comtes d'Urgell*, *Roc Blanc*, and *Hostal Andorra*, moderate, are best.

At **Encamp:** *Univers*, inexpensive.

At **Pas de la Casa:** *Refugi dels Isards*, moderate.

At **Sant Julia de Loria:** *Pol* (M), *Barcelona* (M). *Coma Bella*, moderate, comfortable, is beautifully situated in a forest.

At **Soldeu:** *Hôtel del Tarter* (I), reader-recommended for comfort and value.

ARGELÈS-GAZOST. *Cimes* (I), quiet. *Gabizos* (I), close to park.

AUCH. *France,* (E), with magnificent and justly renowned restaurant *Daguin*, famed for its duck specialties; very expensive. Also has a bar (called *Neuvième*) serving good (I) dishes.

Restaurant. *Toulousy* (M), at **Robinson** south on N21. Good chef.

AUTERIVE. Small *Pyrénées* is an inexpensive hotel-restaurant.

AX-LES-THERMES. Spa. Best is *Royal Thermal*, expensive. *Moderne*, comfortable, moderate. *Terminus* (M), small Logis de France.

BAGNÈRES-DE-BIGORRE. Spa (season, May 15–Oct. 15). *Résidence*, moderate, set in lovely grounds, with pool. *St-Vincent*, inexpensive.

BARÈGES. *Europe* and *Richelieu*, moderate. *Central* (I), small Logis de France with good full-board terms.

CASTRES. *Grand*, moderate.
Restaurant. *La Caravelle* (M), 150 av. Roquecourbe, for regional dishes.

CAUTERETS. Spa (May–Sept.) and winter sports center. *Trois Pics* (M), *Mouré* (M) and *Etche Ona*, moderate. *Peguère* (I), comfortable, and modest *Centre et Poste*. Family *pensions* are numerous. Try *Pont d'Espagne*, at **Pont d'Espagne,** inexpensive. About 5.5 km (3½ miles) south is the pleasant and inexpensive little *Fruitière*, in the national park, with regional cooking.

CONDOM. **Restaurant.** *Table des Cordeliers* (E), in a 14th-cent. building, gives you a sample of regional cooking. Also has 20 rooms in a separate building (called *Logis des Cordeliers*). Relais et Châteaux member.

CORDES. *Grand-Ecuyer* (E), an attractively decorated 14th-cent. house, expensive, with excellent *nouvelle cuisine* in restaurant.

EAUX-BONNES. *Poste* (I), with restaurant.

FOIX. *Hostellerie Barbacane*, moderate, no restaurant. *Audoye* (M).

LOURDES. *Gallia et Londres* (E), comfortable, but restaurant is disappointing. *Grand Hôtel de la Grotte* (E). *Ambassadeurs, Espagne* and *Impérial* (E). *Christina* (M), *Family* (I).
Restaurant. *D'Albret et Taverne de Bigorre* (M), with fixed-price meals in every price range. Also has some rooms.

LOURES-BAROUSSE. *Hostellerie des Vallées* (I), small and quiet with restaurant. **Restaurant.** *Divan* (M).

LUCHON. Spa (May–mid-Oct.) and winter sports resort. Best is *Poste et Golf* with fine restaurant (M), expensive. *Corneille* (E). *Henri-Sors* (I). *Bon Accueil* (I), Logis de France with some kitchenettes.
Restaurants. Your best bet is the restaurant in the *Corneille* hotel (M) or the *Rotonde* (M) in the *Poste et Golf*; both have local specialties.

MIREPOIX. Hotel-restaurant *Commerce*, inexpensive, with good-value restaurant.

MONGIE-TOURMALET. *Mandia* (E). *Crête Blanche* (M), small, shares restaurant with *Sol y Neou* (M).

MONTAUBAN. *Hostellerie Les Coulandrières*, on road to Castelsarrasin, with pool, is expensive. *Midi*, moderate.
Restaurants. *Chapon Fin* (M), 1 pl. St-Orens; *Delmas* (I), 10 rue Michelet. Both good.

NERAC. *Albret* (I), small and busy hotel-restaurant, with filling regional cuisine.

PAU. *Continental*, central, best, expensive. *Roncevaux* (M) and *Bristol* (M), 40 and 27 rooms, no restaurant. *Europe* (M), central but quiet. *Béarn* (I), no restaurant.
At **Lescar,** 7 km (4½ miles) west, *Novotel Pau-Lescar*, with pool.

TOULOUSE AND THE CENTRAL PYRENEES

At **Gelos**, 5 km (3 miles) south on Gan road, *Hostellerie le Bourbail* (I), a pleasant country inn, and at **Uzos**, the *Beau Manoir* (M), with pool.
Restaurants. Best is *Pierre*, 16 rue L.-Barthou, with excellent regional cuisine, (M). *Conti* (E), in Hôtel Continental, again with interesting 'new' dishes. At **Jurançon**, *Chez Ruffet* (M), good *nouvelle cuisine*, pleasant atmosphere.

PLAISANCE. *Ripa Alta* (M), excellent little hotel-restaurant, with good cooking.

RABASTENS. *Pré Vert* (I), delightful little hotel-restaurant on shady promenade des Lices.

RABASTENS-DE-BIGORRE. Restaurant. *Chez Yvonne* (I), rustic décor, good local dishes, friendly.

RÉALMONT. *Noël*, small and moderate but has superb food with local specialties, reasonably priced (M). Advisable to reserve for restaurant.

ST-BETRAND-DE-COMMINGES. *Comminges* (M). *Castex* (I), modest little place, amazing value.

ST-LARY. Popular winter sports center. *Terrasse Fleurie* (no restaurant). *Mir* (I). *Pons Le Dahu*, inexpensive.

SALIES-DE-BÉARN. Spa (season, Apr.–Oct.). *Blason*, inexpensive, has a good restaurant (I). *Larquier* (I), near casino, with restaurant.

SAUVETERRE-DES-COMMINGES. *Hostellerie des 7 Molles*, ringed by mountains, moderate, with excellent restaurant (M), pool and tennis courts.

TARBES. *Président*, with pool, restaurant (M) and grill (I). *Concorde* (M), just out on Lourdes road. *Foch, Normandie* and *Henri IV*, none with restaurant, moderate.
Restaurant. *Caravelle*, at airport (M).

TOULOUSE. *Frantel-Wilson*, in town center, is expensive; no restaurant. *Concorde* is only slightly less luxurious, but cheaper. Also expensive: *Sofitel*, at airport and *Novotel*, quite close to airport, are both modern, functional; *Caravelle* (no restaurant), too, is modern, but is in town center; all these have airconditioning.
Moderate: *Ours Blanc, Raymond IV*, neither with restaurant. Eight km (5 miles) south, on D21 at **Vieille-Toulouse**, is the peaceful *Flânerie*, set in lovely grounds near golf and riding facilities, but with no restaurant; moderate. Eight km (5 miles) west, at **Tournefeuille**, is *Chanterelles* (E), a Relais du Silence.

Restaurants. *Vanel,* 22 rue M.-Fontvieille, has superb regional dishes, as has *Séville,* both (E); *Darroze* (E), 13 rue Castellane, *nouvelle cuisine* versions of typical regional dishes. *Rôtisserie des Carmes* (I), pl. des Carmes; *Frégate* (M), 16 pl. Wilson and *Chez José,* 105 rue A.-Viadieu, are all (M). *Orsi* (M), 13 rue de l'Industrie, specializes in fish. *Cassoulet* (I), 40 rue Peyrolieres.

At **Lacourtensourt,** 8 km (5 miles) north, *La Feuilleraie* (M) is set in attractive grounds and has a pool.

CASINOS. All the spa towns have casinos, and so do various other places, though many of them are open in the summer only. Ax-les-Thermes is closed in winter and offers only boule, as do Bagnères-de-Bigorre (but it is open year-round) and Cauterets (summer only). Luchon (summer only) and Pau (year-round) also have baccara, roulette and blackjack.

WINTER SPORTS. The Pyrenees comprise the second most important ski region in France. Here you have real mountain skiing at lower rates than the more frequented Alps. The weather tends to be warmer and sunnier too. The region is less given to social distinctions than the Alps: fanciest center is Superbagnères, with nearby Luchon. Even there however accommodations are bargain-priced compared with the Alpine centers. The season runs Dec.–Apr., and there are plenty of lifts, ski schools, rinks, etc.

ANDORRA. Some of the finest virgin skiing fields in the Pyrenees, if not in Europe, are to be found in Andorra. Equipment, however, is rather minimal, and a good skier has soon done everything there is to do. Fine cross-country and powder-snow skiing, on the other hand. There are two ski centers, one at Pas de la Casa and Envalira, the other at Soldeu lift. Season: Dec. into June.

THE ATLANTIC COAST

Two thousand years of wine

With well over 640 km (400 miles) of coastline, including long sandy beaches stretching right down to the Spanish border beyond elegant Biarritz and picturesque St-Jean-de-Luz, most of this part of western France is holiday country *par excellence*. The many resorts, catering for every pocketbook, offer an enormous variety of sports opportunities, especially sailing, swimming, fishing, waterskiing and—the latest craze—windsurfing, all of which can be practised both in the sea and on the inland lakes. The magnificent sandy beaches running south from Royan are backed by 1,215,000 hectares (3 million acres) of pine forests, through which snakes a chain of lakes, many of them recently developed (but not over-developed) and equipped with every type of holiday amenity.

Yet the Atlantic coast is far more varied than those who come here merely to soak up the sun can begin to realize. That same sun has been bringing prosperity to the region since the time of the Romans, by ripening the grapes that produce the magnificent clarets that are one of the chief glories of France. Bordeaux, the headquarters of the wine trade, is a large and prosperous town, with many cultural attractions, Arcachon's prosperity stems from its splendid oysters beds, while further north La Rochelle is an important fishing port. Right down in the south, the resort of Biarritz still has a smart summer season, a far cry from the fiercely local traditions of the Basque country and the simple life led in the little farmhouses of the Béarn, in what is now known as the Pyrénées Atlantiques. Inland Poitou, way up in the north of this region, is different again, with much to offer in the way of art and architectural treasures, as well as a haven for seekers of solitude and rural charm.

Beaches and lakes

Let's start by visiting the coast, which has resorts for all tastes and budgets. Until fairly recently this part of France had escaped the attentions of the developers, except of course for the smart resorts down by the Spanish border. But a government program to increase the area's tourist potential has led to many new yacht marinas, golf courses and the like, none of which, needless to say, is popular with nature lovers and the strong ecology lobby in France. Yet development hasn't so far spoilt this coastline and the sea is still clear and clean. Bathing is a delight (though you should bear in mind that in some places the undertow is such that it's dangerous to swim too far out).

If we start in the north we come first to Les Sables d'Olonne, a fast-growing resort in the Vendée that is only 450 km (280 miles) from Paris. This busy little town carries on its important fishing-port activities in addition to catering for its thriving tourist trade. The fine sandy beach is a delightful place on which to bask in the sun. Occasionally you may see, clattering along the streets in their little wooden shoes, the slim, graceful Sablaise women, with their short pleated skirts and their perky winged hats. Walk along the Remblai esplanade by the side of the beach, and observe the carefree crowds, transfigured by the brilliant sunshine and the invigorating sea air. In the evening the casino provides you with concerts, a mild flutter if you are so inclined, and dancing.

A trip by boat through the waterways of the extraordinary salt marshlands takes you to the forest of Olonne, covering nearly 10 km (6 miles), with its serried ranks of stately pines.

The tiny fishing village of Croix de Vie on the coast just north of Les Sables d'Olonne is pleasant for a quiet week on the beach.

Luçon, inland and to the east of Les Sables d'Olonne, has the distinction of having had Richelieu as its bishop. Its 13th-century cathedral of Notre-Dame, with its 85-meter (280-ft) spire, is only the first of the many interesting churches along the Atlantic coast.

La Rochelle

Halfway between Les Sables d'Olonne and Royan is La Rochelle, once one of the most important trading ports of France, through which passed the bulk of the trade with Canada. It was a great Protestant stronghold until its defeat by Cardinal Richelieu, but when France lost Canada to the English, La Rochelle received a blow from which it has never recovered. In 1891 the port of La Pallice was constructed 5 km (3 miles) away, with modern amenities designed to restore the former fortunes of the region. The Germans built their enormous submarine bases at La Pallice during the last war (they can still be seen). The town was heavily bombed by the Allies but has been handsomely restored.

La Rochelle still remains the most important fishing port on the Atlantic coast, and it is also undoubtedly the most interesting from the historic and architectural point of view. It is a delightful old town with its 16th-century town hall, the rue des Merciers with old wooden houses, the covered market in the place du Marché, and the 14th-century towers at the entrance to the old port. Don't forget to visit the Tour de la Chaîne, which used to help support the chain suspended between it and the Tour St-Nicolas, which served as an efficient barrier when it was necessary to close the port. For a magnificent view of the town and surrounding countryside, climb to the summit of the Tour de la Lanterne, formerly a lighthouse. A new museum opened here in 1982: the Musée du Nouveau Monde, which is a must for transatlantic visitors.

There is also a beach, and running down to it, the beautiful Parc Charruyer, through which meanders a stream that forms occasional pools inhabited by swans. You can spend many happy days in La Rochelle, exploring its treasures, or lounging in the old port with its picturesque fishing boats and old towers. A visit to the early-morning fish auction, with bidders shouting their prices, is fascinating.

La Rochelle is also a smart little town with chic boutiques and restaurants. The best season to visit is in the golden days at the beginning of September, when the hordes of hippies and the rather noisy visitors from northern Europe have left.

Take the ferry to the Ile de Ré, a flat and romantically melancholy island with beautiful wide beaches, ranging from sheltered coves where children can bathe safely to great stretches like those in southern California, where the surf comes pounding in—and the currents can be tricky. Pine-covered dunes and woods for hiking and cycling, picturesque fishing villages, a couple of old churches, make this island a favorite with fashionable families from Bordeaux and Paris. But beware August: the camp sites are so crowded you can barely plant a tent pole, and the beaches near the towns get dirty.

South of Rochefort, a magnificent toll bridge leads to the increasingly popular resort island of Oléron, 32 km (20 miles) long and 6 km (4 miles) wide, covered with pine woods, dunes and beaches. Oléron is well provided with hotels for all tastes and purses.

Still farther south, at the mouth of the Gironde, is Royan, almost entirely rebuilt since 1945. From here, a car-ferry service operates all day long to the Médoc peninsula.

Poitiers and Angoulême

On the way to Poitiers from the north and west, there are many artistic and historical sights to be seen, such as the Roman theater in Sanxay; the old donjons of Loudun and Niort; the Romanesque churches of Aulnay-de-Saintonge, St-Généroux, Champdeniers and St-Jouin-de-Marnes; the old stone bridges in Airvault, Parthenay and Châtellerault; a superb 16th-century castle in Oiron; the medieval château of Dampierre-sur-Boutonne; Touffou, a famous Renaissance castle; St-Médard dominated by a 17th-century château, and Thouars with its venerable old houses and 12th-century church. All these little towns and their monuments are charming.

The region known as 'Green Venice', not far from Niort, will provide you with an unforgettable couple of hours, as you move slowly along by boat through tree-shaded canals past fields nearly all separated by strips of water, where the farmer's means of locomotion is a boat instead of a cart. The trip starts from Coulon, a pretty little town on the banks of the slow-flowing river Sèvres-Niortaise.

Poitiers, ancient capital of Poitou where English archers displayed their legendary skill and valor in 1356, is one of the most charming little towns in this part of France. Historically and artistically it has few rivals. Notre-Dame-la-Grande, an interesting Romanesque church with magnificent 12th-century façade and pinecone-shaped towers, is surrounded by a busy open-air market; the immense Gothic cathedral of St-Pierre with steep steps descending to a huge portal has plump gargoyles and tremendous space and luminosity; Ste-Radegonde, adorned by frescoes and colored columns, harbors a dark crypt containing the remains of St Radegonde; St-Hilaire-le-Grand, built on different levels, has a Romanesque exterior and heavily restored interior; St-Porchaire, once an old clock tower, has been converted into a square church with interesting carved capitals. The 4th-century baptistry of St-Jean, one of the oldest Christian buildings in France, stands in the middle of a modern thoroughfare. The Palais de Justice affords the only entrance to the 12th-century Palais des Ducs. In the vast Salle des Pas Perdus, with its late Gothic windows and the three largest fireplaces in France, Joan of Arc was questioned by the doctors of the university on behalf of Charles VII. Here too Richard the Lion Heart was proclaimed duke of Anjou and count of Poitou in 1170.

Angoulême is perched high on its rocky promontory, and from its ramparts you may enjoy the panorama of the valley of the Charente, almost 76 meters (250 ft) below. Its 12th-century cathedral of St-Pierre shows strong Byzantine influence in the dome, but local originality in the bell-tower and the façade with 75 venerable statues, each in a separate niche. The town hall in the center of the old town should not be missed.

Saintes, an ancient Roman city on the river Charente has its magnificent Triumphal Arch of Germanicus, the ruins of a Roman theater, and three beautiful old churches. Close by, Cognac is a small town whose fame is based, of course, on brandy—if your head is strong visit the vaults of Hennessy, Otard, Martell and others. The town has old houses, the lovely park of François I, the Hôtel de Ville, and the ancient but dilapidated château of the Valois family (where Francois I was born in 1494) with a 13th-century tower and a charming Renaissance fountain.

Bordeaux, the wine capital

About 112 km (70 miles) south of Saintes lies Bordeaux. Today the fourth city of France in population, the second in area, Bordeaux is an important center of trade, industry, and culture. The last is the heritage of a past running back 2,000 years, when Bordeaux was a flourishing Roman city and Romans drank Bordeaux wine. A reminder of the Roman era is to be seen in the Palais Gallien, all that remains of the 3rd-century amphitheater. In the 12th century Bordeaux with Aquitaine, of which it was the capital, became English, when Henry Plantagenet, who had married Eleanor, Duchess of Aquitaine, became Henry II of England. The English tongue distorted Aquitaine to Guyenne, and *clairette* (which in French means a sparkling white wine of the south) to claret. Not until 1453 did Bordeaux again become French.

Bordeaux is not primarily a tourist city and may therefore be visited at any time of the year. But its two big events of the year, which attract visitors as well as its own citizens, occur in May, when the International Festival of Music and Dance uses the cathedral, the public gardens, the famous châteaux of the region (including the Château de la Brède where Montesquieu was born) and other convenient buildings as backdrops, and the International Fair moves into the new fair buildings in the Quartier du Lac.

The city itself, rather than any particular points within it, is what you want to see in Bordeaux, to understand why Victor Hugo described it as Versailles plus Antwerp and why the exiled Goya chose to live there until his death in 1828. You might well begin by getting a general view of the city from the Tour St-Michel, if your breath will carry you up the 228 steps to the top. You will need some of your breath when you come down again, for gasping, if you go into the crypt, which is stacked with mummies. It is traditional for the guide to play the light of his lamp on one desiccated figure after another in the otherwise gloomy room, and to take such liberties with the dead as pulling beards and caressing withered breasts. You are hereby warned.

To make your acquaintance with Bordeaux, you should visit the esplanade des Quinconces; walk along the quais, for the life of the port; stroll along the pleasant allées de Tourny and visit the place de la Bourse, whose 18th-century façades are under the protection of the Fine Arts Ministry. If you want to shop, try the Cours de l'Intendance. And when, exhausted, you are ready to sink into a chair on a sidewalk terrace and let the life of the town flow by, pick one along the Cours Georges Clemenceau, Bordeaux's main boulevard.

Among the traditional goals of sightseers, first place undoubtedly goes to the Grand Théâtre, the pride of the city, a building so magnificent that Garnier did not hesitate to borrow details from it when he designed the Opéra in Paris and so elaborately equipped in proportion to its seating capacity of 1,300 that even with every seat filled at every performance it could never possibly pay its own way. The list of the great churches of the city is headed by the cathedral of St-André, part of which goes back to the 11th century; the fine Romanesque church of St-Seurin is also 11th century. The cathedral's fine carved portals and the 15th-century bell-tower, however, are Gothic. The church of Ste-Croix has a splendid Romanesque façade, St-Michel and Ste-Eulalie are Gothic. For an interesting patrician house, see the Hôtel de Labottière.

Museums include the Musée des Beaux-Arts, which owns works by Cranach, Titian, Veronese, Rubens, Chardin, Corot, Delacroix and Rodin; the 18th-century Museum of Decorative Art with furnishings and rare collectors' items of that period; a Natural History Museum; the Museum of Ancient Art; the Musée Jean-Moulin, devoted to the history of the Resistance movement, and the Galerie des Beaux-Arts, which stages excellent temporary exhibits.

Excursions into the wine region

If you are a wine lover, the tourist office in Bordeaux or in the local wine-producing villages will arrange visits to vineyards and cellars.

The easiest way to combine a trip through the vineyards with some interesting sightseeing is to take an excursion to St-Emilion, the fortified hilltop town that gives its name to one of the region's richest wine districts.

Scenically situated on the slopes at the very edge of the town is the Château Ausone, whose wines are officially ranked as the greatest of St-Emilion's 400-odd vintages. The town itself offers many medieval details and several curiosities from times even more remote. Among the latter is the 7th-century hermitage of St-Emilion. Hollowed out of the rock, this contains crude versions of the basic modern conveniences—a bed, a table, a clothes closet, and a fountain more or less in the form of a bathtub. Giggling girls drop two pins into the 'tub'; if the pins land in the form of a cross it is a sure sign that the dropper will be married within the year.

Nearby is the entrance to the 'monolithic' chapel. This underground shrine, whose nave is separated from the aisles by ten roughly square columns, 38 meters (125 ft) long, about 20 meters (65 ft) wide and more than 15 meters (50 ft) high. The dimensions are impressive when you learn that monks, beginning their work some 900 years ago, hacked the whole church out of solid rock. A subterranean passage, once running from the church, leads to partially excavated catacombs containing clumsily carved columns and many skeletons in superimposed tombs of great antiquity. (Guided visits only.)

Worth a visit, to see vineyards as well as castles, are Margaux with its 18th-century château and wine museum, Château Latour with its famous tower, Château Yquem and Château Guiraud.

Arcachon and Le Pyla, and pleasant little Mimizan-Plage south of Bordeaux, offer delightful beaches (not so self-conscious as Biarritz), the highest sand dunes in Europe, and a variety of sports, ranging from wind-surfing and pine-needle skiing, to yacht racing and Basque *pelote*. Don't be misled by this word *'pelote',* however; you won't be in the Basque country until you've crossed the strange sandy plain and marsh of the Landes between Bordeaux and Bayonne. Nowadays, it is mostly pine forest; the result of a vast program of land reclamation and afforestation. The newly set up Regional Park of the Gascony Landes, covering 10,000 acres, has its own museum, the Ecomusée de la Grand-Lande; well worth a visit. You'll see a collection of furnished houses and farm buildings typical of the region, plus exhibits relating to local crafts, all set in a lovely clearing in the forest.

On the southern fringes of the Landes are the beaches of Hossegor and Capbreton, and Dax, an inland spa, the ancient Roman Aquae Tarbellicae. There are many new holiday centers and campsites round the string of lakes running parallel to the coast. At Bombannes, for example, you'll find a well-equipped recreation center.

The Basque country

About 120,000 of the nearly two million Basques live in France. They are handsome in their national dress, characterized by the beret, worn frequently by the men, rope-soled shoes called *espadrilles,* and the *makhila,* which is carried on a thong and serves both as a walking stick and as a weapon.

Much of the Basques' energy is expended in dancing, poetic improvisation, *pelote* and, in recent years, agitation for a measure of autonomy for the Basque provinces in Spain. French Basques rarely have the same craving for autonomy, yet they sympathize with their Spanish brothers and there are strong cultural and linguistic links across the frontier.

While Basque legends and dances have their counterparts in many European countries, the origin of these people remains obscure. The resemblance of their evening call, the *irrinzina,* to that of the Upper Amazon Indians does not solve the mystery; nor does the fact that the Basques reckon in twenties, like the ancient Mayas. Some ethnologists say their language resembles Japanese. It's fascinating, anyhow, to wonder whether they stem from the Berbers of antiquity, or whether they are survivors of the lost continent of Atlantis.

Bayonne, capital of the Basque country

Although Bayonne is the official capital of the Pays Basque, it is not typically Basque. During the August festivities and bullfights the city is a colorful blend of Gascon, Spanish and Basque vivacity.

Bayonne's Basque Museum offers a delightful presentation of life and lore in the little country's three states, Labourd, Basse-Navarre and Soule. The Bonnat Museum houses one of France's richest collections of El Greco, Tintoretto, Dürer, Goya and Bonnat. Don't miss the lovely Gothic cathedral of Ste-Marie.

You'll probably buy a pair of those comfortable Basque *espadrilles,* with the rope soles and the cloth uppers, and you'll need them, if you dance all night in the streets during the popular celebrations. And if you've seen your first bullfight or *pelote* match, you may add to your charm bracelet a small *torero* or a *chistera.* For that matter, a real wicker *chistera* (the wicker bat used in the game) is an amusing and interesting souvenir.

THE ATLANTIC COAST

You'll need several days if you're going to explore the countryside as well as Bayonne's old streets, quays and ramparts. For fine views of the Pyrenees, take a short excursion on foot (one hour for the round trip) to the Hauteurs de St-Etienne, or drive to La Croix de Mouguerre, about 6 km (4 miles) south.

Biarritz, fashionable seaside resort

Smartest and most frequented of France's Atlantic beach resorts is Biarritz, which stands at the entrance to the Pays Basque. It enjoys an unusually favorable year-round climate and a particularly attractive location, where the sandy pine forests of the Landes merge with the craggy Basque coast. Carlist exiles from Spain put Biarritz on the map in 1838. Unable to visit San Sebastian on the Spanish coast, they sought a recreation spot as close as possible to their old stamping ground. Among the exiles was Eugénie de Montijo, destined to become empress of France, with whom Biarritz found special favor.

It was the Empress Eugénie who gave Biarritz its coming out party, changing the town into an international favorite. Visits by Queen Victoria and Edward VII attracted a fashionable British clientele to Biarritz. Half the crowned heads of Europe slept in Eugénie's villa, now the Hôtel du Palais. After 40 years or so of eclipse Biarritz is now modestly coming back into fashion, and celebrities are again appearing. But its true golden age will never return.

Extending from the Hôtel du Palais to the Côte des Basques is a magnificent promenade that is one of Biarritz's main attractions. Visit the Rocher de la Vierge when the sea is rough, for a dramatic view. Follow the lower promenade, along the boulevard du Prince de Galles, for a glimpse of the foaming breakers that beat constantly upon the sands, giving the name of Côte d'Argent (Silver Coast) to the length of the French Basque coast.

The lighthouse is a few minutes' walk beyond the Hôtel Miramar, on the summit of Cap St-Martin, and commands a splendid view. When the tide is low you'll be able to continue on to the Plage de la Chambre d'Amour.

St-Jean-de-Luz, resort town and fishing port

More intimate and picturesque is the resort and fishing-town of St-Jean-de-Luz. Some of its fortified houses are several centuries old. The church of St-Jean is typical Basque architecture, with an aisleless nave, gilded altar screen, and three-tired wooden galleries reserved for men. Reserved, also, since 1660, is the door through which Louis XIV passed to wed Spanish Maria Theresa. (Their marriage contract is in the Musée du Souvenir, in Ducontenia Park.) The door was then sealed to prevent its being used by common folk.

Sailors of St-Jean-de-Luz were the first to fish the Grand Banks off Newfoundland—in 1520—and they supplied most of the ships that broke the English blockade of La Rochelle in 1627. The port suffered a mortal blow when the Grand Banks fishing rights were transferred to Great Britain in 1713, but the new harbor has since become an important sardine-fishing port and center of the French tuna industry. Much of the town's interest is centered on the harbor. In the place Louis XIV is the 17th-century Château Lohobiague (or de Louis XIV), and overlooking the harbor is the turreted Maison de l'Infante, where the Infanta Maria Theresa stayed before her marriage.

The celebration of *Toro del Fuego,* which begins on June 24, is in itself sufficient reason for a visit to the Basque country. For three days and nights the entire populace dances the *fandango,* that stunning exhibition of restrained passion, in the streets. And best of all, the Bull of St-Jean, a crazy, fire-spitting creature made of papier-mâché, is carried about the town, lashing about in a frenzy of pseudo rage and real sparks.

A favorite excursion is to the mountain of La Rhune (898 meters/ 2,950 ft)—you can climb it in three hours—and to the little Basque village of Ascain, where Pierre Loti wrote his novel, *Ramuntcho.* The Col de St-Ignace is the starting point of a cog-wheel railway to La Rhune, a 30-minute trip. Beyond (13 km/8 miles) is another characteristic village, Sare, whose caves are well worth visiting.

Hendaye and the Spanish frontier

At Hendaye, on the Ile-des-Faisans in the middle of the river Bidassoa, which separates France from Spain, François I shamefully purchased his release from Spanish captivity by delivering his two small sons as hostages, with no intention of keeping his side of the bargain. Some hundred years later the island witnessed a scene of great splendor when Louis XIV met his bride, Maria Theresa, and her father, Philip IV of Spain, in an ingenious solution of the precedence problem.

From Hendaye you can look across the Bidassoa to Spanish Fuentarrabia. A scant 24 km (15 miles) away along the magnificent coast is Biarritz's rival, San Sebastian. If you're driving, you can stop to enjoy the panorama that spreads below the Haya, or Mount of Three Crowns, and the curious fortified church of Renteria. And you can wander in the old towns of San Pedro and San Juan, which guard the narrow entrance to the Bay of Pasajes.

Once beyond the coastal villas you find, in the mountain towns, charming Basque houses. Neat, white-washed dwellings, often decorated in peasant fashion, with hearts, flowers and birds, they crowd around the village church, beside which there is always a well for *pelote*. The Basques blithely mingle religion with their beloved national sport; they also have a fine, philosophical attitude toward death. You often see the inscription, *'Orhait hilceaz'*—'Remember death'. Indeed, you can almost feel this peaceful acceptance of fate in the country graveyards, so silent and so timeless, with their strange discoidal tombstones. The finest examples of these faceless antiquities are found in the cemeteries of Bidarray and Urrugne. At the pass of Roncevaux—remember your *Song of Roland?*—is the enchanting town of St-Jean-Pied-de-Port, an ideal place for rambling, fishing, or just sitting in the sun.

Before you leave the Pays Basque you may want to linger in Soule, to see its three-spired churches—especially those of Gotein and Aussurucq—and, if you're lucky the most lavish, as well as the oldest, Basque dance, the *mascarade*. For five centuries this strange tradition has persisted, with the same masques, the most curious of which is that of the *zamalzain,* who wears a wooden horse strapped about his waist. If you happen to be in Itxassou, Bidarray or Louhossoa on the Sunday after Corpus Christi, you will see all this, amidst dancing, singing and popping of shotguns.

PRACTICAL INFORMATION

WHEN TO GO. The height of the tourist season along the coast is July and Aug., when you will find it very crowded. Come in June or Sept. if you can, since bathing is still good then but the resorts are far more peaceful and the countryside is at its best too. Although many of the Basque resorts stage their main folklore festivals in July and Aug., the spring and early summer have their share of events and the weather is delightful, while Biarritz is far smarter in Sept. than in either July or Aug. Sept. is also, of course, the month for Bordeaux and the wine region, though as Bordeaux is a big and busy town with an active cultural life not geared to tourists, you'll find plenty to do there at any time of year.

Special events include Bayonne's Ham Fair, Biarritz's Easter gala season and Royan's contemporary art festival, all in **April**; Bordeaux's International Fair and *Mai Musical* (music, dance and theater festival), Angoulême's puppet festival and La Rochelle's international regatta, in **May**; **June** is the month for wine fairs and all sorts of traditional happenings in both the coastal resorts and the inland vineyard areas of the Gironde; the traditional *Fête-Dieu* procession in the Basque country and the fireworks, dancing in the streets and the *toros de fuego fête* in St-Jean-de-Luz to celebrate the Feast of St John the Baptist on June 24 (and for several days beforehand). In **July** there are festivals of all kinds, including the colorful Tuna Fair in St-Jean-de-Luz, bullfights in Bayonne, the golf season in Arcachon, which also has a one-day regatta, horse races, golf and tennis tournaments, polo, riding events and many other sporting events in Biarritz, more regattas in La Rochelle. **August** sees a continuation of the summer season in all resorts, plus a folklore festival in Bayonne, the traditional France v. Spain *pelote Basque* championship in Arcachon, and a magnificent firework display in Biarritz. In **September** the Basque resorts have a music festival, and the wine region round Bordeaux is busy staging wine fairs and other events to celebrate the new vintage. Poitiers has international show jumping in **October**, while **November** is the month for Bordeaux's famous SIGMA show, devoted to contemporary art of all kinds (dance, theater, music, cinema, painting and sculpture). There is more show-jumping, this time in Bordeaux, in **December**, which also sees the celebrated midnight mass on Christmas Eve in the church of St-Jean-de-Luz.

WHAT TO DO. The coastal regions offer every imaginable kind of sports amenity, with excellent **swimming, sailing, windsurfing, canoeing** on the artificial lakes inland, **waterskiing, fishing** and **underwater swimming.**

THE ATLANTIC COAST

Riding is popular in the delightful countryside of the Charente *département* and you can even hire a horse-drawn caravan for a really leisurely holiday.

The smart resorts near the Spanish border all have **casinos,** with Biarritz's open year-round, and many elegant gala evenings. **Golf,** too, is particularly good here, with five 18-hole courses in the Basque country, and others in the Bordeaux area. Many **tennis** courts have been built recently.

Inquire at the France-Accueil (Welcome Information) tourist office in Bordeaux about visits to vineyards and wine cellars for **wine-tasting.** A new idea is a cruise in a barge or launch through the vinegrowing area of the Bordelais; also **gastronomic** weekends in the Landes.

HOW TO GET ABOUT. By air. *TAT* flies from Paris to Royan and La Rochelle and to Bergerac, and also from Lyon to Poitiers and from Lille, Marseille and Toulouse to Nantes; *Air Inter* from Paris to Bordeaux, Biarritz. Bordeaux and Biarritz also have air links with Marseille, and Bordeaux only with Lille, Lyon, Mulhouse/Bâle, Nice, Strasbourg and Toulouse. If you want to fly direct from Britain, *British Airways* and *Air France* have a total of eight flights weekly to Bordeaux.

By train. *L'Aquitaine* will rush you from Paris to Bordeaux in only 4 hrs (first-class only, with TEE supplement), and there are plenty of other trains too, though they're not quite so fast. Paris–La Rochelle takes about 4½ hrs, Paris–Poitiers about 2¾ hrs. To Bayonne and Hendaye the best way is to travel overnight, as the journey takes a good 7 hrs. All these trains leave from the Gare d'Austerlitz in Paris. Cross-country services include convenient overnight train Bordeaux-Lyon. If you happen to be coming from Spain, there are good trains from Madrid to Bayonne and Hendaye. Car-couchette trains run from Paris to Bordeaux and Biarritz, from Marseille to Bordeaux, and, useful for British visitors, from Boulogne to Biarritz. If you're coming from Germany, there are car-couchettes from Düsseldorf, Cologne, Frankfurt and Saarbrucken to Biarritz, which has a service to Brussels. Toulouse-Bordeaux now takes only 1 hr as the whole line has been electrified.

By bus or coach. There are quite good local bus services, but no long-distance ones. However French Railways (SNCF) do have a combined rail and coach weekend tour to Arcachon from Paris two or three times a year (usually in June and Sept.). If you don't mind a long journey you can travel by coach from London's Victoria bus station to Biarritz.

By car. From Paris the A10 autoroute (called *L'Aquitaine*) takes you through Orléans and Tours to Poitiers and on to Bordeaux. From Poitiers the N11 goes west to La Rochelle; from Niort the N148 for Les Sables-d'Olonne and from Saintes the N150 for Royan. Bordeaux has a motorway ringroad circling the town if you continue on to Biarritz. The Basque Coast motorway (A63) is now in service right across the Landes region. If you're coming from Lyon you take the A7 to Orange, then the A9 to Narbonne and the new A61 to Toulouse and the N124 to Bayonne and Biarritz, or continue on the A61,

508   **THE FACE OF FRANCE**

romantically called the *Autoroute des Deux Mers* (the Mediterranean and the Atlantic) to Bordeaux.

By boat. Visitors from Britain to Biarritz can travel with their car with *Brittany Ferries* to Santander in Spain, then drive up to France.

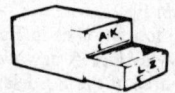

USEFUL ADDRESSES. The *Welcome Information office* for the Aquitaine region is at 12 cours du 30 Juillet, Bordeaux, with the city's own *tourist office* at the same address. The *Regional Tourist Committee* for the Aquitaine is at 24 allées de Tourny, also in Bordeaux. For the Poitou-Charentes region, 11 bis rue des Augustines, 17000 La Rochelle. *Departmental Tourist Committee* for the Landes region: Prefecture, 40011 Mont-de-Marsan.

The Basque country's main *tourist offices* are at 24 av. Foch, Bayonne; sq. d'Ixelles, 64200 Biarritz; Cité Administrative, Biarritz (which also houses the *Touring Club de France's* office); and pl. Maréchal Foch in St-Jean-de-Luz.

American Express, 31 bld Thiers, St-Jean-de-Luz. In Paris: *Maison Poitou-Charentes,* 4 av. de l'Opéra, ler.

Car hire. *Avis,* 1 rue Ste-Ursule, Bayonne; 25 av. Edouard-VII and airport, Biarritz; 59 rue Peyronnet, Bordeaux, and at Mérignac airport; 166 bld Joffre, La Rochelle; 31 bld Thiers, St-Jean-de-Luz. *Hertz,* 95 rue Maubec, Bayonne; 17 av. Foch, Biarritz, and at Parme airport; 7/8 rue Charles-Domercq, Bordeaux, and Mérignac airport; 1 av. Charles-de-Gaulle, La Rochelle. *Europcar,* 32 av. Maréchal-Foch, Biarritz; 1 allées Paulmy, Bayonne.

The *Gironde Departmental Tourist Committee,* 12 cours du 30-Juillet, in Bordeaux has a new teletourist reservation scheme that enables you to find out about all sorts of special holidays (golfing, tennis, riding, *gîtes ruraux,* holiday villages, etc.) without wasting any time; and in summer they also have a camping information service with an automatic telephone-answering machine so that you can ring any hour of the day or night to find out where there are spaces on camp or caravan sites (96-81-33).

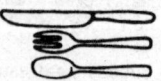

REGIONAL FOOD AND DRINK. Needless to say, the coastal regions specialize in fish dishes, with mussels in cream sauce in the Charentes area, mussels cooked with rice and red peppers in the Basque country, fried or grilled sardines straight from the sea, excellent prawns and *langoustines* (Dublin Bay prawns or scampi), fish stews of various kinds, and stewed squid too.

The Bordeaux region is famous for *cèpes à la bordelaise,* mushrooms stewed in olive oil with parsley and garlic, and for *sauce bordelaise,* which is made with red wine, shallots, beef stock, beef marrow and seasonings. This sauce is often served with kidneys, but is also good with steak, and you may find it with egg dishes too. In the Landes you find all sorts of little birds, such as the famous *ortolan,* served roasted in the oven, as well as delicious goose liver pâtés. The characteristic flavor of much of the cooking of southwestern France comes from the use of goose fat, as in succulent stews such as *daubes* of beef. Another characteristic flavor in the Basque country is the *piment basquais,* made from

THE ATLANTIC COAST

crushed red peppers. Red peppers (or sometimes green ones) are also used for *piperade,* a cross between scrambled eggs and an omelet and also including tomatoes and onions, cooked in goose dripping or olive oil. Other specialties hereabouts are *tioro,* a fish stew strongly flavored with onion, and *chipirones,* baby squid served either stewed with their ink as a sauce or stuffed. *Jambon de Bayonne* is a type of ham; fresh salmon and trout always seem to be available.

The Basque region produces several wines, one of the best-known being *Irouléguy,* but they cannot of course compare with the superb clarets of the Bordeaux region, which include the most famous names in the world. The wines of Bordeaux are classified in five *crus* or growths. Preeminent are the *premier grand cru* wines of the Médoc peninsula, *Château Lafite* and *Château Latour,* at Pauillac, and *Château Margaux,* at Margaux. Equally good is *Château Haut-Brion,* in the Graves district at Pessac. Queen of the white wines is the matchless *Château Yquem,* sweet but never cloying, from the Sauternes district. Also good are the rich wines of St-Emilion and the red and white wines of the Graves district, so-called after the gravelly soil from which they spring. The district of Entre-deux-Mers, between the Dordogne and the Gironde, also produces good quality red and white wines.

The Cognac region naturally produces wonderful brandy, and you'll also find cognac-flavored chocolates here.

HOTELS AND RESTAURANTS. The Atlantic coast can offer accommodations to suit every pocket, ranging from the luxury hotels of resorts like Biarritz to modest but comfortable little hotels in the family resorts and small inns in the inland districts, where prices may be 50% lower than on the coast. Most resort hotels are closed in winter, but not in Bordeaux, which, like all big towns in France, has hotels in every price range. Restaurants referred to as *E, M* or *I* are expensive, moderate or inexpensive.

This is also a good area for camping (ask for the Aquitaine *Guide des Campings* for a full list, available from tourist offices—see addresses section).

AINHOA. *Argi-Eder,* expensive, very comfortable, good cuisine, pool. *Ithurria* (M), historic 17th-century building with excellent regional cuisine and very comfortable rooms.

AIRE-SUR-L'ADOUR. *Commerce* (I), good restaurant. *Domaine du Bassibé* (E), lovely terraces, garden, pool, tennis, is 9 km (5½ miles) away at **Segos.**

ANGLET. *Château de Brindos* (E), pseudo-medieval castle, beautifully situated on lake with pool and good classical cuisine. Close to airport. *Biarritz Golf* (I) at **Chambre d'Amour.**
Restaurants. *Relais de Parme* (M), at the airport, run by Robert Laporte, father of Pierre, who has the Café de Paris in Biarritz. Excellent classical cooking, fine wines.

THE FACE OF FRANCE

ANGOULÊME. Pleasant are *France* (M) and *Trois Piliers* (I), the latter with no restaurant. *Novotel* (M), just outside on the N10. *Motel PM 16* (M), 7 km (4 miles) away on Poitiers road, with good restaurant. *Epi d'Or* and *Palais* are inexpensive. Neither has restaurant.

At **Asnières-sur-Nouère**, 8 km (5 miles) south, is the sumptuous *Moulin du Maine-Brun*, with pool and good cuisine (both classical and 'new'), (E).

Restaurants. *Chamade* (M), best in town; imaginative cuisine. *Petite Auberge* (I), very good value.

ARCACHON. *Arc-Hôtel*, with heated pool, is expensive, as are *Grand Hôtel Richelieu*, no restaurant, and *Roc et Moderne*, close to beach. *Atlantic* (E). Moderate: *Gascogne*, with garden and restaurant, *Plage*, with restaurant. Inexpensive: *Nautic*, no restaurant. *Pergola*, without restaurant.

At **Le Moulleau:** *Les Tamarins*, moderate. *Buissonnets* (M), with goodish restaurant.

Restaurants. *Mareyeur* (E), overlooking sea, inventive cuisine and a pool too. *La Guitoune*, excellent food and service, and *Corniche*, at **Pyla-sur-Mer**, good seafood. Both (M).

ASCAIN. *Rhûne*, moderate, has restaurant and annex with pool. Small *Pont*, high moderate, has excellent food (M).

AUROS. Restaurant. *Chez Simone* (M), friendly, good regional dishes.

BARBÉZIEUX. *Boule d'Or* (I), good restaurant (M).

BAYONNE. *Agora*, moderate. *Loustau* and *Basses Pyrénées*, moderate. *Deux Rivières*, reader-recommended, comfortable, moderate, no restaurant.

Restaurants. *La Tanière*, *Beluga*, both (M), friendly. *Euzkalduna* (M), with good regional cooking.

BERGERAC. *Bordeaux*, moderate, good cuisine; *France*, moderate, no restaurant. *Londres*, modernized, inexpensive. *Cyrano* (M), the name may be obvious but the cooking is unusual and inventive; excellent value, with deliciously light versions of regional recipes. Also has a few rooms.

BIARRITZ. *Palais*, super-deluxe, pool, cabanas. Modern *Loews-Biarritz Miramar* (E), opened 1982, 126 rooms with balconies. Futuristic complex including salt water cure center. Expensive hotels include the elegant *Eurotel-Biarritz*, the *Président*, the *Regina et Golf*, modern *PLM Victoria Surf* and the *Plaza*. *Windsor*, *El Mirador* (good restaurant) and *Edouard VII* (M).

Some 5 km (3 miles) away, at **Lac de Brindos**, *Château de Brindos* (see Anglet entry). Excellent restaurant (E).

Restaurants. Pierre Laporte's *Café de Paris* (E) is the best. Recently converted to the *nouvelle cuisine* with great success, it is also the finest restaurant on

THE ATLANTIC COAST

the whole Atlantic coast. *Coq Hardi,* in El Mirador hotel (E), chic; *Relais Miramar* (M), in Miramar hotel. *L'Alambic* (M), also owned by Pierre Laporte but much less expensive. *Chez Maurice* (M). *Operne* (M), opened 1983, overlooking sea.

BIDART. *Bidartea* (M), with pool is 3 km (2 miles) north.
Restaurant. *Hacienda* (M), with rooms; *Chistera* (M), on N10 road, very attractive.

BORDEAUX. At the Expositions Park, north, are *Sofitel* (E) and *PLM-Aquitania* (E). *Mercure* and *Novotel le Lac,* with pool, restaurant, moderate.
Among the expensive hotels are the *Grand Hôtel de Bordeaux,* pl. de la Comédie, extensively modernized and with goodish restaurant; and *Frantel,* with excellent food, on rue R.-Lateulade.
Moderate: *Normandie,* 7 cours 30 Juillet, and *Majestic,* 2 rue Condé, neither with restaurant; *Royal Médoc,* 3 rue Sèze, and *Teminus,* at St-Jean rail station. *Arcades,* opposite St-Jean station where you pay for your room upon arriving, rue Eugène-le-Roy; *Faisan,* 28 rue Ch.-Domercq; no restaurant. *Français,* 12 rue du Temple, in pedestrian street, no restaurant. *Etche Ona,* 11 rue Mautrec, no restaurant. At the airport is the *Novotel-Mérignac* (E).
Restaurants. Tops: *Dubern* (E), 42 allées de Tourny, with mixture of classical and new cuisine, good wines. Best for nouvelle cuisine, *Christian Clément,* (M), 58 rue du Pas-St-Georges. *Mériadeck* (M), in Frantel hotel; *Jean Ramet* (E), 7 pl. Jean-Jaurès. *Périgord St-Jean* (M), 202 cours de la Marne. Among the best bistrots are *Plantié* (M), 401 bis bld du Pt-Wilson, and *Chez Philippe* (E), 1 pl. du Parlement. Eight km out at **Pessac,** is the very fine *Réserve* (E), outdoor meals. Has 22 (E) rooms.

BRANNE. *France* (M), modest hotel-restaurant.

CASTILLON-LA-BATAILLE. *Bonne Auberge* (M), nice little hotel-restaurant, well placed if you want to sample Entre-Deux-Mers wines.

CHÂTEAUNEUF-SUR-CHARENTE. *Au Soleil d'Or,* inexpensive, good cooking.

CHÂTELAILLON. *Grand* (M), *Hostellerie Select* (M), with good cuisine.
Restaurant. *Océan* (M), 121 bld République, with rooms.

CHOLET. Restaurant. At nearby **Nuaille,** *Baumotel* (M), with pool and good restaurant; reader-recommended.

COGNAC. *François I* (M), no restaurant. *Orléans* (I), modest, modern, no restaurant.
Restaurant. *L'Auberge* (M), good, is also a hotel.

At **Cierzac,** 13 km (8 miles) south, is the lovely *Moulin de Cierzac* (M), one of the pleasantest restaurants in the area. Also has a few (E) rooms.

DAX. Spa (season, all year). *Splendid* (M), pool and gardens. *Régina,* moderate. *Peyroux,* inexpensive. All have restaurants.

Restaurants. *Bois de Boulogne* (M), with local dishes. *Richelieu* (M), with (I) *menus* and a few rooms too.

EUGÉNIE-LES-BAINS. *Les Prés et les Sources d'Eugénie,* in grounds, with pool, deluxe. Its restaurant (E), run by famous chef Michael Guérard (of *Cuisine Minceur* fame), is one of France's best. Special diet menus are so delicious you won't want any others. Closed Nov. through March. *Pension Lalanne* across the street is a modest *pension de famille* with good home cooking (M).

HENDAYE. *Liliac* and *Central,* at the beach, are both moderate. In town, *Chez Antoinette,* inexpensive, with garden and restaurant.

Restaurant. *Bakéa* (M), about 4 km (2 miles) south via D258 at **Biriatou,** well situated, some moderate rooms.

HOSSEGOR. *Mercédès* (E) and *Beauséjour* (E), both with pool, well situated. *Ermitage* and *Plage* (M), the former has dinner only. *Terrasses du Lac* (I) and *Hélianthes* (I), with pool but no restaurant.

Restaurant. *Huitrières du Lac* (M), with a few rooms.

JARNAC. Hotel-restaurant *Terminus,* one of our favorite discoveries in the Cognac region, inexpensive.

LABASTIDE-D'ARMAGNAC. Restaurant. *Loubère* (M), good regional cuisine. Also has rooms.

LACANAU new resort. *Etoile d'Argent,* inexpensive, with restaurant.

LUÇON. *Voyageurs,* inexpensive but comfortable, with restaurant.

MIMIZAN-PLAGE. *Taris,* moderate, family-style, in town. At the beach: *Côte d'Argent* (E), with panoramic restaurant (dinner only) (M). *Parc,* moderate. *France* (I), small and unpretentious but excellent food (full-board terms only in high season).

MONTLUÇON. Restaurants. 1.5 km (1 mile) south, near racetrack is *Château St-Jean* (M), excellent food. A few (E) rooms available. *Bon Coin* (M), deliciously light cuisine, plus lake views and a few peaceful rooms.

MONSÉGUR. *Grand* (I), with restaurant, is a good base for exploring the Entre-Deux-Mers area.

THE ATLANTIC COAST

NIEUIL. *Château de Nieuil,* expensive, a towered castle on Paris–Bordeaux road, near D739. Good restaurant.

NIORT. *Terminus* (good restaurant), a Relais et Châteaux member, and *Brèche;* both moderate.
Restaurants. *Belle Etoile* (M), 115 quai Métayer. *Poêle d'Or* (M), in Terminus hotel. *La Cloche d'Or* (M), handy for lunch, by the Donjon.

ILE DE NOIRMOUTIER. A little out-of-town is the secluded *Les Prateaux,* surrounded by pines, moderate.

OIRON. Restaurant. *Relais du Château* (M), modest but pleasant; also has some (I) rooms.

ILE D'OLÉRON. At **La Rémigeasse,** *Grand Large* (E), with good restaurant (E); at **Plage du Vert-Bois,** *Les Pins du Vert Bois* (E), restaurant, with pool, secluded.
At **Ste-Marie-de-Ré,** *Atalante* (E), pleasant, peaceful, with restaurant, pool and saltwater cures.
At **St-Trojan,** *Novotel* (E). *Les Cleunes* (M).
Restaurant. At **St-Georges,** the *Trois Chapons* is (M).

PARTHENAY. *Nord* (I), typical little French provincial hotel-restaurant in this busy market town; good value home-style cooking.

POITIERS. *France,* expensive, with good restaurant (M); *Novotel,* moderate, 8 km out of town on N10. *Chapon Fin,* moderate.
Restaurants. *Maxime* (M), good value *menus,* inventive cuisine. *Delanné* (M), 10 rue Paul-Guillon, good for *nouvelle cuisine.*

ILE DE RÉ. At **La Flotte,** *Le Richelieu,* expensive, a wonderful little spot with pool, private bungalows, garden; its excellent restaurant (E) specializes in seafood.
At **Le Bois-Plage,** *Les Gollandières,* pleasantly located, moderate.
Restaurant. *St-Hubert* (I), at **St-Martin.**

ROCHEFORT. *Roca Fortis,* moderate, and *France,* inexpensive; neither with restaurant. 8 km away at **Soubise,** *Hôtel Soubise,* with one of the best restaurants in the region (M).
Restaurant. *Tourne-Broche* (M), good regional cooking.

ROCHELLE, LA. *Yachtman* (E), modern and well run, close to harbor, with good restaurant and pool. Relais et Châteaux member. *Champlain* (E), no restaurant, an old manor; *France et Angleterre,* moderate with a very good restaurant (M); *Commerce,* inexpensive, with restaurant (I).

Restaurants. Best is *Pacha* (E), in Yachtman hotel, quai Valin, serving *nouvelle cuisine*. Also good are *Serge* (E), 46 cours des Dames; *Richelieu* (M) in France et Angleterre hotel, and *Vieux Port* (M), 4 pl. de la Chaine.

ROCHE-SUR-YON. *Campanile* (M), modern, well run, with restaurant.

ROYAN. *France, Family Golf Hôtel,* right on the beach, moderate.
At **Pontaillac** are the moderate *Grand Hôtel Pontaillac* and *Miramar* and *Résidence de Saintonge* (M). Only latter has restaurant.

SABLES-D'OLONNE, LES. *Atlantic,* expensive, is best, with pleasant little restaurant called *Sloop. Roches Noires* (M), no restaurant, and *Beau Rivage* (M), comfortable, both right on beach.
Restaurants. *Capitaine* (M), *Pergola* (I), with some rooms.

ST-EMILION. Hotel-restaurant, *Hostellerie de Plaisance* (M), very comfortable, good classical cuisine and fine wines (M).

SAINTES. *Commerce Mancini,* comfortable, moderate. Excellent restaurant (especially fish) is (M).
Restaurant. *Louis* (I), good-value seafood.

ST-JEAN-DE-LUZ. *Chantaco,* at the Chantaco Golf Club, good restaurant, most attractive (closed Oct. to Easter). *Madison,* (M), no restaurant, sea views. *Paris* (no restaurant) is inexpensive. *Hostellerie Ciboure* (I), with pool, at **Ciboure.** About 1.5 km (1 mile) north, at **Pointe Ste-Barbe** are *Motels Basques* (M), restaurant, ocean view.
Restaurants. *Vieille Auberge* (I), 22 rue Tourasse, popular, good; *Petit Grill Basque* (I), 4 rue St-Jacques. *Chez Pablo* (I), 5 rue Mlle.-Etcheto, very simple, delicious food.
Arrantzaleak, in **Ciboure,** has delicious fresh fish served in huge quantities, Basque songs, cheerful atmosphere (M).

ST-JEAN-PIED-DE-PORT. *Pyrénées* (M), with very good restaurant, one of the best in the region. *Central,* moderate. *Etche Ona* (M), small and pleasant for both rooms and meals. *Navarre* (M), no restaurant.

SEIGNOSSE. *Auberge du Lac Blanc* is inexpensive and pleasant. *Soleillade,* moderate, best-known for its good (I) restaurant.

SOULAC-sur-MER. *Pins* (M), at **Amélie-sur-Mer** 4.5 km (2½ miles) southwest, is modern, comfortable, close to beach.

SOUSTONS. *La Bergerie,* like a country home, and *Pavillon Landais,* by lake, both moderate.

THE ATLANTIC COAST

At nearby **Azur,** the tiny *Auberge des Pins* (I), with half or full board only. **Restaurant.** *Pavillon Landais* (M), in hotel (see above).

VILLENEUVE-DE-MARSAN. *Europe* (M), with pool and very good restaurant serving mixture of local specialties and *nouvelle cuisine*.

CASINOS. Biarritz's two casinos are open year-round, giving you a chance to play boule, roulette, 30/40, blackjack or baccara to your heart's content. St-Jean-de-Luz and Hendaye have casinos too, but they're open only in the summer season. Biarritz is the center of nightlife in the **Pays Basque,** with *Chez Albert* and *Il Gatto Verde* both popular. Hosségor and Les Sables d'Olonne have small casinos, and Arcachon's gives you a chance to play blackjack as well as the traditional roulette, boule and baccara.

AROUND THE DORDOGNE

Rural valleys and prehistoric paintings

Not so long ago this region of rural France could be referred to as undiscovered, but as increasing numbers of city dwellers react against the stresses and strains of urban living and head for places where they can adopt a more peaceful rhythm, at least for their holidays, these rural provinces and *départements* are changing rapidly. Yet although voices are constantly being raised to deplore the influx of holidaymakers, the region's new popularity is in many ways to the advantage of the tourist, who finds a wide range of festivals and events staged for his entertainment and pleasure.

The old provinces and regions of the Limousin and the Périgord, the Rouergue and the Quercy; the beautiful river valleys of the Dordogne and the Lot; the wild upland reaches of the Cévennes—all these are ideal holiday territory for those who do not insist on four-star hotels

AROUND THE DORDOGNE

and the latest movies. They offer few internationally known buildings or sights, but their absence is easily compensated for by a wealth of picturesque villages, Romanesque churches, prehistoric remains and lonely castles perched high on sheer cliffs.

Limoges, city of porcelain and enamel

One of the chief cities of the region, Limoges lies directly on the rail and road route to and from Paris. Save a few hours to look briefly at its cathedral of St-Etienne, the Adrien Dubouché Museum (ceramics), the Palais Episcopal or Municipal Museum with samples of Limoges china from the 12th century to the present, and some enchanting 13th-century houses.

In the mid-19th century, an American china retailer boarded a ship in New York, bound for France. His objective was to find a cup to match a broken one brought into his shop. Knowing only that the broken cup had come from France, he began his search, and finally came to Limoges, where he found china that matched the cup. For three-quarters of a century French craftsmen had been producing this delicate porcelain for the French market, using a pure white clay found in St-Yriex, south of Limoges. This clay, called kaolin, had been known for centuries in China, but was discovered in Europe only in the 18th century.

This American, David Haviland, took a bold step—he moved to France, set up his own factory at Limoges and began to produce quality porcelain for the tables of American homes. Rapidly his fame spread, and china bearing the Haviland hallmark became synonymous with some of the finest produced in Europe.

Well worth your while is a tour of one of the porcelain factories and enamel workshops, which can be visited, but only during the summer months. Ask the tourist office for addresses and times when the public is admitted.

Northwest of Limoges is the martyr-village of Oradour-sur-Glane, scene of the worst massacre in occupied France during World War II. On June 10, 1944, a unit of the SS Das Reich Division murdered 650 men, women and children in cold blood and burned their village. The charred remains are preserved today as a memorial, and deserve a visit.

Périgord and the Dordogne valley

Northeast of Bordeaux is the Périgord, known primarily for its prehistoric art and gourmet's cuisine. But there are rich, luxuriant valleys through which flow clear rivers: the Dordogne, the Vézère, the Auvézère, the Isle and the Dronne. Separating the valleys are rugged plateaus of granite and limestone, sharp outcroppings of rock and sheer cliffs.

As you drive through hilly country towards the Dronne valley, you see fortified châteaux perched on every slope. You fleet through brown stone villages roofed in red tile; and you may still see mule-drawn carts or fields being plowed by yoked oxen. You can also take slow-boat trips down the Lot or Dordogne rivers, looking up at the châteaux, or weave in a houseboat or flat-bottomed barge all the way up the Garonne from Bordeaux or Toulouse.

Brantôme on the banks of the Dronne is enchanting, with its crystal-clear canal flanked by balustraded terraces and crossed by lovely old bridges. Interesting are its 11th-century bell tower, its white, 18th-century Benedictine abbey, a 15th-century church, and several fine grottoes. Nearby lies the Renaissance château of Bourdeilles, with a 14th-century fortress, open daily to the public.

Périgueux, capital of the department of Dordogne, is built on the site of an old Roman city, called Vésone after its protectress, the goddess Vesuna. Ruins of a pagan temple erected in her honor still stand. After the city was sacked by barbarians in the 3rd century, it was given back its Gallic name, Pétrocores, and the modern names of both city and region developed from this word.

Starting with the ruins of a Roman arena that dates from the 3rd century, there is scarcely a period of architecture that is not represented in Périgueux. The cathedral of St-Front, believed to have been built between 1125 and 1150, is one of the strangest in France. Built in the shape of a Greek cross, it is primarily Romanesque in style. Its five domes betray Byzantine influence, and understandably so, for Périgueux was on the trade route to the East. St-Etienne, the other domed church in the city, is less ostentatiously restored than St-Front.

A visit to the Périgueux Museum to look at the remarkable prehistoric collections makes a convenient preliminary to trips outside the city and gives you a chance to examine an unusual collection of Gallo-Roman mosaics, ceramics and bronzes. France's first ever Truffle Museum opened at Sorges-en-Dordogne near Périgueux in 1981.

Prehistoric art

Throughout the region are traces of Roman, medieval and Renaissance civilizations, but these are less striking attractions than the caves, caverns and grottoes of the countryside. It is in some of these that archeologists found the bones, utensils and paintings of Cro-Magnon man. The brown, gray and black paintings of racing horses and reindeer, of bison and cows, show a well-developed sense of form and movement.

AROUND THE DORDOGNE

Forty-two km (26 miles) southeast of Périgueux is Les Eyzies. It was here, at the confluence of the Beune and Vézère rivers that Cro-Magnon skeletons were found in 1868. One skeleton remains, under glass. The village lies at the bottom of a 182-meter (600-ft) cliff, and halfway up, under an impressive outcrop of rock, is a 16th-century château that now houses the National Prehistory Museum. On the terrace of the museum stands a statue of Cro-Magnon man as imagined by the sculptor Dardé in 1930.

In the vicinity of Les Eyzies, in the Beune valley, prehistoric paintings may be seen in the Font-de-Gaume grotto; engravings in the Combarelle grotto, and, at the Abri du Cap Blanc, a frieze in bold relief depicting a dozen animal figures.

Near Montignac-sur-Vézère are the Lascaux Caves, discovered in 1940 and containing what have been called the finest prehistoric paintings in Europe, possibly 30,000 years old. Despite precautions taken to preserve the paintings—including airconditioning—it was discovered in 1963 that they had begun to deteriorate, and the caves were closed permanently. An exact replica is to be built, but until then tourists must make do with visiting the various other caves in the region, including those around Les Eyzies and the particularly interesting one near Rouffignac.

Châteaux of Périgord

The surrounding countryside is liberally sprinkled with medieval châteaux. See Beynac-et Cazenac, where the barons of Périgueux once met. From its ramparts the view over the meandering valley of the Dordogne is sensational. Then there's the heavily restored château of Fayrac situated near the impressive ruins of Castelnaud, which overlooks a picturesque village of narrow, winding streets and old houses with an admirable view of the Dordogne valley and the mighty castles of Beynac and Marqueyssac.

The charming village of La Roque-Gageac, wedged between rocky cliffs and the Dordogne, is commanded by the lofty castle of Marqueyssac, renowned for its magnificent terraced gardens, which afford a wide vista over the village to the château of Castelnaud across the river. Just west of La Bachellerie there's the beautiful 18th-century castle of Rastignac, strongly reminiscent of the White House in Washington with its Ionic columns and rounded façade. The château of Biron, begun in the 12th century but including buildings of later periods, dominates the country for miles around.

The imposing château of Hautefort, with its crenellated walls, round towers and drawbridge is worth visiting as well as the 16th-century castle of Puyguilhem with its chubby tower topped by a peaked roof, its Renaissance staircase and carved windows; also Monbazillac famous for its wine as well as its grounds. At Thonac, the 16th-century château of Losse faces the river Vézère, its walls swathed in ivy. It was built by Jean de Losse, governor of the Périgord and a violent enemy of the Huguenots. Visit the massive ruins of the feudal castle of Commarque at Sireuil; also the macabre remains of the château de l'Herm, which was the scene of a family murder.

Climb the mount to the medieval town of Domme with a panoramic view of the valley from its ramparts; see Souillac with its interesting church, a fine 12th-century abbey in the Périgourdin–Romanesque style; and also the ancient abbey of Cadouin founded in 1115; then, St-Céré, a picturesque little town with many 15th, 16th and 17th-century houses. Perched on a hillside nearby is the château of Montal, superbly restored at the beginning of this century. Don't miss the aristocratic old town of Sarlat with many fine houses (guided tours, on foot, are sometimes held on summer evenings). One of the most spectacular feudal castles of the region is Castelnau-Bretenoux, surrounded by vineyards and commanding the river Lot from its high perch. Only the donjon (an oriental-inspired tower built in 1080, with thin columned windows topped by a Moorish spindle), the main walls and corner towers remain of the original structure. A disaster occurred in 1850 when a bankrupt noble heir set fire to the castle hoping to collect the insurance. Later, it was bought and restored by Mouliérat, a famous tenor of the Opéra Comique who left it to the state, complete with tapestries, period furniture and bibelots.

From St-Céré you can make many pleasant excursions to the picturesque little towns and villages dotted about the surrounding countryside—Autuire and its nearby waterfall, Loubressac with its castle, Carennac, perched on the banks of the Dordogne with a Romanesque abbey and peaceful cloister, Martel, which still has many medieval buildings, or Gramat, a pleasant little market town.

A scenic route from St-Céré to the industrial town of Tulle, set deep in the valley, winds high through wild, rugged, uninhabited lands. Tulle was the scene of one of the worst massacres of World War II. On June 9, 1944, 99 young hostages were hanged from balconies in the main streets by the SS, in reprisal for a Communist-led attempt to liberate the town.

Subterranean river

An excellent excursion from Brive, Périgueux or St-Céré is to the Gouffre de Padirac, a well or abyss over 90 meters (300 ft) deep, at the bottom of which is a subterranean river, reached by elevators and stairs. You can travel by boat for about 1 km (½ mile), gliding in and

AROUND THE DORDOGNE

out of vast chambers, one over 82 meters (270 ft) high. The stalagmites and stalactites, the grotesque rock structures and the weird crystalline formations seen in the dimly lit underground passages have earned the Gouffre its reputation as one of the most interesting natural phenomena in France.

Not far from Padirac is Rocamadour, a village set in a narrow gorge of the river Alzou. According to tradition, Zacheus, a publican who had the honor of entertaining Jesus in his home, came to Gaul after the crucifixion and, under the name of Amadour, became a hermit and set up a shrine in the cliff overlooking the river. Since then, other chapels and shrines have been built in the cliff, one of them containing the crypt of St. Amadour. The village consists of a single street of houses built in the Middle Ages to shelter pilgrims who came to honor St Amadour. Rocamadour is still the goal of pilgrimages. On top of the cliff is a 14th-century château, rebuilt during the 19th century, which houses the priests who are in charge of the shrines. There is a magnificent view from here over the village and its setting of spectacular cliffs.

The lively town of Cahors, ancient capital of the province of Quercy, has a Romanesque cathedral in the domed style of Aquitaine, and the beautiful medieval bridge of Valentré, which spans the Lot. Some 8 km (5 miles) away the château of the bishops of Cahors has been converted into a modern hotel, the towered château of Mercuès, overlooking the Lot valley. The Quercy has now been discovered, especially by British visitors, who appreciate the calm friendliness of the inhabitants, the lovely village architecture, the little-known historic monuments—and the reasonable prices.

East to Conques

This damp limestone region, called the Châtaigneraie, was once so fertile that the area became over-populated, but the earth was soon impoverished by a too intensive exploitation of its wealth. The men left, and today the tourist crosses a vast expanse covered with ferns and gorse, firs, pines and wild beeches, only occasionally coming upon one of the poor hamlets of this formerly prosperous region.

Not far from Figeac (which has a good coin museum), but very different from it, is the partly abandoned village of Conques. People come from afar to this wild valley, for here stands one of the most beautiful religious monuments in the south of France. Ste-Foy-de-Conques. It was begun some time near 1050 as one of the four major churches along the pilgrimage way to Santiago de Compostela in Spain.

From Conques delightful side trips can be made through the lovely Lot valley to Entraygues, with its 13th-century bridge and 16th-century houses (along the rue Basse), to the medieval town of Estaing, hugging the banks of the Lot, with its picturesque bridge and old castle; to nearby Espalion, beloved by fishermen, and by artists for its red stone bridge and Renaissance château built on the river's edge; to the tiny fortified village of St-Côme on the Lot with its winding cobbled streets; to Bozouls precariously clinging to the edge of a deep canyon; to the medieval hill town of Rodez with its fortress-like cathedral commanding the main square and, beside it, a 16th-century bell tower of reddish-brown stone graced by late Gothic motifs. Rodez has recently benefited from a state grant designed to help urban renewal and has given itself a face lift: the ramparts have been restored, pedestrian precincts have been built and the place is full of modern hotels and smart boutiques.

In the Causses region—high barren reaches, the realm of solitary winds—visit the near-deserted 14th-century village of La Couvertoirade, once a stop on the road to Santiago de Compostela, and also La Cavalerie, ancient seat of the Knights Templar. What makes the Causses appear even more like a wilderness is the infrequency of villages, but this loneliness is broken in the summer by huge herds of sheep coming up from the Camargue and the plains of Languedoc. The trek is made by tens of thousands of the animals, which come to graze on the short grass of the plateaux.

The Causses are limestone plateaux that were raised at the same time as the Pyrenees. Pressure caused fractures and cleavages that trapped the torrential autumn rains. Over thousands of years the swirling waters ate into the mass of stone, gouging out the canyons, caves, underground rivers and lakes that today delight the tourist, boatman and geologist.

Gorges of the Tarn

The most famous and most impressive of these canyons, the Gorges of the Tarn, separating the Causse Sauveterre from the Causse Méjean, provides more than 48 km (30 miles) of gorges, stretching from Millau, the headquarters for excursions into this strange part of France, all the way to Ste-Enimie. The entire course of the canyon is a wilderness filled with sudden views of breathtaking silhouettes of the red and yellow cliffs, the rocky chaos of landslides that have tumbled into the river, routing the waters swirling around them. Various points along the gorges are floodlit on summer evenings. Though a highway winds its way the length of the canyon, you should also, if possible, go down the Tarn by boat. (During the season there is a regular service between La Malène and the Cirque des Baumes.)

Not far from Millau, at the foot of towering limestone cliffs, lies Roquefort-sur-Soulzon, famous for its ewes'-milk cheese since the time

AROUND THE DORDOGNE

of the Romans. For a tour of Roquefort's caves, inquire at La Société des Caves, Caves de la Rue.

We now turn northward, away from the Gorges of the Tarn towards Mende, just before reaching Florac. Mende, town of the most sparsely populated region of France, is located at the base of a small foothill of the Causse. In July and August canoeists embark from under the old bridge of Notre-Dame-de-Peyrane for a cruise on the Lot, and hosts of campers pitch tents in the country around.

Close to Mende are the Cévennes Mountains, a magnificent region that is becoming increasingly popular with walkers and nature lovers. In them is the Cévennes National Park, a nature reserve with many protected species. On the edge of the park is Villefort, a pleasant little holiday resort with a beautiful artificial lake fringed by heather covered hills. Lovers of Robert Louis Stevenson's *Travels with a Donkey* might like to try following his itinerary (preferably without the donkey!) as more and more tourists have been doing since the centenary of his journey was celebrated in 1978.

PRACTICAL INFORMATION

WHEN TO GO. The main tourist season in this part of France is short—just July and Aug. This is when most of the events and festivals take place, and when you'll be able to attend concerts in the region's churches, for instance. But it can be very hot in these months too, and you may be plagued by mosquitoes. Also the most popular centers are crowded, though it's still relatively easy to get off the beaten tourist track here. Spring is delightful, but can be wet, as can early summer. Sept. is one of the best months, with the temperatures more suitable for exploring than in mid-summer, and in Oct. the trees are magnificent. The region is rarely visited in the winter.

Most of the local festivals take place in the summer months, but picturesque *fêtes* celebrating local patron saints occur throughout the year **January** sees Brive's *Foire des Rois* (Epiphany Fair), with truffles and foie gras for sale. In April, Aubazine has a goat fair. **Easter** sees the beginning of Rocamadour's *son-et-lumière*, which continues right through the summer to October 15. The first major festivals come in **July:** Sarlat's theater festival; Gourdon's international music festival; Brive's folklore event; and in Rodez, a summer festival plus the 'Rouergue cultural week' is staged. Many of these festivals continue into **August,** which is also the month for folklore festivals in Bergerac and in Gourdon, and for an international religious music festival in the little town of St-Céré. In late August and early **September** Périgueux has its *journées de Périgueux,* with all sorts of cultural and folklore events. Also in September, riding competitions are held at Pompadour. And on the first Sunday of the month thousands of Protestants from all over Europe make a pilgrimage to the Musée du Désert at the lonely Mas Soubeyran, to commemorate the martyrdom of the Huguenots, who fought to defend their faith after the Revocation of the Edict of Nantes in 1685. In **October** comes the picturesque *Fête de Notre Dame des Petits Ventres,* in Limoge's delightful rue de la Boucherie; chestnut fairs are often held too.

WHAT TO DO. Exploring the villages and little towns of this still relatively unspoilt area is one of the favorite occupations of those who visit it. But if you prefer to have an active holiday geared to some form of sport you'll find plenty of opportunities here too. **Riding** is one of the most popular pursuits, with riding holidays offered in many places. For instance the Club Méditerranée has a 'village' devoted to riding at Pompadour in the Corrèze. The Aveyron *département* is particularly active in organizing riding holidays at any of its 24 riding establishments (details from the Association Départementale de Tourisme Equestre, Chambre d'Agriculture, route de Moyrazès, 12009 Rodez).

AROUND THE DORDOGNE

In the Lozère the Centre Equestre des Monts d'Aubrac, 48260 Nasbinals, organizes riding parties through the Cévennes and the Aubrac, with accommodation in friendly farmhouses. Horses are also popular here as carriage-pullers —in the Limousin you can have a leisurely holiday in a horse-drawn *calèche*, spending the night in *gîtes* (usually part of farmhouses) or camping (write for details to *Hobby Voyage*, 8 rue de Milan, 75009 Paris). If you prefer Shanks's pony, watch out for the signposted GR footpaths; or if you'd feel happier joining a **walking** party, inquire at the regional tourist offices or write to the Comité National des Sentiers de Grande Randonnée, 92 rue de Clignancourt, 75883 Paris cedex 18. Alternatively, **cycling** is a good way of getting about; here too you can join organized cycling tours, arranged by local clubs or by the tourist offices. For a trout's eye view of the region your best bet is a **canoe**; this region is full of rivers and the possibilities are endless. The Ligue Régionale de Canoë–Kayak, 87120 Eymoutiers, will give you details. **Potholing** is favored by the adventurous, but you shouldn't attempt this without local assistance.

Fishing, too, is a favorite pastime, but you must inquire at the local tourist office about where you are allowed to fish and what sort of permit you need.

The Club Méditerranée village at Pompadour is an ideal spot for **tennis** fans. Elsewhere, towns and villages are increasingly building new courts.

The ancient region of Rouergue has developed a most imaginative scheme of unusual holidays through its *Club des Vacances Insolites*. Local residents who are skilled at some craft, profession or pursuit, volunteer to give courses to holiday makers, for a most reasonable price. Visitors are lodged in modest hotels or *gîtes* . . . or they camp, especially in Aug. when the tiny hotels of the region are full. The courses are varied: sculpture, fossil-hunting, pottery, ceramics, theater, photography, fencing, weaving, stained glass, iron work; but the most fun is living in close contact with the craftsmen and with the people in these tiny, picturesque villages. Write *Maison du Rouergue*, 30 rue Chaussée-d'Antin, 75008 Paris.

HOW TO GET ABOUT. By air. For flights to Bordeaux, see Atlantic coast chapter. *TAT* flies Paris–Rodez and Pairs–Perigueux. Another alternative is Paris–Le Puy, which is served by a small airline called *Compagnie Aerienne du Languedoc*. Flights to Toulouse and Clermont-Ferrand can also be useful (see Pyrenees and Auvergne chapters).

By train. The main rail route to southwest France operates from the Gare d'Austerlitz in Paris, with the famous *Le Capitole* to Toulouse traveling twice a day in each direction on weekdays and stopping at Limoges and Cahors. Journey times are 3-3½ hrs to Limoges and just under 5 hrs to Cahors. The car-sleeper service to Brive-la-Gaillarde will save precious time. The *Barcelona-Talgo* trains now stop at Limoges. The whole area is well served by cross-country trains, which give you a good opportunity to admire the magnificent scenery. Limoges–Brive–Rocamadour–Rodez and then on to Toulouse is particularly interesting. If you want to combine a visit to this region with one to another part of France, there are various possibilities. Here's just one of them:

Nantes–La-Rochelle–Limoges. The SNCF offers packages covering rail fare, full board and accommodations in Najac in the Rouergue, May through September.

By coach. The SNCF have regular 3-day and occasional 9-day tours from Paris in the summer months, usually based in Najac, and visiting the Quercy, Rouergue, the Gorges du Tarn and Gascony. They also have combined coach and rail tours of the Gorges du Tarn from Paris, leaving Fri. evening and returning early on Mon. morning; a tour of the gorges that includes Entraygues, Conques and Rodez; a five-day tour of the Rouergue and Najac. Within the region there are plenty of day- and half-day coach excursions from centers such as Sarlat. *Europe Autocar* have a week's coach tour of Quercy, the Tarn, Perigord and the Dordogne in July and August, and a three day visit to the châteaux and abbeys of the Limousin. Their *Rouergue* trip (1 week in May, June and September) also gives you a chance to visit the Auvergne.

MOTORING. From Paris the fastest route is to take the A10 motorway *(L'Aquitaine)* to Poitiers, then the N147 to Limoges. From here the N21 goes on to Périgueux and Bergerac; and the N20 to Brive and Cahors. For Rocamadour, Figeac and Rodez branch off the N20 on to the N140. For popular Sarlat winding roads (the D60 and D67) leave the N89 between Brive and Périgueux. If you don't want to use the motorway, take the N20 all the way from Paris via Orléans, Vierzon, Châteauroux and Limoges to Uzerches.

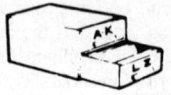

USEFUL ADDRESSES. The *Welcome Information office* for the Limousin and city tourist office are at bld de Fleurus, 87000 Limoges, and the *Regional Tourist Committee* at 8 cours Bugeaud. For the Corrèze write to the *Maison du Tourisme,* quai Baluze, 19000 Tulle. The *Departmental Committee for the Dordogne–Périgord* region is at 16 av. du Président Wilson, 24000 Périgueux; *Departmental Tourist Committee* for Lot-et-Garonne, 4 rue André-Chenier, BP 158, 47005 Agen. *Youth Information Center,* 3 rue Jules-Guesde, 18700 Limoges.

In Paris, the *Maison du Limousin,* 18 bld Haussmann, 9e; *Maison de la Lozère,* 4 rue Hautefeuille, 6e; *Maison du Périgord,* 30 rue Louis-le-Grand, 2e; and the *Maison du Rouergue,* 3 rue Chaussée-d'Antin, 8e. The *Maison du Lot-et-Garonne,* 15-17 passage Choiseul, 75002 Paris, is a useful source of information.

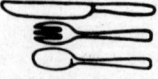

REGIONAL FOOD AND DRINK. Périgord cooking is renowned throughout France. But not until you taste the *cèpes à la périgourdine, cou d'oie farci, confit d'oie* or *galantine de dinde truffée* of Périgord will you really understand what it is. The specialty, and perhaps the secret, is truffles, served with and in most of the dishes of the region. *Foie gras* (goose liver) is another specialty and Périgord cuisine is based on goose fat rather than butter. *Charcut-*

AROUND THE DORDOGNE

erie shops in the Périgord carry shelves of goodies to take home as gifts to less-fortunate friends, such as tins of *foie gras,* truffles preserved in Madeira, *rillettes,* and a selection of canned *pâtés.*

Best known wines are *Monbazillac* white and *Cahors* red. An interesting liqueur is produced locally, *crème de noix,* made from walnuts.

HOTELS AND RESTAURANTS. This is not an area for deluxe accommodations, but you'll find plenty of pleasant country inns and small family hotels. You may even find yourself in a château converted into a charming hotel. For information on *gîtes,* which are very plentiful in this area, see our 'Facts at your Fingertips' section. The Cévennes region is full of holiday villages, grouped in such picturesque localities as Florac, Meyrueis, La-Barre-des-Cévennes; also *gîtes ruraux,* as well as farms that take paying guests. For details, write to Direction du Parc des Cévennes, La Croisette, 48400 Florac.

Restaurants and hotels referred to as *E, M* or *I* are expensive, moderate or inexpensive.

BEAULIEU-SUR-DORDOGNE. *Le Turenne,* an old manor house, plenty of atmosphere, moderate. *Central* (I). Both have good restaurants (M).

BRANTÔME. Small *Moulin de l'Abbaye* (E), restored and converted mill (Relais et Château member), with lots of charm and a very good restaurant (M). *Chabrol,* 21 rooms, good restaurant, moderate.

Restaurant. 6 km (4 miles) northeast at **Champagnac-de-Belair,** *Moulin du Roc* (E), excellent cuisine by a highly talented woman chef; also has a few peaceful rooms.

BRIVE-LA-GAILLARDE. *Truffe Noire* (E). *Montauban,* inexpensive. *Paris,* moderate, but no restaurant.

At **Varetz,** nearby, the 13th-cent. *Château de Castel Novel* (E) is a perfect center for the Dordogne.

Restaurant. *Cremaillère* (M), delicious cuisine, though portions can be a bit on the small side. Also has rooms.

LE BUGUE. *Le Royal Vézère,* expensive; pool, all amenities. Has very good restaurant called *Albuca.*

BUSSIÈRE. *Le Relais,* pleasant and inexpensive little hotel/restaurant; Logis de France.

CAHORS. *Wilson* (E), no restaurant, modern, central. *France* and *Terminus,* neither with restaurant, are pleasant, moderate.

Restaurants. *La Taverne* (M), 41 rue J. B.-Delpech, good.

At nearby **Laroque-des-Arcs,** is the charming *Hostellerie Beau Rivage* (M) with super cuisine, and some rooms.

CARENNAC. *Fénélon* (I), quiet and friendly, good restaurant (M).

CONQUES. *Ste-Foy,* moderate, with more than acceptable restaurant (I). No lunches, though.

CRESSENSAC. Not far from the fortified village of Turenne, a charming country inn, *La Truffière,* moderate.

DOMME. *Esplanade,* moderate, good restaurant.

ENTRAYGUES. *Deux Vallées,* comfortable, moderate. Restaurant is (I).

ESPALION. *Moderne,* quite good regional cooking, moderate.

LES EYZIES. *Cro-Magnon* (M), with pool, and *Centenaire,* moderate, with good restaurants (E), and a few (E) suites. *Les Glycines,* good, moderate.

LIMOGES. *Frantel,* expensive, with good restaurant (E). *Mapotel Luk* (M), modern, comfortable, with restaurant. *Richelieu* (M), no restaurant. *Faisan* (M). *Petit Paris* (I). Just north, *Novotel,* with pool, moderate, and a bit further out, *La Résidence,* moderate, pleasant.
Restaurants. *Petits Ventres* (M) and *Versailles* (I).

LA MALÈNE. *Manoir de Montesquieu* (M), 15th-century manor house, classical cuisine. *Château de la Caze* (E), on banks of Tarn river gorges, about 5.5 km (3 miles) from town, good restaurant (M).

MENDE. *Lion d'Or* (E), with pool. *Remparts* (I), no restaurant.

MEYRUEIS. *Renaissance* (M) and *Europe* (I), with pool, good cuisine.

MEYSSAC. *Relais du Quercy* (I), small, with large garden and regional cuisine.

MILLAU. *International* (E), modern and comfortable, good restaurant. *Musadière* (E), good regional cooking served in generous quantities. *Moderne* (I), shares nearby *International's* restaurant.
Restaurants. *Buffet de France,* at station, and *Capion* both uphold the culinary honor of the Aveyron *département;* both (M).

MOISSAC. *Moulin de Moissac* (E), overlooking river Tarn, excellent restaurant. *Chapon Fin,* in town, moderate, with local specialties in restaurant (M).

MONTCABRIER. Peaceful *Relais de la Dolce* (E), with nice grounds, pool and regional cuisine.

MONTIGNAC-SUR-VÉZÈRE. *Soleil d'Or* (M), with big garden and straightforward cuisine.

NAJAC. *Belle-Rive* (I), lovely location, with pool and restaurant.

PÉRIGUEUX. *Domino* (M), the best in town. Modern *Ibis* (I), is next to the cathedral. *Bristol* (M), no restaurant. 4 miles north, *Regina* (I), no restaurant.
About 6 km (4 miles) south at **Antonne** is the hotel *Ecluse* (M), one of those pleasant inns you often find in the Dordogne.
Restaurants. Best is *Léon*, 18 cours Tourny. *Marcel*, 37 av. de Limoges. Both (M).

ROCAMADOUR. *Ste-Marie* (M), with a terrace, lovely view and good cuisine; *Beau Site et Notre Dame* (M); *Panoramic* (M) is peaceful.
Restaurants. Best is *Ste-Marie* (M) (in hotel). Also *Bellevue* (M), which also has rooms. Outside town on D247 (the Lacave road), *Auberge de la Garenne* (M), good regional cuisine (plenty of truffles!); also has rooms.

RODEZ. Best is *Tour Maje*, 42 rooms, no restaurant, moderate. Then come *Broussy, Moderne*, inexpensive, with restaurant, and *Parc*, moderate, with no restaurant. *Midi* and *Poste* are both inexpensive. 3.5 km (2 miles) away, *Hostellerie de Fontanges* (M), with lovely grounds and pool.
Restaurant. *Le Régent* has good 'new' cooking at reasonable prices (M).

LA ROQUE-GAGEAC. One of the most magnificent locations on the Dordogne. *Gardette* (I), first-rate Périgord cuisine (M).

ST-CÉRÉ. A good place to stay while touring the region. *Paris et du Coq Arlequin*, moderate, very good restaurant, (M). *France* (open only July to mid-Sept.), with good restaurant (M), and *Parc* are both good and inexpensive.

STE-ENIMIE. *Commerce* and *Paris*, both moderate.

SARLAT. *Madeleine*, moderate, good, with restaurant (M). *Verperie* (M), is attractive. Just outside town are two lovely inns: *Hoirie* (M), a handsome old Périgord building, with antique furniture but no restaurant, and *Hostellerie Meysset* (E); both are peaceful.
Restaurants. *St-Albert*, an old favorite (M), in hotel of same name. *Marcel* is also (M).

SIORAC-EN-PÉRIGORD. In the Dordogne. *Scholly*, fine classical cuisine (M).

SOUILLAC. *Ambassadeurs,* very good food. *Grand Hôtel,* pleasant ambiance, reader-recommended. Both moderate.

Restaurant. *Vieille Auberge* (M), excellent, best reserve in summer. Also has rooms.

SOUSCEYRAC. Restaurant. *Déjeuner de Sousceyrac* (M), superb food, good value. Also has rooms.

TRÉMOLAT. *Le Vieux Logis,* an expensive but popular hideout in this typical Dordogne village. *Panoramic* (M) is 2.5 km (1½ miles) northwest via D31.

TULLE. *Limouzi,* in town center, moderate, modernized; good regional cooking.

VILLEFORT. *Balme* (I), modest little hotel-restaurant.

VILLENEUVE-sur-LOT. *Parc* (E), pleasant Logis de France with garden and good restaurant (M).

THE AUVERGNE

France's volcanic heart

The Auvergne is right in the middle of France, in the Massif Central that forms the country's mountainous heartland, with a rich geological heritage fashioned over the centuries by volcanic upheavals. It has six volcanoes as little—geologically speaking—as 10,000 years old, one of them, Sancy, ten times the size of Italy's far more famous Vesuvius. Yet the Auvergne's heritage, in spite of its lakes and mountains, its lush green fields, its gorges and rivers, is not solely nature's responsibility. Few tourists realize that it has as many as 500 châteaux, ranging from imposing fortresses such as Murol to romantic Château Brûlé, ruined 12th-century Tournoël, crushed by Richelieu, and majestic Parentignat, which has been owned by the same family since it was built during the reign of the Sun King.

Visiting the châteaux of the Auvergne has become much more rewarding since 1975, the Year of the Châteaux, when many were opened to the public for the first time (they can usually be visited from about Easter to October). This part of France also has some particularly interesting Romanesque churches, with perhaps the finest at St-Nectaire, Issoire and Orcival.

Yet the Auvergne has much else to offer, especially for those who like outdoor pursuits such as hiking and rambling, riding, fishing or canoeing—plus the sort of filling, rustic dishes that you need after a day in the open air! It is becoming an increasingly important skiing center too, popular with all who are looking for energetic family holidays at reasonable prices, who prefer ski to *après-ski*.

But this is not solely a place for unsophisticated enjoyment, even if many of the French still persist, against all the evidence, in thinking of the sturdy Auvergnats as worthy but dull peasants. Spas are plentiful here (Vichy is the best-known, but La Bourboule, Châtel-Guyon and Royat are all major watering places too). Like spas all over the world, they have a full calendar of galas and concerts, golf championships and tennis tournaments. And, again like all spas, they have casinos. If you want grand hotels and smart restaurants you'll obviously be better off here than in the more rural districts, but you won't necessarily eat better—the hard-working Auvergnats have a tradition of good eating and indeed run many of the best regional restaurants in Paris.

It should be remembered, however, that the Auvergne does have its modern aspect too. Clermont-Ferrand, its capital, has long been the capital of the tyre industry as well: the great Michelin has been here since 1886. There are important hydro-electric plants, harnessing the region's mighty torrents, along with the metallurgical and chemical industries. These new industries have inevitably pushed into the background the region's traditional crafts, chief of which is lace-making, but a recent swing away from mass-produced goods to traditional craftsmanship (this new mood is particularly evident in France, though it is affecting the whole of the Western world) is reviving some of them, and the tourist industry is beginning to realize the potential of craft classes as a magnet for frustrated city-dwellers.

Moulins and Vichy

The Auvergne is usually approached from the north. Old Moulins, with its narrow cobbled streets, has a famous triptych by the Maître de Moulins in its cathedral. To the south lies Vichy, one of the world's most famous watering places, situated on the right bank of the Allier, with its well-kept flower beds and shady parks. Vichy's springs and brilliant season of music and dramatic festivals have always attracted

THE AUVERGNE

visitors. The Romans were the first to appreciate the benefits of Vichy's springs, of which there are nine. The famous Source des Célestins, whose bottled waters enjoy a worldwide reputation, produces over 204,570 liters (45,000 gallons) a day. The waters are strongly alkaline and are particularly recommended for digestive troubles. At the *buvettes*, which are open all year, the water is free. The three thermal establishments, with their baths and other therapeutic treatments, are owned by the state and are open during the season. You can visit the Grand Etablissement Thermal and also the state factory, near the railroad station, where the famous Vichy mineral is bottled.

The triangular Vieux Parc is the fashionable center of Vichy, a favorite promenade before the apèritif hours and during the evening. Past the casino and towards the boulevard des Etats-Unis, in the old part of town, is the striking church of St-Blaise, a modern building of unconventional design built on to the old church. In the interior, notice the glass and the murals of the cathedrals of France. At the 12th–16th-century château of Lapalisse; 19 km (12 miles) north of Vichy, you can watch a *son-et-lumière* performance on summer evenings.

Thiers and Riom

Thiers, 35 km (22 miles) to the southeast and built on the crest of a rocky ravine, has been the cutlery capital of France since the Middle Ages. Every other shop displays knives of every shape and size at most reasonable prices. You can visit the factories by inquiring at the tourist office. The town's many half-timbered houses are a tourist attraction, and so is the picturesque place Pirou dominated by the 15th-century Château Pirou.

Southwest of Vichy, on the road to Clermont-Ferrand, is the small town of Riom, with numerous Gothic and Renaissance art treasures, including the lovely stained-glass windows in the church of St-Pierre and in the Palais de Justice. From the feudal ruins of the château of Tournoël nearby—one of the most romantic sites in Auvergne—there's a spectacular view over three plateaux. Twice nightly during the summer, the château is the setting for a *son-et-lumière* performance. At the château of Chazeron, not far from Riom, you can watch a performance called 'Auvergne, Land of Liberty'.

Clermont-Ferrand and the Puy-de-Dôme

Tens of thousands of tourists each year pass through Clermont-Ferrand, lying at the crossroads of the Massif Central. This lively city of 220,000 is a center of the French rubber industry (Michelin's main factory is here) as well as the capital of Auvergne. It has a famous early

Gothic cathedral, and its 12th-century basilica of Notre-Dame-du-Port, with its curious roof, is an admired example of the Auvergnat Romanesque style. Also worth visiting are the Ranquet Museum, showing regional costumes and art, and the Fontaine d'Amboise.

The outstanding sights of Auvergne are the ruins of the Roman Temple of Mercury and the view from the top of the Puy-de-Dôme. The panorama is really exceptional, with its succession of wooded *puys* (peaks of porous domite) rolling away before the eye. There are crater depressions on the summit of each, mementoes of the days when the volcanoes were active.

The Mont-Dore region, spas and winter sports

The one-street thermal town of St-Nectaire, hedged by wooded hills, boasts a beautiful 12th-century Romanesque church. Nearby is the delightful resort of Murol with its lovely Lake Chambon, its medieval château perched on a small hill, and its splendid view of Mont-Dore.

Excursions from here will take you to Orcival, with its beautiful church, and to Lake Guéry. It is near Besse-en-Chandesse, in the heart of the region of ancient craters, that the beautiful lakes of Pavin, Chauvet, Contat-en-Féniers, St-Amandin and Riom-ès-Montagne are found. Giving off reddish-brown reflections, they are surrounded by blue fir trees, villages of black lava, and enormous cattle farms with buildings made of lava and slate. Le Mont-Dore and La Bourboule are health resorts noted particularly for respiratory troubles, and are starting points for many trips into the mountains.

The top winter sports resort in the Massif Central is Le Mont-Dore. The slopes are gentler than in the great Alps or the Pyrenees, giving them an appeal for beginners as well as for those who prefer quieter places, smaller crowds, and lower prices.

To the south begins the ascent toward the Massif du Cantel, a region that is now being discovered, especially by British visitors. It has all of the striking physical grandeur of a magnified Mont-Dore. Glacier valleys furrow out from the enormous bulk of the range and we can follow one of them straight toward the triangular pyramid of Puy Mary. The view over the chain of hills and peaks is less sharp than that from Mont-Dore. Our way down lies to the south, through the Mandaille valley, a country of pastures and forests.

Salers is a medieval village, unspoiled by neon lights or modern buildings. The permanent population in the beautiful stone houses has shrunk to a little over 600, but summer vacationers, who have just begun to rediscover it, turn the town into a metropolis of 5,000 in summer. Salers is the home of Cantal cheese (you can visit the cheese cooperative). The fortified walls were designed by a Marshall Lafayette,

THE AUVERGNE

an ancestor of the Marquis de Lafayette who fought in the American Revolution.

Nearby is the Barrage de Sarrans, part of an extensive regional hydroelectric scheme on the river Truyère that includes a huge lake and two subsidiary dams.

Le Puy-en-Velay

The N106 from Alès to Le Puy twists mercilessly for miles through the mountains, beside the Gorges de Chassézac, past giant granite rocks and heather-clad hills. In the distance loom the bold red summits of mountains, and panoramic views are plentiful over a russet valley dotted with sparse vegetation. The resort town of Bastide is followed by lonely pine woods. More barren country cut by rock cliffs and rushing streams continues as far as Luc, where the Allier valley begins. Stone fences curb grazing cattle, and the landscape suggests a Chinese painting with a high broad plateau broken by red humped domes or *puys*. In the fertile valley, cultivated yellow and tan squares lie like carpets spread over emerald hills. Here you can still chance upon an aged peasant woman, sitting before a farm or a thatched stable, making lace. Her fingers fly with surprising dexterity, and from distaff and thread there slowly grows a delicate piece of lace.

The location of Le Puy itself is extraordinary: four precipitous volcanic outcrops rise from the narrow plain. On the lowest, guarding the western approach, St-Joseph and the Child; the 11th-century chapel of St-Michel balances precariously on the highest outcrop; on another peak dominating the town and the cathedral, stands a huge statue of the Virgin, Notre-Dame-de-France, erected in 1860 from melted-down Russian cannon taken at Sebastopol during the Crimean War. Atop the fourth pinnacle sits the extraordinary Romanesque cathedral, Notre-Dame-du-Puy, built of polychrome lava. A complicated structure pressed on to its rocky site, it is approached by a long flight of stone steps, affording a wonderful view of the narrow slanted street directly below, and the green landscape that rolls away into the distance. Its nave, also polychrome, is reminiscent of some Islamic mosque; the Black Virgin worshipped here recalls the ancient cult of Isis. Don't miss the elaborately penned bible of Théodulph, one of the most precious specimens of Carolingian calligraphy, or the remarkable fresco of St Michael in the cloisters. The lovely cloisters were much influenced by the Moorish style, with their use of alternating black and white stones. (Note the beautiful Romanesque iron gate). For summer visitors, there is a *son-et-lumière* performance at the great medieval hilltop château of Polignac, 13 km (8 miles) from Le Puy to the west.

Some 40 km (25 miles) further north, in the middle of a plateau that is almost 1,100 meters (3,600 ft) high and covered with woods and pastures, lies the town of Chaise-Dieu, with its famous church of St-Robert. Its frescoes of the *Danse Macabre* have recently been restored and are worth close study. Splendidly drawn in red and black, they represent Death dancing with the nobility, bourgeoisie and working folk. The immense, though badly damaged, cloisters and the choir with its beautiful early 16th-century Brussels and Arras tapestries and carved stalls are also worth seeing.

Due north on the N106, some 8 km (5 miles) from Ambert are ancient paper mills on the Val de Laga, with an interesting museum that records both the history and method of manufacturing handmade paper. Ambert itself has given its name to a blue cheese considered by connoisseurs to be one of the world's best. The small town has retained its 16th-century appearance and atmosphere based on the circular town hall: 'façades everywhere, but without a center,' wrote Jules Romain, whose novels are set mainly in this region he knew so well. He was born only 19 km (12 miles) east of Puy, at the hamlet of La Chapuze: Among the towns and villages described by him are Yssingeaux (Gothic town hall), whence the N103 leads to Tence and the Gorges of the Lignon before climbing to the Col de la Batterie (914 meters/3,000 ft high), the watershed between the Atlantic and the Mediterranean.

On the direct route from Le Puy to Clermont-Ferrand, at Brioude, the meeting place of the Allier valley and the fertile plain of Limagne, is another beautiful church. Here, by making a short detour you can follow the winding green gorge of the river Alagnon north to St-Germain-Lembron. On a nearby hill are the ruins of the château of Nonette, dismantled by Richelieu.

Continuing north we reach the prosperous and cheerful town of Issoire with its remarkable 12th-century church of St-Paul. It is, however, a Lidice of the past, for it was almost completely razed to the ground in 1577, at the time of the religious wars, by order of the duc d'Alençon, son of Henri II. The work done he ordered an inscription put up in the main square reading: 'Here was Issoire'.

THE AUVERGNE

PRACTICAL INFORMATION

WHEN TO GO. May and June are probably the best months to visit the Auvergne, when the countryside is a riot of wild flowers and birdsong yet there is still snow on the highest peaks. July and Aug. can be hot, and campsites and resorts are crowded, but they are the best time for a walking holiday in the mountains, where the air stays fresh and cool. The fall is magnificent, with the forests a blaze of color, but can be wet. Winter is obviously winter-sports time; don't visit the rest of the region then, as roads are often blocked by snow. The spas have a full calendar of events—social, sporting and cultural—all year, but the summer months are the peak time.

January is winter-sports month, with important ski races in the Mont Dore region; the ski season continues in **February** and **March.** The first great religious festival comes on Maundy Thursday (the day before Good Friday), when torchlit processions of hooded penitents wend their way through the streets of Le Puy and Saugues. **May** too has its traditional religious ceremonies—a pilgrimage to Notre-Dame-des-Miracles in Mauriac on the Sunday after May 9, and the famous Notre-Dame-du-Port festival in Clermont-Ferrand, with a huge procession on the Sunday after May 15. Ascension Day sees more pilgrimages and torchlit processions, at Orcival, for instance, and other pilgrimages are made around this period to Marsat, Volvic, Usson and Salers. **June** sees Riom's St-Amable celebrations, with the picturesque processions of 'peasants' in 17th-cent. costume bearing aloft the saint's relics. Besse-en-Chandesse's turn comes in **July**, when it stages its *Fête de la Montée,* during which a statue of the Virgin Mary is ceremoniously carried up to the chapel of Notre-Dame-de-Vassivière, where she spends the summer. **July** and **August** are the height of the summer season at Vichy, with innumerable concerts, sports events and galas of all kinds. The other spas follow suit, though not on quite such a grandiose scale. The Gallea Cup tennis tournament in Vichy (late July or early August) is a particularly important sports event. August 15 (Assumption Day and a public holiday in France) is naturally devoted to the Virgin Mary, the best-known ceremonies being in Le Puy and Thiezac, again with processions through the streets. Many other folklore events crowd the calendar, such as the shepherds' pilgrimage and traditional get-together in La Font-Sainte on the last Thursday of the month, and St-Pourcain's Vine Fair. La Chaise-Dieu's Festival of French Music starts in late August. In **September** the main folklore event is again at Besse-en-Chandesse—the *Dévalade,* the return journey of the Virgin's statue to her winter quarters in town. Vichy's summer season lasts into **October.**

538 THE FACE OF FRANCE

WHAT TO DO. The Auvergne is a sports lover's paradise with **fishing** in the trout- and salmon-filled lakes and rivers; **canoeing** and **kayaking** and even **waterskiing** on the lakes; **riding** (there are hundreds of miles of signposted bridle paths); **hiking** and **rambling** (walking tours are offered by many organizations such as the France-Accueil hotel chain, who have all-in rates); **cycling** along the peaceful roads. Organized sports include **tennis** and **golf**, with many facilities in the spas and big towns, and **swimming pools** are found everywhere. For winter holidaymakers the Mont Dore region is an important **skiing** center.

If you prefer a less energetic holiday, make for one of the **spas**, where there are plenty of cultural and social events. Or you can of course 'take the waters'.

With its long rural past the Auvergne is increasingly becoming a center for the revival of traditional **crafts**, which are being lovingly handed down to French and foreign holidaymakers eager to escape from the uniformity of mass production. You can learn to make lace or pottery, to carve stone, to make beautiful ironwork, to weave baskets, paint on wood, dye fabrics.

Lovers of rural France will be tempted by a week's holiday in a **horse-drawn caravan**, or even a little carriage *(calèche)* if you want to do it in style.

Information on all these activities, and many more, can be obtained from the regional and local tourist offices or the Maison d'Auvergne in Paris (see addresses section).

HOW TO GET ABOUT. By air. *Dan Air* flies from London (Gatwick) to Clermont-Ferrand direct; *TAT* make the same trip once a week from mid-June to early September. There are also several flights a day from Paris and at least once a day from Nice by *Air Inter*. *TAT* flies between Clermont-Ferrand and Bordeaux, Lyon, Marseille and Toulouse, but as these flights are mainly used by businessmen, they are scarce or nonexistent in August. Lyon's Satolas airport isn't far away (see Lyon chapter). Vichy has a small airport too, with flights to and from Nice by *TAT* a few times a week (roughly May-mid-September).

By train. Trains from Paris's Gare de Lyon take 2 hrs 40 mins to Moulins, 3 hrs 15 mins to Vichy, 4 hrs to Clermont-Ferrand, 5 to Issoire, 6½ to Le Puy; for Montluçon (3¾ hrs) and Aurillac (5¾ hrs) you leave from the Gare d'Austerlitz. The Cévenol, one of the SNCF's popular 'tourist trains,' with special route maps, descriptive leaflets covering the places you travel through, and regional specialties in the buffet car, travels daily to and from Paris stopping in places such as La Bastide-Puylaurent (R.L. Stevenson country) and Villefort.

By coach. The SNCF (French railways) has a five-day combined coach and train visit called 'Volcanoes and Lakes in the Auvergne', but it runs only two or three times a year. Local coach tours are organized from all main centers. *Europe Autocar* have various excursions centered on the gastronomy of the Massif Central and the volcanoes in the Auvergne.

THE AUVERGNE

MOTORING. By car. Motorway enthusiasts should take the A6 to Lyon, then the N89 to Clermont-Ferrand (with a stretch of motorway from Thiers to Clermont-Ferrand). Otherwise there's the N7 to Moulins, followed by the N9 to Clermont-Ferrand, Riom and Issoire, the N9 and N209 to Vichy, and the N9 and N102 to Le Puy. You can save driving time by taking the summer carsleeper express from Boulogne to Lyon and then branching off from there.

USEFUL ADDRESSES. Auvergne's *Welcome Information office (France-Accueil)* is at 19 rue du Parc, 13200 Vichy; this is also the address for Vichy's own *tourist office* and *syndicat d'initiative*. The *Comité Régional de Tourisme* is at 45 av. Julien, BP 395, 63011 Clermont-Ferrand and the four departmental tourist offices are: for the Allier, *Syndicat d'initiative*, pl. de l'Hôtel-de-Ville, 03000 Moulins; for Cantal, *Comité Departemental du Tourisme*, Préfecture, 15000 Aurillac; for Haute-Loire, *Office de Tourisme*, pl. de Breuil, 43000 Le Puy; and for Puy-de-Dôme, *Comité Départemental du Tourisme et du Thermalisme*, 69 bld Gergovia, 63038 Clermont-Ferrand.

In Paris the *Maison d'Auvergne* at 194 bis, rue de Rivoli, 1er, is helpful.

For addresses of *Logis de France* and *Gîtes de France* write to the Paris headquarters (see 'Facts at your Fingertips' section) for their special booklets on the Auvergne.

For information on the Auvergne's 19 holiday villages write to *Vacances-Auvergne-Limousin*, 31 rue Eugène-Gilbert, 63000 Clermont-Ferrand.

Car hire. *Avis*, pl. Galliéni and airport, Clermont-Ferrand; 53 av. Paul-Doumer, Vichy. *Hertz*, 71 av. de l'URSS, Clermont-Ferrand; 18 rue Source-de-l'Hôpital, Vichy. *Europcar*, 22 bld Charles-de-Gaulle, Clermont-Ferrand; Zone Industrielle de Corsac, Le Puy; 78 rue de Paris, Vichy.

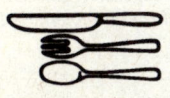

REGIONAL FOOD AND DRINK. Auvergne is an area where the rivers teem with trout and the natives cook it deliciously in butter. Auvergnat *charcuterie* is famous throughout France. It is also the land of cheeses famous throughout the world—Roquefort, St-Nectaire and St-Marcellin. Other specialties that you will encounter are *potée auvergnate* (pickled pork, sausage and vegetables), *coq au vin*, the green lentils of Le Puy, and *boudin* (a white pudding of pork, flavored with fennel and rum and served with russet apples). Desserts include acacia flowers dipped in batter flavored with orange water and fried, and *Milliard* (batter pudding containing black cherries). Although the Auvergne vineyards are not of the first rank, they do produce a number of acceptable wines, such as *Châteaugay, Corent, St-Pourcain* and *Chanturges*.

THE FACE OF FRANCE

HOTELS AND RESTAURANTS. Vichy and some of the other spas are the only places where you'll find deluxe accommodations, but there are plenty of small comfortable hotels and even more modest and charming country inns. Altogether the Auvergne boasts over 800 classified hotels, 390 Logis de France and no fewer than 2000 *gîtes*. The chain of *France-Accueil* hotels, which started in this region, has a successful formula of seven days' room and all meals in any of the chain's hotels (you need not stay in the same one all the time), plus excursions. In 1983, 25 *France Accueil* hotels grouped together to stage an '*Auvergne an Liberté*' campaign offering special rates and including a cassette telling you all about them and their region. Ask for leaflets at tourist offices, or write to the regional tourist committee for information.

Restaurants and hotels are referred to as *E, M* or *I*, signifying expensive, moderate or inexpensive.

AURILLAC. *Thomasse* (M), typical regional style, no restaurant. *Relax* (M), with restaurant.

BESSE-EN-CHANDESSE. Winter sports resort. *Les Mouflons,* moderate, notable cuisine. *Gazelle* (I), small.

LA BOURBOULE. *Russie et Victoria* (M), Logis de France; *Iles Britanniques* (E); *Aviation* (M), Logis de France; *Parc* (M), near the casino, and *Louvre* (M). *Baigneurs* and *Genève* are (I). All have restaurants.

Restaurant. 1.5 km (1 mile) north on D88, the *Tournebride* (M), good, converted farm. Also has 8 rooms.

CHAISE-DIEU, LA. *Echo et Abbaye* (M), peaceful Logis de France with good value restaurant.

CHÂTELGUYON. Spa (season, May–Sept.). *Splendid,* expensive. *Excelsior,* with bungalows, and *International* are both moderate. *Marie-Antoinette* (M), *Métropole,* inexpensive.

CLERMONT-FERRAND. *Arverne* (E), central and with luxury quality but not prices; a member of the PLM chain. *Frantel,* (E), unusually personal service and good restaurant. *Midi* (M), near station, pleasant Logis de France. *Galliéni,* (M), with good restaurant (M). *Ravel,* inexpensive, no restaurant. At **Chamalières,** 3 km (2 miles) west of town, *Radio* (M), peaceful, well run hotel with twenties décor and excellent restaurant—you may even see ex-president Giscard d'Estaing here, as he's mayor of Chamalières.

Restaurant. *Truffe d'Argent* (M). *Buffet de la Gare Routière* (M), at the bus station, is also good.

THE AUVERGNE

ISSOIRE. Best is the modern *Pariou* (M). *Floride* (I) has an agreement with a restaurant nearby. Both are pleasant Logis de France.

LAPALISSE. *Gallard* (I), with excellent restaurant (M).

LIEUTADES. *Boudon* (I), small hotel/restaurant (Logis de France).

LE MONT-DORE. Spa (season, May–Sept.) and winter sports center. *Carlina*, moderate; *Panorama* (M) and *Métropole* (E). *Oise* and *Nouvel-Hôtel* are moderate. *Castelet* (M). Five km (3 miles) from town is the *Puy Ferrand* (M), good value Relais du Silence with good restaurant. There are many other modest family hotels.
Restaurants. *Belle Epoque* (M), good value *menus*. *Pitsounet* at **Genestoux** is small, inexpensive.

MOULINS. *Paris* (E), delightful Relais et Châteaux member in old town, with excellent regional cuisine and good value *menus*. 7 km (4 miles) away at **Coulandon,** attractive *Chalet* (M), a Relais du Silence with family cuisine (but restaurant is closed for lunch and at weekends, except during the school holidays).

MUROL. *Parc*, moderate, with pool and garden.

LE PUY. *Chris'tel*, moderate, 30 rooms, good value. *Cygne*, also moderate. *Grand Cerf* (I), friendly Logis de France.
Restaurant. *Le Petit Vatel* (M), 9 pl. Michelet.

RIOM. *Voyageurs*, moderate, with good restaurant. *Lyon* (no restaurant) is inexpensive.

ROYAT. *Métropole* (E), has some suites; restaurant is (M). *Royal St-Mart*, *Régina*, moderate. *Univers*, inexpensive.
Restaurants. *L'Hostalet* (M) best. *Le Paradis* is also good (M). *La Pépinière* (I), also has rooms.

ST-FLOUR. *Bonne Table* (M), with special rates including ski hire.

ST-NECTAIRE. *Savoy* (M); restaurant isn't open to non-residents. *Paix* (I); *Hermitage* (I), both Logis de France, with restaurants.

SALERS. In this lovely medieval town, the tiny *Remparts*, inexpensive, with good restaurant (I). 6 km (4 miles) away at **Theil**, charming *Hostellerie Marmonne* (M), a Relais du Silence with lovely garden and good food too.

THIERS. *Aigle d'Or*, on rue de Lyon (N89), inexpensive, good restaurant.

VICHY. Spa (season, Jan.–Nov.). *Aletti Thermal Palace, Pavillon Sévigné* (where you may even be given the great marquise's bedroom) are expensive, exceptionally pleasant. *Albert I* (M), elegant. *Novotel* (E), av. Thermale, with 128 airconditioned and soundproofed rooms, has direct access to the Grand Etablissement Thermal. *Hermitage du Pont-Neuf* (M), sq. Albert-ler, *Magenta* (M), av. Walter-Stucki, *Londres,* bld Russie, inexpensive.

Restaurants. *Rotonde du Lac* (E), lovely, *Grillade-Strauss* (M). Also *L'Escargot qui tête* (M).

At nearby **Abrest,** 5 km (3½ miles) away, attractive *Colombière* (M). Also has 4 rooms.

VIC-SUR-CÈRE. *Hôtel des Bains,* moderate, regional dishes (M). *Bel Horizon,* inexpensive, with lovely views.

CASINOS. Vichy has two casinos: the *Elysée Palace Casino* is open year-round, while the *Grand Casino* closes out of the summer season. At both of them you have a choice of boule, baccara, roulette, blackjack and écarté. There are also smaller casinos at Bourbon-l'Archambault, Châtelguyon, Le Mont-Dore, Néris-les-Bains, Royat and St-Nectaire. Apart from the Royat casino, where you can play boule, baccara, roulette and blackjack all year, these are open only in the summer season and offer only boule.

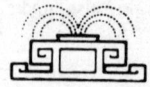

SPAS. Vichy is the major spa and has recently set up a brand-new migraine clinic. Otherwise the main complaints for which people come to the Auvergne's watering places for a cure are: rheumatism, asthma, gout and liver ailments. Bourbon-l'Archambault, Châtelguyon, Chaudes-Aigues, Néris-les-Bains, Royat, Sail-les-Bains, St-Nectaire are the other lowland spas, while Mont-Dore's thermal establishment, up at nearly 1,070 meters (3,500 ft), has recently been modernized and extended (though the main building still contains bits of the original Roman baths).

WINTER SPORTS. The handful of Massif Central resorts attract a largely regional and family clientele, so there is little *après-ski* activity. Slopes are gentler and heights are lower than in the Alps and Pyrenees, with the result that snow conditions are likely to be a bit uncertain as early as Dec. However, the *téléférique* to the Puy de Sancy reaches snowfields over 1,830 m (6,000 ft) high, making a good season of spring skiing possible until mid-April.

Le Mont-Dore (1,050 m/3,450 ft) is the most important and best-equipped center in this region. In addition to the Sancy *téléférique,* the Capucin funicular makes slopes 1,462 m (4,800 ft) high accessible. There is an ample supply of good inexpensive accommodations. Only some 426 km (265 miles) from Paris by road (plows keep the roads snow-free), Le Mont-Dore is also accessible by autorail from Clermont-Ferrand, and by bus from St-Nectaire.

THE AUVERGNE

Cross-country skiing is increasingly popular in this region. St-Flour is a popular center.

 **PARC DES VOLCANS.** This is France's largest natural park, covering 281,000 hectares (702,500 acres), and it offers endless possibilities for hiking, camping, naturewatching and so on. You can camp on selected farms and eat good local dishes in farmhouses. For information, contact *Syndicat Mixte du Parc des Volcans,* Centre d'Information, 28 rue St-Esprit, 63000 Clermont-Ferrand.

CORSICA

The scented isle

Third largest, and perhaps the loveliest, of the Mediterranean islands, Corsica well deserves such titles as 'the Isle of Beauty' and 'the Scented Isle'. Now a *département* of metropolitan France, with a population of about 300,000, Corsica is one of the European vacation spots whose popularity is growing most rapidly.

Corsica's rugged grandeur is a refreshing change after the more 'civilized' delights of Paris and the Riviera. Almost the entire island is covered with jagged, forested mountains. Perched on the sides of peaks and nestled in the valleys are numerous little villages that look like a picture out of the Middle Ages. Many of the smaller bays are still quite inaccessible except by boat, because of the high rocky coastline.

The first thing that will strike you about the island, whether you come by air or sea, will be the mountains, which seem to spring straight

CORSICA

up from the ocean. The highest peak is Monte Cinto (2,700 meters/ 8,890 ft), but it is only 24 km (15 miles) from the sea. The approach by air is superb—Ajaccio resembles an amphitheater, with the port occupying the stage and the houses perched where the seats should be.

Sprawling coastal beaches are fringed with palm trees, ancient buildings, and open-air cafés; Genoese watchtowers dot the coast, and houses and boats sparkle with the wild, bright Corsican reds, greens, yellows, blues. The air is full of the scent of rosemary and thyme, and songs that are half-French, half-Genoese. All combine to give Corsica great individuality.

The hill towns vary in size from a cluster of houses to fairly large towns, but the tall stone houses with their heavy slate roofs, narrow slit windows and heavy doors give the impression of an old fortress. Indeed, the houses were often built to form a solid defensive fortress wall, for the Corsicans fought their Genoese masters for generations before the island was ceded to France. Once upon a time the word *vendetta* was almost synonymous with Corsica. The streets are narrow alleys, built more for donkeys and goats than for modern vehicles.

And there is the wild countryside of Corsica: the chalky cliffs at Bonifacio, where in the 15th century the inhabitants resisted a long Spanish siege, the crimson mountains that rise straight up from the sea at Piana, the fertile vineyards in the valleys. From the dense undergrowth (called *maquis*), the rich scent of myrtle, honeysuckle, lavender, eucalyptus, cyclamen and wild mint carries far out to sea during the spring. 'I would recognize Corsica, eyes closed, only because of its perfume,' said Napoleon.

Although the tourist boom in the past few years has produced many new hotels and newly developed tourist areas, the boom has also resulted in ever-increasing prices. But for the budget-minded, Corsica is an excellent place for camping. The Corsicans can be friendly, but are often cautious with foreigners, and as insular as inhabitants of most islands.

Ajaccio, birthplace of Napoleon

The chief town of the island is Ajaccio, actually a cross between an overgrown village and a modern city, with 52,000 inhabitants. It is a fine winter resort, but you will find it interesting no matter when you are there. Located on a protected gulf, it is surrounded by green mountains and rocky crags covered with snow during the winter.

The place Fesch, opposite the steamer landing, is a good place to start your tour of the town. In the Hôtel de Ville there is a Napoleonic room containing a collection of family portraits, as well as the emperor's baptismal certificate and the bronze deathmask made at St

Helena by his Corsican doctor. Follow the rue Charles to the little street in which stands Napoleon's birthplace, facing a small garden. Here you will see the couch upon which he was born in 1769, his study and bedroom, complete with trap door. At the end of the street is the 16th-century cathedral where he was baptized. In the rue Fesch is the home of Cardinal Fesch, Napoleon's uncle, now a museum. The right wing contains the imperial chapel, the left wing is a museum with an exceptional collection of early Italian paintings (13th to 15th century), as well as 17th-century Roman and Neapolitan paintings. The market on boulevard du Roi Jérôme, behind the Hôtel de Ville, is a good place to buy some of the local *brocciu* cheese, sausages, delicious peaches, fresh almonds by the kilo, and regional pastries. The fish market, right under the building, sells *fruits de mer* in all their colorful glory. Go early to see the full display.

From Ajaccio to Bonifacio

Southward from Ajaccio the (N196) turns and twists, affording wonderful views of the gulf of Ajaccio and the Iles Sanguinaires. On the gulf of Valinco is the busy fishing port and tourist resort of Propriano. Sartène, 82 km (51 miles) from Ajaccio, is a typical old Corsican town, with several streets that retain the atmosphere and style of the Middle Ages. Perched magnificently in the mountains, it has a splendid view of the bay below and the distant mountain ring. West and southwest of Sartène, towards the sea, the countryside is strewn with megalithic dolmens, menhirs and stone circles. For more spectacular scenery, take the southerly route that branches east to Cauro, thence via Zonza and Porto-Vecchio to Bonifacio.

Bonifacio, 37 km (23 miles) further, is an ancient fortress town set spectacularly on high chalk cliffs. It still maintains an active garrison, including some Foreign Legionnaires in their white *képis*. Almost entirely medieval in atmosphere (and, let's face it, in odor), the citadel withstood many sieges, most famous vestiges of which are the steps cut in the high rock face during the 15th century by the troops of Alphonse d'Aragon (take a boat trip outside the harbor to see these, and the famous grottoes). Bonifacio citadel also has a number of old churches, and in the rue Longue you will be able to see the façades of the houses where Emperor Charles V stayed in 1541 and where Napoleon was billeted at one point in his army career. There is a yacht harbor and a sailing school.

Northward from Ajaccio to Bastia

Another side trip from Ajaccio, perhaps even more picturesque than the drive to Bonifacio, takes you north up the western coast to Porto, Calvi and L'Ile-Rousse. The road is frequently steep and twisting, and is not for apprentice drivers, but magnificent panoramas meet the eye at every turn. Along the coast from Piana to Porto, the *calanques (calanches)* or coves of red-tinted rocks form a startling contrast to the vivid blue sea into which they plunge and the verdant greens of the surrounding vegetation. Inland from Porto, a magnificent scenic route (D84) leads to Calvi via Evisa, the Spelunca gorge, Scala di Santa Regina and Ponte-Leccia. Porto, a little fishing town 80 km (50 miles) from Ajaccio on the gulf of Porto, is considered to be the most beautiful corner of Corsica. The mild climate of Calvi (another 77 km/48 miles), its setting on the sea, and the high mountains that surround its landward perimeter have long made it a tourist resort. The old citadel, with its 16th-century walls and narrow streets, is a fine place to wander. In the rue Colombo is the alleged birthplace of Columbus. L'Ile-Rousse, only 24 km (15 miles) from Calvi, has an interesting convent that dates from the end of the 15th century; its climate and its beauty have helped to make it one of the most fashionable resorts in Corsica. Nearby St-Florent has become one of the busiest pleasure-craft harbors on the island.

On the northeast coast is Bastia, the largest town and commercial capital of the island, and the only Corsican city that was badly damaged during World War II. The most interesting part is the old port area. Most of the buildings date from the 17th and 18th centuries, and the citadel was built during the 16th and 17th centuries. Be sure to see the old governor's place (1453); the churches of Ste-Marie, Ste-Croix, St-Roch and la Concepcion, the citadel, and place St-Nicolas.

One of the most beautiful excursions from Bastia is the circuit of Cap Corse, the finger-like peninsula that points north toward France. The road parallels the sea almost to the tip of the cape, and all along there are lovely little bays and coves, and many valleys leading up into the forest-covered mountains that form the backbone of the peninsula. The entire trip is only 127 km (79 miles), but plan on taking a day for the drive, for you will want to stop and admire the scenery at every turn. Old Genoese watchtowers, villas, lime trees and olive groves contrast with rocky fiords and the *maquis,* stunted and warped by the force of the northeast wind called the *libeccio.* The tiny port of Centuri is one of the marvels of the Cap.

From Bastia to Bonifacio

There are several alternative ways to go south from Bastia. The most scenic route goes via Casamozza, Corte, Ghisoni, Ghisonaccia, Solenzara, Zonza and Porto-Vecchio. This road crosses a corner of the coastal plain for 19 km (12 miles), but at Casamozza you turn on to the N193 and climb up into the wonderful Corsican mountains. There are 5 km (3 miles) of mountain roads before you reach Corte, but the scenery more than compensates for the driving difficulties. Overhanging Corte, the island's largest inland town, are the fantastic 15th-century citadel and the brooding crags of Monte Rotondo.

From Corte to Ghisonaccia it is mountain driving most of the way, but at the latter town you return to the coastal plain. At Solenzara the road swings inland once again and takes you over the Col de Bavella to Zonza, considered by many to be the most spectacularly beautiful drive in the island. From Zonza you head through beautiful forested country to Porto-Vecchio on the coast with its granite walls, cork-oak plantations and elegant marina. The country between Porto-Vecchio and Bonifacio is less interesting, but they are only 26 km apart.

One more trip, made by almost every visitor to Corsica, is the drive or train ride from Bastia to Ajaccio via Corte. Of course, you can travel in either direction, but if you start out from Bastia, the drive to Corte is the same as the one mentioned for the Bastia–Bonifacio excursion. After leaving Corte the road flanks several high peaks. It passes through the town of Vivario, the jumping-off point for tours of the Inzecca Gorge, then climbs up into the heavily forested mountain country around the town of Vizzavona, a lovely area. From Vizzavona it is only a little over 48 km (30 miles) to Ajaccio. The road leads past Bocognano, a favorite summer resort of the people of Ajaccio, then runs through a forest of chestnut trees as it drops into the valleys that lead to the gulf of Ajaccio.

Warning. Recent reports in French newspapers suggest that it is extremely unwise for visitors to Corsica to accept invitations—however friendly—to take boat trips or other jaunts with locals they do not know well. There have been a number of incidents in which tourists have been involved, and most of them ended unpleasantly.

PRACTICAL INFORMATION

WHEN TO GO. The best seasons are the late spring (mid-May through June) and fall (Sept.–mid-Oct.). Accommodation is less crowded and the weather excellent. If you wish to holiday in July or Aug. it is wise to reserve hotel space almost a year ahead of time. In May you get the full benefit of 'the scented isle' when the *maquis* is in flower.

Summer weather is hot and dry along the coast, but there are cool breezes at higher levels. Winters are mild and can be rainy, but there is hardly a day without some warming sunshine. Cross-country skiing has recently become popular and attracts many winter visitors.

Among the special celebrations to be observed in Corsica are those held during the Easter season in **March** and **April**, Ajaccio's mid-Lenten festival and carnival and the Good Friday processions at Corte and Sartène. Early in **May**, there are the fair of St-Pancras at Ajaccio and the festival and fair of St-Pascal at Corte. A traditional festival at the chapel of St Restituta, near Calenzana, on May 21 commemorates the successful resistance of the women of that town to the German mercenaries of Genoa in 1732. Following Ajaccio's Music and Drama Festival in **July** comes Calvi's fortnight of yacht races and regattas. Napoleon's birthday, **August** 15, is the excuse for the year's most lavish celebrations. All over the island there are fireworks and parades, with parties and theatrical presentations in the larger towns. In the tiny hamlet of Casmacciola on **September** 8, the curious procession of the Santa du Niola follows a spiral route, in keeping with the ancient rite of the *granitola* or 'dance of the snails', as accompanying shepherds improvise chanted verses. During this month, too, Ile-Rousse holds its colorful trade fair. In **November**, Corsica's Automobile Club runs the 'Rally of the 10,000 Bends'.

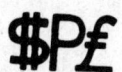

MONEY. It is essential to carry plenty of French francs with you. Opportunities to change travelers checks are few and far between. Some of the first-class hotels will cash checks, but the exchange rate won't be in your favor.

WHAT TO SEE. Corsica has scenic beauty galore—wild, rugged, vividly colorful. In addition, every corner of the island seems to have its share of Napoleonic lore, of castles, towers and bastions left by every invader and inhabitant since the Etruscans. The chief towns are Ajaccio, the capital, superbly situated on a mountain-ringed bay; Corte, the ancient capital in the heart of the mountains; Bastia, chief port and center for touring Cap Corse; Calvi, port and tourist center; Sartène, a delightful medieval country town; the curious fortress town of Bonifacio, on the southern tip of the island.

The west coast is beautiful and rugged; the east coast is flatter and less beautiful. On the west you'll find deserted coves and tiny jewel-like beaches; on the east, wide sandy beaches. The summer resorts are around Porto and Ajaccio on the east, Calvi, Cap Corse and St-Florent in the north, Porto-Vecchio and Bonifacio in the south.

Two of Corsica's top scenic attractions are the tour of Cap Corse from Bastia and the *calanques* (coves) of Piana extending 11 km (7 miles) along the gulf of Porto. Other sights include: the remains of the Roman city of Mutola, near Calvi, and of Mariana, near Bastia; the Spelunca gorges, between Porto and Evisa; the forest of Aïtone and Col de Vergio; the Scala di Santa Regina; the grotto of Sdragonato; Asco, the 'Zermatt of Corsica'; the Inzecca gorge; the Col de Vizzavona; the Col de Bavella, near Zonza; the grotto of the Veaux-Marins. All along the coast you will see the Genoese towers, most of them dating from the 15th cent., whose watchfires served to warn the coastal inhabitants of impending danger. Except for the citadels of Ajaccio, Bastia, Bonifacio, Calvi and Corte, they are the sole vestiges of military architecture still in existence on the island.

Caura and Tizzano, both near Sartène, are famed for their mysterious Bronze-Age *menhirs,* as is Filitosa, 80 km (50 miles) southeast of Ajaccio. At Cucuruzzu, northeast of Propriano, in a strikingly beautiful site, is a remarkably preserved Bronze-Age fortress. Many villages have tiny Romanesque churches where recent restoration has brought to light extraordinary medieval frescoes: Sermano di Bozio, near Corte; the convent of the Alesani valley (south of Bastia); San Michel de Murato; and La Trinité d'Aregno are some of the most interesting. One of the prettiest of baroque churches is at the tiny town of La Porta, south of Bastia.

HOW TO GET ABOUT. By air. *Air France* and *Air Inter* have daily flights from Paris and Marseille to Ajaccio, Calvi and Bastia (under 2 hrs from Paris, 50 mins from Marseille). There are daily flights between Nice or Marseille and Calvi (40 mins), Ajaccio and Bastia. Some of these flights are increased in summer. *British Airways* and *Air France* fly regularly from London. (Air France has substantial reductions on its flight to Corsica from Oct. to June 1). Air-France has popular fly-drive packages. As well as the three major airports, the island has smaller airports at popular Propriano and at Figari, which are now able to receive large aircraft.

The local airline, *Kallistair,* has regular flights year-round between Ajaccio, Calvi, Propriano and Figari. Reductions for children, students, honeymooners and three or more members of one family traveling together.

TAT have extensive services to Corsica from the French mainland in the summer (check dates with your travel agent or locally). They fly to Ajaccio from: Bordeaux, Clermont-Ferrand, Le Havre, Lille, Metz, Mulhouse, Nantes, Strasbourg, Toulon, and Toulouse; to Bastia from: Bordeaux, Lille, Metz, Mulhouse, Nantes, Strasbourg and Toulouse; to Figari from: Geneva, Lille, Lyon, Marseille, Nice, Paris and Toulouse. *SNCF* have occasional 7-day holidays in Marina Viva (cost covers plane travel, accommodations and full-board).

Warning: this information was correct for 1983, but flight schedules to Corsica are notorious for frequent changes, so we recommend that you check with the French Government Tourist Office or your travel agent before making plans for 1984.

By boat. *Société Nationale Maritime Corse-Mediterranée* runs frequent boat services from Marseille, Toulon and Nice to Ajaccio, Calvi, Bastia, Ile-Rousse and to Propriano in summer. Crossing time is 6–10 hrs and there are daily sailings in summer and about twice a week in winter. Not too comfortable unless you take the overnight car ferries *Napoléon* and *Fred Scamaroni,* or the daytime ferries *Corse* and *Comté de Nice.* Book well ahead if traveling in July or Aug. In the UK bookings can be made with *P & O Ferries.* The *SCNM* also has good all-in rates.

Corsica Ferries have sailings from Livorno (Leghorn), San Remo and La Spezia, and Genoa to Bastia in summer. Crossing time is 4½ and 7 hrs respectively. Also regular sailings year-round from Sardinia by *Tirrenia* (three times a week in Aug.).

Boats from the French mainland now have a red, white and blue fare system; from October through May, excluding Easter, (blue period) fares are only 50% of the normal fare (white period), while in most of July and August (red period) they are considerably higher than in the normal period. These fares apply both to passengers and their cars. You can also buy a special air ticket for yourself while sending your car by boat. Also 50% reductions for women over 60 and men over 62.

By bus. Despite the rapid expansion of tourism on the island, public transport facilities are inconvenient from the tourist angle, and for touring a car is essential unless you are prepared to stop overnight in out-of-the-way places. However, traveling by public bus network can be fun—you will meet the people and all the highlights will be pointed out to you (in French).

By coach. Undoubtedly the best way to tour Corsica is by road, and a variety of motorcoach excursions and circular tours is offered during the winter and summer seasons from Bastia, Ajaccio, Calvi and Ile-Rousse, most of them lasting from one to three days. From late March to early Oct., Ajaccio, Calvi and Bastia are points of departure for a six-day tour of Corsica. Seats must be reserved well in advance. There are also numerous half- to one-day excursions by the *Société d'Exploitation d'Autocars en Corse (SNCF).*

Club Méditerranée have introduced a new tour of inland Corsica, in groups driving a total of six cars. It gives a good glimpse of the little-known villages in the interior, but has to be combined with a week in the club's village in Cargèse. *Europe Autocar* have a 1 week trip in April or May which leaves from Paris and includes the flight to Calvi, a tour of the island and flight back from Ajaccio.

By rail. Corsica's railway system is a simple one, consisting of one main route and two branches. It runs from Ajaccio to Ponte Leccia in the northern central part of the island and then divides, one part going to Calvi and the other to Bastia. Entire services are by autorail diesel cars and it is one-class only. Traveling on it certainly is a good way to see local life. Trains are clean and moderately comfortable. Scenery is spectacular along most of the route.

EXCURSIONS. There are a number of delightful trips that may be taken from various centers to nearby points of interest and to those farther afield.

From Ajaccio, the Fontaine du Solario may be reached on foot; then continue to the Chemin des Crêtes for a magnificent view (about 40 mins walking time). From pl. Diamant a car or bus ride takes you along the coast road to the old Chapelle des Grecs and on to La Parata, an old Genoese tower guarding the entrance to the gulf. You can climb up the dizzy heights if you wish. A 45-min. boat trip to Ajaccio harbor will bring you to the Iles Sanguinaires, which continue from La Parata, and allow time for a short exploration before the return trip. Some 16 km miles inland, to the northwest, is the château de la Punta Pozzo di Borgo (780 meters/2,560 feet), commanding a panoramic view of the bays of Ajaccio and Sagone. A long day's drive will allow you to see the gulf of Porto, then to head into the mountains over the spectacular Col de Vergio, which can be snow-covered as late as May, to the ancient capital of Corte, and down to the sea again through lovely chestnut forests.

From Bastia, the tour around Cap Corse is definitely a must, and you will probably want to devote an entire day to it. A magnificent panorama makes the short jaunt (7 km/4½ miles) to the pilgrimage church of Ste-Lucie worthwhile. Some 22 km (14 miles) to the south, off N198, is La Canonica, the most important Romanesque church in Corsica. Also to the south, a scenic route (N843) leads via the Lancone gorge and a side road to the village of Murato with its curious church of St-Michel.

From Calvi, a pleasant road leads to the Maison Forestière de Bonifato, 19 km (12 miles) away, in the center of the forest of Bonifato, framed by a semicircle of mountains. A shorter trip leads to Calenzana with its Romanesque churches of St-Pierre and of St-Restituta (2.5 km/1½ miles away), containing the tomb of that 4th-cent. saint. Excursions by boat may be made to the curious Seals' Cave or Grotto des Veaux-Marins (1 hr), to the Punta della Revellata lighthouse (½ hr), and in summer to Porto (highly recommended), and La Girolata.

From Bonifacio, a 45-min. walk to Cap Pertusato on Corsica's southernmost tip will reward you with a fine view of the town, the straits, and the Sardinian village of Longosardo (may be reached by boat in about 1½ hrs); 6 km (4 miles) to the northeast lies the picturesque gulf of Santa Manza; 5 km (3 miles) to the northwest on the Sartène road, then 15 mins by mule path, brings you to the Ermitage de la Trinité, from which there is another spectacular view. When a west wind is not blowing, the grottoes of Sdragonato may be explored from Bonifacio by boat (1½ hrs; the smaller *camere* or caverns require an additional half hour); the opening in the interior through which the light filters bears a striking resemblance in outline to the map of Corsica.

From Zonza, a magnificent circular tour via forest roads to the Col de Bavella, Solenzara, Porto-Vecchio and back affords some difficult driving as well as the top scenic excursion in southern Corsica.

Corsica now has its own *Wine Roads.* Maps and leaflets from main tourist offices and further information from *Uvacorse,* Chambre d'Agriculture, Résidence Castel-Vecchio, 20000 Ajaccio.

MOTORING. Visitors who prefer to do their own driving will do better to rent a car on the island than bring their own and pay the high shipping charges from the mainland, the only way to transport a car. Scooters can be rented from *Solvet.* We recommend you stick to the internationally known car hire firms. Gasoline is around 10% cheaper than on the French mainland.

The mountainous terrain of Corsica, with its narrow, hairpin bend roads, requires extremely cautious driving. There is hardly a stretch of level or straight road. Don't count on an average of more than 48 kph (30 mph), and remember that hours of driving on those twisting roads can be exhausting. A new idea is to explore Corsica in a motor-home, sleeping two to four people. This is quite ideal for a family—you avoid hotels, have privacy, and Corsica is lovely for camping *(Cox and Kings* or *Havas Voyages).* Minimum, one week.

USEFUL ADDRESSES. The *Comité Régional du Tourisme en Corse* (regional tourist office) is at 38 cours Napoléon, BP 162, 20178 Ajaccio. Main *syndicats d'initiative* or city *tourist offices* at Hôtel de Ville, Ajaccio; 35 bld Paoli, Bastia; chemin de la Plage, Calvi; 2 rue Maréchal-Juin, Porto-Vecchio; 2 av. Napoléon, Propriano.

In Paris the *Maison de la Corse,* at 82 blvd Haussmann, 9e, has a great deal of information and will help you organize your holiday. For information on *Gîtes Ruraux* in Corsica: 22 bld Paoli, Ajaccio. For information on *camping: Fédération Régionale de l'Hôtellerie de Plein Air,* 34 cours Napoléon, 20000 Ajaccio.

For information on scheduled *coach* services ask for the booklet *La Corse: Ile de Beauté,* which gives detailed timetables. For excursions, inquire at local tourist offices.

For *car ferries,* the *Société Nationale Maritime Corse-Méditerranée* has offices at quai Lherminier, Ajaccio; quai Landry, Calvi; av. J.-Calizi, Ile-Rousse; quai Commandant-Lherminier, Propriano. Also at 12 rue Godot-de-Mauroy in Paris 9e; 61 blvd des Dames in Marseille; 3 av. Gustave-V, Nice; and 21 av. de l'Infanterie-de-Marine, Toulon.

For hire of *bicycles* and *scooters;* Station Emmanuelli at 27 cours Impérial, Ajaccio; and rue Joffre, Calvi.

Car hire: Avis, 3 pl. de Gaulle, Ajaccio (also bld Sampiéro and at airport); 2 rue Notre-Dame de Lourdes, Bastia; quai Camparetti, Bonifacio; rue Pasteur, Porto-Vecchio; 22 rue Général-de-Gaulle, Propriano. *Hertz,* 8 cours Grandval, Ajaccio (also at airport); sq. St-Victor and airport, Bastia; 2 rue du Maréchal-

Joffre, Calvi; (and airport); *Europcar,* 16 cours Grandval, Ajaccio (and airport); 30 rue Cesar, Campinchia, Bastia (and airport); airport, Calvi; rue Jean-Nicoli, Porto-Vecchio.

American Express, Auto-Excursions Ollandini, 'Le Tourisme Corse', 3 pl. de Gaulle, Ajaccio.

For *fishing* permits, the *Fédération Départementale de Pêche,* 7 bld Paoli, Bastia.

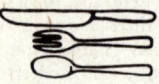 **REGIONAL FOOD AND DRINK.** Corsica does not boast any luxury restaurants and the local cuisine, although tasty and copious, can hardly be called gastronomic. Seafood is abundant and delicious, but many foods have to be imported and restaurant prices are therefore comparatively high. Much of the cooking is done with olive oil, and has a distinctly Italian flavor.

The sea provides the staple diet of Corsica, and you'll be served with all varieties of Mediterranean fish, grilled, baked, broiled or fried. The sardines fried in batter are good, provided you don't mind head, tail, bones and the lot. Shellfish include cockles, limpets, winkles, sea urchins *(oursins),* apart from the delicious oysters and crayfish (sold by weight in restaurants, and an expensive addition to your bill). *Ziminu* is the Corsican *bouillabaisse,* its simpler form being *soupe de poisson. Suppa* is a thick vegetable and herb soup.

The local cheeses are delicious; apart from the *brocciu,* which is used in both sweet and savory dishes, we recommend the mild *bastelicaccia* and the *bleu de Corse.* (The famous Roquefort cheese has, in fact, been made in Corsica for years and only matured in the Aveyron caves.) Omelets filled with cream cheese and mint are delicious.

Among the notable Corsican *charcuterie* products are *figatelli* (small dry sausages made of pork), salami sausage, and pork *lonzu* (filet) or *coppa* (shoulder). You will find pork, lamb (even blackbird) stews, kid or wild boar drenched in herbs, and mushrooms in great variety. Ham, leg of lamb with garlic and a brandy sauce, and artichoke hearts stuffed with chopped meat and topped with *brocciu* are other island specialties.

Corsican confectionery features a whole galaxy of *pisticcine, torta, canestrone, rappi* and *pane biscottu*—fritters, tarts, biscuits, and so on—made with chestnut or wheat flour, raisins, nuts, butter and eggs. The pastries known as *fiadonu, imbrocciatta* and *cocciula* are flavored with *brocciu* and brandy.

Notable wines are the white and *rosé* wines of Patrimonio, in the Bastia region, the *Malvoisie* and *Muscat* of Cap Corse, also *Cédratine* and *Myrtle* liqueur, and *eau de vie* (brandy).

 **HOTELS AND RESTAURANTS.** The tourist boom in Corsica has resulted in much building of new hotels in hitherto undeveloped areas. These are modern and impersonal, clean but occasionally haphazard in service; meals are good and copious. Prices are about the same as on the Riviera, which

means fairly high. Most hotels will provide a packed lunch, in lieu of your midday meal, if you want to be off for the day. There are few hotels that can be called deluxe. It is sometimes obligatory to take full board terms, and is indeed advisable in smaller places, as there are few restaurants, and restaurants are fairly expensive. Best check your hotel or restaurant bill for every item. Many British tour operators offer Corsica packages.

It is possible to rent villas, bungalows and apartments. For addresses, prices, etc., write to the *Office de Tourisme* at Ajaccio, Bastia, Calvi, Ile-Rousse, Porto or Corte. Several British travel agencies offer interesting packages that include air travel, villa rental and self-drive arrangements.

Many hotels are closed from about mid-Oct. to Easter, or for some time during this period. Check in advance. Restaurants and hotels listed *E, M* or *I,* are expensive, moderate or inexpensive.

AJACCIO. For pleasant atmosphere and lovely gardens, *Etrangers* (M); try for a room in the delightful villa annex. *Fesch,* an old house in the heart of the old town, is full of charm, moderate, no restaurant. *Albion* (M), pleasant, central yet peaceful, well run and popular with British visitors, no restaurant. *Impérial* (E) and *San Carlu* (M), no restaurant. *Mouettes,* a little outside, on sea, moderate, no restaurant.

At airport: expensive *Campo dell'Oro.*

On the Sanguinaires road: beautiful *Eden Roc* (E), (full-board only), *Dolce Vita* (M), both with pool. *Cala di Sole* (E), with water-skiing, skin-diving, *Calanches* (E), and *Palm Beach* (M). *Stella di Mare,* moderate.

Restaurants. All round the pl. Fesch, near the port, are pleasant terrace restaurants where you can scan the menu or see what other folk are eating: one is *Palmiers* (M). *Frédante* (E), in narrow side street, delicious local dishes. *La Grange* (I), rue notre-Dame, is quick, open late. *Pardi* (I), which has been on the rue Fesch for as long as anyone can remember. *Café du Golfe* is the most popular drinking spot with locals. *Bec Fin* (I), an old favorite. *St-Hubert* (I), rue Colonel-Colonna-d'Ornano, good fixed-price meals with some local specialties, good range of *menus.*

BASTIA. In town *Bonaparte,* moderate, no restaurant. Just out on the Ajaccio road, *O'Stella,* moderate.

At **Pietranera,** 3 km (2 miles) north, the *Pietracap* (M), with pool, no restaurant, is fairly expensive. *Alivi* (E) pleasant, good cuisine.

At **Miomo,** 5 km (3 miles) out, *Sablettes,* moderate; good restaurant.

Restaurants. *Bistrot du Port* (M), tiny and friendly. *La Taverne* (I). *Chez Assunta* (M), in 17th-century chapel, smart but with good straightforward local cooking and very reasonable prices.

BONIFACIO. All on the port, none in the citadel above. *Solemare* (M), no restaurant but own pool. *Caravelle* (M), pleasant. *Etrangers,* inexpensive, with restaurant.

Restaurant. *Stella d'Oro* (M), in old town.

CALVI. *Grand,* deluxe, no restaurant. *Résidence des Aloës* (E), modern, near beach. *Kallisté,* nicely located, moderate. *Clos des Amandiers* (M), has bungalows, pool, restaurant. On the cliffs above the town, the *St-Christophe.* Recent, moderate, are *St-Erasme, Il Tramonte.*

Just outside Calvi is the attractive *Club de l'Horizon,* moderate, a Franco-British complex with bungalows and apartments, restaurants and sports facilities. Good value, though you must stay a minimum of one week. Open June through mid-September.

Restaurant. *Ile de Beauté* (E), has good local specialties.

CARGÈSE. Best is *Lentisques,* on the beach, with pleasant garden, moderate. *Spelunca,* moderate, and *Hélios,* also moderate, in pretty setting. *Thalassa,* inexpensive, right on the beach.

CORTE. *Paix,* (M), Logis de France, good cuisine. *Sampiero* (M), no restaurant.
Restaurant. *Santucci* (I), family run, delightful, but only open for lunch.

FAVONE. *U Dragulinu* (M), right on beach, pleasant restaurant.

EVISA. *Aïtone,* inexpensive, modest but delightful with good restaurant and lovely views. Higher up the mountainside and run by the same family is *Scopa Rossa,* moderate, very peaceful; again has glorious views.

L'ILE-ROUSSE. The famous *Napoléon Bonaparte* (E), plenty of old style comfort. *Pietra* (E). *La Gare* (I).
Restaurants. *Le Grillon* (M), with rooms, *California, Le Relais* (I).

PIANA. Best is *Capo Rosso* (E), with pool and sea views.

PORTICCIO. Near Ajaccio. *Sofitel-Porticcio* (E), beautifully sited, but under air flight path. Has salt water therapy center and diet restaurant. *Maquis* consists of small bungalows, charmingly decorated in rustic manner. Expensive, with good restaurant serving local specialties (M). Both have private beaches. *Isolella,* 5 km (3 miles) away at **Agnarello,** is inexpensive.
Restaurant. *Dorbera* (M), good pasta, friendly.

PORTO. *Capo d'Orto* (M), with pool and restaurant. *Bella Vista,* inexpensive. At **Porto-Marine,** *Flots Bleus,* moderate with good value restaurant.

A few miles out, at **Serriera-Plage,** *Stella-Marina,* (M), hotel-restaurant close to beach in the Corsica Nature Park, modern rooms, all with bath. Attractive restaurant. Also pleasant is the *Aiglon* (M).

PORTO POLLO. *Kallisté* (I), family-type, good for small children; *Eucalyptus* (M), more selective.

CORSICA

PORTO-VECCHIO. At the beach, *Roches Blanches,* and *Le Goéland,* no restaurant; both moderate. *Cala Verde* (E), *Aiglon* (E), *San Giovanni* (M), modern, attractive, with pool. On road to Palombiaggia, *Ziglione* (E), good restaurant (M). Beautifully sited between the *maquis* and the sea. *Roi Théodore* (M), comfortable, with pool and two restaurants.
Restaurant. *Lucullus* (I), rue Gén.-de-Gaulle. *Troquemuche* (M).

PROPRIANO. *Marinca* (E), is quiet, with good views, 5 km (3 miles) north of town. *Miramar* and *Roc e Mare* are modern. All expensive, have private beaches or are close to public beaches.
Restaurants. *Lido* (M), with rooms, has good fish. *Thalassa* (M), good seafood, always crowded.

SAGONE. *Le Santana,* just across road from beach, modern, moderate.
Restaurant. *La Rascasse* (I), good seafood.

ST-FLORENT. *Europe,* like a charming old-fashioned family home. Peaceful *Treperi* bungalows, just outside town, has good restaurant and good value full-board rates. Also has rooms with kitchenettes.
Restaurant. *La Gaffe* (M), overlooking harbor.

SARTÈNE. Restaurant. *Chaumière* (M), good regional cuisine.

SOLENZARA. *Solenzare* (I), pleasant garden, no restaurant.

TIUCCIA, *Liscia* (M), with bungalows, pool, no restaurant. *Cinarca,* friendly, half-board only or try taking an apartment for 3 people.
At **Calcatoggio,** on the bay of Liscia, is the *Transat Hotel San Bastiano* (E), a beautifully secluded hotel village, full or half board only.

VENACO. *Paesotel E Caselle,* small, shepherd's cottage-style décor, in isolated but beautiful location; fine food, swimming, tennis, high moderate. *Torrent* (M) is 4 km (2½ miles) away.

VIZZAVONA. *Monte d'Oro,* chalet-like hotel in the mountains, inexpensive.

ZONZA. *Tourisme,* inexpensive, with restaurant.

HOLIDAY VILLAGES. Corsica also has a number of holiday villages of varying degrees of comfort and ranging from small (20 beds) to huge (2,000 beds, at Lozari). There are even two naturist villages, if that's your scene. Full list available from regional tourist office in Ajaccio or Maison de Corse in Paris.

VILLA RENTAL. Also popular and less expensive, if you plan to spend several weeks on the island. Various British agencies *(Erna Low, John Morgan*

Travel, Inter-Home) are specialists. Rental sometimes includes a self-drive car. Probably safer to go through a British agency than the Corsican rental agencies: many Corsicans, alas, consider tourists birds to be plucked.

CLIMBING AND CAMPING. Corsica's rugged terrain offers a number of challenging opportunities for mountain climbing. Calacuccia and Asco are the best bases for the ascent of Monte Cinto 2,708 m (8,890 ft), the island's highest peak. Other recommended ascents are: Paglia d'Orba (2,498m/8,200 ft, 5 hrs from Col de Vergio); Monte d'Oro (2,390 m/7,845 ft, 4½ hrs from Vizzavona); Incudine 'the Anvil' (2,135m/7,008 ft, 6 hrs from Zicavo); Rotondo (2,624 m/8,613 ft, 9 hrs from Corte); Monte Renoso (2,356 m/7,733 ft, 7 hrs from Mastelica). Asco is the chief mountain-climbing center. However, freelance mountain climbing can be very dangerous due to the nature of the rock formation. Apply for full information to the Ajaccio tourist office first.

Corsica has become so popular with campers that unauthorized camping is now frowned on by the tourist authorities, who guide enthusiasts toward the 100-odd campsites on the island. No camping is allowed along the seashore and if you're determined to do your own thing inland, you must get permission from the owner of the land or the town hall. The Regional Tourist Office (see *Useful Addresses*) publishes an annual list of camp and caravan/trailer sites.

ENGLISH-FRENCH TOURIST VOCABULARY

EVERYDAY EXPRESSIONS

Can anyone here speak English?	Y a-t-il quelqu'un qui parle anglais?
Do you speak English?	Parlez-vous anglais?
Do you understand?	Comprenez-vous?
Don't mention it	Je vous en prie
I beg your pardon	Pardon!
Good morning . . . day . . . afternoon	Bonjour
Good evening . . . night	Bonsoir
Goodbye	Au revoir
How are you?	Comment allez-vous?
How much . . . many?	Combien?
I don't know	Je ne sais pas
I don't understand	Je ne comprends pas
Yes	Oui
No	Non
Please speak more slowly	Parlez plus lentement, s'il vous plaît
Stop	Arrêtez
Go ahead	Continuez
Hurry	Dépêchez-vous
Wait here	Attendez ici
Come in!	Entrez!
Sit down	Asseyez-vous
Thank you	Merci
Thank you very much	Merci bien
There is, there are	Il y a
Very good . . . well	Très bien
What is this?	Qu'est-ce que c'est?
What do you want?	Que voulez-vous?
Please	S'il vous plaît
I'm sorry	Je regrette
You're welcome	Je vous en prie
What time is it?	Quelle heure est-il?
What is your name?	Comment vous appelez-vous?
With pleasure	Avec plaisir
You are very kind	Vous êtes bien aimable

NUMERALS

1	un	7	sept
2	deux	8	huit
3	trois	9	neuf
4	quatre	10	dix
5	cinq	11	onze
6	six	12	douze

ENGLISH-FRENCH TOURIST VOCABULARY

13 treize	30 trente
14 quatorze	40 quarante
15 quinze	50 cinquante
16 seize	60 soixante
17 dix-sept	70 soixante-dix
18 dix-huit	80 quatre-vingt
19 dix-neuf	90 quatre-vingt-dix
20 vingt	100 cent
21 vingt-et-un	1000 mille

DAYS OF THE WEEK

Sunday	Dimanche
Monday	Lundi
Tuesday	Mardi
Wednesday	Mercredi
Thursday	Jeudi
Friday	Vendredi
Saturday	Samedi

MONTHS

January	janvier
February	février
March	mars
April	avril
May	mai
June	juin
July	juillet
August	août
September	septembre
October	octobre
November	novembre
December	décembre

COMMON QUESTIONS

Is there . . .	Y a-t-il . . .
—a bus for . . . ?	—un autobus pour . . . ?
—a coach for . . . ?	—un car pour . . . ?
—a dining car?	—un wagon-restaurant . . . ?
—an English interpreter?	—un interprète anglais?
—a guide?	—un guide?
—a good hotel at . . . ?	—un bon hôtel á . . . ?
—a good restaurant here?	—un bon restaurant ici?
—a sleeper?	—une place dans le wagon-lit?
—time to get out?	—le temps de descendre?
—a train for . . . ?	—un train pour . . . ?
Where is . . .	Où est (sont-*plural*)
—the airport?	—l'aéroport?
—a bank?	—une banque?

ENGLISH-FRENCH TOURIST VOCABULARY

—the bar?   —le bar?
—the barber's shop?   —le coiffeur?
—the bathroom?   —la salle de bain?
—the ticket (booking) office?   —le guichet?
—a chemist's shop (drugstore)?   —une pharmacie?
—the movies (cinema)?   —le cinéma?
—the cloakroom?   —le vestiaire?
—the British (American) Consulate?   —le consulat d'Angleterre (d'Amérique)?
—the Customs office?   —la douane?
—a garage?   —un garage?
—a hairdresser (barber)?   —un coiffeur?
—the lavatory?   —les toilettes?
—the luggage?   —les bagages?
—the museum?   —le musée?
—the police station?   —la gendarmerie?
—the post office?   —la poste?
—the railway station?   —la gare?
—the theater?   —le théâtre?
—a tobacconist?   —un débit de tabac?

When . . .   Quand . . .
—is lunch?   —le déjeuner est-il servi?
—is dinner?   —le dîner est-il servi?
—is the first (last) bus?   —le premier (dernier) autobus part-il?
—is the first (last) train?   —le premier (dernier) train part-il?
—does the train leave (arrive)?   —le train part-il (arrive-t-il)?
—does the theater open?   —ouvre-t-on le théâtre?
—will it be ready?   —sera-t-il (elle) prêt(e)?
—does the performance begin (end)?   —la séance commence-t-elle (finit-elle)?
—will you be back?   —rentrerez-vous?
—can you return them?   —pouvez-vous me les rendre?
—can I have a bath?   —pourrais-je prendre un bain?

Which is . . .   Quel est . . .
—the way to . . . street?   —Par où va-t-on à la rue . . . ?
—the best hotel at . . . ?   —le meilleur hôtel de . . . ?
—the train (bus) for . . . ?   —le train (autobus) pour . . . ?

What is . . .   Quel est . . .
—the fare to . . . ?   —le prix du billet à . . . ?
—the single fare?   —le prix d'aller?
—the round trip (return) fare?   —le prix aller retour?
—the fare (taxi)?   —Je vous dois combien?
—the price?   —le prix?
—the price per day? per week?   —le prix par jour? par semaine?
—the price per kilo? (2.2 pounds)   Combien le kilo?
—the price per meter? (39½ inches)   Combien le mètre?
—the matter?   Qu'est-ce qu'il y a?
—the French for . . . ?   Comment dit-on . . . en français?

Have you . . .   Avez-vous . . .
—any American (English) cigarettes?   —des cigarettes américaines (anglaises)?

—a timetable?	—un indicateur?
—a room to let?	—une chambre à louer?
—anything ready? (Food)	—quelque chose de prêt?
How often?	Combien de fois?
How long?	Combien de temps

DAILY NEEDS

I want . . .	Je désire . . . Je voudrais . . .
—my bill	—l'addition (la note)
—to buy	—acheter
—cigars, cigarettes	—des cigares, cigarettes
—a dentist	—consulter un dentiste
—a dictionary	—un dictionnaire
—a doctor	—consulter un médecin
—something to drink	—prendre quelque chose à boire
—something to eat	—manger quelque chose
—some American (English) papers	—des journaux américains (anglais)
—a haircut	—me faire couper les cheveux
—a shave	—me faire raser
—to go to	—aller à . . .
—a porter	—un porteur
—to see . . .	—voir . . .
—to send a telegram	—envoyer un télégramme
—some stamps	—des timbres
—a taxi	—un taxi
—to telephone	—téléphoner
—the waiter	—parler avec le garçon
—some beer	—de la bière
—change for . . .	—la monnaie de . . .
—water	—de l'eau
—my key	—ma clé
—razor blades	—des lames de rasoir
—a road map	—une carte routière
—soap	—du savon

MEDICAL

Doctor	Médecin
Nurse	Infirmière
I am ill	Je suis malade
My husband (wife, child, friend) is ill	Mon mari (ma femme, mon enfant, mon ami) est malade
Please call a doctor	Veuillez appeler un mèdecin
Where is a hospital?	Veuillez m'indiquer un hôpital?
There has been an accident	Il y a eu un accident
Do you have . . .	Avez-vous . . .
—bandage or sticking plaster	—un bandage ou pansement gommé
—gauze pads	—des carrés de gaze
—sanitary pads	—serviettes hygiéniques

ENGLISH-FRENCH TOURIST VOCABULARY

—scissors — des ciseaux
—hot water bottle — une bouillotte

MENU TRANSLATOR

MEATS (VIANDE)

agneau	lamb	jambon	ham
biftec	steak	lapin	rabbit
boeuf	beef	lard	bacon
charcuterie	pork cold cuts	mouton	mutton
châteaubriand	fillet steak	porc	pork
côte, côtelette	chop	rosbif	roast beef
entrecôte	rib steak	saucisse	sausage
gigot d'agneau	leg of lamb	saucisson	salami
gibier	game	veau	veal

POULTRY (VOLAILLE)

caille	quail	oie	goose
canard	duck	pintade	guinea hen
caneton	duckling	poulet	chicken
coq	young cock	poussin	spring chicken
faisan	pheasant		

OFFAL (ABATS)

cervelle	brains	langue	tongue
foie	liver	rognon	kidney
tripes	tripe		

FISH (POISSON)

anguille	eel	perche	perch
maquereau	mackerel	saumon	salmon
merlan	whiting	truite	trout
cabillaud	cod		

SHELLFISH (COQUILLAGES, CRUSTACÉS)

bouquet	prawn	homard	lobster
crevettes	shrimp	huîtres	oysters
ecrevisses	crawfish	langouste	spiny rock lobster, crayfish
escargots	snails	langoustines	scampi
fruits de mer	mixed shellfish	moules	mussels
cuisses de grenouilles	frogs' legs	palourdes prairies	clams

ENGLISH-FRENCH TOURIST VOCABULARY

VEGETABLES (LÉGUMES)

aubergine	eggplant, aubergine	haricots verts	french beans
champignons	mushrooms	lentilles	lentils
chou	cabbage	navets	turnips
choufleur	cauliflower	oignons	onions
courgettes	zucchini, courgettes		
cresson	watercress	oseille	sorrel
endive	chicory	pommes de terre	potatoes
épinards	spinach	petits pois	peas
fèves	broad beans	poireaux	leeks
flageolets	kidney beans (green)	riz	rice
haricots blancs	white haricot beans	tomates	tomatoes
		topinambours	Jerusalem artichokes

DESSERTS (DESSERTS)

Beignets	fritters	glace	ice cream
crème caramel	caramel custard	tarte	pie, tart, flan
gâteau	cake		

SAUCES AND STYLES

Aïoli	garlic mayonnaise	bordelaise	prepared with red bordeaux, garlic, onions and mushrooms
bearnaise	sauce of egg, butter and herbs		
bien cuit	well done	à la broche	spit-roasted
chantilly	with whipped cream	pâté	finely chopped and pressed meat
croustade	baked pastry shell		
flambé	with flaming cognac	à point	medium (as in 'a steak medium welldone')
fricassé	braised, fried		
fumé	smoked	rôti	roasted
au gratin	browned under the grill (sometimes with grated cheese)	saignant	rare (as 'a rare steak')
indienne	curried	vinaigrette	with vinegar and oil dressing
niçoise	prepared with oil, garlic, tomatoes and onions		

MISCELLANEOUS

café	small, strong black coffee		
café crème	coffee with milk (or cream)	oeuf	egg
		pain	bread
beurre	butter	potage	soup
fromage	cheese	sucre	sugar
lait	milk	thé	tea

INDEX

INDEX

The letters H and R indicate Hotel and Restaurant listings

GENERAL INFORMATION

Air travel
  airport to Paris 27
  from Britain 22-3
  from N. America 19-20
  from the continent 25
  in France 40
Auto travel
  conversion tables 46-7
  from Britain 23-4
  from the continent 25
  in France 44-7
  package tours 24-5
  rentals 44-5
Bicycling 43
Bus travel 43-4
Camping 13-14, 38
Casinos & gambling 40
Climate 5-6
Costs 3-5
Credit cards 27
Currency 26-7
Customs
  American 49
  British 49-50
  Canadian 50
  French
    arrival 26
    departure 48
Drinking water 39
Electricity 34
Ferries/boat travel
  from Britain 23-4
  in France 47
Festivals 8-9
Food & drink 82-8
Handicapped travelers 48
Health certificates 18
Holidays 6
Hotels & other accommodations 27-30
Hovercraft 24
Information sources 7
Local time 46
Mail 34
Medical services 18-19
Off-season travel 6
Packing & clothing 14-17
Passports and visas
  American 17
  British 17-18
  Canadian 18
Pollution report 36
Public facilities 34
Restaurants 30-2, 82-8
Ship travel
  from N. America 21-2
Spas 39
Special events 7-8
Special interest tours 11-13
Sports 35-9
Student travel 14
Telephones & telegrams 35
Tipping 32-3
Tourist discounts 33
Tours 10
Trailer travel 13-14
Train travel
  Eurailpass 42-3
  from Britain 23
  from the continent 25
  in France 41-3
  to the Riviera 23
Travel agents 9-10
Travelers checks 26-7

Geographical

Abbeville HR299
Abri du Cap Blanc 519
Agay 405, H423
Agde HR471
Aiguebelle H423
Aigues-Mortes 444, HR454
Ainhoa H509
Aire-sur-l'Adour HR509
Aix-en-Provence 450-1, HR454-5
Aix-les-Bains 374, HR385
Ajaccio 545-6, HR555
Albertville HR385
Albi 480, HR490-1
Alençon 263, HR267
Alise-Ste-Reine 346-7
Allevard HR385
Alpe d'Huez 385
Alsace & Lorraine 314-330, HR324-30
  climate 321
  food & drink 324
  information sources 324
  seasonal events 321-2
  sightseeing 322-3
  transportation 323

INDEX

Ambert 536
Amboise 276, HR286-7
Ambonnay HR311
Amélie-les-Bains 462, H471
Amiens 296, HR299
Ammerschwihr HR325
Andorra 485-6, HR491
Andorra-la-Vella 486, HR491
Anet 217
Angers 279-80, HR287
Anglet HR509
Angoulême 499, HR510
Annecy 374, HR385
Annonay HR368
Antibes 407, HR425
Antraigues 364, R368
Aphrodite 464-5
Apt 449, HR455
Arbois 333, HR339
Arcachon 501, HR510
Arcs, Les 375, HR385
Arcy-sur-Cure 344
Ardèche, The 363-4
Ardennes, The 307
Ardres H300
Argelès-Gazost H491
Argelès-sur-Mer 462, HR471
Argentan HR267
Argentière HR385
Arles 445-6, HR455
Arles-sur-Tech 462
Armagnac 480
Arnay-le-Duc HR355
Arras 296, HR300
Arromanches 261, HR267
Ascain 504, HR510
Atlantic Coast 495-15, HR509-15
   climate 506
   food & drink 508-9
   information sources 509
   seasonal events 506
   sports 506-7
   transportation 507-8
Aubenas 364, HR369
Auch 481, HR491
Audierne R248
Aurillac HR540
Auron 379, HR385
Auros R510
Auterive HR491
Autrans HR385
Autuire 520
Autun 349, HR355
Auvergne, The 531-42, HR540-2
   climate 537
   food & drink 539
   information sources 539
   seasonal events 537
   sports 538, 542
   transportation 538-9

Auvilliers-les-Forges HR300
Auxerre 344, HR355
Avallon 347, HR355
Avignon 447-8, HR455
Avoriaz 374-5, H385
Avranches 262, HR267
Ax-les-Thermes H491
Ay 305
Azay-le-Rideau 277-8, HR287

Bagnères-de-Bigorre 483, H491
Bagnoles-de-l'Orne 263, HR268
Bains-les-Bains HR325
Baix HR369
Ballon d'Alsace R325
Bandol 400, HR421
Banyuls-sur-Mer 462, HR471
Barbézieux HR510
Barbizon 220, HR232
Barcelonnette 379, HR386
Barèges 483, H491
Bargemon R425
Bar-le-Duc HR325
Barnville-Carteret 262, HR268
Bar-sur-Aube H311
Basque country 502-3
Bastia 547, HR555
Bastide 535
Batz-sur-Mer HR248
Baule, La 243, HR248
Baume-les-Dames HR339
Baume-les-Messieurs 334, R340
Baux, Les 446, HR455
Bayeux 261, HR268
Bayonne 502-3, HR510
Beaucaire 447
Beaugency HR287
Beaulieu-sur-Dordogne HR527
Beaulieu-sur-Mer 411, HR425
Beaune 348-9, HR355
Beausset, Le HR421
Beauvais 228, HR232
Bec-Hellouin, Le 258, HR268
Beg-Meil 242, H248
Belfort 334-5, HR340
Belle-Ile 243, H248
Benodet 242, H248
Berck-Plage 294, HR300
Bergerac HR510
Bermont 320
Besançon 332-3, HR340
Besançon-la-Mouillière 333
Besse-en-Chandesse 534, HR540
Bétharram 481
Beuil 379, H386
Beuvron-en-Auge R268
Beynac-et-Cazenac 519
Bézards, Les HR287
Béziers 466, HR472
Biarritz 503, HR510-1

INDEX

Bidart HR511
Billiers-Penlan H248
Biot R426
Blain R248
Blérancourt 226, HR232
Blois 280, HR287
Bombannes 502
Bonhomme, Le HR325
Bonifacio 449, H455
Bonnatrait HR386
Bonneval-sur-Arc H386
Bonnieux 449, H455
Bordeaux 499-500, HR511
Bormes-les-Mimosas 401-2, HR423
Bougival 219, HR232
Bouilland HR356
Boulogne 294, HR300
Boulou, Le HR472
Bourboule, La 534, HR540
Bourg-en-Bresse HR369
Bourges 281-2, HR287
Bourget-du-Lac 374, HR386
Bourg-St-Maurice 375-6, H386
Bourlémont 320
Bozouls 522
Bracieux HR287
Branne HR511
Brantôme 518, H527
Brest 241-2, HR248
Breteuil 215
Briançon 377-8, HR386
Brie-Comte-Robert 222, R232
Brignogan-Plage HR248
Brignoles 413, HR456
Brioude 536
Brittany 238-54, HR248-54
    climate 245
    food & drink 247
    information sources 247
    seasonal events 245
    transportation 246-7
Brive-la-Gaillarde HR527
Bugue, Le HR527
Burgundy 344-58, HR354-8
    climate 351
    food & drink 354
    information sources 353
    seasonal events 351
    sightseeing 351-2
    sports 352
    transportation 352-3
Bussang HR325
Bussière HR527
Bussy-Rabutin 346

Cabasson 401
Cabourg 260, HR268
Caen 261, HR268-9
Cagnes 407, HR426
Cahors 521, HR527-8
Calais 293-4, HR300
Calvi 547, HR556
Camargue, The 444-5
Cancale 240, HR248
Canet-en-Roussillon HR472
Cannes 405-6, HR426
Cap d'Agde 465, HR472
Cap d'Ail 412, HR426
Cap d'Antibes HR426
Capendu HR472
Cap Ferrat 410-1, HR429
Cap Martin HR428-9
Carantec H249
Carcassonne 463-4, HR472
Carennac 520, HR528
Carentan HR269
Cargèse H556
Carhaix R249
Carnac 243, HR249
Carpentras 449, H456
Cassis 399, HR421
Castellane 378, H386
Castellet HR421
Castelnau-Bretenoux 520
Castelnaud 519
Castillon-la-Bataille HR511
Castres 480, HR491
Caudebec-en-Caux 258, HR269
Cauterets 483, H491
Cavalaire HR423
Cavalerie, La 514
Cavalière HR423
Centuri 547
Céret 462, H472
Cévennes 523
Chaâlis 224-5
Chablis H356
Chagny HR356
Chaise-Dieu 536, HR540
Chalon-sur-Saône HR356
Chambéry 374, HR386
Chambord 280, HR287
Chamonix-Mont-Blanc 374, HR386
Champagne 304-13, HR311-3
    climate 308
    food & drink 311
    information sources 311
    seasonal events 308
    sightseeing 308-9
    transportation 309-10
Champagnole HR340
Champillon HR311
Champs 223-4
Chantilly 229, HR232-3
Charbonnières-les-Bains HR369
Charleville-Mezières 307, HR311
Charquemont HR340
Chartres 215-6, HR233
Château-Arnoux H456
Château-Chinon HR356

INDEX

Châteaudun HR288
Château Latour 501
Châteaulin HR249
Châteauneuf-du-Pape 449
Châteauneuf-sur-Charente H511
Château-Thierry 223
Châtel HR387
Châtelaillon HR511
Châtelguyon H540
Châtillon-sur-Seine 344-5, HR356
Chaumontel H233
Chaumont-sur-Loire 280
Chaumont-sur-Tharonne H288
Chennevières-sur-Marne 222, R233
Chenonceau 277, HR288
Chenôve 348
Cherbourg 262, HR269
Chesne HR312
Chevery 280
Chevreuse 215, R233
Chinon 278, HR288
Chiry-Ourscamp 226
Cholet HR511
Chorges 378
Ciotat, La 400, HR421
Cirque de Gavarnie 483
Clermont-Ferrand 533-4, HR540
Clos-Vougeot 348
Cluny 349, HR356
Clusaz, La 375, HR387
Cognac 499, HR511
Cogolin 403
Coignières R233
Col de la Faucille HR340
Col de la Schlucht 317, H329
Col du Donon HR325
Colle-sur-Loup HR426
Collioure 462, HR472
Collonges-au-Mont d'Or R369
Colmar 316-7, HR325
Colombey-les-Deux-Eglises 304-5, HR312
Combarelle 519
Combloux 375, HR387
Combourg 244, H249
Compiègne 225-6, HR233
Comps-sur-Issole H456
Concarneau 242-3, HR249
Condamine, La 436
Condé-en-Brie 222
Condom HR492
Conflans-Ste-Honorine R233
Conques 521, HR528
Contamines, Les 375, HR387
Contrexéville 320, HR325-6
Cordes 480, HR492
Corsica 544-58, HR554-8
 climate 549
 currency 549
 food & drink 554

 information sources 553-4
 seasonal events 549
 sightseeing 549-50
 sports 558
 transportation 550-3
Corte 548, HR556
Côte Vermeille 462
Coullons HR288
Coulon 498
Courchevel 375, HR387
Cour-Cheverny HR288
Courseulles-sur-Mer HR269
Coussey 330
Coutainville HR269
Coutances 262, HR269
Coye-la-Forêt R233
Crépy-en-Valois HR233
Cressensac H528
Crest 363
Croisic, Le 243, HR249
Croix-de-Vie 497
Crotoy, Le R300
Cucugnan R473

Dabo 316, HR326
Dampierre 215, HR233
Dax 502, HR512
Deauville 260, HR269
Devinière, La 278
Dieppe 259, HR269-70
Dieulefit 363
Digne 378, HR387
Digoin HR356
Dijon 347-8, HR356
Dinan 240, HR249
Dinard 240, HR249
Dives-sur-Mer R270
Divonne-les-Bains 334, HR340
Dizy 305
Dol-de-Bretagne 240, H249
Dôle 333, HR340
Domfront 263, HR270
Domme 520, HR528
Domrémy 320
Dordogne, The 516-30, HR527-30
 climate 524
 food & drink 526-7
 information sources 526
 seasonal events 524
 sports 524-5
 transportation 525-6
Douai HR300
Douarnenez 242, H249
Dreux 217, HR234
Drôme, The 360, 363
Duclair HR270
Dunkerque (Dunkirk) 293, HR301

Eaux-Bonnes 481, HR492
Eaux-Chaudes 481

INDEX

Ecouen 228
Elne 462
Encamp H491
Enghien-les-Bains 227, HR234
Ensérune 466
Entraygues 521, HR528
Entrecasteaux 451
Epernay 305, HR312
Epinal HR326
Erdevin H249
Ermenonville 224, H234
Esbly R234
Escaldes, Les H491
Espalion 522, H528
Estaing 521-2
Etampes 219, HR234
Etretat 258, HR270
Eugénie-les-Bains HR512
Evisa HR556
Evreux 258, HR270
Eyzies, Les 519, HR528
Eze-Bord-de-Mer 411, H426
Eze-Village 411, HR427

Falaise 263
Faou, Le H249
Favonne HR556
Fayence 413, HR427
Fayrac 519
Fécamp 258-9, HR270
Fère-en-Tardenois HR312
Ferté-sous-Jouarre R234
Figeac 521
Fixin HR357
Flaine HR387
Flassons-sur-Issole H456
Fleury-sur-Ouche R357
Foix 484, HR492
Fontainebleau 220-1, HR234
Fontaine de Vaucluse 449, HR456
Font-de-Gaume 519
Fontenay 345-6
Fontevraud 278-9, HR288
Fontfroide 463
Font-Romeu 461, HR473
Fontvielle 446, HR456
Fôret-Fouesnant, La H249
Forges-les-Eaux 259, HR270
Fos H421
Fougerès 244, H249
Fréjus 404, HR423
French Alps 373-96, HR384-96
   climate 384
   food & drink 384
   information sources 384
   seasonal events 380
   sightseeing 380-2
   sports 391-6
   transportation 382-3
Fumay HR301

Gap 378, HR387
Gargas 484
Gassin 403, HR423
Gavarnie 483
Gemenos HR421
Gérardmer HR326
Gerbier de Jonc 364
Gets, Les 375, H387
Gevrey-Chambertin 348, HR357
Gex HR340
Gien 282, R288
Giverny 263
Givet 307, HR312
Glanum 447
Golfe Juan HR427
Gordes 449, HR456
Gouarec H250
Gouesnière, La H250
Gouffre de Padirac 520-1
Goumois HR341
Gramat 520
Grand Ballon 317, HR326
Grand-Brière 243-4
Grand Canyon due Verdon 413, 451
Grande Chartreuse 376-7
Grande Motte, La 465, HR473
Grand-Pressigny R288
Grange de Meslay 276
Granville 262, HR270-1
Grasse 379, HR427
Grenoble 376, HR388
Grésy-sur-Isere HR388
Grignan 363, H369
Grimaud R423
Gros-Bois 222
Grottes des Demoiselles 466
Gruissan 465, HR473
Guebwiller HR326
Guermantes 223
Guidel H250
Guimiliau 241
Guingamp HR250

Harcourt 258
Hardelot-Plage 293, HR301
Hautefort 519
Haut-Koenigsbourg 318, HR326
Hautvillers 305
Havre, Le 258, HR271
Hay-les-Roses, L' 219
Hédé R249
Hendaye 504, HR512
Hennebont H250
Hesdin HR301
Hohrodberg HR326
Hohwald, Le HR326
Honfleur 259-60, HR271
Hôpitaux-Neufs 334, HR341
Hossegor 502, HR512
Houches, Les HR388

INDEX

Houlgate 260, HR271
Hyères-les-Palmiers 400-1, HR423

Ile de Bendor 400
Ile de France 21-37, HR232-7
  climate 230
  food & drink 231
  seasonal events 230
  sightseeing 230-1
  transportation 231
Ile de Noirmoutier H513
Ile de Porquerolles 401, HR423
Ile de Port Cros 401, H423
Ile de Ré 497-8, HR513
Ile de Sein 242
Ile d'Hyères 401, HR423
Ile du Levant 401
Ile-Rousse, L' 547, HR556
Ile Ste-Honorat 406
Ile Ste-Marguerite 406
Illhausern HR327
Iseran 376
Isle-Adam, L' 228, HR234
Isola 379, H388
Issambres, Les HR423
Issoire 536, HR541

Jarnac HR512
Joigny HR357
Joinville HR312
Josselin 244, H250
Jougne 334, HR341
Joyeuse 364
Juan-les-Pins 406-7, HR427
Jullouville HR271
Jumièges 257, H271
Jura & Franche-Comté 331-43, HR339-42
  climate 336
  food & drink 339
  information sources 338
  seasonal events 336
  sightseeing 336
  sports 336-7, 343
  transportation 337-8

Kayserberg 317, HR327
Kernascléden 244

Labastide-d'Armagnac HR512
Lacanau HR512
Laffrey 377
Lagny 223-4, HR234
Lamastre HR369
Lamballe 240
Lambesc R456
Landersheim R327
Langeais HR288
Languedoc & Roussillon 459-76, HR471-5
  climate 467
  food & drink 470-1
  information sources 470
  seasonal events 467
  sightseeing 468
  sports 468, 475
  transportation 469-70
Laon HR312
Lapallise HR541
Largentière 364
Laruns 481
Lavandou, Le 402, HR423-4
Lecques, Les H421
Lelex HR341
Lembach HR327
Léry R271
Lescar 481
Lézardrieux H250
Lieutades HR541
Liffre R250
Lignon 536
Lille 295-6, HR301
Limoges 517, HR528
Limoux 463, HR473
Lisieux 260, HR271
Loches 277, HR288
Locmaria HR250
Locmariaquer 243
Locranon 242, H250
Loire Valley 274-91, HR286-91
  climate 283
  food & drink 286
  information sources 285
  sightseeing 283-4
  sports 284
  transportation 284-5
Longwy 320
Lons-le-Saunier 333, HR341
Lorient 243, HR250
Loubressac 520
Loudun 498
Lourdes 482, HR492
Loures-Barousse HR492
Louveciennes 219, R234
Luchon 483, HR492
Luçon 497, HR512
Lude, Le 282-3
Lunéville 319, H327
Luxeuil-les-Bains HR341
Luynes HR289
Lyon 360-2, HR369-70, map 361

Mâcon 350, HR357
Maiche H341
Maillane 447
Maintenon 217
Maisonneuve HR370
Maisons-Lafitte 218, R234
Malbuisson HR341
Malène, La HR528

INDEX

Malmaison 218, R234
Malo-les-Bains HR301
Manosque H456
Mans, Le 282, HR289
Mantes 217
Margaux 501
Markstein 317
Marly-le-Roi 219, R234
Marseille 398-9, HR421-2
Martel 520
Mas-d'Azil 484
Massy-Palaiseau H235
Maubeuge HR301
Maussane H456
Meaux 223, HR235
Megève 375, HR388
Méjannes-le-Clap H473
Mende 523, HR528
Menerbes R456
Menton 411-2, HR427
Menuires, Les 375, H388
Mercurey HR357
Méribel-les-Allues 375, H388
Merlimont R302
Mesnil-Val HR271
Mesnuls, Les R235
Métabief 334, HR341
Metz 319-20, HR327
Meulan 218, HR235
Meursalt 349
Meyrargues H456
Meyrueis H528
Meyssac H528
Millau 522, HR528
Milly-la-Fôret R235
Mimizan-Plage 501, HR512
Minerve 466
Mionnay HR370
Miramar HR424
Mirepoix HR492
Moëlan-sur-Mer H250
Moissac HR528
Molitg-les-Bains HR473
Molsheim HR327
Monaco 432-41, HR439-40
   climate 438
   information sources 439
   map 435
   nightlife 440-1
   seasonal events 438
   transportation 438
Monbazillac 520
Monein 481
Mongie-Tourmalet HR492
Montaigu 333
Montal 520
Montauban 480, HR492
Montbard 346
Montbazon H289
Montbéliard HR341

Mont Blanc 373-5
Montbrison HR370
Montcabrier H529
Mont-Dore, Le 534, HR541
Monte-Carlo 436-7, HR439-40
Montélimar 363, HR370
Montgenèvre 378, HR388
Monthermé 307
Montignac-sur-Vézère 519, H529
Montlhéry 219
Montluçon HR512
Montmajour 446
Montmiral HR312
Montmorency 227-8
Montpellier 465, HR473
Montpoupon 277
Montrachet 349
Montrésor 277
Montreuil-sur-Mer 294, HR302
Montrichard HR289
Mont-St-Michel 262-3, HR271-2
Montségur 484-5, HR512
Montsoreau HR289
Moret-sur-Loing 221, HR235
Morez 334, H341
Morlaas 481
Morlaix 241, HR251
Mortain 263
Mortefontaine 224
Morzine 374, HR389
Mougins 406, HR427
Moulins 532, HR541
Moustiers-Ste-Marie 413, 451, H427
Mulhouse 317, HR327-8
Mur-de-Bretagne H251
Mur-de-Sologne HR289
Murol 534, H541

Najac HR529
Nancy 318-9, HR328
Nanterre 218-9
Nantes 244, HR251
Nantua 334, HR342
Napoule, La 405, HR424
Narbonne 462-3, HR473
Nerac HR492
Neufchatel-en-Bray HR272
Nevers HR357
Niaux 484
Nice 407-10, HR428, map 409
Niederbronn-les-Bains HR328
Niedersteinbach HR328
Nieuil HR513
Nîmes 443, HR456-7
Niort 498, HR513
Nolay HR357
Normandy 255-73, HR267-73
   climate 264
   food & drink 267
   information sources 266

seasonal events 264
sightseeing 265-6
transportation 264-5
Northern France 292-303, HR299-303
  climate 297
  food & drink 299
  information sources 299
  seasonal events 297
  sports 297
  transportation 298-9
Noves HR457
Noyon 226
Nuits-St-Georges 348, HR357
Nyons 363

Obernai 318, HR328
Odeillo 461
Oiron 498, HR513
Onzain H289
Oppède-le-Vieux 449
Oradour-sur-Glane 517
Orange 448, HR457
Orbec HR272
Orbey H328
Orchamps-Vennes HR342
Orcival 534
Orléans 281, HR289
Ormesson 222
Ornans 332
Ouistreham 261, HR272
Ozoir-la-Ferrière R235

Paimpol 241, H251
Paimpont 244
Palavas-les-Flots HR474
Paris 91-209, H101-16
  super-deluxe 102-3
  1st-6th arrondissements 103-7
  7th-13th arrondissements 107-13
  14th-18th arrondissements 113-5
  suburbs & airports 116
    Neuilly 115
  R167-86
    1st-6th arrondissements 167-73
    7th-12th arrondissements 173-8
    14th-20th arrondissements 178-82
    Boulogne-Billancourt 182-3
    foreign cuisine 183-5
    wine bistros 185-6
  arrondissements 97-101, map 99
  auto rentals 122
  Bastille, The 155-6
  Bois de Boulogne 153-4
  cemeteries 131-2
  children's entertainment 132-3
  churches 132
  cultural & social info. 135
  currency & exchange 116-7
  Eiffel Tower 152-3
  emergencies 133-4
  Etoile, The 139-40
  exploring 138-64
  food & drink 165-6
  guides 134-5
  handicapped travelers 137
  Hôtel de Ville 159-60
  hours of business 123
  Iles de la Cité & St-Louis 145-6
  information sources 135
  Les Halles/Beaubourg 160-1
  Louvre, The 144-5
  Madeleine, The Opéra 154-5
  mail & telegrams 117
  map 142-3
  Marais, The 157-8
  Montmartre 163-4
  museums 126-30
  Napoleon's Tomb 151
  newspapers & magazines 133
  night life 187-97
  Notre-Dame & the islands 147-8
  Palais-Royal 161-3
  parks & gardens 130-2
  Place de la Concorde 140-4
  Quartier Latin 148-50
  safety precaution 137
  St-Germain-des-Prés 150-1
  Sainte-Chapelle 146
  shopping 198-209
  sightseeing 92-5, 125-6
  sports 123-4
  students & teachers info. 136
  transportation 120-2
    metro map 118-9
Parthenay HR513
Pas de la Casa H491
Pau 480-1, HR492-3
Pégomas H428
Peillon 412, R428
Peïra-Cava 412
Périgueux 518, HR529
Pérouges 362, HR370
Perpignan 461-2, HR474
Perros-Guirec 241, HR251
Peyriac Minervois HR274
Pézenas 466
Piana H556
Pic de St-Loup 466
Pierrefonds 225
Plagne, La 375, H389
Plaisance HR493
Pléhédel H251
Pleneuf-Val-André R251
Pleumeur-Bodou 241
Pléven H251
Pleyben 244
Plombières-les-Bains HR328
Ploudalmézeau H251
Plougastel R251

INDEX 577

Plougastel-Daoulas 242
Ploumanac'h HR251
Plounérin R251
Poët-Laval 363, HR371
Pointe du Raz 242, H251
Poissy 218, R235
Poitiers 498-9, HR513
Poix HR302
Poligny HR342
Pont Audemer HR272
Pont-Aven 243, R252
Pontchartrain HR235
Pont-de-Vaux HR371
Pont-du-Gard 444, HR457
Pont-l'Abbé R252
Pont l'Evêque 260
Ponts-Neufs R252
Pornichet H252
Port-Barcarès 464, R474
Port Camargue 465, HR474
Porté-Puymorens H474
Port Grimaud 403, HR424
Porticcio HR556
Port-Leucate 464, H474
Porto 547, HR556
Porto Pollo H556
Porto-Vecchio 548, HR557
Port Vendres HR474
Pouilly-sur-Loire HR358
Pra-Loup H389
Praz-sur-Arly 375, HR389
Privas 364, HR371
Propriano 546, HR557
Provence & The Carmargue 442-58, HR454-8
  climate 452
  food & drink 454
  information sources 453-4
  seasonal events 452
  transportation 452-3
Provins 221-2, HR235
Puy, Le 535, HR541
Puy-de-Dome 534
Puyguilhem 519-20
Pyla, Le 501

Quarré-les-Tombes H358
Questembert R252
Quiberon 243, HR252
Quillan HR474
Quimper 242, HR252
Quimperlé 243, H252

Rabastens HR493
Rabastens-de-Bigorre R493
Raguenès-Plage H252
Ramatuelle 403, HR424

Rambouillet 215, H235
Rampillon 222
Rastignac 519
Réalmont HR493
Remiremont HR328-9
Rennes 244, HR252
Rethondes 226
Revin 307
Rheims 306-7, HR312-3
Rhône Valley 359-72, HR368-72
  climate 365
  food & drink 367-8
  information sources 367
  seasonal events 365
  sports 366
  transportation 366-7
Ribeauvillé 318, HR329
Riec-sur-Belon HR252
Riez 451
Riom 533, HR541
Riquewihr 318, R329
Rivesaltes H474
Riviera, The 397-431, HR421-30
  climate 414
  costs 420-1
  excursions 418
  food & drink 419-20
  information sources 419
  nightclubs 430-1
  seasonal events 414
  sports 415
  transportation 416-8
Roanne HR371
Rocamadour 521, HR529
Rochefort HR513
Rochegude HR457
Rochelle, La 497, HR513-4
Rochepot, La HR358
Roche-sur-Yon HR514
Rodez 522, HR529
Roncevaux 505
Ronchamp 335, H342
Roquebrune 411, HR428-9
Roquefort-sur-Soulzon 522-3
Roque-Gageac 519, H529
Roscoff H252
Rosiers, Les HR290
Rosporden H253
Rothéneuf 240
Roubaix 295-6, HR302
Rouen 256-7, HR272
Rousillon 449, HR457
Rousses, Les 334, HR342
Royan 498, HR514
Royat HR541
Royaumont 229

Sables-d'Olonne, Les 496, HR514
Sagone HR557
Saillagousse H474

INDEX

St-Amour H342
St-André-de-Corsy R371
St-Benoît-sur-Loire 281
St-Bertrand-de-Comminges 483-4, H493
St-Brieuc 241, HR253
St-Cast 240, H253
St-Céré 520, HR529
St-Claude 332, HR342
St-Cloud 211-2
St-Côme 522
St-Cosme 276
St-Cyprien 464, HR474-5
St-Denis 227
St-Emilion 501, HR514
St-Etienne HR371
St-Fargeau 345
St-Florent 547, HR557
St-Flour H541
St-Germain-en-Laye 218, HR235-6
St-Gervais-les-Bains 375, HR389
St-Gilles 444
St-Girons 484
St-Guénolé HR253
St-Guilhem-le-Désert 466
St-Hippolyte HR329
St-Jacut H253
St-Jean-Cap Ferrat 410, HR429
St-Jean-de-Luz 503-4, HR514
St-Jean-Pied-de-Port 505, HR514
St-Joachim R253
St-Lary HR493
St-Lô HR272
St-Malo 240, HR253
St-Martin-de-Boscherville 257
St-Martin-de-Vésubie 412
St-Martin-du-Canigou 461
St-Maximin-la-Ste-Baume 451
St-Michel-de-Cuxa 461
St-Nazaire 243, HR253
St-Nectaire 534, HR541
St-Omer 294, HR302
St-Paul-de-Vence 412, HR429
St-Pol-de-Léon 241
St-Pons HR475
St-Quentin 296, HR302
St-Raphaël 404, HR424
St-Rémy-de-Provence 446-7, HR457
St-Rémy-les-Chèvreuse R236
St-Thégonnec 241
St-Tropez 402-3, HR424-5
St-Vaast-la-Hougue HR272
St-Wandrille 257
Ste-Anne d'Auray 243, H253
Ste-Anne-la-Palud 242, H253
Ste-Catherine-de-Fierbois 283
Ste-Enimie H529
Ste-Marie-aux-Mines HR329
Ste-Maxime 402-4, HR424
Ste-Odile 318
Saintes 499, HR514
Stes-Maries-de-la-Mer 445, HR457

Salers 534-5, HR541
Salies-de-Béarn HR493
Salins-les-Bains H342
Sallanches HR389
Salon-de-Provence 451, HR457-8
Salses 462, H475
Samoëns 375, H389
Samois-sur-Seine R236
Sanary 400, H422
Santa Coloma HR491
Sant Julia de Loria H491
Sanxay 498
Sare 504
Sarlat 520, HR529
Sartène 546, R557
Saulieu HR358
Saumur 279, HR290
Sauveterre-de-Comminges HR493
Saverne HR329
Sceaux 219
Sedan 307, HR313
Sees HR272
Seguret 458
Seignosse HR514
Seillans HR425
Sémur-en-Auxois HR358
Sénanque 449
Senlis 225, HR236
Senlisse HR236
Sens 345, HR358
Sept-Saulx HR313
Serre-Chevalier 378, HR389
Sète 465, HR475
Sèvres 212
Seynes-les-Alpes 378, HR389
Seyssel HR342
Sézanne HR313
Siorac-en-Périgord H529
Sireuil 520
Sisteron 378, HR389
Soissons 226-7, R236
Soldeu H491
Solenzara 548, H557
Solutré 344
Sospel 412
Souillac 520, HR530
Soulac-sur-Mer H514
Soule 505
Sousceyrac HR530
Soustons HR514-5
Strasbourg 315-6, HR329-30

Tain l'Hermitage 363, HR371
Talloires HR389-90
Tarare HR371
Tarascon 447, HR458
Tarbes 482, HR493
Tarn 522
Théoule 405, HR425
Thiers 533, HR541
Thionville R330

INDEX

Thoiry 217-8, R236
Thoissey HR371
Thonac 520
Thonon-les-Bains 374, HR390
Thoronet 451
Thouars 498
Thury-Harcourt HR273
Tignes 375, HR390
Tiuccia H557
Tonnerre HK358
Toulon 400, HR422
Toulouse 479-80, HR493-4
Toulouse & The Central Pyrenees 477-94, HR490-4
  climate 487
  food & drink 490
  information sources 489-90
  seasonal events 487
  sports 487-8, 494
  transportation 488-9
Touquet-Paris-Plage, Le 294, HR302
Tourcoing HR302
Tournon 363, HR371
Tournus 349-50, HR358
Tours 275-6, HR290
Tours-sur-Marne HR313
Tourtur HR429, HR458
Trayas, Le 405
Trébeurden H253
Tréboul HR253
Tregastel 241, H253
Tréguier 241, H253
Tregunc H254
Tremblay H254
Trevou-Trestel H254
Triel 218
Trois Epis, Les HR330
Trouville 260
Troyes HR313
Tulle 520, H530
Turbie, La 411
Turckheim HR330
Turini HR429

Uriage-les-Bains 377, H390
Ussé 278
Uzès 443-4, H458

Vaison-la-Romaine 449, HR458
Valberg 379, H390
Valbonne 406, R429
Valdahon H342
Val de Laga 536
Val d'Esquières 404
Val d'Isère 375, HR390
Valençay H290
Valence 363
Valenciennes 296, HR303
Valgorge 364, HR371

Vallée des Merveilles 412-3
Valloire H390
Valognes 262
Valras-Plage H475
Vals-les-Bains 364, HR371-2
Val Thorens 375, H390
Vannes 243, HR254
Vans, Les HR372
Varengeville 259
Varennes-Jarcy HR236
Vars-les-Claux H390
Vaucouleurs 320
Vaux-le-Vicomte 222
Veigne HR290
Venaco H557
Vence 412, HR429
Vendôme 282, HR290
Verdun HR313
Verdun-sur-le-Doubs H358
Véretz HR290
Vernet-les-Bains 461, H475
Vernon HR273
Versailles 212-4, HR236-7
Vertus HR313
Vessau 364
Veules-les-Roses R273
Vézelay 347, H358
Vichy 532-3, HR542
Vic-sur-Cère H542
Vienne 362, HR372
Villandry HR291
Villard-de-Lans HR390
Ville d'Avray R237
Villedieu-les-Poêles 262, HR273
Villefort 523, HR530
Villefranche-sur-Mer 410, HR429
Villefranche-sur-Saône 362
Villeneuve-de-Marsan HR515
Villeneuve-lès-Avignon 448, H458
Villeneuve-Loubet HR430
Villeneuve-sur-Lot HR530
Villequier 258, HR273
Villers-Cotterêts 227
Villerville H273
Vincennes 224
Vire HR273
Vironvay HR273
Vitré 244, H254
Vittel HR330
Vizille 377
Vizzavona 548, H557
Vonnas HR372
Vouvray 276, HR291

Wangenbourg 316, HR330
Wimereux HR303
Wissant 303
Wissembourg HR330

Zonza 548, HR557

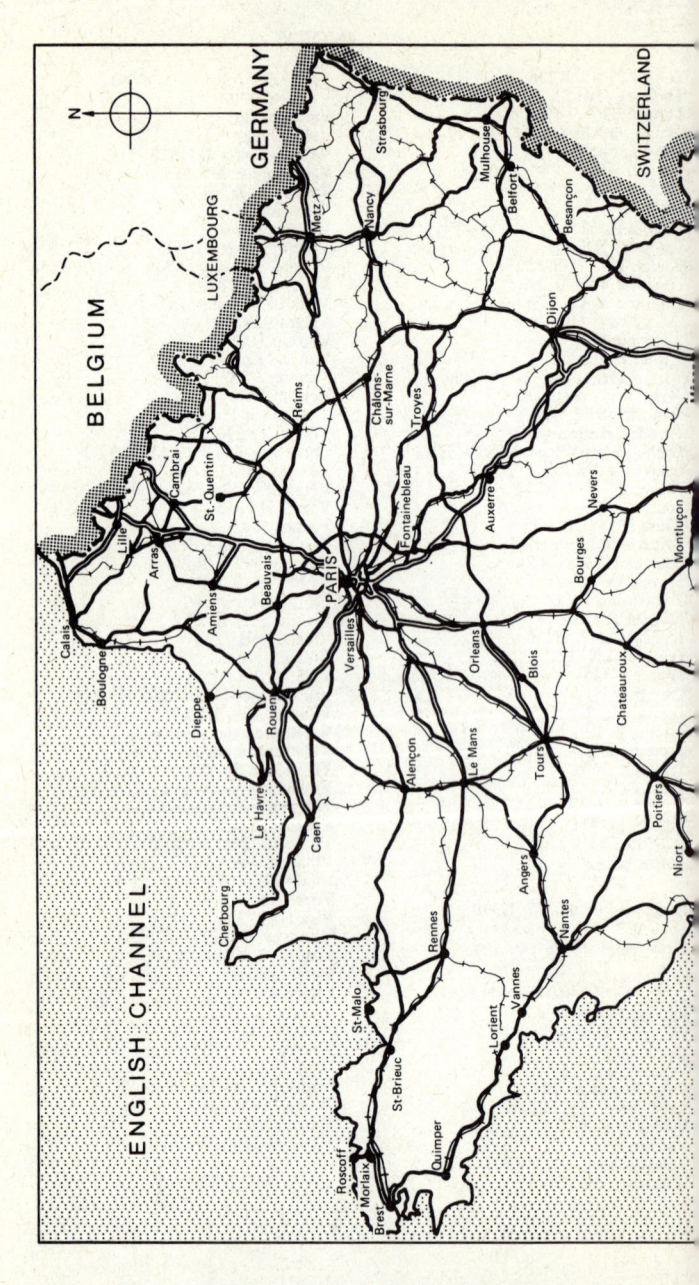

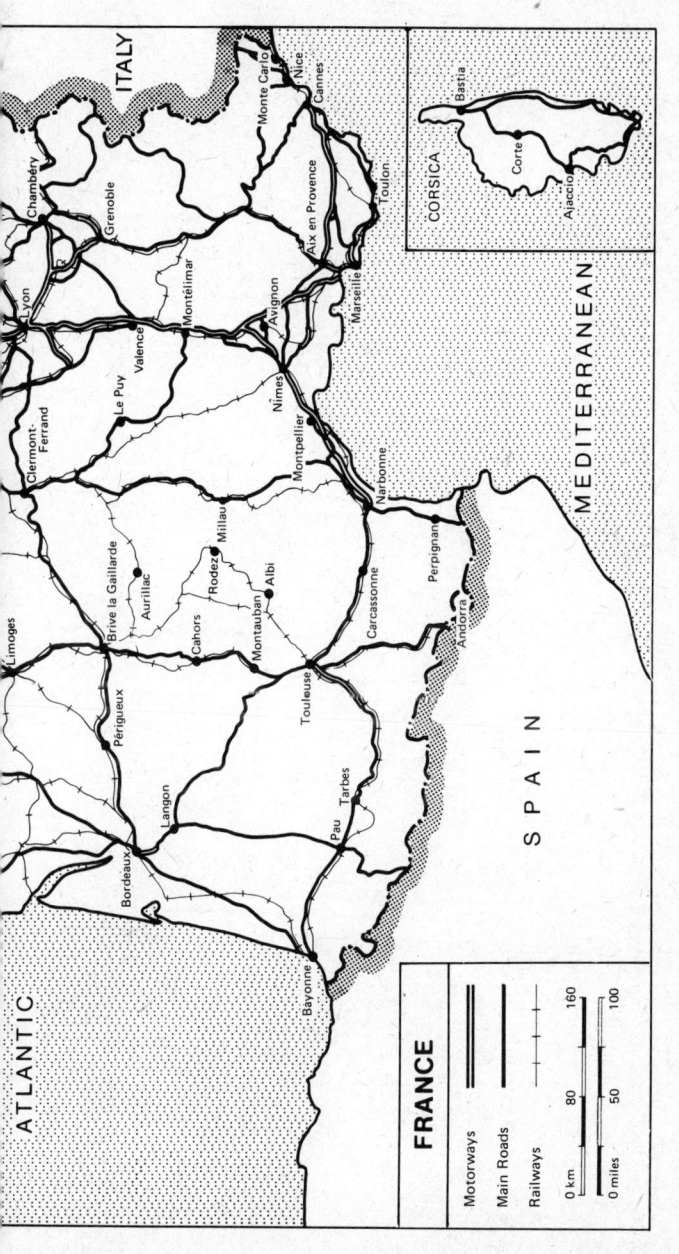